examines Congress's role as watchdog, looking in particular at the **SEC and the financial crisis**. There is expanded discussion on **increasing political polarization** and congressional **oversight and regulation** concerning the oil industry.

- The presidency chapter features the Obama administration throughout, streamlines information on **executive agreements**, and looks at **Obama's picks for the judiciary**. A revised examination of **public approval** looks at how changes in the economy precipitated Obama's approval rating drop.

- A thoroughly revised bureaucracy chapter addresses the **politicization of the bureaucracy** and differing views on **regulation**.

- The courts chapter focuses on the contentious **confirmation process** and the role of partisanship in stalling nominations and also discusses new Supreme Court justices **Sonia Sotomayor and Elena Kagan**.

- The public opinion chapter has been reorganized, with examination of the **sources of division in public opinion** and the connection of this division to partisanship and ideology.

- **National health care reform** leads off the parties and interest groups chapter with updates regarding the **Tea Party movement** and the *Citizens United* case.

- The significance of the *Citizens United* ruling is examined in the new *What's at Stake?* in the voting and elections chapter. Reorganized discussions on **voting and reform** and on **voter turnout attitudes** are also included.

- The **growing role of the Internet** as a news source is explored in the media chapter's new *What's at Stake?*

- The policy chapter includes new discussion of **national health care reform**, the **Dodd-Frank bank reform bill**, and the **federal stimulus bill**, along with an updated *What's at Stake?* that examines the **BP oil spill** within the context of the debate over offshore drilling.

republic-brief.cqpress.com includes chapter summaries; review questions; key term flashcards; crossword puzzles; practice quizzes; interactive exercises; and KTRBlog.

Online Instructor's Resources include a test bank; lecture slides; an instructor's manual; and downloadable, full-color graphics from the full version of *KTR*. To register, go to http://college.cqpress.com/instructors-resources/republic-brief.

CQ Press, a division of SAGE, is the leading publisher of books, directories, periodicals, and electronic products on American government and international affairs, with expanding lists in history and journalism. CQ Press consistently ranks among the top commercial publishers in terms of quality, as evidenced by the numerous awards its products have won over the years. CQ Press owes its existence to Nelson Poynter, former publisher of the *St. Petersburg Times,* and his wife Henrietta, with whom he founded Congressional Quarterly in 1945. Poynter established CQ with the mission of promoting democracy through education and in 1975 founded the Modern Media Institute, renamed The Poynter Institute for Media Studies after his death. The Poynter Institute (www.poynter.org) is a nonprofit organization dedicated to training journalists and media leaders.

In 2008, CQ Press was acquired by SAGE, a leading international publisher of journals, books, and electronic media for academic, educational, and professional markets. Since 1965, SAGE has helped inform and educate a global community of scholars, practitioners, researchers, and students spanning a wide range of subject areas, including business, humanities, social sciences, and science, technology, and medicine. A privately owned corporation, SAGE has offices in Los Angeles, London, New Delhi, and Singapore, in addition to the Washington DC office of CQ Press.

Keeping
the Republic

POWER AND CITIZENSHIP IN AMERICAN POLITICS

FOURTH BRIEF EDITION

Christine Barbour, Indiana University

Gerald C. Wright, Indiana University

A Division of SAGE
Washington, D.C.

CQ Press
2300 N Street, NW, Suite 800
Washington, DC 20037

Phone: 202-729-1900; toll-free, 1-866-4CQ-PRESS (1-866-427-7737)

Web: www.cqpress.com

Cover design: TODA The Office of Design and Architecture
Interior design: Judy Myers
Composition: C&M Digitals (P) Ltd.

♾ The paper used in this publication exceeds the requirements of the American
National Standard for Information Sciences—Permanence of Paper for Printed
Library Materials, ANSI Z39.48-1992.

Printed and bound in the United States of America

14 13 12 11   2 3 4 5

Library of Congress Cataloging-in-Publication Data

Barbour, Christine
  Keeping the republic : power and citizenship in American politics / Christine
Barbour, Gerald C. Wright. — 4th brief ed.
    p. cm.
  Includes bibliographical references and index.
  ISBN 978-1-60871-274-8 (alk. paper)
  1. United States—Politics and government. I. Wright, Gerald C. II. Title.

JK276.B37 2011
320.473—dc22

                                                        2010044427

We dedicate this book with love to our parents,
Patti Barbour and John Barbour, Doris and Gerry Wright,

To our kids, Andrea and Darrin, Monica and Michael,

To our grandkids, Amelia, Elena, Paloma, and Asher,

And to each other.

About the Authors

Christine Barbour teaches in the political science department and the Honors College at Indiana University, where she has become increasingly interested in how teachers of large classes can maximize what their students learn. At Indiana, Professor Barbour has been a Lilly Fellow, working on a project to increase student retention in large introductory courses, and a member of the Freshman Learning Project, a university-wide effort to improve the first-year undergraduate experience. She has served on the *New York Times* College Advisory Board, working with other educators to develop ways to integrate newspaper reading into the undergraduate curriculum. She has won several teaching honors, but the two awarded by her students mean the most to her: the Indiana University Student Alumni Association Award for Outstanding Faculty (1995–1996) and the Indiana University Chapter of the Society of Professional Journalists Brown Derby Award (1997). When not teaching or writing textbooks, Professor Barbour enjoys playing with her dogs, traveling with her coauthor, and writing about food. She is the food editor for *Bloom Magazine* of Bloomington and is a coauthor of *Indiana Cooks!* (2005) and *Home Grown Indiana* (2008). She is currently working on another cookbook and a book about local politics, development, and the fishing industry in Apalachicola, Florida.

Gerald C. Wright has taught political science at Indiana University since 1981. An accomplished scholar of American politics, his books include *Statehouse Democracy: Public Opinion and Policy in the American States* (1993), coauthored with Robert S. Erikson and John P. McIver, and he has published more than fifty articles on elections, public opinion, and state politics. Professor Wright has long studied the relationship among citizens, their preferences, and public policy. He is currently conducting research with grants from the National Science Foundation and the Russell Sage Foundation on the factors that influence the equality of policy representation in the states and in Congress. He is also writing a book about representation in U.S. legislatures. He has been a consultant for Project Vote Smart in the last several elections. Professor Wright is a member of Indiana University's Freshman Learning Project, a university-wide effort to improve the first-year undergraduate experience by focusing on how today's college students learn and how teachers can adapt their pedagogical methods to best teach them. In his nonworking hours, Professor Wright also likes to spend time with his dogs, travel, eat good food, and play golf.

Brief Contents

Contents

Preface

This fourth brief edition of *Keeping the Republic* is designed for those who want a concise, streamlined, inexpensive, and engaging version of its longer, more comprehensive parent. While we have condensed the longer text's account of the American political system, we have taken great pains to preserve the accessibility and enthusiasm of that book. Our goal was to meet the needs of those looking for a shorter text to use with various supplemental readings, as well as those who want broad coverage in a price-sensitive package.

We have also stayed true to our original goal in writing the text: to share the excitement of discovering humankind's capacity to find innovative solutions to those problems that arise from our efforts to live together on a planet too small, with resources too scarce, and with saintliness in too short a supply. In this book we honor the human capacity to manage our collective lives with peace and even, at times, dignity. And, in particular, we celebrate the American political system and the founders' extraordinary contribution to the possibilities of human governance.

This book covers essential topics with clear explanations, but it is also organized thematically, intended to guide students through a wealth of material and to help them make sense of the content both academically and personally. To that end we have developed two themes that run through every chapter: an analytic theme to help students organize the details and connect them to the larger ideas and concepts of American politics, and an evaluative theme to help them find personal meaning in the American political system and develop standards for making judgments about how well the system works. Taken together, these themes provide students with a framework on which to hang the myriad complexities of American politics.

The analytic theme we chose is a classic in political science: politics is a struggle over limited power and resources, as gripping as a sporting event in its final minutes, but much more vital. The rules guiding that struggle influence who will win and who will lose, so that often the struggles with the most at stake are over the rule-making itself. In the words of a very famous political scientist, *politics is about who gets what and how they get it.* This theme runs throughout the narrative of the book and, to reinforce it, we begin and end every chapter with a feature called *What's at Stake?* that asks what people want from politics—what they are struggling to get and how the rules affect who gets it.

For the evaluative theme, we focus on the "who" in the formulation of "who gets what and how." Who are the country's citizens? What are the ways they engage in political life? In order to "keep" a republic, citizens must shoulder responsibilities as well as exercise their rights. We challenge students to view democratic participation among the diverse population as the price of maintaining liberty.

Our citizenship theme has three dimensions. First, in the *Profiles in Citizenship* feature, included in approximately half the chapters, we introduce students to important figures in American politics and ask the subjects why they are involved in public service or some aspect of political life. Based on personal interviews with these people, the profiles model republic-keeping behavior for students, helping them to see what is expected of them as members of a democratic polity. We unabashedly feel that a primary goal of teaching introductory politics is not only to create good scholars but also to create good citizens. Second, at the end of every chapter, the feature *Citizenship and . . .* provides a critical view of what citizens can or cannot do in American politics, evaluating how democratic various aspects of the American system actually are and what possibilities exist for change. Third, we premise this book on the belief that the skills that make good students and good academics are the same skills that make good citizens: the ability to think critically about and process new information and the ability to be actively engaged in one's subject. Accordingly, in our *Consider the Source* feature, we help students examine critically the various kinds of political information they are bombarded with— from information in textbooks like this one, to information from the media or the Internet, to information from their congressperson or political party.

We have long believed that teaching is a two-way street, and we welcome comments, criticisms, or just a pleasant chat about politics or pedagogy. You can email us directly at barbour@indiana.edu and wright1@indiana.edu or write to us at the Department of Political Science, Indiana University, Bloomington, IN 47405.

What's New in the Fourth Brief Edition

Elections are almost as rough on American government textbook authors as they are on the candidates—in order to get books in the bookstores for the new semester we get less than a week to pull all the new information together and update our texts. In the case of 2010 that means that as we write, a couple of House races are still up in the air (which is still better than 2000, when we wrote the election update without knowing who had won the presidency). All considered, this fourth brief edition of *Keeping the Republic* is as current as we can make it.

The 2008 election turned some of our conventional wisdom about who gets what in American politics upside down. Americans elected an African American to the presidency and seriously entertained the idea of a woman president or vice president. Young people, traditionally nonvoters, turned out for the primaries and caucuses, and for the second time in a row they turned out in large numbers for the general election. Changing demographics and the passing of time had blurred the distinction between red states and blue states. In 2010, however, amidst a painfully slow economic recovery, politics looked more like business as usual. The president's party took a midterm beating (President Obama called it a "shellacking"—larger than but similar to what President Bush described in 2006 as a "thumping"). Young people stayed home, and the electoral map was blue at the coasts and red in the center. We have updated the text throughout to reflect the current balance of power in the House and Senate and tried to put the election results into historical perspective.

And that's not all. Writing the fourth brief edition also gave us an opportunity to revise, improve, and update graphics and features to make them more useful and pertinent to both instructors and students. Graphs in every chapter reflect the newest data available, and a majority of the chapters feature new opener images. We've also added photos in each chapter to illustrate particular events discussed in the text. New *What's at Stake?* vignettes examine such topics as the rise of the Tea Party, a state attorney general's effort to prosecute a professor for what he saw as fraudulent scientific research, the use of the filibuster in the Senate to stymie Obama's presidential ambitions, the role of interest groups in the passage of health care reform, the implications for elections of the Supreme Court's decision in *Citizens United v. Federal Election Commission,* the slow demise of the print media in favor of electronic forms of information distribution, and the implications of BP's 2010 oil spill in the Gulf for the future of offshore drilling. Two other *What's at Stake?* vignettes have been updated to reflect the differences between the Obama and the Bush administrations with respect to the use of presidential signing statements and enforcing federal drug laws over state laws permitting the sale of medical marijuana.

Supplements

We know how important good resources can be in the teaching of American government. Our goal has been to create resources that not only support but also enhance the text's themes and features. Also, the book's companion site at http://republic-brief.cqpress.com helps students master each chapter's learning objectives, vocabulary, and conceptual information. We greatly appreciate the efforts of adopter and instructor Heidi Getchell-Bastien of Northern Essex Community College, who has updated and improved the resources that accompany our text.

For Instructors:

- The **KTRblog** will provide news postings, connecting current events to the book's themes and topics.
- Our **Test Bank** has nearly nine hundred test questions, separated into factual and conceptual multiple-choice, short-answer, fill-in-the-blank, and short-essay questions to help you create exams. The test bank is available in *Respondus*—flexible and easy-to-use test-generation software that allows you to build, customize, and even integrate exams into course management systems.

- **PowerPoint Lecture Slides** provide an outline for each chapter, highlighting key concepts and leaving plenty of room for adaptability.
- The online **Instructor's Manual** includes chapter overviews, lecture starters, class activities, and discussion questions, pointing to ways in which the power and citizenship themes can be developed further.
- All of the **Figures, Tables, and Maps** from the full fifth edition, in full color, as well as the graphics from the fourth brief edition, are available as both Power-Point slides and PDFs so that you can easily teach with them in the classroom.
- All features from the full edition are available in PDF form for instructors to assign to students, including the *Consider the Source* critical thinking boxes and a full set of *Profiles in Citizenship* that contain new interviews with Sen. Jon Tester, David Frum, Peter Orszag, Nate Silver, and Andrew Sullivan.
- **A free six-month subscription to *CQ Weekly*** is available through CQ Press to instructors who adopt *Keeping the Republic* (subject to minimum quantities). We use *CQ Weekly* to stay up to date on current developments, and we know many of our colleagues do as well. This is a useful source to animate your lectures with topical and insightful analysis from the same magazine that informs politicians and policymakers in Washington.
- Instructors should go to **http://cqpress.college.com/instructors-resources/republic-brief** to register and download these materials.

For Students:

- A **Study** section offers summaries and learning objectives that encapsulate the most important facts and concepts of each chapter.
- Interactive **Quizzes** allow students to work through approximately fifteen multiple-choice questions per chapter and receive immediate results, both by question type (for example, conceptual, factual, and vocabulary) and by chapter section, so that they can effectively gauge their comprehension of the material. If you would like to track your students' online work, you can have them email their quiz results directly to you.
- Interactive **Flashcards and Crossword Puzzles** are handy ways for students to review the book's key terms. Students can also mark terms they would like to return to as well as shuffle and reset their cards.
- Web-based **Exercises** provide activities that encourage students to apply information, concepts, and principles from the text in a series of interactive questions. Response boxes allow students to email their answers to their instructors for credit or a grade.
- An **Explore** section has annotated web links to facilitate further research.
- Our **Take a Position** feature builds on particular issues or controversies covered in the text, leading students through the critical thinking process so that they can build a balanced, well-argued position on current events.

Acknowledgments

The Africans say that it takes a village to raise a child—it is certainly true that it takes one to write a textbook! We could not have done it without a community of family, friends, colleagues, students, reviewers, and editors, who supported us, nagged us, maddened us, and kept us on our toes. Not only is this a better book because of their help and support, but it would not have been a book at all without them.

In addition to all the folks we gratefully acknowledge in the full edition of this text, some made a particular contribution to this brief edition. We would like to thank the reviewers who have given us their feedback on the past and current brief editions of our book: Jean Abshire, Indiana University Southeast; Vicky Cannon Bollenbacher, Aims Community College; Robert Bradley, Illinois State University; Pam Brunfelt, Vermilion Community College; Matthew T. Christensen, Boise State University; Timothy Dale, University of Wisconsin–Green Bay; Robert L. Dion, University of Evansville; Richard Flanagan, College of Staten Island, the City University of New York; Paul Hain, Texas A&M University–Corpus Christi; Charles A. Hantz, Danville Area Community College; Paul L. Hathaway, Jacksonville State University; Cyrus Hayat, IUPU–Indianapolis; Richard Holtzman, Bryant University; Glen D. Hunt, Austin Community College; Alana Jeydel, American River College; Robert Klotz, University of Southern Maine; Tom McInnis, University of Central Arkansas; Linda Medcalf, South Puget Sound Community College; Jeff Millstone, Austin Community College; Jason C. Myers, California State University Stanislaus; Richard Pacelle, Georgia Southern University; Denise Richardson, Laney College; Thomas A. Schmeling, Rhode Island College; Angela Ugran, Cuyahoga Community College, East Campus; and Ulf Zimmermann, Kennesaw State University.

We are indebted to Pat Haney, who has provided the nuts and bolts of the foreign policy part of Chapter 14 since the first edition. Pat has been a cheerful, tireless collaborator for more than ten years now, and we are so grateful to him. And we'd like to thank all the people at CQ Press who believe in this book and made this edition possible. In this day and age of huge publishing conglomerates, it has been such a pleasure to work with a small, committed team who are dedicated to top-quality work.

Christine Barbour
Gerald C. Wright

To the Student

Suggestions on How to Read This Textbook

1. As they say in Chicago about voting, do it **early and often.** If you open the book for the first time the night before the exam, you will not learn much from it and it won't help your grade. Start reading the chapters in conjunction with the lectures, and reread them all at least once before the exam. A minimum of two readings is necessary for a decent education and a decent grade.

2. Pay attention to the **chapter headings.** They tell you what we think is important, what our basic argument is, and how all the material fits together. Often, chapter subheadings list elements of an argument that may show up on a quiz. Be alert to these clues.

3. **Read actively.** Constantly ask yourself: What does this mean? Why is this important? How do these different facts fit together? What are the broad arguments here? How does this material relate to class lectures? How does it relate to the broad themes of the class? When you stop asking these questions, you are merely moving your eyes over the page, and that is a waste of time.

4. **Highlight or take notes.** Some people prefer highlighting because it's quicker than taking notes, but others think that writing down the most important points helps in recalling them later. Whichever method you choose (and you can do both), be sure you're doing it properly.

- *Highlighting.* Highlight with a pen or marker that enables you to read what's on the page. Do not highlight too much. An entirely highlighted page will not give you any clues about what is important. Read each paragraph and ask yourself: What is the basic idea of this paragraph? Highlight that. Avoid highlighting all the examples and illustrations. You should be able to recall them on your own when you see the main idea. Beware of highlighting too little. If whole pages go by with no marking, you are probably not highlighting enough.
- *Outlining.* Again, the key is to write down enough, but not too much. Recopying a chapter written by someone else is deadly boring—and a waste of time. Go for key ideas, terms, and arguments.

5. Note all **key terms,** including those that appear in chapter headings. Be sure you understand the definition and significance.

6. Do not skip **tables and figures.** These things are there for a purpose, because they convey crucial information or illustrate a point in the text. After you read a chart or graph, make a note in the margin about what it means.

7. Do not skip the *Consider the Source* **boxes** or the *Profiles in Citizenship* **boxes.** They are not filler! The *Consider the Source* boxes provide advice on becoming a critical consumer of the many varieties of political information that come your way. They list questions to ask yourself about the articles you read, the web sites you visit, and the media you consume, among other things. Each *Profiles in Citizenship* box highlights the achievements of a political actor pertinent to that chapter's focus. They model citizen participation and can serve as a beacon for your own political power long after you've completed your American government course.

8. Make use of the book's web site at **http://republic-brief.cqpress.com.** There are chapter summaries, flashcards, and practice quizzes that will help prepare you for exams.

Keeping the Republic

POWER AND CITIZENSHIP IN AMERICAN POLITICS

Chapter 1

Power and Citizenship in American Politics

▶ What's at Stake?

Barack Obama was rocking the vote, big time, but still the talking heads were skeptical. Would younger voters turn out at the polls, giving Obama the electoral edge he needed to win? The conventional wisdom said no.

"Are they going to show up?" asked ABC News's Cokie Roberts back in February. "Probably not. They never have before. By the time November comes, they'll be tired," she added, authoritatively.[1]

But they did show up. They showed up in force on the cold January night in 2008 when Iowans caucused to choose their Democratic nominee for president. They showed up throughout the spring, as state after state racked up delegate totals for Barack Obama. They showed up for rallies and speeches and volunteer efforts throughout the summer in the days after the nomination was clinched, but before the general election campaign was launched on Labor Day. They gave money and signed up on the Internet, and they organized on campuses across the country, registering their peers and preparing to get them to the polls on Election Day. And they showed up on November 4.

Tired? Looks like Roberts had her facts wrong.

Obama was banking on it. Speaking of his campaign in his victory speech after his election as the first African American president in our nation's history, he said, "It drew strength from the young people who rejected the myth of their generation's apathy; who left their homes and their families for jobs that offered little pay and less sleep."

And when the exit poll data came rolling in, it was clear: young voters had played a huge, if uncharacteristic, part in Obama's election. More than half, 51 percent, of young voters showed up to vote in 2008, an increase of 11 percent over 2000 and almost 2 percent over 2004. They made up 17 percent of the electorate, a 2.2 million voter increase over 2004, with turnout especially high in the battleground states where campaigning was fiercest.[2]

Most important for Obama was the fact that the 23 million voters under age thirty broke decisively for him over his Republican opponent, John McCain. Obama carried the youth vote by 66 to 39—a more than two-to-one margin—much higher than the 53-to-46 split among the population as a whole. For an age cohort that politicians usually write off as apathetic, uninformed, and uninvolved, young people came through for Obama in a big way.

These statistics would surely have given considerable peace of mind to Benjamin Franklin, who was keenly aware of the importance of popular attention to the political process. In 1787, when asked by a woman what he and other founders of the Constitution had created, he answered: "A Republic, Madam, if you can keep it." But ever since eighteen-year-olds had been given the vote in 1972, their voting turnout had been low, their efforts to keep the republic distinctly lackluster.

Young people have generally been less interested in politics, and less informed, than their elders. In one 2002 survey, only 51 percent of those aged eighteen to twenty-five could name Dick Cheney as vice president of the United States and only 45 percent said they were interested in local politics, fewer than in any other age group.[3] One writer, noting that Americans of all ages expressed increasingly high levels of distrust in government and dislike for politics, sounded the dire warning that "a nation that hates politics will not long thrive as a democracy."[4]

For those who believe that political engagement is essential to the prosperity of democracy, a critical question is whether 2008 constitutes a lasting change in young people's political attitudes. Perhaps it was a fluke, a one-time thing, tied to vague rumors about the Iraq war, or to an unusually close election, or to extraordinary get-out-the-vote efforts made by the political parties and other activist groups. Is young people's political involvement really such a big deal, or is concern about keeping the republic just an idiosyncrasy of long-deceased founders and hyperactive political science professors? What is really at stake for American democracy in the issue of youthful engagement in the political system? We will be able to address this question better after we explore the meaning of politics and the difference it makes in our lives.

Have you got grand ambitions for your life? Do you want a powerful position in business, influence in high places, money to make things happen? Perhaps you'd like to make a difference in the world, heal the sick, fight for peace, feed the poor. Or maybe all you want from life is a good education, a well-paying job, a comfortable home, and a safe, prosperous, contented existence. Think politics has nothing to do with any of those things? Think again.

The things that make those goals attainable—a strong national defense, education loans or tax deductions for tuition money, economic prosperity, full employment, favorable mortgage rates, time off from work to have kids, secure streets and neighborhoods, cheap and efficient public transportation—are all influenced by or are the products of politics.

Yet if you listen to the news, politics may seem like one long campaign commercial: eternal bickering and finger-pointing by people who feather their nests and those of their cronies at the expense of the voters and who publicly proclaim to be morally upstanding while keeping the tabloids busy with the tawdry details of their private lives. Politics, which we would like to think of as a noble and even morally elevated activity, takes on all the worst characteristics of the business world, where we expect people to take advantage of each other and pursue their own private interests. Can this really be the heritage of Thomas Jefferson and Abraham Lincoln? Can this be the "world's greatest democracy" at work?

In this book we explore that question, getting to the heart of what politics is and how it relates to other concepts such as power, government, rules, economics, and citizenship. We propose that politics can best be understood as the struggle over who gets power and resources in society. Politics produces winners and losers, and much of the reason it can look so ugly is that people fight desperately not to be losers.

Contrary to the way they appear in the media, and maybe even in our own minds, the people who are doing that desperate fighting are not some special breed—more corrupt or self-interested or greedy than the rest of us. They are us—whether they are officials in Washington or mayors of small towns, corporate CEOs or representatives of labor unions, local cops or soldiers in the Middle East, church-goers or atheists, doctors or lawyers, shopkeepers or consumers, professors or students, they are the people that in a democracy we call citizens.

As we will see, it is the beauty of a democracy that all the people, including the everyday people like us, get to fight for what they want. Not everyone can win, of course, and many never come close. There is no denying that some people bring resources to the process that give them an edge, and that the rules give advantages to some groups of people over others. But the people who pay attention and who learn how the rules work can begin to use those rules to increase their chances of getting what they want, whether it is a lower personal tax bill, greater pollution controls, a more aggressive foreign policy, safer streets, a better educated population, or more public parks. If they become very skilled citizens, they can even begin to change the rules so that they can fight more easily for the kind of society they think is important, and so that people like them are more likely to end up winners in the high-stakes game we call politics.

In this chapter we introduce you to this fascinating world of politics, focusing on the meaning of *politics* itself, the varieties of political systems and the roles they endorse for the individuals who live under them, the American founders' ideas about democracy and citizenship, the ideas that hold us together as a nation, the ideas that define our political conflicts, and the themes of power and citizenship that will serve as our framework for understanding American politics.

What Is Politics?

A peaceful means for determining who gets power and influence in society

Over two thousand years ago, the Greek philosopher Aristotle said that we are political animals, and political animals we seem destined to remain. The truth is that politics is a fundamental and complex human activity. In some ways it is our capacity to be political—to cooperate, bargain, and compromise—that helps distinguish us from all the other animals out there. While it certainly has its baser moments (impeachments, indictments, and intelligence abuses come to mind), politics also allows us to reach more exalted heights than we could ever achieve alone—from the dedication of a new public library, to the building of a national highway system, to the stabilization of a crashing economy, to the guarantee of health care to all U.S. citizens.

To explore politics—in all its glory as well as its shame—we need to begin with a clear and neutral definition. One of the most famous definitions, put forth by the well-known political scientist Harold Lasswell, is still one of the best, and we use it to frame our discussion throughout this book. Lasswell defined **politics** as "who gets what, when, and how."[5] Politics is a way of determining, without recourse to violence, who gets the power and resources in society, and how they get them. **Power** is the ability to get other people to do what you want them to do. The resources in question here might be government jobs, tax revenues, laws that help you get your way, or public policies that work to your advantage.

Politics is the process through which we try to arrange our collective lives in some kind of **social order** so that we can live without crashing into each other at every turn, provide ourselves with goods and services we could not obtain alone, and maximize the values and behaviors we think are important. But politics is also about getting our own way. Our own way may be a noble goal for society or it may be pure self-interest, but the struggle we engage in is a political struggle. Because politics is about power and other scarce resources, there will always be winners and losers. If we could always get our own way, politics would disappear. It is because we cannot always get what we want that politics exists.

What would a world without politics be like? There would be no resolution or compromise between conflicting interests, because those are certainly political activities. There would be no agreements struck, bargains made, or alliances formed. Unless there were enough of every valued resource to go around, or unless the world were big enough that we could live our lives without coming into contact with other human beings, life would be constant conflict—what the philosopher Thomas Hobbes (1588–1679) called a "war of all against all." Individuals, unable to cooperate with one another (because cooperation is essentially political), would have no option but to resort to brute force to settle disputes and allocate resources.

Our capacity to be political saves us from that fate. We do have the ability to persuade, cajole, bargain, promise, compromise, cooperate, and even, on occasion, bribe and deceive. We do have the ability to agree on what principles should guide our handling of power and other scarce resources and to live our collective lives according to those principles. Because there are many potential theories about how to manage power—who should have it, how it should be used, how it should be transferred—agreement on which principles are **legitimate**, or accepted as "right," can break down. When agreement on what is legitimate fails, violence often takes its place. Indeed, the human history of warfare attests to the fragility of political life.

Politics and Government

Although the words *politics* and *government* are sometimes used interchangeably, they really refer to different things. Politics is a process or an activity through which power and resources are gained and lost. **Government**, on the other hand, is a system or organization for exercising authority over a body of people.

American *politics* is what happens in the halls of Congress, on the campaign trail, at Washington cocktail parties, and in neighborhood association meetings. It is the making of promises, deals, and laws. American *government* is the Constitution and the institutions set up by the Constitution for the exercise of authority by the American people, over the American people.

Authority is power that citizens view as legitimate, or "right"—power to which we have implicitly consented. You can think of it this way: as children, we probably did as our parents told us or submitted to their punishment if we didn't because we recognized their authority over us. As we became adults, we started to claim that they had less authority over us, that we could do what we wanted. We no longer saw their power as wholly legitimate or appropriate. Governments exercise authority because people recognize them as legitimate, even if they often do not like doing what they are told (paying taxes, for instance). When governments cease to be regarded as legitimate, the result may be revolution or civil war, unless the state is powerful enough to suppress all opposition.

Rules and Institutions

Government is shaped by the process of politics, but it in turn provides the rules and institutions that shape the way politics continues to operate. The rules and institutions of government have a profound effect on how power is distributed and who wins and loses in the political arena. Life is different in other countries not only

Tiffany Benjamin

How do you get to be a delegate to the Democratic National Convention when you are only twenty years old? According to Tiffany Benjamin, all it takes is a dare from a friend, the willingness to take a risk, and a little bit of luck. She doesn't mention that it also takes some uncommon guts and determination, but that's clearly the case.

Tiffany was an undergraduate at Indiana University when she and a friend decided it would be a kick to go to the 2000 Democratic National Convention in Los Angeles, where Al Gore would receive the nomination for president. They were both active in the Democratic Party on campus, so both got emails from the party outlining the steps to winning one of the coveted spots at the national convention.

The chances of getting elected were tiny, they knew, but they badly wanted to go to L.A. "I'll do this if you'll do it," Tiffany told her friend. And he said, "Okay, I dare you," and she said, "I dare *you*," and she went and got all her forms filled in and sent them out on the very last possible day, only to find that her friend had chickened out. "I couldn't do it," he told her. "I was too afraid."

Afraid? If Tiffany's ever heard the word, she doesn't let on. First, she headed off to the Democratic National Convention (yes, she won election as an alternate at-large delegate, only to step into the shoes of a delegate who couldn't go). She had a blast, as she knew she would. Cameras followed her around as one of the youngest delegates, and she attended party after party, meeting famous politicians, listening to speeches, and becoming more deeply inspired with the ideas of these people who believe in the same things she believes in, and who fight for the same things she fights for.

Then it was back to Bloomington for her senior year and a summer as an international exchange student in Mauritius—a tiny country in the middle of the Indian Ocean—before heading off to Harvard Law School.

Maybe Tiffany's intrepid stance toward life in general (and political life in particular) is a self-protective byproduct of growing up with a Republican dad and

because people speak different languages and eat different foods but also because their governments establish rules that cause life to be lived in different ways.

Rules can be thought of as the *how*, in the definition "who gets what, and *how*." They are directives that determine how resources are allocated and how collective a Democratic mom (divorced since she was a baby). Eventually she decided her views were closer to the Democrats'. Looking for activities to get involved in when she arrived at Indiana University, she saw a mass flier advertising a party meeting and went. "And I kind of clicked with some of the people, and it was a cool party. So I decided I would stay."

Stay she did. Tiffany threw herself into the business of politics, active on campus but also volunteering to work on campaigns, starting with John Hamilton's effort to win Indiana's 8th congressional district in 2000. "That was the best experience for me ever, even though we lost. . . . I felt like my views were getting lost, and the issues I really cared about were getting lost." It galvanized her. "From then on I just got severely, actively involved."

And that's where she has been ever since. Reflecting back as a freshly minted lawyer about to move to Washington, D.C., to begin a new career, Tiffany's deep, abrupt chuckle is as contagious and engaging as ever, her eyes just as wickedly full of irony and fun, but there is a core of underlying seriousness that wasn't there before. Working as a student public defender with adult clients and juveniles caught up in the courts, seeing what happens to people who cannot get the system to work for them, has only strengthened the resolve to make a difference that she discovered as a freshman while she was looking for ways to make some friends on campus.

Advice on doing the impossible (like getting to a nominating convention in 2008):
Don't be afraid of anything. Listen to yourself first, because a million people told me I wasn't going to get there. And another thing is, don't take it too seriously. And be sure to have a lot of fun.

On keeping the republic:
Get involved. And that doesn't just mean vote, and it doesn't just mean go to a political party meeting. It means find out what the issues are, think about how you feel about those issues, and then *do* something. . . . Whatever you do, it does absolutely make a difference. Even if you think it doesn't matter, you will be impressed in the ways that, ten years from now, someone will come up to you and tell you that what you did mattered.

action takes place—that is, they determine how we try to get the things we want. We can do it violently, or we can do it politically, according to the rules. Those rules can provide for a single dictator, for a king, for rule by God's representative on earth or by the rich, for rule by a majority of the people, or for any other arrangement. The point of rules is to provide us with a framework for solving—without violence—the problems generated by our collective lives.

Because the rules we choose can influence which people will get what they want most often, understanding the rules is crucial to understanding politics. Consider for a moment the impact a change of rules would have on the outcome of the sport of basketball, for instance. What if the average height of the players could be no more than 5 feet 10 inches? What if the baskets were lowered? What if foul shots counted for two points rather than one? Basketball would be a very different game, and the teams recruited would look quite unlike the teams we now cheer for. So it is with governments and politics: change the people who are allowed to vote or the length of time a person can serve in office, and the political process and the potential winners and losers change drastically.

We can think of **institutions** as the *where* of the political struggle, though Lasswell didn't include a "where" component in his definition. They are the organizations where governmental power is exercised. In the United States, our rules provide for the institutions of a representative democracy, that is, rule by the elected representatives of the people, and for a federal political system. Our Constitution lays the foundation for the institutions of Congress, the presidency, the courts, and the bureaucracy as a stage on which the drama of politics plays itself out. Other systems might call for different institutions, perhaps an all-powerful parliament, or a monarch, or even a committee of rulers.

These complicated systems of rules and institutions do not appear out of thin air. They are carefully designed by the founders of different systems to create the kinds of society they think will be stable and prosperous, but also where people like themselves are likely to be winners. Remember that not only the rules but also the institutions we choose influence which people most easily and most often get their own way.

Politics and Economics

Whereas politics is concerned with the distribution of power and resources in society, **economics** is concerned specifically with the production and distribution of society's wealth—material goods like bread, toothpaste, and housing, and services like medical care, education, and entertainment. Because both politics and economics focus on the distribution of society's resources, political and economic questions often get confused in contemporary life. Questions about how to pay for government, about government's role in the economy, and about whether government or the private sector should provide certain services have political and economic dimensions. Because there are no clear-cut distinctions here, it can be difficult to keep these terms straight. We can begin by examining different economic systems, shown in Figure 1.1.

Capitalism
The economic system most familiar to Americans is capitalism. In a pure **capitalist economy**, all the means that are used to produce material resources (industry,

Figure 1.1

A Comparison of Economic Systems

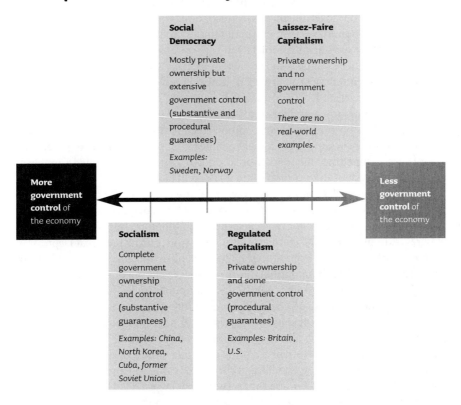

Social Democracy

Mostly private ownership but extensive government control (substantive and procedural guarantees)

Examples: Sweden, Norway

Laissez-Faire Capitalism

Private ownership and no government control

There are no real-world examples.

More government control of the economy

Less government control of the economy

Socialism

Complete government ownership and control (substantive guarantees)

Examples: China, North Korea, Cuba, former Soviet Union

Regulated Capitalism

Private ownership and some government control (procedural guarantees)

Examples: Britain, U.S.

Economic systems are defined largely by the degree to which government owns the means by which material resources are produced (for example, factories and industry) and controls economic decision making. On a scale ranging from socialism—complete government ownership and control of the economy (on the left)—to laissez-faire capitalism—complete individual ownership and control of the economy (on the right)—social democracies would be located in the center. These hybrid systems are characterized by mostly private ownership of the means of production but considerable government control over economic decisions.

business, and land, for instance) are privately owned, and decisions about production and distribution are left to individuals operating through the free-market process. Capitalist economies rely on the market—the process of supply and demand—to decide how much of a given item to produce or how much to charge for it. In capitalist countries, people do not believe that the government is capable of making such judgments; they want to keep such decisions out of the hands of government and in the hands of individuals, whom they believe know best about what they want. The philosophy that corresponds with this belief is called laissez-faire capitalism, from a French term that, loosely translated, means "let people do as they wish." The government has no economic role at all in such a system. However, no economic system today maintains a purely unregulated form of capitalism, with the government completely uninvolved.

Like most other countries today, the United States has a system of **regulated capitalism**. It maintains a capitalist economy, and individual freedom from government interference remains the norm, but it allows government to step in and regulate the economy to guarantee individual rights and to provide **procedural guarantees** that the rules will work smoothly and fairly. Although in theory the market ought to provide everything that people need and want, and should regulate itself as well, sometimes the market breaks down, or fails. In regulated capitalism the government steps in to try to fix it.

Markets have cycles: periods of growth are often followed by periods of slowdown or recession. Individuals and businesses look to government for protection from these cyclical effects—for example, when Franklin Roosevelt created the Works Progress Administration to get Americans back to work during the Great Depression or, more recently, when Congress attempted to stabilize the economy in the wake of the collapse caused by the subprime mortgage crisis in the fall of 2008. Government may also act to ensure the safety of the consumer public and of working people, or to encourage fair business practices (like prevention of monopolies), or to provide goods and services that people have no incentive to produce themselves.

Highways, streetlights, libraries, museums, schools, Social Security, national defense, and a clean environment are some examples of the goods and services that many people are unable or unwilling to produce privately. Consequently government undertakes to provide these things (with money provided by taxpayers) and, in doing so, becomes not only a political but an economic actor as well. To the extent that government gets involved in a capitalist economy, we move away from laissez-faire to regulated capitalism.

Socialism

In a **socialist economy** like that of the former Soviet Union (based loosely on the ideas of German economist Karl Marx), economic decisions are made not by individuals through the market but rather by politicians, based on their judgment of what society needs. Instead of allowing the market to determine the proper distribution of material resources, politicians decide what the distribution ought to be and then create economic policy to bring about that outcome. In other words, they emphasize not procedural guarantees of fair rules and process, but rather **substantive guarantees** of what they believe to be fair outcomes.

According to the basic values of a socialist or communist system (although some theoretical differences exist between the two, they are similar for our purposes here), it is unjust for some people to own more property than others and to have power over them because of it. Consequently, the theory goes, the state or society—not corporations or individuals—should own the property (like land, factories, and corporations). In such systems, the public and private spheres overlap, and politics controls the distribution of all resources. The societies that have tried to put these theories into practice have ended up with very repressive political systems, but Marx hoped that eventually socialism would evolve to a point where each individual had control over his or her own life—a radical form of democracy.

Many theories hold that socialism is possible only after a revolution that thoroughly overthrows the old system to make way for new values and institutions. This is what happened in Russia in 1917 and in China in the 1940s. Since the socialist economies of the former Soviet Union and Eastern Europe have fallen apart, socialism has been left with few supporters, although some nations, like China, North Korea, and Cuba, still claim allegiance to it.

Social Democracy

Some countries in Western Europe, especially the Scandinavian nations of Norway, Denmark, and Sweden, have developed hybrid economic systems. As noted in Figure 1.1, these systems represent something of a middle ground between socialist and capitalist systems. Primarily capitalist, in that they believe most property can be privately held, proponents of **social democracy** nonetheless argue that the values of equality promoted by socialism are attractive and can be brought about by democratic reform rather than revolution. Believing that the economy does not have to be owned by the state for its effects to be controlled by the state, social democratic countries attempt to strike a difficult balance between providing substantive guarantees of fair outcomes and procedural guarantees of fair rules.

Since World War II, the citizens of many western European nations have elected social democrats to office, where they have enacted policies to bring about more equality—for instance, the elimination of poverty and unemployment, better housing, and adequate health care for all. Even where social democratic governments are voted out of office, such programs have proved so popular that it is often difficult for new leaders to alter them.

Political Systems and the Concept of Citizenship

Different ideas about power and the social order,
different models of governing

Just as there are different kinds of economic systems, there are different sorts of political systems, based on different ideas about who should have power and what the social order should be—that is, how much public regulation there should be over individual behavior. For our purposes, we can divide political systems into two types: those in which the government has the power to impose a particular social order, deciding how individuals ought to behave, and those in which individuals exercise personal power over most of their own behavior and ultimately over government as well. These two types of systems are not just different in a theoretical sense—they have very real implications for the people who live in them. Thus the notion of citizenship (or the lack of it) is tied closely to the kind of political system a nation has.

Figure 1.2 offers a comparison of these systems. The first type of system, called authoritarian government, potentially has total power over its subjects; the second type, nonauthoritarian government, permits citizens to limit the state's power by claiming rights that the government must protect. Another way to think about this, to use the terminology we introduced in the previous section, is that in authoritarian systems, government makes substantive decisions about how people ought to live their lives; in nonauthoritarian systems, government merely guarantees that there are fair rules and leaves the rest to individual control. Sometimes governments that exercise substantive decision making in the economic realm also do so with respect to the social order. But, as Figure 1.3 shows, there are several possible combinations of economic and political systems.

Authoritarian Systems

Authoritarian governments give ultimate power to the state rather than to the people to decide how they ought to live their lives. By *authoritarian governments,* we usually mean those in which the people cannot effectively claim rights against the state; where the state chooses to exercise its power, the people have no choice but to submit to its will. Authoritarian governments can take various forms: sovereignty can be vested in an individual (dictatorship or monarchy), in God (theocracy), in the state itself (fascism), or in a ruling class (oligarchy).

When a system combines an authoritarian government with a socialist economy, we say that the system is **totalitarian**. That is, as in the earlier example of the former Soviet Union, it may exercise its power over every part of society—economic, social, political, and moral—leaving little or no private realm for individuals.

An authoritarian state may also limit its own power. In such cases, it may deny individuals rights in those spheres where it chooses to act, but it may leave large areas of society, such as a capitalist economy, free from governmental interference. Singapore is an example of this type of **authoritarian capitalism**; people have considerable economic freedom, but stringent social regulations limit their noneconomic behavior.

Often authoritarian governments pay lip service to the people, but when push comes to shove, as it usually does in such states, the people have no effective power against the government. Again, government does not just provide guarantees of fair processes for individuals; it guarantees a substantive vision of what life will be like—what individuals will believe, how they will act, what they will choose.

Figure 1.2

A Comparison of Political Systems

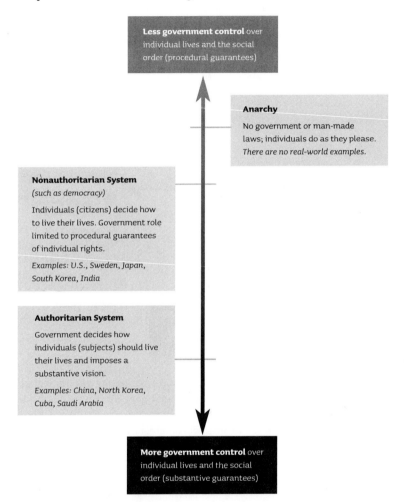

Less government control over individual lives and the social order (procedural guarantees)

Anarchy
No government or man-made laws; individuals do as they please. *There are no real-world examples.*

Nonauthoritarian System
(such as democracy)
Individuals (citizens) decide how to live their lives. Government role limited to procedural guarantees of individual rights.
Examples: U.S., Sweden, Japan, South Korea, India

Authoritarian System
Government decides how individuals (subjects) should live their lives and imposes a substantive vision.
Examples: China, North Korea, Cuba, Saudi Arabia

More government control over individual lives and the social order (substantive guarantees)

Political systems are defined by the extent to which individual citizens or governments decide what the social order should look like, that is, how people should live their collective, noneconomic lives. Except for anarchies, every system allots a role to government to regulate individual behavior, for example, to prohibit murder, rape, and theft. But beyond such basic regulation, political systems differ radically in terms of who gets to determine how individuals live their lives, and whether government's role is simply to provide procedural guarantees that protect individuals' rights to make their own decisions or to provide a much more substantive view of how individuals should behave.

Figure 1.3

Political and Economic Systems

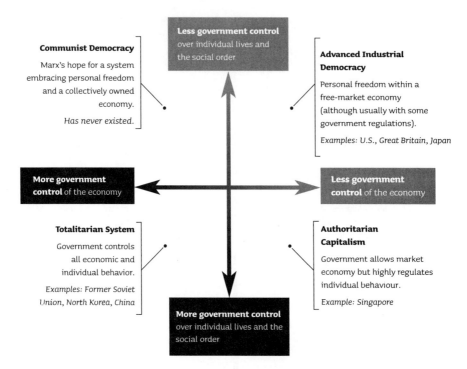

Political systems work in conjunction with economic systems, but government control over the economy does not necessarily translate into tight control over the social order. We have identified four possible combinations of these systems, signified by the labeled points in each quadrant. These points are approximate, however, and some nations cannot be classified so easily. Sweden is an advanced industrial democracy by most measures, for instance, but because of its commitment to substantive economic values, it would be located much closer to the vertical axis.

Democracy and Nonauthoritarian Systems

In nonauthoritarian systems, ultimate power rests with the individuals to make decisions concerning their lives. The most extreme form of nonauthoritarianism is called **anarchy**. Anarchists would do away with government and laws altogether. People advocate anarchy because they value the freedom to do whatever they want more than they value the order and security that governments provide by forbidding or regulating certain kinds of behavior. Few people are true anarchists, however. While anarchy may sound attractive in theory, the inherent difficulties of the position make it hard to practice. For instance, how could you even organize a revolution to get rid of government without some rules about who is to do what and how decisions are to be made?

A less extreme form of nonauthoritarian government, and one much more familiar to us, is **democracy** (from the Greek *demos,* meaning "people"). In democracies, government is not external to the people, as it is in authoritarian systems; in a fundamental sense, government is the people. Recognizing that collective life usually calls for some restrictions on what individuals may do (laws forbidding murder, for instance, or theft), democracies nevertheless try to maximize freedom for the individuals who live under them. Although they generally make decisions through some sort of majority rule, democracies still provide procedural guarantees to preserve individual rights—usually protections of due process (guarantee of a fair trial, right to a lawyer, and so on) and minority rights. This means that if individuals living in a democracy feel their rights have been violated, they have the right to ask government to remedy the situation.

Democracies are based on the principle of **popular sovereignty**; that is, there is no power higher than the people and, in the United States, the document establishing their authority, the Constitution. The central idea here is that no government is considered legitimate unless the governed consent to it, and people are not truly free unless they live under a law of their own making. Theories of democracy vary, however, in how much active control they give to individuals.

- Theorists of **elite democracy** propose that democracy is merely a system of choosing among competing leaders; for the average citizen, input ends after the leader is chosen.[6] Some adherents of this view hold that actual political decisions are made not by elected officials but by the elite in business, the military, the media, and education. In this view, elections are merely symbolic—to perpetuate the illusion that citizens have consented to their government or to convince them they have a stake in the system.
- Advocates of **pluralist democracy** argue that what is important is not so much individual participation but membership in groups that participate in government decision making on their members' behalf, such as labor unions, professional associations, and environmental or business groups.[7] Some pluralists argue that individual citizens have little effective power and that only when they are organized into groups are they truly a force for government to reckon with.
- Supporters of **participatory democracy** claim that more than consent or majority rule in making governmental decisions is needed. Individuals have the right to control all the circumstances of their lives, and direct democratic participation should take place not only in government but in industry, education, and community affairs as well.[8] For advocates of this view, democracy is more than a way to make decisions: it is a way of life, an end in itself.

These theories about how democracy should (or does) work locate the focus of power in individuals, groups, and elites. Real-world examples of democracy probably include elements of more than one of these theories; they are not mutually exclusive.

The people of many Western countries have found the idea of democracy persuasive enough to found their governments on it. In recent years, especially since the mid-1980s, democracy has been spreading rapidly through the rest of the world as the preferred form of government. No longer the primary province of industrialized Western nations, attempts at democratic governance now extend into Asia, Latin America, Africa, Eastern Europe, and the republics of the former Soviet Union. There are many varieties of democracy other than our own. Some democracies make the legislature (the representatives of the people) the most important authority; some retain a monarch with limited powers; some hold referenda at the national level to get direct feedback on how the people want them to act on specific issues.

Most democratic forms of government, because of their commitment to procedural values, practice a capitalist form of economics. Fledgling democracies may rely on a high degree of government economic regulation, but **advanced industrial democracies** combine a considerable amount of personal freedom with a free-market (though still usually regulated) economy. It is rare to find a country that is truly committed to individual political freedom that also tries to regulate the economy heavily. The economist Karl Marx believed that radical democracy would coexist with communally owned property, in a form of **communist democracy**, but such a system has never existed, and most real-world systems fall somewhere along the horizontal continuum shown in Figure 1.3.

The Role of the People

What is important about the political and economic systems we have been sorting out here is that they have a direct impact on the lives of the people who live in them. So far we have given a good deal of attention to the latter parts of Lasswell's definition of politics. But easily as important as the what and the how in Lasswell's formulation is the who. Underlying the different political theories we have looked at are fundamental differences in the powers and opportunities possessed by everyday people.

In authoritarian systems, the people are **subjects** of their government. They possess no rights that protect them from that government; they must do whatever the government says or face the consequences, without any other recourse. They have obligations to the state but no rights or privileges to offset those obligations. They may be winners or losers in government decisions, but they have very little control over which it may be.

Everyday people in democratic systems have a potentially powerful role to play. They are more than mere subjects; they are **citizens**, or members of a political community with rights as well as obligations. Democratic theory says that power is drawn from the people—that the people are sovereign, that they must consent to be governed, and that their government must respond to their will. In practical terms, this may not seem to mean much, since not consenting doesn't necessarily give us the right to disobey government. It does give us the option of leaving, however, and seeking a more congenial set of rules elsewhere. Subjects of authoritarian governments rarely have this freedom.

In democratic systems, the rules of government can provide for all sorts of different roles for citizens. At a minimum, citizens can usually vote in periodic and free elections. They may be able to run for office, subject to certain conditions, like age or residence. They can support candidates for office, organize political groups or parties, attend meetings, write letters to officials or the press, march in protest or support of various causes, even speak out on street corners.

Theoretically, democracies are ruled by "the people," but different democracies have at times been very selective about whom they count as citizens. Beginning with our days as colonists, Americans have excluded many groups of people from citizenship: people of the "wrong" religion, income bracket, race, ethnic group, lifestyle, and gender have all been excluded from enjoying the full rights of colonial or U.S. citizenship at different times. In fact, American history is the story of those various groups fighting to be included as citizens. Just because a system is called a democracy is no guarantee that all or even most of its residents possess the status of citizen.

Citizens in democratic systems are said to possess certain rights or areas where government cannot infringe on their freedom. Just what these rights are varies in different democracies, but they usually include freedom of speech and the press, the right to assemble, and certain legal protections guaranteeing fair treatment in the criminal justice system. Almost all of these rights are designed to allow citizens to criticize their government openly without threat of retribution by that government.

Citizens of democracies also possess obligations or responsibilities to the public realm. They have the obligation to obey the law, for instance, once they have consented to the government (even if that consent amounts only to not leaving). They may also have the obligation to pay taxes, serve in the military, or sit on juries. Some theorists argue that virtuous citizens should put community interests ahead of personal interests. A less extreme version of this view holds that while citizens may go about their own business and pursue their own interests, they must continue to pay attention to their government. Participating in its decisions is the price of maintaining their own liberty and, by extension, the liberty of the whole. Should citizens abdicate this role by tuning out of public life, the safeguards of democracy can disappear, to be replaced with the trappings of authoritarian government. There is nothing automatic about democracy. If left unattended by nonvigilant citizens, the freedoms of democracy can be lost to an all-powerful state, and citizens can become transformed into subjects of the government they failed to keep in check.

This Western notion of citizenship as conferring both rights and responsibilities first became popular in the 1700s, as Europeans emerged from the

Middle Ages and began to reject notions that rulers were put on earth by God to be obeyed unconditionally. Two British philosophers, Thomas Hobbes and John Locke, led the new way of thinking about subjecthood and citizenship. Governments are born not because God ordains them, but because life without government is "solitary, poor, nasty, brutish, and short" in Hobbes's words, and "inconvenient" in Locke's. The foundation of government is reason, not faith, and reason leads people to consent to being governed because they are better off that way.

People have freedom and rights before government exists, declared Locke. When they decide they are better off with government than without it, they enter into a **social contract**, giving up some of those rights in exchange for the protection of the rest of their rights by a government established by the majority. If that government fails to protect their rights, it has broken the contract, and the people are free to form a new government or not, as they please. But the key element here is that for authority to be legitimate, citizens must consent to it. Note, however, that nowhere did Locke suggest that all people ought to participate in politics, or that people are necessarily equal. In fact, he was concerned mostly with the preservation of private property, suggesting that only property owners would have cause to be bothered with government because only they have something concrete to lose.

Meanwhile, as philosophers in Europe were beginning to explore the idea of individual rights and democratic governance, there had long been democratic stirrings on the founders' home continent. The Iroquois Confederacy was an alliance of five (and eventually six) East Coast Native American nations whose constitution, the "Great Law of Peace," impressed such American leaders as Benjamin Franklin with its suggestions of federalism, separation of powers, checks and balances, and consensus-building. While historians are not sure that these ideas had any direct influence on the founders' thinking about American governance, they were clearly part of the stew of ideas that the founders could dip into, and some scholars make the case that their influence was significant.[9]

Democracy in America
Limited participation to limit the impact of a self-interested citizenry

For our purposes, the most important thing about these ideas about politics is that they were prevalent at the same time the American founders were thinking about how to build a new government. Locke particularly influenced the writings of James Madison, a major author of our Constitution. The founders wanted to base their new government on popular consent, but they did not want to go too far. Madison, as we will see, was particularly worried about a system that was too democratic.

The Dangers of Democracy

Enthusiastic popular participation under the government established by the Articles of Confederation—the document that tied the colonies together before the Constitution was drafted—almost ended the new government before it began. Like Locke, Madison thought government had a duty to protect property, and if people who didn't have property could get involved in politics, they might not care about protecting the property of others. Worse, they might form "factions," groups pursuing their own self-interests rather than the public interest, and even try to get some of that property for themselves. So Madison rejected notions of "pure democracy," in which all citizens would have direct power to control government, and opted instead for what he called a "republic."

A **republic**, according to Madison, differs from a democracy mainly in that it employs representation and can work in a large state. Most theorists agree that democracy is impossible in practice if there are a lot of citizens and all have to be heard from. But we do not march to Washington or phone our legislator every time we want to register a political preference. Instead, we choose representatives—members of the House of Representatives, senators, and the president—to represent our views for us. Madison thought this would be a safer system than direct participation (all of us crowding into town halls or the Capitol) because public passions would be cooled off by the process. You might be furious about health care costs when you vote for your senator, but he or she will represent your views with less anger. The founders hoped the representatives would be older, wealthier, and wiser than the average American and that they would be better able to make cool and rational decisions.

Competing Views of Citizenship

The notion of citizenship that emerges from Madison's writings is not a very flattering one for the average American, and it is important to note that it is not the only ideal of citizenship in the American political tradition. Madison's low expectations of the American public were a reaction to an earlier tradition that had put great faith in the ability of democratic man to put the interests of the community ahead of his own, to act with what scholars call "republican virtue." According to this idea, a virtuous citizen could be trusted with the most serious of political decisions because if he (women were not citizens at that time) were properly educated and kept from the influence of scandal and corruption, he would be willing to sacrifice his own advancement for the sake of the whole. His decisions would be guided not by his self-interest but by his public-interested spirit. At the time of the founding, hope was strong that although the court of the British monarch had become corrupt beyond redemption, America was still a land where virtue could triumph over greed. In fact, for many people this was a crucial argument for American independence: severing the ties would prevent that corruption from creeping across the Atlantic and would allow the new country to keep its virtuous political nature free from the British taint.[10]

Pledge allegiance

Military personnel take the oath of allegiance to the United States during a naturalization ceremony. Immigrants may serve in the U.S. military regardless of their citizenship. When becoming naturalized citizens, they renounce their former home and vow to "support and defend" the Constitution and laws of the United States "against all enemies."

When democratic rules that relied on the virtue, or public interestedness, of the American citizen were put into effect, however, especially in the days immediately after independence, these expectations seemed to be doomed. Instead of acting for the good of the community, Americans seemed to be just as self-interested as the British had been. When given nearly free rein to rule themselves, they had no trouble remembering the rights of citizenship but ignored the responsibilities that come with it. They passed laws in state legislatures that canceled debts and contracts and otherwise worked to the advantage of the poor majority of farmers and debtors—and that seriously threatened the economic and political stability of the more well-to-do. It was in this context of national disappointment that Madison devised his notion of the republic. Since people had proved—so he thought—not to be motivated by virtue, he felt that a government must be designed that would produce virtuous results, regardless of the character of the citizens who participated in it.

Today two competing views of citizenship still exist in the United States. One, echoing Madison, sees human nature as self-interested and holds that individual participation in government should be limited, that "too much" democracy is a bad thing. The second view continues to put its faith in the citizen's ability to act virtuously, not just for his or her own good but for the common good. President John F. Kennedy movingly evoked such a view in his inaugural address in 1961, when he urged Americans to "ask not what your country can do for you—ask what you can do for your country." These views of citizenship have coexisted throughout our history. Especially in times of crisis such as war or national tragedy, the second view of individual sacrifice for the public good has seemed more prominent. In the wake of September 11, 2001, citizens freely gave their time and money to help their fellow countrypeople and were more willing to join the military and volunteer for community service. At other times, and particularly at the national level of politics, the dominant view of citizenship has appeared to be one of self-interested actors going about their own business with little regard for the public good. When observers claim, as they often do today, that there is a crisis of American citizenship, they usually mean that civic virtue is taking second place to self-interest as a guiding principle of citizenship.

These two notions of citizenship do not necessarily have to be at loggerheads, however. Where self-interest and public spirit meet in democratic practice is in the process of deliberation, collectively considering and evaluating goals and ideals for communal life and action. Individuals bring their own agendas and interests, but in the process of discussing them with others holding different views, parties can find common ground and turn it into a base for collective action. Conflict can erupt too, of course, but the process of deliberation at least creates a forum from which the possibility of consensus might emerge. Scholar and journalist E. J. Dionne reflects on this possibility: "At the heart of republicanism [remember that this is not a reference to our modern party] is the belief that self-government is not a drab necessity but a joy to be treasured. It is the view that politics is not simply a grubby confrontation of competing interests but an arena in which citizens can learn from each other and discover an 'enlightened self-interest' in common." Despite evidence of a growing American disaffection for politics, Dionne hopes that Americans will find again the "joy" in self-governance because, he warns, "A nation that hates politics will not long thrive as a democracy."[11]

> Where self-interest and public spirit meet in democratic practice is in the process of deliberation. . . .

Who Is a Citizen and Who Is Not?
Native-born and naturalized citizens

Citizenship is not just a normative concept—that is, a prescription for how governments ought to treat residents and how those residents ought to act. It is also a very precise legal status. A fundamental element of democracy is not only the careful specification of the rights granted and the obligations incurred in citizenship but also an equally careful legal description of just who is a citizen and how that status can be acquired by noncitizens.

If you are born in any of the fifty states, in the District of Columbia, or in most of America's overseas territories, such as Puerto Rico or Guam, you are an American citizen, whether your parents are Americans or not. This rule follows the principle of international law called *jus soli*, which means literally "the right of the soil." The exceptions to this rule in the United States are children born to foreign diplomats serving in the United States and children born on foreign ships in U.S. waters. These children would not be considered U.S. citizens. According to another legal principle, *jus sanguinis* ("the right by blood"), if you are born outside the United States to American parents, you are also an American citizen (or you can become one if you are adopted by American parents). Interestingly, if you are born in the United States but one of your parents holds citizenship in another country, depending on that country's laws, you may be able to hold dual citizenship. Most countries, including the United States, require that a child with dual citizenship declare allegiance to one country on turning age eighteen. It is worth noting that requirements for U.S. citizenship, particularly as they affect people born outside the country, have changed frequently over time.

So far, citizenship seems relatively straightforward. But as we know, the United States since before its birth has been attractive to **immigrants**, people who are citizens or subjects of another country who come here to live and work. Today there are strict limitations on the numbers of immigrants who may legally enter the country. There are also strict rules governing the criteria for entry. If immigrants come here legally on permanent resident visas—that is, if they follow the rules and regulations of the U.S. Citizenship and Immigration Services (USCIS)—they may be eligible to apply for citizenship through a process called **naturalization**.

However, many people who come to the United States do not come as legal permanent residents. The USCIS refers to these people as nonimmigrants. Some arrive seeking asylum, or protection. These are political **refugees**, who are allowed into the United States if they face or are threatened with persecution because of their race, religion, nationality, membership in a particular social group, or political opinions. Not everyone who feels threatened is given legal refugee status, however; the USCIS requires that the fear of persecution be "well founded," and it is itself the final judge of a well-founded fear. Refugees may become legal permanent residents after they have lived here continuously for one year (although there are annual limits on the number who may do so), at which time they can begin accumulating the in-residence time required to become a citizen, if they wish to.

Other people who may come to the United States legally but without official permanent resident status include visitors, foreign government officials, students, international representatives, temporary workers, members of foreign media, and exchange visitors. These people are expected to return to their home countries and not take up permanent residence in the United States.

Illegal immigrants have arrived here by avoiding the USCIS regulations, usually because they would not qualify for one reason or another. American laws have become increasingly harsh with respect to illegal immigrants, but people continue to come anyway. Many illegal immigrants act like "citizens," obeying the laws, paying taxes, and sending their children to school. Nonetheless, some areas of the country, particularly those near the Mexican-American border, like Texas, California, and Arizona, often have serious problems brought on by illegal immigration. Even with border controls to regulate the number of new arrivals, communities can find themselves swamped with new residents, often poor and unskilled, looking for a better life. Because their children must be educated and they themselves may be entitled to receive social services, they can pose a significant financial burden on those communities without necessarily increasing the available funds. Although many illegals pay taxes, many also work off the books, meaning they do not contribute to the tax base. Furthermore, most income taxes are federal, and federal money is distributed back to states and localities to fund social services based on the population count in the census. Since illegal immigrants are understandably reluctant to come forward to be counted, their communities are typically under-funded in that respect as well.

Even people without legal permanent resident status have rights and responsi-bilities in the United States, just as U.S. citizens do when they travel to other coun-tries. Immigrants enjoy some rights, primarily legal protections. Not only are they entitled to due process in the courts, but the U.S. Supreme Court has ruled that it is illegal to discriminate against immigrants in the United States.[12] Nevertheless, their rights are limited; they cannot, for instance, vote in our national elections (although some localities, in the hopes of integrating immigrants into their communities, allow them to vote in local elections[13]) or decide to live here permanently without permission (which may or may not be granted). In addition, immigrants, even legal ones, are subject to the decisions of the USCIS, which is empowered by Congress to exercise authority in immigration matters.

What Do American Citizens Believe?
A common culture based on shared values

Making a single nation out of such a diverse people is no easy feat. It is possible only because, despite all our differences, Americans share some fundamental attitudes and beliefs about how the world works and how it should work. These ideas, our political culture, pull us together and, indeed, provide a framework in which we can also disagree politically over who gets what without resorting to vio-lence and civil war.

American Political Culture: Ideas That Unite Us

Political culture refers to the general political orientation or disposition of a nation—the shared values and beliefs about the nature of the political world that give us a common language in which to discuss and debate political ideas. **Values** are ideals or principles that most people agree are important, even though they may disagree on exactly how the value—such as "equality" or "freedom"—ought to be defined. Note that statements about values and beliefs are not descriptive of how the world actually is but rather are prescriptive, or normative, statements about how the value-holders believe the world ought to be. Our culture consists of deep-seated, collectively held ideas about how life should be lived. **Normative** statements aren't true or false but depend for their worth on the arguments that are made to back them up. Often we take our own culture (that is, our common beliefs about how the world should work) so much for granted that we aren't even aware of it. For that reason, it is often easier to see our own political culture by contrasting it to another.

Political culture is shared, although certainly some individuals find themselves at odds with it. When we say, "Americans think . . . ," we mean that most Americans hold those views, not that there is unanimous agreement on them. Political culture is handed down from generation to generation, through families, schools, communities, literature, churches and synagogues, and so on, helping to provide stability for the nation by ensuring that a majority of citizens are well grounded in and committed to the basic values that sustain it. We talk about the process through which values are transferred in Chapter 10, "Public Opinion."

> . . . Americans generally think government should guarantee fair processes—such as a free market to distribute goods, majority rule to make decisions, and due process to determine guilt and innocence. . . .

In American political culture, our expectations of government focus on rules and processes rather than on results. For example, we think government should guarantee a fair playing field but not guarantee equal outcomes for all the players. In addition, we believe that individuals are responsible for their own welfare and that what is good for them is good for society as a whole. Our insistence on fair rules is the same emphasis on *procedural guarantees* we saw in our earlier discussion of capitalism, whereas the belief in the primacy of the individual citizen is called **individualism**. American culture is not wholly procedural and individualistic—indeed, differences on these matters constitute some of the major partisan divisions in American politics—but it tends to be more so than is the case in most other nations.

When we say that American political culture is procedural, we mean that Americans generally think government should guarantee fair processes—such as a free market to distribute goods, majority rule to make decisions, and due process to determine guilt and innocence—rather than specific outcomes. By contrast, people in the social democratic countries of Sweden, Norway, and Denmark typically believe that government should actively seek to realize the values of equality—perhaps to guarantee a certain quality of life for all citizens or to increase equality of income. While American politics does set some substantive goals for public policy, Americans are generally more comfortable ensuring that things are done in a fair and proper way, and trusting that the outcomes will be good ones because the rules are fair. Although the American government does get involved in social programs and welfare, it aims more at helping individuals get on their feet so that they can participate in the market (fair procedures) rather than at cleaning up slums or eliminating poverty (substantive goals).

The individualistic nature of American political culture means that individuals, not government or society, are seen as responsible for their own well-being. This notion contrasts with a collectivist social democratic point of view, which holds that what is good for society may not be the same as what is in the interest of individuals. Thus our politics revolves around the belief that individuals are usually the best judges of what is good for them; we assume that what is good for society will automatically follow. American government rarely asks citizens to make major economic sacrifices for the public good, although individuals often do so privately and voluntarily. Where Americans are asked to make economic sacrifices, like paying taxes, they are unpopular and more modest than in most other countries.

A collective interest that supersedes individual interests is generally invoked in the United States only in times of war or national crisis. This echoes the two American notions of self-interested and public-interested citizenship we discussed earlier.

We can see our American procedural and individualistic perspective when we examine the different meanings of three core American values: democracy, freedom, and equality.

- **Democracy** Democracy in America, as we have seen, means representative democracy, based on consent and majority rule. Basically, American democracy is a procedure for making political decisions, for choosing political leaders, and for selecting policies for the nation. It is seen as a fundamentally just or fair way of making decisions because every individual who cares to participate is heard in the process, and all interests are considered. We don't reject a democratically made decision because it is not fair; it is fair precisely because it is democratically made. Democracy is valued primarily not for the way it makes citizens feel, or the effects it has on them, but for the decisions it produces. Americans see democracy as the appropriate procedure for making public decisions—that is, decisions about government—but generally not for decisions in the private realm. Rarely do employees have a binding vote on company policy, for example, as they do in some Scandinavian countries.

- **Freedom** Americans also put a very high premium on the value of freedom, defined as freedom for the individual from restraint by the state. This view of freedom is procedural in the sense that it holds that no unfair restrictions should be put in the way of your pursuit of what you want, but it does not guarantee you any help in achieving those things. For instance, when Americans say, "We are all free to get a job," we mean that no discriminatory laws or other legal barriers are stopping us from applying for any particular position; a substantive view of freedom would ensure us the training to get a job so that our freedom meant a positive opportunity, not just the absence of restraint. Americans' extraordinary commitment can be seen nowhere so clearly as in the Bill of Rights, the first ten amendments to the U.S. Constitution, which guarantee our basic civil liberties, the areas where government cannot interfere with individual action. (See Chapter 4, "Fundamental American Liberties," for a complete discussion of our civil liberties.) Finally, our proceduralism is echoed in the value we attach to economic freedom, the freedom to participate in the marketplace, to acquire money and property, and to do with those resources pretty much as we please. Americans believe that government should protect our property, not take it away or regulate our use of it too heavily. Our commitment to individualism is apparent here, too. Even if society as a whole would be better off if we paid down the federal debt (the amount our government owes from spending more than it brings in), our individualistic view of economic freedom means that Americans have one of the lowest tax rates in the industrialized world. This reflects our national tendency in normal times to emphasize the rights of citizenship over its obligations.

- **Equality** A third central value in American political culture is equality. For Americans, equality is valued not because we want individuals to be the same but because we want them to be treated the same. Equality in America means government should guarantee equality of treatment, of access, and of opportunity, not equality of result. People should have equal access to run the race, but we don't expect them all to finish in the same place. Thus, we believe in political equality (one person, one vote) and equality before the law—that the law shouldn't make unreasonable distinctions among people the basis for treating them differently, and that all people should have equal access to the legal system. One problem the courts have faced is deciding what counts as a reasonable distinction. Can the law justifiably discriminate between—that is, treat differently—men and women, minorities and white Protestants, rich and poor, young and old? When the rules treat people differently, even if the goal is to make them more equal in the long run, many Americans get very upset. Witness the controversy surrounding affirmative action policies in this country. The point of such policies is to allow special opportunities to members of groups that have been discriminated against in the past, in order to remedy the long-term effects of that discrimination. For many Americans, such policies violate our commitment to procedural solutions. They wonder how treating people unequally can be fair.

American Ideologies: Ideas That Divide Us

Most Americans are united in their commitment to proceduralism and individualism at some level, and to the key values of democracy, freedom, and equality, but a lot of room remains for disagreement on other ideas and issues. The sets of beliefs and opinions about politics, the economy, and society that help people make sense of their world, and that can divide them into opposing camps, are called **ideologies.** Sharing a political culture doesn't mean we don't have ideological differences, but because we share core values about how the world should be, we have a common language in which to debate and resolve our differences, and a set of boundaries that keep those differences from getting out of hand. And again, like the values and beliefs that underlie our culture, our ideologies are based on normative prescriptions. Remember that one of the reasons we can disagree so passionately on political issues is that normative statements about the world are not true or false, good or bad—instead they depend for their force on the arguments we make to defend them. While it might seem clear as a bell to us that our values are right and true, to a person who disagrees with our prescriptions, we are as wrong as they think we are. And so we debate and argue.

But because we share that political culture, the range of debate in the United States is fairly narrow. We have no successful communist or socialist parties here, for instance. The ideologies on which those parties are founded seem unappealing to most Americans because they violate the norms of procedural and individualistic culture. The two main ideological camps in the United States are the liberals (associated, since the 1930s, with the Democratic Party) and the conservatives (with the Republicans), with

Free to Protest
The U.S. Constitution guarantees freedom of speech and assembly. Tea Party demonstrators march in protest of Obama administration policies. One man's feelings are made clear as he wraps himself in a Don't Tread on Me flag with a picture of Obama depicted as the Joker.

many Americans falling somewhere in between. But because we are all part of American political culture, we are still procedural and individualistic, still believe in democracy, freedom, and equality, even if we are also liberals or conservatives.

There are lots of different ways of characterizing American ideologies. In general terms, we can say that **conservatives** tend to be in favor of traditional social values, distrust government action except in matters of national security, are slow to advocate change, and place a priority on the maintenance of social order. **Liberals**, in contrast, value the possibilities of progress and change, trust government, look for innovations as answers to social problems, and focus on the expansion of individual rights and expression. For a more rigorous understanding of ideology in America, we can focus on the two main ideological dimensions of economics and social order issues.

Traditionally we have understood ideology to be centered on differences in economic views, much like those located on our economic continuum (see Figure 1.1). Based on these economic ideological dimensions, we often say that the liberals who take a more positive view of government action and advocate a large role for government in regulating the economy are on the far left, and those conservatives, more suspicious of government, who think government control should be minimal are on the far right. Because we lack any widespread radical socialist traditions in the United States, both American liberals and conservatives are found on the right side of the broader economic continuum.

In the 1980s and 1990s, another ideological dimension became prominent in the United States. Perhaps because, as some researchers have argued, most people are able to meet their basic economic needs, many Americans began to focus less on economic questions and more on issues of morality and quality of life. The new ideological dimension, which is analogous to the social order dimension we discussed earlier, divides people on the question of how much control government should have over the moral and social order—whether government's role should be limited to protecting individual rights and providing procedural guarantees of equality and due process, or whether the government should be involved in making more substantive judgments about how people should live their lives.

While few people in the United States want to go so far as to allow government to make all moral and political decisions for its subjects, there are some who hold that it is the government's job to create and protect a preferred social order, although visions of what that preferred order should be may differ. A conservative view of the preferred social order usually includes an emphasis on religion in public life (prayer in school, public posting of religious documents like the Ten Commandments), a rejection of abortion and physician-assisted suicide, promotion of traditional family values (including a rejection of gay marriage and other gay rights), emphasis on the "American Way" (rejecting the value of diversity for conformity and restricting immigration), and censorship of materials that promote alternative visions of the social order. Conservatives are not the only ones who seek to tell individuals how to live their lives, however. There is also a newer, more liberal vision of the social order that prescribes an expanded government role to regulate individual lives to achieve different substantive ends—the preservation of the environment, for instance (laws that require individuals to recycle or that tax gasoline to encourage conservation), or the creation of a sense of community based on equality and protection of minorities (rules that urge political correctness, affirmative action, and censorship of pornography), or even the promotion of individual safety (laws promoting gun control, seat belts, and motorcycle helmets).

Clearly this social order ideological dimension does not dovetail neatly with the more traditional liberal and conservative orientations toward government action. Figure 1.4 shows some of the ideological positions that are yielded by these two dimensions, though note that this figure shows a detail of the broader political spectrum that we saw in Figure 1.3 and is focused on the narrower spectrum commonly found in an advanced industrial democracy. For instance, **economic liberals**, who are willing to allow government to make substantive decisions about the economy, tend to embrace the top procedural individualistic position on the social order dimension, and so they fall into the upper-left quadrant of the figure. Some economic policies they favor are job training and housing subsidies for the poor, taxation to support social programs, and affirmative action to ensure that opportunities for economic success are truly equal. As far as government regulation of individuals' private lives, however, these liberals favor a hands-off stance, preferring individuals to have maximum freedom over their noneconomic affairs. While they are willing to let government regulate behaviors such as murder, rape, and theft, they believe that most moral issues (such as abortion and the right to die) are questions of individual responsibility. They have an expansive vision of individual rights, valuing diversity and including in the system people who historically have been left out—women, minorities, gays, and immigrants. Their love for their country is tempered by the view that the government should be held to the same strict procedural standard to which individuals are held—laws must be followed, checks and balances must be adhered to in order to limit government power, and individual rights must be protected, even when the individuals are citizens of another country.

Economic conservatives share their liberal counterparts' reluctance to allow government interference in people's private lives, but they combine this with a conviction that government should limit involvement in the economy as well. In the upper-right quadrant of the figure, these economic conservatives prefer government to limit its role in economic decision making to regulation of the market (like changing interest rates and cutting taxes to end recessions), elimination of "unfair" trade practices such as monopolies, and provision of some public goods such as highways and national defense. When it comes to immigration they favor more open policies, since immigrants often work more cheaply and help keep the labor market competitive for business. The most extreme holders of economic conservative views are called **libertarians**, people who believe that only minimal government action in any sphere is acceptable. Consequently, economic conservatives also hold the government accountable for sticking to the constitutional checks and balances that limit its own power.

In the lower-left quadrant of the figure, people tend to favor a substantive government role in achieving a more equal distribution of material resources (such as welfare programs and health care for the poor) but want that equality carried into the social order as well. They are willing, at least to some extent, to allow government to regulate individual behavior to create what they see as a better society. While they continue to want the freedom to make individual moral choices that economic liberals want, **social liberals** are happy to see some government action to realize a substantive vision of what society should be like. This liberal vision is forward looking and adaptive to changing social roles and technological progress. It seeks to regulate the effects of that progress, protecting the physical environment and individual well-being from the hazards of modern life. Government is valued for how well it realizes this vision of substantive fairness, and it is criticized when it falls short. The most extreme adherents of social liberalism are sometimes called **communitarians** for their strong commitment to a community based on radical equality of all people. It is a collectivist, community-based vision that holds that individuals should be expected to make some sacrifices for the betterment of society. Because collectivism is not very popular in the American individualist culture, strong adherents to this view are relatively few in number. Many economic liberals, however, pick up some of the policy prescriptions of social liberals, like environmentalism, gun control, and affirmative action.

To the right of them, and below economic conservatives on the figure, are **social conservatives**. These people share economic conservatives' views on limited government involvement in the economy but with less force and perhaps for different

Figure 1.4

Ideological Beliefs in the United States

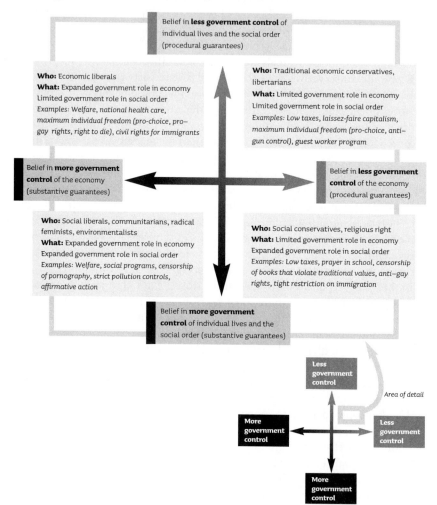

Although committed generally to a procedural and individualistic political culture (this entire figure would fit in the upper-right quadrant of Figure 1.3), Americans still find plenty of room for political disagreement. This figure outlines the two main dimensions of that conflict: beliefs about government's role in the economy and beliefs about government's role in establishing a preferred social order. Those ideological beliefs on the right side of the figure are conservative beliefs, and those on the left side are more liberal. The axes in these figures are continuums and do not represent all-or-nothing positions; most Americans fall somewhere in between.

reasons. (In fact, many social conservatives, as members of the working class, were once liberals under Franklin Roosevelt's New Deal in the 1930s.) Their primary concern is with their vision of the moral tone of life, not economics, and it does not seem incongruous to them that they should want a limited economic role for government while requiring that politicians enact a fairly substantive set of laws to create a particular moral order. Their vision of that order includes an emphasis on fundamentalist religious values and traditional family roles, and a rejection of change or diversity that it sees as destructive to the preferred social order. Immigration is threatening because it brings into the system people who are different and threatens to dilute the majority that keeps the social order in place. Social conservatives seek to protect people's moral character rather than their physical or economic well-being, and embrace a notion of community that emphasizes a hierarchical order (everyone in his or her proper place) rather than equality for all. Since limited political power is not valued here, a large and powerful state is appreciated as being a sign of strength on the international stage. Patriotism for social conservatives is not a matter of holding the government to the highest procedural standards, as it is for those at the top half of Figure 1.4. Less worried about limiting government power over individual lives, they adopt more of a "my country right or wrong," "America First" view that sees criticism of the United States as unpatriotic.

Who Fits Where?

Many people, indeed most of us, might find it difficult to identify ourselves as simply "liberal" or "conservative," because we consider ourselves liberal on some issues, conservative on others. The framework in Figure 1.5 allows us to see ourselves and major groups in society as we might line up if we distinguish between economic and social-moral values. We can see, for instance, the real spatial distance that lies between (1) the religious right (as social conservatives are known), who are very conservative on political and moral issues but who were once part of the coalition of southern blue-collar workers who supported Roosevelt on the New Deal; (2) traditional Republicans, who are very conservative on economic issues but often more libertarian on political and moral issues, wanting government to guarantee procedural fairness and keep the peace but otherwise to leave them alone; and (3) moderate Republicans, who are far less conservative economically and morally. In 2008 Republican presidential candidate John McCain had difficulty holding this coalition together. A moderate Republican himself, he was viewed with suspicion by the social conservatives in his party, and he struggled to find the levels of support that were enjoyed by George W. Bush when he ran in 2000 and 2004.

Similarly, the Democrats must try to respond to the *economic liberals* in the party, very procedural on most political and moral issues (barring affirmative action) but relatively (for Americans) substantive on economic concerns, to *social liberals,* substantive on both economic and social issues, and to newer groups, like the *Democratic Leadership Conference* (DLC), that are fairly procedural on political and moral issues but not very substantive on economic matters at all. It was

President Bill Clinton, as a DLC founder, who helped move his party closer to the mainstream from a position that, we can see in Figure 1.5, is clearly out of alignment with the position taken by most Americans. While Al Gore, himself a DLC-er, faced a threat from the more extreme segments on the left in 2000 (Bill Bradley in the primaries and Ralph Nader in the general election), in the 2004 and 2008 presidential races, dislike of George W. Bush united Democrats across their party's ideological spectrum and neither John Kerry nor Barack Obama had difficulty keeping the Democratic coalition together.

How to Use the Themes and Features in This Book

Our primary goal in this book is to get you thinking critically about American politics—to introduce you to the twin tasks of analysis and evaluation with the aid of the themes of power and citizenship. Lasswell's definition of politics gives us a framework of **analysis** for this book; that is, it outlines how we will break down politics into its component parts in order to understand it. Lasswell's definition provides a strong analytic framework because it focuses our attention on questions we can ask to figure out what is going on in politics.

Accordingly, in this book, we analyze American politics in terms of three sets of questions:

- Who are the parties involved? What resources, powers, and rights do they bring to the struggle?
- What do they have at stake? What do they stand to win or lose? Is it power, influence, position, policy, or values?
- How do the rules shape the outcome? Where do the rules come from? What strategies or tactics do the political actors employ to use the rules to get what they want?

If you know who is involved in a political situation, what is at stake, and how (under what rules) the conflict over resources will eventually be resolved, you will have a pretty good grasp of what is going on, and you will probably be able to figure out new situations, even when your days of taking an American government course are far behind you. To get you in the habit of asking those questions, we have designed two features in this text explicitly to reinforce them.

As you found at the start of your reading, each chapter opens with a *What's at Stake?* feature that analyzes a political situation in terms of what various groups of citizens stand to win or lose. Each chapter ends with a *What's at Stake Revisited* feature, where we return to the issues raised in the introduction, once you have the substantive material of the chapter under your belt. We reinforce the task of analysis with a *Consider the Source* feature appearing in some chapters that discusses ways you can improve your **critical thinking** skills by analyzing (that is, taking apart) different kinds of sources of information about politics.

Figure 1.5

Approximate Ideological Placement of Parties and Groups in U.S. Politics

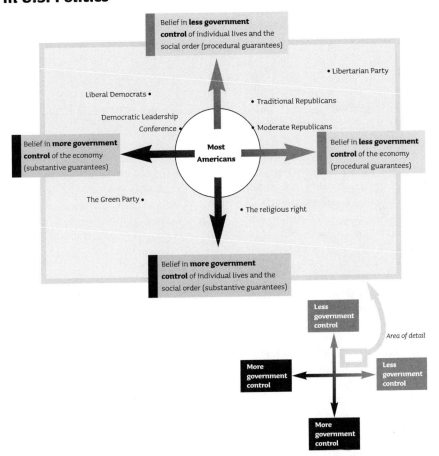

Within the confines of American political culture (remember that this entire figure still fits in the upper-right quadrant of Figure 1.3), American political groups take very divisive positions—many of them outside the mainstream where most Americans are located. The job of a political party—to capture the support of those groups without losing the Americans in the middle—can be a tough one.

As political scientists, however, not only do we want to understand *how* the system works, but we also want to assess *how well* it works. A second task of critical thinking is **evaluation**, or seeing how well something measures up according to a standard or principle. We could choose any number of standards by which

Critical Thinking

The world is full of people who would like to sell us a bill of goods. Our only defense is our capacity to think critically about the conclusions they want us to accept. Make no mistake, critical thinking is hard work. It means not accepting the easy answer, because someone says so, or because that's what we've always been told is true. Critical thinking is challenging the conclusions of others, asking why or why not, turning the accepted wisdom upside down, and exploring alternative interpretations.

Although hard work may not be very appealing, critical thinking can be a vital and enjoyable activity. When we are good at it, it empowers and liberates us. We are not at the mercy of others' conclusions and decisions. We can evaluate facts and arguments for ourselves, upending conventional wisdom and exploring the world of ideas with confidence.

The trick to learning how to think critically is to do it. It helps to have a model to follow, however, and we provide one below. The focus of critical thinking here is understanding political argument. *Argument* in this case refers not to a confrontation or a fight, but rather to a political contention, based on a set of assumptions, supported by evidence, leading to a clear, well-developed conclusion with consequences for how we understand the world.

Critical thinking involves constantly asking questions about the arguments we read about: who has created it, what is the basic case and what values underlie it, what evidence is used to back it up, what conclusions are drawn, and what difference does the whole thing make. To help you remember the questions to ask, we have used a mnemonic device that creates an acronym from the five major steps of critical thinking. Until asking these questions becomes second nature, thinking of them as CLUES to critical thinking about American politics will help you keep them in mind as you read.

This is what CLUES stands for:

Consider the source and the audience
Lay out the argument and the underlying values and assumptions
Uncover the evidence
Evaluate the conclusion
Sort out the political implications

We'll investigate each of these steps in a little more depth.

Consider the source and the audience

Who wrote the argument in question? Where did the item appear? What audience is it directed toward? What do the author or publisher need to do to attract and keep the audience? How might that affect content?

If the person is a mainstream journalist, he or she probably has a reputation as an objective reporter to preserve, and will at least make an honest attempt to provide unbiased information. Even so, knowing the actual news source will help you nail that down. Even in a reputable national paper like the *New York Times* or the *Wall Street Journal*, if the item comes from the editorial pages, you can count on its having an ideological perspective, and opinion magazines will have even more blatant points of view.

Lay out the argument and the underlying values and assumptions

What basic argument does the author want to make? What assumptions about the world does he or she hold? What values about what is important and what government should do? Are all the important terms clearly defined?

If these things aren't clear, the author may be unclear him- or herself. There is a lot of sloppy thinking out there, and being able to identify it and discard it is very valuable. Often we are intimidated by a smart-sounding argument, only to discover on closer examination that it just doesn't hold up. A more insidious case occurs when the author is trying to obscure the point in order to get you to sign on to something you might not otherwise accept. If the argument, values, and assumptions are not perfectly clear and up front, there may be a hidden agenda you should know about.

Uncover the evidence

Has the author done basic research to back up the argument with facts and evidence?

Good arguments cannot be based on gut feelings, rumor, or wishful thinking. They should be based on hard evidence, either empirical, verifiable observations about the world, or solid, logical reasoning. If the argument is worth being held, it should be able to stand up to rigorous examination and the author should be able to defend it on these grounds.

Evaluate the conclusion

Is the argument successful? Does it convince you? Why or why not? Does it change your mind about any beliefs you held previously? Does accepting this argument require you to rethink any of your other beliefs?

Conclusions should follow logically from the assumptions and values of an argument, if solid evidence and reasoning supports it. What is the conclusion here? What is the author asking you to accept as the product of his or her argument? Does it make sense to you? Do you "buy it"? If you do, does it fit with your other ideas or do you need to refine what you previously thought? Have you learned from this argument, or have you merely had your own beliefs reinforced?

Sort out the political implications

What is the political significance of this argument? What difference does it make to your understanding of the way the political world works? How does it affect who gets what scarce resources and how they get them? How does it affect who wins in the political process and who loses?

Political news is valuable if it means something. Otherwise, it wastes your time if it claims to be something more than entertainment. Make the information you get prove its importance, and if it doesn't, find a different news source to rely on.

Source: Adapted from the authors' "Preface to the Student," in Christine Barbour and Matthew J. Streb, *Clued in to Politics: A Critical Thinking Reader in American Government* (Boston: Houghton Mifflin, 2004).

to evaluate American politics, but the most relevant, for most of us, is the principle of democracy and the role of citizens.

We can draw on the two traditions of self-interested and public-interested citizenship we have discussed to evaluate the powers, opportunities, and challenges presented to American citizens by the system of government under which they live. In addition to the two competing threads of citizenship in America, we can also look at the kinds of action that citizens engage in and whether they take advantage of the options available to them. The United States has elements of the elite, pluralist, and participatory ideals of democracy we discussed earlier, and one way to evaluate citizenship in America is to look at what opportunities for participation exist and whether citizens take advantage of them.

To evaluate how democratic the United States is, we will look at the changing concept and practice of citizenship in this country with respect to the subject matter of each chapter in a section called *Citizenship and. . . .* In that section we will look at citizenship from many angles, considering such questions as the following: What role do "the people" have in American politics? How has that role expanded or diminished over time? What kinds of political participation do the rules of American politics (formal and informal) allow, encourage, or require citizens to take? What kinds of political participation are discouraged, limited, or forbidden? Do citizens take advantage of the opportunities for political action that the rules provide them? How do they react to the rules that limit their participation? How do citizens in different times exercise their rights and responsibilities? What do citizens need to do to "keep" the republic? How democratic is the United States?

To put all this in perspective, many chapters include another feature that gives you a more concrete idea of what citizen participation might mean on a personal level. *Profiles in Citizenship* introduce you to individuals who have committed a good part of their lives to public service and focus on what citizenship means to those people and what inspired them to take on a public role.

Each of these features is designed to help you to think critically about American politics either by analyzing power in terms of who gets what, and how, or by evaluating citizenship to determine how well we are keeping Benjamin Franklin's mandate to keep the republic. And remember that further exploration of the book's themes is always available on the text web site at http://republic-brief.cqpress.com.

Citizenship and Politics
The gap between the ideal and the practice of American democracy

Today's American political system, based on a set of values that favor individual rights and fair procedures, bears a pretty close resemblance to Madison's "republican government." Keeping in mind that this system was not meant to be a "pure democracy," it is interesting to note that it has grown more democratic in some ways in the past two hundred years. For one thing, more people can participate now, and, since eighteen-year-olds won the right to vote, the electorate is younger than ever. But in many ways, government remains removed from "the people," even if the definition of "the people" has expanded over time, and voter turnout is low in the United States.

A growing number of educators and social scientists argue that falling levels of involvement, interest, and trust in politics are not something to be explained and dismissed with complacency but instead signal a true civic crisis in American politics. They see a swing from the community-minded citizens of republican virtue to the self-interested citizens of Madisonian theory so severe that the fabric of American political life is threatened. These scholars argue that democracies can survive only with the support and vigilance of citizens and that American citizens are so disengaged as the new century begins as to put democracy itself in danger. They would place the responsibility for low levels of participation in the United States not just on the system but also on the citizens themselves for not availing themselves of the opportunities for engagement that do exist.

While the question of how democratic the United States is may seem to be largely an academic one—that is, one that has little or no relevance to your personal life—it is really a question of who has the power and who is likely to be a winner in the political process. Looked at this way, the question has quite a lot to do with your life, especially as government starts to make more demands on you and you on it. Are you likely to be a winner or a loser? Are you going to get what you want from the political system? How much power do people like you have to get their way in government?

▶ What's at Stake Revisited

We began this chapter by asking whether youthful engagement in politics is really a matter of great importance, and what might be at stake in the question of whether the gains in the youth vote we saw in 2008 turn out to be permanent. Since then we have covered a lot of ground, arguing that politics is fundamental to human life and, in fact, makes life easier for us by giving us a nonviolent way to resolve disputes. We pointed out that politics is a method by which power and resources get distributed in society: politics is who gets what, and how they get it. Citizens who are aware and involved stand a much greater chance of getting what they want from the system than do those who check out or turn away. One clear consequence when young people disregard politics, then, is that they are less likely to get what they want from the political system. This is, in fact, exactly what happens.

There are also consequences for the system as a whole. Democracy is neither inevitable nor self-sustaining. As we will see in this book, the American system is a work of political genius that in many ways takes us as we are. It can accommodate the self-interested citizen, at least some of the time, but it depends for its continued existence on the presence of public-interested citizens as well.

Ironically, the absence of a public-interested spirit among us can be damaging to our own self-interest. People who pay attention to politics learn to use the rules of the system to get the things they want. Many college students complained that the 2000 election, with its focus on prescription drug coverage for the elderly and the financial solvency of Social Security, was "not about them" or the issues they cared about. A glance at voter turnout statistics tells us why: older people vote in far greater numbers than do young people. By not participating, young people ensure that they are not a force that politicians have to reckon with.

The increased youth vote in 2004 and 2008, however, makes it likely that politicians will not soon risk ignoring the areas of government action that matter to young people. "Young voters are back, and politicians will ignore them at their peril," one political science professor told the *Boston Globe*. "I'm convinced that we've turned the corner and that young Americans will continue to be important players in the electoral process."[14]

We always rely on government to provide some things—good schools, safe neighborhoods, well-maintained roads, a stable economy—but in times of war or other national crises, government looms even larger in our lives. We depend on it to protect us, our families, our homes, and our livelihoods. At that point, our failure to be able to use the system to get the things we value becomes far more critical. Consider one issue that has affected many generations of young people during wartime: the draft. From 1948 to 1973, young American men were drafted into compulsory military service. Although the draft ended in 1973, President Jimmy Carter made it mandatory for men aged eighteen to twenty-five to register with the Selective Service. Failure to do so can be punished with a $250,000 fine and five years in jail, and offenders cannot get student loans or government jobs. Although there are no current plans to reinstate the draft, officials moved fast after September 11, 2001, to fill vacancies on Selective Service or draft boards around the country.[15] Before the 2004 election, rumors flew fast and furiously that the Iraq war, almost universally believed to need more manpower, would require a draft.[16] Young people could hardly claim that issue is "not about them."

But it is not just young people who have a stake in their own indifference to politics. All American citizens are at risk, for in a very real sense, the future of the American republic is in the hands of those who are just today learning to keep it. As we have argued in this chapter, keeping the republic requires constant vigilance and critical citizenship. As we proceed through this introduction to American politics, remember what you have at stake in becoming an educated citizen of the U.S. government.

▶ Summary With Key Terms

Politics (4) is the struggle for **power** (4) and resources in society—who gets what, and how they get it. We can use the tools of politics to allocate scarce resources and to establish our favored vision of the **social order** (4), as long as there is agreement that the way power is managed is **legitimate** (5).

Government (5) is an organization set up to exercise **authority** (5) over a body of people. It is shaped by politics and helps provide the **rules** (6) and **institutions** (8) that in turn continue to shape the political process.

Politics is different from **economics** (8), which is a system for distributing society's wealth. Economic systems vary in how much control government has over how that distribution takes place, ranging from a **capitalist economy** (8) (or **regulated capitalism** [10], like that of the United States), where the free market reigns but government may provide **procedural guarantees** (10) that the rules are fair, to a **socialist economy** (10), where government makes **substantive guarantees** (10) of what it holds to be fair distributions of material resources. **Social democracy** (11) is in the middle, a market economy that aims to fulfill substantive goals.

Economic systems vary according to how much control government has over the economy; political systems vary in how much control government has over individuals' lives and the social order. They range from **totalitarian governments** (12), where an **authoritarian government** (12) might make substantive decisions about how lives are to be lived and the social order arranged, to **anarchy** (14), where there is no control over those things at all. Short of anarchy is **democracy** (15), based on **popular sovereignty** (15), where individuals have considerable individual freedom and the social order provides fair processes rather than specified outcomes. Various economic-political systems include **authoritarian capitalism** (12) and **advanced industrial democracy** (16), as well as **communist democracy** (16), a theoretical possibility with no real-world examples.

An authoritarian government might be a monarchy, a theocracy, a fascist government, or an oligarchy. People who live in such systems are **subjects** (16), unable to claim rights against the government. Theories of democracy—**elite democracy** (15), **pluralist democracy** (15), and **participatory democracy** (15)—vary in how much power they believe individuals do or should have, but all individuals who live under democratic systems are **citizens** (16) because they have fundamental rights that government must protect. The idea that government exists to protect the rights of citizens originated with the idea of a **social contract** (18) between rulers and ruled.

The American government is a representative democracy called a **republic** (19). Two visions of citizenship exist in the United States: one puts self-interest first; the other emphasizes the public interest. The first is more common; the latter emerges most often in times of national strife.

Immigrants (22) are citizens or subjects of another country who come to the United States to live and work. Legal immigrants may be eligible to apply for citizenship through the process of **naturalization** (22). Some people arrive here as refugees (22) seeking asylum or protection from persecution, subject to permission from the U.S. Citizenship and Immigration Services.

Americans share a **political culture** (23)—common **values** (23) and beliefs, or **normative** (23) ideas about how life should be lived, that draw them together. The U.S. political culture emphasizes procedural guarantees and **individualism** (24), the idea that individuals know what is best for themselves. The core values of American culture are democracy, freedom, and equality, all defined through a procedural, individualistic lens.

Within the context of our shared political culture, Americans have divergent beliefs and opinions, called **ideologies** (26), about political and economic affairs. Generally these ideologies are referred to as **conservative** (27) and **liberal** (27), but we can be more specific. Depending on their views about the role of government in the economy and in establishing the social order, most Americans can be defined as one of the following: **economic liberals** (28); **economic conservatives** (29), including **libertarians** (29); **social liberals** (29), including **communitarians** (29); and **social conservatives** (29). In a two-party political system like ours, it can be hard for either party to maintain the support of a majority when ideologies are so diverse.

The goal of this book is to teach **critical thinking** (32) about American politics through the tools of **analysis** (32) and **evaluation** (33). We will analyze how American politics works through the framework of our definition of politics—who gets power and resources and how they get them. We will evaluate how well American politics works by focusing on the opportunities and challenges of citizenship.

Explore this subject further with suggested readings, movies, and web sites at http://republic-brief.cqpress.com, where you'll also find study aids, practice quizzes, flash cards, and Internet exercises.

Chapter 2

The Politics of the American Founding

▶ What's at Stake?

It might have been 1773 all over again. Antitax and anti-government, the 2010 Tea Partiers were angry, and if they didn't go as far as to empty shiploads of tea into Boston Harbor, they made their displeasure known in other ways. Though their ire was directed at government in general, they found specific targets in the Bush administration's Troubled Asset Relief Program (TARP) bailouts of big financial institutions in 2008 and other measures taken in response to the economic crisis that began that year, including mortgage assistance for people facing foreclosure, the stimulus bill, and the health reform act, all passed by Congress in 2009 and 2010 with the strong backing of President Barack Obama.

Many of the Tea Partiers were simply focused on airing their aversion to the agenda of President Obama and the Democrats who had swept into office after the 2008 election, and they signaled their intention to vote for more conservative replacements in 2010 and 2012. Other messages were more ominous, rejecting the very legitimacy of the U.S. government—by doubting the citizenship of the president, by claiming that the election that brought him to power had been rigged by groups like ACORN, or by arguing that the government in Washington was tyrannical and it was the job of patriotic citizens to resist it.

The Tea Party movement is a decentralized mix of many groups—most simply frustrated Republicans (the major party that most Tea Partiers identify with or lean toward) but others more extreme. David Barstow of the *New York Times* wrote in early 2010 that a "significant undercurrent within the Tea Party movement" was less like a part of the Republican Party than it was like "the Patriot movement, a brand of politics historically associated with libertarians, militia groups, anti-immigration advocates and those who argue for the abolition of the Federal Reserve."[1] He quotes a Tea Party leader so worried about the impending tyranny threatening her country that she can imagine being called to violence in its defense. "I don't see us being the ones to start it, but I would give up my life for my country. . . . Peaceful means are the best way of going about it. But sometimes you are not given a choice."

Reflecting these same feelings, Tea Party members in Oklahoma City in April 2010 declared their intention to pass a state law to create a militia to defend their state against the federal government.[2] Their announcement came just days before the fifteenth anniversary of the day Timothy McVeigh, holding many similar views about the illegitimacy of the federal government, attacked the federal building in Oklahoma City, killing 168 people, including 19 children.

Like the extreme Tea Partiers quoted above, and even McVeigh and his associates, patriot and militia group members are everyday men and women who say they are the ideological heirs of the American Revolution. They liken themselves to the colonial Sons of Liberty who rejected the authority of the British government and took it upon themselves to enforce the laws they thought were just. The Sons of Liberty instigated the Boston Massacre and the Boston Tea Party, historical events that we celebrate as patriotic but that would be considered treason or terrorism if they took place today— and were considered as such by the British back when they occurred.

Today's so-called Patriot groups claim that the federal government has become as tyrannical as the British government ever was, that it deprives citizens of their liberty and over-regulates their everyday lives. They go so far as to claim that federal authority is illegitimate. Militia members reject federal laws that do everything from limiting the weapons that individual citizens can own, to imposing taxes on income, to requiring the registration of motor vehicles, to creating the Federal Reserve Bank, to reforming the health care system. They maintain that government should stay out of individual lives, providing security at the national level perhaps, but allowing citizens to regulate and protect their own lives.

Some militias go even further. Many militia members, for instance, are convinced that the United Nations is seeking to take over the United States (and that top U.S. officials are letting this happen). Others blend their quests for individual liberty with rigid requirements about who should enjoy that liberty. White supremacist or anti-Semitic groups aim at achieving an all-white continent or see Jewish collaboration behind ominous plots to destroy America.

Although there are some indications that militia membership was down in the wake of the negative publicity surrounding the 1995 Oklahoma City bombing, membership in such groups has surged since Obama's election. Currently there are 127 militias in the United States, among 512 Patriot groups.[3] The groups base their claim to legitimate existence on the Constitution's Second Amendment, which reads,

"A well regulated Militia, being necessary to the security of a free State, the right of the people to keep and bear Arms, shall not be infringed." Members of state militias, and other groups like them, take this amendment literally and absolutely, as did Timothy McVeigh and members of a Michigan militia group, Hutaree, who were arrested by police in March 2010, after their plan to use roadside bombs was discovered. They face charges of sedition and intent to use weapons of mass destruction.[4]

The federal government has reacted strongly to limit the threat presented by state militias and others who believe that its authority is not legitimate. Partly in response to the Oklahoma City bombing, Congress passed an antiterrorism bill signed by President Bill Clinton in 1996 that would make it easier for federal agencies to monitor the activities of such groups. Those powers were broadened in the wake of the September 11, 2001, attack on the United States by foreign terrorists. President George W. Bush gave the Department of Homeland Security a broad mandate to combat terrorism, including the homegrown variety.

Is the federal government responding appropriately to these threats? Are these groups, as they claim, the embodiment of revolutionary patriotism? Do they support the Constitution, or sabotage it? And where do we draw the line between a Tea Party member who wants to sound off against elected officials and policies she doesn't like, and one who advocates resorting to violence to protect her particular reading of the Constitution? Think about these questions as you read this chapter on the founding of the United States. Think about the consequences and implications of revolutionary activity then and now. We return to the question of what's at stake for American politics in the militia movement at the end of the chapter.

Schoolchildren in the United States have had the story of the American founding pounded into their heads. From the moment they start coloring grateful Pilgrims and cutting out construction paper turkeys in grade school, the founding is a recurring focus of their education, and with good reason. Democratic societies, as we saw in Chapter 1, rely on the consent of their citizens to maintain lawful behavior and public order. A commitment to the rules and goals of the American system requires that we feel good about that system. What better way to stir up good feelings and patriotism than by recounting thrilling stories of bravery and derring-do on the part of selfless heroes dedicated to the cause of American liberty? We celebrate the Fourth of July with fireworks and parades, displaying publicly our commitment to American values and our belief that our country is special, in the same way that other nations celebrate their origins all over the world. Bastille Day (July 14) in France, May 17 in Norway, October 1 in China, and July 6 in Malawi all are days on which people rally together to celebrate their common past and their hopes for the future.

Of course, people feel real pride in their countries, and many nations, not only our own, do have amazing stories to tell about their earliest days. But since this is a textbook on politics, not patriotism, we need to look beyond the pride and the amazing stories. As political scientists, we must separate myth from reality. For us, the founding of the United States is central not because it inspires warm feelings of patriotism but because it can teach us about American politics—the struggles for power that forged the political system that continues to shape our collective struggles today.

The history of the American founding has been told from many points of view. You are probably most familiar with this account: the early colonists escaped to America to avoid religious persecution in Europe. Having arrived on the shores of the New World, they built communities that allowed them to practice their religions in peace and to govern themselves as free people. When the tyrannical British king made unreasonable demands on the colonists, they had no choice but to protect their liberty by going to war and by establishing a new government of their own.

But sound historical evidence suggests that the story is more complicated, and more interesting, than that. A closer look shows that early Americans were complex beings with economic and political agendas as well as religious and philosophical motives. After much struggle among themselves, the majority of Americans decided that those agendas could be better and more profitably carried out if they broke their ties with England.[5]

In this chapter we talk a lot about history—the history of the American founding and the creation of the Constitution. Like all authors, we have a particular point of view that affects how we tell the story. True to the basic theme of this book, we are interested in power and citizenship. We want to understand American government in terms of who the winners and losers are likely to be. It makes sense for us to begin by looking at the founding to see who the winners and losers were then. We are also interested in how rules and institutions make it more likely that some people will win and others lose. Certainly an examination of the early debates about rules and institutions will help us understand that. Because we are interested in winners and losers, the *who* of politics, we are interested in understanding how people come to be defined as players in the system in the first place. It was during the founding that many of the initial decisions were made about who "We, the people" would actually be. Finally, we are interested in the product of all this debate—the Constitution of the United States, the ultimate rule book for who gets what in American politics. Consequently our discussion of American political history focuses on these issues. Specifically in this chapter we explore the colonial break with England and the Revolution, the initial attempt at American government—the Articles of Confederation, the Constitutional Convention, the Constitution itself, and the ratification of the Constitution.

The Split From England
Making the transition from British subjects to American citizens

America was a political and military battlefield long before the Revolution. Not only did nature confront the colonists with brutal winters, harsh droughts, disease, and other unanticipated disasters, but the New World was also already inhabited before the British settlers arrived, both by Native Americans and by Spanish and French colonists. These political actors in North America during the seventeenth and early eighteenth centuries had, perhaps, more at stake than they knew. All were trying to lay claim to the same geographical territory; none could have foreseen that that territory would one day become the strongest power in the world. Whoever won the battle for North America would put their stamp on the globe in a major way.

By the late 1700s the eastern colonies of North America were heavily English. For many reasons, life in England had limited opportunities for freedom, for economic gain, and for political power. English settlers arrived in America seeking, first and foremost, new opportunities. But those opportunities were not available to all. "We, the people" had been defined in various ways throughout the 1600s and 1700s, but never had it meant anything like "everybody" or even "every white male." Religious and property qualifications for the vote, and the exclusion of women and blacks from political life, meant that the colonial leaders did not feel that simply living in a place, obeying the laws, or even paying taxes carried with it the right to participate in government. Following the rigid British social hierarchy, they wanted the "right kind" of people to participate—people who could be depended on to make the kind of rules that would ensure their status and maintain the established order. The danger of expanding the vote, of course, was that the new majority might have wanted something very different from what the old majority wanted.

Those colonists who had political power in the second half of the eighteenth century gradually began to question their relationship with England. For much of the history of colonial America, England had left the colonies pretty much alone, and they had learned to live with the colonial governance that Britain exercised. Of course, they were obliged, as colonies, to make England their primary trading partner. Even goods they exported to other European countries had to pass through England, where taxes were collected on them. However, smuggling and corrupt colonial officials had made those obligations less than burdensome. It is important to remember that the colonies received many benefits by virtue of their status: they were settled by corporations and companies funded with British money, such as the Massachusetts Bay Company; they were protected by the British army and navy; and they had a secure market for their agricultural products.

Whether the British government was actually being oppressive in the years before 1776 is open to interpretation. Certainly the colonists thought so. Britain was deeply in debt, having won the **French and Indian War**, which effectively forced the French out of North America and the Spanish to vacate Florida and retreat west of the Mississippi. The war, fought to defend the British colonies and colonists in America, turned into a major and expensive conflict across the Atlantic as well. Britain, having done its protective duty as a colonial power and having taxed British citizens at home heavily to finance the war, turned to its colonies to help pay for their defense. It chose to do that by levying taxes on the colonies and by attempting to enforce more strictly the trade laws that would increase British profits from American resources.

Newt Gingrich

History is anything but dull when it comes from the mouth of the man who has made so much of it. Newt Gingrich was the architect of the Contract With America, a document that helped propel the Republicans into the majority in Congress in 1994 for the first time in forty years, and made him Speaker of the U.S. House of Representatives from 1995 to 1998. As you will see in Chapter 7, his ideas and the policies they generated still inform the terms of political debate in this country more than a decade later.

But sitting at his desk at the American Enterprise Institute, with his distinguished gray head tilted slightly as he listens to a question, his fingertips pressed lightly together as he thinks over the answer, it is hard to forget that long before he revolutionized American politics in the 1990s, Newt Gingrich was a history professor at Western Georgia College. For the last six years he has resumed the work of a scholar in the rarified atmosphere of the American Enterprise Institute, a conservative Washington think tank, where, in addition to being a media commentator and adviser to his party, he can play with ideas and talk to other smart people to his heart's content.

Life as an intellectual clearly suits him. Does it mean Gingrich has given up politics for good? Maybe, but maybe not. The media had a field day speculating on the possibility that he would run for president in 2008, and he says he is considering a run in 2012. It's hard to imagine that all that energy and creativity and leadership potential aren't going to run for something. His 2010 book, *To Save America: Stopping Obama's Secular-Socialist Machine*, certainly hints at his intention to stay active in public life.

It seems to be part of who he is. When he was as young as ten years old, he was flexing his civic muscles by petitioning the Harrisburg (Pennsylvania) City Council to build a zoo. They didn't, but only, he claims with a smile, because his military family moved away before he could persuade them. Given his extraordinary record of public achievement since, it is a good bet he'd have gotten his zoo if the Gingrich family had stayed put.

But they did not. Throughout his junior high years the Gingriches lived in a number of post–World War II European cities—gracious, civilized cities-turned-battlefields that still bore the scars of combat. There was no pretending that the atrocities of war "couldn't happen there"; they had happened, and it was apparent to Gingrich that they could happen at home, too, if serious steps weren't taken. He says, "Out of all that experience I concluded that citizenship was central to our freedom and our safety, and that having civilian leaders who thought about it every day was central to our survival. I spent the summer of 1958 praying about it, and then in August of 1958 [at age 15] I decided to do what I've been doing ever since."

What he does—the short answer—is to study history and glean from it insights about human motivation and behavior, and then use those historical insights to make things happen today. He is committed to crafting new ideas out of old lessons, leading his fellow citizens on a mission he believes will restore the country to fundamental principles.

Ask him to explain just why it's important to study history and he pauses so long you wonder if he's forgotten the question or perhaps thinks it's so obvious that he won't deign to give it an answer. But no, he's just assembling his thoughts; you can almost hear the clicks and whirls of the processors. He opens his mouth and gracefully constructed sentences tumble out, fully formed. No umms, no stumbles; just perfect, elegant prose. Here's what he says:

On why students should study history:
If you've never run out of gas, you may not understand why filling your gas tank matters. And if you've never had your brakes fail, you may not care about having your brakes checked. And if you've never slid on an icy road, you may not understand why learning to drive on ice really matters. For citizens, if you haven't lived in a bombed-out city like Beirut or Baghdad, if you haven't seen a genocidal massacre like Rwanda, if you haven't been in a situation where people were starving to death, like Calcutta, you may not understand why you ought to study history. Because your life is good and it's easy and it's soft.

But for most of the history of the human race, most people, most of the time, have lived as slaves or as subjects to other people. And they lived lives that were short and desperate and where they had very little hope. And the primary breakthroughs have all been historic. It was the Greeks discovering the concept of self-governance, it was the Romans creating the objective sense of law, it was the Jewish tradition of being endowed by God—those came together and fused in Britain with the Magna Carta, and created a sense of rights that we take for granted every day. Because we have several hundred years of history protecting us. And the morning that history disappears, there's no reason to believe we'll be any better than Beirut or Baghdad.

On keeping the republic:
Be responsible, live out your responsibilities as a citizen, dedicate some amount of your time every day or every week to knowing what is going on in the world, be active in campaigns, and if nobody is worthy of your support, run yourself. . . . The whole notion of civil society [is] doing something as a volunteer, doing something, helping your fellow American, being involved with human beings. America only works as an organic society. . . . We're the most stunningly voluntaristic society in the world. And so if voluntarism dries up, in some ways America dries up.

The series of acts passed by the British infuriated the colonists. The Sugar Act of 1764, which imposed customs taxes, or duties, on sugar, was seen as unfair and unduly burdensome in a depressed postwar economy, and the Stamp Act of 1765 incited protests and demonstrations throughout the colonies. Similar to a tax in effect in Great Britain for nearly a century, it required that a tax be paid, in scarce British currency, on every piece of printed matter in the colonies, including newspapers, legal documents, and even playing cards. The colonists claimed that the law was an infringement on their liberty and a violation of their right not to be taxed without their consent. Continued protests and political changes in England resulted in the repeal of the Stamp Act in 1766. The Townshend Acts of 1767, taxing goods imported from England, such as paper, glass, and tea, and the Tea Act of 1773 were seen by the colonists as intolerable violations of their rights. To show their displeasure, they hurled 342 chests of tea into Boston Harbor in the famous Boston Tea Party. Britain responded by passing the Coercive Acts of 1774, designed to punish the citizens of Massachusetts. In the process, Parliament sowed the seeds that would blossom into revolution in just a few years.

Revolution

From the moment the unpopularly taxed tea plunged into Boston Harbor, it became apparent that Americans were not going to settle down and behave like proper and orthodox colonists. Britain was surprised by the colonial reaction, and it could not ignore it. Even before the Boston Tea Party, mobs in many towns were demonstrating and rioting against British control. Calling themselves the Sons of Liberty, and under the guidance of the eccentric and unsteady Sam Adams, cousin of future president John Adams, they routinely caused extensive damage. In early 1770 they provoked the Boston Massacre, an attack by British soldiers that left six civilians dead and further inflamed popular sentiments.

By the time of the December 1773 Boston Tea Party, also incited by the Sons of Liberty, passions were at a fever pitch. The American patriots called a meeting in Philadelphia in September 1774. Known as the First Continental Congress, the meeting declared the Coercive Acts void, announced a plan to stop trade with England, and called for a second meeting in May 1775. Before they could meet again, in the early spring of 1775, the king's army went marching to arrest Sam Adams and another patriot, John Hancock, and to discover the hiding place of the colonists' weapons. Roused by the silversmith Paul Revere, Americans in Lexington and Concord fired the first shots of rebellion at the British, and the Revolution was truly under way.

The Declaration of Independence

In 1776, at the direction of a committee of the Continental Congress, thirty-four-year-old Thomas Jefferson sat down to write a declaration of independence from England. His training as a lawyer at the College of William and Mary and his service as a representative in the Virginia House of Burgesses helped prepare him for his task, but he had an impressive intellect in any case. President John Kennedy once announced to a group of Nobel Prize winners he was entertaining that they were "the most extraordinary collection of talents that has ever gathered at the White House, with the possible exception of when Thomas Jefferson dined alone."[6] A testimony to Jefferson's capabilities is the strategically brilliant document that he produced.

The **Declaration of Independence** is first and foremost a political document. Having decided to make the break with England, the American founders had to convince themselves, their fellow colonists, and the rest of the world that they were doing the right thing. Jefferson did not have to hunt far for a good reason for his revolution. John Locke, whom we discussed in Chapter 1, had handed him one on a silver platter. Remember that Locke said that government is based on a contract between the rulers and the ruled. The ruled agree to obey the laws as long as the rulers protect their basic rights to life, liberty, and property. If the rulers fail to do that, they break the contract, and the ruled are free to set up another government. This is exactly what the second paragraph of the Declaration of Independence says, except that Jefferson changed "property" to "the pursuit of happiness," perhaps to garner the support of those Americans who didn't own enough property to worry about. The rest of the Declaration focuses on documenting the ways in which the colonists believed that England, and particularly George III, had violated their rights and broken the social contract.

". . . That All Men Are Created Equal"

The Declaration of Independence begins with a statement of the equality of all men. Since so much of this document relies heavily on Locke, and since clearly the colonists did *not* mean that all men are created equal, it is worth turning to Locke for some help in seeing exactly what they did mean. In his most famous work, *Second Treatise of Government*, Locke wrote,

> Though I have said above that all men are by nature equal, I cannot be supposed to understand all sorts of equality. Age or virtue may give men a just precedency. Excellency of parts and merit may place others above the common level. Birth may subject some, and alliance or benefits others, to pay an observance to those whom nature, gratitude, or other respects may have made it due.[7]

Men are equal in a natural sense, said Locke, but society quickly establishes many dimensions on which they may be unequal. A particularly sticky point for Locke's ideas on equality was his treatment of slavery. Although he hemmed and hawed about it, ultimately he failed to condemn it. Here, too, our founders would have been in agreement with him.

African Americans and the Revolution

The Revolution was a mixed blessing for American slaves. On the one hand, many slaves won their freedom during the war. Slavery was outlawed north of Maryland, and many slaves in the Upper South were also freed. The British offered freedom in exchange for service in the British army, although the conditions they provided were not always a great improvement over enslavement. The abolitionist, or anti-slavery, movement gathered steam in some northern cities, expressing moral and constitutional objections to the institution of slavery. Whereas before the Revolution only about 5 percent of American blacks were free, the number grew tremendously with the coming of war.[8]

In the aftermath of war, African Americans did not find their lot greatly improved, despite the ringing rhetoric of equality that fed the Revolution. The economic profitability of slave labor still existed in the South, and slaves continued to be imported from Africa in large numbers. The explanatory myth, that all men were created equal but that blacks weren't quite men and thus could be treated unequally, spread throughout the new country, making even free blacks unwelcome in many communities. By 1786 New Jersey prohibited free blacks from entering the state, and within twenty years northern states started passing laws specifically denying free blacks the right to vote.[9] No wonder the well-known black abolitionist Frederick Douglass said, in 1852, "This Fourth of July is yours, not mine. You may rejoice, I must mourn."

> The explanatory myth that all men were created equal but that blacks weren't quite men . . . spread throughout the new country . . .

Native Americans and the Revolution

Native Americans were another group the founders did not consider to be prospective citizens. Not only were they already considered members of their own sovereign nations, but their communal property holding, their nonmonarchical political systems, and their divisions of labor between women working in the fields and men hunting for game were not compatible with European political notions. Pushed farther and farther west by land-hungry colonists, the Indians were actively hostile to the American cause in the Revolution. Knowing this, the British hoped to gain their allegiance in the war. Fortunately for the Revolutionary effort, the colonists, having asked in vain for the Indians to stay out of what they called a "family quarrel," were able to suppress early on the Indians' attempts to get revenge for their treatment at the hands of the settlers.[10] There was certainly no suggestion that the claim of equality at the beginning of the Declaration of Independence might include the peoples who had lived on the continent for centuries before the white man arrived.

Women and the Revolution

Neither was there any question that "all men" might somehow be a generic term for human beings that would include women. Politically, the Revolution proved to be a step backward for women: it was after the war that states began specifically to prohibit women, even those with property, from voting.[11] That doesn't mean, however, that women did not get involved in the war effort. Within the constraints of society, they contributed what they could to the American cause. They boycotted tea and other British imports, sewed flags, made bandages and clothing, nursed and housed soldiers, and collected money to support the Continental Army. Under the name Daughters of Liberty, women in many towns met publicly to discuss the events of the day, spinning and weaving to make the colonies less dependent on imported cotton and woolen goods from England, and drinking herbal tea instead of tea that was taxed by the British. Some women moved beyond such mild patriotic activities to outright political behavior, writing pamphlets urging independence, spying on enemy troops, carrying messages, and even, in isolated instances, fighting on the battlefields.[12]

Men's understanding of women's place in early American politics was nicely put by Thomas Jefferson, writing from Europe to a woman in America in 1788:

> But our good ladies, I trust, have been too wise to wrinkle their foreheads with politics. They are contented to soothe & calm the minds of their husbands returning ruffled from political debate. They have the good sense to value domestic happiness above all others. There is no part of the earth where so much of this is enjoyed as in America.[13]

Women's role with respect to politics is plain. They may be wise and prudent, but their proper sphere is the domestic, not the political, world. They are almost "too good" for politics, representing peace and serenity, moral happiness rather than political dissension, the values of the home over the values of the state. This explanation provides a flattering reason for keeping women in "their place" while allowing men to reign in the world of politics.

The Articles of Confederation
Political and economic instability under the nation's first constitution

In 1777 the Continental Congress met to try to come up with a **constitution**, or a framework that established the rules for the new government. The **Articles of Confederation**, our first constitution, created the kind of government the founders, fresh from their colonial experience, preferred. The rules set up by the Articles of Confederation show the states' jealousy of their power. Having just won their independence from one large national power, the last thing they wanted to do was create another. They were also extremely wary of one another, and much of the debate over the Articles of Confederation reflected wide concern that the rules not give any states preferential treatment. (See the appendix for the text of the Articles of Confederation.)

The Articles established a "firm league of friendship" among the thirteen American states, but they did not empower a central government to act effectively on behalf of those states. The Articles were ultimately replaced because, without a strong central government, they were unable to provide the economic and political stability that the founders wanted. Even so, under this set of rules, some people were better off and some problems, namely the resolution of boundary disputes and the political organization of new territories, were handled extremely well.

The Provisions of the Articles

The government set up by the Articles was called a **confederation** because it established a system in which each state would retain almost all of its own power to do what it wanted. In other words, in a confederation, each state is sovereign and the central government has the job of running only the collective business of the states. It has no independent source of power and resources for its operations. Another characteristic of a confederation is that because it is founded on state sovereignty (authority), it says nothing about individuals. It creates neither rights nor obligations for individual citizens, leaving such matters to be handled by state constitutions.

Under the Articles of Confederation, Congress had many formal powers, including the power to establish and direct the armed forces, to decide matters of war and peace, to coin money, and to enter into treaties. However, its powers were quite limited. For example, although Congress controlled the armed forces, it had no power to draft soldiers or to tax citizens to pay for its military needs. Its inability to tax put Congress—and the central government as a whole—at the mercy of the states. The government could ask for money, but it was up to the states to contribute or not as they chose. Furthermore, Congress lacked the ability to regulate commerce between states, as well as between states and foreign powers. It could not establish a common and stable monetary system. In essence, the Articles allowed the states to be thirteen independent units, printing their own currencies, setting their own tariffs, and establishing their own laws with regard to financial and political matters. In every critical case—national security, national economic prosperity, and the general welfare—the U.S. government had to rely on the voluntary good will and cooperation of the state governments. That meant that the success of the new nation depended on what went on in state legislatures around the country.

Some Winners, Some Losers

The era of American history following the Revolution was dubbed "this critical period" by John Quincy Adams, nephew of patriot Sam Adams, son of John Adams, and himself a future president of the country. During this time, while the states were under the weak union of the Articles, the future of the United States was very much up in the air. The lack of an effective central government meant that the country had difficulty conducting business with other countries and enforcing harmonious trade relations and treaties. Domestic politics was equally difficult. Economic conditions following the war were poor. Many people owed money and could not pay their debts. State taxes were high, and the economy was depressed, offering farmers few opportunities to sell their produce, for example, and hindering those with commercial interests from conducting business as they had before the war.

The radical poverty of some Americans seemed particularly unjust to those hardest hit, especially in light of the rhetoric of the Revolution about equality for all.[14] One of the places the American passion for equality manifested itself was in some of the state legislatures, where laws were passed to ease the burden of debtors and farmers. Often the focus of the laws was property, but rather than preserving property, as Lockean theory said the law should do, it frequently was designed to confiscate or redistribute property instead. The "have-nots" in society, and the people acting on their behalf, were using the law to redress what they saw as injustices in early American life. To relieve postwar suffering, they printed paper money, seized property, and suspended "the ordinary means for the recovery of debts."[15] In other words, in those states, people with debts and mortgages could legally escape or postpone paying the money they owed. With so much economic insecurity, naturally those who owned property would not continue to invest and lend money. The Articles of Confederation, in their effort to preserve power for the states, had provided for no checks or limitations on state legislatures. In fact, such actions would have been seen under the Articles as infringing on the sovereignty of the states.

The political elite in the new country started to grumble about **popular tyranny**. In a monarchy, one feared the unrestrained power of the king, but perhaps in a republican government, one had to fear the unrestrained power of the people. The final straw was **Shays's Rebellion**. Massachusetts was a state whose legislature, dominated by wealthy and secure citizens, had not taken measures to aid the debt-ridden population. Beginning in the summer of 1786, mobs of musket-wielding farmers from western Massachusetts began marching on the Massachusetts courts and disrupting the trials of debtors in an attempt to prevent their land from being foreclosed (taken by those to whom the farmers owed money). The farmers demanded action by a state legislature they saw as biased toward the interests of the rich. Their actions against the state culminated in the January 1787 attack on the Springfield, Massachusetts, federal armory, which housed more than 450 tons of military supplies. Led by a former captain in the Continental Army, Daniel Shays, the mob, now an army of more than 1,500 farmers, stormed the armory. They were turned back, but only after a violent clash with the state militia, raised to counter the uprisings. Such mob action frightened and embarrassed the leaders of the United States, who of course also were the wealthier members of society. The rebellion seemed to foreshadow the failure of their grand experiment in self-governance. In the minds of the nation's leaders, it underscored the importance of discovering what James Madison would call "a republican remedy for those diseases most incident to republican government."[16] In other words, they had to find a way to contain and limit the will of the people in a government that was to be based on that will. If the rules of government were not producing the "right" winners and losers, the rules would have to be changed before the elite lost the power to change them.

The Constitutional Convention
Division and compromise over state power and representation

State delegates were assigned the task of trying to fix the Articles of Confederation, but it was clear that many of the fifty-five men who gathered in May 1787 were not interested in saving the existing framework at all. Many of the delegates represented the elite of American society—wealthy lawyers, speculators, merchants, planters, and investors—and thus they were among those being most injured under the Articles. Members of the delegations met through a sweltering Philadelphia summer to reconstruct the foundations of American government. As the delegates had hoped, the debates at the **Constitutional Convention** produced a very different system of rules than that established by the Articles of Confederation. Many of them were compromises to resolve conflicting interests brought by delegates to the convention.

How Strong a Central Government?

Put yourself in the founders' shoes. Imagine that you get to construct a new government from scratch. You can create all the rules and arrange all the institutions just to your liking. The only hitch is that you have other delegates to work with. Delegate A, for instance, is a merchant with a lot of property. He has big plans for a strong government that can ensure secure conditions for conducting business and can adequately protect property. Delegate B, however, is a planter. In Delegate B's experience, big government is dangerous. Big government is removed from the people, and it is easy for corruption to take root when people can't keep a close eye on what their officials are doing. People like Delegate B think that they will do better if power is decentralized (broken up and localized) and there is no strong central government. In fact, Delegate B would prefer a government like that provided by the Articles of Confederation. How do you reconcile these two very different agendas?

The solution adopted under the Articles of Confederation basically favored Delegate B's position. The new Constitution, given the profiles of the delegates in attendance, was moving strongly in favor of Delegate A's position. Naturally, the agreement of all those who followed Delegate B would be important in ratifying, or getting approval for, the final Constitution, so their concerns could not be ignored. The compromise chosen by the founders at the Constitutional Convention is called **federalism**. Unlike a confederation, in which the states retain the ultimate power over the whole, federalism gives the central government its own source of power, in this case the Constitution of the people of the United States. But unlike a unitary system, which we discuss in Chapter 3, federalism also gives independent power to the states.

Compared to how they fared under the Articles of Confederation, the advocates of states' rights were losers under the new Constitution, but they were better off than they might have been. The states could have had *all* their power stripped away. The economic elite, people like Delegate A, were clear winners under the new rules. This proved to be one of the central issues during the ratification debates. Those who sided with the federalism alternative, who mostly resembled Delegate A, came to be known as **Federalists**. The people like Delegate B, who continued to hold on to the strong-state, weak-central-government option, were called **Anti-Federalists**. We return to them shortly.

Large States, Small States

Once the convention delegates agreed that federalism would provide the framework of the new government, they had to decide how to allot power among the states. Should all states count the same in decision making, or should the large states have more power than the small ones? The rules chosen here would have a crucial impact on the politics of the country. If small states and large states had equal amounts of power in national government, residents of large states such as Virginia, Massachusetts, and New York would actually have less voice in the government than residents of small states like New Jersey and Rhode Island.

Picture two groups of people trying to make a joint decision, each group with one vote to cast. If the first group has fifty people in it and the second has only ten, the individuals in the second group are likely to have more influence on how their single vote is cast than the individuals in the first group. If, however, the first group has five votes to cast and the second only one, the individuals are equally represented, but the second group is effectively reduced in importance when compared to the first. This was the dilemma faced by the representatives of the large and small states at the Constitutional Convention. Each wanted to make sure that the final rules would give the advantage to states like his own.

Two plans were offered by convention delegates to resolve this issue (Table 2.1). The first, the Virginia Plan, was the creation of James Madison. Fearing that his youth and inexperience would hinder the plan's acceptance, he asked fellow Virginian Edmund Randolph to present it to the convention. The Virginia Plan represented the preference of the large, more populous states. This plan proposed a strong national government run by two legislative houses. One house would be elected directly by the people, one indirectly by a combination of the state legislatures and the popularly elected national house. The numbers of representatives would be determined by the taxes paid by the residents of the state, which would reflect the free population in the state. In other words, large states would have more representatives in both houses of the legislature, and national law and policy would be weighted heavily in their favor. Just three large states—Virginia, Massachusetts,

Table 2.1

Distribution of Powers Under the Articles of Confederation, the New Jersey and Virginia Plans, and the U.S. Constitution

Key Questions	Articles of Confederation	New Jersey Plan	Virginia Plan	The Constitution
Who is sovereign?	States	States	People	People
What law is supreme?	State law	State law	National law	National law
What kind of legislature; what is the basis for representation?	Unicameral legislature; equal votes for all states	Unicameral legislature; one vote per state	Bicameral legislature; representation in both houses based on population	Bicameral legislature; equal votes in Senate, representation by population in House
How are laws passed?	Two-thirds vote to pass important measures	Extraordinary majority to pass measures	Majority decision making	Simple majority vote in Congress, presidential veto
What powers are given to Congress?	No congressional power to levy taxes, regulate commerce	Congressional power to regulate commerce and tax	Congressional power to regulate commerce and tax	Congressional power to regulate commerce and tax
What kind of executive is there?	No executive branch; laws executed by congressional committee	Multiple executive	No restriction on strong single executive	Strong executive
What kind of judiciary is there?	No federal court system	No federal court system	National judiciary	Federal court system
How can the document be changed?	All states required to approve amendments	Unanimous approval of amendments by states	Popular ratification	Amendment process less difficult

and Pennsylvania—would be able to form a majority and carry national legislation their way. The **Virginia Plan** also called for a single executive, to see that the laws were carried out, and a national judiciary, both appointed by the legislature, and it gave the national government the power to override state laws.

A different plan, presented by William Paterson of New Jersey, was designed by the small states to offer the convention an alternative that would better protect their interests. The **New Jersey Plan** amounted to a reinforcement, not a replacement, of the Articles of Confederation. It provided for a multiperson executive, so that no one person could possess too much power, and for congressional acts to be the "supreme law of the land." Most significantly, however, the Congress would be much like the one that had existed under the Articles. In its one house, each state would have only one vote. The delegates would be chosen by the state legislatures. Congressional power was stronger than under the Articles, but the national government was still dependent on the states for some of its funding. The large states disliked this plan because the small states together could block what the large states wanted, even though the large states had more people and contributed more revenue.

The prospects for a new government could have foundered on this issue. The stuffy heat of the closed Convention Hall shortened the tempers of the weary delegates, and frustration made compromise difficult. Each side had too much to lose by yielding to the other's plan. The solution finally arrived at was politics at its best. The **Great Compromise** kept much of the framework of the Virginia Plan. It proposed a strong federal structure headed by a central government with sufficient power to tax its citizens, regulate commerce, conduct foreign affairs, organize the military, and exercise other central powers. It called for a single executive and a national judicial system. The compromise that allowed the small states to live with it involved the composition of the legislature. Like the Virginia Plan, it provided for two houses. The House of Representatives would be based on state population, giving the large states the extra clout they felt they deserved, but in the Senate each state would have two votes. This would give the small states much more power in the Senate than in the House of Representatives. Members of the House of Representatives would be elected directly by the people, members of the Senate by the state legislatures. Thus the government would be directly binding on the people as well as on the states. A key to the compromise was that most legislation would need the approval of both houses, so that neither large states nor small states could hold the entire government hostage to their wishes. The small states were sufficiently happy with this plan that most of them voted to ratify the Constitution quickly and easily. See Table 2.1 for a comparison of the Constitution with the Articles of Confederation and the different plans for reform.

North and South

The compromise reconciling the large and small states was not the only one crafted by the delegates. The northern and southern states, which is to say the non-slave-owning

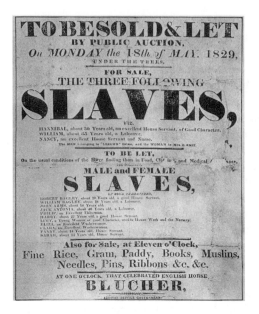

Three-fifths of a person

In 1763 the Confederate Congress devised a formula to allocate tax assessments based on population count. This same formula, in which every five slaves would count as three people, was used to calculate representation in the House under the Constitution. The wording was vague, however, and the word *slavery* was not used until the institution was outlawed by the Thirteenth Amendment, nearly eighty years after the writing of the Constitution.

and the slave-owning states, were at odds over how population was to be determined for purposes of representation in the lower house of Congress. The southern states wanted to count slaves as part of their population when determining how many representatives they got, even though they had no intention of letting the slaves vote. Including slaves would give them more representatives and thus more power in the House of Representatives. For exactly that reason, the northern states said that if slaves could not vote, they should not be counted. The bizarre compromise, also a triumph of politics if not humanity, is known as the **Three-fifths Compromise**. It was based on a formula developed by the Confederation Congress in 1763 to allocate tax assessments among the states. According to this compromise, for representation purposes, each slave would count as three-fifths of a person—that is, every five slaves would count as three people. Interestingly, the actual language in the Constitution is a good deal cagier than this. It says that representatives and taxes shall be determined according to population, figured "by adding to the whole Number of free Persons, including those bound to Service for a Term of Years, and excluding Indians not taxed, three fifths of *all other persons.*"

The issue of slavery was divisive enough for the early Americans that the most politically safe approach was not to mention it explicitly at all and thus to avoid having to endorse or condemn it. Implicitly, of course, their silence had the effect of letting slavery continue. Article I, Section 9, of the Constitution, in similarly vague language, allows that

> The Migration or Importation of such Persons as any of the States now existing shall think proper to admit, shall not be prohibited by Congress prior to the Year one thousand eight hundred and eight, but a Tax or duty may be imposed on such Importation, not exceeding ten dollars for each Person.

Even more damning, Article IV, Section 2, obliquely provides for the return of runaway slaves:

No Person held to Service or Labour in one State under the Laws thereof, escaping into another, shall, in Consequence of any Law or Regulation therein, be discharged from such Service or Labour, but shall be delivered up on Claim of the Party to whom such Service or Labour may be due.

The word *slavery* does not appear in the Constitution until it is expressly outlawed in the Thirteenth Amendment, passed in December 1865, nearly eighty years after the writing of the Constitution.

The Constitution
Three branches—legislative, executive, and judicial—separated and checked

The document produced as a result of these compromises was a political innovation. All governments must have the power to do three things: (1) legislate, or make the laws, (2) administer, or execute the laws, and (3) adjudicate, or interpret the laws. Because of their fear of concentrated power, however, the founders did not give all the power to one institution, but rather provided for separate branches of government to handle it, and then ensured that each branch would have the ability to check the others. In this section we review briefly the U.S. Constitution and the principles that support it.

The Legislative Branch

Legislative power is lawmaking power. The body of government that makes laws is called the **legislature**. The U.S. Congress is a **bicameral legislature**, meaning that there are two chambers—the House of Representatives and the Senate. Article I, by far the lengthiest article of the Constitution, sets out the framework of the legislative branch of government. Since the founders expected the legislature to be the most important part of the new government, they spent the most time specifying its composition, the qualifications for membership, its powers, and its limitations. The best-known part of Article I is the famous Section 8, which spells out the specific powers of Congress. This list is followed by the provision that Congress can do anything "necessary and proper" to carry out its duties. The Supreme Court has interpreted this clause so broadly that there are few effective restrictions on what Congress can do.

The House of Representatives, where representation is based on population, was intended to be truly representative of all the people—the "voice of the common man," as it were. To be elected to the House, a candidate need be only twenty-five years old and a citizen for seven years. Since House terms last two years, members run for reelection often and can be ousted fairly easily, according to public whim. The founders intended this office to be accessible to and easily influenced by citizens, and to reflect frequent changes in public opinion.

The Senate is another matter. Candidates have to be at least thirty years old and citizens for nine years—older, wiser, and, the founders hoped, more stable than the representatives in the House. Because senatorial terms last for six years, senators are not so easily swayed by changes in public sentiment. In addition, senators were originally elected by members of the state legislatures, not directly by the people. (This was changed by constitutional amendment in 1913.) Election by state legislators, themselves a "refinement" of the general public, would ensure that senators were a higher caliber of citizen: older and wiser but also more in tune with "the commercial and monied interest," as Massachusetts delegate Elbridge Gerry put it at the Constitutional Convention.[17] The Senate would thus be a more aristocratic body—that is, it would look more like the British House of Lords, where members are admitted on the basis of their birth or achievement, not by election.

The Executive Branch

The **executive** is the part of government that "executes" the laws, or sees that they are carried out. Although technically executives serve in an administrative role, many end up with some decision-making or legislative power as well. National executives are the leaders of their countries, and they participate, with varying amounts of power, in making laws and policies. That role can range from the U.S. president—who, though not a part of the legislature itself, can propose, encourage, and veto legislation—to European prime ministers, who are part of the legislature and may have, as in the British case, the power to dissolve the entire legislature and call a new election.

The fact that the Articles of Confederation provided for no executive power at all was a testimony to the founders' conviction that such a power threatened their liberty. The chaos that resulted under the Articles, however, made it clear to founders like Alexander Hamilton that a stronger government was called for, not only a stronger legislature but a stronger executive as well. The constitutional debates reveal that many of the founders were haunted by the idea that they might inadvertently reestablish the same tyrannical power over themselves that they had only recently escaped with the Revolution.

The solution finally chosen by the founders is a complicated one, but it satisfied all the concerns raised at the convention. The president, a single executive, would serve an unlimited number of four-year terms. (A constitutional amendment in 1951 limited the president to two elected terms.) But the president would be chosen neither by Congress nor directly by the people. Instead, the Constitution provides for the president's selection by an intermediary body called the **Electoral College**. Citizens vote not for the presidential candidates but for a slate of electors, who in turn cast their votes for the candidates about six weeks after the general election. The founders believed that this procedure would ensure a president elected by well-informed delegates who, having no other lawmaking power, could not be bribed or otherwise influenced by candidates. We say more about how this works in Chapter 12, on elections.

Article II of the Constitution establishes the executive branch. The four sections of that article make the following provisions:

- Section 1 sets out the four-year term and the manner of election (that is, the details of the Electoral College). It also provides for the qualifications for office: that the president must be a natural-born citizen of the United States, at least thirty-five years old, and a resident of the United States for at least fourteen years. The vice president serves if the president cannot, and Congress can make laws about succession if the vice president is incapacitated.
- Section 2 establishes the powers of the chief executive. The president is commander-in-chief of the armed forces and of the state militias when they are serving the nation, and he has the power to grant pardons for offenses against the United States. With the advice and consent of two-thirds of the Senate, the president can make treaties, and with a simple majority vote of the Senate, the president can appoint ambassadors, ministers, consuls, Supreme Court justices, and other U.S. officials whose appointments are not otherwise provided for.
- Section 3 says that the president will periodically tell Congress how the country is doing (the State of the Union address given every January) and will propose to them those measures that he thinks appropriate and necessary. Under extraordinary circumstances, the president can call the Congress into session or, if the two houses of Congress cannot agree on when to end their sessions, can adjourn them. The president also receives ambassadors and public officials, executes the laws, and commissions all military officers of the United States.
- Section 4 specifies that the president, vice president, and other civil officers of the United States (such as Supreme Court justices) can be impeached, tried, and convicted for "Treason, Bribery, or other high Crimes and Misdemeanors."

The Judicial Branch

Judicial power is the power to interpret the laws and to judge whether they have been broken. Naturally, by establishing how a given law is to be understood, the courts (the agents of judicial power) end up making law as well. Our constitutional provisions for the establishment of the judiciary are brief and vague; much of the American federal judiciary under the Supreme Court is left to Congress to arrange. But the founders left plenty of clues as to how they felt about judicial power in their debates and their writings, particularly in *The Federalist Papers*, a series of newspaper editorials written to encourage people to support and vote for the new Constitution.

For instance, the practice of judicial review is introduced through the back door, first mentioned by Hamilton in *Federalist* No. 78 and then institutionalized by the Supreme Court itself with Chief Justice John Marshall's 1803 ruling in *Marbury v. Madison*, a dispute over presidential appointments. **Judicial review** allows the Supreme Court to rule that an act of Congress or the executive branch (or of a state or local government) is unconstitutional—that is, that it runs afoul of constitutional principles. This review process is not an automatic part of lawmaking; the Court does not examine every law that Congress passes or every executive order to be sure that it does not violate the Constitution. Rather, if a law is challenged as unjust or unconstitutional by an individual or a group, and if it is appealed all the way to the Supreme Court, the justices may decide to rule on it.

This remarkable grant of the power to nullify legislation to what Hamilton called the "least dangerous" branch is not in the Constitution. In *Federalist* No. 78, however, Hamilton argued that it was consistent with the Constitution. In response to critics who objected that such a practice would place the unelected Court in a superior position to the elected representatives of the people, Hamilton wrote that, on the contrary, it raised the people, as authors of the Constitution, over the government as a whole. Thus, judicial review enhanced democracy rather than diminished it.

In 1803 Marshall agreed. As the nation's highest law, the Constitution sets the limits on what is acceptable legislation. As the interpreter of the Constitution, the Supreme Court must determine when laws fall outside those limits. It is interesting to note that this gigantic grant of power to the Court was made by the Court itself and remains unchallenged by the other branches. It is ironic that this sort of empire building, which the founders hoped to avoid, appears in the branch that they took the least care to safeguard. We return to *Marbury v. Madison* and judicial review in Chapter 9, on the court system.

Article III of the Constitution is very short. It says that the judicial power of the United States is to be "vested in one Supreme Court, and in such inferior courts as the Congress may from time to time ordain and establish," and that judges serve as long as they demonstrate "good behavior." It also explains that the Supreme Court has original jurisdiction in some types of cases and appellate jurisdiction in others. That is, in some cases the Supreme Court is the only court that can rule. Much more often, however, inferior courts try cases, but their rulings can be appealed to the Supreme Court. Article III provides for jury trials in all criminal cases except impeachment, and it defines the practice of and punishment for acts of treason. Because the Constitution is relatively silent on the role of the courts in America, that role has been left to the definition of Congress and, in some cases, of the courts themselves.

Separation of Powers and Checks and Balances

Separation of powers means that legislative, executive, and judicial powers are not exercised by the same person or group of people, lest they abuse the considerable amount of power they hold. We are indebted to the French Enlightenment philosopher the Baron de Montesquieu for explaining this notion. In his massive book *The Spirit of the Laws*, Montesquieu wrote that liberty could be threatened only if the same group that enacted tyrannical laws also executed them. He said, "There would be an end of everything, were the same man or the same body, whether of nobles or of the people, to exercise those three powers, that of enacting laws, that of executing the public resolutions, and of trying the causes of individuals."[18] Putting all political power into one set of hands is like putting all our eggs in one basket. If the person or body of people entrusted with all the power becomes corrupt or dictatorial, the whole system will go bad. If, however, power is divided so that each branch is in separate hands, one may go bad while leaving the other two intact.

The principle of separation of powers gives each of the branches authority over its own domain. A complementary principle, **checks and balances**, allows each of the branches to police the others, checking any abuses and balancing the powers of government. The purpose of this additional authority is to ensure that no branch can exercise power tyrannically. In America's case, the president can veto an act of Congress; Congress can override a veto; the Supreme Court can declare a law of Congress unconstitutional; Congress can, with the help of the states, amend the Constitution itself; and so on. Figure 2.1 illustrates these relationships.

As we saw, the Constitution establishes separation of powers with articles setting up a different institution for each branch of government. Checks and balances are provided by clauses within these articles.

- Article I sets up a bicameral legislature. Because both houses must agree on all legislation, they can check each other. Article I also describes the presidential veto, with which the president can check Congress, and the override provision, by which two-thirds of Congress can check the president. Congress can also check abuses of the executive or judicial branch with impeachment.
- Article II empowers the president to execute the laws and to share some legislative function by "recommending laws." The president has some checks on the judiciary through his power to appoint judges, but his appointment power is checked by the requirement that a majority of the Senate must confirm his choices. The president can also check the judiciary by granting pardons. The president is commander-in-chief of the armed forces, but his ability to exercise his authority is checked by the Article I provision that only Congress can declare war.
- Article III creates the Supreme Court. The Court's ruling in the case of *Marbury v. Madison* fills in some of the gaps in this vague article by establishing judicial review, a true check on the legislative and executive branches. Congress can countercheck judicial review by amending the Constitution (with the help of the states).

The Constitution wisely ensures that no branch of the government can act independently of the others, yet none is wholly dependent on the others either. This results in a structure of separation of powers and checks and balances that is distinctively American.

Figure 2.1

Separation of Powers and Checks and Balances

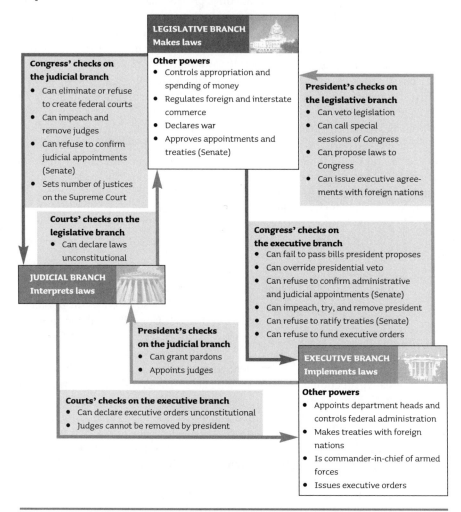

LEGISLATIVE BRANCH
Makes laws

Congress' checks on the judicial branch
- Can eliminate or refuse to create federal courts
- Can impeach and remove judges
- Can refuse to confirm judicial appointments (Senate)
- Sets number of justices on the Supreme Court

Other powers
- Controls appropriation and spending of money
- Regulates foreign and interstate commerce
- Declares war
- Approves appointments and treaties (Senate)

President's checks on the legislative branch
- Can veto legislation
- Can call special sessions of Congress
- Can propose laws to Congress
- Can issue executive agreements with foreign nations

Courts' checks on the legislative branch
- Can declare laws unconstitutional

JUDICIAL BRANCH
Interprets laws

Congress' checks on the executive branch
- Can fail to pass bills president proposes
- Can override presidential veto
- Can refuse to confirm administrative and judicial appointments (Senate)
- Can impeach, try, and remove president
- Can refuse to ratify treaties (Senate)
- Can refuse to fund executive orders

President's checks on the judicial branch
- Can grant pardons
- Appoints judges

EXECUTIVE BRANCH
Implements laws

Courts' checks on the executive branch
- Can declare executive orders unconstitutional
- Judges cannot be removed by president

Other powers
- Appoints department heads and controls federal administration
- Makes treaties with foreign nations
- Is commander-in-chief of armed forces
- Issues executive orders

Amendability

If a constitution is a rule book, then its capacity to be changed over time is critical to its remaining a viable political document. A rigid constitution runs the risk of ceasing to seem legitimate to citizens who have no prospect of changing the rules according to shifting political realities and visions of the public good. A constitution that is too easily revised, on the other hand, can be seen as no more than

Figure 2.2

Amending the Constitution

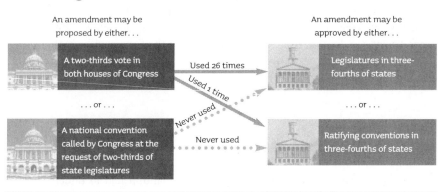

An amendment may be proposed by either...

A two-thirds vote in both houses of Congress

...or...

A national convention called by Congress at the request of two-thirds of state legislatures

Used 26 times

Used 1 time

Never used

Never used

An amendment may be approved by either...

Legislatures in three-fourths of states

...or...

Ratifying conventions in three-fourths of states

a political tool in the hands of the strongest interests in society. A final feature of the U.S. Constitution that deserves mention in this chapter is its **amendability**—the founders' provision for a method of amendment, or change, that allows the Constitution to grow and adapt to new circumstances. In fact, they provided for two methods: the formal amendment process outlined in the Constitution, and an informal process that results from the vagueness of the document and the evolution of the role of the courts (see Figure 2.2).

In the two-hundred-plus years of the U.S. Constitution's existence, more than 10,000 constitutional amendments have been introduced but the Constitution has been amended only 27 times. By contrast, in the course of interpreting the Constitution, the Supreme Court has, for example, extended many of the Bill of Rights protections to state citizens via the Fourteenth Amendment, permitted the national government to regulate business, prohibited child labor, and extended equal protection of the laws to women. In some cases, amendments previously introduced to accomplish these goals (such as the Child Labor Amendment and the Equal Rights Amendment) were not ratified, and in other cases the Court has simply decided to interpret the Constitution in a new way. Judicial interpretation is at times quite controversial. Many scholars and politicians believe that the literal word of the founders should be adhered to, whereas others claim that the founders could not have anticipated all the opportunities and pitfalls of modern life and that the Constitution should be considered a flexible, or "living," document. We return to this controversy when we look more closely at the courts in Chapter 9.

The Constitution is silent on the subject of judicial interpretation, but in part because it is silent, especially in Article III, the courts have been able to create their own role. In contrast, Article V spells out in detail the rather confusing procedures for officially amending the Constitution. These procedures are federal—that is, they require the involvement and approval of the states as well as the national government. The procedures boil down to this: amendments may be proposed either by a two-thirds vote of the House and the Senate or when two-thirds of the states request it by a constitutional convention; they must be approved either by the legislatures of three-fourths of the states or by conventions of three-fourths of the states. Two interesting qualifications are contained in Article V: no amendment affecting slavery could be made before 1808, and no amendment can deprive a state of its equal vote in the Senate without that state's consent. We can easily imagine the North-South and large state–small state conflicts that produced those compromises.

Ratification
Selling the Constitution to Americans

For the Constitution to become the law of the land, it had to undergo **ratification**, that is, it had to be voted on and approved by state conventions in at least nine states. As it happens, the Constitution was eventually ratified by all thirteen states, but not until some major political battles had been fought.

Federalists Versus Anti-Federalists

So strongly partisan were the supporters and opponents of the Constitution that if the battle were taking place today we would probably find them sniping at each other on shows like *The Sean Hannity Show* and *Hardball With Chris Matthews*, and Stephen Colbert would be busy mocking both sides. It was a fierce, lively battle that produced, instead of high television ratings, some of the finest writings for and against the American system. Those in favor of ratification called themselves Federalists. The Federalists, like Delegate A in our earlier hypothetical constitution-building scenario, were mostly men with a considerable economic stake in the new nation. Having fared poorly under the Articles, they were certain that if America were to grow as an economic and world power, it needed to be the kind of country people with property would want to invest in. Security and order were key values, as was popular control. The Federalists thought people like themselves should be in charge of the government, although some of them did not object to an expanded suffrage if government had enough built-in protections. Mostly they were convinced that a good government could be designed if the underlying principles of human behavior were known. If people were ambitious and tended toward corruption, then government should make use of those characteristics to produce good outcomes.

The Anti-Federalists, on the other hand, rejected the notion that ambition and corruption were inevitable parts of human nature. If government could be kept small and local, the stakes not too large and tempting, and popular scrutiny truly vigilant, then Americans could live happy and contented lives without getting involved in the seamier side of politics. America did not need sprawling urban centers of commerce and trade, nor did it need to be a world power. If it did not stray from its rural roots and values, it could permanently avoid the creeping corruption that the Anti-Federalists believed threatened the American polity. The reason the Anti-Federalists found the Articles of Confederation more attractive than the Constitution was that the Articles did not call for a strong central government that, distant from the voters' eyes, could become a hotbed of political intrigue. Instead, the Articles vested power in the state governments, which could be more easily watched and controlled.

Writing under various aliases as well as their own names, the Federalists and Anti-Federalists fired arguments back and forth in pamphlets and newspaper editorials aimed at persuading undecided Americans to come out for or against the Constitution. The Federalists were far more aggressive and organized in their "media blitz," hitting New York newspapers with a series of eloquent editorials, known collectively as *The Federalist Papers*, published under the pen name Publius but really written by Alexander Hamilton, James Madison, and John Jay. These essays were bound and distributed in other states where the ratification struggle was close. *The Federalist Papers* is one of the main texts on early American politics today. In response, the Anti-Federalists published essays under names such as Cato, Brutus, and The Federal Farmer.[19]

The Federalist Papers

Eighty-five essays were written by Publius. In a contemporary introduction to the essays, compiled as a book, one scholar calls them, along with the Declaration of Independence and the Constitution, part of "the sacred writings of American political history."[20] Putting them on a par with holy things is probably a mistake. Far from being divinely inspired, *The Federalist Papers* are quintessentially the work of human beings. They are clever, well thought out, and logical, but they are also tricky and persuasive examples of the "hard sell." Two of the most important essays, numbers 10

and 51, are reprinted in the appendix to this book. Their archaic language makes *The Federalist Papers* generally difficult reading for contemporary students. However, the arguments in support of the Constitution are laid out so beautifully that it is worthwhile to take the trouble to read them. It would be a good idea to turn to them now and read them carefully.

In *Federalist* No. 10, Madison tries to convince Americans that a large country is no more likely to succumb to the effects of special interests than is a small one (preferred by the Anti-Federalists). He explains that the greatest danger to a republic comes from **factions**, what we might call interest groups. Factions are groups of people motivated by a common interest, but one different from the interest of the country as a whole. Farmers, for instance, have an interest in keeping food prices high, even though that would make most Americans worse off. Businesspeople prefer high import duties on foreign goods, even though they make both foreign and domestic goods more expensive for the rest of us. Factions are not a particular problem when they constitute a minority of the population because they are offset by majority rule. They do become problematic, however, when they are a majority. Factions usually have economic roots, the most basic being a difference between the "haves" and "have-nots" in society. One of the majority factions that worried Madison was the mass of propertyless people whose behavior was so threatening to property holders under the Articles of Confederation.

To control the *causes* of factions would be to infringe on individual liberty. But Madison believed that the *effects* of factions are easily managed in a large republic. First of all, representation will dilute the effects of factions, and it is in this essay that Madison makes his famous distinction between "pure democracy" and a "republic." In addition, if the territory is sufficiently large, factions will be neutralized because there will be so many of them that no one is likely to become a majority. Furthermore, it will be difficult for people who share common interests to find one another if some live in South Carolina, for instance, and others live in Maine. (Clearly, Madison never anticipated the invention of the fax machine or electronic mail.) We discuss Madison's argument about factions again when we take up the topic of interest groups, in Chapter 11. In the meantime, however, notice how Madison relies on mechanical elements of politics (size and representation) to remedy a flaw in human nature (the tendency to form divisive factions). This is typical of the Federalists' approach to government and reflects the importance of institutions as well as rules in bringing about desired outcomes in politics.

We see the same emphasis on mechanical solutions to political problems in *Federalist* No. 51. Here Madison argues that the institutions proposed in the Constitution will lead neither to corruption nor to tyranny. The solution is the principles of checks and balances and separation of powers we have already discussed. Again building his case on a potential defect of human character, he says, "Ambition must be made to counteract ambition."[21] If men tend to be ambitious, give two ambitious men the job of watching over each other, and neither will let the other have an advantage.

Federalist No. 84, written by Hamilton, is interesting politically because it failed dismally. The Constitution was ratified despite it, not because of it. In this essay, Hamilton argues that a **Bill of Rights**—a listing of the protections against government infringement of individual rights guaranteed to citizens by government itself—is not necessary in a constitution. The original draft of the Constitution contained no Bill of Rights. Some state constitutions had them, and so the Federalists argued that a federal Bill of Rights would be redundant. Moreover, the limited government set up by the federal Constitution didn't have the power to infringe on individual rights anyway, and many of the rights that would be included in a Bill of

Rights were already in the body of the text. To the Anti-Federalists, already afraid of the invasive power of the national government, this omission was more appalling than any other aspect of the Constitution.

Hamilton explains the Federalist position, that a Bill of Rights was unnecessary. Then he makes the unusual argument that a Bill of Rights would actually be dangerous. As it stands, he says, the national government doesn't have the power to interfere with citizens' lives in many ways, and any interference at all would be suspect. But if the Constitution were prefaced with a list of things government could *not* do to individuals, government would assume it had the power to do anything that wasn't expressly forbidden. Therefore government, instead of being unlikely to trespass on citizens' rights, would be more likely to do so with a Bill of Rights than without. This argument was so unpersuasive to Americans at that time that the Federalists were forced to give in to Anti-Federalist pressure during the ratification process. The price of ratification exacted by several states was the Bill of Rights, really a "Bill of Limits" on the federal government, added to the Constitution as the first ten amendments.

The Final Vote

The small states, gratified by the compromise that gave them equal representation in the Senate and believing they would be better off as part of a strong nation, ratified the Constitution quickly. The vote was unanimous in Delaware, New Jersey, and Georgia. In Connecticut (128–40) and Pennsylvania (46–23), the votes, though not unanimous, were strongly in favor of the Constitution. This may have helped to tip the balance for Massachusetts, voting much more closely to ratify (187–168). Maryland (63–11) and South Carolina (149–73) voted in favor of ratification in the spring of 1788, leaving only one more state to supply the requisite nine to make the Constitution law.

The battles in the remaining states were much fiercer. When the Virginia convention met in June 1788, the Federalists felt that it could provide the decisive vote and threw much of their effort into securing passage. Madison and his Federalist colleagues debated with Anti-Federalist advocates such as George Mason and Patrick Henry, promising as they had in Massachusetts to support a Bill of Rights. Virginia ratified the Constitution by the narrow margin of 89 to 79, preceded by a few days by New Hampshire, voting 57 to 47. Establishment of the Constitution as the law of the land was ensured with the approval of ten states. New York also narrowly passed the Constitution (30–27), but North Carolina defeated it (193–75), and Rhode Island, which had not sent delegates to the Constitutional Convention, refused to call a state convention to put it to a vote. Later both North Carolina and Rhode Island voted to ratify and join the Union, in November 1789 and May 1790, respectively.[22]

Again we can see how important rules are in determining outcomes. The Articles of Confederation had required the approval of all the states. Had the Constitutional Convention chosen a similar rule of unanimity, the Constitution may very well have been defeated. Recognizing that unanimous approval was not probable, however, the Federalists decided to require ratification by only nine of the thirteen states, making adoption of the Constitution far more likely.

Citizenship and the Founding
New rights bring obligations

Citizenship as we know it today was a fledgling creation at the time of the founding. The British had not been citizens of the English government but subjects of the English crown. There is a world of difference between a subject and a citizen, as we pointed out in Chapter 1. The subject has a personal tie to the monarch; the citizen has a legal tie to a national territory. The subject has obligations; the citizen has both obligations and rights.

The new citizens had political power in America, but the leaders of American politics did not entirely trust them. They made their appearance in such episodes as Shays's Rebellion and found their voice in the business of state politics under the Articles of Confederation. They were the soldiers whose support had been vital to winning the Revolution, and they were the citizens whose power Madison feared as he wrote *Federalist* No. 10 about the danger of factions. To some extent, the writing of the Constitution was about reining in the power of the broad concept of citizenship that had been unleashed by the political freedom available under the Articles of Confederation, about checking and balancing the power of the people as well as the power of government.

▶ What's at Stake Revisited

Having read the history of Revolutionary America, what would you say is at stake in the modern militia movement? The existence of state militias and similar groups poses a troubling dilemma for the federal government, and groups, like the Tea Partiers, whose members are mostly benign, are even trickier for the government to deal with. Bill Clinton, who was president when Timothy McVeigh bombed the federal building in Oklahoma City, warned at the time of the fifteenth anniversary of those attacks that "there can be real consequences when what you say animates people who do things you would never do." There are those out there, like Timothy McVeigh, who "were profoundly alienated, disconnected people who bought into this militant antigovernment line."[23]

The dilemma is that, on the one hand, the purpose of government is to protect our rights, and the Constitution surely guarantees Americans freedom of speech and assembly. On the other hand, government must hold the monopoly on the legitimate use of force in society or it will fall, just as the British government fell to the American colonies. If groups are allowed to amass weapons and forcibly resist or even attack U.S. law enforcers, then they constitute "mini-governments," or competing centers of authority, and life for citizens becomes chaotic and dangerous.

The American system was designed to be relatively responsive to the wishes of the American public. Citizens can get involved; they can vote, run for office, change the laws, and amend the Constitution. By permitting these legitimate ways of affecting American politics, the founders hoped to prevent the rise of groups like the Hutaree, who would promote and act toward violence. The founders intended to create a society characterized by political stability, not by revolution, which is why Jefferson's Declaration of Independence is so careful to point out that revolutions should occur only when there is no alternative course of action.

Some militia members reject the idea of working through the system; they say, as did Timothy McVeigh, that they consider themselves at war with the federal government. We call disregard for the law at the individual level "crime," at the group level "terrorism" or "insurrection," and at the majority level "revolution." It is the job of any government worth its salt to prevent all three kinds of activities. Thus it is not the existence or the beliefs but the *activities* of the militia groups that government seeks to control.

What's at stake in the challenges to the legitimacy of government are the very issues of government authority and the rights of individual citizens. It is very difficult to draw the line between the protection of individual rights and the exercise of government authority. In a democracy, we want to respect the rights of all citizens, but this respect can be thwarted when a small number of individuals reject the rules of the game agreed on by the vast majority.

▶ Summary With Key Terms

The battle for America involved a number of groups, including Native Americans, and Spanish, French, and British colonists. By the time the British won the **French and Indian War** (47) to secure the colonists' defense, the colonists, already chafing under British rule, felt secure enough to sever the ties that bound them to the mother country, starting the Revolution and then in 1776 issuing the **Declaration of Independence** (51). Although that document proclaimed the equality of "all men," the American founders clearly did not include African Americans, Native Americans, or women in that category.

Charged with creating a **constitution** (53), the founders drew up the **Articles of Confederation** (53), establishing a **confederation** (54) of sovereign states. The new government wasn't strong enough to provide political stability in the face of popular discontent, however. Worried about **popular tyranny** (55), which they saw threatened in actions like **Shays's Rebellion** (55), the political elite called for a new **Constitutional Convention** (56) in 1787.

The founders rejected a confederal system in favor of **federalism** (56), giving the central government and the states each some power of its own. Those who endorsed this political innovation were known as the **Federalists** (57), and those who opposed it, the **Anti-Federalists** (57). Federalists supported a strong central government in which representation was determined by population—a plan, called the **Virginia Plan** (59), favored by the large states. The Anti-Federalists, suspicious of centralized power, favored the **New Jersey Plan** (59), which limited power and gave each state equal congressional representation regardless of size. These issues were resolved in the **Great Compromise** (59), which created a bicameral legislature, basing representation on population in one house and on equality in the other. The other major conflict among the founders, over how slaves were to be counted for purposes of representation, was resolved by the **Three-fifths Compromise** (60).

The new Constitution was based on **separation of powers** (64) and **checks and balances** (65), keeping the **legislature** (61), the **executive** (62), and the **judicial powers** (63) distinct but allowing each some power over the others. The independence of the branches and the checks between them were enhanced by such institutions as the **bicameral legislature** (61), the **Electoral College** (62), and the practice of **judicial review** (64), though the latter is not mentioned explicitly in the Constitution. The founders provided for **amendability** (67), should circumstances require that the Constitution be changed in the future.

The Federalists and the Anti-Federalists waged a battle over **ratification** (68) of the new Constitution, with the former setting out their case in a series of newspaper editorials known today as *The Federalist Papers* (63). In the most famous of these essays, James Madison argued that the new republic would be well able to handle the danger of **factions** (70), and in another, Alexander Hamilton argued that it would be dangerous to add a **Bill of Rights** (70) to the document. Hamilton ultimately lost the argument, and the Bill of Rights was the price the Anti-Federalists demanded for their agreement to ratify the Constitution.

Explore this subject further with suggested readings, movies, and web sites at http://republic-brief.cqpress.com, where you'll also find study aids, practice quizzes, flash cards, and Internet exercises.

STEPS IN THE ESTABLISHMENT OF A MORE STABLE GOVERNMENT

▶ What's at Stake?

When is an illegal drug not an illegal drug? When a doctor prescribes it for you to cure or alleviate an illness, an injury, or pain. Simple, right?

Not very, as it turns out.

Everyone knows that smoking marijuana is against the law. Among other things, the United States federal Controlled Substances Act says so. Under that law, passed in 1970, marijuana is a "schedule one drug," equivalent, in legal terms, to heroin and LSD.

But some scientists and doctors, as well as their patients, argue that marijuana is a drug, like morphine or codeine, that is beneficial for people who are sick, even though it can be abused by those who are not.

Joseph Kintzel, a Colorado dad who works as a respiratory therapist, is a case in point. After having several back surgeries for herniated disks, Kintzel was out of work for two years due to the severe pain that he tried to control with morphine, Percocet, and Vicodin.

In 2002, with his doctor's authorization, he began treating the pain with regular use of marijuana. He says that in a few months he was off all the narcotic pain killers and was back at work, where he has taken only one sick day in the past four years.[1]

Kintzel can do that because he lives in Colorado, one of twelve states that have passed medical marijuana laws that in different ways protect from prosecution those patients who have documented need for the drug.

But while Kintzel's use of marijuana for medical reasons may be legal in Colorado, it is illegal in the United States. That strange combination is possible because of our federal system, which gives some powers to the states, some to the national government, and some to be shared between them. In the case of medical marijuana laws, the federal government, in the George W. Bush administration, claimed that its law trumped state laws because of the commerce clause, the part of Article 1, Section 8, of the Constitution that gives Congress the power to regulate commerce among the states. In 2005 the Supreme Court, voting six to three in a case concerning a California medical marijuana law, backed that view.[2] Occasionally, federal agents raided local distribution centers, seizing and confiscating quantities of the drug.[3]

Defenders of the laws responded that growing, selling, or smoking marijuana for personal medical use within a single state has nothing to do with interstate commerce. Fourteen states passed laws decriminalizing the use of marijuana for medical purposes by prescription, and slowly, federal law swung in their direction. In May 2009 the Supreme Court refused to hear a case challenging the California law, essentially handing a victory to medical marijuana proponents, and in October, the Justice Department, now under the Obama administration, signaled that, as long as use was consistent with state laws, marijuana use by those holding a prescription for it would not be prosecuted.[4]

Why is this issue so controversial that it made its way twice all the way to the highest court in the land? Why did states continue to defy federal law to allow this practice? And why would the national government change its stance on the issue? Just what is at stake in the use of marijuana to treat medical conditions?

The Federalists and the Anti-Federalists fought intensely over the balance between national and state powers in our federal system. Debates over the Articles of Confederation and the Constitution show that the founders were well aware that the rules dividing the power between the states and the federal government were crucial to determining who would be the winners and losers in the new country. Where decisions are made—in Washington, D.C., or in the state capitals—would make a big difference in "who gets what, and how." Today the same battles are being fought between defenders of state and national powers. The balance of power has swung back and forth several times since the founders came to their own hard-won compromise, but over the past quarter-century there has been a movement, led largely by Republicans, to give more power and responsibility back to the state governments, a process known as **devolution**.

More recently, however, as Republicans became more accustomed to holding the reins of power in Washington with their various congressional majorities and their hold on the presidency from 2000 to 2008, their zeal for returning responsibilities to the states became less urgent, slowing the devolutionary trend. Calls for increased national security in the days after September 11, 2001, have also helped reverse the transfer of power to the states. As the state-federal relationship changes, so too do the arenas in which citizens and their leaders make the decisions that become government policy. Fundamental shifts usually mean changes in the probable winners and losers of American politics.

In this chapter we examine the remarkable power-sharing arrangement that is federalism, exploring its challenges, both historical and contemporary. We look at the definition of federalism and the alternatives the founders rejected when they made this compromise, the ways the balance of power in American federalism has shifted over time, and the structure of federalism today and the ways the national government tries to secure state cooperation.

What Is Federalism?
Balancing power between national and state governments

Federalism is a political system in which authority is divided between different levels of government (the national and state levels, in America's case). Each level has some power independent of the other levels so that no level is entirely dependent on another for its existence. In the United States, federalism was a compromise between those who wanted stronger state governments and those who preferred a stronger national government.

The effects of federalism are all around us. We pay income taxes to the national government, which parcels out the money to the states, under certain conditions, to be spent on programs such as welfare, highways, and education. In most states, local schools are funded by local property taxes and run by local school boards (local governments are created under the authority of the state), and state universities are supported by state taxes and influenced by the state legislature. Even so, both state and local governments are subject to national legislation, such as the requirement that schools be open to students of all races, and both can be affected by national decisions about funding various programs. Sometimes the lines of responsibility can be extremely unclear. Witness the simultaneous presence, in many areas, of city police, county police, state police, and, at the national level, the Federal Bureau of Investigation (FBI), all coordinated, for some purposes, by the national Department of Homeland Security.

Even when a given responsibility lies at the state level, the national government frequently finds a way to enforce its will. For instance, it is up to the states to decide on the minimum drinking age for their citizens. In the 1970s many states required people to be only eighteen or nineteen before they could legally buy alcohol; today all the states have a uniform drinking age of twenty-one. The change came about because interest groups persuaded officials in the federal, that is, national, government that the higher age would lead to fewer alcohol-related highway accidents and greater public safety. The federal government couldn't pass a law setting a nationwide drinking age of twenty-one, but it could control the flow of highway money to the states. By withholding 5 percent of federal highway funds, which every state wants and needs, until a state raised the drinking age to twenty-one, Congress prevailed. This is an example of how the relations between levels of government work when neither level can directly force the other to do what it wants.

Mitch Daniels

Some politicians are born legislators—they like to argue and deliberate and craft careful compromises. Others are natural executives; they focus on solving problems and clearing hurdles. Count Indiana governor Mitch Daniels among the latter group: despite his folksy manner, he likes to get things done.

And Daniels has been getting things done on all levels of government for most of his career, as assistant to the mayor of Indianapolis in the 1970s, as President George W. Bush's director of the Office of Management and Budget (OMB) from January 2001 to June 2003, and as governor of the state of Indiana since 2005. He hasn't exactly been squelching rumors that he might run for president in 2012, either—not surprising, given that it is the ultimate office for getting things done in U.S. politics.

When he took on OMB, Daniels expected his new position to be interesting from the start, but the job took on an unanticipated dimension of high-stakes urgency in the days after September 11. He says, "There was one night that won't be replicated maybe ever again . . . this is probably

> "... if you don't feel grateful for being born into a free society, you better get out and see the world a little bit."

September 13, 14 . . . we're sitting around this long conference table in the Speaker of the House's office with the Speaker of the House, Senator Daschle, the Senate majority leader, and minority—the minority leadership of the House, I'm there for the administration. And I guess a couple of the other committee chairs, or something. And really, in real time, we're hammering out what will be done about the airlines, which are not flying—they're not going back into the air unless we can get them insurance—the Democrats aren't going to agree to insurance unless you compensate the people in New York City, which had never been done—we didn't do it in Oklahoma City, we're going to do it here . . . and on and on . . . and the first steps toward what became a huge expenditure on homeland security and eventually a new cabinet department. All taking shape right there, all those people at one table. Right in the middle of the wee hours, it's an amazing thing. But in an atmosphere, again, that won't happen often, of genuine bipartisanship. Just for a little while they all put their sabers away, and it was astonishing."

Astonishing indeed, and in that emotional, keyed-up, history-shaping moment, it was Daniels's job to keep his head—to hold the costs down, to be sure that compensation offered was reasonable and that they didn't set precedents for the future. How on earth do you prepare for such awesome and humbling responsibility?

Sitting in his huge office in the Indiana statehouse, relaxed and thoughtful, Daniels reflects on the extraordinary journey that has taken an Indiana boy to the heights of national politics and business and brought him back home again to run his state's government. His account is peppered with laughter and self-deprecating anecdotes ("Do you have time for a quick story?" he asks more than once), but they can't hide the hard work, the laser intelligence, and the abiding interest in things political that have gotten him where he is.

It was an early reading of Allen Drury's *Advise and Consent* that hooked him on politics, with its fictionalized account of "the grand theater of the legislative process . . . these large figures and their inner motives and their moments of truth." After his freshman year of college, he was asked by a local precinct committeeman, whose lawn he happened to cut, if he wanted to work on a U.S. Senate campaign. Flattered to be asked, and perhaps with Drury's grand theater in the back of his mind, he said yes.

The campaign put him in touch with Richard Lugar, who went on to become mayor of Indianapolis and U.S. senator. Daniels worked for Lugar (whom he calls "an extraordinary paragon in public service"), mostly as his chief-of-staff, for thirteen years, before deciding he wanted to move back home. Although he detoured to work as a senior adviser in the Reagan White House, he did get back to Indiana, working in the private sector in Indianapolis before heading back to D.C. and the position at OMB. Today he is very happy to be back in Indiana once again, ensconced in the governor's office.

He says, "Governor is the only elected position I can think of that I'd be interested in because it's at a scale big enough to really matter to a lot of people and yet you're in a real position to do things. . . . Things tend to be much more concrete and much more practical, less ideological. Obviously you're closer to the problems here." And solving problems is just what Governor Daniels likes. Other observations:

On citizen wisdom:
In fact, my view has always been that we ought not to have many people spending their entire careers in public life. . . . I think in general people bring the most to

(Continued)

Mitch Daniels (Continued)

public service if they are sort of balanced in their perspective by some other career, or some other professional activity. I think the richness of republican, I'm talking about small "r," republican government comes from the sort of citizen wisdom that you get when people . . . are politicians second and doctors or social workers or small business people or something else as well.

On keeping the republic:

I subscribe to the view that, as somebody once said, giving some time to public affairs is the rent I owe this country. Number one, if you don't feel grateful for being born into a free society, you better get out and see the world a little bit. . . . And then assuming you do feel as grateful as you should, you owe a little rent, you owe a little something to those who made this possible and so that it remains possible for the folks who follow. Now, the way you pay that rent—you've got a lot of choices. And an elected office or even a government job, government service, is only part of it. . . .

The second thing I'd say is that, there are a lot of other ways. . . . The strength of this country to me, maybe the single distinguishing characteristic of American democracy—de Tocqueville sure thought this—is we are joiners in this country and we've got organizations of every kind. . . . And that's every bit as much a way to strengthen a democracy or republic, I think. . . . So I count all of that. Somebody wants to go out and be a leader of the Sierra Club or be a leader of the Heart Association or some civic group, that counts too, to me.

And I guess the last thing is, and I said it before, I don't feel the need at all to consider government service a career choice. If you do, that's honorable but you don't need to. And my personal view is the best citizens of all may be those who are grounded elsewhere, who then try to bring what they've learned to the job of building a better society and a more effective government, without being dependent either professionally, financially, or psychologically on that job.

What Does the Constitution Say?

No single section of the Constitution deals with federalism. Instead, the provisions dividing power between the states and the national government appear throughout the Constitution. As a state matter, local government is not mentioned in the Constitution at all. Most of the Constitution is concerned with establishing the powers of the national government. Since Congress is the main lawmaking arm of the national government, many of the powers of the national government are the powers of Congress. The strongest statement of national power is a list of the **enumerated powers of Congress** (Article I, Section 8). This list is followed by a clause that gives Congress the power to make all laws that are "necessary and proper" to carry out its powers. The **necessary and proper clause** has been used to justify giving Congress many powers never mentioned in the Constitution. National power is also based on the **supremacy clause** of Article VI, which says that the Constitution and laws made in accordance with it are "the supreme law of the land." This means that when national and state laws conflict, the national laws will be followed. The Constitution also sets limitations on the national government. Article I, Section 9, lists some specific powers not granted to Congress, and the Bill of Rights (the first ten amendments to the Constitution) limits the power of the national government over individuals.

The Constitution says considerably less about the powers granted to the states. The Tenth Amendment says that all powers not given to the national government are reserved to the states, although the necessary and proper clause makes it difficult to see which powers are withheld from the national government. The states are given the power to approve the Constitution itself and any amendments to it. The Constitution also limits state powers. Article I, Section 10, denies the states certain powers, mostly the kinds that they possessed under the Articles of Confederation. The Fourteenth Amendment limits the power of the states over individual liberties, essentially a Bill of Rights that protects individuals from state action, since the first ten amendments apply only to the national government.

What these constitutional provisions mean is that the line between the national government and the state governments is not clearly drawn. We can see from Figure 3.1 that the Constitution designates specific powers as national, state, or concurrent. **Concurrent powers** are those that both levels of government may exercise. But the federal relationship is a good deal more complex than this chart would lead us to believe. The Supreme Court has become crucial to establishing the exact limits of provisions such as the necessary and proper clause, the supremacy clause, the Tenth Amendment, and the Fourteenth Amendment. This interpretation has changed over time, especially as historical demands have forced the Court to think about federalism in new ways.

Two Views of Federalism

Political scientists have also changed the way they think about federalism. For many years the prevailing theory was known as **dual federalism**, basically arguing that the relationship between the two levels of government was like a layer cake. That is, the national and state governments were to be understood as two self-contained layers, each essentially separate from the other and carrying out its functions independently. In its own area of power, each level was supreme. Dual federalism reflects the formal distribution of powers in the Constitution, and perhaps it was an accurate portrayal of the judicial interpretation of the federal system for our first hundred years or so.

Figure 3.1

The Constitutional Division of Powers Between the National Government and the States

NATIONAL POWERS	CONCURRENT POWERS	STATE POWERS
• Admit new states into the Union • Coin money • Conduct foreign affairs • Declare war • Establish courts inferior to the Supreme Court • Make laws that are necessary for carrying out the powers vested by the Constitution • Raise and maintain armies, navies • Regulate commerce with foreign nations and among the states	• Borrow and spend money for the general welfare • Charter and regulate banks; charter corporations • Collect taxes • Establish courts • Establish highways • Pass and enforce laws • Take private property for public purposes, with just compensation	**Powers reserved to the states:** • Conduct elections and determine voter qualifications • Establish local governments • Maintain militia (National Guard) • Provide for public health, safety, and morals • Ratify amendments to the federal Constitution • Regulate intrastate commerce **States expressly prohibited from:** • Abridging the privileges or immunities of citizens or denying due process and equal protection of the laws (14th Amendment) • Coining money • Entering into treaties • Keeping troops or navies • Levying import or export taxes on goods • Making war

But this theory was criticized for not describing realistically the way the federal relationship was evolving in the twentieth century. It certainly did not take into account the changes brought about by the New Deal. The layer cake image was replaced by a new bakery metaphor. According to the new theory of **cooperative federalism**, rather than being two distinct layers, the national and state levels were swirled together like the chocolate and vanilla batter in a marble cake.[5] National and state powers were interdependent, and each level required the cooperation of the other to get things done. In fact, federalism came to be seen by political scientists as a partnership, but one in which the dominant partner was, more often than not, the national government.

Possible Alternatives to Federalism

The federal system was not the only alternative available to our founders for organizing the relationship between the central government and the states. In fact, as we know, it wasn't even their first choice as a framework for government. The Articles of

Confederation, which preceded the Constitution, handled the relationship quite differently. We can look at federalism as a compromise system that borrows some attributes from a unitary system and some from a confederal system. Had the founders chosen either of these alternatives, American government would look very different today.

Unitary Systems

In a **unitary system**, the central government ultimately has all the power. Local units (states or counties) may have some power at some time, but basically they are dependent on the central unit, which can alter or even abolish them. Many contemporary countries have unitary systems, among them Britain, France, Japan, Denmark, Norway, Sweden, Hungary, and the Philippines.

Politics in Britain, for example, works very differently from politics in the United States, partly due to the different rules that organize central and local governments. Most important decisions are made in London, from foreign policy to housing policy—even the details of what ought to be included in the school curriculum. Even local taxes are determined centrally. When Margaret Thatcher, then the British prime minister, believed that some municipal units in London were not supportive of her government's policies, she simply dissolved the administrative units. Similarly, in 1972, when the legislature in Northern Ireland (a part of Great Britain) could not resolve its religious conflicts, the central government suspended the local lawmaking body and ruled Northern Ireland from London. These actions are tantamount to a Republican president's dissolving a Democratic state that disagreed with his policies, or the national government's deciding to suspend the state legislature in Alabama and run the state from Washington during the days of segregation. Such an arrangement has been impossible in the United States except during the chaotic state of emergency following the Civil War. What is commonplace under a unitary system is unimaginable under our federal rules.

Confederal Systems

Confederal systems provide an equally sharp contrast to federal systems, even though the names sound quite similar. In **confederal systems**, the local units hold all the power, and the central government is dependent on them for its existence. The local units remain sovereign, and the central government has only as much power as they allow it to have. Examples of confederal systems include America under the Articles of Confederation and associations such as the United Nations and the European Union, twenty-seven European nations that have joined economic and political forces. The European Union has been experiencing problems much like ours after the Revolutionary War, debating whether it ought to move in a more federal direction. Most of the nations involved, jealously guarding their sovereignty, say no.

What Difference Does Federalism Make?

That our founders settled on federalism, rather than a unitary or a confederal system, makes a great deal of difference to American politics. Federalism gave the founders a national government that could take effective action, restore economic stability, and regulate disputes among the states, while allowing the states considerable autonomy. Still, federalism forces the states to continually negotiate their relationships not only with the national government but also with each other. Even though they have the ability to act independently in many respects, they have to be able to cooperate effectively and, frequently, to compete with each other. States are always looking to use their resources in creative ways to win scarce federal benefits, to lure business and economic development opportunities, and to encourage people to relocate within their borders.

Federalism gives both national government and the states a good measure of flexibility when it comes to experimentation with public policy. If all laws and policies need not be uniform across the country, different states may try different solutions to common problems and share the results of their experiments. For instance, in 1994 the state of Oregon began a controversial experiment in the financing of health care by adding many uninsured people to the Medicaid program and paying for the additional number of services covered. Although the plan has suffered some setbacks, it has been politically popular. More time is needed to determine just how successful such a program can be, but Oregon's opportunity to experiment may provide valuable lessons about health care policy for other states and for the national government.[6]

However, it is not only units of government but also individuals who stand to benefit from power sharing between nation and states. Federalism means that there is real power at levels of government that are close to the citizens. Citizens can thus have access to officials and processes of government that they could not have if there were just one distant, effective unit. Federalism allows government to preserve local standards and to respond to local needs—that is, to solve problems at the levels where they occur. Examples include local traffic laws, community school policies, and city and county housing codes.

Federalism is not a perfect system, however, and it has some disadvantages. Where policies are made and enforced locally, all economies of scale are lost. Many functions are also repeated across the country as states administer national programs locally. Most problematic is the fact that federalism permits, even encourages, local prejudices to find their way into law. Until the national government took enforcement of civil rights legislation into its own hands in the 1960s, federalism allowed southern states to practice segregation. Before the passage of the Nineteenth Amendment, women could vote in some states but not others. Similarly, gay Americans do not have the same rights in all localities of the United States today—while they can marry in Massachusetts, Iowa, Vermont, New Hampshire, Connecticut, and the District of Columbia, they do not even have the right to join in civil unions in many other states. To the degree that states have more rather than less power, the uniform enforcement of civil rights cannot be guaranteed.

Overall, federalism has proved to be a flexible and effective compromise for American government. The United States is not the only nation with a federal system, although other countries may distribute power among their various units differently from the way we do. Germany, Canada, Mexico, Australia, and Switzerland are all examples of federal systems.

American Federalism Over Time
Constitutional ambiguity and the role of the
Supreme Court

Although the Constitution provides for both national powers and state powers (as well as some shared powers), several factors have caused the balance between the two to change considerably since it was written. First, because of the founders' disagreement over how power should be distributed in the new country, the final wording about national and state powers was intentionally kept vague, which probably helped the Constitution get ratified. Because it wasn't clear how much power the different levels held, it has been possible ever since for both ardent Federalists and states' rights advocates to find support for their positions in the document.

A second factor that has caused the balance of national and state powers to shift over time has to do with the role given to the Supreme Court to step in and interpret what it thinks the Constitution really means when conflict arises over which level of government should have the final say on a given issue. Those interpretations have varied along with the people sitting on the Court and with historical circumstances. As the context of American life has been transformed through events such as the end of slavery and the Civil War, the process of industrialization and the growth of big business, the economic collapse of the Great Depression in the 1930s and the relative prosperity of the late 1900s, the terror attacks of September 2001 and the recession that began in 2008, the demands made on the different levels of government have shifted, too. When we talk about federalism in the United States, we are talking about specific constitutional rules and provisions, but we are also talking about a fairly continuous evolution of how those rules are understood.

Two trends are apparent when we examine American federalism throughout our history. One is that American government in general is growing in size, at both the state and national levels. We make many more demands of government than did, say, the citizens of George Washington's time, or Abraham Lincoln's, and the apparatus to satisfy those demands has grown accordingly. But within that overall growth, a second trend has been the gradual strengthening of the national government at the expense of the states.

> As the country has grown, so have our expectations of what the government will do for us.

The increase in the size of government shouldn't surprise us. One indisputable truth about the United States is that, over the years, it has gotten bigger, more industrialized, more urban, and more technical. As the country has grown, so have our expectations of what the government will do for us. We want to be protected from the fluctuations of the market, from natural disasters, from unfair business practices, and from unsafe foods and drugs. We want government to protect our "rights," but our concept of those rights has expanded beyond the first ten amendments to include things like economic security in old age, a minimum standard of living for all citizens, a safe interstate highway system, and crime-free neighborhoods. These new demands and expectations create larger government at all levels, but particularly at the national level, where the resources and will to accomplish such broad policy goals are more likely to exist.

The national government has grown so large, so quickly, that the proper balance of power between the national and state governments is a central and controversial political issue today, and one that has traditionally divided the liberals and conservatives we spoke of in Chapter 1. Liberals believe a strong central government can solve society's problems, especially economically, and conservatives believe that "big government" causes more problems than it solves. People in the latter category, like the Anti-Federalists at the founding, would prefer to see power and the distribution of government services located at the state or local level, closer to the people being governed. From 2000 to 2006, however, with Republicans holding the reins of power in both the legislative and the executive branches, the conservative distaste for big government waned somewhat as they were the ones dictating the actions of that government. President Bush's No Child Left Behind Act, for instance, took away many of the prerogatives of local school districts to decide whether to engage in regular testing of students, and yet it enjoyed the support of many conservatives. Also, as we have noted, many conservatives have begun to argue for an expanded national role in regulating morals, if not the economy, and the need to address national security issues after September 11 stepped up conservative calls for bigger government solutions in that arena as well. Some Republicans themselves have noted that, once they come to Washington, conservatives could be "as bad as liberals" about enforcing the national will on states.[7] Once President Obama was elected and the Democrats passed the stimulus bill and health care reform, however, Republicans quickly returned to their traditional views and decried the return of "big government." Both Democrats and Republicans are more willing to entertain the possibility of national government action when they are the ones controlling the national government. We explore this evolving contemporary federalism later in this chapter.

The growth of the national government's power over the states can be traced by looking at four moments in our national history: the early judicial decisions of Chief Justice John Marshall, the Civil War, the New Deal, and the civil rights movement and the expanded use of the Fourteenth Amendment from the 1950s through the 1970s. Since the late 1970s, we have seen increasing opposition to the growth of what is called "big government" on the part of citizens and officials alike, but most of the efforts to cut it back in size and to restore power to the states have been unsuccessful.

John Marshall: Strengthening the Constitutional Powers of the National Government

John Marshall, the third chief justice of the Supreme Court (1801–1835), was a man of decidedly Federalist views. His rulings did much to strengthen the power of the national government both during his lifetime and after. The 1819 case of

McCulloch v. Maryland set the tone. In resolving this dispute about whether Congress had the power to charter a bank and whether the state of Maryland had the power to tax that bank, Marshall had plenty of scope for exercising his preference for a strong national government. Congress did have the power, he ruled, even though the Constitution didn't spell it out, because Congress was empowered to do whatever was necessary and proper to fulfill its constitutional obligations. Marshall did not interpret the word *necessary* to mean "absolutely essential," but rather he took a looser view, holding that Congress had the power to do whatever was "appropriate" to execute its powers. If that meant chartering a bank, then the necessary and proper clause could be stretched to include chartering a bank. Furthermore, Maryland could not tax the federal bank because "the power to tax involves the power to destroy."[8] If Maryland could tax the federal bank, that would imply it had the power to destroy it, making Maryland supreme over the national government and violating the Constitution's supremacy clause, which makes the national government supreme.

Marshall continued this theme in *Gibbons v. Ogden* in 1824.[9] In deciding that New York did not have the right to create a steamboat monopoly on the Hudson River, Marshall focused on the part of Article I, Section 8, that allows Congress to regulate commerce "among the several states." He interpreted commerce very broadly to include almost any kind of business, creating a justification for a national government that could freely regulate business and that was dominant over the states.

Gibbons v. Ogden did not immediately establish national authority over business. Business interests were far too strong to meekly accept government authority, and subsequent Court decisions recognized that strength and a prevailing public philosophy of laissez-faire. The national government's power in general was limited by cases such as *Cooley v. Board of Wardens of Port of Philadelphia* (1851),[10] which gave the states greater power to regulate commerce if local interests outweigh national interests, and *Dred Scott v. Sanford* (1857),[11] which held that Congress did not have the power to outlaw slavery in the territories.

The Civil War: National Domination of the States

The Civil War represented a giant step in the direction of a stronger national government. The war itself was fought for a variety of reasons. Besides the issue of slavery and the conflicting economic and cultural interests of the North and South, the war was fought to resolve the question of national versus state supremacy. When the national government, dominated by the northern states, passed legislation that would have furthered northern interests, the southern states tried to invoke the doctrine of nullification. **Nullification** was the idea that states could render national laws null if they disagreed with them, but the national government never recognized this doctrine. The southern states also seceded, or withdrew from the United States, as a way of rejecting national authority, but the victory of the Union in the ensuing war showed decisively that states did not retain their sovereignty under the Constitution.

The New Deal: National Power Over Business

The Civil War did not settle the question of the proper balance of power between national government and business interests. In the years following the war, the courts struck down both state and national laws regulating business. In 1895 *Pollock v. Farmer's Loan and Trust Co.* held that the federal income tax was unconsti-

Redefining American Government

This highly partisan contemporary cartoon shows President Franklin Roosevelt cheerfully steering the American ship of state toward economic recovery, despite detractors in big business. New Deal policies redefined the scope of both national and state powers.

tutional (until it was legalized by the Sixteenth Amendment to the Constitution in 1913).[12] *Lochner v. New York* (1905) said that states could not regulate working hours for bakers.[13] This ruling was used as the basis for rejecting state and national regulation of business until the middle of the New Deal in the 1930s. *Hammer v. Dagenhart* (1918) said that national laws prohibiting child labor were outside Congress' power to regulate commerce and therefore were unconstitutional.[14]

Throughout the early years of Franklin Roosevelt's New Deal, designed amid the devastation of the Great Depression of the 1930s to recapture economic stability through economic regulations, the Supreme Court maintained its antiregulation stance. But the president berated the Court for striking down his programs, and public opinion backed the New Deal and Roosevelt himself against the interests of big business. Eventually the Court had a change of heart. Once established as constitutional, New Deal policies redefined the purpose of American government and thus the scope of both national and state powers. The relationship between nation and state became more cooperative as the government became employer, provider, and insurer of millions of Americans in times of hardship. Our Social Security system was born during the New Deal, as were many other national programs designed to get America back to work and back on its feet. A sharper contrast to the laissez-faire policies of the early 1900s can hardly be imagined.

Civil Rights: National Protection Against State Abuse

The national government picked up a host of new roles as American society became more complex, including that of guarantor of individual rights against state abuse.

The Fourteenth Amendment to the Constitution was passed after the Civil War to make sure southern states extended all the protections of the Constitution to the newly freed slaves. In the 1950s and 1960s it was used by the Supreme Court to strike down a variety of state laws that maintained segregated, or separate, facilities for whites and African Americans, from railway cars to classrooms. By the 1970s the Court's interpretation of the Fourteenth Amendment had expanded, allowing it to declare unconstitutional many state laws that it said deprived state citizens of their rights as U.S. citizens. For instance, the Court ruled that states had to guarantee those accused of state crimes the same protections that the Bill of Rights guaranteed those accused of federal crimes. As we will see in more detail in Chapter 4, the Fourteenth Amendment has come to be a means for severely limiting the states' powers over their own citizens, sometimes very much against their will.

The trend toward increased national power has not put an end to the debate over federalism, however. In the 1970s and 1980s, Presidents Richard Nixon and Ronald Reagan tried hard to return some responsibilities to the states, mainly by giving them more control over how they spent federal money. In the following section, we look at recent efforts to alter the balance of federal power in favor of the states.

Federalism Today
A continuing struggle

Clearly federalism is a continually renegotiated compromise between advocates of strong national government on the one hand and advocates of state power on the other. Making the job of compromise more complex, however, is the fact that federalism is not a purely ideological issue but also reflects pragmatic politics. If a party dominates the federal government for a long time, its members become accustomed to look to that government to accomplish their aims; those whose party persists in the minority on the federal level tend to look to the states. As one expert put it, "Fundamentally, though, neither federal officials nor most state and local officials values federalism as a constitutional end rather than a political means to partisan ends."[15] In short, most of the time people will fight to have decisions made in the arena (national or state) where they are most likely to prevail, or where the opposition will have the greatest difficulty achieving their policy goals.

The Politics of Contemporary Federalism

Beginning with *Marbury v. Madison*, the Supreme Court has gradually interpreted the Constitution in ways that give the national government more and more power relative to the states. This means that when Congress decides to expand federal policy into new areas, the Supreme Court is unlikely to step in to protect the states. This trend was highlighted in the 1985 case of *Garcia v. San Antonio Metropolitan Transit Authority*,[16] which involved the constitutionality of allowing the federal

Don't Be Fooled by the Op-Ed Pages

"All the news that's fit to print," proclaims the banner of the *New York Times.* But news isn't the only thing you'll find in what readers fondly refer to as "the old gray lady." Some of the most informative, entertaining, and, frequently, infuriating "news" printed in the *New York Times*—and most other newspapers today—can be found in the op-ed pages, where opinion pieces, editorials, and letters to the editor reign supreme. Often the last two inside pages of the first section, the op-ed pages need to be read differently from the rest of the paper. Writers of the standard news pages try to be objective, and while their values and beliefs may sneak in, they attempt to minimize the influence of their opinions on their work.

Writers on the op-ed pages, in contrast, flaunt their opinions, proudly display their biases, and make value-laden claims with abandon. This can make for fascinating reading, and can help you to formulate your own opinions, if you know what you are reading. Op-ed writers include:

- The newspaper's editorial board—editors employed by the paper who take stands on public matters, recommend courses of action to officials, and endorse candidates for office. On the whole, editorial boards are more conservative than liberal (for example, they have endorsed Republican presidential candidates far more often than they have endorsed Democrats)—but they often reflect the ideological tendencies of their reader base. The editors of the *New York Times,* which is read by a liberal urban population, take stances that are on the more liberal side, while the *Wall Street Journal,* subscribed to by the national business community, is more conservative. *USA Today,* which aspires to a broad national circulation, attempts to be more moderate in its outlook.

- Columnists—writers employed by the paper or by a news syndicate (whose work is distributed to many newspapers) who analyze current events from their personal ideological point of view. Columnists can be liberal, like Ellen Goodman (*Boston Globe*) and Molly Ivins (*Fort Worth Star-Telegram*), or conservative, like David Brooks (*New York Times*), George Will (*Washington Post*), and Robert Novak (nationally syndicated). The *Washington Post*'s E. J. Dionne and David Broder, and the *New York Times*'s Maureen Dowd, are all cogent observers and critics of the political scene who defy precise placement on an ideological scale.

While their values tend toward the liberal, they are equally hard on both parties.

- Guest columnists—ranging from the country's elite in the *New York Times* to everyday Americans in *USA Today*—who expound their views on a wide range of issues.
- Readers of the newspaper—who write letters to the editor, responding either to points of news coverage in the newspaper or to other items on the op-ed pages.

Here are some questions to ask yourself as you read the op-ed section of the newspaper:

- Who is the author? What do you know about him or her? As you get used to reading certain newspaper editorial pages and columnists you will know what to expect from them. Guest columnists are harder to gauge. The paper should tell you who they are, but you can always do further research on the web or elsewhere. Figure out how the author's job or achievements might influence his or her views.
- What are the values underlying the piece you are reading? Does the author make his or her values clear? If not, can you figure them out based on what the person writes? Unless you know the values that motivate an author, it is difficult to judge fairly what he or she has to say, and it can be difficult not to be hoodwinked as well.
- Is the author building an argument? If so, are the premises or assumptions that the author makes clear? Does the author cite adequate evidence to back up his or her points? Does the argument make sense? Notice that these are versions of the same questions we set out as guides to critical thinking in Chapter 1. Always think critically when you are reading an op-ed piece, or you are in danger of taking someone's opinions and preferences as fact!
- What kinds of literary devices does the author use that you might not find in a straight news story? Opinion writers, especially columnists, might use sarcasm or irony to expose what they see as the absurdities of politics or political figures, and they might even invent fictional characters. What is the point of these literary devices? Are they effective?
- Has the author persuaded you? Why or why not? Has the author shown you how to look at a familiar situation in a new light, or has he or she merely reinforced your own opinions? Do you feel inspired to write a letter to the editor on the subject? If so, do it!

government to dictate minimum wage standards to municipal governments. (A municipality is a unit of government providing local services for a city or town.) The Court ruled that Congress could regulate municipal salaries and that the Court would not get involved in disputes between the federal government and state and local governments.[17] In other words, the Court would allow the federal government to decide how far to involve itself in state and local matters.

In subsequent decisions, however, the Court has argued that there are some limits to federal encroachment, and the conservative Supreme Court under Chief Justice William Rehnquist passed down a set of decisions beginning in 1991 that signaled a rejection of congressional encroachment on the prerogatives of the states—a power shift dubbed "devolution." However, that movement came to an abrupt stop in 2002 following the attacks of September 11, 2001. The Court continues to have a conservative majority under Chief Justice John Roberts, but its inclinations have tended more toward favoring business than resurrecting federalism.[18]

The Supreme Court's decisions give the federal government great latitude in exercising its powers, but the states are still responsible for the policies that most affect our lives. For instance, the states retain primary responsibility for everything from education to regulation of funeral parlors, from licensing physicians to building roads and telling us how fast we can drive on them. Most questions of contemporary federalism involve the national government trying to influence how the states and localities go about providing the goods and services and regulating the behaviors that have traditionally been within their jurisdictions.

Why should the national government care so much about what the states do? There are several reasons. First, from the perspective of a member of Congress, it is easier to solve many social and economic problems at the national level. Pervasive problems such as race discrimination or air and water pollution do not affect just the populations of individual states. When a political problem does not stop at the state border, it can be easier to conceive of solutions that cross the border as well; such solutions require national coordination. In some instances, national problem solving involves redistributing resources from one state or region to another, which individual states, on their own, would be unwilling or unable to do.

Second, members of Congress gain electoral favor by passing laws and regulations that force the states to do things their supporters prefer. Incumbents have embraced their roles as representatives who can deliver highways; parks; welfare benefits; urban renewal; assistance to farmers, ranchers, miners, and educators; and just about everything else. Doing well by constituents gets incumbents reelected, even if it means getting state and local officials to change how they do their business.[19]

Third, sometimes members of Congress prefer to adopt national legislation to preempt what states may be doing or planning to do. In some cases, they might object to state laws, as Congress did when it passed civil rights legislation against the strong preferences of the southern states. In other cases, they might enact legislation to prevent states from making fifty different regulatory laws for the same product. Here they are being sensitive to the wishes of corporations and businesses—generally large contributors to politicians—to have a single set of laws governing their activities. If Congress makes a set of nationally binding regulations, a business does not have to incur the expense of altering its product (or service) to meet different state standards.

To deliver on their promises, national politicians must have the cooperation of the states. Although some policies, such as Social Security, can be administered easily at the national level, others, such as changing educational policy or altering the drinking age, remain under state authority and cannot be legislated in Washington. It is here that federal policymakers face one of their biggest challenges: how to get the states to do what federal officials have decided they should do.

Let's take the question of mathematics education as an example. Assume that members of Congress have decided that we face a "math crisis" and that more math training needs to take place in our high schools for the nation to remain competitive in the world economy of the twenty-first century. How will they get the education policymakers—that is, the states—to go along with them? One sure way to influence math education would be for the federal government to build and staff a system of "federal schools." Then it could have any kind of a curriculum it wanted. But doing so would be enormously expensive and wasteful, since the states and localities already have schools and already teach math in them. The more efficient alternative would be to try to influence how the states and localities teach math. Here Congress would face the same challenges it does with respect to other policy areas such as health, occupational safety, transportation, and welfare. When Congress wants to act in these areas, it has to find ways to work with the states and localities.

Congressional Strategies for Influencing State Policy

Congress makes two key decisions when it attempts to influence what the states are doing. One is about the character of the rules and regulations that are issued: Will they be broad and allow the states flexibility or narrow and specific to guarantee that policy is executed as Washington wishes? The other is about whether the cost of the new programs they supported will be paid for by the national government and, if so, by how much. The combination of these two decisions yields the four general congressional strategies for influencing the states we see in Table 3.1.

Option One: No Federal Influence
In the period of dual federalism, the federal government left most domestic policy decisions to the states. Precollege education is a good example: the federal government did not provide instructions to the states about curriculum goals (let alone math training), nor did it provide the funds for education. The combination of no instructions and no funding (first row in Table 3.1) yields the outcome of no federal influence. This means the states organized education as they wished. To follow our math example, the outcome of no federal influence would be that some states might concentrate on math, while others might emphasize a different educational issue. Such policy differences are a natural outcome of a situation in which the states, rather than the federal government, have more power in a given policy area.

Table 3.1

How the National Government Influences the States

		Provide Federal Funds?	
		Yes	No
How strict are the rules?	Strict and specific requirements	Categorical Grants: • Good for congressional credit taking. • Ensures state compliance and policy uniformity. • Heavy federal regulatory burden ("red tape"). • National policy requirements may not be appropriate for local conditions.	Unfunded Mandates: • Very cheap for the federal government. • Easy way for members of Congress to garner favor. • States complain about unfairness and burdensome regulations. • Undermines state cooperation.
	No rules or broad grants of power within program areas	Block Grants: • Greater state flexibility, program economy. • State politicians love money without "strings." • Greater program innovation. Undermines congressional credit taking. • Grants become highly vulnerable to federal budget cuts. • Leads to policy diversity and inequality, meeting state rather than national goals.	No federal Influence: • States have autonomy and pay for their own programs. • Results in high diversity of policies, including inequality. Promotes state competition and its outcomes. • Calls for congressional and presidential restraint in exercising their powers.

Option Two: Categorical Grants

In our example, Congress might decide that the nation's long-term economic health depends on massive improvements in high school mathematics education. "No federal influence" is clearly not an option here. Congress could pass a resolution declaring its desire for better math education in high school, but if it wants results, it would have to put some teeth in its "request." If Congress really wants to effect a change, it would have to provide instructions and an incentive for the states to improve math education.

The most popular tool Congress has devised for this purpose is the **categorical grant** (see the second row in Table 3.1), which provides very detailed instructions, regulations, and compliance requirements for the states (and sometimes for local governments, as well) in specific policy areas. If a state complies with the requirements, federal money is released for those specified purposes. If a state doesn't comply with the detailed provisions of the categorical grant, it doesn't get the money. In many cases, the states have to provide some funding themselves. They might, for instance, have to match the amount contributed by the federal government.

To continue with our example, the federal government could pass a math education act that would provide funds on a per-pupil basis for math education in the high schools. The bill might set standards for certain performance or testing levels, requirements for teacher certification in advanced math education training, and perhaps specific goals for decreasing the gender and racial gaps in math performance. School districts and state school boards would have to document their compliance in order to receive their funds.

The states, like most governments, never have enough money to meet all their citizens' demands, so categorical grants can look very attractive, at least on the surface. The grants can be refused, but most of the time they are welcomed. In fact, state and local governments have become so dependent on federal subsidies that these subsidies now make up about 27 percent of all state and local spending.[20] Thus the categorical grant has become a powerful tool for the federal government to use in getting the states to do what it wants.

Use of categorical grants, which are responsible for the large growth in federal influence on the states, blossomed in the 1960s and 1970s, primarily because they are so appealing to Congress. Members of Congress receive credit for sponsoring specific grant programs, which in turn help establish members as national policy leaders, building their reputations with their constituents for bringing "home" federal money. Also, because senators and House members are backed by coalitions of various interest groups, specific program requirements are a way to ensure that a policy actually does what members (and their backers) want—even in states where local political leaders prefer a different course. By contrast, state politicians hate the requirements and all the paperwork that go with reporting compliance with federal regulations. States and localities also frequently argue that federal regulations prevent them from doing a good job. They want the money, but they want more flexibility, too.

Option Three: Block Grants

Conservatives and Republicans have long chafed at the detailed, Washington-centered nature of categorical grants. State politicians understandably want the maximum amount of freedom possible. They want to control their own destinies, not just carry out political deals made in Washington, and they want to please the coalitions of interests and voters that put them in power in the states. Thus, they argue for maintaining federal funding, but with fewer regulations. Their preferred policy tool, the **block grant** (described in the third row of Table 3.1), combines broad (rather than detailed) program requirements and regulations with funding from the federal treasury. Block grants give the states considerable freedom in using the funds in broad policy areas.

Funding Recovery

A sign at a Kentucky construction site credits the expansion work to funds received from the American Recovery and Reinvestment Act of 2009. The act issued grants to states and industries to stimulate growth in an economy hard hit by recession.

In our math education example, the federal government might provide the states with a lump-sum block grant and instructions to spend it on education as each state sees fit. If Congress demanded that the money be spent on math education and insisted on other conditions, the grant would start to look more like a categorical grant and less like a block grant. With an education block grant, members of Congress could not count on their math education problem being solved on a national basis unless it coincidentally resulted from the individual decisions in fifty states and innumerable localities.

One extreme and short-lived form of the block grant was President Nixon's proposal to give money to the states and localities with no strings attached—not in place of categorical grants but largely in addition to existing programs. Beginning in the 1970s under General Revenue Sharing (GRS), the federal government turned over money to all units of lower government automatically. GRS was immensely popular with the governors and mayors, but it never had great congressional backing because members of Congress could neither take credit for nor control how lower governments were spending these federal funds. In practice, GRS never replaced categorical grants; it was just one set of no-strings grants to the subgovernments. Congress did not object when, in 1986, President Reagan suggested abolishing GRS as a way of reducing the deficit.[21]

Less extreme versions of the block grant were pushed by Republican presidents Nixon, Reagan, Gerald Ford, and George W. Bush. However, the largest and most significant block grant was instituted under Democratic president Bill Clinton in 1996 with the passage of the welfare reform act. This reform changed the categorical grant program of Aid to Families with Dependent Children (AFDC) to a welfare block grant to the states, Temporary Assistance to Needy Families (TANF). Under TANF, the states have greater leeway in defining many of the rules of their welfare programs, such as qualifications and work requirements. The states do not get a blank check, however; they must continue to spend at certain levels and to adopt some federal provisions, such as the limits on how long a person can stay on welfare. TANF has ended welfare as an entitlement. Under AFDC, all families who qualified were guaranteed benefits—just as people who qualify for Social Security are assured coverage. This guarantee is not part of TANF. If the states run short of money—for example, if the economy slows down—families who might otherwise qualify may not receive welfare benefits. Such decisions, and their repercussions, are left to the individual states.

Congress has generally resisted the block grant approach for both policy and political reasons. In policy terms, many members of Congress fear that the states will do what they want instead of what Congress intends. One member characterized the idea of putting federal money into block grants as "pouring money down a rat hole"[22] because it is impossible to control how the states deal with particular problems under block grants.

Congress also has political objections to block grants. When federal funds are not attached to specific programs, they lose their electoral appeal for members of Congress, as they can no longer take credit for the programs. From a representative's standpoint, it does not make political sense to take the heat for taxing people's income only to turn those funds over in block grants, so that governors and mayors get the credit for how the money is spent. In addition, interest groups contribute millions of dollars to congressional campaigns when members of Congress have control over program specifics. If Congress allows the states to assume that control, interest groups have less incentive to make congressional campaign contributions. As a result, the tendency has been to place more conditions on block grants with each annual congressional appropriation.[23]

Categorical grants remain the predominant form of federal aid, amounting to about 80 percent of all aid to state and local governments. The change from AFDC to TANF was an important milestone in welfare policy, but it remains to be seen whether Congress will continue this approach in other policy areas.

Option Four: Unfunded Mandates

The politics of federalism yields one more strategy, which is shown in the bottom row of Table 3.1. When the federal government issues an **unfunded mandate**, it imposes specific policy requirements on the states but does not provide a way to pay for those activities. Here Congress either threatens criminal or civil penalties or promises to cut off other, often unrelated, federal funds if the states do not comply with its directions.

A recent example has nearly caused a rebellion in the states. The REAL ID Act was passed by Congress in 2005 following a recommendation of the White House Office of Homeland Security and the 9/11 Commission. This law required regulation of state driver's licenses, typically under control of the states, including verification of an applicant's identity, as well as standardization of watermarks, holograms, and a machine-readable code. These would be required for identification by any citizen doing business with a federal agency, including travelers passing through security at airports. The cost of the program's implementation was estimated at about $23 billion, with the vast majority of it to be shouldered by the states. Although virtually no one opposes the overall goal of national security, the requirements of the law and its cost led to a potential showdown. As of 2009 fourteen states had passed laws prohibiting implementation of the federal law, another ten had passed resolutions denouncing REAL ID, and Congress had postponed its enforcement. The result is that Congress must decide between fulfilling the national security goal of verified identity checks on people and soothing the states' anger and resistance.[24]

In terms of our math education example, the national government might say to the states that at least 45 percent of the students enrolled in advanced high school math courses must be female, and if that quota is not met, the states stand to lose 5 percent of their sewage treatment funds. This requirement could be set with no new federal funding for education at all.

Unfunded mandates are more attractive to members of Congress in periods of ballooning national deficits.[25] Whereas Congress passed unfunded mandates only eleven times from 1931 through the 1960s, it passed fifty-two such mandates in the 1970s and 1980s, a trend that continued into the 1990s.[26] Congress can please interest groups and particular citizen groups by passing such laws, but the laws infuriate state politicians, who have to come up with the money to pay for them. In 1987 South Dakota challenged the law tying federal highway funds to a minimum drinking age, arguing that Congress had exceeded its spending powers. The Supreme Court ruled in favor of the federal government.[27]

President Clinton, working with the Republican majorities in Congress, pushed through the Unfunded Mandate Act of 1995, which promises to reimburse the states for expensive unfunded mandates or to pass a separate law acknowledging the cost of an unfunded mandate. This act, however, may not be enough to dissuade Congress from passing "good laws" with no cost to the U.S. Treasury. Because Congress can define what the states see as an unfunded mandate in several different ways—as a simple "clarification of legislative intent," for example—Congress has continued to push some policy costs on to the states,[28] as in the REAL ID legislation discussed above and the No Child Left Behind Act, which required extensive tests and intervention for failing students and schools. In addition, fears of large unfunded mandates played a role in the debates leading up to health care reform. For instance, a version of the reform that expanded Medicaid for low-income people prompted instant criticism from governors, as Medicaid is paid for largely by state treasuries. Congress later backed down and provided assistance to the states to meet the new policy.

The current status of federalism is a contradictory mix of rhetoric about returning power to the states and new national initiatives (and program requirements) in the areas of health, education, and the environment. Although many in the state and even the national government say they want the states to have more power, the imperatives of effective policy solutions and congressional and presidential electoral calculations combine to create strong pressures for national solutions to our complex of problems.

Advocates for the national government and supporters of the states are engaged in a constant struggle for power as they have been since the days of the Articles of Confederation. The power of the federal government is enhanced through the mechanisms of cooperative federalism, which gives the federal government an increasing role in domestic policy. As the federal government has used the restrictive rules of categorical grants and the economic threats that provide the muscle of unfunded mandates, critics have claimed that cooperative federalism has been transformed into "coercive federalism," in which the states are pressured to adopt national solutions to their local problems with minimal state input.

It is worth remembering, however, that members of Congress who pass the laws are elected in the states and have their primary loyalties to their local constituencies, not to any national audience. States have been only too happy to accept federal funds to meet the needs of their residents (and voters) for everything from education to highways to welfare and health care for the poor. However, they also chafe under the rules and regulations that typically come with federal dollars. The conflict is not likely to end any time soon as the Obama administration takes an activist approach to the massive challenges of the recession and the need to revive the economy, the role of the United States in climate change, and the provision of health care for all Americans.

Citizenship and Federalism
Enhanced opportunities for participation and power at the state and local levels

State and local governments are closer to their citizens than is the federal government. Whereas the federal government may seem to take the form of an elite democracy, run by people far removed from everyday citizens, state and local governments allow far more opportunities for participatory governance, if citizens choose to get involved. Citizens may vote for initiatives and referenda, run for local office, sit on school boards and other advisory boards, or even take part in citizen judicial boards and community-run probation programs.[29]

But there is another way that citizens can shape state and local policies as surely as when they vote at the polls, and that is by voting with their feet. In a kind of political pressure that the federal government almost never has to confront, citizens can move from a state or locality they don't like to one that suits them better. Consider this: few Americans ever think seriously about changing countries.

Other nations may be nice to visit, but most of us, for better or worse, will continue to live under the U.S. government. At the same time, far fewer of us will live in the same state or city throughout our lives. We may move for jobs, for climate, or for a better quality of life. When we relocate, we can often choose where we want to go. Businesses also move—for better facilities, better tax rates, a better labor force, and so on—and they are also in a position to choose where they want to go. This mobility of people and businesses creates incentives for competition and cooperation among states and localities that influence how they operate in important ways. Although we do not conventionally consider the decision to move to be a political act, it affects policy just as much as more traditional forms of citizen participation.

▶ What's at Stake Revisited

As we have seen in this chapter, the issue of what powers go to the federal government and what powers are reserved to the states has been a hotly contested one since the founding, and one that has no clean, crisp, right answer. As the country and the composition of the Supreme Court have changed, so too have interpretations of states' rights and federal power. All of that means that the issue of medical marijuana, which currently is legal in twelve states, though illegal, with the backing of the Supreme Court decision in *Gonzales v. Raich,* nationally, is an excellent example of the messiness that can characterize federal issues in the United States.

For some supporters of the medical marijuana laws, what is at stake is the ability of ill patients to receive the most effective treatment possible. But they are allied with those who want to put limits on national power, some of whom might not approve of medical marijuana on its own merits. In his dissent in the *Raich* case, Justice Thomas said, "No evidence from the founding suggests that 'commerce' included the mere possession of a good or some purely personal activity that did not involve trade or exchange for value. In the early days of the Republic, it would have been unthinkable that Congress could prohibit the local cultivation, possession, and consumption of marijuana." If the national government can regulate this, it can regulate anything.[30]

Opponents of the medical marijuana laws say that as long as the Court has ruled that the state laws violate the commerce clause, the national law should be enforced. Further, some argue that it does touch the issue of interstate commerce because the provision and purchase of medical marijuana "affects the marijuana market generally," and they worry that if the federal government cannot regulate this, then perhaps they will be hampered in other areas, like child pornography, as well.[31]

That there is no clear constitutional resolution of such issues, and that it is possible to imagine the Court ruling differently on this issue some day, explains both how our federal system has found the flexibility to survive so long and so well, and why the debates over where power resides can be so bitterly fought.

► Summary With Key Terms

While the founders of the U.S. Constitution could have created a **unitary** (85) or **confederal system** (85), they instead established a government based on **federalism** (79), in which some powers are held by the national government and some by the states; others, called **concurrent powers** (83), are held by both. Political scientists once held to a theory called **dual federalism** (83) that considered the powers of the two levels to be separate and distinct but now understand their powers to be interrelated, a view known as **cooperative federalism** (84). The Constitution gives a decisive amount of power to the national government via the **enumerated powers of Congress** (83), which concludes with the **necessary and proper clause** (83) and the **supremacy clause** (83).

Federalism reflects a continually changing compromise between advocates of a strong national government and advocates of strong state governments. The balance of power adopted between central and subnational governments directly affects the national government's ability to act on large policy problems and the subnational units' flexibility in responding to local preferences. Although power was concentrated at the national level for much of the twentieth century, we are currently in a phase known as **devolution** (78)—shifting power from the national level to the states.

The growth of national power through much of our history can be traced to the early decisions of Chief Justice John Marshall, notably *McCulloch v. Maryland* (89) and *Gibbons v. Ogden* (89); the constitutional consequences of the Civil War, during which the southern states sought to declare federal laws void within their borders, an unconstitutional process called **nullification** (89); the establishment of national supremacy in economics with the New Deal; and the new national responsibilities in protecting citizens' rights that have been associated with the civil rights movement.

Where states retain power, Congress can use authority and money to encourage state cooperation with its agenda in four ways: it can exercise no influence, letting states have their way; or it can issue **categorical grants** (96), giving states money in exchange for following specific instructions; **block grants** (97), giving states money in exchange for following broad mandates; or **unfunded mandates** (99), giving states no money but expecting compliance with national laws.

Explore this subject further with suggested readings, movies, and web sites at http://republic-brief.cqpress.com, where you'll also find study aids, practice quizzes, flash cards, and Internet exercises.

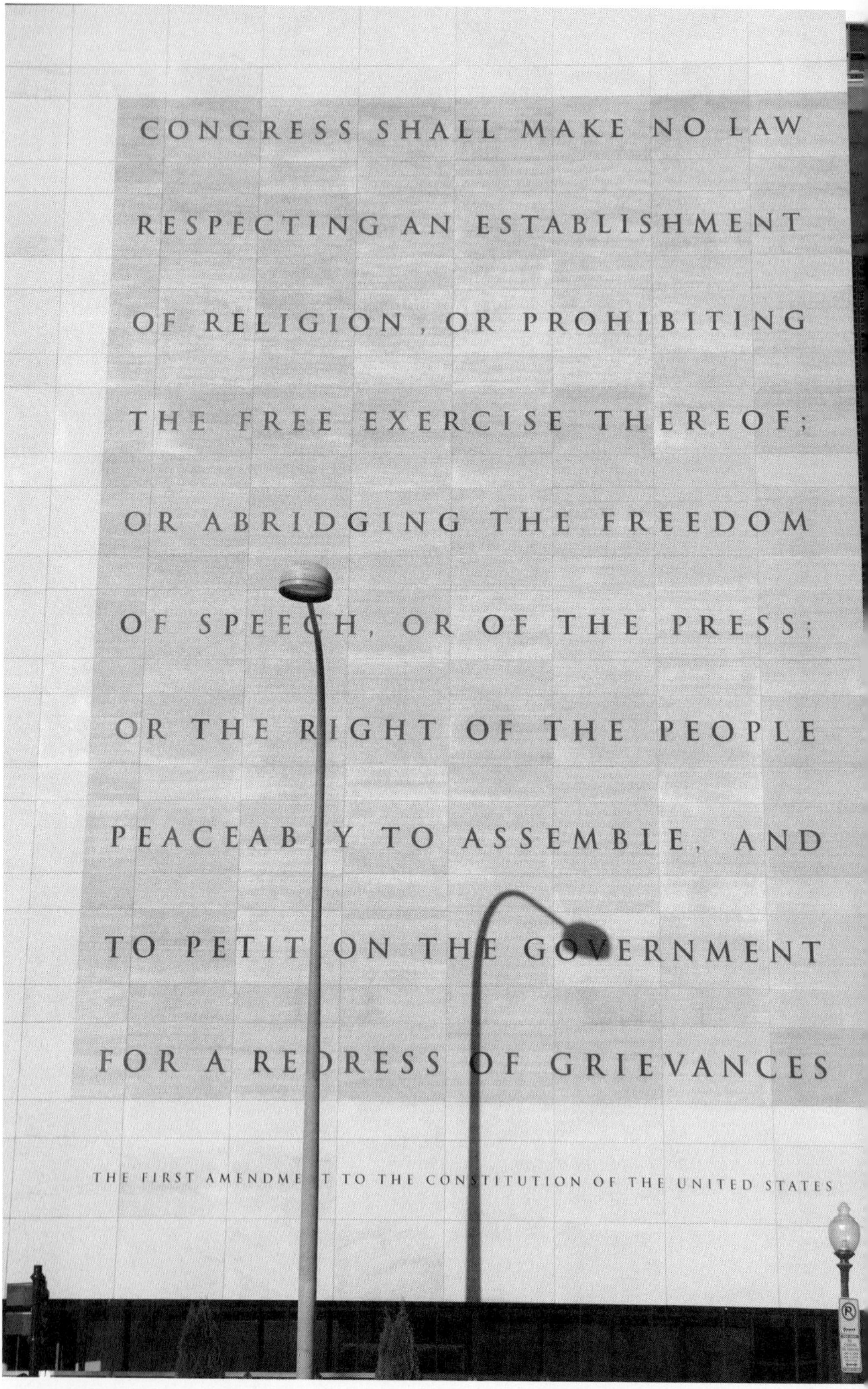

Chapter 4

Fundamental American Liberties

▶ What's at Stake?

It's usually hard to confuse the ivory towers of academia with the mean streets of the criminal underworld, but when Virginia attorney general Ken Cuccinelli set out to investigate the climate research of Professor Michael Mann, that's just where he was headed.

Mann, currently an environmental science professor at Penn State, had been at the University of Virginia from 1999 to 2005, where he obtained several grants of federal and state money to undertake his research on climate change. In 2009, Mann was one of several researchers working in England whose email was hacked by opponents of the idea that human activities were warming the planet. The hacked emails revealed that some of the researchers were resisting attempts by critics to get a hold of their data under the American and British Freedom of Information Acts, and that they had discussed suppressing some of their data that did not support their global warming thesis. Subsequent investigations by the English university Mann was associated with and by Penn State found that there was no evidence that Mann had suppressed or falsified data.[1]

But those investigations were not enough for Cuccinelli, an admitted opponent of climate change science, who wondered if perhaps Mann had deliberately defrauded Virginia taxpayers by using falsified data to obtain state research funds. Cuccinelli sought information from the University of Virginia by issuing "Civil Investigative Demand

Letters" that would require school officials to turn over all of Mann's papers, emails, and other documentation from his time at the university. Fraud, if he found it, meant Cuccinelli could prosecute Mann.

Scholars throughout Virginia and the nation immediately protested. The American Association for the Advancement of Science, the American Association of University Professors, the American Civil Liberties Union of Virginia, and the Union of Concerned Scientists all raised their voices against Cuccinelli's efforts, and the *Washington Post*'s editorial board called the action against Mann "Mr. Cuccinelli's Witch Hunt."[2]

In response to the Civil Investigative Demand Letters, the university's lawyers filed suit, arguing that Cuccinelli's efforts were an unwarranted assault on academic freedom. They wrote:

> Academic freedom is essential to the mission of our Nation's institutions of higher learning and a core First Amendment concern. As Thomas Jefferson intended, the University of Virginia has a long and proud tradition of embracing the "illimitable freedom of the human mind" by fully endorsing and supporting faculty research and scholarly pursuits. Our Nation also has a long and proud tradition of limited government framed by enumerated powers which Jefferson ardently believed was necessary for a civil society to endure. . . .
>
> Unfettered debate and the expression of conflicting ideas without fear of reprisal are the cornerstones of academic freedom; they consequently are carefully guarded First Amendment concerns. Investigating the merits of a university researcher's methodology, results, and conclusions (on climate change or any topic) goes far beyond the attorney general's limited statutory power.[3]

Cuccinelli, for his part, claimed that his investigation had nothing to do with Mann's research. "We're not investigating his academic work," the Virginia attorney general insisted. "That subpoena is directed at the expenditure of dollars. Whether he does a good job, bad job, or I don't like the outcome—and I think everybody already knows his position on some of this is one that I question. But that's not what that's about."[4]

So what *was* it about? Were Cuccinelli's actions just an effort to track down some possible misspent state dollars awarded to a researcher long gone to another state university? Or were they, as critics claimed, an effort to use the power of the state to intimidate researchers whose findings were disagreeable to state officials? Why did the university launch such a strong response in rejecting Cuccinelli's claims, and why did one of the nation's top newspapers speak of Cuccinelli's investigation as a "witch hunt"? Just what is at stake in the issue of academic freedom?

"Give me liberty," declared patriot Patrick Henry at the start of the Revolutionary War, "or give me death." "Live Free or Die," proudly proclaims the New Hampshire license plate. Americans have always put a lot of stock in their freedom. Certain that they live in the least restrictive country in the world, Americans celebrate their freedoms and are proud of the Constitution, the laws, and the traditions that preserve them.

And yet, living collectively under a government means that we aren't free to do whatever we want. There are limits on our freedoms that allow us to live peacefully with our fellows, minimizing the conflict that would result if we all did exactly what we pleased. John Locke said that liberty does not equal license; that is, the freedom to do some things doesn't mean the freedom to do everything. Deciding what rights we give up to join civilized society, and what rights we retain, is one of the great challenges of democratic government.

What are these things called "rights" or "liberties," so precious that some Americans are willing to lay down their lives to preserve them? On the one hand, the answer is very simple. *Rights* and *liberties* are synonyms; they mean freedoms or privileges to which one has a claim. In that respect, we use the words more or less interchangeably. But when prefaced by the word *civil,* both rights and liberties take on a more specific meaning, and they no longer mean quite the same thing.

Our **civil liberties** are individual freedoms that place limitations on the power of government. In general, civil liberties protect our right to think and act without governmental interference. Some of these rights are spelled out in the Constitution, particularly in the Bill of Rights. These include the rights to express ourselves and to choose our own religious beliefs. Others, like the right to privacy, rest on the shakier ground of judicial decision making. Although government is prevented from limiting these freedoms per se, we will see that sometimes one person's freedom—to speak or act in a certain way—may be limited by another person's rights. Government does play a role in resolving the conflicts between individuals' rights.

While civil liberties refer to restrictions on government action, **civil rights** refer to the extension of government action to secure citizenship rights for all members of society. When we speak of civil rights, we most often mean that the government must treat all citizens equally, apply laws fairly, and not discriminate unjustly against certain groups of people. Most of the rights we consider civil rights are guaranteed by the Thirteenth, Fourteenth, Fifteenth, Nineteenth, and Twenty-sixth Amendments. These amendments lay out fundamental rights of citizenship, most notably the right to vote, but also the right to equal treatment before the law and the right to due process of the law. They forbid government from making laws that treat people differently on the basis of race, and they ensure that the right to vote cannot be denied on the basis of race or gender.

Not all people live under governments whose rules guarantee them fundamental liberties. In fact, we argued earlier that one way of distinguishing between authoritarian and nonauthoritarian governments is that nonauthoritarian governments, including democracies, give citizens the power to challenge government if they believe it has denied their basic rights. When we consider our definition of politics as "who gets what, and how," we see that rights are crucial in democratic politics, where a central tension is the power of the individual pitted against the power of the government. What's at stake in democracy is the resolution of that tension. In fact, democracies depend on the existence of rights in at least two ways. First, civil liberties provide rules that keep government limited, so that it cannot become too powerful. Second, civil rights help define who "we, the people" are in a democracy, and they give those people the power necessary to put some controls on their governments.

We will take two chapters to explore in depth the issues of civil liberties and civil rights. In this chapter we begin with a general discussion of the meaning of rights or liberties in a democracy and then focus on the traditional civil liberties that provide a check on the power of government. In Chapter 5 we focus on civil rights and the continuing struggle of some groups of Americans—like women, African Americans, and other minorities—to be fully counted and empowered in American politics.

As an introduction to the basic civil liberties guaranteed to Americans, in this chapter you will learn about the meaning of rights in a democratic society, the Bill of Rights as part of the federal Constitution and its relationship to the states, and several specific rights that it details—freedom of religion, speech, and the press; the right to bear arms; the rights of people accused of crimes; and the right to privacy.

Rights in a Democracy
Limiting government to empower people

The freedoms we consider indispensable to the working of a democracy are part of the everyday language of politics in America. We take many of them for granted: we speak confidently of our freedoms of speech, of the press, of religion, and of our rights to bear arms, to a fair trial, and to privacy. There is nothing inevitable about these freedoms, however.

In fact, there is nothing inevitable about the idea of rights at all. Until the writing of such Enlightenment figures as John Locke, it was rare for individuals to talk about claiming rights against government. Governments were assumed to have all the power, their subjects only such privileges as government was willing to bestow. Locke argued that the rights to life, liberty, and the pursuit of property were conferred on individuals by nature, and that one of the primary purposes of government was to preserve the natural rights of its citizens.

This notion of natural rights and limited government was central to the founders of the American system. In the Declaration of Independence, Thomas Jefferson wrote that men are "endowed by their Creator with certain inalienable rights; that among these are life, liberty, and the pursuit of happiness; that, to secure these rights, governments are instituted among men." John Locke could not have said it better himself.

Practically speaking, of course, any government can make its citizens do anything it wishes, regardless of their rights, as long as it is in charge of the military and the police. But in nonauthoritarian governments, public opinion is usually outraged at the invasion of individual rights. Unless the government is willing to dispense with its reputation as a democracy, it must respond in some way to pacify public opinion. Public opinion can be a powerful guardian of citizens' rights in a democracy.

Just as rights limit government, they also empower its citizens. A person who can successfully claim that he or she has rights that must be respected by government is a citizen of that government. A person who is under the authority of a government but cannot claim rights is merely a subject, bound by the laws but without any power to challenge or change them. This does not mean, as we will see, that a citizen can always have things his or her own way. Nor does it mean that noncitizens have no rights in a democracy. It *does* mean that citizens have special protections and powers that allow them to stand up to government and plead their cases when they believe an injustice is being done.

However, because rights represent power, they are, like all other forms of power, subject to conflict and controversy. Often for one person to get his or her own way, someone else must lose out. People clash over rights in two ways. First, individuals' rights conflict with each other; for instance, one person's right to share a prayer with classmates at the start of the school day conflicts with another student's right not to be subjected to a religious practice against his or her will. Second, individuals' rights can conflict with society's needs and the demands of collective living; for instance, an individual's right to decide whether or not to wear a motorcycle helmet conflicts with society's need to protect its citizens. Since the terror attacks of September 11, 2001, this latter conflict between individual rights and social needs has been thrown into sharp relief, as measures to protect the population have increased the government's ability to do such things as screen airline passengers, intercept email and conduct roving wiretaps, and gain access to library records and bookstore purchases—all at the expense of individual freedom. The balancing of public safety with individuals' rights is complex. We could ensure our safety from most threats, perhaps, if we were willing to give up all of our freedom, but the ultimate problem, of course, is that without our civil liberties, we have no protection from government itself.

Although conflicts over rights sometimes lead to violence, usually they are resolved in the United States through politics—through the process of arguing, bargaining, and compromising over who gets what and how. All this wrangling takes place within the institutions of American politics, primarily in Congress and the courts, but also in the White House, at the state and local levels, and throughout our daily lives.

The Bill of Rights and the States
Keeping Congress and the states in check

The Bill of Rights looms large in any discussion of American civil liberties, but the document that today seems so inseparable from American citizenship had a stormy birth. Controversy raged over whether a bill of rights was necessary in the first place, deepening the split between Federalists and Anti-Federalists during the founding. And the controversy did not end once it was firmly established as the first ten amendments to the Constitution. Over a century passed before the Supreme Court agreed that at least some of the restrictions imposed on the national government by the Bill of Rights should be applied to the states as well.

Why Is a Bill of Rights Valuable?

Recall from Chapter 2 that we came very close to not having any Bill of Rights in the Constitution at all. The Federalists had argued that the Constitution itself was a bill of rights, that individual rights were already protected by many of the state constitutions, and that to list the powers that the national government did *not* have was dangerous, as it implied that it *did* have every other power.

To some extent they were correct in calling the Constitution a bill of rights in itself. Protection of some very specific rights is contained in the text of the document. The national government may not suspend writs of **habeas corpus**, which means that it cannot fail to bring prisoners, at their request, before a judge and inform the court why they are being held and what evidence is against them. This provision protects people from being imprisoned solely for political reasons. Both the national and the state governments are forbidden to pass **bills of attainder**, which are laws that single out a person or group as guilty and impose punishment without trial. Neither can they pass **ex post facto laws**, which are laws that make an action a crime after the fact, even though it was legal when carried out. States may not impair or negate the obligation of contracts; here the founders obviously had in mind the failings of the Articles of Confederation. And the citizens of each state are entitled to "the privileges and immunities of the several states," which prevents any state from discriminating against citizens of other states. This provision protects a nonresident's right to travel freely, conduct business, and have access to state courts while visiting another state.[5] Of course, nonresidents are discriminated against when they have to pay a higher nonresident tuition to attend a state college or university, but the Supreme Court has ruled that this type of "discrimination" is not a violation of the privileges and immunities clause.

Some Federalists, however, including James Madison, came to agree with such Anti-Federalists as Thomas Jefferson, who wrote, "A bill of rights is what the people are entitled to against every government on earth."[6] Even though, as the Federalists argued, the national government was limited in principle by popular sovereignty (the concept that ultimate authority rests with the people), it could not hurt to limit it in practice as well. A specific list of the rights held by the people would give the judiciary a more effective check on the other branches.

Applying the Bill of Rights to the States

If you look closely at the Bill of Rights, you'll see that most of the limitations on government action are directed toward Congress. "Congress shall make no law . . . ," begins the First Amendment. Until about the turn of the twentieth century, the Supreme Court clearly stipulated that the Bill of Rights applied only to the national government and not to the states.[7]

Not until the passage of the Fourteenth Amendment in 1868 did the Constitution make it possible for the Court to require that states protect their citizens' basic liberties. That post–Civil War amendment was designed specifically to force southern states to extend the rights of citizenship to African Americans, but its wording left it open to other interpretations. The amendment says, in part,

> No state shall make or enforce any law which shall abridge the privileges and immunities of citizens of the United States; nor shall any state deprive any person of life, liberty, or property, without due process of the law; nor deny to any person within its jurisdiction the equal protection of the laws.

In 1897 the Supreme Court tentatively began the process of nationalization, or **incorporation**, of most (but not all) of the protections of the Bill of Rights into the states' Fourteenth Amendment obligations to guarantee their citizens due process of the law.[8]

Not until the case of *Gitlow v. New York* (1925), however, did the Court begin to articulate a clear theory of incorporation. In *Gitlow*, Justice Edward Sanford wrote, "We may and do assume that freedom of speech and of the press . . . are among the fundamental rights and liberties protected . . . from impairment by the states."[9] Without any great fanfare, the Court reversed almost a century of ruling by assuming that some rights are so fundamental that they deserve protection by the states as well as the federal government. This approach meant that all rights did not necessarily qualify for incorporation; the Court had to consider each right on a case-by-case basis to see how fundamental it was. This was a tactic that Justice Benjamin N. Cardozo called **selective incorporation**. Over the years the Court has switched between a theory of selective incorporation and total incorporation. As a result, almost all of the rights in the first ten amendments have been incorporated, with some notable exceptions, such as the Second Amendment (see Table 4.1).

Keep in mind that since incorporation is a matter of interpretation rather than an absolute constitutional principle, it is a judicial creation. What justices create they can also "uncreate" if they change their minds or if the composition of the Court changes. Like all other judicial creations, the process of incorporation is subject to reversal, and it is possible that such a reversal may currently be under way as today's more conservative Court narrows its understanding of the rights that states must protect.

Table 4.1

Applying the Bill of Rights to the States

Amendment	Addresses	Case	Year
Fifth	Just compensation	Chicago, Burlington & Quincy v. Chicago	1897
First	Freedom of speech	Gilbert v. Minnesota	1920
		Gitlow v. New York	1925
		Fiske v. Kansas	1927
	Freedom of the press	Near v. Minnesota	1931
Sixth	Counsel in capital cases	Powell v. Alabama	1932
First	Religious freedom (generally)	Hamilton v. Regents of California	1934
	Freedom of assembly	DeJonge v. Oregon	1937
	Free exercise	Cantwell v. Connecticut	1940
	Religious establishment	Everson v. Board of Education	1947
Sixth	Public trial	In re Oliver	1948
Fourth	Unreasonable search and seizure	Wolf v. Colorado	1949
	Exclusionary rule	Mapp v. Ohio	1961
Eighth	Cruel and unusual punishment	Robinson v. California	1962
Sixth	Counsel in felony cases	Gideon v. Wainwright	1963
Fifth	Self-incrimination	Malloy v. Hogan	1964
Sixth	Impartial jury	Parker v. Gladden	1966
	Speedy trial	Klopfer v. North Carolina	1967
	Jury trial in serious crimes	Duncan v. Louisiana	1968
Fifth	Double jeopardy	Benton v. Maryland	1969

Freedom of Religion
Limiting Congress to protect both church and state, and the individual's right to believe

The First Amendment reads, "Congress shall make no law respecting an establishment of religion, or prohibiting the free exercise thereof; or abridging the freedom of speech, or of the press; or the right of the people peaceably to assemble, and to petition the government for a redress of grievances." These are the "democratic freedoms," the liberties that the founders believed to be necessary to maintain a representative democracy by ensuring a free and unfettered people. For all that, none of these liberties has escaped controversy, and none has been interpreted by the Supreme Court to be absolute or unlimited.

Why Is Religious Freedom Valuable?

The briefest look around the world tells us what happens when politics and religion are allowed to mix. When it comes to conflicts over religion, over our fundamental beliefs about the world and the way life should be lived, the stakes are enormous. Passions run deep, and compromise is difficult. In the United States, where a majority of people are religious, religious battles tend to take place in the courts, under the guidelines set out by the First Amendment.

While not all the founders endorsed religious freedom for everyone, some of them, notably Thomas Jefferson and James Madison, cherished the notion of a universal freedom of conscience—the right of all individuals to believe as they pleased. Jefferson wrote that the First Amendment built "a wall of separation between church and State."[10] The founders based their view of religious freedom on three main arguments. First, history has shown, from the Holy Roman Empire to the Church of England, that when church and state are linked, all individual freedoms are in jeopardy. After all, if government is merely the arm of God, what power of government cannot be justified? A second argument for practicing religious freedom is based on the effect that politics can have on religious concerns. Early champions of a separation between politics and religion worried that the spiritual purity and sanctity of religion would be ruined if it was mixed with the worldly realm of politics, with its emphasis on power and influence.[11] Finally, as politics can have negative effects on religion, so too can religion have negative effects on politics, dividing society into the factions that Madison saw as the primary threat to republican government.

The Establishment Clause

The beginning of the First Amendment, forbidding Congress to make laws that would establish an official religion, is known as the **establishment clause**. Americans have fought over the meaning of the establishment clause almost since its inception. While founders like Jefferson and Madison were clear on their position that church and state should be separate realms, other early Americans were not.

A similar division continues today between the **separationists**, who believe that a "wall" should exist between church and state, and the nonpreferentialists, or **accommodationists**, who contend that the state should not be separate from religion but rather should accommodate it, without showing a preference for one religion over another. Accommodationists argue that the First Amendment should not prevent governmental aid to religious groups, prayer in school or in public

Figure 4.1

Our Religious Beliefs Compared to Other Nations

Our Religious Beliefs Compared to Other Nations: Americans take religion very seriously.

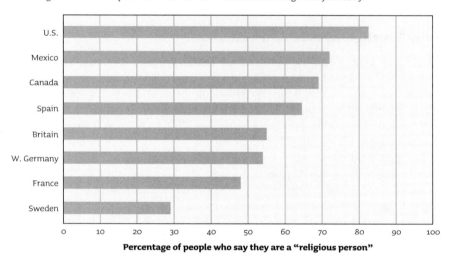

Percentage of people who say they are a "religious person"

Source: *The Public Perspective*, October/November 1997. Survey by the World Values Study Group, 1990–1993.

ceremonies, public aid to parochial schools, the posting of religious documents such as the Ten Commandments in public places, or the teaching of the Bible's story of creation along with evolution in public schools. Adherents of this position claim that a rigid interpretation of separation of church and state amounts to intolerance of their religious rights or, in the words of Supreme Court Justice Anthony Kennedy, to "unjustified hostility to religion."[12] Presidents Ronald Reagan, George H. W. Bush, and George W. Bush, and many other Republicans have shared this view, as have many powerful interest groups such as the Christian Coalition.

A lot is clearly at stake in the battle between the separationists and the accommodationists. On one side of the dispute is the separationists' image of a society in which the rights of all citizens, including minorities, receive equal protection under the law. In this society, religions abound, but they remain private, not matters for public action or support. Very different is the view of the accommodationists, which emphasizes the sharing of community values, determined by the majority and built into the fabric of society and political life.

Today U.S. practice stands somewhere between these two images. Sessions of Congress open with prayers, for instance, but a schoolchild's day does not. Religion is not kept completely out of our public lives, but the Court has generally leaned toward a separationist stance. In the 1960s the Court tried to cement this stance, refining a test that made it unconstitutional for the government to pass laws that affect religion unless the laws have a "secular intent" (that is, a nonreligious intent) and "a primary effect that neither advances nor inhibits religion."[13] In two separate cases the Court decided that laws requiring prayer or the reading of biblical verses in public schools violated the Constitution, and that permitting children to be excused did not reduce the unconstitutionality of the original laws.[14] In an earlier case the Court had ruled that even nondenominational prayer could not be required of children in public schools,[15] and in 1968 the Court struck down an Arkansas law prohibiting the teaching of evolution in public schools.[16] With these rulings the Court was aligning itself firmly with the separationist interpretation of the establishment clause.

As the more conservative appointments of Republican presidents Richard Nixon and Reagan began to shape the Court, the Court's rulings moved in a more accommodationist direction. In *Lemon v. Kurtzman* (1971), the Court added to the old test a third provision that a law not foster "an excessive government entanglement with religion."[17] Under the new **Lemon test** the justices had to decide how much entanglement there was between politics and religion, leaving much to their own discretion.

As the current rule in deciding establishment cases, the *Lemon* test is not used consistently, primarily because the justices have not settled among themselves the underlying issue of whether religion and politics should be separate, or whether state support of religion is permissible.[18] While the justices still lean in a separationist direction, their rulings occasionally nod at accommodationism.

The Free Exercise Clause

Another fundamental question about religious freedom that divides the public and justices alike is what to do when religious beliefs and practices conflict with state goals. The second part of the First Amendment grant of religious freedom guarantees that Congress shall make no law prohibiting the free exercise of religion. The **free exercise clause**, as it is called, has generated as much controversy as the establishment clause. When is the state justified in regulating religion? While Americans have an absolute right to believe whatever they want, their freedom to act is subject to government regulation.[19] The state's **police power** allows it to regulate behavior in order to protect its citizens and to provide social order and security. These two valued goods of religious freedom and social order are bound to conflict, and the Court has had an uneasy time trying to draw the line between them.

The Court's ambivalence can be seen in two cases, three years apart, concerning the obligation to salute the flag. In *Minersville School District v. Gobitis* (1940), two children of a Jehovah's Witness family were expelled from school for violating a rule that required them to salute the flag each day.[20] For a Jehovah's Witness, saluting the flag would amount to worshiping a graven image (idol), which their religion forbids. Their father brought suit, claiming that the rule violated his children's freedom of religion. The Court rejected his claim, arguing that children are required to salute the flag to promote national unity, which in turn fosters national security. Within three years, however, the composition of the Court had changed, and several members had changed their minds. In *West Virginia State Board of Education v. Barnette* (1943), children of Jehovah's Witnesses were again expelled for refusing to salute the flag, but this time the Court overturned the school board's rule requiring the salute.[21]

While *Barnette* still holds, the Court has gone back and forth on other religious freedom issues as it has struggled to define what actions the state might legitimately seek to regulate. Under their police power, states have been allowed to require that businesses close on Sundays, or that certain merchandise not be sold then. In *The Blue Law Cases,* the Court argued that the states are within their rights to require Sunday closings as a provision for a day of rest, and that the Sunday closing laws, while religious in origin, no longer contain religious intent.[22] In *Sherbert v. Verner* (1963), however, the Court seemed to contradict itself. A Seventh Day Adventist, for whom Saturday is the Sabbath, was fired from a company for refusing to work on Saturday and was denied unemployment compensation when she refused to take other jobs with compulsory Saturday hours. A lower court ruled in favor of the woman, and the case was appealed to the Supreme Court. The Court upheld *Sherbert,* finding the denial of benefits to be a clear violation of her constitutional rights. The Court wrote that any incidental burden placed on religious freedom must be justified by a **compelling state interest**. In other words, the state must show that it is absolutely necessary for some fundamental state purpose that religious freedom be limited.[23] How the Court determines what is and what is not a compelling state interest is examined in Chapter 5.

The Court rejected this compelling state interest test, however, in *Employment Division, Department of Human Resources v. Smith* (1990), when it upheld a law denying state unemployment benefits to employees of a drug rehabilitation organization who were fired for using peyote, a hallucinogenic drug, for sacramental purposes in religious ceremonies.[24] Here the Court abandoned its ruling in *Sherbert* and held that if the infringement on religion is not intentional but is rather the byproduct of a general law prohibiting socially harmful conduct, applied equally to all religions, then it is not unconstitutional. It found that the compelling state interest test, while necessary for cases dealing with matters of race and free speech, was inappropriate for religious freedom issues. Under the *Smith* ruling, a number of religious practices have been declared illegal by state laws on the grounds that the laws do not unfairly burden any particular religion.

Religious groups consider the *Smith* ruling a major blow to religious freedom because it places the burden of proof on the individual or church to show that its religious practices should not be punished, rather than on the state to show that the interference with religious practice is absolutely necessary. In response to the *Smith* decision, Congress in 1993 passed the Religious Freedom Restoration Act (RFRA). This act, supported by a coalition of ninety religious groups, restored the compelling state interest test for state action limiting religious practice and required that when the state did restrict religious practice, it be carried out in the least burdensome way. However, in the 1997 case of *City of Boerne v. Flores,* the Court held that the RFRA was an unconstitutional exercise of congressional power and that it constituted too great an intrusion on government power.[25] Congress amended the act in 2003 to apply only to the federal government, and many states passed their own RFRAs to protect religious practices at the state level. In 2006 the Supreme Court affirmed the amended federal RFRA when it ruled that the act protected a New Mexico church's use of tea containing an illegal substance for sacramental purposes, reinstating the compelling state interest test.[26]

Freedom of Expression
Checking government by protecting speech and the press

Among the most cherished of American values is the right to free speech. The First Amendment reads that "Congress shall make no law . . . abridging the freedoms of speech, or of the press" and, at least theoretically, most Americans agree.[27] When it comes to actually practicing free speech, however, our national record is less impressive. In fact, time and again, Congress has made laws abridging freedom of expression, often with the enthusiastic support of much of the American public. As a nation we have never had a great deal of difficulty restricting speech we don't like, admire, or respect. The challenge of the First Amendment is to protect the speech we despise.

Why Is Freedom of Expression Valuable?

Freedom of expression is valuable in a democratic society for several important reasons. First, free speech is important because citizens are responsible for participating in their government's decisions and they need information provided by a free and independent press to protect them from government manipulation. A second, and related, reason to value free speech is that it can limit government corruption. By being free to voice criticism of government, to investigate its actions, and to debate its decisions, both citizens and journalists are able to exercise an additional check on government that supplements our valued principle of checks and balances.

A third reason for allowing free speech—even (or especially) speech of which we do not approve—is the danger of setting a precedent of censorship. Censorship in a democracy usually allows the voice of the majority to prevail. One of the reasons to support minority rights as well as majority rule, however, is that we never know when we may fall into the minority on an issue.

A fourth reason that free speech is valuable comes from the nineteenth-century English philosopher John Stuart Mill, who argued that there should be no limits on speech because only by allowing the free traffic of all ideas—those known to be true as well as those suspected to be false—can we ensure the vigorous protection of the truth. By allowing the expression of all speech, we discover truths we had previously believed to be false (the earth is not flat after all), and we develop strong defenses

against known falsehoods like racist and sexist ideas.

Freedom of speech, it can thus be argued, is important for making democracy function well, for preventing corruption and tyranny in government, for preserving minorities against the power of majorities, and for strengthening and defending the truth. Why, then, is it so controversial? Like freedom of religion, free speech requires tolerance of ideas and beliefs other than our own, even ideas and beliefs that we find personally repugnant. Those who are convinced that their views are eternally true often see no real reason to practice tolerance. Many people believe that, in a democracy, the majority should determine the prevailing views and the minority, having lost the vote, so to speak, should shut up.

Without Rights

Thomas Jefferson wrote, "A bill of rights is what the people are entitled to against every government on earth," but many nations do not provide these rights for their people. Protestors from the Free Burma Coalition demonstrate in 2010 with a poster of Aung San Suu Kyi, who was prevented from taking power after winning elections in Burma (Myanmar) in 1990. She has been under house arrest for two decades.

Speech That Criticizes the Government

Sedition, speech that criticizes the government to incite rebellion, has long been a target of restrictive legislation, and most of the founders were quite content that it should be so. Of course, all of the founders had engaged daily in the practice of criticizing their government when they were in the process of inciting their countrymen to revolution against England, so they were well aware of the potential consequences of seditious activity. Now that the shoe was on the other foot and they were the government, many were far less willing to encourage dissent. Especially during wartime, it was felt, criticism of the government undermined authority and destroyed patriotism.

It didn't take long for American "revolutionaries" to pass the Alien and Sedition Acts of 1798, which outlawed "any false, scandalous writing against the government of the United States." Throughout the 1800s and into the next century, all levels of government, with the support and encouragement of public opinion, squashed the views of radical political groups, labor activists, religious sects, and other minorities.

By the end of World War I, thirty-two of forty-eight states had laws against sedition, which essentially prohibited the advocacy of the use of violence or force to bring about industrial or political change. In 1917 the U.S. Congress passed the Espionage Act, which made it a crime to "willfully obstruct the recruiting or enlistment service of the United States," and a 1918 amendment to the act spelled out what that meant. It became a crime to engage in "any disloyal . . . scurrilous, or abusive language about the form of government of the United States, . . . or any language intended to bring the form of government of the United States . . . into contempt, scorn, contumely, or disrepute."[28] Such sweeping prohibitions made it possible to arrest people on the flimsiest of pretexts.

Those arrested and imprisoned under the new sedition laws looked to the Supreme Court to protect their freedom to criticize the government, but they were doomed to disappointment. The Court did not dispute the idea that speech criticizing the government could be punished. The question it dealt with was just how bad the speech had to be before it could be prohibited. The history of freedom of speech cases is a history of the Court devising tests for itself to determine whether certain speech should be protected or could be legitimately outlawed.

In two cases upholding the Espionage Act, *Schenck v. United States* (1919) and *Abrams v. United States* (1919), Justice Oliver Wendell Holmes began to articulate what he called the **clear and present danger test**.[29] This test, as Holmes conceived it, focused on the circumstances under which language was used. If there were no immediately threatening circumstances, the language in question would be protected, and Congress could not regulate it. But Holmes's views did not represent the majority opinion of the Court, and the clear and present danger test was slow to catch on.

With the tensions that led to World War II, Congress again began to fear the power of foreign ideas, especially communism. The Smith Act of 1940 made it illegal to advocate the violent overthrow of the government or to belong to an organization that did so. The McCarran Act of 1950 required members of the Communist Party to register with the U.S. attorney general. At the same time, Senator Joseph McCarthy was conducting investigations of American citizens to search out communists, and the House Un-American Activities Committee was doing the same thing. The suspicion or accusation of being involved in communism was enough to stain a person's reputation irreparably, even if there was no evidence to back up the claim. Many careers and lives were ruined in the process.

Again, the Supreme Court did not weigh in on the side of civil liberties. Convictions under the Smith and McCarran Acts were upheld. The Court had used the clear and present danger test intermittently in the years since 1919 but usually not as Justices Holmes and Louis D. Brandeis intended, to limit speech only in the rarest and most dire circumstances. Instead, the clear and present danger test had come to be seen as a kind of balancing act in which the interests of society in prohibiting the speech were weighed against the value of free speech. The emphasis on an obvious and immediate danger was lost.

The Court's record as a supporter of sedition laws finally ended with the personnel changes that brought Earl Warren to the position of chief justice. In 1969 the

Bill Maher

Bill Maher is a big fan of the First Amendment. That's because he says what few of us dare to say, what most of us dare not even think. The gasp of laughter that follows the comedian's one-liners is not just shocked amusement, it's shocked recognition that, uncomfortable, unflattering, unpalatable as his observations are, they're often right on target. Maher has made a career out of mocking the emperor's anatomy, while most of us are still oohing and aahing over the splendor of his new clothes. Usually the First Amendment saves his bacon.

And sometimes it doesn't. On September 17, 2001, he went on his ABC comedy show, *Politically Incorrect,* and said, about the suicide bombing of the World Trade Center: "We have been the cowards, lobbing cruise missiles from 2,000 miles away. That's cowardly. Staying in the airplane when it hits the building—say what you want about it, it's not cowardly."

Predictably, in those shaky days of national trouble, all hell broke loose. Asked about Maher's comment at a White House press briefing, then–press secretary Ari Fleischer replied: "All Americans . . . need to watch what they say, watch what they do." Advertisers balked, and Maher's show was canceled.

> "... if you want to teach somebody something, it's got to be like a pill in the dog's food."

He's back now, with a cable show called *Real Time With Bill Maher,* where he continues to speak his mind. Still, there are limits. He says: "I can't get up there every week and just rail about the environment and global warming and whatever is going on that I think is most important. But I push it as far as I can. You've got to try to find entertaining ways to get the message through. I always say, in America if you want to teach somebody something, it's got to be like a pill in the dog's food. You've got to wrap it in the bologna . . . stick it right at the back of his throat so he doesn't even know it's there."

The trouble, as he sees it, is that Americans want to fit their beliefs into tidy categories of "liberal" and "conservative" as if that sums up the whole debate. Maher wants us to dig our way out of our comfortable platitudes to reach new truths, even if they're unpopular. He recalls getting booed once on the *Tonight Show* after he berated an animal trainer who had appeared with his tiger. "They're like, please, Mr. Comedown. We just enjoyed a delightful animal show, and I pointed out that animals really don't want to be in show business." New rule, as Maher would say today.

Maher is a libertarian, but, true to his own creed, he is also a bit of everything else, believing fiercely in causes like animal rights, the environment, personal responsibility, and civic education. Today, he says, we've lost the thread to the things that matter. Raised by parents who served in World War II, Maher grew up thinking that there was a common good worth sacrificing for, "that the world had been to the brink and good citizenship was responsible for saving it. And we have nothing like that today. Nothing." Here's more Maher:

On patriotism:
Well, it means being loyal to your country above other countries. And I am. . . . [But] it has to be put in context and also it has to be put side by side with a greater humanity. . . . Americans who say, "This is the greatest country in the world," without having any clue what goes on in any other countries are just pulling it out of nowhere. There are many things that I'm proud of in this country. I'm proud of how my parents and other people stopped fascism and communism. I'm certainly proud of what we started in 1776. It was a new dawn of freedom and liberty in the world. But I'm not proud of slavery. I'm not proud of the genocide of the Indians. I'm not proud of much of what goes on today. So I still believe in the promise of America, but most of America looks at itself through rose-colored glasses. And that's not healthy.

On keeping the republic:
Take it upon [yourself] to learn the basics. . . . [K]ids need . . . to learn history. Because kids say to me all the time when I say something from history: "How should I know about that, I wasn't born." Oh, really? So nothing happened before you were born? . . . Kids need to learn history so they can put themselves in the proper place, which is of great insignificance. . . . The problem with kids today is not too little self-esteem, it's too much. And history, I think, learning a big picture, is very important in that.

Court overturned the conviction of Charles Brandenburg, a Ku Klux Klan leader who had been arrested under Ohio's criminal syndicalism law. In this case the Court ruled that abstract teaching of violence is not the same as incitement to violence. In other words, political speech could be restricted only if it was aimed at producing or was likely to produce "imminent lawless action." Mere advocacy of specific illegal acts was protected unless it led to immediate illegal activity. In a concurring opinion, Justice William O. Douglas pointed out that it was time to get rid of the clear and present danger test because it was so subject to misuse and manipulation. Speech, except when linked with action, he said, should be immune from prosecution.[30] The **imminent lawless action test** continues to be the standard for regulating political speech today.

Symbolic Speech

The question of what to do when speech is linked to action remained. Many forms of expression go beyond mere speech or writing. No one disputes that government has the right to regulate actions and behavior if it believes it has sufficient cause, but what happens when that behavior is also expression? Is burning a draft card, wearing an armband to protest a war, or torching the American flag an action or an expression? The Supreme Court, generally speaking, has been more willing to allow regulation of symbolic speech than of speech alone, especially if such regulation is not a direct attempt to curtail the speech.

We already saw, under freedom of religion, that the Court has decided that the Constitution protects some symbolic expression, such as saluting or not saluting the American flag. But drawing the line between what is and is not protected has been extremely difficult for the Court. In *United States v. O'Brien* (1968), the Court held that burning a draft card at a rally protesting the Vietnam War was not protected speech because the law against burning draft cards was not aimed at restricting expression and fulfilled an important government interest.[31] Following that reasoning, the Court in 1969 struck down a school rule forbidding students to wear black armbands as an expression of their opposition to the Vietnam War, arguing that the fear of a disturbance was not a sufficient state interest to warrant the suppression.[32]

One of the most divisive issues of symbolic speech that has confronted the Supreme Court, and indeed the American public, concerns that ultimate symbol of our country, the American flag. There is probably no more effective way of showing one's dissatisfaction with the United States or its policies than burning the Stars and Stripes. Emotions ride high on this issue. In 1969 the Court split five to four when it overturned the conviction of a person who had broken a New York law making it illegal to deface or show disrespect for the flag (he had burned it).[33] Twenty years later, with a more conservative Court in place, the issue was raised again. Again the Court divided five to four, voting to protect the burning of the flag as symbolic expression.[34] Because the patriotic feelings of so many Americans were fired up by this ruling, Congress passed the federal Flag Protection Act in 1989, making it a crime to desecrate the flag. In *United States v. Eichmann,* the Court declared the federal law unconstitutional for the same reasons it had overturned the state laws earlier: all were aimed specifically at "suppressing expression."[35] The only way to get around a Supreme Court ruling of unconstitutionality is to amend the Constitution. Efforts to pass an amendment have failed in the House and Senate, meaning that despite the strong feeling of the majority to the contrary, flag burning is still considered protected speech in the United States.

The Court has recently proved willing to restrict symbolic speech, however, if it finds that the speech goes beyond expression of a view. In a 2003 ruling, the Court held that cross burning, a favored practice of the Ku Klux Klan and other segregationists that it had previously held to be protected speech, was not protected under the First Amendment if it was intended as a threat of violence.[36] The Court noted that cross burning would still be protected as symbolic speech in certain cases, such as at a political rally.

Freedom of Assembly

Closely related to symbolic speech is an additional First Amendment guarantee, **freedom of assembly**, or "the right of the people peaceably to assemble, and to petition the government for a redress of grievances." The courts have interpreted this provision to mean not only that people can meet and express their views collectively, but also that their very association is protected as a form of political expression. So, for instance, they have ruled that associations like the NAACP (National Association for the Advancement of Colored People) cannot be required to make their membership lists public[37] (although groups deemed to have unlawful purposes do not have such protection) and that teachers do not have to reveal the associations to which they belong.[38] In addition, the Court has basically upheld people's right to associate with whom they please, although it held that public[39] and, in some circumstances, private groups cannot discriminate on the basis of race or sex.[40]

Obscenity and Pornography

Of all the forms of expression, obscenity has probably presented the Court with its biggest headaches. In attempting to define it in 1964, Justice Potter Stewart could only conclude, "I know it when I see it."[41] The Court has used a variety of tests for determining whether material is obscene, but until the early 1970s, only the most hard-core pornography was regulated.

Coming into office in 1969, however, President Nixon made it one of his administration's goals to control pornography in America. Once the Court began to reflect the ideological change that came with Nixon's appointees, rulings became more restrictive. In 1973 the Court developed the **Miller test**, which returned more control over the definition of obscenity to state legislatures and local standards. Under the *Miller* test, the Court asks "whether the work depicts or describes, in a patently offensive way, sexual conduct specifically defined by state law" and "whether the work, taken as a whole, lacks serious literary, artistic, political or scientific value" (called the SLAPS test).[42] These provisions have also been open to interpretation, and the Court has tried to refine them over time. The emphasis on local standards has meant that pornographers can look for those places with the most lenient definitions of obscenity in which to produce and market their work, and the Court has let this practice go on.

The question of whether obscenity should be protected speech raises some fundamental issues and has created some unlikely alliances. Justice John Marshall Harlan was quite right when he wrote that "one man's vulgarity is another man's lyric."[43] People offended by what they consider to be obscenity believe that their values should be represented in their communities. If that means banning adult bookstores, nude dancing at bars, and naked women on magazine covers at the supermarket, then so be it. But opponents argue that what is obscene to one person may be art or enjoyment to another. The problem of majorities enforcing decisions on minorities is inescapable here. A second issue that has generated debate over these cases is the feminist critique of pornography: that it represents aggression toward women and should be banned primarily because it perpetuates stereotypes and breeds violence. Thus radical feminists, usually on the left end of the political spectrum, have found themselves in alliance with conservatives on the right. There is a real contradiction here for feminists, who are more often likely to argue for the expansion of rights, particularly as they apply to women. Feminists advocating restrictions on pornography reconcile the contradiction by arguing that the proliferation of pornography ultimately limits women's rights by making life more threatening and fundamentally unequal.

Fighting Words and Offensive Speech

Among the categories of speech the Court has ruled may be regulated is one called **fighting words,** words whose express purpose is to create a disturbance and incite violence in the person who hears the speech.[44] However, the Court rarely upholds legislation designed to limit fighting words unless the law is written very carefully and specifically. Consequently, it has held that threatening and provocative language is protected unless it is likely to "produce a clear and present danger of serious substantive evil that rises far above public inconvenience, annoyance, or unrest."[45] It has also ruled that offensive language, though not protected by the First Amendment, may occasionally contain a political message, in which case constitutional protection applies.[46]

These rulings have taken on modern-day significance in the wake of the **political correctness** movement that swept the country in the late 1980s and 1990s, especially on college campuses. Political correctness refers to an ideology, held primarily by some liberals, including some civil rights activists and feminists, that language shapes society in critical ways and, therefore, that racist, sexist, homophobic, or any other language that demeans any group of individuals should be silenced to minimize its social effects. An outgrowth of the political correctness movement was the passing of speech codes on college campuses that ban speech that might be offensive to women or ethnic and other minorities. Critics of speech codes, and of political correctness in general, argue that such practices unfairly repress free speech, which should flourish on, of all places, college campuses. In 1989 and 1991, federal district court judges agreed, finding speech codes on two campuses, the University of Michigan and the University of Wisconsin, in violation of students' First Amendment rights.[47] Neither school appealed. The Supreme Court spoke on a related issue in 1992 when it struck down a Minnesota "hate crime law." The Court held that it is unconstitutional to outlaw broad categories of speech based on its content. The prohibition against activities that "arouse anger, alarm or resentment in others on the basis of race, color, creed, religion or gender" was too sweeping and thus unconstitutional.[48]

Freedom of the Press

The First Amendment covers not only freedom of speech but also freedom of the press. Many of the controversial issues we have already covered apply to both of these areas, but some problems are confronted exclusively, or primarily, by the press: the issue of prior restraint, libel restrictions, and the conflict between a free press and a fair trial.

Prior Restraint

Prior restraint, a restriction on the press before its message is actually published, was the primary target of the founders when they drew up the First Amendment. The Supreme Court has shared the founders' concern that prior restraint is a particularly dangerous form of censorship and has almost never permitted it. Two classic judgments illustrate their view. In *Near v. Minnesota*, Jay Near's newspaper, the *Saturday Press,* was critical of African Americans, Jews, Catholics, and organized labor. His paper was shut down in 1927 under a Minnesota law that prohibited any publication of "malicious, scandalous and defamatory" material. If he had continued to publish the paper, he would have been subject to a $1,000 fine or a year in jail. The Court held that the Minnesota law infringed on Near's freedom of the press. Although an extreme emergency, such as war, might justify previous restraint on the press, wrote Justice Charles Evans Hughes, the purpose of the First Amendment is to limit it to those rare circumstances.[49] Similarly and more recently, in *New York Times Company v. United States,* the Court prevented the Nixon administration from stopping the publication by the *New York Times* and the *Washington Post* of a "top-secret" document about U.S. involvement in Vietnam. The so-called Pentagon Papers were claimed by the government to be too sensitive to national security to be published. The Court held that "security" is too vague a concept to be allowed to excuse the violation of the First Amendment. To grant such power to the president, it ruled, would be to run the risk of destroying the liberty that the government is trying to secure.[50]

Libel

Freedom of the press also collides with the issue of **libel**, the written defamation of character (verbal defamation is called *slander*). Obviously, it is crucial to the watchdog and information-providing roles of the press that journalists be able to speak freely about the character and actions of those in public service. But at the same time, because careers and reputations are ruined easily by rumors and innuendoes, journalists ought to be required to "speak" responsibly. The Supreme Court addressed this issue in *New York Times v. Sullivan,* in which it ruled that public officials, as opposed to private individuals, when suing for libel, must show that a publication acted with "actual malice," which means not that the paper had an evil intent but that it acted with "knowledge that [what it printed] was false or with reckless disregard for whether it was false or not."[51] Shortly thereafter, the Court extended the ruling to include public figures other than officials. Public figures might include movie or television stars, sports celebrities, or musicians, as well as other people whose actions put them in a public position—a candidate running for office, an author promoting her book, or the host of a radio talk show.

The Court's rulings attempt to give the press some leeway in its actions. Without *Sullivan,* investigative journalism would never have been able to uncover the role of the United States in Vietnam, for instance, or the Watergate cover-up. Freedom of the press, and thus the public's interest in keeping a critical eye on government, are clearly the winners here. The Court's view is that when individuals put themselves in the public domain, the public's interest in the truth outweighs the protection of their privacy.

The Right to a Fair Trial

Freedom of the press also confronts head-on another Bill of Rights guarantee, the right to a fair trial. Media coverage of a crime can make it very difficult to find an "impartial jury," as required by the Sixth Amendment. On the other side of this conflict, however, is the "public's right to know." The Sixth Amendment promises a "speedy and public trial," and many journalists interpret this provision to mean that the proceedings ought to be open. The courts, on the other hand, have usually held that this amendment protects the rights of the accused, not of the public. But while the Court has overturned a murder verdict because a judge failed to control the media circus in his courtroom,[52] on the whole it has ruled in favor of media access to most stages of legal proceedings. Likewise, courts have been extremely reluctant to uphold gag orders, which would impose prior restraint on the press during those proceedings.[53]

Censorship on the Internet

Lawmakers do not always know how to deal with new outlets for expression as they become available. Modern technology has presented the judiciary with a host of free speech issues the founders never anticipated. The latest to make it to the courts is the question of censorship on the Internet. Some web sites contain explicit sexual material, obscene language, and other content that many people find objectionable. Because children often find their way onto the Internet on their own, parents and groups of other concerned citizens have clamored for regulation of this medium. Congress obliged in 1996 with the Communications Decency Act, which made it illegal to knowingly send or display indecent material over the Internet. In 1997 the Supreme Court ruled that such provisions constituted a violation of free speech, and that communication over the Internet, which it called a modern "town crier," is subject to the same protections as nonelectronic expression.[54] When Congress tried again with a more narrowly tailored bill, the Child Online Protection Act, the Court struck it down, too.[55]

The Court has not always ruled on the side of a completely unregulated Internet. While not restricting the creation of content, in 2003 the Supreme Court did uphold the Children's Internet Protection Act, which required public libraries that received federal funds to use filtering software to block material that is deemed harmful to minors, such as pornography.[56] However, these filters can create some problems. Many companies and institutions use them to screen offensive incoming email, but such filters often have unwanted consequences. Since the filters cannot evaluate the material passing through, they can end up blocking even legitimate messages and publications. One editor of a newsletter on technology has resorted to intentionally misspelling words (for example, writing "sez" instead of "sex") to avoid the automatic sensors that screen many of his readers' mail.[57]

The Internet can also have the effect of freeing people from censorship, however. As many people who have worked on their high school newspapers know, the Court has ruled that student publications are subject to censorship by school officials if the restrictions serve an educational purpose. The Internet, however, offers students an alternate medium of publication that the courts say is not subject to censorship. As a result, students have been able to publish such matters as the results of investigations into school elections and campus violence that have been excluded from the hard-copy newspaper.[58] We can probably expect some flux in the laws on Internet censorship as the courts become more familiar with the medium itself and the issues surrounding it. (See "*Consider the Source:* Don't Be Fooled by the World Wide Web" in Chapter 5 for some tips on how to evaluate what you find on the Internet.)

The Right to Bear Arms
Providing for militias to secure the state or
securing an individual right?

The Second Amendment to the Constitution reads, "A well regulated militia, being necessary to the security of a free state, the right of the people to keep and bear arms, shall not be infringed." This amendment has been the subject of some of the fiercest debates in American politics. Originally it was a seemingly straightforward effort by opponents of the Constitution to keep the federal government in check by limiting the power of standing, or permanent, armies. Over time it has become a rallying point for those who want to engage in sporting activities involving guns, those who believe that firearms are necessary for self-defense, those who oppose contemporary American policy and want to use revolution to return to what they think were the goals of the founders, and those who simply don't believe that it is government's business to make decisions about who can own guns.

Why Is the Right to Bear Arms Valuable?

During the earliest days of American independence, the chief source of national stability was the state militia system—armies of able-bodied men who could be counted on to assemble, with their own guns, to defend their country from external and internal threats, whether from the British, Native Americans, or local insurrection. Local militias were seen as far less dangerous to the fledgling republic than a standing army under national leadership. Such an army could seize control and create a military dictatorship, depriving citizens of their hard-won rights.

The restructuring of the U.S. military and the growing evidence that under civilian control it did not pose a threat to the liberties of American citizens caused many people to view the Second Amendment as obsolete. But although the militia system that gave rise to the amendment is now defunct, supporters of rights for gun owners, such as the National Rifle Association (NRA), argue that the amendment is as relevant as ever because hunting and other leisure activities involving guns do not hurt anybody (except, of course, the hunted) and are an important part of American culture; because possession of guns is necessary for self-defense; because citizens should have the right to arm themselves to protect their families and property from a potentially tyrannical government; and because the federal government does not have the power to regulate gun use.

Opponents of these views, such as Handgun Control, Inc., and the Coalition to Stop Gun Violence, counter that none of these claims has anything to do with the Second Amendment, which refers only to the use and ownership of guns by state militia members; that countries with stricter gun control laws have less violence and fewer gun deaths; that none of the rights of Americans, even such fundamental ones as freedom of speech and the press, is absolute; and that it is ironic to claim the protection of the Constitution to own weapons that could be used to overturn the government based on that Constitution.[59]

Legislation and Judicial Decisions

Although various kinds of gun control legislation have been passed at the state and local levels, powerful interest groups like the NRA have kept it to a minimum at the federal level. The 1990s, however, saw the passage of three federal bills that affect the right to bear arms: the 1993 Brady Bill, requiring background checks on potential handgun purchasers; the 1994 Crime Bill, barring semiautomatic assault weapons; and a 1995 bill making it illegal to carry a gun near a school. The 1995 law and the interim provisions of the Brady Bill, which imposed a five-day waiting period for all gun sales, with local background checks until a national background check system could be established, were struck down by the Supreme Court on the grounds that they were unconstitutional infringements of the national government into the realm of state power.[60] In September 2004 Congress let the ban on semiautomatic weapons expire, largely at the urging of then–House majority leader Tom DeLay. While some Democrats in Congress promised to reintroduce the ban, many members have been reluctant to act, possibly because the NRA continues to target gun control candidates for defeat in reelections.

Until 2008 the Supreme Court had ruled on only a handful of cases that had an impact on gun rights and the Second Amendment, mostly interpreting the Second Amendment as intending to arm state militias, and letting state gun-related legislation stand.[61] The Supreme Court did strike down the legislation concerning possession of guns near schools and reversed one provision of the Brady Bill on federalism, not Second Amendment, grounds. In the close Brady case, four dissenters argued that the burden put on the localities was not disproportionate to the good done by addressing what they called an "epidemic of gun violence."[62] In 2004 the Court let stand a lower court's ruling that supported a California ban on assault rifles on the grounds that the Second Amendment did not protect individual gun owners. The ruling applies only to those states in the Ninth Circuit, however, and does not require a state to ban assault rifles.

In 2008, however, the Supreme Court heard arguments for the first time since 1939 on whether the Constitution guarantees an individual the right to bear arms. In a five-to-four decision, the Court held that it did, striking down a Washington, D.C., law that banned handgun possession in the home. While the Court held that the D.C. law violated an individual's right to own a gun for self-protection, the majority was careful to say that the right to own guns is not unlimited. For instance, it does not encompass military-grade weapons, and it does not extend to felons and the mentally ill.[63] In 2010 the Court took the ruling a step further, holding that not only could the federal government not violate an individual's right to bear arms, as it had in the D.C. case, but neither could a state government.[64] Writing for the Court in a five-to-four decision, Justice Samuel Alito said, "It is clear that the Framers . . . counted the right to keep and bear arms among those fundamental rights necessary to our system of ordered liberty."[65] Further cases will determine exactly what the parameters of this interpretation are—which state laws violate the right and which do not—but gun rights advocates are hoping to see it applied broadly, as evidenced by the Virginia law, passed just days after the Supreme Court ruling, that allows bar patrons to carry concealed weapons as long as they are not drinking.[66]

The Rights of Criminal Defendants
Protecting the accused from an arbitrary government

Half of the amendments in the Bill of Rights and several clauses in the Constitution itself are devoted to protecting the rights of people who are suspected or accused of committing crimes. The Fourth through Eighth Amendments protect people against unreasonable searches and seizures, self-incrimination, and cruel and unusual punishment, and they guarantee people accused of a crime the right to legal advice, the right to a speedy and public trial, and various other procedural protections.

Why Are the Rights of Criminal Defendants Valuable?

As we indicated, a primary reason for protecting the rights of the accused is to limit government power. One way governments can stop criticism of their actions is by eliminating the opposition, imprisoning them, or worse. The guarantees in the Bill of Rights provide checks on government's ability to prosecute its enemies.

Another reason for guaranteeing rights to those accused of crimes is the strong tradition in American culture, coming from our English roots, that a person is innocent until proven guilty. An innocent person, naturally, still has the full protection of the Constitution, and even a guilty person is protected to some degree, for instance, against cruel and unusual punishment. All Americans are entitled to what the Fifth and Fourteenth Amendments call **due process of the law,** which means that laws must be reasonable and fair, and that those accused of breaking the law—and who stand to lose life, liberty, or property as a consequence—have the right to appear before their judges to hear the charges and evidence against them, to have legal counsel, and to present any contradictory evidence in their defense. Due process means essentially that those accused of a crime have a right to a fair trial.

During the 1960s and 1970s the Supreme Court expanded the protection of the rights of the accused and incorporated them so that the states had to protect them as well. Yet the more conservative 1980s and 1990s witnessed a considerable backlash against a legal system perceived as having gone soft on crime—overly concerned with the rights of criminals at the expense of safe streets, neighborhoods, and cities, and deaf to the claims of victims of violent crimes. We want to protect the innocent, but when the seemingly guilty go free because of a technicality, the public is often incensed. The Supreme Court has had the heavy responsibility of drawing the line between the rights of defendants and the rights of society.

Protection Against Unreasonable Searches and Seizures

The Fourth Amendment guards against "unreasonable searches and seizures" and requires "probable cause" to obtain a warrant. The founders were particularly sensitive on this question because the king of England had had the right to order the homes of his subjects searched without cause, looking for any evidence of criminal activity. For the most part this amendment has been interpreted by the Court to mean that a person's home is private and cannot be invaded by police without a warrant, obtainable only if they have very good reason to think that criminal evidence lies within.

What's Reasonable?

Under the Fourth Amendment, there are a few exceptions to the rule that searches require warrants. Automobiles present a special case, for example, since by their nature they are likely to be gone by the time an officer appears with a warrant. Cars can be searched without warrants if the officer has probable cause to think a law has been broken, and the Court has gradually widened the scope of the search so that it can include luggage or closed containers in the car.

Modern innovations like wiretapping and electronic surveillance presented more difficult problems for the Court because previous law had not allowed for them. A "search" was understood legally to require some physical trespass, and a "seizure" involved taking some tangible object. Listening in on a conversation—electronically from afar—was simply not covered by the law. In fact, in the first case in which bugging was addressed, the Court held that it did not constitute a search.[67] That ruling held for forty years, until the case of *Katz v. United States* (1967), when it was overturned by a Court that required, for the first time, that a warrant be obtained before phones could be tapped.[68] In the same year, the Court ruled that conversations were included under Fourth Amendment protection.[69] A search warrant is thus needed to tap a phone, although the 2001 Patriot Act makes it a good deal easier to get a warrant, and in 2005 it was revealed that President Bush had been allowing the National Security Agency to bypass even those minimal requirements. In early 2006 the Congressional Research Service suggested that Bush had exceeded his authority, and scholars and politicians continue to debate the power of the executive to waive basic protections of civil liberties.[70]

Yet another modern area in which the Court has had to determine the legality of searches is mandatory random testing for drug or alcohol use, usually by urine or blood tests. These are arguably a very unreasonable kind of search, but the Court has tended to allow them where the violation of privacy is outweighed by a good purpose, for instance, discovering the cause of a train accident,[71] preventing drug use in schools,[72] or preserving the public safety by requiring drug tests of train conductors and airline pilots.

The Exclusionary Rule

By far the most controversial part of the Fourth Amendment rulings has been the exclusionary rule. In a 1914 case, *Weeks v. United States*, the Court confronted the question of what to do with evidence that had, in fact, been obtained illegally. It decided that such evidence should be excluded from use in the defendant's trial.[73] This **exclusionary rule**, as it came to be known, meant that even though the police might have concrete evidence of criminal activity, if obtained unlawfully, the evidence could not be used to gain a conviction of the culprit.

The exclusionary rule has been controversial from the start. In some countries, including England, illegally obtained evidence can be used at trial, but the defendant is allowed to sue the police in a civil suit or bring criminal charges against them. The object is clearly to deter misbehavior on the part of the police, while not allowing guilty people to go free. But the exclusionary rule, while it does serve as a deterrent to police, helps criminals avoid punishment. The Court itself has occasionally seemed uneasy about the rule. When the Fourth Amendment was incorporated, in *Wolf v. Colorado,* the exclusionary rule was not extended to the states. The Court ruled that it was a judicial creation, not a constitutionally protected right.[74] Not until the 1961 case of *Mapp v. Ohio* was the exclusionary rule finally incorporated into state as well as federal practice.[75]

But extending the reach of the exclusionary rule did not end the controversy. Although the Warren Court (1953–1969) continued to uphold it, the Burger and Rehnquist Courts (1969–2005) cut back on the protections it offered. In 1974 they ruled that the exclusionary rule was to be a deterrent to abuse by the police, not a constitutional right of the accused.[76] The Court subsequently ruled that illegally seized evidence could be used in civil trials[77] and came to carve out what it called a *good faith exception,* whereby evidence is admitted to a criminal trial, even if obtained illegally, if the police are relying on a warrant that appears to be valid at the time or on a law that appears to be constitutional (though either may turn out to be defective),[78] or on a warrant that is obtained in error. In 2009 the Roberts Court ruled that to trigger the exclusionary rule, the police conduct must be deliberate.[79] The Court's more conservative turn on this issue has not silenced the debate, however. Some observers are appalled at the reduction in the protection of individual rights, whereas others do not believe that the Court has gone far enough in protecting society against criminals.

Protection Against Self-Incrimination

No less controversial than the rulings on illegally seized evidence are the Court's decisions on unconstitutionally obtained confessions. The Fifth Amendment provides for a number of protections for individuals, among them that no person "shall be compelled in any criminal case to be a witness against himself." The Supreme Court has expanded the scope of the protection against self-incrimination from criminal trials, as the amendment dictates, to grand jury proceedings, legislative investigations, and even police interrogations. It is this last extension that has proved most controversial.

In 1966 the Warren Court ruled, in *Miranda v. Arizona,* that police had to inform suspects of their rights to remain silent and to have a lawyer present during questioning to prevent them from incriminating themselves. The *Miranda* rights are familiar to viewers of police dramas: "You have the right to remain silent. Anything you say can and will be used against you. . . ." If a lawyer could show that a defendant had not been "read" his or her rights, information gained in the police interrogation would not be admissible in court. Like the exclusionary rule, the

Miranda ruling could and did result in criminals going free even though the evidence existed to convict them.

Reacting to public and political accusations that the Warren Court was soft on crime, Congress passed the Crime Control and Safe Streets Act of 1968, which allowed confessions to be used in federal courts not according to the *Miranda* ruling, but according to the "totality of the circumstances" surrounding the confession. In 2000, despite the fact that some justices had been highly critical of the *Miranda* ruling over the years, the Court upheld the 1966 decision, stating that it had become an established part of the culture, and held the 1968 Crime Control Act to be unconstitutional.[80]

Right to Counsel

Closely related to the *Miranda* decision, which upholds the right to a lawyer during police questioning, is the Sixth Amendment declaration that the accused shall "have the assistance of counsel for his defense." The founders' intentions are fairly clear from the 1790 Federal Crimes Act, which required courts to provide counsel for poor defendants only in capital cases—that is, those punishable by death. Defendants in other trials had a right to counsel, but the government had no obligation to provide it. The Supreme Court's decisions were in line with that act until 1938, when, in *Johnson v. Zerbst*, it extended the government's obligation to provide counsel to impoverished defendants in all criminal proceedings in federal courts.[81] Only federal crimes carried that obligation until 1963. Then, in one of the most dramatic tales of courtroom appeals (so exciting that it was made into both a book and a movie called *Gideon's Trumpet*), a poor man named Clarence Earl Gideon was convicted of breaking and entering a pool hall and stealing money from the vending machine. Gideon asked the judge for a lawyer, but the judge told him that the state of Florida was not obligated to give him one. He tried to defend the case himself but lost to the far more skilled and knowledgeable prosecutor. Serving five years in prison for a crime he swore he did not commit, he filed a handwritten appeal with the Supreme Court. In a landmark decision, *Gideon v. Wainwright*, the Court incorporated the Sixth Amendment right to counsel.[82]

The *Gideon* decision was a tremendous financial and administrative burden for the states, which had to retry or release many prisoners. Conservatives believed that *Gideon* went far beyond the founders' intentions. Both the Burger and Rehnquist Courts succeeded in rolling back some of the protections won by *Gideon*, ruling, for instance, that the right to a court-appointed attorney does not extend beyond the filing of one round of appeals, even if the convicted indigent person is on death row.[83]

Protection Against Cruel and Unusual Punishment

The Eighth Amendment, which says, in part, that "cruel and unusual punishments" shall not be inflicted, has generated some major political controversies. Like some of the earlier amendments, this guarantee reflects a concern of English law, which

In The Supreme Court of The United States
Washington D.C.

Clarence Earl Gideon
  Petitioner
vs.
H.G. Cochran, Jr., as
Director, Divisions
of corrections state
of Florida

Petition for a writ
of Certiorari Directed
To The Supreme Court
State of Florida.

No. — 890 Misc.

OCT. TERM 1961

U.S. Supreme Court

To. The Honorable Earl Warren, Chief Justice of the United States

Comes now The petitioner, Clarence Earl Gideon, a citizen of The United States of America, in proper person, and appearing as his own counsel. Who petitions this Honorable Court for a Writ of Certiorari directed To The Supreme Court of The State of Florida, To review the order and Judgement of the court below denying The petitioner a writ of Habeus Corpus.

Petitioner submits That The Supreme Court of The United States has The authority and jurisdiction to review The final Judgement of The Supreme Court of The State of Florida The highest court of The State Under sec. 344 (B) Title 28 U.S.C.A. and Because The "Due process clause" of the

Rights of the Accused
Clarence Earl Gideon spent much of his time in prison studying the law. His handwritten appeal to the Supreme Court resulted in the landmark decision *Gideon v. Wainwright*, which granted those accused of crimes the right to counsel.

sought to protect British subjects from torture and inhumane treatment by the king. It is easy to see why it would be controversial, however. What is "cruel," and what is "unusual"? Despite intense lobbying on the part of impassioned interest groups, however, the Court has not ruled that the death penalty itself is cruel or unusual (except in the case of mentally retarded individuals, juveniles, and crimes against an individual that do not result in the death of the victim),[84] and most states have death penalty laws.

The strongest attack on the death penalty began in the 1970s, when the NAACP Legal Defense Fund joined with the American Civil Liberties Union and the American Bar Association to argue that the death penalty was disproportionately given to African Americans, especially those convicted of rape. They argued that this was a violation of the Eighth Amendment and of the Fourteenth Amendment guarantee of equal protection of the law. Part of the problem was that state laws differed about what constituted grounds for imposing the death penalty, and juries had no uniform standards to rely on. Consequently, unequal patterns of application of the penalty developed.

In *Furman v. Georgia* (1972) and two related cases, the Court ruled that Georgia's and Texas's capital punishment laws were unconstitutional, but the justices were so far from agreement that they all filed separate opinions, totaling 231 pages.[85] Thirty-five states passed new laws trying to meet the Court's objections and to clarify the standards for capital punishment. By 1976 six hundred inmates waited on death row for the Court to approve the new laws. That year the Court ruled in several cases that the death penalty was not unconstitutional, although it struck down laws requiring the death penalty for certain crimes.[86] The Court remained divided over the issue. In 1977 Gary Gilmore became the first person executed after a ten-year break.

In 1987 *McClesky v. Kemp* raised the race issue again, but by then the Court was growing more conservative. It held, five to four, that statistics showing that blacks who murder whites received the death penalty more frequently than whites who murder blacks did not prove a racial bias in the law or in how it was being applied.[87] The Rehnquist Court continued to knock down procedural barriers to imposing the death penalty. In 2006 the Roberts Court held that death-row inmates could challenge state lethal injection procedures in lower courts on cruel and unusual punishment grounds. Several of those courts came to different conclusions. In 2008, in *Baze v. Rees*,[88] the Supreme Court upheld Kentucky's lethal injection practice, and other states, waiting for a sign from the Court, went ahead with their own practices.

Public support for capital punishment appears to be softening in recent years, not because of opposition in principle but because of fears that the system might be putting innocent people on death row. This feeling grew as DNA testing cleared some death row residents, and careful investigation showed that others, too, were innocent. After thirteen death row convicts in his state were exonerated between 1977 and 2000, Illinois governor George Ryan, a moderate Republican who supported the death penalty in principle, called for a statewide halt to executions. "I cannot support a system, which, in its administration, has proven so fraught with error," Ryan explained, "and has come so close to the ultimate nightmare, the state's taking of an innocent life."[89] Following his lead, then–Maryland governor Parris Glendening issued a moratorium in 2002, but that action was quickly reversed by the new governor, Robert Ehrlich, in January 2003. In 2007 the New Jersey legislature banned the death penalty in the state—the first state to do so since the Supreme Court declared capital punishment constitutional in 1976.[90] Despite misgivings, the American public continues to favor capital punishment. In a recent Gallup poll, only 31 percent opposed it, even though only 57 percent thought that it was applied fairly.[91]

> Despite misgivings, the American public continues to favor capital punishment.

The Right to Privacy
The personal meets the political

One of the most controversial rights in America is not even mentioned in the Constitution or the Bill of Rights: the right to privacy. This right is at the heart of one of the deepest divisions in American politics, the split over abortion rights and contraceptive use, and is fundamental to two other controversial areas of civil liberties: gay rights and the right to die.

Why Is the Right to Privacy Valuable?

Although the right to privacy is not spelled out in the Bill of Rights, it goes hand in hand with the founders' insistence on limited government. Their goal was to keep government from getting too powerful and interfering with the lives and affairs of individual citizens. They certainly implied a right to privacy, and perhaps even assumed such a right, but they did not make it explicit.

The right to privacy, to be left alone to do what we want, is so clearly desirable that it scarcely needs a defense. The problem, of course, is that a right to privacy without any limits is anarchy, the absence of government altogether. Clearly, government has an interest in preventing some kinds of individual behavior—murder, theft, and rape, for example. But what about other, more subtle behaviors that do not directly affect the public safety but arguably have serious consequences for the public good—such as prostitution, drug use, and gambling? Should these behaviors fall under the right to privacy, or should the state be able to regulate them?

Reproductive Rights

Throughout the 1940s, people had tried to challenge state laws that made it a crime to use birth control, or even to give out information about how to prevent pregnancies. The Supreme Court routinely refused to hear these cases until the 1965 case of *Griswold v. Connecticut* challenged a Connecticut law making it illegal to use contraceptive devices or to distribute information about them. The Court held that while the right to privacy is not explicit in the Constitution, a number of other rights, notably those in Amendments One, Three, Four, Five, and Nine, create a "zone of privacy" in which lie marriage and the decision to use contraception. It said that the specific guarantees in the Bill of Rights have "penumbras," or outlying shadowy areas, in which can be found a right to privacy. The Fourteenth Amendment applies that right to the states, and so Connecticut's law was unconstitutional.[92]

Because of the Court's insistence that reproductive matters are not the concern of the government, abortion rights advocates saw an opportunity to use the *Griswold* ruling to strike down state laws prohibiting or limiting abortion. The Court had tried to avoid ruling on the abortion issue, but by 1973 it had become hard to escape. In *Roe v. Wade*, the justices held that the right to privacy did indeed encompass the right to abortion. It tried to balance a woman's right to privacy in reproductive matters with the state's interest in protecting human life, however, by treating the three trimesters of pregnancy differently. In the first three months of pregnancy, it held, there can be no compelling state interest that offsets a woman's privacy rights. In the second three months, the state can regulate access to abortions if it does so reasonably. In the last trimester, the state's interest becomes far more compelling, and a state can limit or even prohibit abortions as long as the mother's life is not in danger.[93]

The *Roe* decision launched the United States into an intense and divisive battle over abortion. States continued to try to limit abortions by requiring the consent of husbands or parents, by outlawing clinic advertising, by imposing waiting periods, and by erecting other roadblocks. The Court struck down most of these efforts, at least until 1977 when it allowed some state limitations. But the battle was not confined to statehouses. Congress, having failed to pass a constitutional amendment banning abortions, passed over thirty laws restricting access to abortions in various ways. For instance, it limited federal funding for abortions through Medicaid, a move the Supreme Court upheld in 1980.[94] Presidents got into the fray as well. President Reagan and the first President Bush were staunch opponents of *Roe* and worked hard to get it overturned. Reagan appointed only antiabortion judges to federal courts, and his administration was active in pushing litigation that would challenge *Roe*.

The balance on the Supreme Court was crucial. *Roe* had been decided by a seven-to-two vote, but many in the majority were facing retirement. When Burger retired, Reagan elevated Rehnquist, one of the two dissenters, to chief justice, and appointed conservative Antonin Scalia in his place. Reagan's appointees did finally turn the Court in a more conservative direction, but even they were not willing to completely overturn *Roe*, though it has been limited in some respects, including a 2007 decision by the Roberts Court that upheld a ban on partial birth abortion.[95]

In any case, the debate over abortion in this country is certainly not over. It has long been a rallying point for the Christian Right, which has become a powerful part of the Republican Party. Since 1980 the Republicans have included a commitment to a constitutional amendment banning abortion in their presidential party platform. And while President Obama has expressed support for a woman's right to choose, some Democrats oppose abortion rights as well. In 2010 Michigan Rep. Bart Stupak initially refused to support the health care reform bill passed by the Senate because he did not feel it had stringent enough restrictions on the use of federal funds for abortion, though he was able to secure an agreement from the White House that the reform would not change existing law. With Americans nearly evenly split on the question of abortion, it is likely to remain a divisive issue in American politics for some time to come.[96]

Gay Rights

The *Griswold* and *Roe* rulings have opened up a variety of difficult issues for the Supreme Court. If there is a right to privacy, what might be included under it?

On the whole, the Court has been very restrictive in expanding it beyond the reproductive rights of the original cases. Most controversial was its ruling in *Bowers v. Hardwick* (1986).[97]

Michael Hardwick was arrested under a Georgia law outlawing heterosexual and homosexual sodomy. Hardwick challenged the law (although he wasn't prosecuted under it), claiming that it violated his right to privacy. The Court disagreed. Looking at the case from the perspective of whether there was a constitutional right to engage in sodomy, rather than from the dissenting view that what took place between consenting adults was none of their business, the Court held five to four that the state of Georgia had a legitimate interest in regulating such behavior. Justice Lewis Powell, who provided the fifth vote for the majority, said after his retirement that he regretted his vote in the *Bowers* decision, but by then, of course, it was too late. Several states have also been critical of the Court's ruling. The Georgia Supreme Court struck down Georgia's sodomy law in 1998 on privacy grounds, but in a case involving heterosexual rather than homosexual activity. Not until 2003, in *Lawrence v. Texas,* did the Court, in a six-to-three decision, finally overturn *Bowers* on privacy grounds.[98] Interestingly, despite its longtime reluctance to overturn *Bowers,* the Court in 1996 used the equal protection clause of the Fourteenth Amendment to strike down a Colorado law that would have made it difficult for gays to use the Colorado courts to fight discrimination.[99] Thus the Court can pursue several constitutional avenues to expand the rights of gay Americans, should it want to do so. Although it is likely in the near future to have to rule on California's Proposition 8 overturning gay marriage in that state, that ruling is more likely to be decided on equal protection grounds rather than on privacy rights.

The Right to Die

A final right-to-privacy issue that has stirred up controversy for the Court is the so-called right to die. In 1990 the Court upheld the state of Missouri's refusal to allow the parents of a woman who had been in a vegetative state and on life-support systems for seven years to withdraw her life support, because they said the daughter's wishes were not clear. But the Court held that when an individual's wishes were made clear in advance, either in person or via a living will, that person's right to terminate medical treatment was protected under the Fourteenth Amendment's due process clause.[100]

The right-to-die issue surged back into national prominence in 2005 with a case involving Terri Schiavo, a young woman who had been in a persistent vegetative state for over fifteen years. Claiming that Schiavo had not wished to be kept alive by artificial measures, her husband asked a state court to have her feeding tube removed. Her parents challenged the decision, but after numerous appeals the court ordered the tube removed in accordance with the precedent set in the 1990 case. Social conservatives in Congress tried to block the action, but all federal courts, including the Supreme Court, refused to intervene and Schiavo died soon after. Angered by their inability to overturn the state court ruling, conservative groups vowed to fight for federal judicial appointees who would be more likely to intervene in such cases.

The Schiavo case did not change the prevailing legal principles—that this is a matter for individuals to decide and that when their wishes are known they should be respected by the doctors and the courts. In this matter, at least, public opinion seems to be consistent with the law. Polls showed the public strongly opposed to Congress intervention to prevent Schiavo's death, and large majorities supported the removal of her feeding tube. In the wake of the case, 70 percent of Americans said they were thinking about getting their own living wills.[101]

The question of a person's right to suspend treatment is different from another legal issue—whether individuals have the right to have assistance ending their lives when they are terminally ill and in severe pain. Oregon provided the first test of this policy. In 1997 it passed a referendum allowing doctors under certain circumstances to provide lethal doses of medication to enable terminally ill patients to end their lives. In late 2001 U.S. attorney general John Ashcroft effectively blocked the law by announcing that doctors who participated in assisted suicides would lose their licenses to prescribe federally regulated medications, an essential part of medical practice. In 2004 a federal appellate court ruled that Ashcroft overstepped his authority under federal law, and in early 2006 the Supreme Court upheld the Oregon law.

Citizenship and Civil Liberties
Individual rights yield a collective benefit

I n the United States, we are accustomed to thinking about citizenship as a status that confers on us certain rights. But although obligation without rights is an authoritarian dictatorship, rights without obligation leads to a state of nature—anarchy—with no government at all. Plainly, the status of a citizen in a democracy requires both rights and duties in order to "keep the Republic."

The final section of a chapter on civil liberties is an interesting place to speculate about the duties attached to American citizenship. We have explored the Bill of Rights; what might a "bill of obligations" look like? The Constitution itself suggests the basics. Obligations are very much the flip side of rights: for every right guaranteed, there is a corresponding duty to use it. For example:

- The provisions for elected office and the right to vote imply a duty to vote.
- Congress is authorized to collect taxes, duties, and excises, including an income tax. Citizens are obligated to pay those taxes.
- Congress can raise and support armies, provide and maintain navies, and provide for and govern militias. Americans have a duty to serve in the military.
- The Fifth and Sixth Amendments guarantee grand juries and jury trials to those accused of crimes. Citizens must serve on those juries.

But Americans are notoriously lax in fulfilling some of these obligations. We turn out to vote in low numbers, we like to avoid paying taxes, and the draft, like jury duty, is an obligation many Americans have actively sought to escape. It might be worthwhile considering what the political consequences are for a democratic republic when the emphasis on preserving civil liberties is not balanced by a corresponding commitment to fulfilling political obligations.

▶ What's at Stake Revisited

When Virginia attorney general Ken Cuccinelli attempted to investigate the grants obtained by a former University of Virginia professor whose research findings he disagreed with, he was the darling of conservative opponents of the science of global warming but the object of attacks by academics and liberal critics who warned that his efforts could have a "chilling effect" on academic research. For these critics, the freedom to pursue academic research and studies is a First Amendment issue, and academia requires an atmosphere of open debate in order for it to police itself. The *Washington Post's* editorial board wrote,

> By equating controversial results with legal fraud, Mr. Cuccinelli demonstrates a dangerous disregard for scientific method and academic freedom. The remedy for unsatisfactory data or analysis is public criticism from peers and more data, not a politically tinged witch hunt or, worse, a civil penalty. Scientists and other academics inevitably will get things wrong, and they will use public funds in the process, because failure is as important to producing good scholarship as success.[102]

Numerous academic investigations into Professor Mann's research and the efforts of fellow researchers to replicate and test his findings found no evidence of fraud and so, the academics believed, that should be the end of it. Political opponents of Mann's findings believed that fellow academics could not be trusted to police Mann's work and sought to discredit his research using the apparatus of the state, something that University of Virginia lawyers pointed out went way beyond the founders' notion of a limited government.

Clearly, the idea of academic freedom is destined to be a controversial one. Academic freedom—traditionally understood as the right of faculty to teach, research, and write about what they think is important without fear of reprisal[103]— is gradually being redefined by both conservatives and liberals on campus as the right not to have to teach or be taught ideas they disagree with or find offensive. Both sides say the issue is about basic civil liberties and each accuses the other of wanting to indoctrinate students rather than to teach them. The two sets of beliefs are on a collision course, and they may be crashing into each other on a college campus, and maybe even in a state legislature, near you.

Liberal critics of campus culture in the late twentieth century have argued that academia was dominated by white middle-class males who perpetuated a Euro-centric view of the world. These critics demanded that college curricula, hiring practices, admissions standards, and campus life generally should acknowledge the growing diversity of the United States. Multiculturalism and the political cor-rectness movement (see p. 124 in this chapter) are two of the consequences of that effort to make colleges and universities more representative of American diversity.

But increasingly, conservatives argue that the pendulum has swung way too far in that direction. They say that many college professors are too liberal, that students are captive audiences in classes where they are told only one side of the story, and that they are then graded on whether they support the professor's position. They also argue that because students are still developing their opinions about politics and the world, their exposure to liberal professors makes them more likely to leave college with liberal ideas.

Conservative activist David Horowitz feels so strongly about the issue that he created Students for Academic Freedom, an organization that is chartered on more than 130 college campuses and that aims to expose professors who promote their personal beliefs in the classroom. One of the group's goals is to get state legisla-tures and the U.S. Congress to pass an "Academic Bill of Rights" that urges univer-sities to recognize and promote intellectual diversity on college campuses by promoting ideological diversity in the classroom and encouraging schools to hire more conservative professors.[104] The group has had some success. For instance, the Georgia Senate passed a resolution "encouraging public colleges and universi-ties to refrain from discriminating against students because of their political or religious beliefs."[105]

Not surprisingly, these groups have met with criticism in their own turn. Many students disagree that professors are pushing their views in the classroom. Further-more, university faculty and administrators claim that the conservative organiza-tions are engaging in a witch hunt to stifle thought and limit speech. The American Association of University Professors opposes the bills pushed by Students for Aca-demic Freedom on the grounds that these bills infringe on what they call academic freedom—that it imposes political standards for hiring, for instance, instead of the standards of academic rigor they believe are important, and places external controls over what can be taught in the classroom.

What are liberals and conservatives really battling over? In a sense, each side has grown in response to the other. Each wants to restrict research or speech in the classroom that they find offensive. Liberals want open, honest debate on the failings of the Bush administration's American foreign policy, for instance, but want to limit speech that some minorities might find offensive. Conservatives want open, honest debate on issues such as affirmative action but want to limit speech that suggests that current business practices are environmentally unsustainable. Each side wants to censor the other in the name of academic freedom, but neither of these two sides is really so much about academic freedom as it is about freedom to tell one's story as the dominant story. It's not surprising that college campuses, filled with bright young minds and youthful energy, should have become battle-grounds in this fight, but the stakes there are unusually high. If either side manages to "win" the war, the losers, if John Stuart Mill is to be believed, will be critical thinking, the ability to find and defend the truth, and ultimately, the fate of democracy itself.

▶ Summary With Key Terms

Civil liberties (107) and civil rights (107) define the powers that we as citizens have in a democratic polity. Our civil liberties are individual freedoms that place limitations on the power of government. Most of these rights are spelled out in the text of the Constitution—for instance, that government may not suspend habeas corpus (110) or pass bills of attainder (110) or ex post facto laws (110)—or in its first ten amendments, the Bill of Rights. But some rights have developed over the years through judicial decision making. The rights in the Bill of Rights limit only the national government's action, but through a process of incorporation (111)—specifically selective incorporation (111)—the Supreme Court has made some of them applicable to the states.

According to the establishment clause (113) and free exercise clause (115) of the First Amendment, citizens of the United States have the right not to be coerced to practice a religion in which they do not believe, as well as the right not to be prevented from practicing the religion they espouse. Because these rights can conflict, separationists (113) and accommodationists (113) have fought over the meaning of religious freedom since the founding. The courts have played a significant role in navigating the stormy waters of religious expression since then, applying the *Lemon* test (115) to determine whether government is entangled with religion, and using the compelling state interest (116) test to see if laws affecting religion go beyond the legitimate use of the government's police power (115).

Freedom of expression, also provided for in the First Amendment, is often considered the hallmark of our democratic government. Freedom of expression and freedom of assembly (123) help limit corruption, protect minorities, and promote a vigorous defense of the truth. Again, it has been left to the courts to balance freedom of expression with social and moral order, for instance by applying the clear and present danger test (119) and the imminent lawless action test (122) to see if sedition (118) laws restrict speech unconstitutionally, and by applying the *Miller* test (123) to determine what is obscene. The Court has allowed the regulation of some speech, such as fighting words (124), although it has been reluctant to follow codes of **political correctness** (124), to allow **prior restraint** (125), or to ease the laws of **libel** (126).

The right to bear arms, supported by the Second Amendment, has also been hotly debated. Most often the debate over gun laws is carried out in state legislatures.

The founders believed that to limit government power, people needed to retain **due process of the law** (130) throughout the process of being accused, tried, and punished for criminal activities. Thus they devoted some of the text of the Constitution as well as the Bill of Rights to a variety of procedural protections, including the right to a speedy and public trial, protection from unreasonable search and seizure—including the judge-made **exclusionary rule** (131), and the right to legal advice.

Though the right to privacy is not mentioned in either the Constitution or the Bill of Rights—and did not even enter the American legal system until the late 1800s—it has become a fiercely debated right on a number of levels, including reproductive rights, gay rights, and the right to die.

Explore this subject further with suggested readings, movies, and web sites at http://republic-brief.cqpress.com, where you'll also find study aids, practice quizzes, flash cards, and Internet exercises.

Chapter 5

The Struggle for Equal Rights

▶ What's at Stake?

The face of presidential politics underwent a sea change in 2008. The lineup on the Democratic primary debate stage said it all. In years past, almost without exception, debate participants, regardless of party, were white men. Sometimes, more recently, black men like Jesse Jackson or Alan Keyes found their way into the mix, but never for long; and everyone watching knew they didn't really have the political backing to be serious contenders for the presidency. Some women had taken a shot at the White House, one as early as 1872 (though women did not win the right to vote until 1920). But while Republican senator Elizabeth Dole made a serious effort in 2000, only Democrat Carol Moseley Braun (2004) made it to the debate stage, and she, an African American, was not seen as having a real chance at the nomination either. And Hispanics for president? Not usually, and never in a debate.

So the participants on the Democratic primary stage as the campaign got under way in 2007 were an arresting sight. The front-runner was New York senator Hillary Rodham Clinton, a woman with, for the first time, a real opportunity to take her candidacy all the way to the White House. Close behind her in the polls was Illinois senator Barack Obama, whose political backing, particularly among young voters, also gave him a serious chance to win the nomination and the presidency. New Mexico governor Bill Richardson was not running as well in the polls, but he too, with an impressive resume, seemed like a person who might pull it off, which made him the first serious Hispanic candidate for the presidency.

In the Democrats' apparent eagerness for change, the white men on the stage, John Edwards, Joe Biden, and Chris Dodd, seemed a little unexciting, a little too business-as-usual. Seeming to struggle with a sense that he couldn't compete with the exotic novelty of his opponents as the field narrowed, Edwards began to cite his status as "the white male candidate," almost as if he were the one running at a disadvantage once the field had narrowed to three.[1]

Media commentary focused on whether the country was ready for a female or a black president. A Democratic pollster, writing in February 2008, wasn't sure. He compared a 1958 poll, in which 53 percent of Americans said they would be unwilling to vote for an African American president and 41 percent said they would not vote for a woman, with recent data in which only 5 percent said they would not support an African American and 11 percent said they would not back a woman. He noted, however, that it was much less socially acceptable to voice one's prejudices today than it used to be, and wondered if the change the polls reflected was a sincere and lasting one.[2]

Certainly there were many complaints about sexism in the media's coverage of the campaign. Clinton supporters (and many Obama supporters as well) noted that Senator Clinton was frequently called "Hillary"; that her wardrobe and makeup were often the subject of discussion and critique; that her laugh was referred to by some as a "cackle," evoking a witch-like image; and that media commentators compared her to everything from a "she-devil" to "everyone's first wife standing outside a probate court."[3] Clinton's campaign drew attention to these slights, hoping to hold the media accountable, but little changed. When John McCain named Sarah Palin as his running mate at the start of the general election, accusations of sexism again flew fast and furious.

Critical observers claimed that there was racism in the campaign, too. A Republican congressman from Kentucky called the then-forty-six-year-old Obama a "boy."[4] His patriotism and his commitment to Christianity were frequently the subject of Internet rumor and were even questioned in debates, and his opponents occasionally got caught uttering phrases that seemed to feed into racial stereotypes. For example, then-senator Joe Biden praised him as "the first mainstream African-American who is articulate, bright and clean,"[5] former president Bill Clinton seemed to devalue Obama's win in the South Carolina primary by comparing it to Jesse Jackson's,[6] and Senator Clinton made a pitch for support by telling USA Today that a poll had found that "Senator Obama's support among working, hard working Americans, white Americans, is weakening again, and . . . whites in both states who had not completed college were supporting [her]."[7] The Obama campaign itself sent confusing signals. Cautious about alienating white voters, they played down incidents of racism even as they decried them, leading some observers to claim that they themselves were playing "a race card."[8] Midway through the primary season, media obsession with controversial remarks made by the pastor of his church led Obama to give an entire speech on race in an effort to put the issue behind him; the attempt was only partly successful.

As the prevalence of sexism and racism in the 2008 Democratic primary and the accompanying media coverage suggest, neither has been eradicated from American culture. Nonetheless, both Clinton and Palin claimed that their candidacies had made major inroads for future women candidates, and Obama's eventual victory over McCain certainly suggests that racism, too, is on the wane. How did that come about? How did the diversity of the electoral field help to change the way Americans saw both gender and race? What was at stake for American civil rights in the 2008 Democratic primary?

When you consider where we started, the progress toward racial equality in the United States can look pretty impressive. Just over fifty years ago, it was illegal for most blacks and whites to go to the same schools in the American South or to use the same public facilities, like swimming pools and drinking fountains. Today, for most of us, the segregated South is a distant memory. On August 28, 2008, forty years from the day that civil rights leader Martin Luther King Jr. declared that he had a dream that one day a child would be judged on the content of his character rather than the color of his skin, the nation watched as Barack Obama, born of a white mother from Kansas and an African father from Kenya, accepted the Democratic Party's nomination to the presidency. Obama went on to become the first African American president of the United States. Such moments, caught in the media spotlight, illuminate a stark contrast between now and then.

But in some ways, the changes highlighted at such moments are only superficial. Though black cabinet members are not uncommon—George W. Bush had two African American secretaries of state, Colin Powell and Condoleezza Rice, and Obama appointed the first black attorney general, Eric Holder—there have been remarkably few blacks in national elected office. *USA Today* pointed out in 2002 that "if the US Senate and the National Governors Association were private clubs, their membership rosters would be a scandal. They're virtually lily white,"[9] and not much has changed since then. Since Reconstruction, only three elected governors and three U.S. senators have been African Americans. Ironically, Obama's election to the presidency in 2008 removed the only black senator serving at the time, although the Illinois governor eventually appointed another African American to replace him.

Blacks fare poorly on other measures as well. On average, blacks are less educated and much poorer than whites, they experience higher crime rates, they live disproportionately in poverty-stricken areas, they score lower on standardized tests, and they rank near the bottom of most social measurements. Life expectancy is lower for African American men and women than for their white counterparts, and a greater percentage of African American children live in single-parent homes than do white or Hispanic children. The statistics illustrate what we suggested in Chapter 4—that rights equal power, and long-term deprivation of rights results in powerlessness. Unfortunately, the granting of formal **civil rights**, which we defined in Chapter 4 as the citizenship rights guaranteed by the Thirteenth,

Fourteenth, Fifteenth, Nineteenth, and Twenty-sixth Amendments, does not immediately bring about change in social and economic status.

African Americans are not the only group that shows the effects of having been deprived of its civil rights. Native Americans, Hispanics, and Asian Americans have all faced or face unequal treatment in the legal system, the job market, and in schools. Women, making up over half the population of the United States, have long struggled to gain economic parity with men. People in America are also denied rights, and consequently power, on the basis of their sexual orientation, their age, and their physical abilities. A country once praised by French observer Alexis de Tocqueville as a place of extraordinary equality, the United States today is haunted by traditions of unequal treatment and intolerance that it cannot entirely shake.

In this chapter we look at the struggles of these groups to gain equal rights and the power to enforce those rights. The struggles are different because the groups themselves, and the political avenues open to them, vary in important ways. To understand how groups can use different political strategies to change the rules and win power, in this chapter you will learn more about the meaning of political inequality, the struggle of African Americans to claim rights denied to them because of race, the struggle of Native Americans, Hispanics, and Asian Americans to claim rights denied to them because of race or ethnicity, women's battle for rights denied to them on the basis of gender, and the fight by other groups in society to claim rights denied to them on a variety of bases.

The Meaning of Political Inequality
When is different treatment okay?

Despite the deeply held American expectation that the law should treat all people equally, laws by nature must treat some people differently from others. Not only are laws designed in the first place to discriminate *between* those who abide by society's rules and those who don't,[10] but the laws can also legally treat criminals differently once they are convicted. For instance, in all but two states, Maine and Vermont, felons are denied the right to vote for some length of time and in two, Virginia and Kentucky, felons forfeit voting rights permanently.[11] But when particular groups are treated differently because of some characteristic like race, religion, gender, sexual orientation, age, or wealth, we say that the law discriminates *against* them, that they are denied equal protection of the laws. Throughout our history, legislatures, both state and national, have passed laws treating groups differently based on characteristics such as these. Sometimes those laws have seemed just and reasonable, but often they have not. Deciding which characteristics may fairly be the basis of unequal treatment is the job of all three branches of our government, but especially of our court system.

The Supreme Court has expended considerable energy and ink on this problem, and its answers have changed over time as various groups have waged the battle for equal rights, against a backdrop of ever-changing American values, public opinion, and politics. Before we look at the struggles those groups have endured in their pursuit of equal treatment by the law, we should understand the Court's current formula for determining what sorts of discrimination need what sorts of legal remedy.

When Can the Law Treat People Differently?

The Supreme Court has divided the laws that treat people differently into three tiers (see Table 5.1). The top tier refers to those ways of classifying people that are so rarely constitutional that they are immediately "suspect." **Suspect classifications** require that the government have a compelling state interest for treating people differently. Race is a suspect classification. To determine whether a law making a suspect classification is constitutional, the Court subjects the law to a heightened standard of review called **strict scrutiny**, which means that the Court looks very carefully at the law and the government interest involved.

The next tier refers to *quasisuspect classifications,* which the Court views as less potentially dangerous and which may or may not be legitimate grounds for treating people differently. These classifications are subject not to strict scrutiny, but to an **intermediate standard of review**. That is, the Court looks to see whether the law requiring different treatment of people bears a substantial relationship to an important state interest. An "important interest" test is not as hard to meet as a "compelling interest" test. Laws that treat women differently from men fall into this category.

Finally, the least scrutinized tier consists *of nonsuspect classifications;* these are subject to the **minimum rationality test**. The Court asks whether the government had a rational basis for making a law that treats a given class of people differently. A law that discriminates on the basis of age, such as a curfew for young people, or on the basis of economic level, such as a higher tax rate for a certain income bracket, need not stem from compelling or important government interests. The government must merely have had a rational basis for making the law, which is fairly easy for a legislature to show.

The significance of the three tiers of classification and the three review standards is that all groups who feel discriminated against want the Court to view them as a suspect class so that they will be treated as a protected group. Civil rights laws might cover them anyway, and the Fourteenth Amendment, which guarantees equal protection of the laws, may also formally protect them. However, once a group is designated as a suspect class, the Supreme Court is very unlikely to permit *any* laws to treat them differently. Thus gaining suspect status is crucial in the struggle for equal rights.

After over one hundred years of decisions that effectively allowed people to be treated differently because of their race, the Court finally agreed in the 1950s that race is a suspect class. Women's groups, however, have failed to convince the Court, or to amend the Constitution, to make gender a suspect classification. The intermediate standard of review was devised by the Court to express its view that it is a little more dangerous to classify people by gender than by age or wealth, but not

Table 5.1

When Can the Law Treat People Differently?

Legal Classification	When laws treat people differently because of . . .	The court applies . . .	The court asks . . .	Example: Test used to uphold a classification	Example: Test used to strike down a classification
Suspect	Race (or legislation that infringes on some fundamental rights)	Strict scrutiny standard of review	Is there a *compelling state interest* in this classification?	Government had a compelling state interest (national security) in relocating Japanese Americans from the West Coast during World War II. *Korematsu v. United States* (1944)	State government had no compelling reason to segregate schools to achieve state purpose of educating children. *Brown v. Board of Education* (1954)
Quasisuspect	Gender	Intermediate standard of review	Is there an *important state purpose* for this classification, and are the means used by the law substantially related to the ends?	Court upheld federal law requiring males but not females to register for military service (the draft). *Rostker v. Goldberg* (1981)	Court struck down an Alabama law requiring husbands but not wives to pay alimony after divorce. *Orr v. Orr* (1979)
Nonsuspect	Age, wealth, sexual orientation	Minimum rationality standard of review	Is there a *rational basis* for this classification?	Court found a Missouri law requiring public officials to retire at age 70 to have a rational basis. *Gregory v. Ashcroft* (1991)	Court struck down an amendment to the Colorado constitution that banned legislation to protect people's rights on the basis of their sexual orientation because it had no rational relation to a legitimate state goal. *Romer v. Evans* (1996)

as dangerous as classifying them by race or religion. Some groups in America—homosexuals, for instance—have not even managed to get the Court to consider them in the quasisuspect category. Although some states and localities have passed legislation to prevent discrimination on the basis of sexual orientation, gays can be treated differently by law as long as the state can demonstrate a rational basis for the law.

These standards of review make a real difference in American politics—they are part of the rules of politics that determine society's winners and losers. Americans who are treated unequally by the laws consequently have less power to use the democratic system to get what they need and want (like legislation to protect and further their interests), to secure the resources available through the system (like education and other government benefits), and to gain new resources (like jobs and material goods). People who cannot claim their political rights have little if any standing in a democratic society.

Different Kinds of Equality

The notion of equality is very controversial in America. The disputes arise in part because we often think that *equal* must mean "identical" or "the same." Thus equality can seem threatening to the American value system, which prizes people's freedom to be different, to be unique individuals. We can better understand the controversies over the attempts to create political equality in this country if we return briefly to a distinction we made in Chapter 1 between substantive and procedural equality.

In American political culture, we prefer to rely on government to guarantee fair treatment and equal opportunity (a *procedural* view), rather than to manipulate fair and equal outcomes (a *substantive* view). We want government to treat everyone the same, and we want people to be free to be different, but we do not want government to treat people differently in order to make them equal at the end. This distinction poses a problem for the civil rights movement in America, the effort to achieve equal treatment by the laws for all Americans. When the laws are changed, which is a procedural solution, substantive action may still be necessary to ensure equal treatment in the future.

Rights Denied on the Basis of Race
The battle to end the legacy of slavery and racism, fought mainly in the courts

We cannot separate the history of our race relations from the history of the United States. Americans have struggled for centuries to come to terms with the fact that citizens of African nations were kidnapped, packed into sailing vessels, exported to America, and sold, often at great profit, into a life that destroyed their families, their spirit, and their human dignity. The stories of white supremacy and black inferiority, told to numb the sensibilities of European Americans to the horror of their own behavior, have been almost as damaging as slavery itself and have lived on in the American psyche—and in political institutions—much longer than the practice they justified. **Racism**, institutionalized power inequalities in society based on the perception of racial differences, is not a "southern problem" or a "black problem"; it is an American problem, and one that we have not yet managed to eradicate from national culture.

Not only has racism had a decisive influence on American culture, it has also been central to American politics. From the start, those with power in America have been torn by the issue of race. The framers of the Constitution were so ambivalent that they would not use the word *slavery*, even while that document legalized its existence. Although some early politicians were morally opposed to the institution of slavery, they were, in the end, more reluctant to offend their southern colleagues by taking an antislavery stand. Even the Northwest Ordinance of 1787, which prohibited slavery in the northwestern territories, contained the concession to the South that fugitive slaves could legally be seized and returned to their owners. The accumulated tensions associated with slavery exploded in the American Civil War.

The Civil War and Its Aftermath: Winners and Losers

We can't begin to speculate here on all the causes of the Civil War. Suffice it to say that the war was not fought simply over the moral evil of slavery. Slavery was an economic and political issue as well as an ethical one. The southern economy depended on slavery, and when, in an effort to hold the Union together in 1863, President Abraham Lincoln issued the Emancipation Proclamation, he was not simply taking a moral stand; he was trying to use economic pressure to keep the country intact. The proclamation, in fact, did not free all slaves, only those in states rebelling against the Union.[12]

It is hard to find any real "winners" in the American Civil War. Indeed the war took such a toll on North and South that neither world war in the twentieth century would claim as many American casualties. The North "won" the war, in that the Union was restored, but the costs would be paid for decades afterward. Politically, the northern Republicans, the party of Lincoln, were in the ascendance, controlling both the House and the Senate, but their will was often thwarted by President Andrew Johnson, a Democrat from Tennessee who was sympathetic toward the South.

The Thirteenth Amendment, banning slavery, was passed and ratified in 1865. In retaliation, and to ensure that their political and social dominance of southern society would continue, the southern white state governments legislated **black codes**. Black codes were laws that essentially sought to keep blacks in a subservient economic and political position by restoring as many of the conditions of slavery as possible. As one scholar describes it, "Twenty years after freedom, a former slave was apt to be a black peasant, apathetically scratching a crop out of exhausted soil not his own, with scrawny mules and rusted plows and hoes that he had neither the incentive nor the means to improve."[13] In all likelihood, he was still working for, or at least on the land of, his former master. "Freedom" did not make a great deal of difference in the lives of most former slaves after the war.

Congress, led by northern Republicans, tried to check southern obstruction of its will by instituting a period of federal control of southern politics called **Reconstruction**, which began in 1865. In an attempt to make the black codes unconstitutional, the Fourteenth Amendment was passed, guaranteeing all people born or naturalized in the United States the rights of citizenship. Further, no state could deprive any person of life, liberty, or property without due process of the law, or deny any person equal protection of the law. As we saw in Chapter 4, the Supreme Court has made varied use of this amendment, but its original intent was to bring some semblance of civil rights to southern blacks. The Fifteenth Amendment followed in 1870, effectively extending the right to vote to all adult males.

At first, Reconstruction worked as the North had hoped. Under northern supervision, southern life began to change. Blacks voted, were elected to some local posts, and cemented Republican dominance with their support. But soon southern whites responded with violence. Groups like the Ku Klux Klan terrorized blacks in the South and made them reluctant to claim the rights to which they were legally entitled for fear of reprisals. Lynchings, arson, assaults, and beatings made claiming one's rights or associating with Republicans a risky business. Congress fought back vigorously and suppressed the reign of terror for a while, but its efforts earned accusations of military tyranny, and the Reconstruction project began to run out of steam. Plagued by political problems of their own, the Republicans were losing electoral strength and seats in Congress. Meanwhile, the Democrats were gradually reasserting their power in the southern states. Reconstruction was effectively over by 1876, and shortly after that southern whites set about the business of disenfranchising blacks, or taking away their newfound political power.

Without the protection of the northern Republicans, disenfranchisement turned out to be easy to accomplish. The strategy chosen by the Democrats, who now controlled the southern state governments, was a sly one. Under the Fifteenth Amendment the vote could not be denied on the basis of race, color, or previous condition of servitude, so they set out to deny it on legal bases that would have the primary effect of targeting blacks. **Poll taxes**, which required the payment of a small tax before voters could cast their votes, effectively took the right to vote away from the many blacks who were too poor to pay, and **literacy tests**, which required potential voters to demonstrate some reading skills, excluded most blacks who, denied an education, could not read. Even African Americans who were literate were often kept from voting because a white registrar administered the test unfairly. To permit illiterate whites to vote, literacy tests were combined with **grandfather clauses**, which required passage of such tests only by those prospective voters whose grandfathers had not been allowed to vote before 1867. Thus, unlike the black codes, these new laws, called **Jim Crow laws**, obeyed the letter of the Fifteenth Amendment, never explicitly saying that they were denying blacks the right to vote because of their race, color, or previous condition of servitude. This strategy proved devastatingly effective, and by 1910, registration of black voters had dropped dramatically, and registration of poor, illiterate whites had fallen as well.[14] Southern Democrats were back in power and had eliminated the possibility of competition.

Jim Crow laws were not just about voting but also concerned many other dimensions of southern life. The 1900s launched a half-century of **segregation** in the South, that is, of separate facilities for blacks and whites for leisure, business, travel, education, and other activities. The Civil Rights Act of 1875 had guaranteed that all people, regardless of race, color, or previous condition of servitude, were to have full and equal accommodation in "inns, public conveyances on land or water, theaters, and other places of public amusement," but the Supreme Court struck down the law, arguing that the Fourteenth Amendment restricted the behavior only of states, not of private individuals.[15] Having survived the legal test of the Constitution, Jim Crow laws continued to divide the southern world in two. But it was not a world of equal halves. The whites-only facilities were invariably superior to those intended for blacks; they were newer, cleaner, more comfortable. Before long, the laws were challenged by blacks who asked why equal protection of the law shouldn't translate into some real equality in their lives.

> Having survived the legal test of the Constitution, Jim Crow laws continued to divide the southern world in two.

One Jim Crow law, a Louisiana statute passed in 1890, required separate accommodations in all trains passing through the state. Homer Plessy, traveling through Louisiana, chose to sit in the white section. Although Plessy often passed as a white person, he was in fact one-eighth black, which made him a black man according to Louisiana law. When he refused to sit in the "Colored Only" section, Plessy was arrested. He appealed his conviction all the way to the Supreme Court, which ruled against him in 1896. In *Plessy v. Ferguson*, the Court held that enforced separation of the races did not mean that one race was inferior to the other. As long as the facilities provided were equal, states were within their rights to require them to be separate. Rejecting the majority view, Justice John Marshall Harlan wrote in a famous dissent, "Our Constitution is color-blind, and neither knows nor tolerates classes among citizens."[16] It would be over fifty years before a majority on the Court shared his view. In the meantime, everyone immediately embraced the "separate," and forgot the "equal," part of the ruling. Segregated facilities for whites and blacks had received the Supreme Court's seal of approval.

The Long Battle to Overturn *Plessy*: The NAACP and Its Legal Strategy

The years following the *Plessy* decision were bleak ones for African American civil rights. The formal rules of politics giving blacks their rights had been enacted at the national level, but no branch of government at any level was willing to enforce them. The Supreme Court had firmly rejected attempts to give the Fourteenth Amendment more teeth. Congress was not inclined to help since the Republican fervor for reform had worn off. Nor were the southern state governments likely to support black rights.

The **National Association for the Advancement of Colored People (NAACP)**, founded in 1910, aimed to help individual blacks, to raise white society's awareness of the atrocities of contemporary race relations, and most important, to change laws and court rulings that kept blacks from true equality. The NAACP, over time, was able to develop a legal strategy that was finally the undoing of Jim Crow and the segregated South.

Beginning with a challenge to segregation in law schools, a form of discrimination that Supreme Court justices would be most likely to see as dangerous, NAACP lawyers made the case that separate could not be equal in education. A series of victories over legal education set the stage for tackling the issue of education more broadly.

The NAACP had four cases pending that concerned the segregation of educational facilities in the South and the Midwest. In 1954 the Court ruled on all of them under the case name *Brown v. Board of Education of Topeka.* In their now-familiar arguments, NAACP lawyers emphasized the intangible aspects of education, including how it made black students feel to be made to go to a separate school. They cited sociological evidence of the low self-esteem of black schoolchildren, and they argued that it resulted from a system that made black children feel inferior by treating them differently.

Under the new leadership of Chief Justice Earl Warren, the Court ruled unanimously in favor of Linda Brown and the other black students. Without explicitly denouncing segregation or overturning *Plessy,* lest the South erupt in violent outrage again, the Warren Court held that separate schools, by their very definition, could never be equal because it was the fact of separation itself that made black children feel unequal. Segregation in education was inherently unconstitutional.[17] The principle of "separate but equal" was not yet dead, but it had suffered serious injury.

The *Brown* decision did not bring instant relief to the southern school system. The Court, in a 1955 follow-up to *Brown,* ruled that school desegregation had to take place "with all deliberate speed."[18] Such an ambiguous direction was asking for school districts to drag their feet. The most public and blatant attempt to avoid compliance took place in Little Rock, Arkansas, in September 1957, when Governor Orval Faubus posted the National Guard at the local high school to prevent the attendance of nine African American children. Rioting white parents, filmed for the nightly news, showed the rest of the country the faces of southern bigotry. Finally, President Dwight Eisenhower sent one thousand federal troops to guarantee the safe passage of the nine black children through the angry mob of white parents who threatened to lynch them rather than let them enter the school. The *Brown* case and the attempts to enforce it proved to be catalysts for a civil rights movement that would change the whole country.

The Civil Rights Movement

In the same year that the Court ordered school desegregation to proceed "with all deliberate speed," a woman named Rosa Parks sat down on a bus in Montgomery, Alabama, and started a chain of events that would end with a Court order to stop segregation in all aspects of southern life. As law required, Parks sat in the black section at the back of the bus. As the bus filled, all the white seats were taken, and the driver ordered Parks and the other blacks in her row to stand. Tired from a fatiguing day as a seamstress, Parks refused. She was arrested and sent to jail.

Overnight, local groups in the black community organized a boycott of the Montgomery bus system. A **boycott** seeks to put economic pressure on a business to do something by encouraging people to stop purchasing its goods or services. Montgomery blacks, who formed the base of the bus company's clientele, wanted the bus company to lose so much money that it would force the local government to change the bus laws. Against all expectations, the bus boycott continued for over a year. In the meantime the case wound its way through the legal system, and a little over a year after

Defying the Jaws of Injustice

A seventeen-year-old demonstrator in Birmingham, Alabama, is attacked by a police dog after defying a city anti-parade ordinance on May 3, 1963. This photograph ran on the cover of the New York Times the next day and drew the attention of President John Kennedy. As images and stories of other similar events spread, more people increasingly demanded that the violence end and that blacks be given equal rights and opportunities.

the boycott began, the Supreme Court affirmed a lower court's judgment that Montgomery's law was unconstitutional.[19] Separate bus accommodations were not equal.

Two Kinds of Discrimination

The civil rights movement launched by the Montgomery bus boycott confronted two different types of discrimination. **De jure discrimination** (discrimination by law) is created by laws that treat people differently based on some characteristic like race. This is the sort of discrimination most blacks in the South faced. Especially in rural areas, blacks and whites lived and worked side by side, but by law they used separate facilities. Although the process of changing the laws was excruciatingly painful, once the laws were changed and the new laws were enforced, the result was integration.

The second sort of discrimination, called **de facto discrimination** (discrimination in fact), however, produces a kind of segregation that is much more difficult to eliminate. Segregation in the North was of this type because blacks and whites did not live and work in the same places to begin with. It was not laws that kept them apart, but past discrimination, tradition, custom, economic status, and residential patterns. This kind of segregation is so hard to remedy because there are no laws to change; the segregation is woven more complexly into the fabric of society.

We can look at the civil rights movement in America as having two stages. The initial stage involved the battle to change the laws so that blacks and whites would be equally protected by the laws, as the Fourteenth Amendment guarantees. The second stage, and one that is ongoing today, is the fight against the aftereffects of those laws, and of centuries of discrimination, that leave many blacks and whites still living in communities that are worlds apart.

Changing the Rules: Fighting De Jure Discrimination

Rosa Parks and the Montgomery bus boycott launched a new strategy in blacks' fight for equal rights. Although it took the power of a court judgment to move the city officials, blacks themselves had exercised considerable power through peaceful protest and massive resistance to the will of whites. One of the leaders of the boycott was a young Baptist minister named Martin Luther King Jr. A founding member of the Southern Christian Leadership Conference, a group of black clergy committed to expanding civil rights, King became known for his nonviolent approach to political protest. This philosophy of peacefully resisting enforcement of laws perceived to be unjust, and marching or "sitting in" to express political views, captured the imagination of supporters of black civil rights in both the South and the North. Black college students, occasionally joined by whites, staged peaceful demonstrations, called sit-ins, to desegregate lunch counters in southern department stores and other facilities. The protest movement was important for the practices it challenged directly—such as segregation in motels and restaurants, on beaches, and in other recreational facilities—but also for the pressure it brought to bear on elected officials and the effect it had on public opinion, particularly in the North, which had been largely unaware of southern problems.

The nonviolent resistance movement, in conjunction with the growing political power of northern blacks, brought about remarkable social and political change in the 1960s. The administration of Democratic president John F. Kennedy, not wanting to alienate the support of southern Democrats, tried at first to limit its active involvement in civil rights work. But the political pressure of black interest groups forced Kennedy to take a more visible stand. The Reverend King was using his tactics of nonviolent protest to great advantage in the spring of 1963. Kennedy responded to the political pressure, so deftly orchestrated by King, by sending to Birmingham federal mediators to negotiate an end to segregation, and then by sending to Congress a massive package of civil rights legislation.

Kennedy did not live to see his proposals become law, but they became the top priority of his successor, Lyndon Johnson. During the Johnson years, the president, majorities in Congress, and the Supreme Court were in agreement on civil rights issues, and their joint legacy is impressive. The Kennedy-initiated Civil Rights Bill of 1964 reinforced the voting laws, allowed the attorney general to file school desegregation lawsuits, permitted the president to deny federal money to state and local programs that practiced discrimination, prohibited discrimination in public accommodations and in employment, and set up the Equal Employment Opportunity Commission (EEOC) to investigate complaints about job discrimination. Johnson also sent to Congress the Voting Rights Act of 1965, which, when passed, disallowed discriminatory tests like literacy tests and provided for federal examiners to register voters throughout much of the South. The Supreme Court, still the liberal Warren Court that had ruled in *Brown,* backed up this new legislation.[20] In addition, the Twenty-fourth Amendment, outlawing poll taxes in federal elections, was ratified in 1964.

Because of the unusual cooperation among the three branches of government, by the end of the 1960s, life in the South—though far from perfect—was radically different for blacks. In 1968, 18 percent of southern black students went to schools with a majority of white students; in 1970 the percentage rose to 39 and in 1972 to 46. The comparable figure for black students in the North was only 28 percent in 1972.[21] Voter registration had also improved dramatically: from 1964 to 1969, black voter registration in the South nearly doubled, from 36 to 65 percent of adult blacks.[22]

Changing the Outcomes: Fighting De Facto Discrimination

Political and educational advances did not translate into substantial economic gains for blacks. As a group, they remained at the very bottom of the economic hierarchy, and ironically the problem was most severe not in the rural South but in the industrialized North. Many southern blacks who had migrated to the North in search of jobs and a better quality of life found conditions not much different from those they had left behind. Abject poverty, discrimination in employment, and segregated schools and housing led to frustration and inflamed tempers. In the summers of 1966 and 1967, race riots flashed across the northern urban landscape. Impatient with the passive resistance of the nonviolent protest movement in the South, many blacks became more militant in their insistence on social and economic change. The Black Muslims, led by Malcolm X until his assassination in 1965; the Black Panthers; and the Student Nonviolent Coordinating Committee all demanded "black power" and radical change. These activists rejected the King philosophy of working peacefully through existing political institutions to bring about gradual change.

Northern whites who had applauded the desegregation of the South grew increasingly nervous as angry African Americans began to target segregation in the North. The de facto segregation there meant that black inner-city schools and white suburban schools were often as segregated as if the hand of Jim Crow had been at work. In the 1970s the courts and some politicians, believing that they had a duty not only to end segregation laws in education but also to integrate the schools, instituted a policy of **busing** in some northern cities. Students from majority-white schools would be bused to mostly black schools, and vice versa. The policy was immediately controversial; riots in South Boston in 1974 resembled those in Little Rock seventeen years earlier.

Not all opponents of busing were reacting from racist motives. Busing students from their homes to a distant school strikes many Americans as fundamentally unjust. Parents seek to move to better neighborhoods so that they can send their children to better schools, only to see those children bused back to the old schools, and they fear for the safety of their children when they are bused into poverty-stricken areas with high crime rates. Parents of both races want their children to be part of a local community and its activities, which is hard when the children must leave the community for the better part of each day.

The Supreme Court has shared America's ambivalence about busing. Although it endorsed busing as a remedy for segregated schools in 1971,[23] three years later it ruled that busing plans could not merge inner-city and suburban districts unless officials could prove that the district lines had been drawn in a racially discriminatory manner.[24] Since many whites were moving out of the cities, there were fewer white students to bus, and busing did not really succeed in integrating schools in many urban areas. Fifty years after the *Brown* decision, many schools, especially those in urban areas, remain largely segregated.[25]

The example of busing highlights a problem faced by civil rights workers and policymakers: deciding whether the Fourteenth Amendment guarantee of equal protection simply requires that the states not sanction discrimination or imposes an active obligation on them to integrate blacks and whites. As the northern experience shows, the absence of legal discrimination does not mean equality. In 1965 President Johnson issued an executive order that not only prohibited discrimination in firms doing business with the government but also ordered them to take **affirmative action** to compensate for past discrimination. In other words, if a firm had no black employees, it wasn't enough not to have a policy against hiring them; the firm now had to actively recruit and hire blacks. The test would not be federal law or company policy, but the actual racial mix of employees.

Johnson's call for affirmative action was taken seriously not only in employment situations but also in university decisions. Patterns of discrimination in employment and higher education showed the results of decades of decisions by white males to hire or admit other white males. Blacks, as well as other minorities and women, were relegated to low-paying, low-status jobs. After Johnson's executive order, the EEOC decided that the percentage of blacks working in firms should reflect the percentage of blacks in the labor force. Many colleges and universities reserved space on their admissions lists for minorities, sometimes accepting minority applicants with grades and test scores lower than those of whites.

We have talked about the tension in American politics between procedural and substantive equality, between equality of treatment and equality of results. That is precisely the tension that arises when Americans are faced with policies of busing and affirmative action, both of which are instances of American policy attempting to bring about substantive equality. The end results seem attractive, but the means to get there—treating people differently—seem inherently unfair in the American value system. The Supreme Court reflected the public's unease with affirmative action policies but did not reject the idea, holding in 1978 that schools can have a legitimate interest in having a diversified student body and that they can take race into account in admissions decisions, just as they can consider geographic location, for instance.[26]

Few of the presidents after Kennedy and Johnson took strong pro–civil rights positions, but none effected a real reversal in policy until Ronald Reagan. Reagan's strong conservatism led him to regret the power that had been taken from the states by the Supreme Court's broad interpretation of the Fourteenth Amendment, and he particularly disliked race-based remedies for discrimination, like busing and affirmative action. The Reagan administration lobbied the Court strenuously to get it to change its rulings on the constitutionality of those policies, but it wasn't until the end of Reagan's second term, when the effect of his conservative appointments to the Court kicked in, that a true change in policy occurred.

In 1989 the Court fulfilled civil rights advocates' most pessimistic expectations. In a series of rulings, it held that the Fourteenth Amendment did not protect workers from racial harassment on the job,[27] that the burden of proof in claims of employment discrimination was on the worker,[28] and that affirmative action was on shaky constitutional ground.[29] The Democratic-led Congress sought to undo some of the Court's late-1980s rulings by passing the Civil Rights Bill of 1991, which made it easier for workers to seek redress against employers who discriminate.

Blacks in Contemporary American Politics

The Supreme Court's use of strict scrutiny on laws that discriminate on the basis of race has put an end to most de jure discrimination, but much de facto discrimination remains. Affirmative action, one of the few remedies for de facto discrimination, continues to be a controversial policy in America. In 1996, voters in California declared affirmative action illegal in their state, and voters in Washington did the same in 1998. Michigan voted in 2006 to ban affirmative action in the state's public colleges and government contracting, and in 2008, affirmative action was struck down by voters in Nebraska. Despite the controversy, however, there remains considerable support for affirmative action in the United States. Efforts to end affirmative action have failed in state legislatures in New Jersey, Michigan, Arizona, Colorado, and almost a dozen other states. Still, as the 2006 success of the so-called Michigan Civil Rights Initiative and the 2008 defeat of affirmative action in Nebraska show, campaigns in the public can succeed where the legislature may balk. The American public remains divided: opinion polls show support for the ideals behind affirmative action but not if it is perceived to be giving minorities preferential treatment.[30]

The federal courts, while still supportive of the spirit of affirmative action, have taken the notion that race is a suspect classification to mean that any laws treating people differently according to race must be given strict scrutiny, even if their intent is to benefit rather than harm the group they single out. So, for instance, in 2003 the Supreme Court threw out the University of Michigan's undergraduate admissions policy because it was tantamount to racial quotas,[31] but in another case that year the Court held, five to four, that the law school's holistic approach of taking into account the race of the applicant was constitutional because of the importance of creating a diverse student body.[32]

One of the consequences of the continued de facto discrimination in the United States is a gap between the income and wealth of whites and blacks (see Figure 5.1). We began this chapter noting that blacks fall behind whites on most socioeconomic indicators, although we should not disregard the existence of a growing black middle class. The median household income for African Americans in 2008 was $34,218; for whites it was $53,312.[33]

Because people of lower income and education levels are less likely to vote, African Americans' economic disadvantage translates into a political limitation as well. And although voting discrimination is clearly illegal, some racial patterns in disenfranchisement still need further examination. The most notorious case in point is the 2000 presidential election vote in Florida. Numerous studies show that many people's votes ultimately went uncounted in Florida, with African American, Hispanic, and elderly voters especially hard hit.[34]

African Americans have had difficulty overcoming barriers not just on the voting side of the democratic equation. Although the numbers are more encouraging at the local level, where blacks tend to elect other blacks to office, as the constituencies grow larger and more diverse, the task of black candidates gets tougher. In the 112th Congress, elected in 2010, 44 of 435 members of the House of Representatives were black, and there were no black senators, none having been elected since Barack Obama, who became only the sixth African American senator in U.S. history. In 2008 there were 642 black mayors.[35] There is currently one African American governor, Deval Patrick of Massachusetts, who won re-election in 2010. And though there have been several important black cabinet members, those are appointed, not elected, positions.

Indeed, public opinion polls had indicated that more than 140 years after the end of the Civil War, Americans were ready to elect a black president,[36] and in 2008, of course, they did just that. Barack Obama is the nation's first African American

Figure 5.1

Mean Earnings in 2007, by Highest Degree Earned, by Race and Hispanic Origin

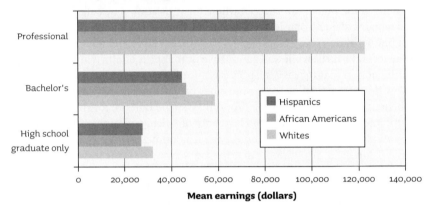

Mean earnings (dollars)

Source: U.S. Census Bureau, *Statistical Abstract of the United States*, 2010, Table 227.

president, elected in a campaign that was remarkably free of racial overtones, although Obama did give one speech during the primary campaign that dealt explicitly with race. Obama's administration promised to usher in a much more relaxed attitude toward race (he jokingly referred to himself, in his first press conference after his election, as a "mutt"). Although that approach to a subject that has been difficult for Americans to talk about may help to create more ease in the long run, in the short term a disconcerting amount of criticism of the new administration, especially from such rightwing entertainers-commentators as Rush Limbaugh, and conservative provocateurs such as Andrew Breitbart, comes with a racial tinge.

But it's still an open question whether this dramatic movement at the top of the ticket will have an effect on the overall numbers of African Americans in American politics. In 2008, black turnout at the polls rose to 16.1 million voters, 2 million more than turned out in 2004.[37] That change, if lasting, might send more black candidates to political office. And in the wake of Obama's election, African Americans appeared to be more optimistic about black progress; a majority (53 percent) said life will be better for blacks in the future (compared to 44 percent who said so in 2007), and 54 percent of blacks said Obama's election has improved race relations.[38] But in general, African American candidates continue to face a reality that is daunting. They attribute their difficulties achieving statewide and national office to four factors: the scarcity of blacks in lesser state offices, from which statewide candidates are often recruited; the fact that many good black politicians are mayors, who traditionally have trouble translating urban political success to statewide success; the fact that black politicians have fewer deep pockets from which to raise funds, since they often represent lower-income areas; and "old fashioned prejudice"—their belief that nonblacks are less likely to vote for them and that party officials are less likely to encourage them to run for higher office because of that.[39]

Rights Denied on the Basis of Race and Ethnicity
Different paths to equality for Native Americans, Hispanics, and Asian Americans

African Americans are by no means the only Americans whose civil rights have been denied on racial or ethnic grounds. Native Americans, Hispanics, and Asian Americans have all faced their own particular kind of discrimination. For historical and cultural reasons, these groups have had different political resources available to them, and thus their struggles have taken shape in different ways.

Native Americans

Native Americans of various tribes shared the so-called New World for centuries before it was discovered by Europeans. The relationship between the original inhabitants of this continent and the European colonists and their governments was difficult, marked by the new arrivals' clear intent to settle and develop the Native Americans' ancestral lands, and complicated by the Europeans' failure to understand the Indians' cultural, spiritual, and political heritage. The lingering effects of these centuries-old conflicts continue to color the political, social, and economic experience of Native Americans today.

The precise status of Native American tribes in American politics and in constitutional law is complicated. The Indians always saw themselves as sovereign independent nations, making treaties, waging war, and otherwise dealing with the early Americans from a position of strength and equality. But that sovereignty has not consistently been recognized by the U.S. government, and many of the treaties that the government made with Indian tribes were broken as the tribes were forced off their native lands. The commerce clause of the Constitution (Article I, Section 8) gives Congress the power to regulate trade "with foreign nations, among the several states, and with the Indian tribes," but it also has been interpreted as giving Congress guardianship over Indian affairs. The creation of the Bureau of Indian Affairs in 1824 as part of the Department of War (moved to the Department of the Interior in 1849) institutionalized that guardian role.

Modern congressional policy toward the Native Americans has varied from trying to assimilate them into the broader, European-based culture to encouraging them to develop economic independence and self-government. The combination of these two strategies—stripping them of their native lands and cultural identity, and reducing their federal funding to encourage more independence—has resulted in tremendous social and economic dislocation in the Indian communities. Poverty, joblessness, and alcoholism have built communities of despair and frustration for many Native Americans. Their situation has been aggravated as Congress has denied them many of the rights promised in their treaties in order to exploit the natural resources so abundant in the western lands they have been forced onto, or as they have been forced to sell rights to those resources in order to survive.

The political environment in which Native Americans found themselves in the mid-twentieth century was very different from the one faced by African Americans. Essentially, Native American tribes find themselves in a relationship with the national government that mimics elements of federalism—what some scholars have called "fry-bread federalism."[40] Although that relationship has evolved over time, the gist of it is that American Indians are citizens of tribes as well as citizens of the United States, with rights coming from each. It was not clear what strategy the Native Americans should follow in trying to get their U.S. rights recognized. Denied them was not simply formal rights, or their enforcement, but the fulfillment of old promises and the preservation of a culture that did not easily coexist with modern American economic and political beliefs and practices. State politics did not provide any remedies, not merely because of local prejudice, but because Indian reservations are separate legal entities under the federal government. Because Congress itself was largely responsible for denying the rights of Native Americans, it was not a likely source of support for their expansion. Nor were the courts anxious to extend rights to Native Americans.

Like many other groups shut out from access to political institutions, Native Americans took their political fate into their own hands. Focusing on working outside the system to change public opinion and to persuade Congress to alter public policy, the Indians formed interest groups like the National Congress of American Indians (NCAI), founded in 1944, and the American Indian Movement (AIM), founded in 1968, to fight for their cause. But for all the militant activism of the sixties and seventies, Native Americans have made no giant strides in redressing the centuries of dominance by white people. They remain at the bottom of the income scale in America, earning less than African Americans on average, and their living conditions are often poor. In 2008, 24.2 percent of American Indians lived in poverty, compared to only 13.2 percent of the total U.S. population.[41] And in 2009 the high school graduation rate of Native Americans was only 51 percent, compared to 70 percent of the overall population.[42]

Since the 1980s, however, an ironic twist of legal interpretation has enabled some Native Americans to parlay their status as semisovereign nations into a foundation for economic prosperity. Close to thirty states now allow gambling on Indian reservations, many of whose casinos rival Las Vegas in gaudy splendor, and the money is pouring into their coffers. Close to thirty states now allow Indian gambling casinos, and in 2008 they brought in more than $26 billion, more than Native Americans received in federal aid.[43] In 2006 Native American gaming revenue represented 42 percent of all casino gambling revenue nationwide,[44] although many tribes and individuals have no share in it. Casino gambling is controversial on several counts among Native Americans themselves, some of whom see it as their economic salvation and others as spiritually ruinous, and among other Americans, many of whom object for economic reasons. Regardless of the moral and economic questions unleashed by the casino boom, Native Americans argue that it is a way to recoup at least some of the resources that have been taken from them in the past.

Politically, there has been some improvement as well. While recent Supreme Court cases failed to support religious freedom for Native Americans, some lower court orders have supported their rights. In 1996 President Bill Clinton issued an executive order that requires federal agencies to protect and provide access to sacred religious sites of American Indians, which has been a major point of contention in Indian-federal relations. Until the Supreme Court ruled in 1996 that electoral districts could not be drawn to enhance the power of particular racial groups, Native Americans had been gaining strength at the polls, to better defend their local interests. Still, the number of American Indian state representatives has increased slightly in the past few years, although only one American Indian, Tom Cole of Oklahoma, is currently serving in the House of Representatives. There are no American Indians in the Senate now that Senator Ben Nighthorse Campbell of Colorado retired after his term expired in 2005.

Hispanic Americans

Hispanic Americans, also called Latinos, are a diverse group with yet another story of discrimination in the United States. Among the reasons the Hispanic experience is different from that of other groups we discuss are the diversity within the Hispanic population; the language barrier that many face; and the political reaction to immigration, particularly illegal immigration, from Mexico into the United States.

Hispanics are the largest minority group in the United States today, making up over 15 percent of the population. Their numbers have more than tripled in the past twenty-plus years, from 14.6 million in 1980 to 46.8 million in 2008.[45] Since 1990 the Hispanic population has grown by 103 percent, compared with an increase of 13.3 percent among non-Hispanics. This population growth is strikingly diverse; Hispanics' roots may be in Mexico, Puerto Rico, Cuba, Central and South America, as well as other Spanish-speaking parts of the world. These groups have settled in different parts of the country as well. Mexican Americans are located largely in California, Texas, Arizona, and New Mexico. Puerto Ricans live primarily in New York, New Jersey, and other northern cities. Cubans tend to be clustered in South Florida.

These groups differ in more than place of origin and settlement. Cubans are much more likely to have been political refugees, escaping the communist government of Fidel Castro, whereas those from other countries tend to be economic refugees looking for a better life. Because educated, professional Cubans are the ones who fled, they have largely regained their higher socioeconomic status in this country. For instance, almost 25.1 percent of Cuban Americans are college educated, a percentage matching that found in the U.S. population as a whole, but only 8.6 percent of Mexican Americans and 15.6 percent of Puerto Ricans are college graduates.[46] Consequently, Cuban Americans also hold more professional and managerial jobs, and their standard of living, on average, is much higher. While their numbers suggest that if they acted together they would wield considerable clout, their diversity has led to fragmentation and powerlessness.

Language has also presented a special challenge to Hispanics. The United States today ranks sixth in the world in the number of people who consider Spanish a first language, with an active and important Spanish-language media of radio, television, and press. This preponderance of Spanish speakers is probably due less to a refusal on the part of Hispanics to learn English than to the fact that new immigrants are continually streaming into this country.[47] Nonetheless, especially in areas with large Hispanic populations, white Anglos feel threatened by what they see as the encroachment of Spanish, and many communities have launched **English-only movements** to make English the official language, precluding foreign languages from appearing on ballots and official documents.

A final concern that makes the Hispanic struggle for civil rights unique in America is the reaction against immigration, particularly illegal immigration from Mexico. A backlash against illegal immigration has some serious consequences for Hispanic American citizens, who may be indistinguishable in appearance, name, and language from recent immigrants. All of this makes acceptance into American society more difficult for Hispanics; encourages segregation; and makes the subtle denial of equal rights in employment, housing, and education, for instance, easier to carry out.

Though Hispanics face formidable barriers to assimilation, their political position is improving. Like African Americans, they have had some success in organizing and calling public attention to their circumstances. Cesar Chavez, as leader of the United Farm Workers in the 1960s, drew national attention to the conditions under which farm workers labored. Following the principles of the civil rights movement, he highlighted concerns of social justice in his call for a nationwide boycott of grapes and lettuce picked by nonunion labor, and in the process he became a symbol of the Hispanic struggle for equal rights. Groups like the Mexican American Legal Defense and Education Fund (MALDEF) and the League of United Latin American Citizens (LULAC) continue to lobby to end discrimination against Hispanic Americans.

There were twenty-seven Hispanic representatives in the 111th Congress and three Hispanic senators. There is one Hispanic governor (Bill Richardson of New Mexico). In 2004 President Bush appointed Alberto Gonzales to be the first Hispanic attorney general, and in 2008 President Obama appointed Sonia Sotomayor to be the first Hispanic justice on the U.S. Supreme Court. Many Hispanics have been appointed to high-level state offices as well. The voter turnout rate for Hispanics has traditionally been low because they are disproportionately poor and poor people are less likely to vote, but this situation is changing. Where the socioeconomic status of Hispanics is high and where their numbers are concentrated, as in South Florida, their political clout is considerable, as the intense controversy over the custody of young Cuban refugee Elian Gonzalez in 1999–2000 made clear.

Presidential candidates, mindful of Florida's twenty-seven electoral votes, regularly make pilgrimages to South Florida to denounce Cuba's communist policies, a position popular among the Cuban American voters there. Grassroots political organization has also paid off for Hispanic communities. In Texas, for instance, local groups called Communities Organized for Public Service (COPS) have brought politicians to Hispanic neighborhoods so that poor citizens can meet their representatives and voice their concerns. Citizens who feel that they are being listened to are more likely to vote, and COPS was able to organize voter registration drives that boosted Hispanic participation. Similarly, the Southwest Voter Registration Project has led over one thousand voter registration drives in several states, including California, Texas, and New Mexico. Such movements have increased registration of Hispanic voters by more than 50 percent. In 2000, Hispanics made up 14 percent of California's 11 million registered voters. Nationally, in 2008, Hispanics made up 7 percent of all registered voters. Fifty percent of all Latinos voted that year, compared to only 45 percent in 2000.[48]

Because of the increase in the number of potential Hispanic voters, and because of the prominence of the Hispanic population in battleground states such as Florida, New Mexico, Colorado, and Nevada, and even in places such as Iowa, where one might not expect a significant Hispanic population, both Barack Obama and John McCain actively courted Hispanic voters in the 2008 presidential election. Each candidate ran several advertisements entirely in Spanish, and Obama considered choosing New Mexico governor Bill Richardson as his running mate.

Asian Americans

Asian Americans share some of the experiences of Hispanics, facing cultural prejudice as well as racism and absorbing some of the public backlash against immigration. Yet the history of Asian American immigration, the explosive events of World War II, and the impressive educational and economic success of many Asian Americans mean that the Asian experience is also in many ways unique.

Like Hispanics, the Asian American population is diverse. There are Americans with roots in China, Japan, Korea, the Philippines, India, Vietnam, Laos, and Cambodia, to name just a few. Today Asian Americans live in every region of the United States. In 2008 Asian Americans comprised 55.3 percent of the population in Hawaii and 12.1 percent of that in California.[49] New York City has the largest Chinese community outside China. The more recent immigrants are spread throughout the country, with the Asian population in the South especially fast growing.[50]

Asians have faced discrimination in the United States since their arrival. The fact that they are identifiable by their appearance has made assimilation into the larger European American population difficult. While most immigrants dream of becoming citizens in their new country, and eventually gaining political influence through the right to vote, that option was not open to Asians. The Naturalization Act of 1790 provided for only white immigrants to become naturalized citizens, and

► Consider the Source

Don't Be Fooled by the World Wide Web

P. T. Barnum said there's a sucker born every minute—and that was decades *before* the advent of the Internet. He would have rubbed his hands in glee over the gullibility of people in the electronic age. While freedom of speech is a powerful liberty, as we saw in Chapter 4, one consequence is that it makes it very difficult to silence those making fraudulent or misleading claims. We regulate radio and television, of course, but that is because these media were originally (before the days of cable and satellites) held to be scarce resources that belonged to the public. Private publishers can enforce standards of excellence, or accuracy, or style, on what they publish, but when a medium is quasipublic, like the Internet, and access to it is easy and cheap, it is impossible to restrict the views and ideas that are published without also doing some serious damage to freedom of speech. Consequently, anything goes, and it is up to us as consumers to sort the grain from the chaff. Here are some tips to help you become a savvy surfer of the World Wide Web:

- **Find out the source of the web site.** Examine the web address, or URL, for clues. Web addresses end with .com, .org, .gov, .net, or .edu to indicate, respectively, commercial, nonprofit, government, network, or educational sites. Sites from other countries end with abbreviations of the nation. For example, .kr indicates the site is from Korea and .fr indicates France. If a tilde (~) appears in the address, it is likely to be a personal home page rather than an official site.[1] Remember, however, that anyone can purchase rights to a web address; an official-looking address does not necessarily confer legitimacy on a site.
- **Check out the author of the site.** Sometimes the author is not who he or she seems to be—many authors try to disguise the source of their sites to gain respectability for their ideas or to lure users further in, or they may seem to support groups or individuals who turn out to be their targets.
- **If something about a site does not look right (what one author calls the "J.D.L.R.," or the Just Doesn't Look Right, test), investigate more closely.**[2] Be suspicious if, for example, you notice lots of misspellings or grammatical errors, or if the site has an odd design. Analyze the site's tone and approach. A very shrill or combative tone could signal a lack of objectivity. When a familiar site doesn't look the way you expect it to, consider the possibility that hackers have broken into it and changed its content.

- **Find out who is footing the bill.** Whoever said there is no such thing as a free lunch might have been speaking of the Internet. Ultimately our access to the glorious world of cyberspace must be paid for, and since we as consumers seem to be singularly unwilling to pay for the information we find, providers of that information are increasingly looking to advertisers to pick up the bill.[3] Commercial interests can shape the content of what we find on the web in any number of ways: links to sponsors' pages may appear prominently on a web page, web sites may promote the products of their advertisers as if they were objectively recommending them without making the financial relationship clear, or the commercial bias may be even more subtle.

- **Use the Internet to evaluate the Internet.** You can find out who runs a site by going to www.internic.net and using the "whois" search function. This will give you names and contact information but is not, warns Tina Kelly of the *New York Times*, conclusive. Similarly, she suggests running authors' names through a search engine or groups-beta.google.com, which searches newsgroups, to see what you can find out about them. Some browsers will tell you when a site was last updated. On Netscape, for instance, you can get this information by clicking on the View option and going to Page Info or Document Info. And remember that you can always e-mail authors of a site and ask for their credentials.[4] If no contact information for the author is available on the site itself, that alone can tell you something about its reliability. For more information on how to evaluate various types of web sites, check out the Widener University Wolfgram Memorial Library's "Evaluate Web Pages" at www.widener.edu/?pageId=480 and click on "Evaluate Web Pages."

- **Note the other kinds of information the site directs you to.** If you are in doubt about a site's legitimacy, check some of its links to external sites. Are they up to date and well maintained? Do they help you identify ideological, commercial, or other bias the site may contain? If there are no links to other sites, ask yourself what this might mean.

---

1. Tina Kelly, "Whales in the Minnesota River? Only on the Web, Where Skepticism Is a Required Navigational Aid," *New York Times*, March 4, 1999, D9.

2. Kelly, D1.

3. Saul Hansell and Amy Harmon, "Caveat Emptor on the Web: Ad and Editorial Lines Blur," *New York Times*, February 26, 1999, A1.

4. Kelly, D9.

with few exceptions—for Filipino soldiers in the U.S. Army during World War II, for example—the act was in force until 1952. Exclusionary immigration reflected this country's long-standing hostility toward Asians, but anti-Asian sentiment was especially evident in the white American reaction to Japanese Americans during World War II. In 1942 the U.S. government rounded up Japanese Americans, forced them to abandon or sell their property, and put them in detention camps for purposes of "national security." The government was worried about security threats posed by people with Japanese sympathies, but two-thirds of the 120,000 people incarcerated were American citizens. Perhaps the greatest insult was the Supreme Court's approval of curfews and detention camps for Japanese Americans.[51] Although the government later reversed its policy and, in 1988, paid $1.25 billion in reparations to survivors of the ordeal, Japanese American internment is an ugly scar on America's civil rights record.

One unusual feature of the Asian American experience is their overall academic success and corresponding economic prosperity. High school and college graduation rates are higher among Asian Americans than among other ethnic groups and are at least as high as, and in some places higher than, those of whites. In 2009, 13 percent of the students at Harvard were Asian, as were 22.5 percent at Stanford, 26 percent at MIT, and 45 percent at the University of California, Berkeley.[52] Although all Asian groups have not been equally successful (groups that have immigrated primarily as refugees—like the Vietnamese—have higher rates of poverty than do others), median household income in 2008 was $65,637 for Asian and Pacific Islanders, compared with $52,312 for whites, $37,913 for Hispanics, and $34,218 for blacks.[53] A number of factors probably account for this success. Forced out of wage labor in the West in the 1880s by resentful white workers, Asian immigrants developed entrepreneurial skills and many came to own their own businesses and restaurants. A cultural emphasis on hard work and high achievement lent itself particularly well to success in the American education system and culture of equality of opportunity. Furthermore, many Asian immigrants were highly skilled and professional workers in their own countries and passed on the values of their achievements to their children.

According to all our conventional understanding of what makes people vote in the United States, participation among Asian Americans ought to be quite high. Voter turnout usually rises along with education and income levels, yet Asian American voter registration and turnout rates have been among the lowest in the nation. Particularly in states with a sizable number of Asian Americans such as California, their political representation and influence do not reflect their numbers. Political observers account for this lack of participation in several ways. Until after World War II, as we saw, immigration laws restricted the citizenship rights of Asian Americans. In addition, the political systems that many Asian immigrants left behind did not have traditions of democratic political participation. Finally, many Asian Americans came to the United States for economic reasons and have focused their attentions on building economic security rather than learning to navigate an unfamiliar political system.[54]

Some evidence indicates, however, that this trend of nonparticipation is changing. Researchers have found that where Asian Americans do register, they tend to vote at rates higher than those of other groups.[55] In the 1996 election, concerted efforts were made to register and turn out Asian Americans by a national coalition of Asian American interest groups seeking to maximize their impact at the polls. The results included the election of Gary Locke as the first Asian American governor of a mainland state (Washington). Today Locke is President Obama's secretary of commerce. In 2010 there was one Asian American governor (Bobby Jindal of Louisiana), eight Asian American members of the House of Representatives, and three Asian American senators. One reason for the increasing participation of Asian Americans, in addition to the voter registration drives, is that many Asian Americans are finding themselves more and more affected by public policies. Welfare reform that strips many elderly legal immigrants of their benefits, changes in immigration laws, and affirmative action are among the issues driving Asian Americans to the polls. However, even continued efforts to register this group are unlikely to bring about electoral results as dramatic as those that we are starting to see for Hispanics, because Asian Americans tend to split their votes more or less equally between Democrats and Republicans.[56] Interestingly, a recent survey of Asian Americans found that an astonishing 50 percent of Asians claim no partisan affiliation.[57]

Rights Denied on the Basis of Gender
Fighting the early battles for equality at the state level

Of all the battles fought for equal rights in the American political system, the women's struggle has been perhaps the most peculiar, for women, while certainly denied most imaginable civil and economic rights, were not outside the system in the same way that racial and ethnic groups have been. Most women lived with their husbands or fathers, and many shared their view that men, not women, should have power in the political world. Women's realm, after all, was the home, and the prevailing belief was that women were too good, too pure, too chaste, to deal with the sordid world outside. As a New Jersey senator argued in the late 1800s, women should not be allowed to vote because they have "a higher and holier mission. . . . Their mission is at home."[58] Today there are still some women as well as men who agree with the gist of this sentiment. That means that the struggle for women's rights not only has failed to win the support of all women but also has been actively opposed by some, as well as by many men whose power, standing, and worldview it has threatened.

The legal and economic position of women in the early nineteenth century, though not exactly "slavery," in some ways was not much different. According to English common law, on which our system was based, when a woman married, she merged her legal identity with her husband's, which is to say in practical terms, she no longer had one. Once married, she could not be a party to a contract, bring a lawsuit, own or inherit property, earn wages for any service, gain custody of her children in case of divorce, or initiate divorce from an abusive husband. If her husband were not a U.S. citizen, she lost her own citizenship. Neither married nor unmarried women could vote. In exchange for the legal identity his wife gave up, a husband was expected to provide security for her, and if he died without a will, she was entitled to one-third of his estate. If he made a will and left her out of it, however, she had no legal recourse to protect herself and her children.[59]

The Struggle for Suffrage

Although individual women may have rebelled at this state of affairs, the women's movement itself is commonly dated from an 1848 convention on women's rights held in Seneca Falls, New York. At the convention, propositions that were enthusiastically and unanimously approved included calls for the right to own property, to have access to higher education, and to receive custody of children after divorce. The only resolution not to receive unanimous support, even among the supporters of women's rights at the convention, was one calling for women's right to vote.

The women's movement picked up steam after Seneca Falls, but it had yet to settle on a political strategy. The courts were closed to women, since they had no independent legal identity. For a long time, women's rights advocates worked closely with the antislavery movement, assuming that when blacks received their rights, they and the Republican Party would rally to the women's cause. Not only did that fail to happen, but the passage of the Fourteenth Amendment marked the first time the word *male* appeared in the Constitution, causing a bitter split between the two movements.

Regularly, from 1878 to 1896 and again after 1913, a federal women's suffrage amendment called the Susan B. Anthony Amendment, named after an early advocate of women's rights, was introduced into Congress but failed to pass. Other women's rights advocates focused efforts at the state level, taking on the more practical task of changing state electoral laws. It was this state strategy that would finally create the conditions under which the Nineteenth Amendment would be passed and ratified in 1920.

Going to the Dance

With the Nineteenth Amendment headed toward final ratification in 1919, women began to sense the first signs of real political power.

The state strategy was a smart one for women. Unlike the situation blacks faced after the war, the national government was not behind their cause. It was possible for women to have an impact on state governments, however, even those where discrimination was a problem. Different states have different cultures and traditions, and the Constitution allows them to decide who may legally vote. Women were able to target states that were sympathetic to them, and then gradually gain enough political clout that their demands were listened to on the national level.

Women were able to vote beginning in 1869 in the Territory of Wyoming, and when Wyoming was admitted to the Union in 1890, it was the first state to give women the vote. Wyoming's experience did not prove contagious, however. From 1870 to 1910, women waged 480 suffrage campaigns in thirty-three states, caused seventeen referenda to be held in eleven states, and won in only two of them—Colorado (1893) and Idaho (1896). In 1910 women began to refine their state strategy and were soon able to win two more referenda, in Washington (1910) and California (1911). By 1912, with the addition of Arizona, Kansas, Oregon, and Illinois, women could vote in states that controlled 74 of the 483 Electoral College votes that decided the presidency.

In 1914 an impatient, militant offshoot of the women's movement began to work at the national level again, picketing the White House and targeting the presidential party, contributing to the defeat of twenty-three of forty-three Democratic candidates in the western states where women could vote. The appearance of political power lent momentum to the state efforts. In 1917 North Dakota gave women presidential suffrage. Ohio, Indiana, Rhode Island, Nebraska, and Michigan soon followed suit. Arkansas and New York joined the list later that year. A major women's rights group issued a statement to Congress that if it would not pass the Susan B. Anthony Amendment, its members would work to defeat every legislator who opposed it. The amendment passed in the House but not the Senate, and the group targeted four senators. Two were defeated, and two held on to their seats by a narrow margin. Nine more states gave women the right to vote in presidential elections.

In 1919 the Susan B. Anthony Amendment was reintroduced into Congress with the support of President Woodrow Wilson and passed by the necessary two-thirds majority in both houses. When, in August 1920, Tennessee became the thirty-sixth state to ratify the Nineteenth Amendment, women finally had the vote nationwide. Unlike the situation faced by African Americans after the passage of the Fifteenth Amendment, the legal victory ended the women's suffrage battle. Although many women were not inclined to use their newly won right, enforcement of women's suffrage was not as difficult as enforcement of black suffrage. But right to the end, opposition to women's suffrage had been petty and virulent, and the victory was only narrowly won.

The debate over women's suffrage, like the fight over black civil rights, was bitter because so much was at stake. If women were to acquire political rights, opponents feared, an entire way of life would end. In many ways, of course, they were right. The opposition to women's suffrage came from a number of different directions. In the South, white men rejected it for fear that women would encourage enforcement of the Civil War amendments, giving political power to blacks. And if women could vote, then of course black women could vote, further weakening the white male position. In the West, and especially the Midwest, brewing interests fought suffrage, believing that women would force temperance on the nation. Liquor interests fought the women's campaign vigorously, stuffing ballot boxes and pouring huge sums of money into antisuffrage efforts. In the East, women's opponents were industrial and business interests, who were concerned that voting women would pass enlightened labor legislation and would organize for higher wages and better working conditions. Antisuffrage women's groups, usually representing upper-class women, claimed that women's duties at home were more than enough for them to handle and that suffrage was unnecessary because men represented and watched out for women's interests.[60] For well-to-do women, the status quo was comfortable, and changing expectations about women's roles could only threaten that security.

Everything these opponents feared eventually came to pass, though not necessarily as a result of women voting. Although women's rights advocates were clear winners in the suffrage fight, it took a long time for all the benefits of victory to materialize. As the battle over the Equal Rights Amendment would show, attitudes toward women were changing at a glacial pace.

The Equal Rights Amendment

The Nineteenth Amendment gave women the right to vote, but it did not ensure the constitutional protection against discrimination that the Fourteenth Amendment had provided for African Americans. It was unconstitutional to treat people differently on account of race but not on account of gender. Following ratification of the Nineteenth Amendment in 1920, some women's groups turned their attention to the passage of an **Equal Rights Amendment (ERA)**, which would ban discrimination on the basis of gender and guarantee women equal protection under the law. Objections to the proposed amendment again came from many different directions. Traditionalists, both men and women, opposed changing the status quo and giving more power to the federal government. But even some supporters of women's rights feared that requiring laws to treat men and women the same would actually make women worse off by nullifying legislation that sought to protect women. Many social reformers, for instance, had worked for laws that limited working hours or established minimum wages for women, and these laws would now be in jeopardy. Opponents also feared that the ERA would strike down laws preventing women from being drafted and sent into combat. Many laws in American society treated men and women differently, and few would survive under the ERA.

In the early 1970s, several pieces of legislation signaling that public opinion was favorable to the idea of expanding women's rights were passed. Among these was Title IX of the Education Amendments, which in 1972 banned gender discrimination in schools receiving federal funds. This meant, among other things, that schools had to provide girls with an equal opportunity and equal support to play sports. The ERA was, however, less successful.

The House of Representatives finally passed the ERA in 1970, but the Senate spent the next two years refining the language of the amendment. Finally, on March 22, 1972, the Senate passed the amendment, and the process of getting the approval of three-quarters of the state legislatures began. By early 1973, thirty states had ratified the amendment, but over the next four years, only five more states voted for ratification, bringing the total to thirty-five states, three short of the necessary thirty-eight. Despite the extension of the ratification deadline from 1979 to 1982, the amendment died unratified.

The ERA failed to pass for several reasons. First, although most people supported the idea of women's rights in the abstract, they weren't sure what the consequences of such an amendment would be, and they feared the possibility of radical social change. Second, the ERA came to be identified in the public's mind with the 1973 Supreme Court ruling in *Roe v. Wade*, ensuring women's abortion rights in the first trimester of a pregnancy, a ruling that, as we saw in Chapter 4, remains controversial today.[61] Finally, the Supreme Court had been striking down some (though not all) laws that treated women differently from men, using the equal protection clause of the Fourteenth Amendment. According to some opponents, this made the ERA unnecessary.[62]

Gender Discrimination Today

Despite the failure of the ERA, most of the legal barriers to women's equality in this country have been eliminated. But because the ERA did not pass and there is no constitutional amendment specifically guaranteeing equal protection of the law regardless of gender, the Supreme Court has not been willing to treat gender as a suspect classification, although it has come close at times. Laws that treat men and women differently are subject only to the intermediate standard of review, not the strict scrutiny test.

Having achieved formal equality, women still face some striking discrimination in the workplace. They earn only seventy-seven cents for every dollar earned by men (see Figure 5.2), and the National Committee on Pay Equity, a nonprofit group in Washington, D.C., calculates that the pay gap may cost some women almost half a million dollars over their work lives.[63] Women's ability to seek remedies for this discrimination has been limited by law. In 2007 the U.S. Supreme Court ruled in a five-to-four decision that a female worker's right to sue for discrimination was constrained by the statutes of limitations in existing civil rights law.[64] On January 29, 2009, the first bill signed into law by President Obama was the Lilly Ledbetter Act, extending the time frame so that workers could still sue even if the wage discrimination against them revealed itself over time. A companion piece to this legislation, the Paycheck Fairness Act, would prohibit discrimination and retaliation against workers who bring discrimination claims. It passed in the House but remained stalled in the Senate as of 2010.

Figure 5.2

Changes in Median Income, by Sex

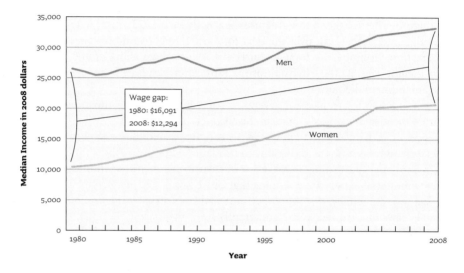

Source: U.S. Census Bureau, *Historical Income Tables*, Table P-8, retrieved from www.census.gov/hhes/www/income/histinc/incpertoc.html.

In addition to earning lower wages, women are tremendously underrepresented at the upper levels of corporate management and academic administration, as well as in other positions of power. Some people argue that the reason women earn less than men and wield less power is that many women leave and enter the job market several times or put their careers on hold to have children. Such interruptions prevent them from accruing the kind of seniority that pays dividends for men. The so-called mommy track has been blamed for much of the disparity between men's and women's positions in the world. Others argue that there is an enduring difference in the hiring and salary patterns of women that has nothing to do with childbearing or that reflects male inflexibility when it comes to integrating motherhood and corporate responsibility. These critics claim that there is a "glass ceiling" in the corporate world, invisible to the eye but impenetrable, which prevents women from realizing their full potential. The Civil Rights Act of 1991 created the Glass Ceiling Commission to study this phenomenon, and among the commission's conclusions was the observation that business is depriving itself of a large pool of talent by denying leadership positions to women.

Some analysts have argued that the glass ceiling is a phenomenon that affects relatively few women. Most women today are less preoccupied with moving up the corporate ladder than with making a decent living, or getting off what one observer has called the "sticky floor" of low-paying jobs.[65] Although the wage gap between men and women with advanced education is narrowing, women still tend to be excluded from the more lucrative blue-collar positions in manufacturing, construction, communication, and transportation.[66]

Women in Contemporary Politics

Women still face discrimination not only in the boardroom but in politics as well. While more women today hold elected office than at any other time in history, women still remain the most underrepresented group in Congress and the state legislatures. In the 111th Congress, only 73 of 435 members of the House of Representatives were female. There are currently seventeen female senators and six female governors. As of 2009, 33 cities with populations of more than 100,000 had female mayors.[67] In an April 2008 poll, only 63 percent of those surveyed agreed that the United States was ready for a woman president.[68]

However, the representation of women in government is clearly better than it was. Hillary Clinton came very close to winning the Democratic nomination for president in 2008, and polls at the time indicated that she could have beaten Republican John McCain. McCain himself chose a woman for his running mate. Nancy Pelosi became the first female Speaker of the House in 2006, and three of the last four U.S. secretaries of state have been women. In fact, in 2010, the second and fourth officials in the line of succession to the president of the United States were women (the Speaker of the House follows the vice president, and the secretary of state comes after the president pro tem of the Senate). In 1971 women comprised only 2 percent of Congress members and less than 5 percent of state legislators. Today 18 percent of Congress members and 24.5 percent of state legislators are female, both all-time highs. Women held 22.9 percent of all statewide executive offices in 2010, including six governorships and nine lieutenant governorships.[69] Although this percentage is below the high of 27.6 in 2001, it is a substantial increase from the 11 percent in 1979.[70] In 2008, women entered four of the thirty-three gubernatorial races on a major-party ticket (two won, giving the United States a total of eight women governors).[71]

Rights Denied on Other Bases
Challenging other classifications in the courts

Race, gender, and ethnicity, of course, are not the only grounds on which the laws treat people differently in the United States. Three other classifications that provide interesting insights into the politics of rights in America are sexual orientation, age, and disability.

Sexual Orientation

Gays and lesbians have faced two kinds of legal discrimination in this country. On the one hand, overt discrimination simply prohibits some behaviors: gays cannot serve openly in the military, for instance, and in some states they cannot adopt children or teach in public schools. But a more subtle kind of discrimination doesn't forbid their actions or behavior; it simply fails to recognize them legally. Thus in most states gays cannot marry or claim the rights that married people share, such as collecting their partner's Social Security, being covered by a partner's insurance plan, being each other's next of kin, or having a family. Some of these rights can be mimicked with complicated and expensive legal arrangements; some are possible because of the good will of particular companies toward their employees; but others, under the current laws, are out of reach. Being gay, unlike being black or female or Asian, is something that can be hidden from public view; and until the 1970s many gays escaped overt discrimination by denying or concealing who they were, but that too, many people argue, is a serious deprivation of civil rights.[72]

The legal status of gays in America was spelled out in the case of *Bowers v. Hardwick,* discussed in Chapter 4.[73] Here the Supreme Court argued that there was no constitutionally protected right to engage in homosexual behavior, nor any reason why the states could not regulate or outlaw it. The Court did not require that a law that treated people differently on the basis of sexual orientation fulfill either a compelling or an important state purpose; it merely had to be a reasonable use of state power. The *Bowers* judgment remained more or less intact until 1996, when a bitterly split Court struck down an amendment to the Colorado constitution that would have prevented gays from suing for discrimination in housing and employment. The Court ruled that gays could not be singled out and denied the fundamental protection of the law—that "a state cannot deem a class of persons a stranger to its laws." Although the majority on the Court did not rule that sexual orientation was a suspect classification, it did hint at greater protection than the minimum rationality test would warrant.[74] For the first time, it treated gay rights as a civil rights issue.

The two biggest victories for gays and lesbians in a court of law came in 2003. First, in *Lawrence v. Texas,* the Supreme Court overturned the *Bowers* decision, ruling that state sodomy laws were a violation of the right to privacy.[75] The gay and lesbian movement received another unexpected legal victory in 2003, when the Massachusetts Supreme Judicial Court ruled, in an extremely controversial four-to-three decision, that marriage was a civil right and that the state's law banning homosexual marriage violated the equal protection and due process clauses in the Massachusetts constitution.[76] The Massachusetts court ruling sent shockwaves throughout the country as the nation's first legal gay marriages were performed in Massachusetts. Critics charged that the courts had overstepped their bounds, and legislatures in eleven states took steps to ban gay marriage. Almost immediately after the ruling, President George W. Bush announced his support for an amendment to the Constitution defining marriage as a union between a man and a woman. However, because Congress had already passed a Defense of Marriage Act (DOMA) in 1996 stating that states need not recognize gay marriages performed in other states, the amendment failed to garner much immediate congressional support. Should the Supreme Court strike down DOMA in the future, that may change. Also, in reaction to the Massachusetts Supreme Court ruling, eleven states overwhelmingly passed propositions in 2004 that banned same-sex marriage and a total of twenty-six states currently ban gay marriage by constitutional amendment and forty-three by statute.

Despite the popular backlash in some places, efforts to amend the Massachusetts constitution to ban same-sex marriage were defeated by the state legislature in 2007, and in 2008 the California Supreme Court struck down that state's ban on gay marriage, arguing that the state constitution protected a fundamental right to marry. Unlike the Massachusetts decision, which allowed only residents of that state to marry there, California's decision also allowed nonresidents to marry. In the immediate aftermath of the California decision, New York governor David Paterson instructed all of his state's agencies to recognize same-sex marriages performed elsewhere, clearing the way for New Yorkers marrying in Massachusetts, California, or Canada to have their marriages considered legitimate in New York. While challenges to Governor Paterson's action are in the works, and California voters amended their constitution to ban gay marriage in 2008, there has clearly been some movement toward an expansion of marriage rights at the state level. Gay marriage is currently legal in Connecticut, Iowa, Massachusetts, New Hampshire, Vermont, and Washington, D.C., and is recognized in New York, Rhode Island, and Maryland.

The courts are not the only political avenue open to gays in their struggle for equal rights. Gays have also been effective in parlaying their relatively small numbers into a force to be reckoned with electorally. Gays began to organize politically in 1969, after riots following police harassment at a gay bar in New York City, the Stonewall Inn. Today many interest groups are organized around issues of concern to the gay community. The largest, the Human Rights Campaign, made a total contribution to campaigns of nearly $4.5 million in 2008, with $1.3 million going to federal candidates.[77] While in the past gays have primarily supported the Democratic Party, a growing number identify themselves as independents, and a group of conservative gays calling themselves the Log Cabin Republicans have become active on the political right. Openly gay members of Congress have been elected from both sides of the partisan divide.

One area in which gay voters have had some impact is the issue of gays in the military. In 1992, acting on a campaign promise made to gays, President Clinton decided to end the ban on gays in the military with an executive order, much as President Harry Truman had ordered the racial integration of the armed forces in 1948. Clinton, however, badly miscalculated the public reaction to his move. The Christian Right and other conservative and military groups were outraged. In the ensuing storm, Clinton backed off his support for ending the ban and settled instead for a "don't ask, don't tell" (DADT) policy. Members of the armed forces need not disclose their sexual orientation, but if they reveal it, or the military otherwise finds out, they can still be disciplined or discharged. In 2008 Barack Obama campaigned on the repeal of DADT, and in 2010 his administration signaled its intention to examine and repeal the policy banning gays in the military, while loosening its enforcement in the meantime.[78] Fearing the loss of a Democratic majority in the November 2010 midterm elections, Democrats in the House and Senate decided not to wait until the Pentagon's examination of the transition had taken place and crafted a compromise bill with the White House that would end DADT once certain benchmarks had been met. The bill passed in the House and in the Senate Armed Services Committee in May 2010, needing to be passed in the Senate to become law.[79]

The issue of gay rights has come to the forefront of the American political agenda not only because of gays' increasing political power but also because of the fierce opposition of the Christian Right. Their determination to banish what they see as an unnatural and sinful lifestyle—and their conviction that protection of the basic rights of homosexuals means that they will be given "special privileges"—has focused tremendous public attention on issues that most of the public would rather have had remain private. The spread of AIDS and the political efforts of gay groups to fight for increased resources to battle the disease have also heightened public awareness of gay issues. Public opinion remains mixed on the subject, but tolerance is increasing. In 2010, 8 in 10 Americans favored lifting the ban on gays in the military and 46 percent favored permitting gays to adopt (up from 38 percent in 1999).[80] Still, in 2009, 54 percent opposed gay marriage. Interestingly, young people consistently support issues of gay and lesbian rights in far greater numbers than their elders, an indication that change may be on the horizon. For example, whereas 64 percent of those aged 65 years or older opposed gay marriage, only 45 percent of those aged 18–29 years did so.[81]

Age

In 1976 the Supreme Court ruled that age is not a suspect classification.[82] That means that if governments have rational reasons for doing so, they may pass laws that treat younger or older people differently from the rest of the population, and courts do not have to use strict scrutiny when reviewing those laws. Young people are often not granted the full array of rights of adult citizens, being subject to curfews or locker searches at school, nor are they subject to the laws of adult justice if they commit a crime. Some observers have argued that children should have expanded rights to protect them in dealings with their parents.

Older people face discrimination most often in the area of employment. Compulsory retirement at a certain age regardless of an individual's capabilities or health may be said to violate basic civil rights. The Court has generally upheld mandatory retirement requirements.[83] Congress, however, has sought to prevent age discrimination with the Age Discrimination Act of 1967, outlawing discrimination against people up to seventy years of age in employment or in the provision of benefits, unless age can be shown to be relevant to the job in question. In 1978 the act was amended to prohibit mandatory retirement before age seventy, and in 1986 all mandatory retirement policies were banned except in special occupations.

Unlike younger people, who can't vote until they are eighteen and don't vote in great numbers after that, older people defend their interests very effectively. Voter participation rates rise with age, and older Americans are also extremely well organized politically. AARP (formerly the American Association of Retired Persons), a powerful interest group with over 30 million members, has been active in pressuring government to preserve policies that benefit elderly people. In the debates in the mid-1990s about cutting government services, AARP was very much present, and in the face of the organization's advice and voting power, programs like Social Security and Medicare (providing health care for older Americans) remained virtually untouched.

Disability

People with physical and mental disabilities have also organized politically to fight for their civil rights. Advocates for the disabled include people with disabilities themselves, people who work in the social services catering to the disabled, and veterans' groups. Even though laws do not prevent disabled people from voting, staying in hotels, or using public phones, circumstances often do. Inaccessible buildings, public transportation, and other facilities can pose barriers as insurmountable as the law, as can public attitudes toward and discomfort around disabled people.

The 1990 Americans with Disabilities Act (ADA), modeled on the civil rights legislation that empowers racial and gender groups, protects the rights of the more than 44 million mentally and physically disabled people in this country. Disabilities covered under the act need not be as dramatic or obvious as confinement to a wheelchair or blindness. People with AIDS, recovering drug and alcohol addicts, and heart disease and diabetes patients are among those covered. The act provides detailed guidelines for access to buildings, mass transit, public facilities, and communication systems. It also guarantees protection from bias in employment; the EEOC is authorized to handle cases of job discrimination because of disabilities, as well as race and gender. The act was controversial because many of the required changes in physical accommodations, such as ramps and elevators, are extremely expensive to install. Advocates for the disabled respond that these expenses will be offset by increased business from disabled people and by the added productivity and skills that the disabled bring to the workplace. The reach of the act was limited in 2001, when the Supreme Court ruled that state employees could not sue their states for damages under the ADA because of the seldom discussed, but extremely important, Eleventh Amendment, which limits lawsuits that can be filed against the states.[84] The Court's five-to-four decision was criticized by disability rights advocates as severely limiting the ADA.

Citizenship and Civil Rights Today
The power of group action

It should be clear that the stories of America's civil rights struggles are the stories of citizen action. Of the three models of democratic participation that we discussed in Chapter 1—elite, pluralist, and participatory—the pluralist model best describes the actions citizens have taken to gain protection of their civil rights from government. Pluralism emphasizes the ways that citizens can increase their individual power by organizing into groups. The civil rights movements in the United States have been group movements. Groups succeeded in gaining rights where individual action and pleas for government action were unavailing. To the extent that groups in America have been unable to organize effectively to advance their interests, their civil rights progress has been correspondingly slowed.

▶ What's at Stake Revisited

In this chapter we have learned that the long and difficult battle for civil rights in this country is not yet over. Nonetheless, we began with the observation that the very fact that one of the major parties' slate of candidates included a woman, an African American, and a Hispanic, and that the other party fielded a female vice-presidential candidate, was itself a step forward for equality. How could the fact that these individuals ran make a difference, even though only one of them reached the White House? What was at stake in these high-profile candidacies?

America has always been proud to be a nation of equal opportunity, where "any child can grow up to be president." Through more than fifty presidential elections, however, "any child" has turned out to mean any white male child. Girls or kids from other races may have had aspirations, but when they looked at the long lineup of candidates through the years, white male faces were all that they saw. History offered them few or no role models for their hopes for running for president.

In 2008 that changed. As the long primary season drew to an end in the spring of 2008, the candidates and political commentators reflected on what those candidacies had meant.

In closing her concession speech, for instance, Clinton stopped to consider the impact her campaign had had on race and gender in America:

> Think how much progress we have already made. When we first started, people everywhere asked the same questions:
>
> Could a woman really serve as commander-in-chief? Well, I think we answered that one.
>
> And could an African American really be our president? Senator Obama has answered that one.

Together Senator Obama and I achieved milestones essential to our progress as a nation, part of our perpetual duty to form a more perfect union.

Now, on a personal note—when I was asked what it means to be a woman running for president, I always gave the same answer: that I was proud to be running as a woman but I was running because I thought I'd be the best president. But I am a woman, and like millions of women, I know there are still barriers and biases out there, often unconscious.

I want to build an America that respects and embraces the potential of every last one of us.

I ran as a daughter who benefited from opportunities my mother never dreamed of. I ran as a mother who worries about my daughter's future and a mother who wants to lead all children to brighter tomorrows. To build that future I see, we must make sure that women and men alike understand the struggles of their grandmothers and mothers, and that women enjoy equal opportunities, equal pay, and equal respect. Let us resolve and work toward achieving some very simple propositions: There are no acceptable limits and there are no acceptable prejudices in the twenty-first century.

You can be so proud that, from now on, it will be unremarkable for a woman to win primary state victories, unremarkable to have a woman in a close race to be our nominee, unremarkable to think that a woman can be the president of the United States. And that is truly remarkable.[85]

Although Obama himself did not refer explicitly to race when he claimed the nomination, fellow African Americans did. Writing in the *Washington Post*, Pulitzer Prize–winning columnist Eugene Robinson, like Hillary Clinton, took "a moment to contemplate the mind-bending improbability of what just happened." He wrote:

A young, black first-term senator—a man whose father was from Kenya, whose mother was from Kansas and whose name sounds as if it might have come from the roster of Guantánamo detainees—has won a marathon of primaries and caucuses to become the presidential nominee of the Democratic Party. To reach this point, he had to do more than outduel the party's most powerful and resourceful political machine. He also had to defy, and ultimately defeat, 389 years of history. . . . Whether he wins or loses, history has been made. Maybe there's more to come, maybe not; but already—after 389 long years—it's safe to say that this nation will never be the same.[86]

The Obama, Clinton, and Richardson candidacies are not important just for what they measure about racism and sexism in America today, but for the impact they will have on generations just coming of age. A diarist on the liberal blog *Daily Kos* pointed out that "my kids will grow up in a world that has always had (in their memories, at least) an African-American as the standard bearer for a major political party,"[87] and the novel experience of seeing people just like themselves at the heights of American politics will be had not only by black kids, but by Hispanic children and girls as well—something that has never before been true in American politics. And that, in Senator Clinton's words, is truly remarkable.

▶ Summary With Key Terms

Throughout U.S. history, various groups, because of some characteristic beyond their control, have been denied their **civil rights** (147) and have fought for equal treatment under the law. All laws treat people differently on some basis, and the Supreme Court has come up with a formula to determine when that discrimination is constitutional. When a law treats people differently according to race or religion, the Court rules that it is making a **suspect classification** (149), which is subject to **strict scrutiny** (149) to see if the state has a compelling purpose to pass the law. If not, the law is struck down. Laws that discriminate according to gender are subject to an easier standard called an **intermediate standard of review** (149); those that discriminate according to age, wealth, or sexual orientation are subject to the easiest standard for the state to meet, the **minimum rationality test** (149).

African Americans have experienced two kinds of **segregation** (154): that created by **de jure discrimination** (157), laws that treat people differently; and that created by **de facto discrimination** (157), which occurs when societal tradition and habit lead to social segregation. De jure discrimination, now illegal, included the passage of **black codes** (152) prior to the Civil War and then, after **Reconstruction** (153), **poll taxes** (153), **literacy tests** (153), **grandfather clauses** (153), and other **Jim Crow laws** (153) designed to return the south to the pre–Civil War days. By forming interest groups such as the **National Association for the Advancement of Colored People (NAACP)** (155) and developing strategies of nonviolent resistance such as sit-ins and **boycotts** (156), African Americans eventually defeated de jure discrimination. De facto discrimination persists in America, signified by the education and wage gap between African Americans and whites. Programs like **busing** (159) and **affirmative action** (159), which could remedy such discrimination, remain controversial. Although African Americans have made great strides in the past fifty years, **racism** (152) is a persistent problem, and much inequality remains.

Native Americans, Hispanics, and Asian Americans have also fought to gain economic and social equality. Congressional control over their lands has led Native Americans to assert economic power through the development of casinos. Using boycotts and voter education drives, Hispanics have worked to stem the success of **English-only movements** (166) and anti-immigration efforts. Despite their smaller numbers, Asian Americans also aim for equal political clout, but it is through a cultural emphasis on scholarly achievement that they have gained considerable economic power.

Women's rights movements represented challenges to power, to a traditional way of life, and to economic profit. Early activists found success through state politics because they were restricted from using the courts and Congress, and they were finally able to earn women the right to vote in 1920. After repeated efforts to pass the **Equal Rights Amendment (ERA)** (174) failed, current efforts focus on the courts to give women greater protection under the law.

Gays, youth, the elderly, and the disabled enjoy the most fundamental civil rights, but they still face de jure and de facto discrimination. While moral concerns motivate laws against gays, social order and cost-efficiency concerns mark the restrictions against youth, the elderly, and disabled Americans.

Explore this subject further with suggested readings, movies, and web sites at http://republic-brief.cqpress.com, where you'll also find study aids, practice quizzes, flash cards, and Internet exercises.

Chapter 6

Congress

▶ What's at Stake?

In the summer of 2009, with the passage of health care reform in sight, the Democratic Party was on the brink of an historic achievement and Republicans wanted to stop it. Senator Jim DeMint, a Republican from South Carolina, said, "If we are able to stop Obama on this it will be his Waterloo. It will break him."[1]

But the Democrats were equally determined to get the bill through, especially Senator Ted Kennedy, who had been working for years to pass his signature issue of health care reform. With a Democratic president in the White House and Democratic majorities in the House and Senate, reform was nearly a done deal when Kennedy died on August 25, 2009, succumbing to the brain tumor he had been diagnosed with a little more than a year earlier. Massachusetts governor Deval Patrick appointed a Democrat to hold the seat until a special election could be held the following January and the Senate passed a health care bill on December 24, 2009, by a vote of 60 to 39. All that remained was for the House of Representatives to pass its version of the bill, and then for the two versions to be resolved into a single bill, a final step that would require another vote in each chamber.

In an irony that was not lost on any observers of American politics, Kennedy's death precipitated an event that appeared to give DeMint and his fellow Republicans just the opening they wanted to kill the bill. When the special election took place in January 2010, it was Republican Scott Brown who won the seat that Kennedy had held for almost forty-seven years. The Democrats still had a healthy majority in the Senate—there were still fifty-nine

of them after Brown was elected, to only forty-one Republicans—but thanks to a rule called the filibuster, in the Senate fewer than sixty seats might as well be a minority for all the good it does the majority political party.

A filibuster lets a group of senators prevent a vote from taking place on the Senate floor by allowing them to hold an extended debate—essentially "talking a bill to death." And it is death, unless three-fifths of the chamber (that's sixty senators) votes for cloture, which ends the debate and allows the vote to proceed. The end result is that if a minority of the Senate is passionate or ornery enough it can thwart the will of the majority, and of the voters who chose them. With Brown's election depriving the Democrats of their sixtieth vote, Republicans were celebrating Obama's Waterloo.

Democrats, however, were reluctant to see this chance slip away. Unable to muster sixty votes in the Senate in the face of united Republican opposition, the Democratic leadership scrambled and came up with a Plan B. Instead of passing its own bill and then sending it along with the Senate bill to a committee whose job it would be to hammer out a compromise, a step that would require a further vote in the now-unfriendly Senate, the House of Representatives simply passed the Senate's bill on March 21, 2010. The move frustrated many House Democrats who wanted the chamber to pass a more liberal bill, but it enabled President Obama to sign the bill into law, preserving his signature legislation and giving him a major political victory. The House then made the changes it wanted by passing a second bill. Unable to break a filibuster on the second bill, Senate majority leader Harry Reid sent the changes through as part of the budget reconciliation process (all the changes had to be budget related), which required only a simple majority vote. By the skin of its legislative teeth, the U.S. Congress passed reform guaranteeing health care to almost all Americans.

In the aftermath, the filibuster came in for heavy criticism by Democrats even as it was hailed by Republicans. Nancy Pelosi, the Speaker of the U.S. House of Representatives, called it "the 60-vote stranglehold on the future."[2] But Republicans stood by the words of Senate minority leader Mitch McConnell, R-Ky., who said shortly after the Republicans lost their majority in the Senate, "I think we can stipulate once again for the umpteenth time that matters that have any level of controversy about it in the Senate will require 60 votes."[3] Sure enough, Republicans proceeded to block as much of President Obama's agenda as they could, employing the filibuster when they could summon the votes and blocking votes on presidential appointments as well as on policies such as an extension of unemployment benefits during the recession and the 2010 National Defense Authorization Act; the latter would have meant a conditional end to the policy of Don't Ask Don't Tell that has kept gays from serving openly in the military.

Which side is right here? Is the filibuster a good thing, or a bad thing, or does it just depend on where you stand on any particular issue that faces a filibuster? What is at stake in the filibuster, anyway? We'll be able to look at this issue more carefully after we have a better understanding of how Congress works.

The U.S. Congress is the longest-running and most powerful democratic legislature in the world. The Capitol in Washington, D.C., home to both the House of Representatives and the Senate, is as much a symbol of America's democracy as the Stars and Stripes or the White House. We might expect Americans to express considerable pride in their national legislature, with its long tradition of serving democratic government. But if we did, we would be wrong. Congress is generally distrusted, seen by the American public as incompetent, corrupt, torn by partisanship, and at the beck and call of special interests.[4] Yet, despite their contempt for the institution of Congress as a whole, Americans typically revere their representatives and senators and reelect them so often that critics have long been calling for term limits to get new people into office. How can we understand this bizarre paradox?[5]

If politics is about who gets what and how, then Congress is arguably the center of American national politics. Not only does it often decide exactly who gets what, but it also has the power to alter many of the rules (or the how) that determine who wins and who loses in American political life. Within this context, there are two main reasons for America's love-hate relationship with Congress. The first is that citizens have conflicting goals when it comes to the operation of their national legislature. On the one hand, they want an advocate in Washington to take care of their local or state interests and to ensure that their home district gets a fair share of national resources such as highway funds, military expenditures, and agricultural support. On the other hand, citizens also want Congress to take care of the nation's business. This can pose a quandary for legislators, because what is good for the home district, like price supports for tobacco farmers or keeping a redundant military base open, might not be good for the nation as a whole. The second reason for citizens' love-hate relationship with Congress is that the rules that determine how Congress works were designed by the founders to produce slow, careful lawmaking that can seem motionless to an impatient public. When citizens are looking to Congress to produce policies that they favor or to distribute national resources, the built-in slowness can look like intentional foot-dragging and partisan bickering.

These twin themes, Congress's conflicting goals and its institutionalized slowness, will take us a long way toward understanding our mixed feelings about our national legislature. In this chapter we focus on who—including citizens, other politicians, and members of Congress themselves—gets the results they want from Congress, and how the rules of legislative politics help or hinder them. You will learn about the clash between representation and lawmaking, the powers and responsibilities of Congress, congressional membership and elections, the organization of Congress, and the rules of congressional operation.

Representation and Lawmaking in Congress
An institutional tension between two roles

We count on our elected representatives in both the House and the Senate to perform two major functions: representation and lawmaking. By **representation**, we mean that those we elect should represent, or look out for, our local interests and carry out our will. At the same time, we expect our legislators to address the country's social and economic problems by **national lawmaking**—passing laws that serve the interests of the entire nation.

The functions of representation and lawmaking often conflict. What is good for us and our local community may not serve the national good. One of the chief lessons of this chapter is that the rules under which Congress operates make it likely that when these primary functions do conflict, members of Congress will usually favor their jobs as representatives. That is, a member of Congress will usually do what the local district wants. Thus national problems go unaddressed while local problems get attention, resources, and solutions. No wonder we love our individual representatives but think poorly of the job done by Congress as a national policy-making institution.

Representation means working on behalf of one's **constituency**, the folks back home in the district who voted for the member as well as those who did not. To help us understand this complex job, political scientists often speak about four types of representation.[6] Most members of Congress try to excel at all four functions so that constituents will rate them highly and reelect them.

- **Policy representation** refers to congressional work for laws that advance the economic and social interests of the constituency. For example, House members and senators from petroleum-producing states can be safely predicted to vote in ways favorable to the profitability of the oil companies, members from the Plains states try to protect subsidies for wheat farmers, and so on.
- Voters have also come to expect a certain amount of **allocative representation**, in which the congressperson gets projects and grants for the district. Such perks are called **pork barrel** benefits, paid for by all the taxpayers but enjoyed by just a few. Congress members who are good at getting pork barrel projects for their districts (for example, highway construction or the establishment of a research institution) are said to "bring home the bacon."
- Senators and representatives also represent their states or districts by taking care of the individual problems of constituents, especially problems that involve the federal bureaucracy. This kind of representation is called **casework**, or constituency service, and it covers things such as finding out why a constituent's Social Security check has not shown up, sending a flag that has flown over the nation's capitol to a high school in the district, or helping with immigration and naturalization problems.

- A fourth kind of representation is called **symbolic representation**. In this elusive but important function, the member of Congress represents many of the positive values Americans associate with public life and government. Thus members are glad to serve as commencement speakers at high school graduations or to attend town meetings to explain what is happening in Washington.

But representation is not the only business of our senators and representatives. A considerable part of their job involves working with one another in Washington to define and solve the nation's problems. We expect Congress to create laws that serve the common good. One scholar calls this view of effective lawmaking "collective responsibility."[7] By this he means that Congress should be responsible for the effectiveness of its laws in solving national problems. A variety of factors go into a representative's calculation of how to vote on matters of national interest. He or she might be guided by conscience or ideology, by what opinion polls say the local constituents want, or by party position. And these considerations may very well be at odds with the four kinds of representation just described, frequently making it difficult, if not impossible, for members to fulfill their collective responsibility.

Congressional Powers and Responsibilities
Expansive powers held in check by the Constitution

The Constitution gives the U.S. Congress enormous powers, although it is safe to say that the founders could not have imagined the scope of contemporary congressional power since they never anticipated the growth of the federal government to today's size. As we will see, they were less concerned with the conflict between local and national interests we have been discussing than they were with the representation of short-term popular opinion versus long-term national interests. The basic powers of Congress are laid out in Article I, Section 8, of the Constitution (see Chapter 2 and the Appendix). They include the powers to tax, to pay debts, and to provide for the common defense and welfare of the United States, among many other things.

Differences Between the House and the Senate

The term *Congress* refers to the institution that is formally made up of the U.S. House of Representatives and the U.S. Senate. Congresses are numbered so that we can talk about them over time in a coherent way. Each congress covers a two-year election cycle. The 112th Congress was elected in November 2010, and its term runs from January 2011 through the end of 2012. The **bicameral** (two-house) **legislature** is laid out in the Constitution. As we discussed in earlier chapters, the founders wanted two chambers so that they could serve as a restraint on each other, strengthening the principle of checks and balances. The framers' hope was that the smaller, more elite Senate would "cool the passions" of the people represented in the House. Accordingly, while the two houses are equal in their overall power—both can initiate legislation (although tax bills must originate in the House), and both must pass every bill in identical form before it can be signed by the president to become law—there are also some key differences, particularly in the extra responsibilities assigned to the Senate. In addition, the two chambers operate differently, and they have distinct histories and norms of conduct (that is, informal rules and expectations of behavior).[8] Some of the major differences are outlined in Table 6.1.

The single biggest factor determining differences between the House and the Senate is size. With 100 members, the Senate is less formal; the 435-person House needs more rules and hierarchy in order to function efficiently. The Constitution also provides for differences in terms: two years for the House, six for the Senate (on a staggered basis—all senators do not come up for reelection at the same time). In the modern context, this means that House members (also referred to as congresspersons or members of Congress, a term that sometimes applies to senators as well) never stop campaigning. Senators, in contrast, can suspend their preoccupation with the next campaign for the first four or five years of their terms and thus, at least in theory, have more time to spend on the affairs of the nation. The minimum age of the candidates is different as well: members of the House must be at least twenty-five years old, senators thirty. This again reflects the founders' expectation that the Senate would be older, wiser, and better able to deal with national lawmaking. This distinction was reinforced in the constitutional provision that senators be elected not directly by the people, as were members of the House, but by state legislatures. Although this provision was changed by constitutional amendment in 1913, its presence in the original Constitution reflects the convictions of its authors that the Senate was a special chamber, one step removed from the people.

Budget bills are initiated in the House of Representatives. In practice this is not particularly significant since the Senate has to pass budget bills as well, and most of the time differences are negotiated between the two houses. The budget process has gotten quite complicated, as demonstrated by congressional struggles to deal with the deficit, which called for reductions in spending at the same time that constituencies and interest groups were pleading for expensive new programs. The budget process illustrates once again the constant tension for members of Congress between being responsive to local or particular interests and at the same time trying to make laws in the interest of the nation as a whole.

Other differences between the House and the Senate include the division of power on impeachment of public figures such as presidents and Supreme Court justices. The House impeaches, or charges the official with "treason, bribery, or other high crimes and misdemeanors," and the Senate tries the official. Both Andrew Johnson and Bill Clinton were impeached by the House, but in both cases the Senate failed to find the president guilty of the charges brought by the House. In addition, only the Senate is given the responsibility of confirming appointments to the executive and judicial branches, and of sharing the treaty-making power with the president.

Table 6.1

Differences Between the House and the Senate

	House	Senate
Constitutional Differences		
Term length	2 years	6 years
Minimum age	25	30
Citizenship required	7 years	9 years
Residency	In state	In state
Apportionment	Changes with population	Fixed; entire state
Impeachment	Impeaches official	Tries the impeached official
Treaty-making power	No authority	2/3 approval
Presidential appointments	No authority	Majority approval
Organizational Differences		
Size	435 members	100 members
Number of standing committees	20	16
Total committee assignments per member	Approx. 6	Approx. 11
Rules Committee	Yes	No
Limits on floor debate	Yes	No (filibuster possible)
Electoral Differences, 2008		
Average winners spent	$1.37 million	$8.5 million
Average losers spent	$493,000	$4.1 million
Most expensive campaign	$7.3 million	$21.8 million
Incumbency advantage	95% reelected	83% reelected
	(93.4% 50-year average)	(80.4% 50-year average)

Source: Roger H. Davidson and Walter J. Oleszek, *Congress and Its Members*, 11th ed. (Washington, D.C.: CQ Press, 2008), 63, 209; Federal Election Commission data compiled by Center for Responsive Politics; Gary C. Jacobson, "Congress: The Second Democratic Wave" in Michael Nelson, ed., *The Elections of 2008* (Washington, D.C.: CQ Press, 2010), Table 5-1.

Congressional Checks and Balances

The founders were concerned generally about the abuse of power, but since they were most anxious to avoid executive tyranny, they granted Congress an impressive array of powers. Keeping Congress at the center of national policymaking are the power to regulate commerce; the exclusive power to raise and to spend money for the national government; the power to provide for economic infrastructure (roads, postal service, money, patents); and significant powers in foreign policy, including the power to declare war, to ratify treaties, and to raise and support the armed forces. But the Constitution also limits congressional powers through the protection of individual rights and by the watchful eye of the other two branches of government, with which Congress shares power.

Our system of checks and balances means that to exercise its powers, each branch has to have the cooperation of the others. Thus Congress has the responsibility for passing bills, but the bills do not become law unless (1) the president signs them or, more passively, refrains from vetoing them, or (2) both houses of Congress are able to muster a full two-thirds majority to override a presidential veto. While the president cannot vote on legislation or even introduce bills, the Constitution gives the chief executive a powerful policy formulation role in calling for the president's annual State of the Union address and in inviting the president to recommend to Congress "such measures as he shall judge necessary and expedient."

One of the important functions of Congress is **congressional oversight** of the executive—of the president and the agencies of the bureaucracy that fall under the executive branch. This is usually done through hearings and selective investigations of executive actions whereby Congress attempts to ensure that the president and bureaucracy are carrying out the laws as Congress intended. How the president implements the laws passed by Congress is almost always a point of friction between the two branches.

During the George W. Bush administration, the job of oversight became more critical to the maintenance of checks and balances because the administration believed that the presidency had been diminished by Congress in the thirty-five or so years since Watergate, and President Bush used a number of devices to limit what the administration saw as unconstitutional congressional interference in the workings of the executive branch.[9] For most of President Bush's two terms, he had a cooperative Republican majority in Congress that was loath to cross the president in his interpretation of the powers of his office, so congressional oversight was neglected. Democrats, however, were chomping at the bit to investigate what they saw as Bush's executive excesses and abuse of power. When, in 2006, Republicans lost their majorities in the House and the Senate, the new Democratic leadership of both houses immediately began to hold hearings to investigate the administration's actions.

Oversight also comes in to play when Congress delegates authority to regulatory agencies in the executive branch. Often the agencies do what they are supposed to do, which can make the job of keeping an eye on them boring and unrewarding. But if Congress does not keep watch, the agencies can develop unhealthy relationships with those they are supposed to be regulating. This was the case with the Securities and Exchange Commission, which failed to protect us from the risky investment practices that resulted in the economic meltdown in late 2008, as well as with the Minerals Management Service, whose failure to adequately police offshore drilling procedures contributed to the ecological disaster in the Gulf of Mexico following the 2010 explosion of BP's *Deepwater Horizon* drilling platform. Since these relationships develop far from public scrutiny, we rely on Congress to ensure, through oversight, that agencies do the job they were set up to do, though there is a strong temptation for members to slight congressional responsibility here in favor of splashier and more electorally rewarding activities.

Another congressional check on the executive is the requirement that major presidential appointments, for instance to cabinet posts, ambassadorships, and the federal courts, must be confirmed by the Senate. Historically, most presidential appointments have proceeded without incident, but in recent administrations, appointments have become increasingly political. Senators sometimes use their confirmation powers to do more than "advise and consent" on the appointment at hand. They can, and do, tie up appointments, either because they oppose the nominee on account of his or her ideology or because they wish to extract promises and commitments from the president. In today's highly polarized Congress, senators of the minority party are quick to object to many of a president's appointees. The result is that many appointments languish and high offices in the federal government go unfilled for months or even years.

A continuing source of institutional conflict between Congress and the president is the difference in constituencies. The president looks at each policy in terms of a national constituency and his own policy program, whereas members of Congress necessarily take a narrower view. For example, the president may decide that clean air should be a national priority whereas for some members of Congress a clean air bill might mean closing factories in their districts.

Checks and balances, of course, require the cooperation of Congress not only with the executive branch but also with the judiciary. The constitutional relationship between the federal courts and Congress is simple in principle: Congress makes the laws, and the courts interpret them. The Supreme Court also has the lofty job of deciding whether laws and procedures are consistent with the Constitution, although this power of judicial review is not mentioned in the Constitution.

We think of the judiciary as independent of the other branches, but this self-sufficiency is only a matter of degree. Congress, for example, is charged with setting up the lower federal courts and determining the salaries for judges, with the interesting constitutional provision that a judge's salary cannot be cut. Congress also has considerable powers in establishing some issues of jurisdiction—that is, deciding which courts hear which cases (Article III, Section 2)—and in limiting the courts' discretion to rule or impose the sentences judges think best. And, as we just indicated, in accepting and rejecting presidential Supreme Court and federal court nominees, the Senate influences the long-term operation of the courts.[10]

Congressional Elections
Political calculations to define districts and
determine who will run

The first set of rules a future congressperson or senator has to contend with are those that govern congressional elections. These, more than any others, are the rules that determine the winners and losers in congressional politics. With House elections every two years and Senate elections every six years, much of the legislator's life is spent running for reelection.

The Politics of Defining Congressional Districts

As a result of the Great Compromise in 1787, the Constitution provides that each state will have two senators and that seats in the House of Representatives will be allocated on the basis of population. Two important political processes regulate the way House seats are awarded on this basis. One is **reapportionment**, in which the 435 House seats are reallocated among the states after each ten-year census. States whose populations grow gain seats, which are taken from those whose populations decline or remain steady. The winners are mostly in the rapidly growing Sun Belt states of the South and Southwest; the losers are largely in the Northeast and Midwest.

The second process deals with the way that districts are drawn in each state. Until the 1960s the states often suffered from malapportionment, the unequal distribution of population among the districts so that some had many fewer residents than others (perhaps, for instance, because people moved from rural areas to cities within the same state). This, in effect, gave greater representation to those living in lower population districts. This difference is built in to the Constitution in the case of the U.S. Senate, but the Supreme Court decided in 1964 that for the U.S. House of Representatives as well as for both houses of the state legislatures, Americans should be represented under the principle of "one person, one vote" and that the districts therefore must have equal populations.[11] The average size of a House district in the year 2000 was 646,952.[12] Districts are equalized following the census through a political process called **redistricting**, or the redrawing of district lines in states with more than one representative. This procedure, which is carried out by the state legislators (or by commissions they empower), can turn into a bitter political battle because how the district lines are drawn will have a lot to do with who has, gets, and keeps power in the states.

Gerrymandering is the process of drawing district lines to benefit one group or another, and it can result in some extremely strange shapes by the time the state politicians are through. Gerrymandering usually is one of three kinds. Pro-incumbent gerrymandering takes place when a state legislature is so closely divided that members can't agree to give an advantage to one party or the other, so they agree to create districts that reinforce the current power structure by favoring the people who already hold the seats.[13] A second kind of gerrymandering is partisan gerrymandering. Generally, the goal of the

The First Gerrymander

In 1812, during Massachusetts governor Elbridge Gerry's administration, district lines for the state senate were drawn to concentrate Federalist Party support in a few districts, thereby helping to elect more Democratic-Republicans. This contemporary cartoon likened one particularly convoluted district to a long-necked monster.

party controlling the redistricting process in a particular state legislature is to draw districts to maximize the number of House seats their party can win.

Finally, **racial gerrymandering** occurs when district lines are drawn to favor or disadvantage an ethnic or a racial group. For many years, states in the Deep South drew district lines to ensure that black voters would not constitute a majority that could elect an African American to Congress. Since the 1982 Voting Rights Act, the drawing of such lines has been used to maximize the likelihood that African Americans will be elected to Congress. Both Republicans and African American political activists have backed the formation of *majority-minority districts,* in which African Americans or Hispanics constitute majorities. This has the effect of concentrating enough minority citizens to elect one of their own, and at the same time, it takes these (usually Democratic) voters out of the pool of voters in other districts, thus making it easier for nonminority districts to be won by Republicans.[14] The boundaries for the First and Twelfth Districts of North Carolina, for instance, were redrawn after the 1990 census to consolidate the state's African American population. The Twelfth District was particularly oddly shaped, snaking for over 160 miles along a narrow stretch of Interstate 85. The gerrymandering accomplished its purpose: two African Americans—the first since 1889—were elected to represent North Carolina in Congress in 1992.[15]

Racial gerrymandering, however, remains highly controversial. While politicians and racial and ethnic group leaders continue to jockey for the best district boundaries for their own interests, the courts struggle to find a "fair" set of rules for drawing district lines. In recent cases the Supreme Court declared that race cannot be the predominant factor in drawing congressional districts. It can be taken into account, but so must other factors, such as neighborhood and community preservation. Since, as we discussed in Chapter 5, race is a suspect classification, it is subject to *strict scrutiny* whenever the law uses it to treat citizens differently, and the law must fulfill a compelling state purpose, whether it penalizes them or benefits them.[16] After holding an earlier effort unconstitutional, the Court allowed a later redrawing of the North Carolina district to stand, arguing that where black voters are mostly Democrats, disentangling race from politics can be difficult, and that race can be a legitimate concern in redistricting as long as it is not the "dominant and controlling" consideration.[17]

Deciding to Run

Imagine that your interest in politics is piqued as a result of your American politics class. You think the representative from your district is out of touch with the people, too wrapped up in Washington-centered politics, and you start day-dreaming about running for office. What sorts of things should you consider? What would you have to do to win?

The formal qualifications for Congress are not difficult to meet. In addition to the age and citizenship requirements listed in Table 6.1, the Constitution requires that you live in the state you want to represent, although state laws vary on how long or when you have to have lived there. Custom also dictates that if you are running for the House, you live in the district you want to represent. There are no educational requirements for Congress.

While constitutionally the qualifications for Congress are looser than those for many other jobs you may apply for when you graduate, in fact, most members of Congress have gone to college, three-quarters have graduate degrees, nearly half are lawyers, many are businesspeople, and quite a few are millionaires. By most estimations, Congress comprises an educational, occupational, and economic elite. Congress is also an overwhelmingly white male institution. White males make up 40 percent of the U.S. population, but they account for more than 80 percent of the members of the U.S. Congress. Congress is, however, more representative today than it has been through most of our history, though its progress is slow.

Like most prospective members of Congress, if you decide to run you are probably motivated by a desire to serve the public. These days, if you are contemplating a run for Congress you are also increasingly likely to be motivated by your ideology—that is, you are probably a conservative Republican or a liberal Democrat who wants to run from a sense of personal conviction and commitment to enact policy that represents your particular strongly held values. But your wish to run for Congress may also be enhanced by the fact that it is a very attractive job in its own right. First, there is all the fun of being in Washington, living a life that is undeniably exciting and powerful. The salary, $174,000 in 2010, puts representatives and senators among the top wage earners in the nation, and the "perks" of office are rather nice as well. These include generous travel allowances, ample staff, franking privileges (the ability to send mailings to constituents free of charge), free parking at Reagan National Airport, health and life insurance, and substantial pensions.[18] Offsetting these enviable aspects of serving in Congress are the facts that the work is awfully hard, it is expensive to keep up two homes (one in D.C. and one in the home district), and the job security is nonexistent.

To have an outside chance of winning, nonincumbent candidates for Congress need political and financial assets, and they must be strategic politicians. Strategic politicians act rationally and carefully in deciding when to run and what office to run for. As a strategic candidate yourself, consider these questions:

Is this a district or state I can win? People want to vote for and be represented by people like themselves, so determine whether you and the district are compatible. Liberals do not do well in conservative parts of the South, African Americans have great difficulty getting elected in predominantly white districts, Republicans have a hard time in areas that are mostly Democratic, and so forth.

Can I beat my opponent? Whether your opponent is vulnerable is governed largely by the **incumbency advantage**, which refers to the edge in visibility, experience, organization, and fundraising ability possessed by the people who already hold the job. It can make them hard to defeat. Three possibilities exist:

- An incumbent of your party already holds the seat. In this case, winning the nomination is a real long shot. From 1984 through 2008, only fifty-four incumbents lost in primary battles to determine a party's nominee, or about 1 percent of all those seeking reelection.[19]

- An incumbent of the opposite party holds the seat. In this case, winning the primary to get your party's nomination may be easier, but the odds are against winning in the general election unless the incumbent has been weakened by scandal, redistricting, or a challenge from within his or her party. Over 96 percent of incumbents running won in their general election contests from 1984 to 2008.[20]
- The incumbent is not running. This is an "open seat," your best chance for success. However, because others know this as well, both the primary and the general elections are likely to be hard fought by high-quality candidates.

Can I get the funds necessary to run a winning campaign? Modern political campaigns are expensive, and campaigns run on a budget and a prayer are hardly ever successful. Winning nonincumbents over the past decade have spent, on average, over four times as much as nonincumbents who did not win, and even then the winning nonincumbents could not keep up with the spending of incumbents.[21] Incumbents have access to a lot more political action committee (PAC) money and other contributions than do nonincumbents. (PACs are money-raising organizations devoted to a particular interest group, such as a labor union or trade association; they make donations to candidates that best represent their interests. We'll hear more about PACs in Chapter 11, on interest groups.) As a nonincumbent, you should probably aim at a minimum to raise $1.19 million—the average for challengers who defeated incumbents in 2008.[22] Senate contests, with their much larger constituencies, cost much more.

How are the national tides running? Some years are good for Democrats, some for Republicans. These tides are a result of such things as presidential popularity, the state of the economy, scandals, and military engagements abroad. If it is a presidential election year, a popular presidential candidate of your party might sweep you to victory on his or her coattails. The **coattail effect**, less significant in recent elections, refers to the added votes congressional candidates of the winning presidential party receive in a presidential election year as voters generalize their enthusiasm for the national candidate to the whole party.

While the strength of coattails might be declining, there is no arguing with the phenomenon of the **midterm loss**. This is the striking regularity with which the presidential party loses seats in Congress in the midterm elections, also called "off-year" elections—those congressional elections that fall in between presidential election years. The 1994 election that brought Republicans to power in Congress for the first time in forty years was a striking example of the midterm loss: fifty-three seats changed from Democratic to Republican control, making it the largest change of this sort in fifty years.[23] In general, the presidential party losses depend on the president's standing with the public and the state of the economy; an unpopular president and a sour economy spell bad news for congressional candidates of the presidential party in an off-year election.[24] Before 1998 the presidential party had lost seats in the House of Representatives in every midterm election of the twentieth century except in 1934. For different reasons, 1998 and 2002 have proved to be exceptions to the midterm loss rule, but in 2006 the midterm loss returned true to

Russ Feingold

The conference room in Senator Russ Feingold's Middleton, Wisconsin, office is papered with posters showing his listening sessions—one for every year he's been in office. Seventy-two town meetings a year, that's one per county, times thirteen years in office, that's more than 900 so far. And boy is he proud of that. He made a campaign promise when he first ran for the Senate that he would make the visits to keep in touch with his constituents, about which one journalist said, "What a stupid pledge. He'll never be able to do it." That reporter has since had to eat his words because if there is one thing you can say about Russ Feingold, he believes in keeping his promises.

Leaning back in his chair, relaxed and casual in a green golf shirt, Feingold explains how it came about. "[T]he reason I'm doing all these [sessions] is that people kept saying to me, when I was running and nobody really knew who I was, 'Hey you seem like a nice guy but we know how this works. You're going to get elected, you go out there and we never see you again.' And I thought, 'OK, how can I break that image? How can I change peoples' feeling about their representative by doing something that will guarantee them access?' So I made this pledge. Kind of a crazy pledge, but everybody in this state knows that in their county every year, they can come talk to me, they can say whatever they want to me, in their own home county without an appointment, without making a campaign contribution."

Compared to most of us, whose senators are protected by barricades of staff and protocol, Feingold's constituents have amazing access. He has clearly given a lot of thought to what it means to be a representative, and says it this way: "I work for the people of Wisconsin. And they're my boss. They've elected me to listen to them and to try to agree with them and help them with their views if I can justify them as being a good thing for Wisconsin and America. And they expect me to lead."

That clarity about what his job is and who he answers to has given Feingold the courage to take some strong, unconventional but principled stands. One, of course, is the pledge on the listening tours. Another was the cosponsorship, with the Republican senator from Arizona, John McCain, of the campaign finance legislation that was enacted in 2002. Another was the refusal to accept any soft money from his party in his reelection campaign in 1998—an election he almost lost and in which the money he turned down would have come in mighty handy. Then there was the Patriot Act—in the frightening days after September 11, Feingold was the only senator to vote against it. And in the summer of 2005, he was the first senator to demand a timetable for finishing the war in Iraq.

Feingold has the courage to stand on his convictions because he believes his constituents trust him, counting on him to do his homework, to tell the truth, and to keep his promises, even where they might disagree with some of his views.

"I'm not afraid of people being mad at me in Washington, or any of that, because what matters to me is that people think I'm doing a good job."

Feingold clearly relishes the job he is doing—not surprising since being in politics is what he's wanted to do since he was a kid. His lawyer dad was one of a handful of progressive Democrats in a county of Wisconsin Republicans, and fascinating people, stalwarts in the Progressive tradition, came through the family home, firing young Russ with a desire to share the excitement of politics. He can remember clearly being seven when John F. Kennedy became president, and determining that he, too, would like to be president one day (an ambition his family and childhood friends don't let him forget). Growing up in a turbulent, stimulating time—civil rights, the environment, the women's movement, Vietnam—helped shape his consciousness and propelled him into a life of public service. He's there because he believes deeply in the issues he works for and feels the weight of having to make the right calls in the troubled times we live in. But, push him a little, and he admits that it's a lot of fun as well. He says with a grin, "And of course, I like the excitement. I don't like to be bored and I'm not bored in this shop." Here's what else he has to say:

On living in interesting times:
But to me, to love history, to be involved as it's occurring is a very exciting thing. [A]s I studied great, frightening events in human history and what it means to be involved in foreign policy, what I didn't anticipate is that the most interesting times are also the most upsetting. And that those are really truly tragic times. And what 9/11 really made me realize [is] that the most exquisitely interesting questions are raised at a time when you're almost devastated by the difficulties that this country is going through. So, you know, some say it's Confucius, some say it's Scottish, but the sentiment "may you live in interesting times" is a curse.

On keeping the republic:
Obviously John F. Kennedy said it best in his inaugural address. And that greatly inspired all of us because he gave all of us a clean phrase. "Ask not what your country can do for you, ask what you can do for your country. . . ." It's an invitation to pick something that you can do, that you'll enjoy, but that'll help this nation get through this difficult period and continue to be the great nation that it is. It's a wonderful feeling. It's part of feeling good about yourself. And I want young people to think of it that way. It's not just about doing your duty. It feels good to help this country move forward. It's good for your family, it's good for everybody around you, it's good for you. . . . I love that expression. In fact, when we were trying to stop this ridiculous attempt to take away the filibuster about the judges, that was the quote that was used. Because Thomas Jefferson said that the Senate was supposed to be the cooling saucer and that's what Franklin was talking about. It's a republic. It's not a direct democracy. It is a republic if you can keep it.

form. President Bush's approval ratings were lower than any president's ratings save for Richard Nixon's on the eve of his impeachment, and the president's party paid the price as the Democrats won back control of both houses of Congress. Similarly, in 2010, a sputtering economic recovery, high unemployment, and President Obama's correspondingly low approval ratings cost the Democrats the majority in the House. The GOP gain of more than 60 House seats was the largest for that party in six decades, eclipsing the historic 1994 victory and easily wiping out the Democrats' gains in the previous two election cycles. The Democrats were especially vulnerable because they had won in a large number of Republican districts in 2006 and again in 2008. With fewer seats at stake in the Senate, the Democrats lost only six seats, keeping majority control in that chamber, but not by much.

The 112th Congress

Whereas the elections of 2006 and 2008 were big wins for the Democrats, in 2010 the political winds strongly favored Republicans. The combination of the earlier Democratic wins, which had many Democrats defending House seats in Republican or swing districts; unified Democratic control of both houses of Congress and the presidency; and a lingering recession that still produced an unemployment rate of nearly 10 percent made the Democrats an easy target for voters. Disgruntled and angry Republicans and independents turned out in force while disheartened Democrats stayed home. The Republicans took control of the House with a sizable majority, the Democrats retained a bare majority in the Senate, and the prospects were for political gridlock in Washington.

The demographic profile of the Congress shifted in ways that are consistent with a large Republican win. The number of women dropped by four, to seventy-three, in the House and by two, to fifteen, in the Senate. The number of Hispanics also decreased to two from three in the Senate and to twenty-three from twenty-seven in the House. No African Americans have been elected to the Senate since President Barack Obama held a seat representing Illinois, but in the House their numbers increased, including the election of two black Republicans from Florida and South Carolina. The one Native American continued in the House, as did the two Asians in the Senate. The number of Asians in the House increased by two, to a total of nine.

The intense ideological polarization of the parties appears to have increased. Many Republican candidates were backed by the strongly anti-Washington Tea Party movement, drawing them further to the right. Also, because several moderate Republicans lost in the primaries, even those from more competitive districts were discouraged from positioning themselves in the political center. As many of the Democrats who lost were moderates from competitive and Republican districts, the remaining Democrats are a more homogeneously liberal group. Still, as has been usual in the recent past, there is more ideological diversity in the Democratic Party, evidenced by the election of Joe Manchin III, who won the Senate seat in West Virginia by running against much of the Democratic program in Washington. After the election, Manchin became a prime target for Republicans hoping to persuade him to switch parties and join their ranks. The election presents huge challenges for the parties' leaders to govern. Each party has, in both Congress and the electorate, strongly committed bases that will resist any significant compromise.

Congressional Organization
The key role of political parties and congressional committees

In spite of the imperatives of reelection and the demands of constituency service, the primary business of Congress is making laws. Lawmaking is influenced a great deal by the organization of Congress—that is, the rules of the institution that determine where the power is and who can exercise it.

The Central Role of Party

Political parties are central to how Congress functions for several reasons. First, Congress is organized along party lines. In each chamber, the party with the most members—the **majority party**—decides the rules for each chamber and gets the top leadership posts, such as the Speaker of the House, the majority leader in the Senate, and the chairmanships of all the committees and subcommittees.

Party is also important in Congress because it is the mechanism for members' advancement. Because all positions are determined by the parties, members have to advance within their party to achieve positions of power in the House or the Senate, whether as a committee chair or in the party leadership.

> [A]lthough Americans like to downplay the importance of parties in their own lives, political parties are fundamental to the operation of Congress and, hence, to what the national government does.

Finally, party control of Congress matters because the parties stand for very different things. Across a wide range of issues, Democrats embrace more policies, whereas Republicans advocate more conservative ones. Upon winning office, these candidates vote very differently from each other. Thus, although Americans like to downplay the importance of parties in their own lives, political parties are fundamental to the operation of Congress and, hence, to what the national government does.

Parties have become much more significant in Congress in recent years due to the process of **party polarization**. This refers to the growing ideological differences between the two parties and the greater ideological agreement within the parties. Today, almost all the Democrats in Congress are pretty liberal, and to an even greater extent, the vast majority of congressional Republicans are very conservative. This makes it harder for the parties to work together because their members are committed to such divergent positions across the whole range of issues that Congress must deal with.

Polarization has also been a significant factor in the growing intensity of conflict and rancor that is characteristic of recent congresses. Republican opposition to President Obama's proposals has been quite solid, whereas he has been able to count on the support of most congressional Democrats. As we will see later in this chapter, this means the president has been successful in getting his priorities enacted by the House of Representatives only because there are enough Democrats there to get his bills passed even in the face of united Republican opposition. It has been much more difficult for the president to get his policies passed in the Senate, where for most of his term so far the Democrats have not been able to command sixty votes to break a filibuster without the cooperation of at least one Republican.

The Leadership

The majority and minority parties in each house elect their own leaders, who are, in turn, the leaders of Congress. Strong, centralized leadership allows Congress to be more efficient in enacting party or presidential programs, but it gives less independence to members to take care of their own constituencies or to pursue their own policy preferences.[25] Although the nature of leadership in the House of Representatives has varied over time, the current era is one of considerable centralization of power. Because the Senate is a smaller chamber and thus easier to manage, its power is more decentralized.

The Constitution provides for the election of some specific congressional officers, but Congress itself determines how much power the leaders of each chamber will have. The main leadership offices in the House of Representatives are the Speaker of the House, the majority leader, the minority leader, and the whips. The real political choice about who the party leader should be occurs within the party groupings in each chamber. The **Speaker of the House** is elected by the majority party and, as the person who presides over floor deliberations, is the most powerful House member. The House majority leader, second in command, is given wide-ranging responsibilities to assist the Speaker.

The leadership organization in the Senate is similar but not as elaborate. The presiding officer of the Senate is the vice president of the United States, who can cast a tie-breaking vote when necessary but otherwise does not vote. When the vice president is not present, which is almost always the case, the president pro tempore of the Senate officially presides, although the role is almost always performed by a junior senator. Because of the Senate's much freer rules for deliberation on the floor, the presiding officer has less power than in the House, where debate is generally tightly controlled. The locus of real leadership in the Senate is the majority leader and the minority leader. Each is advised by party committees on both policy and personnel matters, such as committee appointments.

In both chambers, Democratic and Republican leaders are assisted by party whips. (The term *whip* comes from an old English hunting expression; the "whipper in" was charged with keeping the dogs together in pursuit of the fox.) Elected by party members, whips find out how people intend to vote so that on important party bills, the leaders can adjust the legislation, negotiate acceptable amendments, or employ favors (or, occasionally, threats) to line up support. Whips work to persuade party members to support the party on key bills, and they are active in making sure favorable members are available to vote when needed.

Leaders can exercise only the powers that their party members give them. From the members' standpoint, the advantage of a strong leader is that he or she can move legislation along, get the party program passed, do favors for members, and improve the party's standing. The disadvantage is that a strong party leader can pursue national party (or presidential) goals at the expense of members' pet projects and constituency interests, and he or she can withhold favors.

The power of the Speaker of the House has changed dramatically over time. At the turn of the century, the strong "boss rule" of Speaker Joe Cannon greatly centralized power in the House. Members rebelled at this and moved to the **seniority system**, which vested great power in committee chairs instead of the Speaker. Power followed

The Treatment

As Senate majority leader and later as president, Lyndon B. Johnson was legendary for his ability to cajole, charm, bully, and—by any and all means necessary—persuade others to see things his way. Supreme Court justice Abe Fortas shares a laugh with Johnson here as he is subjected to "the treatment."

seniority, or length of service on a committee, so that once a person assumed the chairmanship of a committee, business was run very much at the pleasure of the chair.[26] The seniority system itself was reformed in the 1970s by a movement that weakened the grip of chairs and gave some power back to the Speaker and the party caucuses, as well as to members of the committees and, especially, subcommittees.[27]

The Speaker's powers were further enhanced with the Republican congressional victories in the 1994 election, when Rep. Newt Gingrich, R-Ga., became Speaker (see the *Profiles in Citizenship* feature in Chapter 2). Gingrich quickly became the most powerful Speaker since the era of boss rule. His House Republican colleagues were willing to give him new powers because his leadership enabled them to take control of the House and to enact the well-publicized conservative agenda that they called the *Contract With America*.[28] Gingrich continued as the powerful Republican congressional spokesperson and leader until he resigned in the wake of the almost unprecedented reversal of the 1998 midterm loss, to be replaced by Dennis Hastert, a Republican from Illinois.

When the Democrats won control of the House in 2006, Nancy Pelosi was elected Speaker, the first woman to hold that position. In response to those who wondered if Pelosi could wield power as effectively as her male counterparts, Pelosi herself stated, "Anybody who's ever dealt with me knows not to mess with me."[29] That proved to be an accurate foreshadowing of how she has managed the office. As leader, she was, according to one political analyst, a pragmatist who is unafraid to disappoint her liberal base in the cause of maintaining or even expanding her party's House majority."[30] Pelosi's role in passing Obama's health care reform bill was decisive, and she was effective at maintaining the support and discipline of her Democratic majority in the House, holding on to her leadership position in the party even after the Republicans regained the majority in 2010.[31] John Boehner's lot as Speaker will be more difficult in many ways. His leadership skills will be tested by the challenge of holding his party together as his caucus is divided between traditional Republicans and the newly elected Tea Partiers who come to Congress determined not to compromise in accomplishing their ambitious agenda.

The leaders of the Senate have never had as much formal authority as those in the House. The traditions of the Senate, with its much smaller size, allow each senator to speak or to offer amendments at will. The highly individualistic Senate would not accept the kind of control that some Speakers wield in the House. But though the Senate majority leader cannot control senators, he or she can influence the scheduling of legislation, a factor that can be crucial to a bill's success. The current majority leader, Harry Reid of Nevada, proved to be a highly effective manager in the biggest legislative victories of Obama's first years as president, shepherding the health care bill through the Senate and securing sixty votes to pass financial regulation.

The Committee System

Meeting as full bodies, the House and the Senate would not be able to consider and deliberate on all of the 10,000 bills and 100,000 nominations they receive every two years.[32] Hence, the work is broken up and handled by smaller groups called committees.

The Constitution says nothing about congressional committees; they are completely creatures of the chambers of Congress they serve. The committee system has developed to meet the needs of a growing nation as well as the evolving goals of members of Congress. Initially, congressional committees formed to consider specific issues and pieces of legislation; after they made their recommendations to the full body, they dispersed. As the nation grew, and with it the number of bills to be considered, this ad hoc system became unwieldy and Congress formed a system of more permanent committees. Longer service on a committee permitted members to develop expertise and specialization in a particular policy area, and thus bills could be considered more efficiently. Committees also provide members with a principal source of institutional power and the primary position from which they can influence national policy.

What Committees Do

It is at the committee and, even more, the subcommittee stages that the nitty-gritty details of legislation are worked out. Committees and subcommittees do the hard work of considering alternatives and drafting legislation. Committees are the primary information gatherers for Congress. Through hearings, staff reports, and investigations, members gather information on policy alternatives and discover who will support different policy options. Thus committees act as the eyes, ears, and workhorses of Congress in considering, drafting, and redrafting proposed legislation.

Committees do more, however, than write laws. Committees also undertake the congressional oversight we discussed earlier in this chapter. That is, they check to see that executive agencies are carrying out the laws as Congress intended them to. Committee members gather information about agencies from the media, constituents, interest groups, staff, and special investigations. A lot of what is learned in oversight is reflected in changes to the laws giving agencies their power and operating funds.

Members and the general public all agree strongly on the importance of congressional oversight; it is part of the "continuous watchfulness" that Congress mandated for itself in the Legislative Reorganization Act of 1946 and reiterated in its Legislative Reorganization Act of 1970. Nevertheless, oversight tends to be slighted in the congressional process. The reasons are not hard to find. Oversight takes a lot of time, and the rewards to individual members are less certain than from other activities like fundraising or grabbing a headline in the district with a new pork project. Consequently, oversight most often takes the form of "fire-alarm" oversight, in which some scandal or upsurge of public interest directs congressional attention to a problem in the bureaucracy rather than careful and systematic reviews of agencies' implementation of congressional policies.[33]

Types of Committees

Congress has four types of committees: standing, select, joint, and conference. The vast majority of work is done by the **standing committees**. These are permanent committees, created by statute, that carry over from one session of Congress to the next. They review most pieces of legislation that are introduced to Congress. So powerful are the standing committees that they scrutinize, hold hearings on, amend, and, frequently, kill legislation before the full Congress ever gets the chance to discuss it.

The standing committees deal with issues in specific policy areas, such as agriculture, foreign relations, or justice. Each committee is typically divided into several subcommittees that focus on detailed areas of policy. There are 20 standing committees and 101 subcommittees in the House. The Senate has 17 committees and 70 subcommittees. Not surprisingly, committees are larger in the House, with membership rising to more than seventy on some committees, compared to fewer than thirty on the Senate committees. The size of the committees and the ratio of majority to minority party members on each are determined at the start of each Congress by the majority leadership in the House and by negotiations between the majority and minority leaders in the Senate. Standing committee membership is relatively stable as seniority on the committee is a major factor in gaining subcommittee or committee chairs; the chairs wield considerable power and are coveted positions.

The policy areas represented by the standing committees of the two houses roughly parallel each other, but the **House Rules Committee** exists only in the House of Representatives. (There is a Senate Rules and Administration Committee, but it does not have equivalent powers.) The House Rules Committee provides a "rule" for each bill that specifies when it will be debated, how long debate can last, how it can be amended, and so on. Because the House is so large, debate would quickly become chaotic without the organization and structure provided by the Rules Committee. Such structure is not neutral in its effects on legislation, however. Since the committees are controlled by the majority party in the House, and especially by the Speaker, the rule that structures a given debate will reflect the priorities of the majority party.

When a problem before Congress does not fall into the jurisdiction of a standing committee, a **select committee** may be appointed. These committees are usually temporary and do not recommend legislation per se. They are used to gather information on specific issues, like the Select Committee on Homeland Security did after the September 11 terror attacks, or to conduct an investigation, as did the Select Bipartisan Committee to Investigate the Preparation for and Response to Hurricane Katrina.

Joint committees are made up of members of both houses of Congress. While each house generally considers bills independently (making for a lot of duplication of effort and staff), in some areas they have coordinated activities to expedite consideration of legislation. The joint committees in the 111th Congress were on printing, economics, taxation, and the Library of Congress.

Before a bill can become law, it must be passed by both houses of Congress in exactly the same form. But because the legislative process in each house often subjects bills to different pressures, they may be very different by the time they are debated and passed. **Conference committees** are temporary committees made up of members of both houses of Congress commissioned to resolve these differences, after which the bills go back to each house for a final vote. Members of the conference committees are appointed by the presiding officer of each chamber, who usually taps the senior members, especially the chair, of the committees that considered the bill. Most often the conferees are members of those committees.

In the past, conference committees have tended to be small (five to ten members). In recent years, however, as Congress has tried to work within severe budget restrictions, it has taken to passing huge "megabills" that collect many proposals into one. Conference committees have expanded in turn, sometimes ballooning into gigantic affairs with many "subconferences."[34] In rare cases, like the passing of health care reform in 2010, congressional leaders will forgo the formal conference committee if they think opponents of a bill may try to block it there. Both chambers of Congress still need to approve the same version of the bill, however, so an alternate mechanism of bringing them together must be found.[35]

Committee Assignments

Getting on the right standing committee is vital for all members of Congress because so much of what members want to accomplish is realized through their work on these committees. Members who like to focus on national lawmaking might try to get assigned to committees like Commerce or Foreign Affairs, which have broad jurisdictions and often deal with weighty, high-profile concerns. The House Ways and Means Committee and the Senate Finance Committee, because they deal with taxation—a topic of interest to nearly everyone—are highly prized committee assignments, as are the Senate Appropriations, Armed Services, and Foreign Relations Committees.[36]

Decisions on who gets on what committee vary by party and chamber. Although occasionally the awarding of committee assignments has been used by the parties to reward those who support party positions, in general both the Democrats and the Republicans accommodate their members when they can, since the goal of both parties is to support their ranks and help them be successful.

Committee Chairs

For much of the twentieth century, congressional power rested with the chairmen and chairwomen of the committees of Congress; their power was unquestioned under the seniority system. Today, seniority remains important, but chairs serve at the pleasure of their party caucuses and the party leadership. The committees, under this system, are expected to reflect more faithfully the preferences of the average party member rather than just those of the committee chair or current members.[37]

Congressional Resources

For Congress to guide government lawmaking, it needs expertise and information. Members find, however, that alone they are no match for the enormous amount of information generated by the executive branch, on the one hand, or the sheer informational demands of the policy process—economic, social, military, and foreign affairs—on the other. The need for independent, expert information, along with the ever-present reelection imperative, has led to a big growth in what we call the congressional bureaucracy. Congress has over 22,000 employees, paid for by the federal government. This makes it by far the largest staffed legislature in the world.

The vast majority of congressional staff—secretaries, computer personnel, clericals, and professionals—work for individual members or committees. The staff handle mailings; meet visiting constituents; answer mail, phone calls, faxes, and email messages; create and maintain member web sites; and contact the executive agencies on behalf of constituents. They arrange meetings for members in their constituencies, and they set up local media events. House members have an average staff of eighteen per member, while the Senate averages twice that, with the sizes of Senate staff varying with state population.

The committees' staffs (about 2,200 in the House and 1,200 in the Senate) do much of the committee work, from honing ideas, suggesting policy options to members, scheduling hearings, and recruiting witnesses, to actually drafting legislation.[38] In most committees each party also has its own staff. Following the 1994 election, committee staffs were cut by one-third; however, members did not force any cuts in the sizes of their personal staffs.

Reflecting a reluctance dating from Vietnam and Watergate to be dependent on the executive branch for information, Congress also has nonpartisan staff that run research organizations and agencies to facilitate its work, providing expert advice and technical assistance. The Congressional Research Service (CRS), a unit of the Library of Congress, employs over eight hundred people to do research for members of Congress. For example, if Congress is considering a bill to relax air quality standards in factories, it can have the CRS determine what is known about the effects of air quality on worker health. The Government Accountability Office (formerly the General Accounting Office but still known as the GAO), with its 3,200 employees, audits the books of executive departments and conducts policy evaluation and analysis. The Congressional Budget Office (CBO) is Congress' economic adviser, providing members with economic estimates about the budget, the deficit or surplus, and the national debt, and forecasts of how they will be influenced by different tax and spending policies. Congress has a stronger and more independent role in the policy process when it is not completely dependent on the executive branch for information and expertise.

How Congress Works
An already complex process, complicated further
by internal and external forces

The policies passed by Congress are a result of both external and internal forces. The external environment includes the problems that are important to citizens at any given time—sometimes the economy, sometimes foreign affairs, at other times national security or the federal deficit or the plight of the homeless and so forth. The policy preferences of the president loom large in this external environment as well. It is often said, with some exaggeration but a bit of truth, that "the president proposes, the Congress disposes" of important legislation. Parties, always important, have been increasing their influence in the policymaking arena, and organized interests play a significant role, too.

The Context of Congressional Policymaking

Congress also has a distinct internal institutional environment that shapes the way it carries out its business. Three characteristics of this environment are especially important. First, Congress is bicameral. Almost all congressional policy has to be passed, in identical form, by both houses. This requirement, laid out by the founders in the Constitution, makes the policy process difficult because the two houses serve different constituencies and operate under different decision-making procedures. The House, for example, because of its size and traditions, is much more hierarchically organized. The leadership has a good deal of influence over committees and particularly over how legislation is considered. The Senate is more egalitarian and its debate wide-open; the leadership has less control and fewer powers.

Because the houses are different, getting legislation through both is difficult. Interests that oppose a bill and lose in one chamber can often be successful at defeating the bill in the other. The opposition only has to stop a bill in one place to win, but the proponents of a bill have to win in both houses. In Congress, it is much easier to play defense than offense.

The second overriding feature of the institutional environment of Congress as a policymaking institution is its fragmentation. As you read the next section on how a bill becomes a law, think about the piecemeal nature of the policy process in Congress. Legislation is broken into bits, each considered individually in committees. It is very difficult to coordinate a bill with those laws that are already on the books or with what another committee might be doing in a closely related area. Thus Congress does such seemingly nonsensical things as subsidizing both tobacco growers and antismoking campaigns. This fragmentation increases opportunities for constituencies and individual members, in addition to well-organized groups, to influence policy on issues they really care about. It also makes it very hard for national policymakers—the president or congressional leaders—to take a large-scale, coordinated approach to major policy problems.

The third institutional influence on Congress are congressional norms— informal rules of procedure that are learned quickly by newcomers when they enter Congress. Norms include the idea that members should work hard, develop a specialization, treat other members with the utmost courtesy, reciprocate favors, and take pride in their respective chambers and in Congress as a whole. The purpose of congressional norms is to constrain conflict and personal animosity in an arena where disagreements are inevitable, but they also aid in getting business done. Although congressional norms continue to be important, they are less constraining on members today than they were in the 1950s and 1960s.[39] The current norms allow for more individualistic, media-oriented, and conflictual behavior than in the past.

How a Bill Becomes a Law—Some of the Time

When we see something that seems unfair in business or in the workplace, when disaster strikes and causes much suffering, when workers go on strike and disrupt our lives—whenever a crisis occurs, we demand that government do something to solve the problem that we cannot solve on our own. This means government must have a policy, a set of laws, to deal with the problem. We consider two aspects of congressional policy here: (1) the agenda, or the source of ideas for new policies; and (2) the legislative process, or the steps a bill goes through to become law. Very few proposed policies, as it turns out, actually make it into law, and those that do have a difficult path to follow.

Setting the Agenda

Before a law can be passed, it must be among the things that Congress thinks it ought to do. There is no official list of actions that Congress needs to take, but when a bill is proposed that would result in a significant change in policy, it must seem like a reasonable thing for members to turn their attention to—a problem that is possible, appropriate, and timely for them to try to solve with a new policy. That is, it must be on the **legislative agenda**. Potential new laws can get on Congress' agenda in several ways. First, because public attention is focused so intently on presidential elections and campaigns, new presidents are especially effective at setting the congressional agenda. Their proposals may be efforts to fulfill campaign promises, to pay political debts, to realize ideological commitments, or to deal with a crisis.

A second way an issue gets on the legislative agenda is when it is triggered by a well-publicized event, even if the problem it highlights is not a new one at all. For example, the 2010 explosion of BP's oil drilling platform *Deepwater Horizon* and the subsequent release of millions of barrels of crude oil into the Gulf of Mexico drew the nation's attention to energy policy, the adequacy of regulatory procedures, and the need to protect the environment. What leaders in Washington will actually do in response to such an event is hard to predict, especially in circumstances in which they are unable to do much of anything (the federal government had neither the technical know-how nor the equipment to plug the oil well, for instance). Nonetheless, such events create a public demand that the government "do something!"

A third way an idea gets on the agenda is for some member or members to find it in their own interests, either political or ideological, to invest time and political resources in pushing the policy. Many members of Congress want to prove their legislative skills to their constituents, key supporters, the media, and fellow lawmakers. The search for the right issue to push at the right time is called **policy entrepreneurship**. Most members of Congress to greater or lesser degrees are policy entrepreneurs. Those with ambition, vision, and luck choose the issues that matter in our lives and that can bring them significant policy influence and recognition, but most successful policy entrepreneurs are not widely recognized outside of the policy communities in which they operate.[40] Policy entrepreneurship by members is important in setting the congressional policy agenda, and it can reap considerable political benefits for those associated with important initiatives.

Legislative Process

Bills, even those widely recognized as representing the president's legislative program, must be introduced by members of Congress. The formal introduction is

Figure 6.1

How a Bill Becomes Law: Neat and Tidy Version

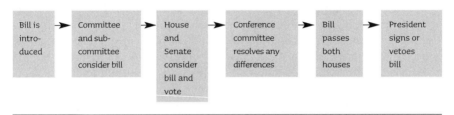

done by putting a bill in the "hopper" (a wooden box) in the House, where it goes to the clerk of the House, or by giving it to the presiding officer in the Senate. The bill is then given a number (for example, HR932 in the House or S953 in the Senate) and begins the long journey that *might* result in its becoming law. Figure 6.1 shows the much-simplified, general route for a bill once it is introduced in either the House or the Senate, but the actual details can get messy, and there are exceptions. A bill introduced in the House goes first through the House and then on to the Senate, and vice versa. However, bills may be considered simultaneously in both houses.

The initial stages of committee consideration are similar for the House and the Senate. The bill first has to be referred to committee. This is largely automatic for most bills; they go to the standing committee with jurisdiction over the content of the bill. A bill to change the way agricultural subsidies on cotton are considered would start, for example, with the House Committee on Agriculture. In some cases, a bill might logically fall into more than one committee's jurisdiction, and here the Speaker exercises a good deal of power. He or she can choose the committee that will consider the bill or even refer the same bill to more than one committee. This gives the Speaker important leverage in the House because he or she often knows which committees are likely to be more or less favorable to different bills. Senators do not worry quite as much about where bills are referred because they have much greater opportunity to make changes later in the process than do representatives. We'll see why when we discuss floor consideration.

Bills then move on to subcommittees, where they may, or may not, get serious consideration. Most bills die in committee because the committee members either don't care about the issue (it isn't on their agenda) or actively want to block it. Even if the bill's life is brief, the member who introduced it can still campaign as its champion. In fact, a motivation for the introduction of many bills is not that the member seriously believes they have a chance of passing but that the member wants to be seen back home as taking some action on the issue.

When a subcommittee decides to consider a bill, it will hold hearings—testimony from experts, interest groups, executive department secretaries and undersecretaries, and even other members of Congress. The subcommittee deliberates and votes the bill back to the full committee. There the committee further considers the bill and makes changes and revisions in a process called *markup*. If the committee votes in favor of the final version of the bill, it goes forward to the floor. Here, however, a crucial difference exists between the House and the Senate.

In the House, bills go from the standing committee to the Rules Committee. This committee, highly responsive to the Speaker of the House, gives each bill a "rule," which includes when and how the bill will be considered. Some bills go out under an "open rule," which means that any amendments can be proposed and added as long as they are germane, or relevant, to the legislation under consideration. More typically, especially for important bills, the House leadership gains more control by imposing restrictive rules that limit the time for debate and restrict the amendments that can be offered. For example, if the leadership knows that there is a lot of sentiment in favor of action on a tax cut, it can control the form of the tax cut by having a restrictive rule that prohibits any amendments to the committee's bill. In this way, even members who would like to vote for a different kind of tax cut face pressure to go along with the bill because they can't amend it; it is either this tax cut or none at all, and they don't want to vote against a tax cut. Thus, for some bills, not only can the House Rules Committee make or break the bill, but it can also influence the bill's final content.

Unlike the House, the Senate generally guarantees all bills an "open rule" by default and there is no germane rule that says that an amendment must logically relate to the policy being considered. The majority leader, usually in consultation with the minority leader, schedules legislation for consideration. Their control, however, is fairly weak because any senator can introduce any proposal as an amendment to any bill, sometimes called a rider, and get a vote on it. Thus senators have access to the floor for whatever they want in a way that is denied to representatives. Furthermore, whereas in the House the rule for each bill stipulates how long a member can debate, the Senate's tradition of "unlimited debate," as we saw in the *What's at Stake?* that opened this chapter, means a member can talk indefinitely. Senators opposed to a bill can **filibuster**, in an effort to tie up the floor of the Senate in nonstop debate to stop the Senate from voting on a bill. A filibuster can be stopped only by **cloture**. Cloture, a vote to cut off debate and end a filibuster, requires an extraordinary three-fifths majority, or sixty votes. A dramatic example of a filibuster occurred when southern senators attempted to derail Minnesota senator Hubert Humphrey's efforts to pass the Civil Rights Act of 1964. First, they filibustered Humphrey's attempt to bypass the Judiciary Committee, whose chair, a southern Democrat, opposed the bill. This was known as the "minibuster" and it stopped Senate business for sixteen days.[41] It was considered "mini" because from March 30 to June 30, 1964, these same southern Democrats filibustered the Civil Rights Act and created a twenty-week backlog of legislation.[42] Often these senators resorted to reading the telephone book in order to adhere to the rules of constant debate. The consequence of a filibuster, as this example suggests, is that a minority in the Senate is able to thwart the will of the majority. Even one single senator can halt action on a bill by placing a hold on the legislation, notifying the majority party's leadership that he or she plans to filibuster a bill. That threat alone often keeps the leadership from going forward with the legislation.[43]

Recent congressional sessions have seen a striking increase in the use of the filibuster. Rarely used until the 1960s, when southern Democrats unpacked it to derail civil rights legislation, it has become increasingly popular, with congresses now averaging around forty attempts at cloture. Only about a third of these have been successful in mustering the necessary sixty votes, so a minority has prevailed over the majority most of the time. The use of the filibuster is considered hardball politics; its greater use in the past fifteen to twenty years reflects the growing party polarization we discussed earlier. In the highly charged partisan atmosphere of the U.S. Senate today, use of the filibuster and the consequent cloture motions reached an all-time high in the 110th Congress (2006–2008) with little prospect for change.[44]

A Bill Becomes a Law

Clearly, a bill must survive a number of challenges to get out of Congress alive. A bill can be killed, or just left to die, in a subcommittee, the full committee, the House Rules Committee, or any of the corresponding committees in the Senate, and, of course, it has to pass votes on the floors of both houses.

There are multiple ways for the House of Representatives to vote, including a simple voice vote ("all in favor say 'aye'"), but most important legislation requires each member to explicitly vote "yea" or "nay" in what are called **roll call votes**. These are a matter of public record and are monitored by the media, interest groups, and sometimes even constituents. A variety of influences come to bear on the senator or member of Congress as he or she decides how to vote. Studies have long shown that party affiliation is the most important factor in determining roll call voting, but constituency also plays a big role, as does presidential politics. Busy representatives often take cues from other members whom they respect and generally agree with.[45] They also consult with their staff, some of whom may be very knowledgeable about certain legislation. Finally, interest groups have an effect on how a member of Congress votes, but studies suggest that their impact is much less than we usually imagine. Lobbying and campaign contributions buy access to members so that the lobbyists can try to make their case, but they do not actually buy votes.[46]

The congressperson or senator who is committed to passing or defeating a particular bill cannot do so alone, however, and he or she looks to find like-minded members for political support. Once a representative or senator knows where he or she stands on a bill, there are a variety of methods for influencing the fate of that bill, many of them effective long before the floor vote takes place. Congressional politics—using the rules to get what one wants—can entail many complex strategies, including controlling the agenda (whether a bill ever reaches the floor), proposing amendments to a bill, influencing its timing, and forming coalitions with other members to pass or block a bill. Knowing how to use the rules makes a huge difference in congressional politics.

If a bill emerges from the roll call process in both houses relatively intact, it goes to the president, unless the chambers passed different versions. If the bills differ, then the two versions go to a conference committee made up of members of both houses, usually the senior members of the standing committees that reported the bills. If the conferees can reach an agreement on a revision, then the revised bill goes back to each house to be voted up or down; no amendments are permitted at this point. If the bill is rejected, that chamber sends it back to the conference committee for a second try.

Finally, any bill still alive at this point moves to the president's desk. He has several choices of action. The simplest choice is that he signs the bill and it becomes law. If he doesn't like it, however, he can veto it. In that case, the president sends it back to the originating house of Congress with a short explanation of what he does not like about the bill. Congress can then attempt a **veto override**, which requires a two-thirds vote of both houses. Because the president can usually count on the support of *at least* one-third of *one* of the houses, the veto is a powerful negative tool; it is hard for Congress to accomplish legislative goals that are opposed by the president. They can, however, bundle policies together, so that the bill that arrives on the president's desk contains elements that he would normally want to veto along with legislation that is very hard for him to turn down.

The president can also kill a bill with the **pocket veto**, which occurs when Congress sends a bill to the president within ten days of the end of a session and the president does not sign it. The bill fails simply because Congress is not in session to consider a veto override. The president might choose this option when he wants to veto a bill without drawing much public attention to it. Similarly, the president can do nothing, and if Congress remains in session, a bill will automatically become law in ten days, excluding Sundays. This seldom-used option signals presidential dislike for a bill but not enough dislike for him to use his veto power.

The striking aspect of our legislative process is how many factors have to fall into place for a bill to become law. At every step there are ways to kill bills, and a well-organized group of members in the relatively decentralized Congress has a good chance, in most cases, of blocking a bill to which these members strongly object. In terms of procedures, Congress is better set up to ensure that bills do not impinge on organized interests than it is to facilitate coherent, well-coordinated attacks on the nation's problems. Once again, we see a balance between representation and effective lawmaking, with the procedures of passage tilted toward the forces for representation.

Citizenship and Congress
Public frustration with a slow-moving institution

Since 1974, periodic Gallup polls have showed that from half to less than a third of the public "approves of the way Congress is handling its job," with levels of approval dipping to 16 percent in 2010. At least four factors help to explain why citizens are not always very happy with Congress. First, some candidates encourage a negative image of the institution they want to join—running for Congress by running against it, and declaring their intention to fight against special interests, bureaucrats, and the general incompetence of Washington.[47] Second, in the post-Watergate wave of investigative reporting, media coverage of Congress has gotten more negative, even though impartial observers say that Congress is probably less corrupt than ever before. Third, since the 1970s, the law requires that information about how much campaigns cost and who contributes to them must be made public, casting a shadow of suspicion on the entire process and raising the concern that congressional influence can be bought. Finally, citizens are turned off by what they see as the incessant bickering and partisanship in Congress.[48]

Given the reasons why many Americans are unhappy with Congress, many of the reforms currently on the agenda are not likely to change their minds. One of the most popular reforms being advocated is term limits. The specific proposals vary, but the intent is to limit the number of terms a member of Congress can serve, usually to somewhere between eight and twelve years. Term limits might work if there were evidence that serving in Congress corrupts good people, but there is no evidence of this at all. It just puts them in the public eye.

Other reforms, however, might make a difference in public support for Congress. Campaign finance reform, for instance, could have a significant impact. Institutional reforms might be able to speed up congressional lawmaking and reduce the need to compromise on details.

Such reforms, however, will probably not fundamentally change how the public feels about Congress. Congress does have the power to act, and when it is unified and sufficiently motivated, it usually does. When Congress reflects a sharply divided society, however, it has a harder time getting things done. It is unable to act *because it is a representative institution,* not because members are inattentive to their districts or in the grip of special interests. Furthermore, Congress has more incentives on a daily basis to be a representative institution than a national lawmaking body. It is important to remember, too, that this is not entirely an accident. It was the founders' intention to create a legislature that would not move hastily or without deliberation. The irony is that the founders' mixed bag of incentives works so well that Congress today often does not move very much at all.

The truth is that democracy is messy. Bickering arises in Congress because members represent many different Americans with varied interests and goals. It is precisely our bickering, our inefficiency, and our willingness to compromise, to give and take, that preserve the freedoms Americans hold dear. It is the nature of representative government.[49]

We conclude where we began. Congress has the dual goals of lawmaking and representation. These goals often and necessarily conflict. The practice of congressional politics is fascinating to many close-up observers but looks less appealing to average citizens, watching the nightly news and following political campaigns from afar. It is important to understand that this view of Congress stems from the conflicting expectations we place on the body more than the failings of the people we send to Washington.

▶ What's at Stake Revisited

We've learned enough about politics to know that Congress is a rule-based institution, and as always, the rules determine who wins and who loses. One of the trickier rules is the filibuster, which as we saw in the *What's at Stake?* earlier in this chapter, has its ardent foes as well as its passionate defenders.

But what is true here, of course, is that the opponents and defenders change sides with their electoral fortunes. Republicans love the filibuster when they are in the minority and it enables them to block a Democratic majority, but not so much when it's the other way around. In 2005, Republican Senate majority leader Bill Frist was so frustrated with Democratic filibusters of President Bush's judicial nominees that he threatened to use what Republicans were calling the "nuclear option." Essentially, Frist would have called on the presiding officer of the Senate for a ruling on the constitutionality of the use of the judicial filibuster and that officer (probably Bush's vice president, Dick Cheney) would have ruled it unconstitutional. Moderate Republicans warned that their party would not always be in the majority and that they would someday regret it if they eliminated the traditional protection for a Senate minority. Along with moderate Democrats, they crafted a compromise that averted the nuclear option. And as that example makes clear, Democrats are not nearly as opposed to the filibuster when they are in the minority as Speaker Pelosi's comments that the filibuster is a "60-vote stranglehold on the future"[50] would suggest.

The filibuster is a rule that gives the minority power, and both parties are aware that one or the other of them will always be in the minority. As we have seen, however, the use of the filibuster has skyrocketed in the recent past, making it the norm even for routine legislation in the Senate. Rather than debating a bill and registering their disapproval by voting against it, opposing senators prevent the debate from happening in the first place. In summer 2010, Democratic senator Russ Feingold from Wisconsin actually joined a Republican filibuster of financial regulatory reform. Republicans were opposed to the bill because they felt it infringed on the rights of business, and Feingold opposed it because he felt that it didn't infringe enough on the rights of business, but no matter. Politics makes strange bedfellows, and it wasn't until Majority Leader Harry Reid peeled off the support of a couple of Republicans that the vote went through.

Americans are advocates of the idea of supporting a downtrodden minority against a tyrannical majority, but in the case of the filibuster, it is the minority that threatens to become tyrannical, holding a majority of senators and, by implication, the voters who elected them, hostage. One of the reasons that Americans don't like their Congress is because so often legislative business gets mired down in partisan wrangling; the filibuster is one more rule by which this can take place.

In 2007, when the Democrats had only a 51–49 majority in the Senate, former Democratic congressman David Obey said: "They [the public] think we have control of the Senate while we merely have custody. They think that we can control the

Senate when in fact we are nine votes short of having the 60 votes that you need to actually run the Senate. So the Senate is a choke point on everything."[51]

Fearing rapid political change, the American founders built a good deal of gridlock into their constitutional design, with checks and balances slowing the policy-making process down to a snail's pace under the best of circumstances. The filibuster can grind the snail's pace to a complete halt. Norm Ornstein, of the conservative American Enterprise Institute, says, "This is a sharp increase in the use of a filibuster as a routine mechanism. The Senate is set up culturally not to act on anything quickly. That's a good thing. But there can be too much of a good thing."[52]

Politicians, though, are unlikely to agree. Although Democrats have tried to weaken it, changing the number of votes needed for cloture from sixty-seven to an easier-to-achieve sixty in 1975, and although they talk of exercising a nuclear option of their own, the chances of reform are slim. One thing is sure in American politics: although the Democrats didn't lose the majority in the 2010 election, they will lose it someday, and the filibuster will seem like a route to righteous opposition when they do.

▶ Summary With Key Terms

Members of Congress are responsible for both **representation** (190) and **national lawmaking** (190). These two duties are often at odds because what is good for a local **constituency** (190) may not be beneficial for the country as a whole.

Representation style takes four forms—**policy representation** (190), **allocative representation** (190) (including the infamous **pork barrel** [190] spending), **casework** (190), and **symbolic representation** (191)—and congresspersons attempt to excel at all four. However, since the legislative process designed by the founders is meant to be very slow, representatives have fewer incentives to concentrate on national lawmaking when reelection interests, and therefore local interests, are more pressing.

The founders created our government with a structure of checks and balances centered around our **bicameral legislature** (191). Not only do the two houses check each other, but Congress can check the other two branches, including the prerogative of **congressional oversight** (194), which allows Congress to keep tabs on the executive, and the House and the Senate may be checked by either the president or the courts. Congress can be very powerful but must demonstrate unusual strength and consensus to override presidential vetoes and to amend the Constitution.

Citizens and representatives interact in congressional elections. Seats are allocated among states through the process of **reapportionment** (196), and the districts are drawn up through **redistricting** (196) to correct for malapportionment. **Gerrymandering** (196) and **racial gerrymandering** (197) make redistricting a highly political process. Congressional races can be influenced, among other things, by the powerful **incumbency advantage** (198), the presidential **coattail effect** (199), and the phenomenon of the **midterm loss** (199).

Congress is organized by the political parties, which are characterized by increasing degrees of **party polarization** (203). The **majority party** (203) in each house has considerable power because it selects the leadership positions, including the **Speaker of the House** (204), filled by the party caucuses. The business of Congress—crafting legislation and engaging in oversight—is done in committees where the leadership is determined by party leaders and by the **seniority system** (205). **Standing committees** (207), including the powerful **House Rules Committee** (208), do most of the work, although **select committees** (208), **joint committees** (208), and **conference committees** (208) are key as well.

Laws get placed on the **legislative agenda** (212) in a variety of ways, often through the efforts of **policy entrepreneurship** (212). They go first to committee before being reported onto the floor, where they are discussed, debated, and subject to a **roll call vote** (215). In the Senate, the **filibuster** (214) can prevent a vote unless **cloture** (214) is obtained. When the bill emerges from Congress it goes to the president, who can sign it or veto it (or kill it with the less public **pocket veto** [216]), subject to a **veto override** (216) by both houses.

Explore this subject further with suggested readings, movies, and web sites at http://republic-brief.cqpress.com, where you'll also find study aids, practice quizzes, flash cards, and Internet exercises.

Chapter 7

The Presidency

▶ What's at Stake?

When President George W. Bush signed the newly passed reauthorization of the Patriot Act in March 2006, he did so with a public and patriotic flourish. Sitting at a desk behind a banner with the words "Protecting the Homeland" on a red, white, and blue background, he proclaimed that this legislation was "vital to win the war on terror and to protect the American people."[1]

The news cameras that day showed a bunch of men smiling for the cameras. Bush was happy because he had gotten what he wanted from Congress on this bill—among other things, beefed-up police powers for the Federal Bureau of Investigation. Congress was happy because the bill contained carefully crafted oversight provisions to keep those new powers in check: the Justice Department, part of the executive branch, was required to keep Congress informed about how the FBI was using the powers granted to them by the bill. Everyone was happy as they grinned for the cameras while the president wielded his pen.

But out of sight of public view, something was happening that was going to make Congress, or at least the members of it who did not belong to the president's party, extremely unhappy, indeed.

Very quietly, without the public display that greeted the bill's signing, the White House issued a document saying that the president didn't really consider himself bound by the requirement that Congress be kept informed, and he reserved the right to withhold information if he deemed that it would "impair foreign relations, national security, the deliberative process of the executive, or the performance of the executive's constitutional duties."[2]

This document, known as a signing statement, was intended to "clarify" the president's understanding of what a bill meant and how he believed it ought to be enforced. Most people in Congress didn't even notice that the signing statement had been added, but those who did were furious. Democratic senator Patrick Leahy from Vermont called the signing statement "nothing short of a radical effort to manipulate the constitutional separation of powers and evade accountability and responsibility for following the law." He added, "The president's constitutional duty is to faithfully execute the laws as written by the Congress, not cherry-pick the laws he decides he wants to follow. It is our duty to ensure, by means of congressional oversight, that he does so."[3]

Bush did not invent the signing statement. Since the 1800s, presidents had been issuing statements if they thought a part of a bill they signed was unconstitutional, especially if they thought it unconstitutionally restricted executive power, but these signing statements, recorded in the *Federal Register,* along with the legislation they refer to, had been used only sparingly. Typically presidents used the presidential veto to block legislation they didn't like, whereupon Congress could override the veto if the bill had sufficient support.

But unlike his predecessors, Bush had not vetoed a single bill by the time he issued the Patriot Act signing statement, after more than five years in office. Instead he had issued a huge number of signing statements, over 750, compared to 232 by his father in his four years in the White House, and only 140 issued by Bill Clinton in his eight years. Bush's successor, President Barack Obama, would veto two bills and issue only about a dozen signing statements in his first two years in office.

Many of Bush's signing statements reflected a strong commitment to the theory of the *unitary executive,* a controversial legal view held by members of the administration that the Constitution requires that all executive power be held only by the president and, therefore, cannot be delegated to or wielded by any other branch. Consequently Bush's signing statements reserved the right to ignore, among other things, an anti-torture law, a law forbidding him to order troops into combat in Colombia, a law requiring him to inform Congress if he wanted to divert funds from congressionally authorized programs to start up secret operations, a law preventing the military from using intelligence about Americans that was gathered unconstitutionally, a law that required the Justice Department to inform Congress about how the FBI was using domestic wiretapping, laws that created whistleblower protection for federal employees, and laws that required the federal government to follow affirmative action principles.[4]

Critics of the Bush administration howled when they realized what was going on, accusing Bush of doing an end run around Congress and claiming that he was setting up himself, and thus the executive branch, as the ultimate decider of what is constitutional, a function generally thought to belong to the Supreme Court. "There is no question that this administration has been involved in a very carefully thought-out, systematic process of expanding presidential power at the expense of the other branches of government," said one scholar.[5]

Defenders advised calm, saying that Bush didn't actually violate all those laws, but he simply reserved the right to do so as a way of letting Congress and the bureaucracy know how he interprets the legislation he has signed. One law professor who used to work for the Bush administration said of signing statements, "Nobody reads them. They have no significance. Nothing in the world changes by the publication of a signing statement."[6]

Who is right here, critics or champions? Are signing statements terribly damaging wounds to the Constitution, or meaningless pieces of paper? Are all signing statements equal? What exactly was at stake in Bush's expanded use of the tactic, and in his adherence to the unitary theory of the executive? We return to these questions after we look more closely at the powers and limitations of the U.S. president.

Ask just about anyone who the most powerful person in the world is and the answer will probably be "the president of the United States." He, or perhaps someday soon, she, is the elected leader of the nation that has one of the most powerful economies, one of the greatest military forces, and the longest-running representative government that the world has ever seen. Media coverage enforces this belief in the importance of the U.S. president. The networks and news services all have full-time reporters assigned to the White House. The evening news tells us what the president has been doing that day; even if he only went to church or played a round of golf, his activities are news. This attention is what one scholar calls the presidency's "monopolization of the public space."[7] It means that the president is the first person the citizens and the media think of when anything of significance happens, whether it is a terrorist attack, a natural disaster, or a big drop in the stock market. We look to the president to solve our problems and to represent the nation in our times of struggle, tragedy, and triumph. The irony is that the U.S. Constitution provides for a relatively weak chief executive, and the American public's and, indeed, the world's expectations of the president constitute a major challenge for modern presidents.

The challenge of meeting the public's expectations is made all the more difficult because so many political actors have something at stake in the office of the presidency. Obviously, the president himself wants to widen his authority to act so that he can deliver on campaign promises and extend the base of support for himself and his party. Although the formal rules of American politics create only limited presidential powers, informal rules help him expand them. Citizens, both individually and in groups, often have high expectations of what the president will do for them and for the country, and they may be willing to allow him more expanded powers to act. An unpopular president, however, will face a public eager to limit his options and ready to complain about any perceived step beyond the restrictive constitutional bounds. Congress, too, stands to gain or lose based on the president's success. Members of the president's party will share some of his popularity, but in general the more power the president has, the less Congress has. This is especially true if the majority party in Congress is different from the president's. So Congress has a stake in limiting what the president may do.

This chapter tells the story of who gets what from the American presidency and how they get it. You will learn about the double expectations gap between what Americans want the president to do and what he can deliver, the evolution of the American presidency from its constitutional origins to the modern presidency, the president's struggle for power, the organization and functioning of the executive office, and the role of presidential style.

The Double Expectations Gap
Public expectations and the reality of what the president actually can do

Presidential scholars note that one of the most remarkable things about the modern presidency is how much the office has become intertwined with public expectations and perceptions. The implication, of course, is that we expect one thing and get something less—that there is a gap between our expectations and reality. In fact, we can identify two different expectations gaps when it comes to popular perceptions of the presidency. One is between the very great promises that presidents make, and that we want them to keep, on the one hand, and the president's limited constitutional power to fulfill those promises on the other. The second gap is between two conflicting roles that the president is expected to play, between the formal and largely symbolic role of head of state and the far more political role of head of government. These two expectations gaps form a framework for much of our discussion of the American presidency.

The Gap Between Presidential Promises and the Powers of the Office

The first gap between what the public expects the president to do and what he can actually accomplish is of relatively recent vintage. Through the 1930s the presidency in the United States was pretty much the office the founders had planned, an administrative position dwarfed by the extensive legislative power of Congress. During Franklin Roosevelt's New Deal, however, public expectations of the president changed. Roosevelt did not act like an administrator with limited powers; he acted like a leader whose strength and imagination could be relied on by an entire nation of citizens to rescue them from the crisis of the Great Depression. Over the course of Roosevelt's four terms in office, the public became used to seeing the president in just this light, and future presidential candidates promised similarly grand visions of policy in their efforts to win supporters. Rather than strengthening the office to allow presidents to deliver on such promises, however, the only constitutional change in the presidency weakened it. In reaction to Roosevelt's four elections, the Twenty-second Amendment was passed, limiting the number of terms a president can serve to two.

Today's presidents suffer the consequences of this history. On the one hand, we voters demand that they woo us with promises to change the course of the country, to solve our problems, and to enact visionary policy. On the other hand, we have not increased the powers of the office to meet this greatly expanded job description. Thus, to meet our expectations, the president must wheel, deal, bargain, and otherwise gather the support needed to overcome his constitutional limitations. And if the president doesn't meet our expectations, or if the country doesn't thrive the way we think it should, even if it isn't his fault and there's nothing he could have done to change things, we hold him accountable and vote him out of office. Some evidence of this can be seen in the fates of the past nine presidents. Only four have been reelected to a second term, and of those, Nixon resigned after Watergate, Ronald Reagan faced the Iran-contra scandal and his party lost its majority in the Senate, Bill Clinton was impeached, and George W. Bush won reelection by the smallest margin of any reelected president and left office with the lowest level of public approval of any president finishing two full terms. The inability of some of our most skilled politicians to survive for even two full terms of office suggests that our expectations of what can be done potentially outstrip the resources and powers of the position.

The Gap Between Conflicting Roles

The second expectations gap that presidents face is in part a product of the first. Since we now expect our presidents to perform as high-level legislators as well as administrators, holders of this office need to be adept politicians. That is, today's presidents need to be able to get their hands dirty in the day-to-day political activities of the nation or, as we just said, to wheel, deal, and bargain. As **head of government**, the president is supposed to run the government, make law, and function as the head of a political party, all functions that will result in some citizens winning more than others, some losing, and some becoming angry. These political functions have expanded greatly since Roosevelt's time.

> Some countries, like Britain, separate the head of state . . . from the head of government . . . but in the United States we expect the president to juggle both roles.

Even so, the image of their president as a politician—an occupational class not held in high esteem by most Americans— often doesn't sit well with citizens who also want their president to be **head of state**, a role above politics in which he serves as a unifying symbol of all that is good and noble about America. In this capacity, the president performs functions such as greeting other heads of state, attending state funerals, tossing out the first baseball of the season, hosting the annual Easter egg hunt on the White House lawn, and consoling survivors of national tragedies. Some countries, like Britain, separate the head of state (the queen) from the head of government (the prime minister), allowing each to do his or her job untarnished by comparisons with the other, but in the United States we expect the president to juggle both roles.

Thus not only must the president contend with a job in which he is required to do far more than he is given the power to do, but he also must cultivate the talents to perform two very contradictory roles: the essentially political head of government, who makes decisions about who will get scarce resources, and the elevated and apolitical head of state, who should unify rather than divide the public. Few presidents are skilled enough to carry off both roles with aplomb; the very talents that make someone adept in one role often disqualify him from being good in the other.

The Evolution of the American Presidency
From restrained administrator to energetic problem-solver

The framers designed a much more limited presidency than the one we have today. The constitutional provisions give most of the policymaking powers to Congress, or at least require power sharing and cooperation. For most of our history, this arrangement was not a problem. As leaders of a rural nation with a relatively restrained governmental apparatus, presidents through the nineteenth century were largely content with a limited authority that rested on the grants of powers provided in the Constitution. But the presidency of Franklin Roosevelt, beginning in 1932, ushered in a new era in presidential politics.

The Framers' Design for a Limited Executive

The presidency was not a preoccupation of the framers when they met in Philadelphia in 1787, since the legislature was presumed by all to be the real engine of the national political system. The breakdown of the national government under the Articles of Confederation demonstrated the need for some form of a central executive, however. Nervous about trusting the general public to choose the executive, the founders provided for an electoral college, a group of people who would be chosen by the states for the sole purpose of electing the president. The assumption was that this body would be made up of leading citizens who would exercise care and good judgment in casting their ballots and who would not make postelection claims on him. Because of their experience with King George III, the founders also wished to avoid the concentration of power that could be abused by a strong executive. Their compromise was a relatively limited scope of presidential authority as laid out in the Constitution.

Qualifications and Conditions of Office

The framers' conception of a limited presidency can be seen in the brief attention the office receives in the Constitution. Article II is short and not very precise. It provides some basic details on the office of the presidency:

- The president is chosen by the Electoral College to serve four-year terms. The number of terms was unlimited until 1951 when, in reaction to Roosevelt's unprecedented four terms in office, the Constitution was amended to limit the president to two terms.
- The president must be a natural-born citizen of the United States, at least thirty-five years old, and a resident for at least fourteen years.
- The president is succeeded by the vice president if he dies or is removed from office. The Constitution does not specify who becomes president in the event that the vice president, too, is unable to serve, but in 1947 Congress passed the Presidential Succession Act, which establishes the order of succession after the vice president: Speaker of the House, president pro tempore of the Senate, and the cabinet secretaries in the order in which their offices were established.
- The president can be removed from office by impeachment and conviction by the House of Representatives and the Senate for "treason, bribery, or other high crimes and misdemeanors." The process of removal involves two steps: First, after an in-depth investigation, the House votes to impeach by a simple majority vote, which charges the president with a crime. Second, the Senate tries the president on the articles of impeachment and can convict by a two-thirds majority vote. Only two American presidents, Andrew Johnson and Bill Clinton, have been impeached (in 1868 and 1998, respectively), but neither was convicted. The power of impeachment is meant to be a check on the president, but it is often used for partisan purposes. Impeachment resolutions were filed against Reagan (over the invasion of Grenada and the Iran-contra affair), George H. W. Bush (over Iran-contra), and George W. Bush (for a host of offenses from falsifying evidence justifying the war in Iraq to condoning torture to failing to respond adequately to Hurricane Katrina). Republicans have talked about impeaching President Obama for various causes—from allegedly offering a job to a Senate candidate to encourage him not to run, to encouraging manipulation of legislative procedures in order to get health care reform passed.[8] To date, none of the Obama charges have been filed as impeachment resolutions, however, and few of the resolutions filed about other presidents made it to the floor for a vote in the House, in part because such actions virtually bring governing to a halt and are not popular with the public.[9]

The Constitutional Powers of the President

The Constitution uses vague language to discuss some presidential powers and is silent on the range and limits of others. It is precisely this ambiguity that allowed the Constitution to be ratified by both those who wanted a strong executive power and those who did not. In addition, this vagueness has allowed the powers of the president to expand over time without constitutional amendment. We can think of the president's constitutional powers as falling into three areas: executive authority to administer government, and legislative and judicial power to check the other two branches.

Executive Powers

Article II, Section 1, of the Constitution begins, "The executive power shall be vested in a president of the United States of America." However, the document does not explain exactly what "executive power" entails, and scholars and presidents through much of our history have debated the extent of these powers.[10] Section 3 states the president "shall take care that the laws be faithfully executed." Herein lies much of the executive authority; the president is the **chief administrator** of the nation's laws. This means that he is the chief executive officer of the country, the person who, more than anyone else, is held responsible for agencies of the national government and the implementation of national policy.

The Constitution also specifies that the president, with the approval of the majority of the Senate, will appoint the heads of departments, who will oversee the work of implementation. These heads, who have come to be known collectively as the **cabinet**, report to the president. Today the president is responsible for the appointments of more than four thousand federal employees: cabinet and lower administrative officers, federal judges, military officers, and members of the diplomatic corp. His responsibilities place him at the top of a vast federal bureaucracy. But his control of the federal bureaucracy is limited because, even though he can make a large number of appointments, he is not able to fire many of the people he hires.

Other constitutional powers place the president, as **commander-in-chief**, at the head of the command structure for the entire military establishment. The Constitution gives Congress the power to declare war, but as the commander-in-chief, the president has the practical ability to wage war. These two powers, meant to check each other, instead provide for a battleground on which Congress and the president struggle for the power to control military operations. After the controversial Vietnam War, which was waged by Presidents Lyndon Johnson and Richard Nixon but never officially declared by Congress, Congress passed the War Powers Act of 1973, which was intended to limit the president's power to send troops abroad without congressional approval. Most presidents have ignored the act, however, when they wished to engage in military action abroad, and since public opinion tends to rally around the president at such times, Congress has declined to challenge popular presidential actions. The War Powers Act remains more powerful on paper than in reality.

Finally, under his executive powers, the president is the **chief foreign policy maker**. This role is not spelled out in the Constitution, but the foundation for it is laid in the provision that the president negotiates **treaties**—formal international agreements with other nations—with the approval of two-thirds of the Senate. The president also appoints ambassadors and receives ambassadors of other nations, a power that essentially amounts to determining what nations the United States will recognize.

While the requirement of Senate approval for treaties is meant to check the president's foreign policy power, much of U.S. foreign policy is made by the president through **executive agreements** with other heads of state, which avoids the slower and more cumbersome route of treaty-making.[11] Executive agreements are used much more frequently; over 10,000 have been executed since 1970, compared to fewer than 1,000 treaties.[12] This heavy reliance on executive agreements gives the president considerable power and flexibility in foreign policy. However, even though the executive agreement is a useful and much-used tool, Congress may still thwart the president's intentions by refusing to approve the funds needed to put an agreement into action.

Legislative Powers

Even though the president is the head of the executive branch of government, the Constitution also gives him some legislative power to check Congress. He "shall from time to time give to the Congress information of the state of the union, and recommend to their consideration such measures as he shall judge necessary and expedient." Although the framers' vision of this activity was quite limited, today the president's **State of the Union address**, delivered before the full Congress every January, is a major statement of the president's policy agenda.

The Constitution gives the president the nominal power to convene Congress and, when there is a dispute about when to disband, to adjourn it as well. Before Congress met regularly, this power, though limited, actually meant something. Today we rarely see it invoked. Some executives, such as British prime ministers who can dissolve Parliament and call new elections, have a much more formidable convening power than that available to the U.S. president.

The principal legislative power given the president by the Constitution is the **presidential veto**. If the president objects to a bill passed by the House and the Senate, he can veto it, sending it back to Congress with a message indicating his reasons. Congress can override a veto with a two-thirds vote in each house, but because mustering the two-thirds support is quite difficult, the presidential veto is a substantial power. Even the threat of a presidential veto can have a major impact on getting congressional legislation to fall in line with the administration's preferences.[13] The elder President Bush was particularly successful in using the veto—he used it often against the Democratic Congress and was overridden only once (see Table 7.1). President Clinton never used the veto in 1993 and 1994, when he had Democratic majorities in Congress. However, over his remaining six years in office, when he faced a mostly Republican Congress, he attempted to stop thirty-six bills; Congress was able to override him only twice.

With Republican majorities in the House and the Senate for most of his first term; the unusual atmosphere of bipartisanship that appeared in Washington after

Table 7.1

Presidential Vetoes, Roosevelt to Obama

Years	President	Total vetoes	Regular vetoes	Pocket vetoes	Vetoes over-ridden	Veto success rate
1933–1945	Franklin Roosevelt	635	372	263	9	97.6%
1945–1953	Harry Truman	250	180	70	12	93.3
1953–1961	Dwight Eisenhower	181	73	108	2	97.3
1961–1963	John Kennedy	21	12	9	0	100.0
1963–1969	Lyndon Johnson	30	16	14	0	100.0
1969–1974	Richard Nixon	43	26	17	7	73.1
1974–1977	Gerald Ford	66	48	18	12	75.0
1977–1981	Jimmy Carter	31	13	18	2	84.6
1981–1989	Ronald Reagan	78	39	39	9	76.9
1989–1993	George H. W. Bush	46	29	17*	1	96.6
1993–2001	Bill Clinton	37	36	1	2	94.4
2001–2009	George W. Bush	12	11	1	4	66.7
2009–	Barack Obama	2	1	1	0	100.0

*Although they are counted here, Congress did not recognize two of Bush's pocket vetoes and considered the legislation enacted.

Source: Mitchel A. Sollenberger, "The Presidential Veto and Congressional Procedure" in CRS Report for Congress, updated February 27, 2004, 4. Retrieved from www.senate.gov/reference/resources/pdf/RS21750.pdf; Joseph J. Schatz, "With a Deft and Light Touch, Bush Finds Ways to Win," CQ Weekly, December 11, 2004, 2900–2904; 2005–2008 data from CRS Report, "Regular Vetoes and Pocket Vetoes: An Overview," www.senate.gov/reference/resources/pdf/RS22188.pdf, July 18, 2008. Veto success rate calculated by authors.

September 11, 2001; and his practice, noted in *What's at Stake?*, of using signing statements to signal his displeasure with parts of the legislation he signed, George W. Bush joined John Quincy Adams and Thomas Jefferson as the only presidents who did not veto a bill during their first term.[14] With the switch of congressional control to the Democratic Party following the 2006 election, however, things changed, and Bush had vetoed a dozen bills by July 2008, a third of which were overridden by Congress. With a Democratic Congress during his first years in office, President Obama had little cause to veto bills; the only veto he issued in his first year and a half in office was one that rejected a spending bill similar to one he had already signed, what the White House described as "a housekeeping move."[15] Congress has regularly sought to get around the obstacle of presidential vetoes by packaging a number of items together in a bill. Traditionally, presidents have had to sign a complete bill or reject the whole thing. Thus, for example, Congress regularly adds such things as a building project or a tax break for a state industry onto, say, a military appropriations bill that the president wants. Often presidents calculate that it is best to accept such add-ons, even if they think them unjustified or wasteful, in order to get passed what they judge to be important legislation.

Another of the president's key legislative powers comes from the vice president's role as presiding officer of the Senate. Although the vice president rarely actually presides over the Senate, Article I, Section 3, says that the he may cast a tie-breaking vote when the 100-member Senate is evenly divided. The fact that a president can count on his vice president to break a tie when the Senate is split over controversial legislation is an often underappreciated legislative power.

Although the Constitution does not grant the president the power to make law, his power to do so has grown over time and now is generally accepted. Presidents can issue **executive orders** (not to be confused with the executive agreements he can make with other nations), which are supposed to be clarifications of how laws passed by Congress are to be implemented by specific agencies. Some of the most significant presidential actions have come from executive orders, including President Franklin Roosevelt's order to hold Japanese Americans in internment camps in World War II, President Truman's order that black and white military troops be integrated, President Kennedy's and President Johnson's affirmative action programs, and many of the post–September 11 security measures, such as the establishment of military tribunals for cases against terrorists. Since executive orders are not Congress-made laws, a new president can reverse any of his predecessor's orders that he wants to, something George W. Bush did more thoroughly than previous presidents.[16] After the Democrats lost their filibuster-proof majority in the Senate in 2010, President Obama made contingency plans to execute some parts of his agenda concerning energy, the environment, and fiscal responsibility via executive order.[17]

Judicial Powers

Presidents can have tremendous long-term impact on the judiciary, but in the short run their powers over the courts are meager. Their continuing impact comes from nominating judges to the federal courts, including the Supreme Court. The political philosophies of individual judges influence significantly how they interpret the law, and this is especially important for Supreme Court justices, who are the final arbiters of constitutional meaning. Since judges serve for life, presidential appointments have a long-lasting effect. For instance, today's Supreme Court is considered to be distinctly more conservative than its immediate predecessors, due to the appointments made by Presidents Reagan and Bush in the 1980s and early 1990s. Moreover, President Reagan is credited by many with having ushered in a "judicial revolution." He, together with his successor, George H. W. Bush, appointed 550 of the 837 federal judges, most of them conservatives. Clinton appointed moderates to the courts, angering many Democrats, who felt that his appointees should have been more liberal. President George W. Bush revived the conservative trend that was halted under Clinton.[18] Although President Obama's pick of Sonia Sotomayor for the Supreme Court pleased liberals, his nomination of Elena Kagan caused some to worry that his selections would follow Clinton's more moderate record.[19] In general, Obama's choices for the judiciary are fairly liberal, but because he has been slower than Bush to make appointments and the appointments he has made have often been blocked by Republicans in the Senate, he has not yet made as distinctive a mark on the courts.[20]

The presidential power to appoint is limited to an extent by the constitutional requirement for Senate approval of federal judges. Traditionally, most nominees have been approved, with occasional exceptions. Sometimes rejection stems from questions about the candidate's competence, but in other instances rejection is based more on style and judicial philosophy. The Democratic-led Senate's rejection of President Reagan's very conservative Supreme Court nominee Robert Bork in 1987 is one of the more controversial cases.[21] Some observers believe that the battle over the Bork nomination signaled the end of deference to presidents and opened up the approval process to endless challenges and partisan bickering.[22] Today the increased party polarization in Congress, the frequent threat of the filibuster, and the use of anonymous holds in the Senate allow the party opposing the president to hold up nominations so that many federal judgeships remain open, causing a backlog of cases. Both parties play the game as they try to prevent undesired ideological shifts in the federal courts.[23]

A president's choice of judges for the federal district courts is also limited by the tradition of **senatorial courtesy**, whereby senior senators of the president's party from the states in which the appointees reside have what amounts to a veto power over the president's choice. If presidents should ignore the custom of senatorial courtesy and push a nomination unpopular with one of the home state senators, fellow senators will generally honor one another's requests and refuse to confirm the appointee.

The least controversial way a president can try to influence a court decision is to have the Justice Department invest resources in arguing a case. The third-ranking member of the Justice Department, the **solicitor general**, is a presidential appointee whose job it is to argue cases for the government before the Supreme Court. The solicitor general is thus a bridge between the executive and the judiciary, not only deciding which cases the government will appeal to the Court, but also filing petitions stating the government's (usually the president's) position on cases to which the government is not even a party. These petitions, called *amicus curiae* ("friend of the court") briefs, are taken very seriously by the Court. The government is successful in its litigation more often than any other litigant, winning over two-thirds of its cases in the past half-century, and often having its arguments cited by the justices themselves in their opinions.[24]

One additional judicial power granted to the president by the Constitution is the **pardoning power**, which allows a president to exempt a person, convicted or not, from punishment for a crime. This power descends from a traditional power of kings as the court of last resort and thus a check on the courts. Pardons are usually not controversial, although they have occasionally backfired in dramatic ways when they are seen as partisan moves rather than disinterested checks on the judiciary.[25] For instance, after President Gerald Ford's post-Watergate pardon of Richard Nixon, Ford experienced a tremendous backlash that may have contributed to his 1976 loss to Jimmy Carter. Similarly, President George H. W. Bush's pardon—after he had already lost to Bill Clinton in 1992—of the people who could conceivably have been charged with wrongdoing in the Iran-contra affair was received extremely negatively. Clinton's turn came in 2001 when, shortly after he left office, he was investigated for trading political favors and contributions for pardons.

The Traditional Presidency

The presidency that the founders created and outlined in the Constitution is not the presidency of today. In fact, so clearly have the effective rules governing the presidency changed that scholars speak of the era of the traditional presidency, from the founding to the 1930s, and the era of the modern presidency, from the thirties to the present. Although the constitutional powers of the president have been identical in both eras, the interpretation of how far the president can go beyond his constitutional powers has changed dramatically.

The founders' limited vision of the office survived more or less intact for a little over one hundred years, although several early presidents exceeded the powers granted in the Constitution. George Washington expanded the president's foreign policy powers, for instance; Jefferson entered into an agreement for the Louisiana Purchase; Andrew Jackson developed the role of president as popular leader; and Abraham Lincoln, during the emergency conditions of the Civil War, stepped outside his constitutional role to try to save the Union.

These presidents believed that they had what modern scholars call **inherent powers** to fulfill their constitutional duty to "take care that the laws be faithfully executed." Some presidents, like Lincoln, claimed that national security required a broader presidential role. Others held that the president, as our sole representative in foreign affairs, needed a stronger hand abroad than at home. Inherent powers are not listed explicitly in the Constitution but are implied by the powers that are granted, and they have been supported, to some extent, by the Supreme Court.[26] But most nineteenth- and early-twentieth-century presidents, conforming to the founders' expectations, took a more retiring role, causing one observer to claim that "twenty of the twenty-five presidents of the nineteenth century were lords of passivity."[27] The job of the presidency was seen as a primarily administrative office, in which presidential will was clearly subordinate to the will of Congress.

The Modern Presidency

The rural nature of life in the United States changed rapidly in the century and a half after the founding. Government in the nineteenth century sought bit by bit to respond to the new challenges of its changing people and economy, and as it responded, it grew beyond the bounds of the rudimentary administrative structure supervised by George Washington. The crisis of the Great Depression and Franklin Roosevelt's New Deal solution exploded the size of government and changed popular ideas of what government was all about.

Nothing in their prior experience had prepared Americans for the calamity of the Great Depression. Following the stock market crash of October 1929, the economy went into a tailspin. Unemployment soared to 25 percent, and the gross national product (GNP) plunged from around $100 billion in 1928 to less than $60 billion in 1932.[28] President Herbert Hoover held that the U.S. government had only limited powers and responsibility to deal with what was, he believed, a private economic crisis. There was no widespread presumption, as there is today, that the government was responsible for the state of the economy or for alleviating the suffering of its citizens.

The election of Franklin Roosevelt in 1932, and his three reelections, initiated an entirely new level of government activism. For the first time, the national

Stumbling Block to Power
Under the modern presidency, presidents like Richard Nixon wielded extensive powers, such as the unofficial waging of war in Vietnam. The abuses of power revealed in the Watergate scandal, however, and Nixon's subsequent resignation contributed to the diminishment of powers reflected in today's executive.

government assumed responsibility for the economic well-being of its citizens on a substantial scale. Relying on the theory mentioned earlier, that foreign affairs are thought to justify greater presidential powers than domestic affairs, Roosevelt portrayed himself as waging war against the Depression and sought from Congress the powers "that would be given to me if we were in fact invaded by a foreign foe."[29] The New Deal programs he put in place tremendously increased the size of the federal establishment and its budget. The number of civilians (nonmilitary personnel) working for the federal government increased by more than 50 percent during Roosevelt's first two terms (1933–1939). The crisis of the Great Depression created the conditions for extraordinary action, and Roosevelt's leadership created new responsibilities and opportunities for the federal government. Congress delegated a vast amount of discretionary power to Roosevelt so that he could implement his New Deal programs.

The legacy of the New Deal is that Americans now look to the president and the government to regulate the economy, solve social problems, and provide political inspiration. No president has had such a profound impact on how Americans live their lives today.[30] Roosevelt's New Deal was followed by Truman's Fair Deal. Eisenhower's presidency was less activist, but it was followed by Kennedy's New Frontier and Johnson's Great Society. All of these comprehensive policy programs did less than they promised, but they reinforced Americans' belief that it is the government's, and in particular the president's, job to make ambitious promises. That, combined with the ascendance of the United States as a world power, its engagement in the Cold War, and its participation in undeclared wars such as Korea and Vietnam, made the office very powerful indeed—what historian Arthur Schlesinger called, in a 1973 book, "the imperial presidency."[31] The philosophy behind the imperial presidency was summed up neatly by Richard Nixon, ironically several years after he was forced to resign, when he declared, "When the president does it, that means it's not illegal."[32]

The modern presidency, bolstered by court rulings that supported the president's inherent powers in foreign affairs, generated something of a backlash in Congress over the belief that neither the Johnson nor the Nixon administrations had been sufficiently forthcoming over the Vietnam War. Frustration with that, as well as with Nixon's abuse of his powers during Watergate and his unwillingness to spend budgeted money as Congress had appropriated it, led Congress to pass the War Powers Act (1973), which we discussed earlier; the Foreign Intelligence and Surveillance Act (1978), designed to put a check the government's ability to spy on people within the United States; and the Independent Counsel Act of 1978, which was intended to provide an impartial check on a president's activities but which was ultimately left open to abuse by his opponents.

The Presidency Today

The modern presidency had been so diminished by post-Watergate developments and the Clinton impeachment that when the George W. Bush administration came to power, Bush and his vice president, Dick Cheney, were determined to restore the luster and power of the office. In January 2002, Vice President Cheney remarked that the presidency is "weaker today as an institution because of the unwise compromises that have been made over the last 30 to 35 years," and he highlighted the "erosion of the powers and the ability of the president" of the United States to do his job.[33] Indeed, many of Bush's executive orders were designed to reinstate those powers, as were the claims of executive privilege made by his administration (see, for example, the *What's at Stake?* discussion that opens this chapter).

The terrorist attacks of September 11, 2001, provided Bush and Cheney with a strong and persuasive rationale for their desire to create a more muscular presidency. Citing concern about future attacks, the Bush administration increased its efforts to make the office more powerful. Signing statements, as we noted earlier, were used to impose the president's interpretation of legislation over that of Congress; the Foreign Intelligence and Surveillance Act was ignored as the administration undertook an illegal wiretapping program on U.S. soil to detect possible terrorist activity; decisions were taken to torture prisoners of war; the prison camp at Guantánamo Bay, Cuba, was established to hold enemy combatants indefinitely; and military tribunals were set up so that terror suspects could be tried without being given the legal protections of a civil trial. Many of these actions relied on the theory of the unitary executive discussed in *What's at Stake?*

Bush's extraordinarily high approval ratings in the days following September 11 made Congress unwilling to take him on. The Republicans in Congress were supportive of the administration's efforts, and the Democrats feared being seen as soft on terrorism and so went along with Bush's plans. The Patriot Act passed handily in 2001, and only the Supreme Court, in the 2004 case *Hamdi v. Rumsfeld* and the 2006 case *Hamdan v. Rumsfeld*, attempted to put on the brakes. As we argue in this chapter, high approval ratings can give a president more power than the Constitution allows him, and Bush used that power throughout his first term not only to wage the war on terror in Afghanistan but also to take the war effort to Iraq, for reasons that were later shown to have been largely exaggerated and fabricated.

Only after Bush's reelection in 2004, with waning approval ratings, was he seen as vulnerable enough for Congress to criticize him seriously. By 2006 his public approval was so low that Democrats easily won back control of both the House and the Senate and began to undertake the job of congressional oversight that had been largely lacking for the previous six years.

Overall, it is unlikely that the Bush-Cheney efforts to bulk up the executive will have lasting effect. Obama will no doubt wrestle with the same challenges of office as have all presidents in the modern age, but he is on record as supporting the traditional checks and balances that limit a president's power. As we saw in the *What's at Stake?* feature at the beginning of this chapter, Obama has continued the use of signing statements, though only on a limited basis to protect a president's constitutional prerogatives.[34] Although liberal critics have called out his use of these statements, as well as his failure to close the prison at Guantánamo Bay, his efforts to pursue the war in Afghanistan, and his continuance of some of the Bush administration's national security practices (like secret wiretapping) that they claim infringe on civil liberties,[35] in general Obama has rejected his predecessor's bulked-up presidential aspirations. A former constitutional law professor, Obama seems more aware than many presidents of the necessity of maintaining checks and balances, and he shows no signs of embracing the Bush philosophy of the unitary executive. Scholars and critics on both sides of the ideological divide will watch his administration through the remainder of his term to see whether he feels the need to push the envelope of presidential power or to operate within the limits of the post-Watergate presidency.[36]

Presidential Politics
The struggle for power in a constitutionally limited office

Presidential responsibilities and the public's expectations of what the president can accomplish have increased greatly since the start of the twentieth century, but as we have discussed, the Constitution has not been altered to give the president more power. To avoid failure, presidents have to seek power beyond that which is explicitly granted by the Constitution, and even beyond what they can claim as part of their inherent powers, and they do that with varying degrees of success.

The Expectations Gap and the Need for Persuasive Power

Even those presidents who have drawn enthusiastically on their inherent powers to protect national security or conduct foreign policy or who support the theory of the unitary executive cannot summon the official clout to ensure that their legislation gets through Congress, that the Senate approves their appointments, and that other aspects of their campaign promises are fulfilled. Some scholars believe that presidents should be given the power necessary to do the job correctly. Others argue that no one can do the job; it is not a lack of power that is the problem, but rather that no human being is up to the task of solving everyone's problems on all fronts. The solution, according to this view, is to lower expectations and return the presidency to a position of less prominence.[37]

New presidents quickly face the dilemma of high visibility and status and limited constitutional authority. Yet people continue to run for and serve as president, and, as we have seen, they deal with the expectations gap by attempting to augment their power with executive orders, executive agreements, claims of executive privilege, signing statements, and the like. All of these give the president some ability to act unilaterally. However, to be successful with larger policy initiatives, presidents seek to develop their primary extraconstitutional power, which is, in one scholar's phrase, the **power to persuade**.[38] To achieve what is expected of them, the argument goes, presidents must persuade others to cooperate with their agendas—most often members of Congress, but also the courts, the media, state and local officials, bureaucrats, foreign leaders, and especially the American public. Other scholars, however, doubt that it is really persuasion alone that allows a president to get things done. They argue that there is not a great deal of evidence that presidents are able to influence important actors, or even the public, to change their policy priorities or preferences, and that presidents' substantial policy successes are primarily due to their ability to see and exploit existing opportunities.[39] Whether they seek to persuade or to take advantage of potential opportunities, presidents have to go beyond their relatively modest constitutional powers if they want to fulfill voter expectations and bring about major policy changes in America.

Going Public

One central strategy that presidents follow in their efforts to influence people "inside the Beltway" (that is, the Washington insiders) to go along with their agenda is to reach out and appeal to the public directly for support. This strategy of **going public** is based on the expectation that public support will put pressure on other politicians to give the president what he wants.[40] Presidents use their powers as both head of government and head of state to appeal to the public.[41] A president's effort to go public can include a trip to an international summit, a town-meeting-style debate on a controversial issue, or even the president's annual State of the Union address or other nationally televised speeches.

At the simplest level of the strategy of going public, the president just takes his case to the people. Consequently, presidential public appearances have increased greatly in the era of the modern presidency. Recent presidents have had some sort of public appearance almost every day of the week, year round. Knowing that the White House press corps will almost always get some airtime on network news, presidents want that coverage to be favorable. Shaping news coverage so that it generates favorable public opinion for the president is now standard operating procedure.[42]

Naturally, only a popular president can use the strategy of going public effectively, so popularity ratings become crucial to how successful a president can be. Since the 1930s the Gallup organization has been asking people, "Do you approve or disapprove of the way [the current president] is handling his job as president?" The public's rating of the president—that is, the percentage saying they approve of how the president is handling his job—varies from one president to the next and also typically rises and falls within any single presidential term. The president's ratings are a kind of political barometer: the higher they are, the more effective the president is with other political and economic actors; the lower they are, the harder he finds it to get people to go along. For the modern presidency, the all-important power to persuade is intimately tied to presidential popularity.

Three factors in particular can affect a president's popularity: the cycle effect, the economy, and unifying or divisive current events.[43] The **cycle effect** refers to the tendency for presidents to begin their terms of office with relatively high popularity ratings, which decline as they move through their four-year terms (see Figure 7.1).

Figure 7.1

Average Quarterly Presidential Approval Ratings, From Eisenhower to Obama

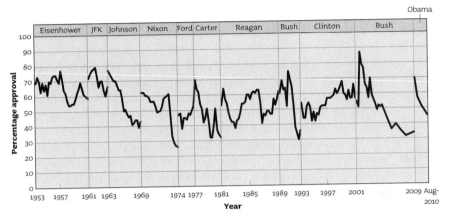

Source: Quarterly data from 1953 to 2000 provided by Robert S. Erikson; developed for Robert S. Erikson, James A. Stimson, and Michael B. MacKuen, *The Macro Polity* (Cambridge: Cambridge University Press, 2002); data for 2000 to 2010 calculated by authors from the Gallup Organization.

During the very early months of this cycle, often called the **honeymoon period**, presidents are frequently most effective with Congress. Often, but not always, presidential ratings rise going into their second terms, but this seldom approaches the popularity they had immediately after being elected the first time. The posthoneymoon drop in approval may be explained by the fact that by then presidents have begun to try to fulfill the handsome promises on which they campaigned. Fulfilling promises requires political action, and as presidents exercise their head-of-government responsibilities, they lose the head-of-state glow they bring with them from the election. Political change seldom favors everyone equally, and when someone wins, someone else usually loses. The cycle effect means that presidents need to present their programs early, while they enjoy popular support. Unfortunately, much opportunity available during the honeymoon period can be squandered because of inexperience, as it was for Bill Clinton. George W. Bush avoided the pitfalls of the early Clinton administration by bringing an experienced staff to the White House with him, but by summer 2001, there were definite signs that Bush's honeymoon, too, was over. Only the surge in support for the president following the September 11 attacks allowed him to break the usual cycle effect in his first term. Similarly, President Obama chose as his first chief of staff veteran White House staffer (from the Clinton administration) and congressman Rahm Emanuel (see *Profiles in Citizenship*), who helped him to accomplish an unusually ambitious legislative agenda in his first two years.

The second important factor that consistently influences presidential approval is the state of the economy. At least since Roosevelt, the government has taken an active role in regulating the national economy, and every president promises economic prosperity. In practice, presidential power over the economy is quite limited, but we nevertheless hold our presidents accountable for economic performance. George H. W. Bush lost the presidency in large measure because of the prolonged recession in the latter part of his administration. Clinton won it with a campaign focused on his plan for economic recovery. The economy was troubled for most of President George W. Bush's first term. Growth was slow, especially after the 2001 attacks, and because of his tax cuts and the cost of the wars that followed the attacks, the Clinton surplus had turned into the Bush deficit. Bush's approval ratings soared in the wake of the September 11 attacks and the early days of the Iraq war but dropped throughout the remainder of his presidency as the public became more pessimistic about the war and the economy cratered toward the end of 2008. As a result of the economic downturn, President Obama came into office during the worst economic recession to hit the nation since the Great Depression of the 1930s. Although his ratings reflected a traditional honeymoon effect, they collapsed as unemployment rose and the economic recovery dragged on.

Newsworthy events can influence presidential approval. Even those over which the president has no control can be opportunities for him to demonstrate leadership. Besides being tests of a president's leadership, newsworthy events can be both divisive and unifying. Political controversy, almost by definition, is divisive and generally hurts presidential ratings. And, of course, controversy in politics is unavoidable even though the public at large is reluctant to accept this fact of democratic governance.[44] This is part of the reason that presidents' approval ratings seldom maintain their honeymoon highs. Eventually presidents must veto bills, take stands on abortion or stem cell research, raise taxes or oppose a tax break, or call for more, or less, regulation. These everyday acts of governing give rise to political friction, which wears down the ratings of a public who prefer not to see their president as a politicking head of government. The drop in ratings for Barack Obama, who was unusually successful in getting his legislative agenda passed, is a textbook example of what happens when a president takes on a political role. Knowing that their cooperation would only bolster Obama, congressional Republicans made a concerted effort to deny him support whenever they could, ensuring that bills that passed on a party-line vote would look controversial and thus unpopular. Whereas divisive events hurt the president, unifying events can help him. Unifying events tend to be those that focus attention on the president's head-of-state role, making him "look presidential," or that deal with perceived threats to the nation. For instance, President George H. W. Bush's ratings soared during the Gulf War, and his high profile was topped by his son's ratings following the terrorist attacks of 2001. Seeking to capitalize on his high approval ratings, Bush took care to frame political issues as if they were about the war, even though many of them (for instance, his tax cut, energy policy, and military spending) were on his agenda prior to September 11 and had nothing to do with national security.

Thus modern presidents necessarily play the ratings game.[45] Those who choose not to play suffer the consequences: Truman, Johnson, and Ford tended not to heed the polls so closely, and they either had a hard time in office or were not reelected.[46] George W. Bush's plunge in the polls meant that his policy initiatives and preferences were largely ignored by both Congress and the media, especially after his bad poll ratings contributed so heavily to the Democrats' winning control of Congress in 2006.

Working With Congress

Presidents do not always try to influence Congress by going public. Sometimes they deal directly with Congress itself, and sometimes they combine strategies and deal with the public and Congress at the same time. The Constitution gives the primary lawmaking powers to Congress. Thus, to be successful with his policy agenda, the president has to have congressional cooperation. This depends in part on the reputation he has with members of that institution and other Washington elites for being an effective leader.[47] Such success varies with several factors, including the compatibility of the president's and Congress's goals and the party composition of Congress.

Presidents usually conflict with Congress in defining the nation's problems and their solutions. In addition to the philosophical and partisan differences that may exist between the president and members of Congress, each has different constituencies to please. The president, as the one leader elected by the whole nation, needs to take a wider, more encompassing view of the national interest. Members of Congress have relatively narrow constituencies and tend to represent their particular interests. Thus, in many cases, members of Congress do not want the same things the president does.

What can the president do to get his legislation through a Congress made up of members whose primary concern is with their individual constituencies? For one thing, presidents have a staff of assistants to work with Congress. The **legislative liaison** office specializes in determining what members of Congress are most concerned about, what they need, and how legislation can be tailored to get their support. In some cases, members just want their views to be heard; they do not want to be taken for granted. In other cases, the details of the president's program have to be explained adequately. It is electorally useful for members to have this done in person, by the president, complete with photo opportunities for release to the papers back home.

When the president and the majority of Congress are of the same party, the president is more successful at getting his programs passed. When the president faces **divided government**—that is, when he is of a different party than the majority in one or both houses—he usually does not do as well.[48] The problem is not just that members of one party act to spite a president of the other party, although that does occur at times. Rather, members of different parties stand for different approaches and solutions to the nation's problems. Democratic presidents and members of Congress tend to be more liberal than the average citizen, and Republican presidents and members of Congress tend to be more conservative. Under a divided government, presidential success is likely to falter, as history has shown (see Figure 7.2).

Figure 7.2

Presidential Success Under Unified and Divided Government, Eisenhower to Obama

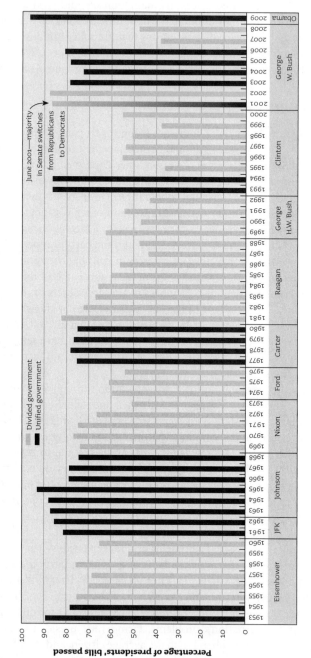

When the president faces a divided government—that is, when the opposing party controls one or both houses of Congress—he usually finds it harder to get his bills passed.

Source: Shawn Zeller, "Historic Success, at No Small Cost," *CQ Weekly,* January 11, 2010, 112.

A dramatic example of the impact of divided government can be seen in the Clinton administrations. For his first two years in office, Clinton worked with a Democratic majority in both houses, and Congress passed 86 percent of the bills he supported. The next two years (1995–1996) the Republicans had a majority in both houses, and Clinton's success rate dropped to 46 percent.[49] Bush enjoyed impressive success, with his favored bills averaging over three-quarters enacted into law, when he had Republican majorities in Congress. But when he had to deal with a Democratic Congress after the 2006 midterm election, his success rate dropped dramatically. With a success rate of 96.7 percent, Obama had the best year of any president in the fifty-six years that *Congressional Quarterly* has been measuring presidential success. This success is attributable to the large Democratic majorities in the House and the Senate coupled with an ambitious agenda and a tanking economy that required action.[50] The 2010 midterm elections, which replaced the Democratic majority in the House of Representatives with a conservative Republican majority, inevitably spelled an end to Obama's high rate of success. Whether he can persuade Republicans to work with him, as Clinton did, seems unlikely, given the increased polarization in Congress.

Divided government, however, does not doom Washington to inaction. When national needs are pressing or the public mood seems to demand action, the president and opposition majorities have managed to pass important legislation.[51] For example, the government was divided with a Democrat in the White House and Republicans in control of both houses of Congress when major welfare reform was passed with the Personal Responsibility and Work Opportunity Act of 1996.

Managing the Presidential Establishment
The challenges of supervising an unwieldy bureaucracy

The modern president is one individual at the top of a large and complex organization called the presidency, which itself heads the even larger executive branch of government. George Washington got by with no staff to speak of and consulted with his small cabinet of just three department heads, but citizens' expectations of government, and consequently the sheer size of the government, have grown considerably since then, and so has the machinery designed to manage that government. Today the executive branch is composed of the cabinet with its fifteen departments, the Executive Office of the President, and the White House staff, amounting altogether to hundreds of agencies and two million civilian employees and almost a million and a half active-duty military employees. The modern president requires a vast bureaucracy to help him make the complex decisions he faces daily, but at the same time the bureaucracy itself presents a major management challenge for the president. The reality of the modern presidency is that the president is limited in his ability to accomplish what he wants by the necessity of dealing with this complex bureaucracy. The executive bureaucracy becomes part of the "how" through which the president tries to get what he wants—for the country, his party, or himself as a politician. But at the same time it becomes another "who," a player in government that goes after its own goals and whose goals can conflict with those of the president.

The Cabinet

Each department in the executive branch is headed by a presidential appointee; collectively, these appointees form the president's cabinet. Today the cabinet comprises fifteen posts heading up fifteen departments. The newest cabinet-level department is the Department of Homeland Security, which was created in 2003. The cabinet is not explicitly set up in the Constitution, though that document does make various references to the executive departments, indicating that the founders were well aware that the president would need specialty advisers in certain areas. President Washington's cabinet included just secretaries of state, treasury, and war (now called the secretary of defense). The original idea was for the cabinet members to be the president's men overseeing areas for which the president was responsible but that he was unable to supervise personally.

All of that has changed. Today the president considers the demands of organized interests and political groups and the stature of his administration in putting his cabinet together. The number of departments has grown as various interests (for example, farmers, veterans, workers) have pressed for cabinet-level representation. Appointments to the cabinet have come to serve presidential political goals after the election rather than the goal of helping run the government. Thus the cabinet secretaries typically are chosen to please—or at least not alienate—the organized interests of the constituencies most affected by the departments. Presidents may also seek ethnic and gender balance in their cabinet choices. Bill Clinton made good on his promise to appoint a cabinet of exceptional diversity, and George W. Bush and Barack Obama followed suit. In addition, the president chooses cabinet members who have independent stature and reputation before their appointments. President Obama borrowed from Abraham Lincoln's notion of building a "team of rivals" when he appointed Hillary Clinton to be his secretary of state and when he retained Bush's secretary of defense, Robert Gates. The president's sense of legitimacy is underscored by having top-quality people working in his administration. Last, but certainly not least, a president wants people who are ideologically similar to him in the policy areas they will be handling.[52] This is not easily achieved (and may not be possible) given the other considerations presidents must weigh.

The combination of these factors in making cabinet choices—political payoffs to organized interests, and the legitimacy provided by top people in the area—often results in a "team" that may not necessarily be focused on carrying out the president's agenda. There are exceptions to the typically guarded relationship between cabinet members and the president, but the political considerations of their appointment, coupled with their independent outlook, generally mean that cabinet members will provide the president with a wide variety of views and perspectives.

They do not usually, as a group, place loyalty to the president's agenda above other considerations in their advice to the president. Consequently, presidents tend to centralize their decision making by relying more on their advisers in the Executive Office of the President for advice they can trust.[53]

Executive Office of the President

The **Executive Office of the President** (**EOP**) is a collection of organizations that form the president's own bureaucracy. Instituted by Franklin Roosevelt in 1939, the EOP was designed specifically to serve the president's interests, supply information, and provide expert advice.[54] Among the organizations established in the EOP is the **Office of Management and Budget** (**OMB**), which helps the president exert control over the departments and agencies of the federal bureaucracy by overseeing all their budgets. The director of OMB works to ensure that the president's budget reflects his own policy agenda. Potential regulations created by the agencies of the national government must be approved by OMB before going into effect. This provides the president an additional measure of control over what the bureaucracy does.

Because modern presidents are held responsible for the performance of the economy, all presidents attempt to bring about healthy economic conditions. The job of the **Council of Economic Advisers** is to predict for presidents where the economy is going and to suggest ways to achieve economic growth without much inflation.

Other departments in the EOP include the **National Security Council** (**NSC**), which gives the president daily updates about events around the world. The NSC's job is to provide the president with information and advice about foreign affairs; however, the council's role has expanded at times into actually carrying out policy— sometimes illegally, as in the Iran-contra affair.[55] When the existing federal bureaucracy is less than fully cooperative with the president's wishes, some presidents have simply bypassed the agencies by running policy from the White House. One strategy that presidents since Nixon have followed is to appoint so-called policy czars who have responsibility for supervising policy across agencies. Obama has used this strategy extensively to coordinate policy in such areas as health care, energy, and the economy. He made over 30 of these appointments in his first two years to establish firm White House control over the bureaucracy. [56]

White House Staff

Closest to the president, both personally and politically, are the members of the **White House Office,** which is included as a separate unit of the EOP. White House staffers have offices in the White House, and their appointments do not have to be confirmed by the Senate. Just as the public focus on the presidency has grown, so has the size of the president's staff. The White House staff, around 60 members under Roosevelt, grew to the 300–400 range under Eisenhower and in 2010 rested at about 469.[57]

Rahm Emanuel

As the first appointment that president-elect Barack Obama made for his new administration, Illinois representative Rahm Emanuel got lots of media attention, particularly as it took him a couple of days to decide to take the job of White House chief of staff, which he held until October 2010. But Emanuel had worked in the White House before, as a policy adviser for Bill Clinton, and it had been an all-consuming job. And he'd been single at the time. Now with a young family, he had to think twice about returning to the nonstop adrenaline rush that is working in the White House.

Life was simpler, if not less hectic, when we interviewed him in 2005, on a busy day between votes in the House. The clock on the wall buzzed intermittently, signifying an imminent vote in the U.S. House of Representatives. Congressman Rahm Emanuel didn't want to miss it, and as he chatted with us, one part of his mind was calculating exactly how much longer he could talk before heading to the House floor from his office in the Longworth House Office Building.

> "... I don't believe every disagreement is partisan. ..."

But part of his attention was wholly focused on recounting the course his career in public life had taken, this son of an immigrant doctor in Chicago who became a student of child psychology in college, then a player in Chicago politics, a fund-raiser for the Clinton campaign in 1992, a senior presidential adviser with an office next to the Oval Office (and, reportedly, the model for Josh Lyman in the television show *The West Wing*), an investment banker, and now (2005, remember) a member of Congress and chair of the DCCC—the Democratic Congressional Campaign Committee.

And all this before he had turned forty-five years old. It should have been astounding, but it wasn't. Emanuel seems to live his life at a faster pace than the rest of us, packing more in and pushing more limits in his impatience and fervor to get things done. He even talks fast, answering questions by telling stories, leaving his listeners to draw their own conclusions as he moves quickly on to his next idea.

Maybe that passion and drive come from his Chicago childhood, where he and his two brothers would read the newspapers to prepare for dinner-table conversation with their parents. The family went to civil rights rallies (his mom ran Chicago CORE—the Congress for Racial Equality), they went to cultural events, and they argued politics at the top of their lungs. (It's an Eastern European–Jewish family thing, Emanuel says. "The decibel level of eight is probably your normal conversation mode.")

In one memorable high-octane family debate in the sixties, Emanuel's mother and maternal grandfather got into a huge argument over a man named Wallace, who young Rahm took to be Alabama governor George Wallace. Nope, his dad told him, the argument was over Henry Wallace, circa 1948. His family was arguing passionately over a political controversy twenty years old, as if it had just taken place yesterday.

Those are some serious political genes, and they propelled Emanuel into Chicago politics, where he worked closely with Mayor Richard Daley and Senator Paul Simon, and then into Clinton's 1992 campaign for the presidency.

How did he get to the White House while still in his thirties? "I was thirty, thirty-one, single, and I figured you want to do politics and you want to play for the big leagues, the presidential is it. . . . I wanted to be in the White House." So he signed on as a fund-raiser for the campaign, and when, against all odds, Clinton won, Emanuel found himself right where he wanted to be.

Okay, so he's clearly driven and goal oriented and ambitious, but it does not appear to be power or, at least, not power for its own sake that drives him. He is dedicated to bringing about a certain community-based vision of society, and the White House was the best platform from which to do it. "In politics and policy [being in the White House] is the Super Bowl. And so there are things that I care about and if you want to make an impact, that's a place you can make a big impact." And a big impact is exactly what he had as he worked on welfare reform, children's health insurance, the Crime Bill, the assault weapons ban, NAFTA, and the balanced budget.

He made the same impact as a representative from Illinois and the guy who took on the job, via the DCCC, of increasing his party's representation in Congress. But though it was his job to strengthen the Democratic Party, Emanuel is cautious about using the word partisanship, believing that the media is too quick to chalk up differences to party conflict rather than honest debate and diversity of opinion. It's natural for democracy to be messy and for people to have huge debates about what government should do, but all too often we treat it as pathology rather than a sign of a healthy, functioning democratic system.

Some Republicans criticized his appointment as Obama's first chief of staff, claiming that he was too partisan and that he didn't signal the kind of transformational politics that Obama had talked about. But Emanuel practices what he preaches about party. He can have strong ideological differences with people, but it isn't personal. He has good friends on both sides of the aisle and is respected by many Republicans as well as Democrats.

(Continued)

Rahm Emanuel (Continued)

Without disagreement, politics can't solve problems. Take the issue of Social Security that Congress dealt with shortly after the 2004 election. Emanuel suggests that when the media labels a debate as partisan, they trivialize it. But the debate Congress had about Social Security was not mere partisan bickering—it was essential to policymaking. He says, "We're not having a partisan debate about Social Security. We're having an honest-to-God disagreement. They [Republicans] think Social Security should go one way, and we [Democrats] think another, and we're not going to get there with everybody sitting around singing 'Kum Ba Yah.' An honest fight and debate about that is a good and strong thing. What happens is it gets reported as a partisan fight and just some petty talk. When it's petty and it's partisan, call it. But not every disagreement is partisan."

An Obama White House with Rahm Emanuel as chief of staff may not have been as peaceful as the No Drama Obama presidential campaign, but it was highly effective at accomplishing Obama's political agenda. As Obama said in a statement announcing the pick of his old friend from Illinois, "And no one I know is better at getting things done than Rahm Emanuel." But, he continued, "[t]hough Rahm understands how to get things done in Washington, he still looks at the world from the perspective of his neighbors and constituents on the northwest side of Chicago, who work long and hard, and ask only that their government stand on their side and honor their values." For his part, Emanuel responded, "I'm leaving a job I love to join your White House for one simple reason—like the record amount of voters who cast their ballot over the last month, I want to do everything I can to help deliver the change America needs." Here's what he has to say on partisanship and participation:

Central to the White House Office is the president's **chief of staff**, who is responsible for the operation of all White House personnel. Depending on how much power the president delegates, the chief of staff may decide who gets appointments with the president and whose memoranda he reads. The chief of staff also has a big hand in hiring and firing decisions at the White House. Critics claim that the chief of staff isolates the president by removing him from the day-to-day control of his administration, but demands on the president have grown to the point that now a chief of staff is considered a necessity. Presidents Carter and Ford tried to get by without a chief of staff, but each gave up and appointed one in the middle of his term to make his political life more manageable.[58]

On the difference between partisanship and honest political disagreement:
Maybe it comes from growing up in a Jewish home where screaming was the decibel you used, but I don't believe every disagreement is partisan. . . . Now if I say, "Hey, you're a jerk," that's partisan. And that's getting into personal. But what happens is, and no disrespect, but the elite media makes every disagreement a partisan disagreement. It isn't partisan, it's a real policy. And what you can't do, nor should you ever do, is drive politics out of politics. That'd be just bureaucracy. Politics is a good thing. It's how we settle our differences. And through this homogenization of debate, we're saying that every debate is a partisan debate. It isn't. It's a political debate about political differences.

On keeping the republic:
First of all you want to do something with your life. You never know when the Good Lord is going to call your number up. And this is one place in the world, one society where you can leave your thumbprint on this and try to make the world a little better—in your own view better. Second, I see and believe that public service is community service. And when you see the kind of practice my father built and what my mother did, and where I came from and also my grandfather and grandmother on both sides, giving something back to your country and this community is central. . . . Get involved in public service. That could mean a community group, that could be a neighborhood group, that could mean an interest group on some issue, that could mean public office. A campaign. But get involved in your public life. We spend enough time with our iPods, TVs, computers—being individuals. Somewhere else in your life find a way to be part of your community . . . and I think you'll find something that's enriching and also something that allows you to contribute. That's different from anything else you're ever going to do in your life.

The chief of staff and the other top assistants to the president have to be his eyes and ears, and they act on his behalf every day. The criteria for a good staffer are very different from those for a cabinet selection. First and foremost, the president demands loyalty. This loyalty is developed from men and women who have hitched their careers to the president's. That is why presidents typically bring along old friends and close campaign staff as personal assistants. For instance, Barack Obama brought with him not only Rahm Emanuel, a longtime friend and colleague from Chicago politics, as his first chief of staff, but also three senior advisers, David Axelrod, Valerie Jarrett, and Pete Rouse, longtime and close associates who played key roles in his 2008 campaign and in his Senate career.

The different backgrounds and perspectives of the White House staff and the cabinet mean that the two groups are often at odds. The cabinet secretaries, dedicated to large departmental missions, want presidential attention for those efforts; the staff want the departments to put the president's immediate political goals ahead of their departmental interests. As a result, the past several decades have seen more and more centralization of important policymaking in the White House, and more decisions have been taken away from the traditional turf of the departments.[59]

The Vice President

For most of our history, vice presidents have not been important actors in presidential administrations. Because the original Constitution awarded the vice presidency to the second-place presidential candidate, these officials were seen as potential rivals to the president and were excluded from most decisions and any meaningful policy responsibility. That was corrected with the Twelfth Amendment (1804), which provided for electors to select both the president and the vice president. However, custom for most of the period since then has put a premium on balancing the ticket in terms of regional, ideological, or political interests, which has meant that the person in the second spot is typically not close to the president. In fact, the vice president has sometimes been a rival even in modern times, as when John Kennedy appointed Lyndon Johnson, the Senate majority leader from Texas, as his vice president in 1960 in an effort to gain support from the southern states.

Since the Constitution provides only that the vice president act as president of the Senate, which carries no power unless there is a tie vote, most vice presidents have tried to make small, largely insignificant jobs seem important, often admitting that theirs was not an enviable post. Thomas Marshall, Woodrow Wilson's vice president, observed in his inaugural address that "I believe I'm entitled to make a few remarks because I'm about to enter a four-year period of silence."[60] Roosevelt's first vice president, John Nance Garner, expressed his disdain for the office even more forcefully, saying that the job "is not worth a pitcher of warm piss."[61]

Ultimately, however, the job of vice president is what the president wants it to be. President Reagan largely ignored George H. W. Bush, for instance, whereas Al Gore, serving under President Clinton, had a central advisory role.[62] Dick Cheney also brought a good deal of Washington experience upon which President George W. Bush relied heavily; Cheney had a stronger résumé than many presidents bring to office and wielded much more power than previous vice presidents. President Obama's vice president, Joe Biden, also brought the heft of a lengthy résumé from six terms in the U.S. Senate and his longtime service on the Senate Foreign Relations Committee. Obama is not likely to relinquish as much authority to his vice president as Bush did, but before agreeing to take the job, Biden made a point of getting assurances that he would have an active role. He has said he sees himself as the "advisor in chief," willing to weigh in with blunt and candid opinions, especially on foreign policy.[63]

Thus, even though the office of the vice presidency is not a powerful one, vice presidents who establish a relationship of trust with the president can have a significant impact on public policy. The office is important as well, of course, because it is the vice president who assumes the presidency if the president dies, is incapacitated, resigns, or is impeached. Many vice presidents also find the office a good launching pad for a presidential bid. Four of the last ten vice presidents—Lyndon Johnson, Richard Nixon, Gerald Ford, and George H. W. Bush—ended up in the Oval Office, although Al Gore did not enjoy similar success in 2000.

The First Spouse

The office of the first lady (even the term seems strangely antiquated) is undergoing immense changes that reflect the tremendous flux in Americans' perceptions of the appropriate roles for men and women. But the office of the first lady has always contained controversial elements, partly the result of conflict over the role of women in politics, but also because the intimate relationship between husband and wife gives the presidential spouse, an unelected position, unique insight into and access to the president's mind and decision-making processes. For all the checks and balances in the American system, there is no way to check the influence of the first spouse. It will be interesting to see whether first "gentlemen" become as controversial as their female counterparts.

Since the 1960s and the advent of the women's movement, the role of the first lady has been seen by the public as less an issue of individual personality and quirks, and more a national commentary on how women in general should behave. As a surrogate for our cultural confusion on what role women should play, the office of the first lady has come under uncommon scrutiny, especially when she takes on a more overtly political role, as did Rosalyn Carter, who even attended cabinet meetings at her husband's request. Public objections to her activities and her position as informal presidential adviser showed that the role of the first lady was controversial even in the late 1970s. Hillary Rodham Clinton shook up public

Promoting Health
First Lady Michelle Obama helps two children harvest sweet potatoes. The first lady speaks publicly to promote healthy living and combat obesity in America, particularly among young children. She has chosen a less active policy-making role than some of her predecessors, but she continues to draw public attention to the issues that matter to her.

expectations of the first lady's role even more. A successful lawyer who essentially earned the family income while her husband, Bill, served four low-paid terms as governor of Arkansas, Hillary was the target of both public acclaim and public hatred. Her nontraditional tenure as first lady was capped in 2000, at the end of her husband's second term, by her election as the junior senator from New York, followed by her own nearly successful run for the Democratic nomination for president in 2008 and her appointment as Obama's secretary of state.

The politically safest strategy for a first lady appears to be to stick with a noncontroversial moral issue and ask people to do what we all agree they ought to do. Lady Bird Johnson beseeched us to support highway beautification; Nancy Reagan suggested, less successfully, that we "just say no" to drugs; and Laura Bush focused on the issues of education, youth, and literacy.

First Lady Michelle Obama has said flatly that she does not intend to take on an active policymaking role, with a West Wing office and extensive staff to match. "I can't do everything," she explains. A committed and active mother to two young children, she wants to keep their lives as normal as possible while living in the White House. In so far as she takes on a public role, it has been in the noncontroversial style of Reagan and Bush, as an advocate for working parents, and particularly those in the military, who juggle career loads with the demands of raising families, and as a strong supporter of a healthy diet as an antidote to rising childhood obesity rates.[64]

The Presidential Personality
Translating leadership style and image into presidential power

Effective management of the executive branch is one feature of a successful presidency, but there are many others. Historians and presidential observers regularly distinguish presidential success and failure, even to the extent of actually rating presidential greatness.[65] Political scientists also assess presidential success, usually in terms of how frequently presidents can get their legislative programs passed by Congress.[66] In addition to the material assets and management skills they bring to the office, the personal resources of a president can also help lead to success or contribute to failure.

Most presidents share some personality characteristics—giant ambition and large egos, for instance—but this does not mean that they are carbon copies of one another. They clearly differ in fundamental ways. A number of scholars have developed classification schemes of presidential personalities. Each of these schemes is based on the expectation that knowing key dimensions of individual presidential personalities will help explain, or even predict, how presidents will behave in certain circumstances. The most famous of these schemes was developed by James David Barber, who classifies presidents on two dimensions: their energy level (passive or active) and their orientation toward life (positive or negative).[67]

Some of our best and most popular presidents have been active-positives. They have had great energy and a very positive orientation toward the job of being president. Franklin Roosevelt, Bill Clinton, and Barack Obama represent this type. Others have had less energy (passives) or have been burdened by the job of being president (negatives). They have acted out their roles, according to Barber, as they thought they should, out of duty or obligation. Ronald Reagan and George W. Bush fit the model of the passive-positive president. They liked being leaders but believed that their job was one of delegating and setting the tone rather than of taking an active policymaking role. Richard Nixon is usually offered as one of the clearest examples of an active-negative president; he had lots of energy but could not enjoy the job of being president.

Assessing individual personalities is a fascinating enterprise, but it is fraught with danger. Few politicians fit neatly into Barber's boxes (or the categories of other personality theorists) in an unambiguous way. Although some scholars find that personality analysis adds greatly to their understanding of the differences between presidencies, others discount it altogether, claiming that it leads one to overlook the ways in which rules and external forces have shaped the modern presidency.[68]

In addition to their personality differences, each president strives to create a **presidential style**, or an image that symbolically captures who he is for the American people and for leaders of other nations. These personal differences in how presidents present themselves are real, but they are also carefully cultivated.[69]

For example, Harry Truman was known for his straight, sometimes profane, talk and no-nonsense decision making. In contrast, Dwight Eisenhower developed his "Victorious General" image as a statesman above the fray of petty day-to-day politics. John Kennedy, whose term followed Eisenhower's, evoked a theme of "getting the country moving again" and embodied this with a personal image of youth and energy.

Bill Clinton's style combined the image of the highly intellectual Rhodes scholar with that of a compassionate leader, famous for "feeling America's pain." That carefully managed image could not disguise the fact that Clinton was also a man of large appetites, however, from his jogging breaks to eat at McDonald's to his extramarital affairs. While people approved of Clinton's leadership through the end of his presidency, a majority of citizens noted concerns about his honesty and moral character.

George W. Bush came into office with an opposite set of characteristics. Widely perceived as a nonintellectual who joked that C students could grow up to be president, he cultivated the image of the chief executive officer he was: a president interested primarily in results, not academic debates, who was willing to set a course and leave others to get the job done. Despite a reputation for hard drinking and high living in his youth, including a drunk driving arrest, his pledge of abstinence, traditional marriage, and frequent references to Jesus Christ helped to put a moral tone on his presidency that Clinton's had lacked.

Barack Obama brings a placid disposition to the White House. His calm demeanor (symbolized by his unofficial campaign slogan—No Drama Obama) has remained consistent through the economic and environmental crises of the first two years of his presidency. As he says of himself, "I don't get too high when things are going well and I don't get too low when things are going tough." Obama's image incorporates elements of the styles of several of his predecessors, combining Ronald Reagan's optimism, Bill Clinton's braininess, and George W. Bush's faith and commitment to family.[70]

Presidential style is an important but subtle means by which presidents communicate. It can be an opportunity for enhancing public support and thereby the president's ability to deal effectively with Congress and the media. But any style has its limitations, and the same behavioral and attitudinal characteristics of a style that help a president at one juncture can prove a liability later. Furthermore, as Clinton's experience shows, the president does not always have total control over the image of him that the public sees. Political enemies and an investigative press can combine to counter the image the president wants to project. Because public perception is tied so closely to leadership ability, a significant portion of the president's staffers end up concerning themselves with "image management."

Citizenship and the Presidency
"Rolling election" by public opinion poll

Although the Constitution does not say so, the citizens of the United States have the ultimate power over the president. We elect him (and someday her), it is true, but our power goes beyond a once-every-four-years vote of approval or disapproval. Modern polling techniques, as we have seen, allow us to conduct a "rolling election," as the media and the politicians themselves track popular approval of the president throughout his term. The presidential strategy of going public is made possible by the fact that all Americans—citizens, the president, and members of Congress—know just where the president stands with the public and how much political capital he has to spend.

In 1998 and 1999, we saw perhaps the clearest example of the power that citizens' support can give to a president, in the fate of Bill Clinton's imperiled presidency. As we indicated, President Clinton had the same problems with the polls in his early years as every other president. By 1996, however, he had hit his political stride and was reelected with 49 percent of the vote. His approval ratings were at normal levels through the first year of his second term, fluctuating between 54 and 62 percent. Once he was under threat of removal from office, however, his ratings soared, hitting a peak of 73 percent on December 19, 1998, the day the House voted to impeach him. Questioned on specifics, people said they disapproved of Clinton's moral character and found his behavior repellent, but that they thought the impeachment movement was politically motivated and that his private behavior had no impact on his ability to do his job. Of course, we know the end of the story. Clinton went on to be acquitted in the Senate. Once he was no longer under threat,

Clinton's ratings dropped to the more typical levels of a popular president near the end of his second term.

It is arguable that these polls saved Clinton's political life. Had they fallen during the impeachment process, it would have been much harder for his supporters to defend him, especially if Democrats and moderates in the House and Senate felt they were risking their own political futures to do so. It is safe to say that if his approval ratings had fallen, the president may well have lost his job. The institution of the American presidency, like most of the government designed by the framers, was meant to be insulated from the whims of the public. It is an irony that in contemporary American politics, the president is more indebted to the citizens for his power than to the Electoral College, Congress, the courts, or any of the political elites the founders trusted to stabilize American government.

▶ What's at Stake Revisited

The Constitution may be a study in ambiguity on some issues, but on others it is crystal clear. Congress makes the laws, for instance. Presidents can veto or they can sign, but when they do the latter, it is their job to enforce the law that Congress passed. The principle of checks and balances depends on this back-and-forth power-wielding arrangement. If one branch could impose its will on the others without limit, checks and balances would disappear.

Still, controversy remains about how strong the executive power should be. When George W. Bush started using signing statements to aggressively challenge congressional will, he was putting the brakes on checks and balances. By refusing to veto legislation he didn't like and instead issuing signing statements that enabled him to ignore parts of laws he didn't consider to be constitutional, Bush was bypassing Congress, which then could not exercise its option of overriding a veto, and the courts, which were unable to play their role as the ultimate determinant of what is constitutional. Bush's defenders claimed that the signing statements were just "political chest thumping" that didn't really mean anything,[71] but in fact, the nonpartisan Government Accountability Office found that Bush failed to comply with congressional legislation multiple times.[72]

Many actors have high stakes in such actions. For the Bush administration, what was at stake was a more muscular presidency, one that wasn't, as they thought, emasculated in the wake of the Watergate scandal, and one that was premised on the unitary theory of the executive that said that executive power belongs to the president alone. As we have seen, signing statements were not the only strategy pursued to strengthen the office, but they were a clear attempt to move the presidency beyond its constitutional limits. Other presidents have used signing statements to assert their right to preserve their constitutional powers, but they have not used the statements to expand them.[73]

For Congress, the stakes were painfully high. We have seen what goes into crafting legislation—the compromise, skill, and bargaining involved in creating laws that the people's representatives feel they can sign on to. Bush's signing statements essentially allowed the executive to rewrite the bills, ignoring what he didn't like and keeping what he did, with no way for Congress to guarantee that its actions would count.

And, of course, the stakes could not have been higher for the American public. The point of checks and balances was to limit the power wielded by any one branch, so that the government as a whole would stay limited in power, and to ensure that individual liberties would be safe from government encroachment. The substance of the legislation that Bush felt he could ignore indicates just how much the public stood to lose from his actions; safeguards against wiretapping and torture, and whistleblower protection were jeopardized, among other things.

Citizens also had a stake in the accountability of their elected officials and the smooth running of their democracy. When Congress passes a bill, or overrides a presidential veto, voters have a check. They can hold their representatives accountable and vote them out of office if they don't like what they do. But if the executive alters the laws on the quiet, the lines of accountability are muddied and democracy itself is endangered.

As Bruce Fein, a former official in the Reagan Justice Department, said, "This is an attempt by the president to have the final word on his own constitutional powers, which eliminates the checks and balances that keep the country a democracy. There is no way for an independent judiciary to check his assertions of power, and Congress isn't doing it either. So this is moving us toward an unlimited executive power."[74] Very high stakes, indeed.

▶ Summary With Key Terms

Presidents face a double expectations gap when it comes to their relationship with the American public: one between what the president must promise in order to gain office and the limitations put on the president by the powers granted by the Constitution and the other between the conflicting roles of **head of government** (227) and **head of state** (227).

Disagreeing about how much power the executive should have, the founders devised rules that both empowered and limited the office, in terms of its ability to check, and be checked by, the other branches. As the executive the president is the **chief administrator** (230), appointing federal employees including members of the **cabinet** (230); the **commander-in-chief** (230); and the **chief foreign policy maker** (230), with the power to execute **treaties** (230) (shared with the Senate) and **executive agreements** (231). His legislative powers include the ability to set his agenda through the **State of the Union address** (231), to wield the **presidential veto** (231) over legislation he dislikes, and to issue **executive orders** (233). His judicial powers include the power to appoint federal judges—tempered by **senatorial courtesy** (234)—to influence court decisions via the **solicitor general** (234), and to exercise the **pardoning power** (235).

Until the 1930s, the era of the traditional presidency described chief executives who mainly lived within the limits of their constitutional powers, although testing the limits of their **inherent powers** (235) in times of crisis. Since the expansion of government in Franklin Roosevelt's New Deal, the modern presidency has seen a more complex relationship in which the public looks to the president to solve their problems, but the president's formal powers remain unchanged.

Under pressure from the public, but with limited constitutional powers to satisfy their demands, the modern president must resort to the **power to persuade** (239), **going public** (240) to convince Americans to pressure their representatives to give him what he wants. Thus, due to the **cycle effect** (240), the president's best opportunities to get his programs passed come during the **honeymoon period** (241), before public and press become disillusioned. Although he employs a **legislative liaison** (243) to smooth his way with Congress, getting his way can be difficult, especially if he is part of a **divided government** (243).

The president presides over a vast bureaucracy, including the cabinet, the **Executive Office of the President** (247)—which encompasses the **Office of Management and Budget** (247), the **Council of Economic Advisers** (247), and the **National Security Council** (247)—and the **White House Office** (247) headed up by his **chief of staff** (250). The president's closest advisers are generally focused on his interests, but the variety of other staff and agency heads—often with their own agendas and often difficult to control—can make life difficult for the chief executive.

Presidential success is the product of many factors including political savvy and management skills, but also of the more intangible resource of character. In part, that character is revealed through **presidential style** (255)—the image the president projects of how he would like to be perceived by the public.

Explore this subject further with suggested readings, movies, and web sites at http://republic-brief.cqpress.com, where you'll also find study aids, practice quizzes, flash cards, and Internet exercises.

Chapter 8

The Bureaucracy

▶ What's at Stake?

What did the chicken that laid your breakfast egg have for *its* breakfast? Was your hamburger once on drugs? And just what is the pedigree of the french fries you ate at lunch? Do you care? Some people do. Those who worry about eating vegetables that have been grown with the aid of pesticides or chemical fertilizers, or meat from animals that were given hormones or antibiotics, or who are concerned about the environmental effects of such practices, form part of a growing number of consumers who look for the label *organic* before they buy food. One estimate says that Americans spent more than $26 billion on organic foods in 2009.[1]

What does it mean to be organic? There is no standardized definition, so states, localities, and private agencies are free to define *organic* as they wish. Usually the standards are stringent. For example, many groups require organic farmers to use land on which no artificial or synthetic fertilizers, pesticides, or herbicides have been used for five years. Such farming techniques favor the small, committed organic farmer and are difficult for large agribusinesses to apply.[2]

In an effort to eliminate the patchwork of local regulations and to assure consumers that organic food purchased anywhere in the country was equally safe, the organic food industry repeatedly asked the U.S. Department of Agriculture (USDA) to nationalize standards. When the USDA revealed its standardized definition of *organic*, however, it was a definition traditional organic farmers and consumers didn't recognize. USDA standards proposed in December 1997 would have allowed the use

of genetic engineering, irradiation, antibiotics and hormones, and sewage sludge—techniques that run directly counter to the values of organic farming—in the production of foods to be labeled *organic*. Though strongly supported by the conventional food manufacturers and the developers of biotechnology, these standards were bitterly opposed by the organic food industry and its consumers.

Before they issue new regulations, however, all federal agencies must give interested parties and the public the opportunity to be heard. In the battle to win USDA support, the conventional food industry and the food preparers associations had—and used—all the resources of big business; the organic food industry had none. Searching for another strategy for influencing the enormous bureaucracy of the USDA, they began a grassroots campaign, encouraging consumers to write to the USDA objecting to the new standards. Natural food stores posted information and distributed fliers on the proposed regulation, and Horizon Organic Dairy used the back panels of its milk cartons to pass on the information and urge consumer action.[3]

The campaign was successful. Nearly 300,000 letters and emails opposing the proposal were received by the USDA. Even Congress went on record against it.[4] The result was that Secretary of Agriculture Dan Glickman eliminated the provision allowing genetic engineering, crop irradiation, and the use of sewage sludge as fertilizer. Said Glickman, "Democracy will work. We will listen to the comments and will, I am sure, make modifications to the rule."[5]

Depending on where you stand, the moral of this story varies. It might be a David-and-Goliath success, or just a quirky tale about a handful of food fanatics. What is really at stake in the issue of whether the organic food industry should be regulated by the USDA?

Kids have dramatic aspirations for their futures: they want to be adventurers or sports stars, doctors or lawyers, even president of the United States. Almost no one aspires to be what so many of us become: bureaucrats. But bureaucrats are the people who make national, state, and local government work for us. They are the people who give us our driving tests and renew our licenses, who deliver our mail, who maintain our parks, who order books for our libraries. Bureaucrats send us our Social Security checks, find us jobs through the unemployment office, process our student loans, and ensure we get our military benefits. In fact, bureaucrats defend our country from foreign enemies, chase our crooks at home, and get us aid in times of natural disasters. We know them as individuals. We greet them, make small talk, laugh with them. They may be our neighbors or friends. But civil servants are seldom much admired or esteemed in this country. Indeed, they are often the target of scorn or jokes, and the people who work in the organizations we call bureaucracies are derided as lazy, incompetent, power hungry, and uncaring.

Such a jaded view, like most other negative stereotypes, is based on a few well-publicized bureaucratic snafus and the frustrating experiences we all have at times with the bureaucracy. Waiting in endless lines at the post office or driver's license bureau, expecting a government check in the mail that never arrives, reading about USDA definitions of *organic* that seem preposterous—all these things can drive us crazy. In addition, as demonstrated by the organic foods example, the bureaucracy is the source of many of the rules that can help us get what we want from government but that often irritate us with their seeming arbitrariness and rigidity. Though they aren't elected, bureaucrats can have a great deal of power over our lives.

Bureaucracies are essential to running a government. Bureaucracy, in fact, is often the only ground on which citizens and politics meet, the only contact many Americans have with government except for their periodic trips to the voting booth. Bureaucrats are often called "civil servants" because, ultimately, their job is to serve the civil society in which we all live. In this chapter—as we give bureaucracy a closer look—you will learn about the definition of *bureaucracy*; the evolution, organization, and roles of the federal bureaucracy; politics inside the bureaucracy; and the relationship between the federal bureaucracy and the branches of the federal government.

What Is Bureaucracy?
A top-down organizational system aiming for competence and fairness

In simplest terms, a **bureaucracy** is any organization that is hierarchically structured—that is, in which orders are given at the top, by those with responsibility for the success of the organization, and followed by those on the bottom. The classic definition comes to us from German sociologist Max Weber. Weber's model of bureaucracy features the following four characteristics:[6]

- *Hierarchy.* A clear chain of command exists in which all employees know who their bosses or supervisors are, as well as for whom they are in turn responsible.
- *Specialization.* The effectiveness of the bureaucracy is accomplished by having tasks divided and handled by expert and experienced full-time professional staffs.
- *Explicit rules.* Bureaucratic jobs are governed by rules rather than by bureaucrats' own feelings or judgments about how the job should be done. Thus bureaucrats are limited in the discretion they have, and one person in a given job is expected to make pretty much the same decisions as another. This leads to standardization and predictability.
- *Merit.* Hiring and promotions are often based on examinations but also on experience or other objective criteria. Politics, in the form of political loyalty, party affiliation, or dating the boss's son or daughter, is not supposed to play a part.

As governments make their bureaucracies look more like Weber's model, we say the closer they are to achieving "neutral competence."[7] **Neutral competence** represents the effort to depoliticize the bureaucracy, or to take politics out of administration, by having the work of government done expertly, according to explicit standards rather than personal preferences or party loyalties. The bureaucracy in this view should not be a political arm of the president or of Congress, but rather it should be neutral, administering the laws of the land in a fair, evenhanded, efficient, and professional way.

The Spoils System

Americans have not always been so concerned with the norm of neutral competence in the bureaucracy. Under a form of bureaucratic organization called the **spoils system**, practiced through most of the nineteenth century, elected executives—the president, governors, and mayors—were given wide latitude to hire their friends, family, and political supporters to work in their administrations (a practice known as **patronage**). The spoils system is often said to have begun with the administration of President Andrew Jackson and gets its name from the adage "To the victor belong the spoils of the enemy." But Jackson was neither the first nor the last politician to see the acquisition of public office as a means of feathering his cronies' nests.

Filling the bureaucracy with political appointees almost guarantees incompetence, because those who get jobs for political reasons are more likely to be politically motivated than genuinely skilled in a specific area. America's disgust with the corruption and inefficiency of the spoils system, as well as our collective distrust of placing too much power in the hands of any one person, led Congress to institute various reforms of the American **civil service**, as it is sometimes called, aimed at achieving a very different sort of organization.

One of the first reforms, and certainly one of the most significant, was the Civil Service Reform Act of 1883. This act, usually referred to as the **Pendleton Act**, created the initial Civil Service Commission, under which federal employees would be hired and promoted on the basis of merit rather than patronage. It prohibited firing employees for failure to contribute to political parties or candidates.

Protection of the civil service from partisan politicians got another boost in 1939 with the passage of the **Hatch Act**, designed to take the pressure off civil servants to work for the election of parties and candidates. They cannot run for federal political office, head up an election campaign, or make contributions or public speeches on behalf of candidates, although they can get involved in election activities that do not focus on just one candidate or party. The Hatch Act was an attempt to neutralize the political effects of the bureaucracy, but in doing so it denies federal employees a number of activities that are open to other citizens.

Bureaucracy and Democracy

Much of the world is organized bureaucratically. Large tasks require organization and specialization. The Wright brothers may have been able to construct a rudimentary airplane, but no two people or even small group could put together a Boeing 747. Similarly, though we idolize individual American heroes, we know that military undertakings like the D-Day invasion of Europe or the war on terrorism take enormous coordination and planning. Less glamorous, but still necessary, are routine tasks like delivering the mail, evaluating welfare applications, ensuring that Social Security recipients get their checks, and processing student loans.

> The existence of bureaucratic decision making . . . may seem like a real puzzle in a country that prides itself on its democratic traditions.

Obviously many bureaucracies are public, like those that form part of our government. But the private sector has the same demand for efficient expertise to manage large organizations. Corporations and businesses are bureaucracies, as are universities and hospitals. It is not being public or private that distinguishes a bureaucracy; rather, it is the need for a structure of hierarchical, expert decision making. Naturally, in this chapter we focus on public bureaucracies.

The existence of bureaucratic decision making, where hierarchy and specialization count and decisions are often made behind closed doors, may seem like a real puzzle in a country that prides itself on its democratic traditions. Consider, however, that democracy may not be the best way to make every kind of decision. If we want to ensure that many voices are heard, democracy is an appropriate way to make decisions. But those decisions will be made slowly (it takes a long time to poll many people on what they want to do), and although they are likely to be popular, they are not necessarily made by people who know what they are doing. When we're deciding whether to have open-heart surgery, we don't want to poll the American people, or even the hospital employees. Instead, we want an expert, a heart surgeon, who can make the "right" decision, not the popular decision, and make it quickly.

Democracy could not have designed the rocket ships that formed the basis of America's space program, decided the level of toxic emissions allowable from a factory smokestack, or determined the temperature at which beef must be cooked in restaurants to prevent food poisoning. Bureaucratic decision making, by which decisions are made at upper levels of an organization and carried out at lower levels, is essential when we require expertise and dispatch.

Accountability and Rules

Bureaucratic decision making does leave open the problem of **accountability**: Who is in charge, and to whom does that person answer? Where does the buck stop? Unlike private bureaucracies, where the need to turn a profit usually keeps bureaucrats relatively accountable, the lines of accountability are less clear in public bureaucracies. Because the Constitution does not provide specific rules for the operation of the bureaucracy, Congress has filled in a piecemeal framework for the bureaucracy that, generally speaking, ends up promoting the goals of members of Congress and the interests they represent.[8] The president of the United States, nominally the head of the executive branch of government, also has goals and objectives he would like the bureaucracy to serve. Thus at the very highest level, the public bureaucracy must answer to several bosses who often have conflicting goals.

The problem of accountability exists at a lower level as well. Even if the lines of authority from the bureaucracy to the executive and legislative branches were crystal clear, no president or congressional committee has the interest or time to supervise the day-to-day details of bureaucratic workings. To solve the problem of accountability within the bureaucracy and to prevent the abuse of public power at all levels, we again resort to rules. If the rules of bureaucratic policy are clearly defined and well publicized, it is easier to tell if a given bureaucrat is doing his or her job and not taking advantage of the power that comes with it.

There can also be negative consequences associated with the bureaucratic reliance on rules. Bureaucrats' jobs can quickly become rule-bound—that is, deviations from the rules become unacceptable, and individuality and creativity are stifled. Sometimes the rules that bind bureaucrats do not seem relevant to the immediate task at hand, and the workers are rewarded for following the rules, not for fulfilling the goals of the organization. Furthermore, compliance with rules has to be monitored, and the best way we have developed to guarantee compliance is to generate a paper or an electronic record of what has been done—thus the endless forms for which the bureaucracy is so famous.

For the individual citizen applying for a driver's license, a student loan, or food stamps, the process can become a morass of seemingly unnecessary rules, regulations, constraints, forms, and hearings. We call these bureaucratic hurdles **red tape**, after the red tape that seventeenth-century English officials used to bind legal documents. Citizens may feel that they are treated as little more than numbers, that the system is impersonal and alienating. These excessive and anonymous procedures cause citizens to think poorly of the bureaucracy, even while they value many of the services that it provides.

Rules thus generate one of the great tradeoffs of bureaucratic life. If we want strict fairness and accountability, we must tie the bureaucrat to a tight set of rules. If we allow the bureaucrat discretion to try to reach goals with a looser set of rules or to waive a rule when doing so seems appropriate, we may gain some efficiency but lose accountability. Given the vast numbers of people who work for the federal government, we have opted for accountability, even while we howl with frustration at the inconvenience of the rules.

The American Federal Bureaucracy
A patchwork of agencies and commissions to meet growing public demands

In 2008, almost two million civilians worked for the federal government, excluding U.S. Postal Service employees, with another million and a half or so in the armed forces. Only a relative handful, 3.3 percent of federal workers, work in the legislative branch or the judiciary. The rest—97 percent of federal workers—are in the executive branch, home of the federal bureaucracy.[9] In this section we look at the evolution of the federal bureaucracy, its present-day organization, and its basic functions.

Evolution of the Federal Bureaucracy

The central characteristic of the federal bureaucracy is that most of its parts developed independently of the others in a piecemeal and political fashion, rather than emerging from a coherent plan. The picture that emerges is more like a patchwork quilt than the streamlined, efficient government structure we would like to have.[10] We can understand federal agencies as falling into three categories:[11]

- *Some government departments deal with fundamental activities.* For example, the Departments of State, War, and the Treasury were the first cabinet offices because the activities they handle are essential to the smooth functioning of government. The Department of State exists to handle diplomatic relations with other nations. The Department of Defense (formerly War) supervises the air force, army, navy, marines, and, in time of war, the coast guard. The Department of the Treasury, which oversees the Internal Revenue Service (IRS), performs the key tax collection function, prints the money we use, and oversees the horrendous job of managing the national debt.
- *Other government departments developed in response to national problems* and to meet the changing needs of the country as it industrialized and evolved into an urban society. For instance, the Department of the Interior was created in 1848 to deal with some of the unforeseen effects of westward expansion. The Interstate Commerce Commission, Federal Trade Commission, Federal Reserve System, and other agencies were created to regulate the burgeoning American marketplace. The Social Security Administration was designed to supplement inadequate and failed old-age pensions during a time of economic hardship. The Office of Economic Opportunity (1964) and the Department of Housing and Urban Development (1965) were intended to cope with the poverty that continued to exist as America prospered after the New Deal. The National Science Foundation and the National Aeronautics and Space Administration (NASA) were crafted to help America respond to the intellectual challenges of the Cold War. Much more recently, the September 11, 2001, terror attacks on the United States led to the establishment of the cabinet-level Department of Homeland Security to coordinate efforts to protect the country.
- *Still other government departments develop in response to different **clientele groups**,* which want government to do something for them. These may include interest groups—groups of citizens, businesses, or industry members who are affected by the regulatory action of the government and who organize to try to influence policy. Or they may include unorganized groups, such as poor people, to which the government has decided to respond. Departments in these areas are sensitive to the concerns of specific groups

rather than focusing on what is good for the nation as a whole. The USDA, among the first of these departments, was set up in 1862 to assist U.S. agricultural interests. It began by providing research information to farmers and later arranged subsidies and developed markets for agricultural products. Politicians in today's budget-cutting climate talk about cutting back on agricultural subsidies, but no one expects the USDA to change its focus of looking out, first and foremost, for the farmer. Other agencies that have been created in response to the demands of clientele groups include the Departments of Commerce (businesspeople), Labor (workers), Education (teachers), and Veterans Affairs (veterans).

Organization of the Federal Bureaucracy

The federal bureaucracy consists of four types of organizations: (1) cabinet-level departments, (2) independent agencies, (3) regulatory agencies, and (4) government corporations. Making the job of understanding the bureaucracy more complicated, some agencies can fit into more than one of those classifications. The difficulty in classifying an agency as one type or another stems partly from Congress' habit of creating hybrids: agencies that act like government corporations, for instance, or cabinet-level departments that regulate. The overall organizational chart of the U.S. government (see Figure 8.1) makes this complex bureaucracy look reasonably orderly. To a large extent the impression of order is an illusion.

Departments

The federal government currently has fifteen **departments**. The heads of departments are known as secretaries—for example, the secretary of state or the secretary of defense—except for the head of the Department of Justice, who is called the attorney general. These department heads collectively make up the president's cabinet, appointed by the president, with the consent of the Senate, to provide advice on critical areas of government affairs such as foreign relations, agriculture, education, and so on. These areas are not fixed, and presidents may propose different cabinet offices. Although the secretaries are political appointees who usually change when the administration changes (or even more frequently), they sit at the heads of the large, more or less permanent, bureaucracies we call departments. Cabinet heads may not have any more actual power than other agency leaders, but their posts do carry more status and prestige.

Independent Agencies

Congress has established a host of agencies outside the cabinet departments. The **independent agencies** are structured like the cabinet departments, with a single head appointed by the president. Their areas of jurisdiction tend to be narrower than those of the cabinet departments. Congress does not follow a blueprint for how to make an independent agency or a department. Instead, it expands the bureaucracy to fit the case at hand, given the mix of political forces of the moment—that

Figure 8.1

Organizational Chart of the U.S. Government

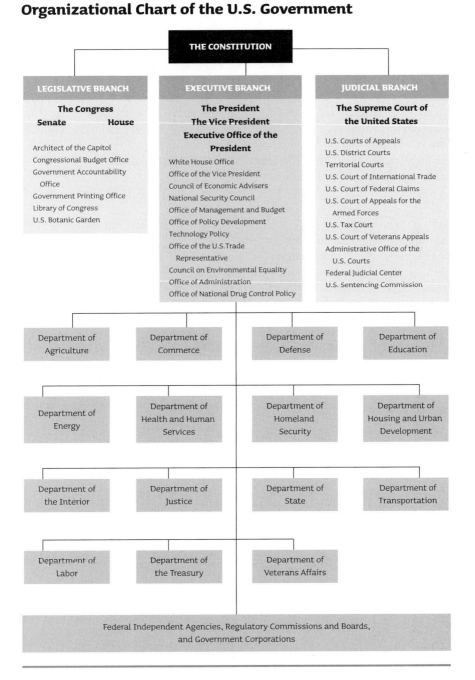

THE CONSTITUTION

LEGISLATIVE BRANCH

The Congress

Senate   House

Architect of the Capitol
Congressional Budget Office
Government Accountability
   Office
Government Printing Office
Library of Congress
U.S. Botanic Garden

EXECUTIVE BRANCH

The President
The Vice President
Executive Office of the President

White House Office
Office of the Vice President
Council of Economic Advisers
National Security Council
Office of Management and Budget
Office of Policy Development
Technology Policy
Office of the U.S.Trade
   Representative
Council on Environmental Equality
Office of Administration
Office of National Drug Control Policy

JUDICIAL BRANCH

The Supreme Court of the United States

U.S. Courts of Appeals
U.S. District Courts
Territorial Courts
U.S. Court of International Trade
U.S. Court of Federal Claims
U.S. Court of Appeals for the
   Armed Forces
U.S. Tax Court
U.S. Court of Veterans Appeals
Administrative Office of the
   U.S. Courts
Federal Judicial Center
U.S. Sentencing Commission

Department of Agriculture

Department of Commerce

Department of Defense

Department of Education

Department of Energy

Department of Health and Human Services

Department of Homeland Security

Department of Housing and Urban Development

Department of the Interior

Department of Justice

Department of State

Department of Transportation

Department of Labor

Department of the Treasury

Department of Veterans Affairs

Federal Independent Agencies, Regulatory Commissions and Boards, and Government Corporations is, given what groups are demanding what action, and with what resources. As a result, the independent agencies vary tremendously in size, from fewer than 400 employees in the Federal Election Commission to over 65,000 for the Social Security Administration. While agencies are called independent because of their independence from cabinet departments, they vary in their independence from the president. This is not accidental but political. When Congress is not in agreement with the current president, they tend to insulate a new agency from presidential control by making the appointments for fixed terms that do not overlap with the president's, or they remove budgetary oversight from the Office of Management and Budget.[12] Thus some agency heads serve at the president's discretion and can be fired at any time; others serve fixed terms, and the president can appoint a new head or commissioner only when a vacancy occurs. Independent agencies also vary in their freedom from judicial review. Congress has established that some agencies' rulings cannot be challenged in the courts, whereas others' can be.[13]

Independent Regulatory Boards and Commissions

Independent regulatory boards and commissions make regulations for various industries, businesses, and sectors of the economy. **Regulations** are simply limitations or restrictions on the behavior of an individual or a business; they are bureaucratically determined prescriptions for how business is to take place. This chapter opened with the battle over a regulation: the guidelines that must be followed for a product to be labeled *organic*. Regulations usually seek to protect the public from some industrial or economic danger or uncertainty. The Securities and Exchange Commission, for example, regulates the trading of stocks and bonds on the nation's stock markets, while the Food and Drug Administration regulates such things as how drugs must be tested before they can be safely marketed and what information must appear on the labels of processed foods and beverages sold throughout the country. Regulation usually pits the individual's freedom to do what he or she wants, or a business's drive to make a profit, against some vision of what is good for the public.

There are thirty-eight agencies of the federal government whose principal job is to issue and enforce regulations about what citizens and businesses can do, and how they have to do it. This effort employs nearly 207,000 people and cost $41 billion in 2005.[14] Given the size of the enterprise, it is not surprising that regulation occasionally gets out of hand. If an agency exists to regulate, regulate it probably will, whether or not a clear case can be made for restricting action. The average cheeseburger in America, for instance, is the subject of over 40,000 federal and state regulations, specifying everything from the vitamin content of the flour in the bun, to the age and fat content of the cheese, to the temperature at which it must be cooked, to the speed at which the ketchup must flow to be certified Grade A Fancy.[15] Some of these rules are undoubtedly crucial; we all want to be able to buy a cheeseburger without risking food poisoning and possible death. Others are informative; those of us on restrictive diets need to know what we are eating, and none of us likes to be ripped off by getting something other than what we think we are paying for. Others seem merely silly; when we consider that adult federal employees are paid to measure the speed of ketchup, we readily sympathize with those who claim that the regulatory function is getting out of hand in American government.

The regulatory agencies are set up to be largely independent of political influence, though some are bureaus within cabinet departments—the federal Food and Drug Administration, for example, is located in the Department of Health and Human Services. Most independent regulatory agencies are run by a commission of three or more people who serve overlapping terms, and the terms of office, usually between three and fourteen years, are set so that they do not coincide with presidential terms. Commission members are nominated by the president and confirmed by Congress, often with a bipartisan vote. Unlike cabinet secretaries and some agency heads, the heads of the regulatory boards and commissions cannot be fired by the president. All of these aspects of their organization are intended to insulate them from political pressures, including presidential influence, in the expectation that they will regulate in the public interest unaffected by current partisan preferences. The number of such agencies is growing, which places the national bureaucracy increasingly beyond the president's control, even as most Americans expect the president to be able to manage the bureaucracy to get things done.[16]

Congress wants to limit presidential influence on the regulatory agencies because not all presidential administrations view regulation the same way, and as they approach the job of appointing regulatory officials accordingly, presidents can have an impact on how the agencies operate during their tenures in office. As holders of a conservative ideology that, in general, prefers to see less regulation and to leave control of industry to the market, Republican presidents tend to appoint businesspeople and others sympathetic to the industries being regulated. Democrats, on the other hand, believe that regulation by impartial experts can smooth out many of the externalities of an unregulated market and tend to appoint those with a record of regulatory accomplishment and scientific expertise.[17]

Government Corporations

We do not often think of the government as a business, but public enterprises are, in fact, big business. The U.S. Postal Service, a **government corporation**, is one of the larger businesses in the nation in terms of sales and personnel. The Tennessee Valley Authority and the Bonneville Power Administration of the northwestern states are both in the business of generating electricity and selling it to citizens throughout their regions. If you ride the rails as a passenger, you travel by Amtrak (technically called the National Railroad Passenger Corporation). All of these businesses are set up to be largely independent of both congressional and presidential influence. This independence is not insignificant. Consider, for example, how angry citizens are when the postal rates go up. Because the Postal Commission is independent, both the president and Congress avoid the political heat for such unpopular decisions.

Roles of the Federal Bureaucracy

Federal bureaucrats at the broadest level are responsible for helping the president to administer the laws, policies, and regulations of government. Bureaucrats are not confined to administering the laws, however. Although the principle of separation of powers—by which the functions of making, administering, and interpreting the laws are carried out by the executive, legislative, and judicial branches—applies at the highest level of government, it tends to dissolve at the level of the bureaucracy. In practice, the bureaucracy is an all-in-one policymaker. It administers the laws, but it also effectively makes and judges compliance with laws.

Bureaucracy as Administrator

We expect the agencies of the federal government to implement the laws passed by Congress and signed by the president. Operating under the ideal of neutral competence, a public bureaucracy serves the political branches of government in a professional, unbiased, and efficient manner. In many cases this is exactly what happens, and with admirable ability and dedication. The rangers in the national parks help citizens enjoy our natural resources, police officers enforce the statutes of criminal law, social workers check for compliance with welfare regulations, and postal workers deliver letters and packages in a timely way. All these bureaucrats are simply carrying out the laws that have been made elsewhere in government.

Bureaucracy as Rule Maker

The picture of the bureaucrat as an impartial administrator removed from political decision making is a partial and unrealistic one. The bureaucracy has a great deal of latitude in administering national policy. Because it often lacks the time, the technical expertise, and the political coherence and leverage to write clear and detailed legislation, Congress frequently passes laws that are vague, contradictory, and overly general. In order to carry out or administer the laws, the bureaucracy must first fill in the gaps. Congress has essentially delegated some of its legislative power to the bureaucracy. Its role here is called **bureaucratic discretion**. Top bureaucrats must use their own judgment, which under the ideal of neutral competence should remain minimal, in order to carry out the laws of Congress. Congress does not say how many park rangers should be assigned to Yosemite versus Yellowstone, for instance; the Park Service has to interpret the broad intent of the law and make decisions on this and thousands of other specifics. Bureaucratic discretion is not limited to allocating personnel and other "minor" administrative details. Congress cannot make decisions on specifications for military aircraft, dictate the advice the agricultural extension agents should give to farmers, or determine whether the latest sugar substitute is safe for our soft drinks. The appropriate bureaucracy must fill in all those details.

The procedures of administrative rule making are not completely insulated from the outside world, however. Before they become effective, all new regulations must first be publicized in the *Federal Register,* which is a primary source of information for thousands of interests affected by decisions in Washington. Before

OTHER BUREAUCRATS WEIGH IN ON USDA'S NEW FOOD PYRAMID

adopting the rules, agencies must give outsiders—the public and interest groups—a chance to be heard, as we saw in the examination of organic farming regulation that began this chapter.

Bureaucracy as Judge

The third major function of governments is adjudication, or the process of interpreting the law in specific cases for potential violations and deciding the appropriate penalties when violations are found. This is what the courts do. However, a great deal of adjudication in America is carried out by the bureaucracy. For example, regulatory agencies not only make many of the rules that govern the conduct of business but also are responsible for seeing that individuals, but more often businesses, comply with their regulations. Tax courts, under the IRS, for instance, handle violations of the tax codes, and their decisions have the full force of law.

Who Are the Federal Bureaucrats?

The full civilian work force of the federal bureaucracy reflects the general population fairly accurately. For example, 45.7 percent of the U.S. civilian labor force is female and 43.9 percent of the civil service is female. African Americans make up 10 percent of the civilian workforce and 17.6 percent of the civil service.[18] The distributions are similar for other demographic characteristics such as ethnic origin or level of education. This representative picture is disturbed, however, by the fact that not all bureaucratic positions are equal. Policymaking is done primarily at the highest levels, and the upper grades are staffed predominantly by well-educated white males. Women and minorities are distinctly underrepresented in the policymaking (and higher-paying) levels of the bureaucracy.[19]

Politics Inside the Bureaucracy

Power struggles between political appointees and professional bureaucrats, constrained by cultural norms

Politicians and bureaucrats alike are wary about the effects of politics on decision making. They act as if fairness and efficiency could always be achieved if only the struggle over competing interests could be set aside through an emphasis on strict rules and hierarchical organization. We know, of course, that the struggle can't be set aside. As a fundamental human activity, politics is always with us, and it is always shaped by the particular rules and institutions in which it is played out. Politics within bureaucracies is a subset of politics generally, but it takes on its own cast according to the context in which it takes place.

Bureaucratic Culture

The particular context in which internal bureaucratic politics is shaped is called **bureaucratic culture**—the accepted values and procedures of an organization. Consider any place you may have been employed. When you began your job, the accepted standards of behavior may not have been clear, but over time you figured out who had power, what your role was, which rules could be bent and which had to be followed strictly, and what the goals of the enterprise were. Chances are you came to share some of the values of your colleagues, at least with respect to your work. Those things add up to the culture of the workplace. Bureaucratic culture is just a specific instance of workplace culture.

Knowing the four main elements of bureaucratic culture—policy commitment, adoption of bureaucratic behavior, specialization and expertise, and identification with the agency—will take us a long way toward understanding why bureaucrats and bureaucracies behave the way they do. Essentially these elements define what is at stake within a bureaucracy, and what bureaucrats need to do to ensure that they are winners and not losers in the bureaucratic world. To explore bureaucratic culture, let's imagine that you have landed a job working in the USDA. Over time, if you are successful in your job, you will come to share the values and beliefs of others working in your department; that is, you will come to share their bureaucratic culture.

As a good bureaucrat in training, the first thing you will do is develop a commitment to the policy issues of agriculture. No matter if you've never thought much about farming before. As an employee of the USDA, you will eventually come to believe that agricultural issues are among the most important facing the country, just as those working at NASA place a priority on investigating outer space, and bureaucrats at the National Institutes of Health believe fervently in health research. You share a commitment to your policy area not only because your job depends on it but also because all the people around you believe in it.

Not long after you join your department, you will start to see the logic of behaving bureaucratically. You may even start to sound like a bureaucrat. Bureaucratese, the formal and often (to outsiders) amusing way that bureaucrats sometimes speak in their effort to convey information without controversy, may become your second tongue (see *Consider the Source* in this chapter). The elaborate rule structure that defines the bureaucracy will come to seem quite normal to you; you will even depend on it because relying on the rules relieves you of the responsibility of relying on your own judgment. The hierarchical organization of authority will also make a good deal of sense, and you will, in fact, find yourself spending a lot of your time helping to make your superiors look good to their superiors, even as the people working under you will be helping you to look good to your bosses. As you become committed to the bureaucratic structure, you learn that conformity to the rules and norms of the enterprise is the name of the game.

Early on in your career, you will realize that departments, agencies, and bureaus have specialized areas of responsibility and expertise. There is not a great deal of interagency hopping; most bureaucrats spend their whole professional lives working in the same area, often in the same department. The lawyers in the Justice Department, scientists at the National Science Foundation, physicians at the National Institutes of Health, and even you as a soybean expert at the USDA all have specialized knowledge as the base of your power.

All three of the characteristics of bureaucratic culture discussed so far lead to the fourth: identification with and protection of the agency. As you become attached to the interests of agriculture, committed to the rules and structures of the bureaucracy, concerned with the fortunes of your superiors, and appreciative of your own and your colleagues' specialized knowledge, your estimation of the USDA rises also. You begin to think that what is good for Agriculture is good for you, and that threats to the department's well-being become threats to you. You identify with the department, not just because your job depends on it but because you believe in what it does.

This pervasive bureaucratic culture breeds a number of political consequences. On the plus side, it holds the bureaucracy together, fostering values of commitment and loyalty to what could otherwise be seen as an impersonal and alienating work environment. It means that the people who work in the federal government, for the most part, really believe in what they do.

But bureaucratic culture can lead to negative consequences as well. As former FBI agent Coleen Rowley pointed out in testimony before the Senate Judiciary Committee in June 2002, this culture very likely had a role in the failure of our law enforcement and intelligence agencies to foresee and prevent the attacks of September 11, 2001. Rowley's office, in Minneapolis, had known that a possible terrorist,

Don't Be Fooled by Bureaucratese

The tortured and twisted language our government bureaucrats seem to love can be so awful that it's actually amusing—if you have nothing at stake in figuring out what it means. Try this on for size: "The metropolitan Washington region's transportation system will promote economic sustainability and quality of life through a facilitation of inter- and intra-jurisdictional connectivity of employment and population centers, with a comprehensive multi-modal approach to mobility and utilize available tools to reduce congestion."[1] What a windy way to say that the Washington transportation system will relieve traffic jams by using a variety of methods of transit!

It's no wonder that people have trouble taking what their government says seriously. But what might be merely irritating, or laughable, or just plain stupid when it comes to transportation can assume a lot more importance when it's something we need to know about. Take taxes: failing to accurately calculate and pay one's taxes can lead to a financial penalty, or worse. But what's a taxpayer to do when confronted with something like this? "If the taxpayer's passive activity gross income from significant participation passive activities (within the meaning of section 1.469-2T-(f)(2)(ii)) for the taxable year (determined without regard to section 1.469-2T-(f)(2) through (4)) exceeds the taxpayer's passive activity deductions from such activities for the taxable year, such activities shall be treated, solely for purposes of applying this paragraph (f)(2)(i) for the taxable year, as a single activity that does not have a loss for such taxable year." Even a nationwide poll of accountants gave this Internal Revenue Service rule the "Most Incomprehensible Government Regulation" award.[2]

The truth is, translating bureaucratese, the bewildering way that government officials often speak, can be quite a project. It would be nice if we could just avoid dealing with government language altogether, but most of us can't. At some time in our lives we register a car, apply for a student loan, get a marriage license, or file a building permit. We may need to register for Social Security benefits or apply for Medicaid or food stamps. We may fill out a passport application or a form to bring purchases back through customs after traveling abroad. We may want to read a report from the local school committee or the public transportation board. And one thing is certain: we all have to pay taxes. Here are a few hints for deciphering government jargon:

1. **Translate overly complicated terms that refer to common objects and events.** In bureaucratese, "means of egress" are exits, a "grade separation structure" can turn out to be a bridge, "rail movements" are train trips, "agricultural specialists" are farmers, and an application for an "unenclosed

premise permit" is a request to build a patio.[3] Such language may result from an effort to be more specific, from a wish to be less specific, or just from a desire to make something sound more important than it is. Don't be fooled by lofty or euphemistic language.

2. **Watch out for the use of the passive voice.** Bureaucrats often speak passively: "Action is taken," or "Resources are acquisitioned." The passive voice allows the author to avoid saying who is taking the action or acquiring the resources, often key pieces of information you need or want to know.

3. **Don't be intimidated by the insider language bureaucrats may create for themselves.** Be sure you understand what you are reading or being told. When officials at the Department of Housing and Urban Development in Washington talk about having a "pony to ride," they aren't referring to a childhood pet but to a "senior inside official who would walk a controversial project through various obstacles in the department, much like a pony express rider could deliver the mails in the Old West."[4] At the local level, "public assistance benefits insurance" (itself a mouthful of bureaucratese) is called "Benny" or, even more obscurely, "Jack Benny" by county welfare agents in Buffalo, New York. There is no end to the creative shorthand employed by bureaucrats. If you do not understand what you are told, ask.

4. **Eliminate redundancy—it can make a relatively simple concept sound incredibly complicated.** Bureaucrats are not the only ones guilty of this. An article on writing for lawyers (many of whom go on to work in the government, of course) points out that it is unnecessary to say "green in color," "consensus of opinion," "free gift," or "final outcome."[5] Such wordiness is not only wrong, but it clutters up the language, making it hard to understand what is being said.

5. **Look for nouns that have been turned into verbs.** Bureaucrats are famous for this. *Impact, acquisition,* and *dialogue,* for instance, are used as nouns in everyday language but as verbs in bureaucratese. If a word seems out of place, it probably is. Think creatively when translating government documents.

6. **Never speak or write like this yourself!** Bureaucratese is bad enough coming from bureaucrats and lawyers. There is no substitute for good, clear, crisp writing.

Reading and understanding the bloated jargon of government bureaucratese can be quite a challenge. Those of you with a sweet tooth can practice on Official Government Bureaucracy Cookies.[6]

(Continued)

Don't Be Fooled by Bureaucratese (Continued)

Official Government Bureaucracy Cookies

Output: six dozen cookie units

Inputs: 1 cup packed brown sugar
1/2 cup butter, softened
2 eggs
2 1/2 cups all purpose flour
1/2 teaspoon salt
1 cup chopped pecans or walnuts
1/2 cup white sugar
1/2 cup shortening
1 1/2 teaspoons vanilla
1 teaspoon baking soda
12 ounces semisweet chocolate chips

Guidance:

After procurement actions, decontainerize inputs. Perform measurement tasks on a case-by-case basis:

1. In a mixing-type bowl, impact heavily on brown sugar, white sugar, butter, and shortening. Coordinate the interface of eggs and vanilla, avoiding an overrun scenario to the best of your skills and abilities.

2. At this point in time, leverage flour, baking soda, and salt into a bowl and aggregate. Equalize with prior mixture and develop intense and continuous

Zacarias Moussaoui, was seeking to take flying lessons. Finding his activities suspicious and worrisome, Minneapolis agents tried to get a warrant to search his computer but were unable to do so. In her testimony, Rowley targeted the FBI's hierarchical culture, with its implicit norm that said field agents did not go over the heads of their superiors, who frequently second-guessed their judgment.[20]

Not only did bureaucratic culture keep the FBI from knowing what information it had prior to September 11, but it also kept the FBI and the Central Intelligence Agency (CIA) from communicating with each other about the various pieces of the puzzle they had found. Between them they had much of the information needed to have discovered the plot, but no one connected the dots. Why? The cultures are different. The FBI is primarily a law enforcement agency; agents are rewarded for making arrests. Its antiterrorist activities prior to September 11 were focused on after-the-fact investigations of terrorist attacks (leading to convictions) but not on preventing such attacks against domestic targets.[21]

liaison among inputs until well coordinated. Associate with chocolate and nut subsystems and execute stirring options.

3. Within this time frame, take action to prepare the heating environment for throughput by manually setting the oven baking unit to a temperature of 375 degrees F.

4. Drop mixture in an ongoing fashion from a teaspoon implement onto an ungreased cookie sheet at intervals sufficiently apart to permit total and permanent throughputs to the maximum extent particular under operating conditions. Position cookie sheet in a bake situation for 8 to 10 minutes or until cooking action terminates.

5. Initiate coordination of outputs with the cooling rack function. Containerize, wrap in red tape, and disseminate to authorized staff personnel on a timely and expeditious basis.

---

1. Walden Siew, "Ready Readers Respond to Our Gibberish Alert," *Washington Times,* December 1, 1997, 1, web version.

2. "Have You Hugged Your 1040 Today?" *Washington Times,* April 15, 1991, D2.

3. Laurel Walker, "Functionaries Should Better Utilize Lexicon: Why Do Bureaucrats Insist on Using So Much Unintelligible Jargon?" *Milwaukee Journal Sentinel,* July 5, 1997, 1–2.

4. Bill McAllister and Maralee Schwartz, "'A Pony to Ride': Freshly Minted Bureaucratese," *Washington Post,* May 8, 1990, 1.

5. Tom Goldstein and Jethro K. Lieberman, "Double Negative Use Is Not Unavoidable," *Texas Lawyer,* May 28, 1990, 2.

6. Laura Robin, "Fluent in Bureaucratese? Output These Food Units," *The Ottawa Citizen,* February 18, 1998, 2–3. Reprinted by permission.

The CIA, on the other hand, is focused on clandestine activity to develop information about non-American groups and nations. It is more secretive and less rule-bound, more focused on plans and intentions than on after-the-fact evidence and convictions. Agents focus on relationships, not individual achievement. One reporter covering the two agencies wrote that though the two agencies need to work with each other, "they have such different approaches to life that they remain worlds apart. In fact, they speak such different languages that they can barely even communicate."[22]

When an agency is charged with making the rules, enforcing them, and even adjudicating them, it is relatively easy to cover up less catastrophic agency blunders. If Congress, the media, or the public had sufficient information and the expertise to interpret it, this would not be as big a problem. However, specialization necessarily concentrates the expertise and information in the hands of the agencies. Congress and the media are generalists. They can tell something has gone wrong when terrorists attack the United States seemingly without warning, but they cannot evaluate the hundreds of less obvious problems that may have led to the failure to warn that only an expert would even recognize.

Congress has tried to check the temptation for bureaucrats to cover up their mistakes by offering protection to whistleblowers. **Whistleblowers**, like Coleen Rowley in the earlier example, are employees who expose instances or patterns of error, corruption, or waste in their agencies, whose consciences will not permit them to protect their agencies and superiors at the expense of what they believe to be the public good. The Whistleblower Protection Act of 1989 established an independent agency to protect employees from being fired, demoted, or otherwise punished for exposing wrongdoing. The act's intention to protect whistleblowers is certainly a step in the direction of countering a negative tendency of organizational behavior, but it does little to offset the pervasive pressure to protect the programs and the agencies from harm, embarrassment, and budget cuts. Because the agency that rules in these cases usually sides with the bureaucracy over the whistleblower, the law hasn't worked quite as its authors intended.[23]

Presidential Appointees and the Career Civil Service

Another aspect of internal bureaucratic politics worth noting is the giant gulf between those at the very top of the department or agency who are appointed by the president and those in the lower ranks who are long-term civil service employees. Of the two million civilian employees in the U.S. civil service, about 3,500 are appointed by the president or his immediate subordinates.

The presidential appointees are sometimes considered "birds of passage" by the career service because of the regularity with which they come and go.[24] Though generally quite experienced in the agency's policy area, appointees have their own careers or the president's agenda as their primary objective rather than the long-established mission of the agency. The professional civil servants, in contrast, have worked in their agencies for many years, and expect to remain there.[25] Chances are they were there before the current president was elected, and they will be there after he leaves office. They are wholly committed to their agencies.

Minor clashes are frequent, but they can intensify into major rifts when the ideology of a newly elected president varies sharply from the central values of the operating agency. Nevertheless, even though the political appointees have the advantage of higher positions of authority, the career bureaucrats have time working on their side. Not surprisingly, the bureaucrat's best strategy when the political appointee presses for a new but unpopular policy direction is to stall. This is easily achieved by consulting the experts on feasibility, writing reports, drawing up implementation plans, commissioning further study, doing cost-benefit analyses, consulting advisory panels of citizens, and on and on.

Given the difficulty that presidents and their appointees can have in dealing with the entrenched bureaucracy, presidents who want to institute an innovative program are better off starting a new agency than trying to get an old one to adapt to new tasks. In the 1960s, when President John Kennedy wanted to start the Peace Corps, a largely volunteer organization that provided assistance to developing countries by working at the grassroots level with the people themselves, he could have added it to any number of existing departments. The problem was that either these existing agencies were unlikely to accept the idea that nonprofessional volunteers could do anything useful, or they were likely to subvert them to their own purposes, such as spying or managing aid. Thus President Kennedy was easily persuaded to have the Peace Corps set up as an independent agency, a frequent occurrence in the change-resistant world of bureaucratic politics.[26]

External Bureaucratic Politics
Turf wars among agencies and with the three branches of government

Politics affects relationships not only within bureaucratic agencies but also between those agencies and other institutions. While the bureaucracy is not one of the official branches of government, since it falls technically within the executive branch, it is often called the fourth branch of government because it wields so much power. It can be checked by other agencies, by the executive, by Congress, or even by the public, but it is not wholly under the authority of any of those entities. In this section we examine the political relationships that exist between the bureaucracy and the other main actors in American politics.

Interagency Politics

As we have seen, agencies are fiercely committed to their policy areas, their rules and norms, and their own continued existence. The government consists of a host of agencies, all competing intensely for a limited amount of federal resources and political support. They all want to protect themselves and their programs, and they want to grow, or at least to avoid cuts in personnel and budgets.

To appreciate the agencies' political plight, we need to see their situation *as they see it*. Bureaucrats are a favorite target of the media and elected officials. Their budgets are periodically up for review by congressional committees and the president's budget department. Consequently agencies are compelled to work for their survival and growth. They have to act positively in an uncertain and changing political environment in order to keep their programs and their jobs.

One way agencies compete to survive is by building groups of supporters. Members of Congress are sensitive to voters' wishes, and because of this, support among the general public as well as interest groups is important for agencies. As a result, agencies try to control some services or products that are crucial to important groups. In most cases, the groups are obvious, as with the clientele groups of, say, the USDA. Department of Agriculture employees work hard for farming interests, not just because they believe in the programs but also because they need strong support from agricultural clientele to survive. Agencies whose work does not earn them a lot of fans, like the IRS, whose mission is tax collection, have few groups to support them. When Congress decided to reform the IRS in 1998, there were no defenders to halt the changes.[27] The survival incentives for bureaucratic agencies do not encourage agencies to work for the broader public interest but rather to cultivate special interests that are likely to be more politically active and powerful.

Even independent regulatory commissions run into this problem. Numerous observers have noted the phenomenon of **agency capture**, whereby commissions tend to become creatures of the very interests they are supposed to regulate. In other words, as the regulatory bureaucrats become more and more immersed in a policy area, they come to share the views of the regulated industries. The larger public's preferences tend to be less well formed and certainly less well expressed because the general public does not hire teams of lawyers, consultants, and lobbyists to represent its interests. An excellent case in point is the USDA's proposed definition of *organic,* which seemed designed to benefit big food industries and agribusiness rather than the public and small farmers. The regulated industries have a tremendous amount at stake. Over time, regulatory agencies' actions may become so favorable to regulated industries that in some cases the industries themselves have fought deregulation, as did the airlines when Congress and the Civil Aeronautics Board deregulated air travel in the 1980s.[28]

Agencies also compete and survive by offering services that no other agency provides. Departments and agencies are set up to deal with the problems of fairly specific areas. They do not want to overlap with other agencies because duplication of services might indicate that one of them was unnecessary, inviting congressional cuts. Thus, in many instances, agencies reach explicit agreements about dividing up the policy turf to avoid competition and duplication. This turf jealousy can undermine good public policy. Take, for example, the military: for years, the armed services successfully resisted a unified weapons procurement, command, and control system. Each branch wanted to maintain its traditional independence in weapons development, logistics, and communications technologies, costing the taxpayers millions of dollars. Getting the branches to give up control of their turf was politically difficult, although it was accomplished eventually.

The Bureaucracy and the President

As we discussed in Chapter 7, one of the president's several jobs is that of chief administrator. In fact, organizational charts of departments and agencies suggest a clear chain of command with the cabinet secretary at the top reporting directly to the president. But in this case, being "the boss" does not mean that the boss always, or even usually, gets his way. The long history of the relationship between the president and the bureaucracy is largely one of presidential frustration.

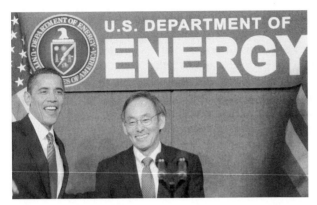

Expert Advisers
President Barack Obama is known for appointing advisers and department heads, such as Energy secretary Steven Chu, more because of their expertise than their ideological views. In contrast, George W. Bush was at times criticized for politicizing the bureaucracy.

President Kennedy voiced this exasperation when he said that dealing with the bureaucracy "is like trying to nail jelly to the wall." The reasons for presidential frustration lie in the fact that, although the president has some authority over the bureaucracy, the bureaucracy's different perspectives and goals often thwart the chief administrator's plans.

Presidents have some substantial powers at their disposal for controlling the bureaucracy. The first is the power of appointment. Presidents appoint the heads and the next layer or two of undersecretaries and deputy secretaries of the departments, and of quite a few of the independent agencies. These cabinet secretaries and agency administrators are responsible for running the departments and agencies. The president's formal power, though quite significant, is often watered down by the political realities of the appointment and policymaking processes.

The appointment process begins at the start of the president's administration when he is working to gain support for his overall program, so he doesn't want his choices to be too controversial. This desire for early widespread support means presidents tend to play it safe and to nominate individuals with extensive experience in the policy areas they will oversee. Their backgrounds mean that the president's men and women are only partially his. They arrive on the job with some sympathy for the special interests and agencies they are to supervise on the president's behalf as well as with loyalty to the president.

Recent presidents have sought to achieve political control over agencies by expanding the numbers of their appointees at the top levels of agencies, especially those agencies whose missions are not consistent with the administration's policy agenda.[29] President George W. Bush was especially adept at this "politicalization" of the bureaucracy. For instance, in his second term, he appointed one of his most trusted personal advisers to head the Department of Justice. Officials in that department then fired existing U.S. attorneys and replaced them with conservatives who would be more sympathetic to Republican policy concerns, which blunted the agency's traditionally aggressive enforcement of civil rights laws.[30] President Obama's appointees, on the other hand, have been named with less of an eye to their ideological views than to their scientific expertise. As a Democrat, Obama has attempted to reinvigorate the regulatory purpose and effective competence of the agencies in the bureaucracy, and his appointees have been notable for their experience and credentials rather than their political views or personal loyalty.[31]

The president's second major power in dealing with the bureaucracy is his key role in the budget process. About fifteen months before a budget request goes to Congress, the agencies send their preferred budget requests to the Office of Management and Budget (a White House agency serving the preferences of the president), which can lower, or raise, departmental budget requests. Thus the president's budget, which is sent to Congress, is a good statement of the president's overall program for the national government. It reflects his priorities, new initiatives, and intended cutbacks. His political appointees and the civil servants who testify before Congress are expected to defend the president's budget.

And they do defend the president's budget, at least in their prepared statements. However, civil servants have contacts with interest group leaders, congressional staff, the media, and members of Congress themselves. Regardless of what the president wants, the agencies' real preferences are made known to sympathetic members of the key authorizations and appropriations committees. Thus the president's budget is a beginning bargaining point, but Congress can freely add to or cut back presidential requests, and most of the time it does so. The president's budget powers, while not insignificant, are no match for an agency with strong interest group and congressional support. Presidential influence over the bureaucratic budget is generally more effective in terminating an activity that the president opposes than in implementing a program that the agency opposes.[32]

The third major power of the president is the veto. As we argued in Chapter 6, the presidential veto can be an effective weapon for derailing legislation, but it is a rather blunt tool for influencing the bureaucracy. First, many spending bills are bundled together. The president may want a different set of funding priorities for, say, mass transit systems, but such funding may be buried in a multibillion-dollar multiagency appropriation. The president may not like everything in the bill, but he does not want to risk shutting down the government or starting a public battle. The veto can be used only as a threat in political bargaining. By itself, it does not guarantee the president what he wants.

In addition to his other efforts, the president can try to reorganize the bureaucracy, combining some agencies, eliminating others, and generally restructuring the way government responsibilities are handled. Such reorganization efforts have become a passion with some presidents, but they are limited in their efforts by the need for congressional approval.[33]

One recent effort at reorganization was the creation of the Department of Homeland Security in response to the terrorist attacks of September 11, 2001. The goal of the department is to refocus the activities of multiple agencies whose jurisdictions touched on security issues, bringing them under the leadership of a single organization. More typical of reorganization efforts in the sense that it was intended to make government leaner and more efficient was President Clinton's National Performance Review (NPR), which later became the National Partnership for Reinventing Government. The goal of this commission, headed by then–vice president Al Gore, was to trim the federal payroll by a quarter of a million jobs and to produce savings of $100 billion by decentralizing, deregulating, and freeing government employees to show more initiative in getting their jobs done.

The president's final major power over the bureaucracy is an informal one, the prestige of the office itself. The Office of the President impresses just about everyone. If the president is intent on change in an agency, his powers of persuasion and the sheer weight of the office can produce results. Few bureaucrats could stand face to face with the president of the United States and ignore a legal order. But the president's time is limited, his political pressures are many, and he needs to choose his priorities very carefully. The media, for example, will not permit him to spend a good part of every day worrying about a little program that they think is trivial. He will be publicly criticized for wasting time on "minor matters." Thus the president and his top White House staff have to move on to other things. The temptation for a bureaucracy that does not want to cooperate with a presidential initiative is to wait it out, to take the matter under study, to be "able" to accomplish only a minor part of the president's agenda. The agency or department can then begin the process of regaining whatever ground it lost. It, after all, will be there long after the president leaves office.

The Bureaucracy and Congress

Relationships between the bureaucracy and Congress are not any more clear-cut than those between the agencies and the president, but in the long run individual members of Congress, if not the whole institution itself, have more control over what specific bureaucracies do than does the executive branch. This is not due to any particular grant of power by the Constitution but rather to informal policymaking relationships that have grown up over time and are now all but institutionalized.

Much of the effective power in making policy in Washington is lodged in what political scientists call **iron triangles**. An iron triangle is a tight alliance between congressional committees, interest groups or representatives of regulated industries, and bureaucratic agencies, in which policy comes to be made for the benefit of the shared interests of all three, not for the benefit of the greater public. Politicians are themselves quite aware of the pervasive triangular monopoly of power. Former secretary of Health, Education, and Welfare John Gardner once declared before the Senate Government Operations Committee, "As everyone in this room knows but few people outside of Washington understand, questions of public policy nominally lodged with the Secretary are often decided far beyond the Secretary's reach by a trinity—not exactly a holy trinity—consisting of (1) representatives of an outside lobby, (2) middle-level bureaucrats, and (3) selected members of Congress."[34]

Figure 8.2

Oil-BOEMRE Iron Triangle

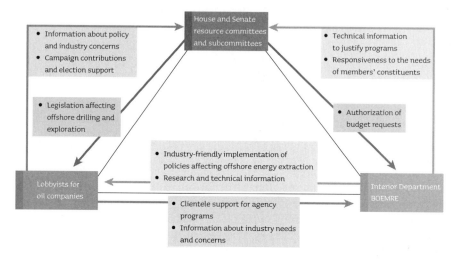

Iron triangles (involving Congress, the bureaucracy, and special interest groups) exist on nearly every subgovernment level. In this example, you can see how the BOEMRE (the Bureau of Ocean Energy Management, Regulation and Enforcement, which depends on the House and Senate for its budget) influences and is influenced by oil company lobbyists, who in turn influence and are influenced by House and Senate committees and subcommittees. This mutual interdependence represents a powerful monopoly of power.

A good example of an iron triangle is the natural resources policy shown in Figure 8.2. In 2010, as oil gushed into the Gulf of Mexico from the ruined oil rig *Deepwater Horizon,* the Minerals Management Service (MMS), an obscure agency that few citizens had heard of, was blasted into the news. The MMS, which was in charge of issuing leases, collecting royalties, and overseeing the dangerous work of offshore drilling for oil and gas on America's continental shelf, was accused of having cozy and even illegal relationships with the industry it was charged with regulating. Agency employees were said to have accepted meals, gifts, and sporting trips from the oil industry, and some agency staff were accused of having had sex and using drugs with industry employees. How could this happen?

At the agency's top sat people like J. Steven Griles, who had worked as an oil industry lobbyist before joining the government. In middle management, the line between the industry and its regulators in the field was blurred.[35] As one MMS district manager put it, "Obviously we're all oil industry. . . . We're all from the same part of the country. Almost all our inspectors have worked for oil companies out on the [Gulf] platforms. They grew up in the same towns."[36] The industry and agency shared a goal of maximizing oil and gas production with hardly more than a whisper of concern for the effects of what was believed to be an unlikely accident. Not surprisingly, many key congressional leaders of the committees with jurisdiction over oil and gas drilling policies are from states with large petroleum interests. The House Committee on Natural Resources and its subcommittee on Energy and Mineral Resources have several members whose districts have major financial interests in oil and gas production, and most of these members receive substantial contributions from the oil and gas industry. The oil- and gas-producing states of Louisiana, Texas, Oklahoma, Colorado, and New Mexico all have members of Congress who receive major contributions from oil and gas industry sources.[37]

Thus the oil industry, the MMS, and members of Congress with responsibility for overseeing the agency all possessed interests in protecting energy production that reinforced one another in a cozy triangle and disregarded the general public's interests in avoiding environmental catastrophe and receiving the appropriate royalties from oil and gas use. The drug and sex scandals, along with the media's relentless coverage of the *Deepwater Horizon* disaster, focused national attention on the problem and spurred the Obama administration to reorganize the agency, now called the Bureau of Ocean Energy Management, Regulation and Enforcement (BOEMRE). However, the forces that created this situation—that is, the intertwined interests among members of Congress who serve on committees that oversee agencies that regulate the industries that affect voters in their districts—are a fundamental part of our political-economic system. As long as citizens and industry are free to "petition Congress for redress of grievances," iron triangles will remain.

The metaphor of the iron triangle has been refined by scholars, who speak instead of **issue networks**.[38] The iron triangle suggests a particular relationship among a fixed interest group and fixed agencies and fixed subcommittees. The network idea suggests that the relationships are more complex than a simple triangle. There are really clusters of interest groups, policy specialists, consultants, and research institutes ("think tanks") that are influential in the policy areas. To continue with the offshore drilling example, environmental groups such as the League of Conservation Voters monitor the environmental records of members of Congress, and outside groups use existing laws to force agencies like the MMS to change their procedures. So, for example, the Center for Biological Diversity sought to sue the Department of the Interior (of which the MMS was part) for failing to get appropriate environmental permits required by the Marine Mammal Protection Act and the Endangered Species Act.[39] Thus "outsiders" can use the courts, and they often lobby sympathetic members of Congress to contest the relationships that develop as iron triangles. Their participation shows that the concept of an iron triangle does not always incorporate all the actors in a particular policy area. That is, although the relationships identified by the iron triangle remain important, the full range of politics is frequently captured better by the concept of issue networks.

Congressional control of the bureaucracy is found more in the impact of congressional committees and subcommittees than in the actions of the institution as a whole. Congress, of course, passes the laws that create the agencies, assigns them their responsibilities, and funds their operations. Furthermore, Congress can, and frequently does, change the laws under which the agencies operate. Thus Congress clearly has the formal power to control the bureaucracy. It also has access to a good deal of information that helps members monitor the bureaucracy. This process is called **congressional oversight**. Members learn about agency behavior through required reports, oversight hearings, reports by congressional agencies such as the Office of Technology Assessment and the Government Accountability Office, and from constituents and organized interests. But Congress is itself often divided about what it wants to do and is unable to set clear guidelines for agencies. During the first six years of the Bush administration, the Republican majority was more intent on supporting the president than on protecting congressional prerogatives in the policy process. This aided the president's expansion of control of the bureaucracy.[40] Only when a congressional consensus exists on what an agency should be doing is congressional control fully effective.

The Bureaucracy and the Courts

Agencies can be sued by individuals and businesses for not following the law. If a citizen disagrees with an agency ruling on welfare eligibility, or the adequacy of inspections of poultry processing plants, or even a ruling by the IRS, he or she can take the case to the courts. In some cases the courts have been important. A highly controversial example involves the timber industry. Environmentalists sued the Department of the Interior and the U.S. Forest Service to prevent logging in some of the old-growth forests of the Pacific Northwest. They sought protection for the spotted owl under the terms of the Endangered Species Act. After a decade-long struggle, logging was greatly restricted in the area in 1992, despite opposition by the economically important timbering interests of the region. However, under the more business-friendly Bush administration, the issue was once again on the agenda and, as the timber industry gained ground, the environmental groups were back in court. In 2009 the Obama administration reversed the Bush administration policy that had doubled the amount of logging allowed.[41]

More often, though, the courts play only a modest role in controlling the bureaucracy. One of the reasons for this limited role is that, since the Administrative Procedures Act of 1946, the courts have tended to defer to the expertise of the bureaucrats when agency decisions are appealed. That is, unless a clear principle of law is violated, the courts usually support administrative rulings.[42] So, for example, while the Supreme Court did restrict some aspects of the Bush administration's policies of unlimited detention of "enemy combatants" held in Guantánamo Bay, it did not go nearly as far as civil liberties advocates wanted.[43]

Another reason is that Congress explicitly puts the decisions of numerous agencies, such as the Department of Veterans Affairs, beyond the reach of the courts. They do this, of course, when members expect they will agree with the decisions of an agency but are uncertain about what the courts might do. Finally, even without these restrictions, the courts' time is extremely limited. The departments and independent agencies make thousands and thousands of important decisions each year; the courts can act on only those decisions about which someone feels sufficiently aggrieved to take the agency to court. Court proceedings can drag on for years, and meanwhile the agencies go about their business making new decisions. In short, the courts can, in specific instances, decide cases that influence how the bureaucracy operates, but such instances are the exception rather than the rule.

Citizenship and the Bureaucracy
The tension between transparency and efficiency

To help increase bureaucratic responsiveness and sensitivity to the public, Congress has made citizen participation a central feature of the policymaking of many agencies. This frequently takes the form of **citizen advisory councils** that, by statute, subject key policy decisions of agencies to outside consideration by members of the public. There are more than 1,200 such committees and councils in the executive branch. The people who serve on these councils are not representative of the general public. Rather, they are typically chosen by the agency and have special credentials or interests relevant to the agency's work.

Other reforms have attempted to make the bureaucracy more accessible to the public. Citizen access has been enhanced by the passage of **sunshine laws**, which require that meetings of policymakers be open to the public. However, most national security and personnel meetings, as well as many criminal investigation meetings, are exempt. The right to attend a meeting is of little use if one doesn't know that it is being held in the first place. The Administrative Procedures Act requires advance published notice of all hearings, proposed rules, and new regulations so that the public can attend and comment on decisions that might affect them. These announcements appear in the *Federal Register*.

A related point of access is the **Freedom of Information Act** (**FOIA**), which was passed in 1966 and has been amended several times since. This act provides citizens with the right to copies of most public records held by federal agencies. Citizens also receive protection under the **Privacy Act of 1974**, which gives them the right to find out what information government agencies have about them. It also sets up procedures so that erroneous information can be corrected and ensures the confidentiality of Social Security, tax, and related records.

These reforms may provide little practical access for most citizens, however. Few of us have the time, the knowledge, or the energy to plow through the *Federal Register* and to attend meetings regularly. Similarly, while many citizens no doubt feel that they are not getting the full story from government agencies, they have little idea of what it is they don't know. Hence few of us ever use the FOIA.

▶ What's at Stake Revisited

Let's go back to the question of what's at stake in the dispute over the USDA's organic food regulation. Remember that regulations are a form of rules, and rules determine who the winners and losers are likely to be. Regulations can serve a variety of interests. They could serve the public interest, simply making it easier for consumers to buy organic food by standardizing what it means to be organic. But regulations can also serve interests besides the public interest. In this case, there were competing business interests as well. Agribusiness and the food preparation industry wanted to use regulations to break into a lucrative market previously closed to them because of the labor-intensive nature of organic farming. For the traditional organic farmers, the proposed regulations spelled disaster.

As far as big business was concerned, this case was like many others. Businesses in the United States are able to lobby the government freely to try to get rules and regulations passed that enhance their positions, and to try to stop those that will hurt them. As we will see in Chapter 11's discussion of interest groups, the larger sums of money that big business can bring to the lobbying effort usually give them an edge in influencing government. If the larger businesses were allowed to compete as organic food producers, the small businesses would lose the only advantage they had, and they would have been forced out of business. In this case, the small businesses were aided by citizen action. This example shows that it is possible to energize a public audience to respond to the bureaucracy. Because those consumers who choose to eat organic foods were a focused, committed, and assertive segment of the population, they were able to follow through with political action.

▶ Summary With Key Terms

Bureaucracy (263), a form of hierarchical organization that aspires to **neutral competence** (264), is everywhere today, in the private as well as the public sphere. Bureaucratic decision making can be more efficient and expert in many cases than democratic decision making. The central problem of bureaucracy is **accountability** (265). The **Pendleton Act** (264) and the **Hatch Act** (264) have moved the federal bureaucracy from the **patronage**-based (264) **spoils system** (264) of the nineteenth century to a **civil service** (264) based on merit. **Red tape** (266), though cumbersome and irritating, also helps increase accountability by providing a paper trail and eliminating the discretion of lower-level bureaucrats to do their jobs in an idiosyncratic way.

The U.S. bureaucracy has grown from just three cabinet **departments** (268) at the founding to a gigantic apparatus of fifteen cabinet-level departments and hundreds of **independent agencies** (268), **independent regulatory boards and commissions** (270), and **government corporations** (271). This growth has been in response to the expansion of the nation, the politics of special economic and social **clientele groups** (267), and the emergence of new problems that require solutions and **regulations** (270). Sometimes agencies identify so thoroughly with the industries they are designed to regulate that we speak of **agency capture** (282).

Many observers believe that the bureaucracy should simply administer the laws the political branches have enacted. In reality, the agencies of the bureaucracy make government policy, using **bureaucratic discretion** (272) to interpret the laws of Congress and to make new regulations, which are then published in the *Federal Register* (272), and they play the roles of judge and jury in enforcing those policies.

Bureaucratic culture (274) refers to how agencies operate—their assumptions, values, and habits, including their reliance on a formal and confusing language called bureaucratese. The bureaucratic culture increases employees' belief in the programs they administer, their commitment to the survival and growth of their agencies, and the tendency to rely on rules and procedures rather than goals, but it can also lead to the kinds of mistakes and conflicts of interest sometimes exposed by **whistleblowers** (280).

Agencies work actively for their political survival. They attempt to establish strong support outside the agency, to avoid direct competition with other agencies, and to jealously guard their own policy jurisdictions. Presidential powers are only modestly effective in controlling the bureaucracy. The affected clientele groups working in close cooperation with the agencies and the congressional committees that oversee them form powerful **iron triangles** (285) and **issue networks** (287). Congress exercises control through the process of **congressional oversight** (288).

Regardless of what the public may think, the U.S. bureaucracy is actually quite responsive and competent when compared with the bureaucracies of other countries. Citizens can increase this responsiveness by taking advantage of opportunities for gaining access to bureaucratic decision making, such as **citizen advisory councils** (289), **sunshine laws** (289), the **Freedom of Information Act** (289), and the **Privacy Act of 1974** (289).

Explore this subject further with suggested readings, movies, and web sites at http://republic-brief.cqpress.com, where you'll also find study aids, practice quizzes, flash cards, and Internet exercises.

Chapter 9

The American Legal System and the Courts

▶ What's at Stake?

The 2000 presidential election must have set Alexander Hamilton spinning in his grave. In *The Federalist Papers* the American founder confidently wrote that the Supreme Court would be the least dangerous branch of government. Having the power of neither the sword nor the purse, it could do little other than judge, and Hamilton blithely assumed that those judgments would remain legal ones, not matters of raw power politics.

More than two hundred years later, however, without military might or budgetary power, the Supreme Court took into its own hands the very political task of deciding who would be the next president of the United States and, what's more, made that decision right down party lines. On a five-to-four vote (five more conservative justices versus four more liberal ones), the Supreme Court overturned the decision of the Florida Supreme Court to allow a recount of votes in the contested Florida election and awarded electoral victory to Republican George W. Bush.

How did it come to this? The presidential vote in Florida was virtually tied, recounts were required by law in some locations, and voting snafus in several other counties had left untold votes uncounted. Whether those votes should, or even could, be counted or whether voter error and system failure had rendered them invalid was in dispute. Believing that a count of the disputed ballots would give him the few hundred votes he needed for victory, Al Gore wanted the recount. Bush did not. The Florida secretary of state, a Republican appointed by the governor, Bush's brother, ordered the vote counting finished. The Florida Supreme Court, heavily dominated by Democrats, ruled instead that a recount should go forward.

Bush appealed to the Supreme Court, asking it to overturn the Florida Supreme Court's decision and to stay, or suspend, the recount pending its decision. A divided Court issued the stay. Justice John Paul Stevens took the unusual route of writing a dissent from the stay, arguing that it was unwise to "stop the counting of legal votes." Justice Antonin Scalia wrote in response that the recount would pose "irreparable harm" to Bush by "casting a cloud on what he claims to be the legitimacy of his election."

The split between the justices, so apparent in the order for the stay, reappeared in the final decision, where six separate opinions ended up being written. On a five-to-four vote, the majority claimed that if the recount went forward under the Florida Supreme Court's order with different standards for counting the vote in different counties, it would amount to a denial of equal protection of the laws. The amount of work required to bring about a fair recount could not be accomplished before the December 12 deadline. A three-person subset of the majority added that the Florida court's order was illegal in the first place.

The dissenters argued instead that the December 12 deadline was not fixed and that the recount could have taken place up to the meeting of the Electoral College on December 18, that there was no equal protection issue, that the Supreme Court should defer to the Florida Supreme Court on issues of state law, and that by involving itself in the political case, the Court risked losing public trust. While the winner of the election was in dispute, wrote Stevens, "the loser is perfectly clear. It is the nation's confidence in the judge as an impartial guardian of the rule of law."

Who was right here? The issue was debated by everyone from angry demonstrators outside the Court to learned commentators in scholarly journals, from families at the dinner table to editorial writers in the nation's press. Was Scalia correct that Bush had really already won and that it was up to the Court to save the legitimacy of his claim to power? Or was Stevens right: that by engaging in politics so blatantly, the Court had done itself irremediable damage in the eyes of the public? What was really at stake for the Court and for America in the five-to-four decision of *Bush v. Gore*?

Imagine a world without laws. You careen down the road in your car, at any speed that takes your fancy. You park where you please and enter a store that sells drugs of all sorts, from Prozac to LSD to vodka and beer. You purchase what you like—no one asks you for proof of your age or for a prescription—and there are no restrictions on what or how much you buy. There are no rules governing the production or usage of currency, either, so you hope that the dealer will accept what you have to offer in trade.

Life is looking pretty good as you head back out to the street, only to find that your car is no longer there. Theft is not illegal, and you curse yourself for forgetting to set the car alarm and for not using your wheel lock. There are no police to call, and even if there were, tracking down your car would be virtually impossible since there are no vehicle registration laws to prove you own it in the first place.

Rather than walk—these streets are quite dangerous, after all—you spot a likely car to get you home. You have to wrestle with the occupant, who manages to clout you over the head before you drive away. It isn't much of a prize, covered with dents and nicks from innumerable clashes with other cars jockeying for position at intersections where there are neither stop signs nor lights and the right of the fastest prevails. Arriving home to enjoy your beer in peace and to gain a respite from the war zone you call your local community, you find that another family has moved in while you were shopping. Groaning with frustration, you think that surely there must be a better way!

And there is. As often as we might rail against restrictions on our freedom, such as not being able to buy beer if we are under twenty-one, or having to wear a motorcycle helmet, or not being able to speed down an empty highway, laws actually do us much more good than harm. British philosophers Thomas Hobbes and John Locke, whom we discussed in Chapter 1, both imagined a "prepolitical" world without laws. Inhabitants of Hobbes's state of nature found life without laws to be dismal or, as he put it, "solitary, poor, nasty, brutish and short." And although residents of Locke's state of nature merely found the lawless life to be "inconvenient," they had to mount a constant defense of their possessions and their lives. One of the reasons both Hobbes and Locke thought people would be willing to leave the state of nature for civil society, and to give up their freedom to do whatever they wanted, was to gain security, order, and predictability in life. Because we tend to focus on the laws that stop us from doing the things we want to do, or that require us to do things we don't want to do, we often forget the full array of laws that make it possible for us to live together in relative peace and to leave behind the brutishness of Hobbes's state of nature and the inconveniences of Locke's.

Laws occupy a central position in any political society, but especially in a democracy, where the rule is ultimately by law and not the whim of a tyrant. Laws are the "how" in the formulation of politics as "who gets what, and how"—they dictate how our collective lives are to be organized, what rights we can claim, what principles we should live by, and how we can use the system to get what we want. Laws can also be the "what" in the formulation, as citizens and political actors use the existing rules to create new rules that produce even more favorable outcomes.

In this chapter you will learn about the notion of law and the role that it plays in democratic society in general and in the American legal system in particular, the constitutional basis for the American judicial system, the dual system of state and federal courts in the United States, and the Supreme Court and the politics that surround and support it.

Law and the American Legal System
Rules of the game that make collective living possible

Thinking about the law can be confusing. On the one hand, laws are the sorts of rules we have been discussing: limits and restrictions that get in our way, or that make life a little easier. But on the other hand, we would like to think that our legal system is founded on rules that represent basic and enduring principles of justice, that create for us a higher level of civilization. Laws are products of the political process, created by political human beings to help them get valuable resources. Those resources may be civil peace and security, or a particular moral order, or power and influence, or even goods or entitlements. Thus, for security, we have laws that eliminate traffic chaos, enforce contracts, and ban violence. For moral order (and for security as well!), we have laws against murder, incest, and rape. And for political advantage, we have laws like those that give large states greater power in the process of electing a president and those that allow electoral districts to be drawn by the majority party. Laws dealing with more concrete resources are those that, for example, give tax breaks to homeowners or subsidize dairy farmers.

For the purpose of understanding the role of law in democratic political systems, we can focus on five important functions of laws:[1]

- The first, and most obvious, function follows directly from Hobbes and Locke: laws *provide security* (for people and their property) so that we may go about our daily lives in relative harmony.
- Laws *provide predictability,* allowing us to plan our activities and go about our business without fearing a random judgment that tells us we have broken a law we didn't know existed.
- The fact that laws are known in advance and identify punishable behaviors leads to the third function of laws in a democracy, that of *conflict resolution,* through neutral third parties known as **courts**—institutions that resolve conflicts according to the law.
- A fourth function of laws in a democratic society is *to reflect and enforce conformity to society's values*—for instance, that murder is wrong or that parents should not be allowed to abuse their children.
- A fifth function of laws in a democracy is *to distribute the benefits and rewards society has to offer and to allocate the costs of those good things,* whether they are welfare benefits, civil rights protection, or tax breaks.

The American Legal Tradition

The U.S. legal system, and that of all fifty states except Louisiana, is based on common law, which developed in Great Britain and the countries that once formed the British Empire. The **common law tradition** relied on royal judges making decisions based on their own judgment and on previous legal decisions, which were applied uniformly, or *commonly*, across the land. The emphasis was on preserving the decisions that had been made before, what is called relying on **precedent**, or *stare decisis* (Latin for "let the decision stand"). Judges in such a system have far more power in determining what the law is than do judges in civil law systems, and their job is to determine and apply the law as an impartial referee, not to take an active role in discovering the truth.

> American legislators . . . are less concerned with creating such a coherent body of law than with responding to the various needs and demands of their constituents. As a result, American laws have a somewhat haphazard and hodgepodge character.

The legal system in the United States, however, is not a pure common law system. Legislatures do make laws, and attempts have been made to codify, or organize, them into a coherent body of law. American legislators, however, are less concerned with creating such a coherent body of law than with responding to the various needs and demands of their constituents. As a result, American laws have a somewhat haphazard and hodgepodge character. But the common law nature of the legal system is reinforced by the fact that American judges still use their considerable discretion to decide what the laws mean, and they rely heavily on precedent and the principle of *stare decisis*. Thus, when a judge decides a case, he or she will look at the relevant law but will also consult previous rulings on the issue before making a ruling of his or her own.

Kinds of Law

Laws are not all of the same type, and distinguishing among them can be very difficult. It's not important that we understand all the shades of legal meaning; in fact, it often seems that lawyers speak a language all their own. Nevertheless, most of us will have several encounters with the law in our lifetime, and it's important that we know what laws regulate what sorts of behavior.

We have used the terms *substantive* and *procedural* elsewhere in this book to refer to political culture, but the words also have precise legal meanings that describe specific kinds of laws. **Substantive laws** are those whose actual content or "substance" defines what we can and cannot legally do. **Procedural laws**, on the other hand, establish the procedures used to conduct the law—that is, how the law is used, or applied, and enforced. Thus a substantive law spells out what behaviors are restricted, for instance, driving over a certain speed or killing someone. Procedural laws refer to how legal proceedings are to take place: how evidence will be gathered and used, how defendants will be treated, and what juries can be told during a trial. Because our founders were concerned with limiting the power of government to prevent tyranny, our laws are filled with procedural protections for those who must deal with the legal system—what we call guarantees of **procedural due process**. Given their different purposes, these two types of laws sometimes clash. For instance, someone guilty of breaking a substantive law might be spared punishment if procedural laws meant to protect him or her were violated because the police failed to read the accused his or her rights or searched the accused's home without a warrant. Such situations are complicated by the fact that not all judges interpret procedural guarantees in the same way.

Another important distinction in the American system is between criminal and civil law. **Criminal laws** prohibit specific behaviors that the government (state, federal, or both) has determined are not conducive to the public peace, behaviors as heinous as murder or as relatively innocuous as stealing an apple. Since these laws refer to crimes against the state, it is the government that prosecutes these cases rather than the family of the murder victim—or the owner of the apple. The penalty, if the person is found guilty, will be some form of payment to the public, for example, community service, jail time, or even death, depending on the severity of the crime and the provisions of the law. In fact, we speak of criminals having to pay their "debt to society," because in a real sense, their actions are seen as a harm to society.

Civil laws, on the other hand, regulate interactions between individuals. If one person sues another for damaging his or her property, or for causing physical harm, or for failing to fulfill the terms of a contract, it is not a crime against the state that is alleged but rather an injury to a specific individual. A violation of civil law is called a *tort* instead of a crime. The government's purpose here is not to prosecute a harm to society but to provide individuals with a forum in which they can peacefully resolve their differences. Apart from peaceful conflict resolution, government has no stake in the outcome.

Sometimes a person will face both criminal charges and a civil lawsuit for the same action. An example might be a person who drives while drunk and causes an accident that seriously injures a person in another car. The drunk driver would face criminal charges for breaking laws against driving while intoxicated and might also be sued by the injured party to receive compensation for medical expenses, missed income, and pain and suffering. Such damages are called *compensatory damages*. The injured person might also sue the bar that served the alcohol to the drunk driver in the first place; this is because people suing for compensation often target the involved party with the deepest pockets, that is, the one with the best ability to pay. A civil suit may also include a fine intended to punish the individual for causing the injury. These damages are called *punitive damages*.

Another kind of law, which we have discussed often in this book so far, is **constitutional law**. This refers, of course, to the laws in the Constitution that establish the basic powers of and limitations on governmental institutions and their interrelationships, and that guarantee the basic rights of citizens. In addition, constitutional law refers to the many decisions that have been made by lower court judges in America, as well as by the justices on the Supreme Court, in their attempts to decide precisely what the Constitution means and how it should be interpreted. Because of our common law tradition, these decisions, once made, become part of the vast foundation of American constitutional law. All of the civil liberties and civil rights cases we have discussed are part of the constitutional law of this country. As we have seen, constitutional law evolves over time as circumstances change, justices are replaced, cases are overturned, and precedent is reversed.

Most laws in the country are not written in the Constitution, however, but rather are made by Congress and the state legislatures, by the bureaucracy under the authority of Congress, and even by the president. **Statutory laws** are those laws that legislatures make at either the state or the national level. Statutes reflect the will of the bodies elected to represent the people, and they can address virtually any behavior. Statutes tell us to wear seatbelts, pay taxes, and stay home from work on Memorial Day. According to the principle of judicial review, judges may declare statutes unconstitutional if they conflict with the basic principles of government or the rights of citizens established in the Constitution.

Because legislatures cannot be experts on all matters, they frequently delegate some of their lawmaking power to bureaucratic agencies and departments. When these bureaucratic actors exercise their lawmaking power on behalf of Congress, they are making **administrative law**. Administrative laws include the thousands of regulations that agencies make concerning how much coloring and other additives can be in the food we buy, how airports will monitor air traffic, what kind of material can be used to make pajamas for children, and what deductions can be taken legally when figuring your income tax. These laws, although made under the authority of elected representatives, are not, in fact, made by people who are directly accountable to the citizens of America. The implications of the undemocratic nature of bureaucratic decision making were discussed in Chapter 8.

Finally, some laws, called **executive orders**, are made by the president himself. These, as we explained in Chapter 7, are laws made without any participation by Congress, and they need be binding only during the issuing president's administration. Famous executive orders include President Harry Truman's desegregation of the armed forces in 1948 and President Lyndon Johnson's initiation of affirmative action programs for companies doing business with the federal government in 1967.

Constitutional Provisions and the Development of Judicial Review
The role of Congress and the courts in establishing the judiciary

Americans may owe a lot of our philosophy of law (called *jurisprudence*) to the British, but the court system we set up to administer that law is uniquely our own. Like every other part of the Constitution, the nature of the judiciary was the subject of hot debate during the nation's founding. Large states were comfortable with a strong court system as part of the strong national government they advocated; small states, cringing at the prospect of national dominance, preferred a weak judiciary. Choosing a typically astute way out of their quandary, the authors of the Constitution postponed it, leaving it to Congress to settle later.

Article III, Section 1, of the Constitution says simply this about the establishment of the court system: "The judicial power of the United States, shall be vested in one supreme court, and in such inferior courts as Congress may from time to time ordain and establish." It goes on to say that judges will hold their jobs as long as they demonstrate "good behavior"—that is, they are appointed for life—and that they will be paid regularly and cannot have their pay reduced while they are in office. The Constitution does not spell out the powers of the Supreme Court. It only specifies which cases must come directly to the Supreme Court (cases affecting ambassadors, public ministers and consuls, and states); all other cases come to it only on appeal. It was left to Congress to say how. By dropping the issue of court structure and power into the lap of a future Congress, the writers of the Constitution neatly sidestepped the brewing controversy. It would require an act of Congress, the Federal Judiciary Act of 1789, to begin to fill in the gaps on how the court system would be organized.

The Least Dangerous Branch

The idea of an independent judiciary headed by a supreme court was a new one to the founders. No other country had one, not even England. Britain's highest court was also its Parliament, or legislature. To those who put their faith in the ideas of separation of powers and checks and balances, an independent judiciary was an

Exercising Judgment
Nominated for life terms, the justices of the U.S. Supreme Court usually serve long after the president who appointed them has left office. The current court is, back row, from left: Sonia Sotomayor, Stephen G. Breyer, Samuel Alito, and Elena Kagan; front row, from left: Clarence Thomas, Antonin Scalia, Chief Justice John G. Roberts Jr., Anthony M. Kennedy, and Ruth Bader Ginsberg.

ideal way to check the power of the president and the Congress. But to others it represented an unknown threat. To put those fears to rest, Alexander Hamilton penned *Federalist* No. 78, arguing that the judiciary was the least dangerous branch of government. It lacked the teeth of the other branches; it had neither the power of the sword (the executive power) nor the power of the purse (the legislative budget power), and consequently it could exercise "neither force nor will, but merely judgment."[2]

John Marshall and Judicial Review

The low prestige of the Supreme Court was not to last for long, however, and its elevation was due almost single-handedly to the work of one man. John Marshall was the third chief justice and an enthusiastic Federalist. During his tenure in office, he found several ways to strengthen the Court's power, the most important of which was having the Court create the power of **judicial review**—the power that allows the Court to review acts of the other branches of government and to invalidate them if they are found to run counter to the principles in the Constitution.

The Constitution does not give the power of judicial review to the Court, but it doesn't forbid the Court to have that power either, and Hamilton had supported the idea in *Federalist* No. 78. Chief Justice Marshall shrewdly engineered the adoption of the power of judicial review in *Marbury v. Madison* in 1803. This case involved a series of judicial appointments to federal courts made by President John Adams in the final hours of his administration. Most of those appointments were executed by Adams's secretary of state, but the letter appointing William Marbury to be justice of the peace for the District of Columbia was overlooked and not delivered. (In an interesting twist, John Marshall, who was finishing up his job as Adams's secretary of state, had just been sworn in as chief justice of the Supreme Court; he would later hear the case that developed over his own incomplete appointment of Marbury.) These "midnight" (last-minute) appointments irritated the new president, Thomas Jefferson, who wanted to appoint his own candidates, so he had his secretary of state, James Madison, throw out the overlooked Marbury letter, along with several other appointment letters. According to the Judiciary Act of 1789, it was up to the Supreme Court to decide whether Marbury got his appointment, which put Marshall in a fix. If he exercised his power under the act and Jefferson ignored him, the Court's already low prestige would be severely damaged. If he failed to order the appointment, the Court would still look weak.

From a legal point of view, Marshall's solution was breathtaking. Instead of ruling on the question of Marbury's appointment, which was a no-win situation for him, he focused on the part of the act that gave the Court the authority to make the decision. This he found to go beyond what the Constitution had intended. That is, according to the Constitution, Congress didn't have the power to give the Court that authority. So Marshall ruled that although he thought Marbury should get the appointment (he had originally made it, after all), he could not enforce it because the relevant part of the Judiciary Act of 1789 was unconstitutional and therefore void. He justified the Court's power to decide what the Constitution meant by saying "it is emphatically the province of the judicial department to say what the law is."[3]

In making this ruling, Marshall chose to lose a small battle in order to win a very large war. By creating the power of judicial review, he vastly expanded the potential influence of the Court and set it on the road to being the powerful institution it is today. While Congress and the president still have some checks on the judiciary through the powers to appoint, to change the number of members and the jurisdiction of the Court, to impeach justices, and to amend the Constitution, the Court now has the ultimate check over the other two branches: the power to declare what they do to be null and void. What is especially striking about the gain of this enormous power is that the Court gave it to itself. What would have been the public reaction if Congress had voted to make itself the final judge of what is constitutional?

Aware of just how substantially their power was increased by the addition of judicial review, justices have tended to use it sparingly. The power was not used from its inception in 1803 until 1857, when the Court struck down the Missouri Compromise.[4] Since then it has been used only about 158 times to strike down acts of Congress, although much more frequently (1,261 times) to invalidate acts of the state legislatures.[5]

Federalism and the American Courts
The structure and organization of the dual court system

In response to the Constitution's open invitation to design a federal court system, Congress immediately got busy putting together the Federal Judiciary Act of 1789. The system created by this act was too simple to handle the complex legal needs and the growing number of cases in the new nation, however, and it was gradually crafted by Congress into the very complex network of federal courts we have today. But understanding just the federal system is not enough. Our federal system of government requires that we have two separate court systems, state and national, and in fact most of the legal actions in this country take place at the state level. Because of the diversity that exists among the state courts, some people argue that in truth we have fifty-one court systems. Since we cannot look into each of the fifty state court systems, we will take the "two-system" perspective and consider the state court system as a whole (see Figure 9.1).

Understanding Jurisdiction

A key concept in understanding our dual court system is the issue of **jurisdiction**, the courts' authority to hear particular cases. Not all courts can hear all cases. In fact, the rules regulating which courts have jurisdiction over which cases are very

Figure 9.1

The Dual Court System

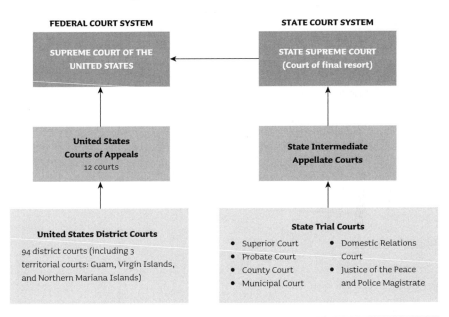

FEDERAL COURT SYSTEM   STATE COURT SYSTEM

SUPREME COURT OF THE ← STATE SUPREME COURT
UNITED STATES (Court of final resort)

United States
Courts of Appeals
12 courts

State Intermediate
Appellate Courts

United States District Courts

94 district courts (including 3
territorial courts: Guam, Virgin Islands,
and Northern Mariana Islands)

State Trial Courts

- Superior Court
- Probate Court
- County Court
- Municipal Court
- Domestic Relations
  Court
- Justice of the Peace
  and Police Magistrate

specific. Most cases in the United States fall under the jurisdiction of state courts. As we will see, cases go to federal courts only if they qualify by virtue of the kind of question raised or the parties involved.

The choice of a court, though dictated in large part by constitutional rule and statutory law (both state and federal), still leaves room for political maneuvering. Four basic characteristics of a case help determine which court has jurisdiction over it: the involvement of the federal government (through treaties or federal statutes) or the Constitution, the parties to the case (if, for instance, states are involved), where the case arose, and how serious an offense it involves.[6]

Once a case is in either the state court system or the federal court system, it almost always remains within that system. It is extremely rare for a case to start out in one system and end up in the other. Just about the only time this occurs is when a case in the highest state court is appealed to the U.S. Supreme Court, and this can happen only for cases involving a question of federal law.

Cases come to state and federal courts under either their original jurisdiction or their appellate jurisdiction. A court's **original jurisdiction** refers to those cases that can come straight to it without being heard by any other court first. The rules and factors just discussed refer to original jurisdiction. **Appellate jurisdiction** refers to those cases that a court can hear on **appeal**—that is, when one of the parties to a case believes that some point of law was not applied properly at a lower court and asks a higher court to review it. Almost all the cases heard by the U.S. Supreme Court come to it on appeal. The Court's original jurisdiction is limited to cases that concern ambassadors and public ministers and to cases in which a state is a party—usually amounting to no more than two or three cases a year.

All parties in U.S. lawsuits are entitled to an appeal, although more than 90 percent of losers in federal cases accept their verdicts without appeal. After the first appeal, further appeals are at the discretion of the higher court; that is, the court can choose to hear them or not. The highest court of appeals in the United States is the U.S. Supreme Court, but its appellate jurisdiction is also discretionary. When the Court refuses to hear a case, it may mean, among other things, that the Court regards the case as frivolous or that it agrees with the lower court's judgment. Just because the Court agrees to hear a case, though, does not mean that it is going to overturn the lower court's ruling, although it does so about 70 percent of the time. Sometimes the Court hears a case in order to rule that it agrees with the lower court and to set a precedent that other courts will have to follow.

State Courts

Although each state has its own constitution, and therefore its own set of rules and procedures for structuring and organizing its court system, the state court systems are remarkably similar to each other in appearance and function. State courts generally fall into three tiers, or layers. The lowest, or first, layer is the trial court, including major trial courts and courts where less serious offenses are heard. The names of these courts vary—for example, they may be called county and municipal courts at the minor level and superior or district courts at the major level. Here cases are heard for the first time, under original jurisdiction, and most of them end here as well.

Occasionally, however, a case is appealed to a higher decision-making body. In about three-fourths of the states, intermediate courts of appeals hear cases appealed from the lower trial courts. In terms of geographic organization, subject matter jurisdiction, and number of judges, courts of appeals vary greatly from state to state. The one constant is that these courts all hear appeals directly from the major trial courts and, on very rare occasions, directly from the minor courts as well.

Each of the fifty states has a state supreme court, although again the names vary. Since they are appeals courts, no questions of fact can arise, and there are no juries. Rather, a panel of five to nine *justices,* as supreme court judges are called, meet to discuss the case, make a decision, and issue an opinion. As the name suggests, a state's supreme court is the court of last resort, or the final court of appeals, in the state. All decisions rendered by these courts are final unless a case involves a federal question and can be heard on further appeal in the federal court system.

Judges in state courts are chosen through a variety of procedures specified in the individual state constitutions. The procedures range from appointment by the governor or election by the state legislature to the more democratic method of election by the state population as a whole. Thirty-nine states hold elections for at least some of their judges, but this procedure is controversial as critics argue that judicial elections can create a conflict of interest, that few people are able to cast educated votes in judicial elections, and that the threat of defeat may influence judges' rulings.

Federal Courts

The federal system is also three-tiered. There is an entry-level tier, called the district courts, an appellate level, and the Supreme Court at the very top. In this section we discuss the lower two tiers and how the judges for those courts are chosen. Given the importance of the Supreme Court in the American political system, we discuss it separately in the next section.

The lowest level of the federal judiciary hierarchy consists of ninety-four U.S. federal district courts. These courts are distributed so that each state has at least one and the largest states each have four. The district courts have original jurisdiction over all cases involving any question of a federal nature or any issue that involves the Constitution, Congress, or any other aspect of the federal government. Such issues are wide ranging but might include, for example, criminal charges resulting from a violation of the federal anticarjacking statute or a lawsuit against the Environmental Protection Agency.

The district courts hear both criminal and civil law cases. In trials at the district level, evidence is presented, and witnesses are called to testify and are questioned and cross-examined by the attorneys representing both sides. In criminal cases the government is always represented by a U.S. attorney. U.S. attorneys, one per district, are appointed by the president, with the consent of the Senate. In district courts, juries are responsible for returning the final verdict.

Any case appealed beyond the district court level is slated to appear in one of the U.S. courts of appeals. These courts are arranged in twelve circuits, essentially large superdistricts that encompass several of the district court territories, except for the twelfth, which covers just Washington, D.C. This twelfth circuit court hears all appeals involving government agencies, and so its caseload is quite large even though its territory is small. (A thirteenth Federal Circuit court hears cases on such specialized issues as patents and copyrights.) Cases are heard in the circuit that includes the district court where the case was heard originally. Therefore, a case that was tried initially in Miami, in the southern district in Florida, would be appealed to the court of appeals in the Eleventh Circuit, located in Atlanta, Georgia.

The jurisdiction of the courts of appeals, as their name suggests, is entirely appellate in nature. The sole function of these courts is to hear appeals from the lower federal district courts and to review the legal reasoning behind the decisions reached there. As a result, the proceedings involved in the appeals process differ markedly from those at the district court level. No evidence is presented, no new witnesses called, and no jury impaneled. Instead, the lawyers for both sides present written briefs summarizing their arguments and make oral arguments as well. The legal reasoning used to reach the decision in the district court is scrutinized, but the facts of the case are assumed to be the truth and are not debated.

The decisions in the courts of appeals are made by a rotating panel of three judges who sit to hear the case. Although many more than three judges are assigned to each federal appeals circuit (the Court of Appeals for the Ninth Circuit, based in San Francisco, has forty-seven), the judges rotate in order to provide a decision-making body that is as unbiased as possible. In rare cases when a decision is of crucial social importance, all the judges in a circuit will meet together, or *en banc*, to render a decision. Having all the judges present, not just three, gives a decision more legitimacy and sends a message that the decision was made carefully.

The Constitution is silent about the qualifications of judges for the federal courts. It specifies only that they shall be appointed by the president, with the advice and consent of the Senate, and that they shall serve lifetime terms under good behavior. They can be removed from office only if impeached and convicted by the House of Representatives and the Senate, a process that has resulted in only thirteen impeachments and seven convictions in more than two hundred years.

Traditionally, federal judgeships have been awarded on the basis of several criteria, not the least of which has been to reward political friendship and support and to cultivate future political support, whether of a particular politician or an entire gender or ethnic or racial group. An increasingly important qualification for the job of federal judge is the ideological or policy position of the appointee. Since the 1970s, politicians have become more aware of the political influence of these courts.

Consequently, politicians can have quite an impact in shaping the U.S. judicial system by the appointments they make, and as they have taken advantage of that opportunity, the Senate confirmation process has become more rancorous. Together, Republican presidents Ronald Reagan and George H. W. Bush appointed more than 60 percent of all federal judges, and they made a conscious effort to redirect what they saw as the liberal tenor of court appointments in the years since the New Deal. Even though Democratic president Bill Clinton appointed many judges as well, the moderate ideology of most of his appointees means that the courts have not swung back in a radically liberal direction.[7] He renewed a commitment made by President Jimmy Carter to create diversity on the federal bench. More than half of Clinton's appointees were women and minorities, compared to 37 percent under Carter, 14 percent under Reagan, 30 percent under the first Bush, and 39 percent under George W. Bush. Clinton's appointees also were what one observer called "militantly moderate"—more liberal than Reagan's and Bush's, but less liberal than Carter's, and similar ideologically to the appointments of Republican president Gerald Ford (see Table 9.1).[8] That, in conjunction with the fact that by the end of George W. Bush's second term, 56.2 percent of the authorized judicial positions had been filled by Republicans,[9] means that today's federal bench tilts in a solidly conservative direction.

The increasing politicization of the confirmation process means that many of a president's nominees face a grueling battle in the Senate, and even if they get through the Senate Judiciary Committee hearings, they are lucky if they can get as far as a vote on the floor. Senators of the opposing party can put a hold on a nomination, requiring a vote of sixty senators to bring the nomination to a vote. While both parties use this tactic to stall those nominations of the other party's president to which they object, the Republicans have recently been more effective. Observers chalk this up to the greater discipline among Republican senators. Says one liberal advocate, "Republican senators have voted in lock step to confirm every judge that Bush has nominated. The Democrats have often broken ranks."[10] That Republican unity has continued into the Obama years. While the politicization of the process means that each party has objected to the more ideological appointments of the other side, in 2009 and 2010 Republicans were blocking votes on all Obama nominations, even moderate ones that would typically have enjoyed bipartisan support, in order to stall the Obama administration's efforts and to gain leverage for other things they wanted.[11] Ironically, when those nominations do eventually come to a vote, they pass with the support of many of the Republicans who supported a filibuster to delay the vote in the first place. While these delay tactics may help the party score a short-term political victory, many federal judgeships are going unfilled as a consequence, contributing to a backlog of cases in the courts.

Another, and related, influence on the appointment of federal judges is the principle of **senatorial courtesy**, which we discussed in Chapter 7. In reality, senators do most of the nominating of district court judges, often aided by applications made by lawyers and state judges. Traditionally, a president who nominated a candidate who failed to meet with the approval of the state's senior senator was highly unlikely to gain Senate confirmation of that candidate, even if he was lucky enough to get the Senate Judiciary Committee to hold a hearing on the nomination. In recent years the practice of senatorial courtesy was weakened somewhat by the Bush administration and Senate Republicans who forced confirmation hearings despite the objections of Democratic home state senators.[12] But once President Barack Obama was elected, Senate Republicans sought to restore the policy, sending a letter to the White House promising to block any appointments that didn't meet with the home state senator's approval.[13]

The growing influence of politics in the selection of federal judges does not mean that merit is unimportant. As the nation's largest legal professional association, the American Bar Association (ABA) has had the informal role since 1946 of evaluating the legal qualifications of potential nominees. While poorly rated candidates are occasionally nominated and confirmed, perhaps because of the pressure of a senator or a president, most federal judges receive the ABA's professional blessing. The ABA's role has become more controversial in recent years, as Republicans are convinced that it has a liberal bias. The Bush administration announced in 2001 that it would no longer seek the ABA's ratings of its nominees, breaking a tradition that went back to Eisenhower. The ABA continued to rate the nominees (and the Bush White House boasted that 99 percent of its nominees had been rated "qualified" or "well qualified"), but it did so independently.[14] In March 2009 the Obama administration restored the ABA's traditional role in the nomination process.

Table 9.1

Characteristics of Presidential Appointees to U.S. District Court Judgeships (by presidential administration, 1963–2008)

	Lyndon Johnson (1963–1968) (N = 122)	Richard Nixon (1969–1974) (N = 179)	Gerald Ford (1974–1976) (N = 52)	Jimmy Carter (1977–1980) (N = 202)
Sex				
Male	98.4%	99.4%	98.1%	85.6%
Female	1.6	0.6	1.9	14.4
Ethnicity				
White	93.4	95.5	88.5	78.7
Black	4.1	3.4	5.8	13.9
Hispanic	2.5	1.1	1.9	6.9
Asian	0.0	0.0	3.9	0.5
Native American	n/a	n/a	n/a	n/a
Religion				
Protestant	58.2	73.2	73.1	60.4
Catholic	31.1	18.4	17.3	27.7
Jewish	10.7	8.4	9.6	11.9
Political Party				
Democrat	94.3	7.3	21.2	91.1
Republican	5.7	92.7	78.8	4.5
Independent/Other	0.0	0.0	0.0	4.5
ABA Rating				
Exceptionally well/ well qualified	48.4	45.3	46.1	50.9
Qualified	49.2	54.8	53.8	47.5
Not qualified	2.5	0.0	0.0	1.5

Note: Percentages may not add up to 100 because of rounding. ABA = American Bar Association; n/a = not available.

Source: Sheldon Goldman, "Reagan's Judicial Legacy: Completing the Puzzle and Summing Up," *Judicature* 72 (April–May 1989): 320, 321, Table 1; and Sheldon Goldman and Elliot Slotnick, "Clinton's First Term Judiciary:

	Ronald Reagan (1981–1988) (N = 290)	George W. Bush (1989–1992) (N = 148)	Bill Clinton (1993–2000) (N = 305)	George W. Bush (2001–2008) (N = 261)
Sex				
Male	91.7%	80.4%	71.5%	79.3%
Female	8.3	19.6	28.5	20.7
Ethnicity				
White	92.4	89.2	75.1	81.6
Black	2.1	6.8	17.4	6.9
Hispanic	4.8	4.0	5.9	10.1
Asian	0.7	0.0	1.3	1.5
Native American	n/a	n/a	0.3	0.0
Religion				
Protestant	60.3	64.2	n/a	n/a
Catholic	30.0	28.4	n/a	n/a
Jewish	9.3	7.4	n/a	n/a
Political Party				
Democrat	4.8	6.1	87.5	8.1
Republican	91.7	88.5	6.2	83.1
Independent/Other	3.4	5.4	6.2	3.4
ABA Rating				
Exceptionally well/ well qualified	53.5	57.4	59.0	70.1
Qualified	46.6	42.6	34.4	28.4
Not qualified	0.0	0.0	1.1	1.5

Many Bridges to Cross," *Judicature* 80 (May–June 1997): 261. Table adapted by Sourcebook staff, Bureau of Justice Statistics, *Sourcebook of Criminal Justice Statistics, 1996* (Washington, D.C.: U.S. Dept. of Justice, 1996), Table 1.77, p. 62; Harold W. Stanley and Richard G. Niemi, *Vital Statistics on American Politics, 2007–2008* (Washington, D.C.: CQ Press, 2008), 281–282, Sheldon Goldman, Sara Schiavoni, and Elliott Slotnick, "George W. Bush's Judicial Legacy: Mission Accomplished," *Judicature*, May/June 2009, 92, 6, p. 279.

The Supreme Court
A political institution

At the very top of the nation's judicial system reigns the Supreme Court. While the nine justices do not wear the elaborate wigs of their British colleagues in the House of Lords, the highest court of appeals in Britain, they do don long black robes to hear their cases and sit against a majestic background of red silk, perhaps the closest thing to the pomp and circumstance of royalty that we have in American government. Polls show that even after its role in the contested presidential election of 2000, the Court gets higher ratings from the public than does Congress or the president, and that it doesn't suffer as much from the popular cynicism about government that afflicts the other branches.[15]

The American public seems to believe that the Supreme Court is indeed above politics, as the founders wished it to be. Such a view, while gratifying to those who want to believe in the purity and wisdom of at least one aspect of their government, is not strictly accurate. The members of the Court themselves are preserved by the rule of lifetime tenure from continually having to seek reelection or reappointment, but they are not removed from the political world around them. It is more useful, and closer to reality, to regard the Supreme Court as an intensely political institution. In at least three critical areas—how its members are chosen, how they make decisions, and the effects of the decisions they make—the Court is a decisive allocator of who gets what, when, and how.

How Members of the Court Are Selected

In a perfect world, the wisest and most intelligent jurists in the country would be appointed to make the all-important constitutional decisions daily faced by members of the Supreme Court. In a political world, however, the need for wise and intelligent justices has to be balanced against the demands of a system that makes those justices the choice of an elected president, confirmed by elected senators. The need of these elected officials to be responsive to their constituencies means that the nomination process for Supreme Court justices is often a battleground of competing views of the public good. Merit is certainly important, but it is tempered by other considerations resulting from a democratic selection process.

On paper, the process of choosing justices for the Supreme Court is not a great deal different from the selection of other federal judges, though no tradition of senatorial courtesy exists at the high court level. Far too much is at stake in Supreme Court appointments to even consider giving any individual senator veto power. The Constitution, silent on so much concerning the Supreme Court, does not give the president any handy list of criteria for making these critical appointments. But the demands of his job suggest that merit, shared ideology, political reward, and demographic representation all play a role in this choice.[16]

Merit

The president will certainly want to appoint the most qualified person and the person with the highest ethical standards who also meets the other prerequisites. Scholars agree that most of the people who have served the Court over the years have been among the best legal minds available, but they also know that sometimes presidents have nominated people whose reputations have proved questionable.[17] The ABA passes judgment on candidates for the Supreme Court, as it does for the lower courts, issuing verdicts of "well qualified," "qualified," "not opposed," and "not qualified." The FBI also checks out each nominee's background.

Political Ideology

Although a president wants to appoint a well-qualified candidate to the Court, he is constrained by the desire to find a candidate who shares his views on politics and the law. Political ideology here involves a couple of dimensions. One is the traditional liberal–conservative dimension. Supreme Court justices, like all other human beings, have views on the role of government, the rights of individuals, and the relationship between the two. Presidents want to appoint justices who look at the world the same way they do, although they are occasionally surprised when their nominee's ideological stripes turn out to be different from what they had anticipated. Republican president Dwight Eisenhower called the appointment of Chief Justice Earl Warren, who turned out to be quite liberal in his legal judgments, "the biggest damn fool mistake I ever made."[18] Although there have been notable exceptions, most presidents appoint members of their own parties in an attempt to get ideologically compatible justices. Overall, roughly 90 percent of Supreme Court nominees belong to the president's party.

But ideology has another dimension when it refers to the law. Justices can take the view that the Constitution means exactly what it says it means and that all interpretations of it must be informed by the founders' intentions. This approach, called **strict constructionism**, holds that if the meaning of the Constitution is to be changed, it must be done by amendment, not by judicial interpretation. Judge Robert Bork, a Reagan nominee who failed to be confirmed by the Senate, was a strict constructionist. During his confirmation hearings, when he was asked about the famous reapportionment ruling in *Baker v. Carr,* that the Constitution effectively guarantees every citizen one vote, Bork replied that if the people of the United States wanted their Constitution to guarantee "one man one vote," they were free to amend the document to say so. In Bork's judgment, without that amendment, the principle was simply the result of justices' rewriting the Constitution. When the senators asked him about the right to privacy, another right enforced by the Court but not specified in the Constitution, Bork simply laughed.[19] The opposite position to strict constructionism, what might be called **judicial interpretivism**, holds that the Constitution is a living document, that the founders could not possibly have anticipated all possible future circumstances, and that justices should interpret the Constitution in light of social changes. When the Court, in *Griswold v. Connecticut,* ruled that while there is no right to privacy in the Constitution, the Bill of Rights can be understood to imply such a right, it was engaging in judicial interpretation. Strict constructionists would deny that there is a constitutional right to privacy.

While interpretivism tends to be a liberal position because of its emphasis on change, and strict constructionism tends to be a conservative position because of its adherence to the status quo, the two ideological scales do not necessarily go hand in hand. For instance, even though the Second Amendment refers to the right to bear arms in the context of militia membership, many conservatives would argue that this needs to be understood to protect the right to bear arms in a modern context, when militias are no longer necessary or practical—not a strict constructionist reading of the Constitution. Liberals, on the other hand, tend to rely on a strict reading of the Second Amendment to support their calls for tighter gun controls.

In the George W. Bush administration, another ideological element rose in importance along with the strict constructionist-interpretivist divide. Bush was concerned with finding nominees who not only would interpret the Constitution strictly but also would support a strengthening of executive power. As we saw in Chapter 7, many members of the Bush administration supported the unitary theory of the executive, which claims that the Constitution permits only the president to wield executive power. Under this theory, efforts by Congress to create independent agencies outside of the president's purview are unconstitutional. The administration also objected to efforts by Congress and the courts to limit or interpret executive power in matters of national security. For both of his nominations to the Court, John Roberts and Samuel Alito, Bush chose candidates who were supporters of a strong executive office.

President Obama's Supreme Court nominees will likely reflect his own center-left, interpretivist ideology. His first nomination, Sonia Sotomayor, who joined the Court in September 2009, was more controversial for remarks she had made about her ethnicity and gender than for her judicial views. When former solicitor general Elena Kagan was nominated by Obama for the Court in 2010, however, her lack of a history of clear judicial rulings left her ideology something of a mystery, and many liberals feared that she would end up being a moderate voice on the court.[20]

Reward

More than half of the people who have been nominated to the Supreme Court have been personally acquainted with the president.[21] Often nominees are either friends of the president, or his political allies, or other people he wishes to reward in an impressive fashion. Harry Truman knew and had worked with all four of the men he appointed to the Court, Franklin Roosevelt appointed people he knew (and who were loyal to his New Deal), John Kennedy appointed his longtime friend and associate Byron White, and Lyndon Johnson appointed his good friend Abe Fortas.[22] While several FOBs (Friends of Bill) appeared on Clinton's short lists for his appointments, none was actually appointed. Though George W. Bush tried to appoint his friend and White House Counsel Harriet Meiers to the Court, she was forced to withdraw her name amid criticism that she wasn't sufficiently qualified.

Barack Obama had a longtime working relationship with one of his nominees, Elena Kagan, who had been his first solicitor general.

Representation

Finally, the president wants to appoint people who represent groups he feels should be included in the political process, or whose support he wants to gain. Lyndon Johnson appointed Thurgood Marshall at least in part because he wanted to appoint an African American to the Court. After Marshall retired, President George H. W. Bush appointed Clarence Thomas to fill his seat. While he declared that he was making the appointment because Thomas was the person best qualified for the job, and not because he was black, few believed him. In earlier years, presidents also felt compelled to ensure that there was at least one Catholic and one Jew on the Court. This necessity has lost much of its force today as interest groups seem more concerned with the political than the denominational views of appointees, but Hispanic groups rejoiced when President Obama made Sonia Sotomayor the first Hispanic member of the Court in 2009. The issue of ethnic representation on the Court was put front and center during Sotomayor's confirmation hearings when she drew fire from Republicans who noted a line in a speech she had given in 2001, where she had argued that "I would hope that a wise Latina woman with the richness of her experiences would more often than not reach a better conclusion than a white male who hasn't lived that life."[23]

The current composition of the Supreme Court does not reflect the population of the United States, although it can certainly be argued that it comes closer than it ever has before. There are six men on the Court and three women. Six justices are Catholic, and three Jewish; only Judeo-Christian religions have been represented on the Court so far. Five of the justices were appointed by Republicans, four by Democrats. They have attended an elite array of undergraduate institutions and law schools. In 2010 their ages ranged from 50 to 77, with the average being 64. There have never been any Native Americans or Asian Americans on the Court, and only a total of two African Americans, whose terms did not overlap, and one Hispanic. The overwhelmingly elite white male Christian character of the Court raises interesting questions. We naturally want our highest judges to have excellent legal educations (although John Marshall barely had any). But should the nation's highest court represent demographically the people whose Constitution it guards? Some observers (including Justice Sotomayor) have suggested that women judges may be sensitive to issues that have not been salient to men and may alter behavior in the courtroom; the same may be true of minority judges as well. In a different vein, what message is sent to citizens when the custodians of national justice are composed primarily of a group that is itself fast becoming a minority in America?

Confirmation by the Senate

As with the lower courts, the Senate must approve presidential appointments to the Supreme Court. As always in judicial matters, the Senate Judiciary Committee plays the largest role, holding hearings and inviting the nominee, colleagues, and concerned interest groups to testify. Sometimes the hearings, and the subsequent vote in the Senate, are mere formalities, but increasingly, as the appointments have become more ideological and when the Senate majority party is not the party of the president, the hearings have had the potential to become political battlefields. Even when the president's party controls the Senate, the minority party can still influence the choice through the filibuster, although the Senate Republicans in 2005 threatened to halt this tradition.

The Bork and Thomas hearings are excellent examples of what can happen when interest groups and public opinion get heavily involved in a controversial confirmation battle. These political clashes are so grueling because so much is at stake.

How the Court Makes Decisions

As it was with the selection process, it is tempting to idealize the way justices make decisions—to believe that the decisions made by the Court are simply a matter of nine wise and learned people consulting eternal principles of wisdom in order to choose the best way to resolve conflicts. We know by now that what happens is more complicated than that. As the justices decide which cases to hear, make decisions about how those cases should be resolved, and write their opinions, they are subject to the same kinds of political forces that influenced their appointments and confirmations.

Choosing Which Cases to Hear

The Supreme Court could not possibly hear the roughly eight thousand petitions it receives each year.[24] Intensive screening is necessary to reduce the number to the more manageable 80 to 90 that the Court finally hears (see Figure 9.2). This screening process is a political one; having one's case heard by the Supreme Court is a scarce resource. What rules and which people determine who gets this resource and who doesn't?

Almost all the cases heard by the Court come from its appellate, not its original, jurisdiction, and of these virtually all arrive at the Court in the form of petitions for **writs of certiorari**, in which the losing party in a lower court case explains in writing why the Supreme Court should hear its case. Petitions to the Court are subject to strict length, form, and style requirements and must be accompanied by a $300 filing fee. Those too poor to pay the filing fee are allowed to petition the Court *in forma pauperis,* which exempts them not only from the filing fee but also from the stringent style and form rules. In the 2008 term, 6,142 of the 7,738 case filings were *in forma pauperis.*[25] The Court's jurisdiction here is discretionary; it can either grant or deny a writ of certiorari. If it decides to grant certiorari and review the case, then the records of the case will be called up from the lower court where it was last heard.

Law clerks, usually recent graduates from law school who have served a year as clerk to a judge on a lower court, have tremendous responsibility over certiorari

Figure 9.2

Pathway to and through the Supreme Court

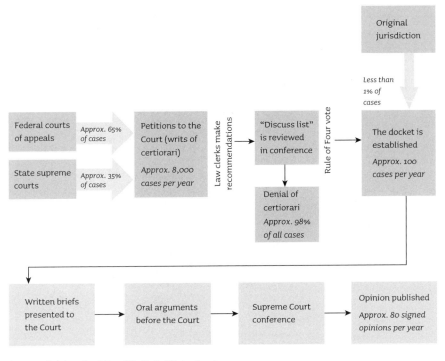

Source: Administrative Office of the United States Courts.

petitions, or "cert pets," as they call them. They must read all the petitions (thirty pages in length plus appendixes) and summarize each in a two- to five-page memo that includes a recommendation to the justices on whether to hear the case, all with minimal guidance or counsel from their justices.[26] The memos are circulated to the justices' offices, where clerks read them again and make comments on the advisability of hearing the cases. The memos, with the clerks' comments, go on to the justices, who decide which cases they think should be granted cert and which denied. The chief justice circulates a weekly list of the cases he thinks should be discussed, which is known unimaginatively as the "discuss list." Other justices can add to that list the cases they think should be discussed in their Friday afternoon meetings.

Once a case is on the discuss list, it takes a vote of four justices to agree to grant it certiorari. This **Rule of Four** means that it takes fewer people to decide to hear a case than it will eventually take to decide the case itself, and thus it gives some

Sandra Day O'Connor

Even though she's told the story many times, Sandra Day O'Connor's voice still echoes with the frustration of that first job hunt. But there is irony in her voice, too—after all, the story has a happy ending, though it's one she never imagined when she graduated from law school back in 1952.

Really, all she wanted then was to work as a lawyer. She was getting married that summer and her husband-to-be still had a year left in law school. Since, she says dryly, they both liked to eat, she thought getting a job would be a good idea.

But she reckoned without the prejudice against hiring women that pervaded the country in those days. There were positions galore posted on the jobs board at Stanford Law School, where she'd graduated third in her class of 102, but none of the firms was willing to hire a woman. She'd even parlayed an undergraduate friendship into an interview at a friend's father's firm, but all that resulted were questions about her office skills.

The Supreme Court justice's story sounds both ludicrous and poignant today, as she recalls it in her impressive law chambers, with their rich polished woods and warm leather furniture, the walls lined with thick volumes of legal wisdom. As this most distinguished of American women recounts that long-ago interview in her precise, forceful voice,

> **"[E]very new generation has to learn all over again the foundations of our government . . . and . . . every individual's role in it."**

her snowy white hair and soft blue suit not blunting at all the effect of the power she radiates, it's hard not to find the incongruity a little amusing, even as one imagines the bitter disappointment of the young lawyer she once was.

"Well, Miss Day, how do you type?" asked the partner who interviewed her. Just so-so, she replied. "If you can type well enough, maybe I can get you a job here as a legal secretary," he suggested. "But, Miss Day, our firm has never hired a woman as a lawyer. I don't see the day when we will—our clients wouldn't accept it."

Having run into a brick wall in the private sector, Sandra Day, soon to be Sandra Day O'Connor, set to work convincing the San Mateo County attorney to hire her; because he was engaged in public law, "he wasn't afraid to have a woman in his office." With that first job—initially undertaken without pay and in a shared office—she launched herself on a public career that coursed through years in the state attorney general's office in Arizona, the Arizona state Senate, and the state bench and would finally hit its dramatic peak twenty-nine years later, when President Ronald Reagan appointed her as the first female justice on the U.S. Supreme Court.

Don't you just wish you could have seen her girlfriend's father's partner's face when that announcement was made?

But maybe it's too easy to blame Sandra Day O'Connor's extraordinary career in public law on the stubborn sexism of the private legal profession in 1950s America.

She might have taken that path anyway—her decision to go to law school in the first place was in part idealistic, inspired by a professor she'd taken a law class from as an undergraduate. "He was the first one who persuaded me that the individual could make a difference in this big world of ours," she remembers. By "the individual" he meant not just a president or governor or other person with power, but even someone "at the bottom of the totem pole." "The person at the bottom will sometimes have the best understanding of how to make something work. If you are sincere about it and determined enough, you can hang in there and see to it that it happens."

And those are the recurring themes in the life of Sandra Day O'Connor: sincerity in her efforts, determination to make a difference, persistence in the face of opposition, and independence in charting her path.

Perhaps all these qualities were honed from an early age, as she grew up on her family's Lazy B Ranch on the border of New Mexico and Arizona. There the fact that their herd grazed on federal land taught her early about the interrelationship between citizens and government. The harsh, isolated beauty of the land taught her other things as well. As she has written, the ranch was "a place where the wind always blows, the sky forms a dome overhead, and the clouds make changing patterns against the blue, and where the stars at night are brilliant and constant, a place to see the sunrise and sunset, and always to be reminded how small we are in the universe but, even so, how one small voice can make a difference."[1]

And there is that idealism again, an optimism about the potential of human beings that is tempered, when she talks, with a strong no-nonsense manner and a brisk practicality, a moderation and pragmatism that is reflected in her judgments on the Court. She clearly doesn't suffer fools gladly but at the same time is not without hope that we can save ourselves from foolishness. Here is some of her advice:

On what she'd tell today's students about how one person can make a difference:
Of course [you] have to have courage, you have to learn to believe in yourself, and to do that you have to develop some skills. So learn to read fast, and to write well, that's what you need to learn to do as a student. I have to read something like 1,500 pages a day. Now I couldn't do that if I hadn't taken speed reading. And that's important. I'm serious. You don't realize how important it is to be able to read fast. Because if you can read fast, think of all you can learn. . . . And then have courage to believe that, yes, you are equipped to do something, and go do it.

On keeping the republic:
You know, I've always said that we don't inherit our knowledge and understanding through the gene pool. And every new generation has to learn all over again the foundations of our government, how it was set up and why, and what is every individual's role in it. And we have to convey that to every generation . . . [i]f every young generation of citizens [doesn't] have an understanding of this, we can't keep our nation in decent order for the future.

---

1. Sandra Day O'Connor and H. Alan Day, *Lazy B: Growing Up on a Cattle Ranch in the American Southwest* (New York: Random House, 2002), 302.

power to a minority on the Court. The denial of certiorari does not necessarily signal that the Court endorses a lower court's ruling. Rather, it simply means that the case was not seen as important or special enough to be heard by the highest court. Justices who believe strongly that a case should not be denied have, increasingly in recent years, engaged in the practice of "dissenting from the denial," in an effort to persuade other justices to go along with them (since dissension at this stage makes the Court look less consensual) and to put their views on record. Fewer than 5 percent of cases appealed to the Supreme Court survive the screening process to be heard by the Court.

One factor that influences whether a case is heard by the Court is whether the United States, under the representation of its lawyer, the **solicitor general**, is party to it. Between 70 and 80 percent of the appeals filed by the federal government are granted cert by the justices, a far greater proportion than for any other group.[27] Researchers speculate that this is because of the stature of the federal government's interests, the justices' trust in the solicitor general's ability to weed out frivolous lawsuits, and the experience the solicitor general brings to the job.[28] Justices are also influenced by **amicus curiae briefs**, or "friend of the court" documents, that are filed in support of about 8 percent of petitions for certiorari by interest groups that want to encourage the Court to grant or deny cert. The amicus briefs do seem to affect the likelihood that the Court will agree to hear a case, and since economic interest groups are more likely to be active here than are other kinds of groups, it is their interests that most often influence the justices to grant cert.[29] As we will see, amicus curiae briefs are also used further on in the process.

Deciding Cases

Once a case is on the docket, the parties are notified and they prepare their written briefs and oral arguments for their Supreme Court appearance. Lawyers for each side get only a half-hour to make their cases verbally in front of the Court, and they are often interrupted by justices who seek clarification, criticize points, or offer supportive arguments. The actual decision-making process occurs before and during the Supreme Court conference meeting. Conference debates and discussions take place in private, although justices have often made revealing comments in their letters and memoirs that give insight into the dynamics of conference decision making. A variety of factors affect the justices as they make decisions on the cases they hear. Some of those factors come from within the justices—their attitudes, values, and beliefs—and some are external.

Justices' attitudes toward the Constitution and how literally it is to be taken are clearly important, as we saw earlier in our discussion of strict constructionism and interpretivism. Judges are also influenced by the view they hold of the role of the Court: whether it should be an active law- and policymaker, or should keep its rulings narrow and leave lawmaking to the elected branches of government. Those who adhere to **judicial activism** are quite comfortable with the idea of overturning precedents, exercising judicial review, and otherwise making decisions that shape government policy. Practitioners of **judicial restraint**, on the other hand, believe more strongly in the principle of *stare decisis* and reject any active lawmaking by the Court as unconstitutional.

These positions seem at first to line up with the positions of interpretivism and strict constructionism, and they often do. But exceptions exist, as when liberal justice Thurgood Marshall, who had once used the Constitution in activist and interpretivist ways to change civil rights laws, pleaded for restraint among his newer and more conservative colleagues who were eager to roll back some of the earlier decisions by overturning precedent and creating more conservative law.[30]

In recent years, especially in the wake of a Massachusetts Supreme Court decision that said forbidding gays the right to marry violates the Massachusetts constitution, conservatives have lambasted what they call the activism or "legislating from the bench" of courts who they say take decision making out of the hands of the people. But activism is not necessarily a liberal stance, and restraint is not necessarily conservative. Activism or restraint often seems to be more a function of whether a justice likes the status quo than it is of any steady point of principle.[31] A justice seeking to overturn the *Roe v. Wade* ruling allowing women to have abortions during the first trimester of pregnancy would be an activist conservative justice; Justice Thurgood Marshall ended his term on the Court as a liberal restraintist.

Justices are also influenced by external factors.[32] Despite the founders' efforts to make justices immune to politics and the pressures of public opinion by giving them lifetime tenure, political scientists have found that justices usually tend to make decisions that are consistent with majority opinion in the United States. Of course, this doesn't mean that justices are reading public opinion polls over breakfast and incorporating their findings into judicial decisions after lunch. Rather, the same forces that shape public opinion also shape the justices' opinions, and people who are elected by the public choose the justices they hope will help them carry out their agenda, usually one that is responsive to what the public wants.

Other political forces than public opinion exert an influence on the Court, however. The influence of the executive branch, discussed earlier, contributes to the high success rate of the solicitor general. Interest groups also put enormous pressure on the Supreme Court, although with varying success. Interest groups are influential in the process of nomination and confirmation of the justices, they file amicus curiae briefs to try to shape the decisions on the certiorari petitions, and they file an increasingly large number of briefs in support of one or the other side when the case is actually reviewed by the Court. According to one scholar, the number of amicus briefs filed by interest groups is increasing.[33] Interest groups also have a role in sponsoring cases when individual petitioners do not have the resources to bring a case before the Supreme Court.

A final influence on the justices worth discussing here is the justices' relationships with each other. While they usually (at least in recent years) arrive at their conference meeting with their minds already made up, they cannot afford to ignore one another. It takes five votes to decide a case, and the justices need each other as allies. One scholar who has looked at the disputes among justices over decisions, and who has evaluated the characterization of the Court as "nine scorpions in a bottle," says that the number of disagreements is not noteworthy.[34] On the contrary, what is truly remarkable is how well the justices tend to cooperate, given their close working relationship, the seriousness of their undertaking, and the varied and strong personalities and ideologies that go into the mix.

Writing Opinions

Once a decision is reached, or sometimes as it is being reached, the writing of the opinion is assigned. The **opinion** is the written part of the decision that states the judgment of the majority of the Court; it is the lasting part of the process, read by law students, lawyers, judges, and future justices. As the living legacy of the case, the written opinions are vitally important for how the nation will understand what the decision means. If, for instance, the opinion is written by the least enthusiastic member of the majority, it will be weaker and less authoritative than if it is written by the most passionate member. The same decision can be portrayed in different ways, can be stated broadly or narrowly, with implications for many future cases or for fewer. If the chief justice is in the majority, it is his or her job to assign the opinion-writing task. Otherwise, the senior member in the majority assigns the opinion. So important is the task that chief justices are known to manipulate their votes, voting with a majority they do not agree with in order to keep the privilege of assigning the opinion to the justice who would write the weakest version of the majority's conclusion.[35] Those justices who agree with the general decision, but for reasons other than or in addition to those stated in the majority opinion, may write **concurring opinions**, and those who disagree may write **dissenting opinions**. These other opinions often have lasting impact as well, especially if the Court changes its mind, as it often does over time and as its composition changes. When such a reversal occurs, the reasons for the about-face are sometimes to be found in the dissent or the concurrence for the original decision.

The Political Effects of Judicial Decisions

The last area in which we can see the Supreme Court as a political actor is in the effects of the decisions it makes. These decisions, despite the best intentions of those who adhere to the philosophy of judicial restraint, often amount to the creation of public policies as surely as do the acts of Congress. Chapters 4 and 5, on civil liberties and the struggle for equal rights, make clear that the Supreme Court, at certain points in its history, has taken an active lawmaking role. The history of the Supreme Court's policymaking role is the history of the United States, and we cannot possibly recount it here, but a few examples should show that rulings of the Court have had the effect of distributing scarce and valued resources among people, affecting decisively who gets what, when, and how.[36]

It was the Court, for instance, under the early leadership of John Marshall, that greatly enhanced the power of the federal government over the states by declaring that the Court itself has the power to invalidate state laws (and acts of the Congress as well) if they conflict with the Constitution;[37] that state law is invalid if it conflicts with

Judicial Impact

Supreme Court decisions frequently influence policymaking, as in the case of *Roe v. Wade*, which legalized abortion. The issue remains hotly contested both in politics and in public and often serves as a litmus test when people assess new nominees to the Court. Here, demonstrators for and against abortion rights face off against one another during a Washington, D.C., event.

national law;[38] that Congress' powers go beyond those listed in Article I, Section 8, of the Constitution;[39] and that the federal government can regulate interstate commerce.[40] In the early years of the twentieth century, the Supreme Court was an ardent defender of the right of business not to be regulated by the federal government, striking down laws providing for maximum working hours,[41] regulation of child labor,[42] and minimum wages.[43] The role of the Court in making civil rights policy is well known. In 1857 it decided that slaves, even freed slaves, could never be citizens;[44] in 1896 it decided that separate accommodations for whites and blacks were constitutional;[45] and then it reversed itself, declaring separate but equal to be unconstitutional in 1954.[46] It is the Supreme Court that has been responsible for the expansion of due process protection for criminal defendants,[47] for instituting the principle of one person–one vote in drawing legislative districts,[48] and for creating the right of a woman to have an abortion in the first trimester of pregnancy.[49] In 2010 the Court ruled that campaign finance legislation could not limit the money spent by corporations on electioneering broadcasts because corporations have First Amendment protections.[50] And, of course, there was the case of *Bush v. Gore*, with which we began this chapter. Each of these actions has altered the distribution of power in American society in ways that some would argue should be done only by an elected body.

Citizenship and the Courts
Equal treatment and equal access?

In this chapter we have argued that the legal system and the American courts are central to the maintenance of social order and conflict resolution and are also a fundamental component of American politics—who gets what, and how they get it. This means that a crucial question for American democracy is: Who takes advantage of this powerful system for allocating resources and values in society? An important component of American political culture is the principle of equality before the law, which we commonly take to mean that all citizens should be treated equally *by* the law, but which also implies that all citizens should have equal access *to* the law. In this concluding section we look at the questions of equal treatment *and* equal access.

In Chapter 5, on civil rights, we examined in depth the issue of equality before the law in a constitutional sense. But what about the day-to-day treatment of citizens by the law enforcement and legal systems? Citizens *are* treated differently by these systems according to their race, their income level, and the kinds of crimes they commit. African Americans and white Americans do not experience our criminal justice system in the same ways, beginning with what is often the initial contact with the system, the police. In a poll taken during the O. J. Simpson criminal trial, months before the verdict was reached, only 33 percent of blacks said they believed the police testify truthfully, and only 18 percent said they would believe the police over other witnesses at a trial. Sixty-six percent of blacks said they thought the criminal justice system was racist, as opposed to only 37 percent of whites.[51] Blacks are often harassed by police or treated with suspicion simply because they are black, and they tend to perceive the police as persecutors rather than protectors. In fact, blacks are more likely to be arrested than whites, and they are more likely to go to jail, where they serve harsher sentences. In part, this is because blacks are more likely to be poor and urban, and to belong to a socioeconomic class where crime not only doesn't carry the popular sanctions that it does for the middle class, but where it may provide some of the only opportunities for economic advancement. But studies show that racial bias and stereotyping also play a role in the racial disparities in the criminal justice system.[52]

Race is not the only factor that divides American citizens in their experience of the criminal justice system. Income also creates a barrier to equal treatment by the law. Over half of those accused of felonies in the United States have court-appointed lawyers. These lawyers are likely to be less than enthusiastic about these assignments: pay is modest and sometimes irregular. Many lawyers do not like to provide free services *pro bono publico* ("for the public good") because they are afraid it will offend their regular corporate clients. Consequently the quality of the legal representation available to the poor is not the same standard available to those who can afford to pay well. Yale law professor John H. Langbein is scathing on the role of money in determining the legal fate of Americans. He says, "Money is the defining element of our modern American criminal-justice system." The wealthy can afford crackerjack lawyers who can use the "defense lawyer's bag of tricks for sowing doubts, casting aspersions, and coaching witnesses," but "if you are not a person of means, if you cannot afford to engage the elite defense-lawyer industry—and that means most of us—you will be cast into a different system, in which the financial advantages of the state will overpower you and leave you effectively at the mercy of prosecutorial whim."[53]

Whereas the issue with respect to the *criminal* justice system is equal treatment, the issue for the *civil* justice system is equal access. Although the Supreme Court has ruled that low-income defendants must be provided with legal assistance in state and federal criminal cases, there is no such guarantee for civil cases. That doesn't mean, however, that less affluent citizens have no recourse for their legal problems. Both public and private legal aid programs exist. Among others, the Legal Services Corporation (LSC), created by Congress in 1974, is a nonprofit organization that provides resources to over 138 legal aid programs around the country with more than 900 local offices. The LSC helps citizens and some immigrants with legal problems such as those concerning housing, employment, family issues, finances, and immigration. Every year LSC programs handle approximately a million cases and provide other legal help to five million more people.[54] This program has been controversial, as conservatives have feared that it has a left-wing agenda, and Republican administrations have threatened its funding.

These arguments do not mean that the U.S. justice system has made no progress toward a more equal dispensation of justice. Without doubt, we have made enormous strides since the days of *Dred Scott,* when the Supreme Court ruled that blacks did not have the standing to bring cases to court, and since the days when lynch mobs dispensed their brand of vigilante justice in the South. The goal of equal treatment by and equal access to the legal system in America, however, is still some way off.

▶ What's at Stake Revisited

Since the divisive outcome of *Bush v. Gore,* the nation has calmed down. The pickets and the angry voices are quiet. The stunning national crisis that began with the terrorist attacks on September 11, 2001, has put things into a broader perspective, and a Court-decided election no longer seems as great a danger as the possibility of being caught without any elected leader at all at a critical time. Public opinion polls show that trust in all institutions of government, including the Supreme Court, ran high after September 11, and Bush's legitimacy no longer rested with the Court's narrow majority but rather with the approval ratings that hit unprecedented heights in the aftermath of the terrorist attacks and with his successful reelection in 2004.

But changed national circumstances and subsequent elections do not mean that the Court's unusual and controversial move in resolving the 2000 election should go unanalyzed. What was at stake in this extraordinary case?

First, as Justice Stevens pointed out, the long-term consequences of people's attitudes toward the Court are unknown. The Court, as we have seen, has often engaged in policymaking, and to believe that it is not a political institution would be a serious mistake. But part of its own legitimacy has come from the fact that most people do not perceive it as political, and it is far more difficult now to maintain that illusion. In the immediate aftermath of the decision, the justices, speaking around the country, tried to contain the damage and reassure Americans; some of the dissenting justices emphasized that the decision was not made on political or ideological grounds. Only in the longer term will we see if that case was persuasive to the American public. It would be ironic indeed if the Court moved to ensure Bush's legitimacy at the expense of its own.

Also at stake in such a deeply divided decision was the Court's own internal stability and ability to work together. While the confidentiality of the justices' discussions in arriving at the decision has been well guarded, the decision itself shows that they were acrimonious. Again, in the aftermath, the justices have tried to put a unified front on what was clearly a bitter split. Members of the majority have continued to socialize with dissenters, and as Justice Scalia himself told one audience, "If you can't disagree without hating each other, you better find another profession other than the law."[55] While the stakes in this case may have been more directly political than in most other cases, the members of the Supreme Court are used to disagreeing over important issues and probably handle the level of conflict more easily than do the Americans who look up to them as diviners of truth and right.

Another stake in the pivotal decision was the fundamental issue of federalism itself. The federal courts, as Justice Ruth Bader Ginsburg wrote in her dissent, have a long tradition of deferring to state courts on issues of state law. Indeed, many observers were astounded that the Court agreed to hear the case in the first place, assuming that the justices would have sent it back to be settled in Florida. Normally it would have been the ardent conservatives on the Court—Rehnquist, Scalia, and Thomas—whom one would have expected to leap to the defense of states' rights. It has been made clear, however, that the *Bush v. Gore* decision did not signal a reversal on their part. If the opinions of the Court about federalism have changed at all since 2000, it will probably be due more to the imperatives of the war on terrorism, as we suggested in Chapter 2, than to the dictates of the election case.

Some observers argue that the majority of the Court saw something else at stake that led them to set aside their strong beliefs in states' rights and to run the risk that they might be seen as more Machiavelli than King Solomon, more interested in power than wisdom. The majority saw the very security and stability of the nation at stake. Anticipating a long recount of the votes that might even then be inconclusive, they thought it was better to act decisively at the start rather than to wait until a circus-like atmosphere had rendered impossible the most important decision a voting public can make. Whether they were right in doing so, and whether the stakes justified the risks they took, politicians, partisans, and historians will be debating for years to come.

▶ Summary With Key Terms

Laws serve five main functions in a democratic society. They offer security, supply predictability, provide for conflict resolution through the **courts** (296), reinforce society's values, and provide for the distribution of social costs and benefits. American law is based on legislation, but its practice has evolved from a **common law tradition** (297) and the use of **precedent** (297) by judges.

Laws serve many purposes and are classified in different ways. **Substantive law** (297) covers what we can or cannot do, while **procedural law** (297) establishes the procedures used to enforce law generally and guarantees us **procedural due process** (298). **Criminal law** (298) concerns specific behaviors considered undesirable by the government, while **civil law** (298) covers interactions between individuals. **Constitutional law** (298) refers to laws included in the Constitution as well as the precedents established over time by judicial decisions relating to these laws. **Statutory law** (299), **administrative law** (299), and **executive orders** (299) are established by Congress and state legislatures, the bureaucracy, and the president, respectively.

The founders were deliberately vague in setting up a court system so as to avoid controversy during the ratification process. The Constitution never stated that courts could decide the constitutionality of legislation. The courts gained the extra-constitutional power of **judicial review** (301) when Chief Justice John Marshall created it in *Marbury v. Madison.*

The United States has a dual court system, with state and federal courts each having different **jurisdictions** (302). Cases come directly to a court through its **original jurisdiction** (303) or on **appeal** (304) if it has **appellate jurisdiction** (303). Both court systems have three tiers; the federal courts range from district courts to the U.S. courts of appeals to the Supreme Court. Judges are appointed to the federal courts by a political process involving the president and the Senate and, often, the principle of **senatorial courtesy** (307).

The U.S. Supreme Court reigns at the top of the American court system. It is a powerful institution, revered by the American public, but as political an institution as the other two branches of government. Politics is involved in how the Court is chosen—a process that considers merit; ideology, especially focusing on whether the justices are believers in **strict constructionism** (311), **judicial interpretivism** (311), **judicial activism** (318), or **judicial restraint** (318); reward; and representation. The work of the Court is also political, as the justices decide whether to issue **writs of certiorari** (314) based on the application of the **Rule of Four** (315), and decide cases influenced by their own values, the **solicitor general** (318), and a variety of **amicus curiae briefs** (318). These influences show up in the writing of the **opinion** (320), and both **concurring** (320) and **dissenting opinions** (320). These opinions are decisive in determining who gets what in American politics.

Explore this subject further with suggested readings, movies, and web sites at http://republic-brief.cqpress.com, where you'll also find study aids, practice quizzes, flash cards, and Internet exercises.

Chapter 10

Public Opinion

▶ What's at Stake?

How much responsibility do you want to take for the way you are governed? Most of us are pretty comfortable with the idea that we should vote for our *rulers* (although we don't all jump at the chance to do it), but how about voting on the *rules*? Citizens of some states—California, for instance—have become used to being asked for their votes on new state laws through referenda and voter initiatives. But what about national politics—do you know enough or care enough to vote on laws for the country as a whole, just as if you were a member of Congress or a senator? Should we be governed more by public opinion than by the opinions of our elected leaders? This is the question that drives the debate about whether U.S. citizens should be able to participate in such forms of direct democracy as the national referendum or initiative.

Not only do many states (twenty-seven out of fifty) employ some form of direct democracy, but many other countries do as well. In the past several years alone, voters in Slovenia were asked to decide about the establishment of a tribunal to resolve a border dispute with Croatia, in Bolivia about whether there should be limits to individual landholdings, in Azerbaijan about amending the constitution, in Sierra Leone about choosing a president (in the first democratic elections since 1967), and in Iceland about terms of payment on the national debt.

In 1995 former senator Mike Gravel, D-Alaska, proposed that the United States join many of the world's nations in adopting a national *plebiscite,* or popular vote on policy. He argued that Americans should support a national initiative he called "Philadelphia II" (to evoke "Philadelphia I," which was, of course, the Constitutional Convention), which would set up procedures for direct popular participation in national lawmaking.[1] Such participation could take place through the ballot box (the Swiss go to the polls four times a year to vote on national policy) or even electronically, as some have suggested, with people voting on issues by computer at home. Experts agree that the technology exists for at-home participation in government. And public opinion is overwhelmingly in favor of proposals to let Americans vote for or against major national issues before they become law.[2]

Do you agree with Gravel and the roughly three-quarters of Americans who support more direct democracy at the national level? Should we have rule by public opinion in the United States? How would the founders have responded to this proposal? And what would be the consequences for American government if a national plebiscite were passed? Just what is at stake in the issue of direct democracy at the national level?

I t is fashionable these days to denounce the public opinion polls that claim to tell us what the American public thinks about this or that political issue. The American people themselves are skeptical—65 percent of them think that the polls are "right only some of the time" or "hardly ever right."[3] (You might believe that finding, or you might not.) Politicians can be leery of polls, too—or even downright scornful of them. Disdainful of the Clinton years, when the president's team of pollsters openly tested the public on various issues, including his approval ratings, the Bush administration was cagey about the fact that they watched polls at all. Bush himself frequently said things like, "I really don't worry about polls or focus groups; I do what I think is right."[4] Matthew Dowd, the Bush administration's chief of polling at the Republican National Committee, echoed that stance with an emphatic "We don't poll policy positions. Ever."[5]

Of course, the Bush administration did look at polls, and conducted them, too, just like every other administration since the advent of modern polling. When in 2002 a reporter visited Karl Rove, Bush's chief political adviser, and asked about the impact of the corporate scandals of the time on Bush's effectiveness as president, Rove pulled out a bundle of polls and started reading off data to support his claim that people continued to support Bush. Then he caught the reporter's quizzical look. "'Not that we spend a lot of time on these,' he said quickly. . . ."[6]

These reactions to public opinion raise an interesting question. What is so bad about being ruled by the polls in a democracy, which, after all, is supposed to be ruled by the people? If politics is about who gets what, and how they get it, shouldn't we care about what the "who" thinks? **Public opinion** is just what the public thinks. It is the aggregation, or collection, of individual attitudes and beliefs on one or more issues at any given time. **Public opinion polls** are nothing more than scientific efforts to measure that opinion—to estimate what an entire group of people thinks about an issue by asking a smaller sample of the group for their opinions. If the sample is large enough and chosen properly, we have every reason to believe that it will provide a reliable estimate of the whole. Today's technology gives us the ability to keep a constant finger on the pulse of America, and to know what its citizens are thinking at almost any given time. And yet, at least some Americans seem torn about the role of public opinion in government today. On the one hand, we want to believe that what we think matters, but on the other hand, we'd like to think that our elected officials are guided by unwavering standards and principles.

In this chapter we argue that public opinion *is* important for the proper functioning of democracy, that the expression of what citizens think and what they want is a prerequisite for their ability to use the system and its rules to get what they want from it. But the quality of the public's opinion on politics, and the ways that it actually influences policy, may surprise us greatly. Specifically, in this chapter you will learn about the role of public opinion in a democracy, how public opinion can be measured, where our opinions come from, and what our opinions are—whether we think like the "ideal democratic citizen."

The Role of Public Opinion in a Democracy
Keeping the government of the people informed by the people

Public opinion is important in a democracy for at least two reasons. The first reason is normative: we believe public opinion *should* influence what government does. The second is empirical: a lot of people actually behave as though public opinion does matter, and to the degree that they measure, record, and react to it, it does indeed become a factor in American politics.

Why Public Opinion *Ought* to Matter

The presence of "the people" is pervasive in the documents that created and support the American government. In the Declaration of Independence, Thomas Jefferson wrote that a just government must get its powers from "the consent of the governed." Our Constitution begins, "We, the People. . . ." And Abraham Lincoln's Gettysburg Address hails our nation as "government of the people, by the people, and for the people." What all of this tells us is that the very legitimacy of the U.S. government, like that of all other democracies, rests on the idea that government exists to serve the interests of its citizens. As political scientist V. O. Key observed, "Unless mass views have some place in the shaping of policy, all talk about democracy is nonsense."[7]

But how to determine whose views should be heard? As we saw in Chapter 1, different theories of democracy prescribe different roles for "the people," in part because these theories disagree about how competent the citizens of a country are to govern themselves. Elitists suspect that citizens are too ignorant or ill informed to be trusted with major political decisions; pluralists trust groups of citizens to be competent on those issues in which they have a stake, but they think that individuals may be too busy to gather all the information they need to make informed decisions; and proponents of participatory democracy have faith that the people are both smart enough and able to gather enough information to be effective decision makers.

As Americans, we are also somewhat confused about what we think the role of the democratic citizen should be. We introduced these conflicting notions of citizenship in Chapter 1. One view, which describes what we might call the *ideal democratic citizen,* is founded on the vision of a virtuous citizen activated by concern for the common good, who recognizes that democracy carries obligations as well as rights. In this familiar model a citizen should be attentive to and informed about politics, exhibit political tolerance and a willingness to compromise, and practice high levels of participation in civic activities.

A competing view of American citizenship holds that Americans are *apolitical, self-interested actors.* According to this view, Americans are almost the opposite of the ideal citizen: inattentive and ill informed, politically intolerant and rigid, and unlikely to get involved in political life.

We argue in this chapter, as we have earlier, that the American public displays both of these visions of citizenship. But we also argue that mechanisms in American politics buffer the impact of apolitical, self-interested behavior, so that government by public opinion does not have disastrous effects on the American polity. Although it may seem like some kind of magician's act, we show that Americans as a *group* often behave as ideal citizens, even though as *individuals* they do not.

Why Public Opinion *Does* Matter

Politicians and media leaders act as though they agree with Key's conclusion, which is the practical reason why public opinion matters in American politics. Elected politicians, for example, overwhelmingly believe that the public is keeping tabs on them. When voting on major bills, members of Congress worry quite a lot about public opinion in their districts.[8] Presidents, too, pay close attention to public opinion. In fact, recent presidents have invested major resources in having an in-house public opinion expert whose regular polls are used as an important part of presidential political strategies. And, indeed, the belief that the public is paying attention is not totally unfounded. Although the public does not often act as if it pays attention or cares very much about politics, it can change its mind and act decisively if the provocation is sufficient. For instance, in the 2006 midterm election, voters showed their frustration with Republicans' support for the war in Iraq (despite polls that said a majority of

> Although it may seem like some kind of magician's act, . . . Americans as a *group* often behave as ideal citizens, even though as *individuals* they do not.

Americans had come to oppose the war) by handing the Democrats enough seats in the House and the Senate to give them control in both chambers.[9]

Politicians are not alone in their tendency to monitor public opinion as they do their jobs. Leaders of the media also focus on public opinion, making huge investments in polls and devoting considerable coverage to reporting what the public is thinking. Polls are used to measure public attitudes toward all sorts of things. Of course, we are familiar with "horse-race" polls that ask about people's voting intentions and lend drama to media coverage of electoral races. Sometimes these polls themselves become the story the media covers. With the availability of a twenty-four-hour news cycle and the need to find something to report on all the time, it is not surprising that the media have fastened on their own polling as a newsworthy subject. Public opinion, or talk about it, seems to pervade the modern political arena.

Citizen Values
American reality far from the ideal

At the beginning of this chapter we reminded you of the two competing visions of citizenship in America: one, the *ideal democratic citizen* who is attentive and informed, is tolerant and participates in politics; and two, the apolitical self-interested actor who does not meet this ideal. As we might expect from the fact that Americans hold two such different views of what citizenship is all about, our behavior falls somewhere in the middle. For instance, some citizens tune out political news but are tolerant of others and vote regularly. Many activist citizens are informed, opinionated, and participatory but are intolerant of others' views, which can make the give and take of democratic politics difficult. We are not ideal democratic citizens, but we know our founders did not expect us to be. As we will see by the end of this chapter, our democracy survives fairly well despite our lapses.

The ideal democratic citizen understands how government works, who the main actors are, and what major principles underlie the operation of the political system. Public opinion pollsters periodically take readings on what the public actually knows about politics, and the conclusion is always the same: Americans are not very well informed about their political system.[10]

Knowledge of key figures in politics is important for knowing whom to thank—or blame—for government policy, key information if we are to hold our officials accountable. For instance, virtually everyone (99 percent of Americans) can name the president, but only about one-quarter of the public can name both senators of their state, and before the Supreme Court's decisive role in resolving the 2000 election, only 16 percent could name the chief justice (the percentage rose to 31 percent afterward).[11] Americans have a reasonable understanding of the most prominent aspects of the governmental system and the most visible leaders but are ignorant about other central actors and key principles of American political life.

Interest in politics is also highly variable in the United States. For example, just 44 percent of the electorate in 2008 said they were "very much interested" in

Don't Be Fooled By the Polls

In the heat of the Clinton impeachment hearings, angry conservative Republicans could not believe the polls: over 65 percent of Americans still approved of the job the president was doing and did not want to see him removed from office. Their conclusion? The polls were simply wrong. "The polls are targeted to get a certain answer," said one Floridian. "There are even T-shirts in South Florida that say 'I haven't been polled.'"[1]

Do we need to know people personally who have been polled in order to trust poll results? Of course not. But there are lots of polls out there, not only those done carefully and responsibly by reputable polling organizations but also polls done for marketing and overtly political purposes—polls with an agenda, we might say. How are we, as good scholars and citizens, to know which results are reliable indications of what the public thinks, and which are not? One thing we can do is bring our critical thinking skills to bear by asking some questions about the polls reported in the media. Try these.[2]

1. **Who is the poll's sponsor?** Even if the poll was conducted by a professional polling company, it may still have been commissioned on behalf of a candidate or company. Does the sponsor have an agenda? How might that agenda influence the poll, the question wording, or the sponsor's interpretation of events?

2. **Is the sample representative?** That is, were proper sampling techniques followed? What is the margin of error?

3. **From what population was the sample taken?** There is a big difference, for instance, between the preference of the *general public* for a presidential candidate and the preference of *likely voters*, especially if one is interested in predicting the election's outcome! Read the fine print. Sometimes a polling organization will weight responses according to the likelihood that the respondent will actually vote in order to come up with a better prediction of the election result. Some polls survey only the members of one party, or the readers of a particular magazine, or people of a certain age, depending on

the election campaign while 41 percent were only "somewhat interested."[12] Taken together, the moderate levels of political knowledge interest indicate that the American public does not approach the high levels of civic engagement recommended by civics texts, but neither are they totally ignorant and unconcerned. In fact, as we will see, the public separates itself into different strata of political the information they are seeking to discover. Be sure the sample is not self-selected. Always check the population being sampled, and do not assume it is the general public.

4. **How are the questions worded?** Are loaded, problematic, or vague terms used? Could the questions be confusing to the average citizen? Are the questions available with the poll results? If not, why not? Do the questions seem to lead you to respond one way or the other? Do they oversimplify issues or complicate them? If the survey claims to have detected change over time, be sure the same questions were used consistently. All these things could change the way people respond.

5. **Are the survey topics ones that people are likely to have information and opinions about?** Respondents rarely admit that they don't know how to answer a question, so responses on obscure or technical topics are likely to be more suspect than others.

6. **What is the poll's response rate?** A lot of "don't knows," "no opinions," or refusals to answer can have a decided effect on the results.

7. **Do the poll results differ from those of other polls, and if so, why?** Don't necessarily assume that public opinion has changed. What is it about this poll that might have caused the discrepancy?

8. **What do the results mean?** Who is doing the interpreting? What are that person's motives? For instance, pollsters who work for the Democratic Party will have an interpretation of the results that is favorable to Democrats, and Republican interpretation will favor Republicans. Try interpreting the results yourself.

---

1. Melinda Henneberger, "Where G.O.P. Gathers, Frustration Does Too," *New York Times*, February 1, 1999, 3.
2. Some of these questions are based in part on similar advice given to poll watchers in Herbert Asher, *Polling and the Public: What Every Citizen Should Know*, 7th ed. (Washington, D.C.: CQ Press, 2007), 206–209.

engagement with only a minority who are seriously involved in following and trying to influence politics and government.

Another key value for our ideal citizen is tolerance. In a democracy, with many people jockeying for position and many competing visions of the common good, tolerance for ideas different from one's own and respect for the rights of others provide oil to keep the democratic machinery running smoothly. It is also a prereq-uisite for compromise, an essential component of politics generally, and democratic politics particularly.

How do Americans measure up on the important democratic requirement of respect for others' rights? The record is mixed. As we saw in Chapter 5, America has a history of denying basic civil rights to some groups, but clearly tolerance has been on the increase since the civil rights movement of the 1960s. Small pockets of intol-erance persist, primarily among such extremist groups as those who advocate vio-lence against doctors who perform abortions, the burning of black churches in the South, or anti-Arab and anti-Muslim incidents following the terrorist attacks on the World Trade Center and the Pentagon on September 11, 2001.[13] Such extremism, however, is the exception rather than the rule in contemporary American politics.

In terms of general principles, almost all Americans support the values of free-dom of speech, freedom of religion, and political equality. For instance, 90 percent of respondents told researchers that they believed in "free speech for all, no matter what their views might be." However, when citizens are asked to apply these principles to particular situations in which specific groups have to be tolerated (especially unpop-ular groups like the American Nazi Party preaching race hatred or atheists preaching against God and religion), the levels of political tolerance drop dramatically.[14]

In studies of political tolerance, the least politically tolerant are consistently the less educated and less politically sophisticated. For example, one study found that on a civil liberties scale designed to measure overall support for First Amendment rights, only 24 percent of high school graduates earned high scores, compared with 52 percent of college graduates.[15]

Many such findings have led some observers to argue that elites are the protec-tors of our democratic values. According to this view, the highly educated and politi-cally active are the ones who guard the democratic process from the mass of citizens who would easily follow undemocratic demagogues (like Adolf Hitler). Critics of this theory, however, say that educated people simply know what the politically cor-rect responses to polls are and so can hide their intolerance better. In practice, the mass public's record has not been bad, and some of the worst offenses of intolerance in our history, from slavery to the incarceration of the Japanese in America during World War II, were led by elites, not the mass public. Nevertheless, the weight of the evidence does indicate that democratic political tolerance increases with education.

A final characteristic of ideal citizens is, not surprisingly, that they participate in the system. One of the most consistent criticisms of Americans by those concerned with the democratic health of the nation is that we do not participate enough. And indeed, as participation is usually measured, the critics are right. For instance, among industrialized nations, the United States ranks last in voter turnout (see Figure 10.1). Various explanations have been offered for the low U.S. turnout, including the failure of parties to work to mobilize turnout and obstacles to participation such as restric-tive registration laws, limited voting hours, and the frequency of elections. We exam-ine who votes and why in Chapter 12, but for now the fact remains that voter turnout in national elections is the lowest, or among the lowest, of the industrialized nations.

Figure 10.1

Comparison of Voter Turnout Among Select Nations

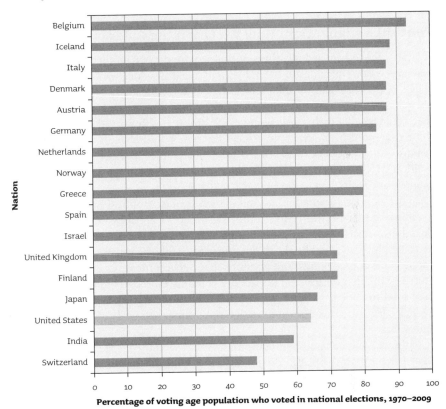

Percentage of voting age population who voted in national elections, 1970–2009

Source: Calculated by authors with data from from the Institute for Democracy and Electoral Assistance, www.idea .int/vt/.

What Influences Our Opinions About Politics?
Sources of continuity and division in the American public

Clearly many, but by no means all, Americans exhibit the characteristics of our so-called ideal democratic citizen, and the traits of ideal democratic citizenship are not distributed equally across the population. But the fact that education and socioeconomic status have something to do with our political opinions and behaviors still does not tell us where our opinions come from. In this section we look at several sources of public opinion: political socialization, economic self-interest, ideology, education, age, gender, race, religion, and geographic region of residence. All these things affect the way we come to see politics, what we believe we have at stake in the political process, and the kind of citizenship we practice.

Political Socialization: How We Learn the Rules of the Game

Democracies and, indeed, all other political systems depend for their survival on each new generation's picking up the values and allegiances of previous generations—beliefs in the legitimacy of the political system and its leaders, and a willingness to obey the laws and the commands of those leaders. You can well imagine the chaos that would result if each new generation of citizens, freshly arrived at adulthood, had to be convinced from scratch to respect the system and obey its laws. In fact, that doesn't happen because we all learn from our cradles to value and support our political systems, which is why the children in France or China support their leaders as surely as the children of the United States support theirs. The process by which we learn our political orientations and allegiances is called **political socialization**.

Political socialization works through a variety of agents. Chief among these is the family, which has a tremendous opportunity to influence the political development of children. Preschool-age children are highly receptive to messages from parents and older siblings, and learning about government begins at an early age. Studies show that the greatest impact of the family is on party identification. Children tend to choose the same political party as their parents.[16] The family has a weaker effect on attitudes about social and political issues such as race relations and welfare.[17]

Schools, where many children begin their day with the Pledge of Allegiance and where an emphasis is placed on getting along with the group, are also important agents of political learning and the development of citizen orientations. Most school districts include as part of their explicit missions that the schools should foster good citizenship,[18] and many require the teaching of American government or civics.

Churches, neighborhoods, and workplaces can be central in the development of political beliefs. This can be traced in part to the ways people select themselves into groups, but beliefs are reinforced by social contacts. The processes of talking, working, and worshiping together lead people to see the world similarly.[19]

Peer groups in general have a lot of influence on individuals' social and political attitudes. Most people want to be like their fellows, and few of us like to stand out as different. In many contexts, when there is a clearly perceived majority position, those holding minority positions tend not to speak up or defend their views. This relative silence tends to embolden the advocates of the majority opinion to speak even more confidently. Thus what may begin as a bare majority for a group's position can become the overwhelming voice of the group.[20]

The major political and social events we live through can also have a profound impact on our political orientations. Some examples include the New Deal realignment that came out of the Great Depression, the political optimism following World War II and the prosperity of the 1950s, the political activism surrounding the civil rights movement and the unpopular Vietnam War in the 1960s and 1970s, and the drop in political trust that resulted from the Watergate scandal and the resignation of President Richard Nixon.[21]

The partisan politics of the 1990s, including the impeachment of President Clinton and the contested presidential election of 2000, should have caused levels of trust to fall even further. That they did not probably reflects citizens' generally positive assessment of government's role in the economic prosperity of the era. The events of September 11, 2001, and the ensuing war on terror caused Americans to see their government in an even more positive light, although as Americans' attention focused on domestic issues and partisan politics returned to business as usual, expressions of trust fell to their pre–September 11 level.[22]

Sources of Divisions in Public Opinion

Political socialization produces a citizenry that largely agrees with the rules of the game and accepts the outcomes of the national political process as legitimate. That does not mean, however, that we are a nation in agreement on most or even very many things. There is a considerable range of disagreement in the policy preferences of Americans, and those disagreements stem in part from citizens' interests, ideology, education, age, gender, race, and religion—even the area of the country in which they live.

Self-Interest
People's political preferences often come from an assessment of what is best for them economically, from asking, "What's in it for me?" So, for instance, those in the lowest income brackets are the least likely to agree that too much is being spent on welfare, while those with more income are more likely to agree. Similarly, as incomes increase so does the feeling that one is paying too much in taxes.[23] These patterns are only tendencies, however. Some wealthy people favor the redistribution of wealth and more spending on welfare; some people living in poverty oppose these policies. Even on these straightforward economic questions, other factors are at work.

Partisanship and Ideology
Much of the division in contemporary American public opinion can be described in ideological (liberal-conservative) or partisan (Democrat or Republican) terms. How we adopt the labels of current political conflict has a good deal of influence on the policy positions we take, and even how we perceive political personalities and events.

As we saw in Chapter 1, ideologies are sets of ideas about politics, the economy, and society that help us deal with the political world. For many Americans today, liberalism stands for faith in government action to bring about equitable outcomes and social tolerance while conservatism for many represents a preference for limited government and traditional social values. A whole host of policy controversies in contemporary American politics are widely discussed in liberal-conservative terms.

Party identification, as we will see in Chapter 11, refers to our relatively enduring allegiances to one of the major political parties; for many of us it is part of what defines us.[24] Party labels provide mental cues that we use in interpreting and responding to personalities and news.

Identification as a Democrat or Republican strongly influences how we see the political world. Research shows that uncertainty about new policies or personalities is usually resolved to be consistent with our partisanship. Even our view of objective events is affected by partisanship. Toward the end of Republican president Ronald Reagan's second term in office, a poll asked Americans whether inflation and unemployment had gotten better or worse over the eight years of his administration. In fact, both had improved, but Democrats and Republicans were miles apart in their perceptions of the objective facts: a majority of the Democrats said inflation was worse and only 8 percent acknowledged it was better. Among Republicans only 13 percent thought it had gotten worse, and fully 47 percent thought it improved.[25] In a more recent example, just fourteen days into the Obama administration, a poll asked if Americans approved or disapproved of the way Obama was handling his job as president. Objectively, it would be hard for anyone to tell much after only two weeks, but partisans had formed their opinions: fully half of the Republicans already disapproved, compared to only 2 percent of Democrats.[26] We clearly do see the world through a partisan lens.

Because party elites and candidates have become ideologically polarized in recent decades—that is, Republicans are increasingly associated with a very conservative ideology and Democrats with a liberal one, with less and less common ground in the middle—citizens find it increasingly easy to sort themselves into one party or the other.[27] As a result, average Democrats and Republicans are much farther apart ideologically than was the case in previous decades. The result for politics is that fewer people are likely to swing between candidates because fewer come to contemporary elections with a fully open mind. Most voters are predisposed by the combination of ideological and partisan identifications one way or the other.

An important ideological group in the electorate comprises those who are "philosophical conservatives" but "operational liberals." When asked, they identify themselves as conservatives, attached to the concept of limited government and an unregulated market, but they also support many of the programs that accompany contemporary liberalism, such as Social Security, Medicare, and environmental protection. Of course, politicians try to play on this, with Republicans appealing their loyalty to "conservative principles" while Democrats avoid ideological labels and try to focus attention on specific favored programs.

Education

As we suggested earlier in our discussion of the ideal democratic citizen, a number of political orientations change as a person attains more education. Better-educated citizens are more likely to be tolerant and committed to democratic principles and

Figure 10.2

The Effects of Education on Democratic Enlightenment and Engagement

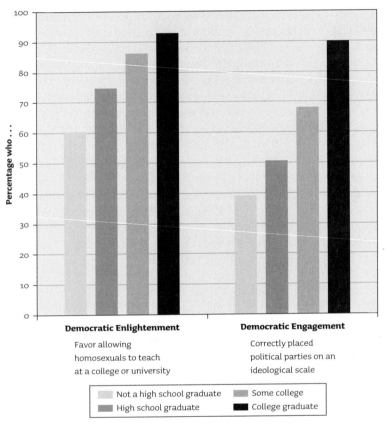

Democratic Enlightenment
Favor allowing
homosexuals to teach
at a college or university

Democratic Engagement
Correctly placed
political parties on an
ideological scale

Legend:
- Not a high school graduate
- High school graduate
- Some college
- College graduate

Source: Calculated by the authors with data from the General Social Survey, 2008, and the American National Election Study, 2008.

are more likely to vote, to be informed about politics, and to participate at all levels of the political system (see Figure 10.2).[28] In short, those who graduate from college have many more of the attributes of the idealized active democratic citizen than do those who do not graduate from high school.

Age

We might expect that people change their opinions as they age, but there is precious little evidence for the common view that masses of people progress from youthful idealism to mature conservatism. Indeed, extensive research shows that on most political issues, only small differences in policy preferences are related to age.[29] One exception is the finding of consistent age differences in political engagement. Middle-age and older citizens are typically more attentive to and more active in politics: they report more frequent efforts to persuade others, they vote more often, and they are more likely to write letters to public officials and to contribute to political campaigns. It seems that acting out one's political role may be part and parcel of the array of activities that we associate with "settling down," such as marrying, having children, and establishing a career. This exception was mitigated somewhat in 2008 with the unusual response of young people to Barack Obama's candidacy for president. The Obama candidacy brought record numbers of young people to the polls, and at the same time created one of the sharpest age-vote relationships we have seen, with younger voters supporting Obama in overwhelming numbers.[30]

Gender

For many years, one's gender had almost no predictive power in explaining opinions and behavior—except that women were less active in politics and usually less warlike in their political attitudes. As women gained more education and entered the work force, however, they also increased their levels of participation in politics; and as men and women approached equality in their levels of electoral participation, their attitudes on issues diverged. This tendency for men and women to take different issue positions or to evaluate political figures differently is called the **gender gap**. In almost all cases, it means that women are more liberal than men. The ideological stances of women overall have not changed significantly since the 1970s, but those of men have shifted steadily, as more call themselves conservatives (see Figure 10.3).[31] In general, the gender gap has been found to be especially large on issues that deal with violence.[32] The gender gap also has electoral consequences. Women are more likely than men to vote for Democratic candidates. In fact, in every presidential election from 1980 to 2008, women have been more supportive of the Democratic candidate than men. Clearly there is something of a gender divide in U.S. national elections.[33]

The differences between men and women might be explained by their different socialization experiences and by the different life situations they face. The impact of one's life situation has emerged recently in what observers are calling the **marriage gap**. This refers to the tendency for different opinions to be expressed by those who are married or widowed versus those who have never been married. "Marrieds" tend toward more traditional and conservative values; "never marrieds" tend to have a more liberal perspective. The "never marrieds" are now sufficiently numerous that in many localities they constitute an important group that politicians must heed in deciding which issues to support.

Race and Ethnicity

Race has been a perennial cleavage in American politics. Only in recent decades have blacks achieved the same political rights as the white majority, and yet disparity in

Figure 10.3

The Effect of Gender on Political Ideology

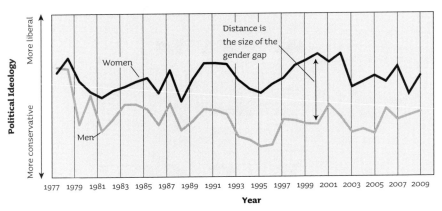

Source: Calculated by the authors from CBS News/*New York Times* national polls, 1976–2009.

income between whites and blacks continues. When we compare by race the answers to a question about spending to improve the condition of blacks, the responses are quite different. African Americans are more favorable to such spending than are whites. We see a similar pattern in whether respondents would support a community bill to bar discrimination in housing. African Americans tend to favor such a law; whites are more likely to side with the owner's right to sell a house to whomever he or she chooses. These differences, some of which are shown in Figure 10.4, are typical of a general pattern. On issues of economic policy and race, African Americans are substantially more liberal than whites. However, on social issues like abortion and prayer in schools, the racial differences are more muted.

The root of the differences between political attitudes of blacks and whites most certainly lies in the racial discrimination historically experienced by African Americans. Blacks tend to see much higher levels of discrimination and racial bias in the criminal justice system, in education, and in the job market. There is undeniably a very large gulf between the races in their perceptions about the continuing frequency and severity of racial discrimination.[34]

Finally, reflecting the very different stands on racial and economic issues the parties have taken, African Americans are the most solidly Democratic group in terms of both party identification and voting. Interestingly, as income and other status indicators rise for whites, they become more conservative and Republican. This does not happen among African Americans. Better-educated and higher-income blacks actually have stronger racial identifications, which results in distinctly liberal positions on economic and racial issues and solid support for Democratic candidates.[35] In recent years, however, the increasing numbers of black

Figure 10.4

Differences in Policy Views, by Race and Ethnicity

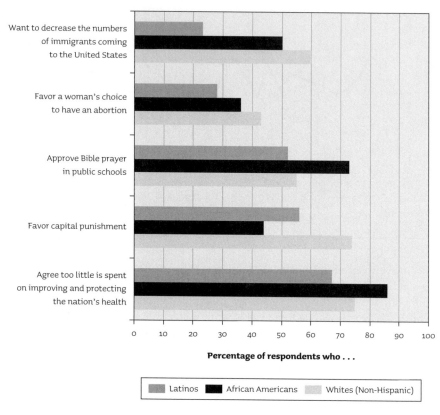

Percentage of respondents who . . .

Latinos   African Americans   Whites (Non-Hispanic)

Source: General Social Survey, 2008.

conservatives, exemplified by such high-profile figures as former secretary of state Condoleezza Rice, former chairman of the Joint Chiefs of Staff and secretary of state Colin Powell, Supreme Court Justice Clarence Thomas, former California Board of Regents member Ward Connerly, and Michael Steele, the head of the Republican National Committee, show that the assumptions once made about African Americans and the Democratic Party are not universally true. Nevertheless, the rise of Democrat Barack Obama to become the first black president of the United States has undoubtedly reinforced the bond between African Americans and the Democratic Party.

Blacks are not, of course, the only minority group in the country. When it comes to public opinion, many other groups, like Hispanics and Asian Americans, do not

A Matter of Morals

Many political issues touch on moral values, which may be rooted in differing religious convictions. While some people feel the government should have no role in setting moral standards, others, particularly conservatives, favor government policies that reflect traditional values.

turn out to be dramatically different from the majority-non-Hispanic whites on most issues. There is so much diversity of opinion within these broad groupings that it can be misleading to talk about a "Hispanic" or an "Asian" opinion.[36]

Religion

Many political issues touch on matters of deep moral conviction or values. In these cases the motivation for action or opinion formation is not self-interest but one's view of what is morally right. The question of morals and government, however, is tricky. Many people argue that it is not the government's business to set moral standards, although it is increasingly becoming the position of conservatives that government policy ought to reflect traditional moral values. In addition, government gets into the morals business by virtue of establishing policies on issues of moral controversy, like abortion, assisted suicide, and organ transplants. These questions are often referred to as social issues, as opposed to economic issues, which center more on how to divide the economic pie.

Our views of morality and social issues are often rooted in our differing religious convictions and the values with which we were raised. We often think of religion in terms of the three major faiths in America: Protestantism, Catholicism, and Judaism. Following the New Deal realignment, there were major political differences in the preferences of these groups, with non-southern Protestants being predominantly Republican, and Catholics and Jews being much more likely to be Democrats and to call themselves liberals. Over the years those differences have softened quite a bit, but today Catholics are less conservative than Protestants, and more Democratic, while Jews and the not religious are clearly more liberal and Democratic than the other groups.[37] Interestingly, Muslims are more liberal than Protestants and Catholics but are more conservative than Jews.[38]

Specific religious affiliations may no longer be the most important religious cleavage for understanding citizen opinions on social issues. Since the 1970s a new distinction has emerged in U.S. politics, between those in whose lives traditional religion plays a central role and those for whom it is less important. In this alignment, those who adhere to traditional religious beliefs and practices (frequent churchgoers, regular Bible readers, "born-again Christians") tend to take conservative positions on an array of social issues (like homosexuality and abortion), compared with more liberal positions taken on those issues by what may be called "seculars."[39]

Geographical Region

Where we live matters in terms of our political beliefs. People in the Farm Belt talk about different things than do city dwellers on the streets of Manhattan. Texans appreciate subtle assumptions that are not shared by Minnesotans. Politicians who come from these areas represent people with different preferences, and much of the politics in Congress is about being responsive to differing geography-based opinions.[40] Whether we live in the city, the suburbs, or the country also has an effect on our opinions. City dwellers are more Democratic in their political preferences and more liberal on issues like spending to help minorities and to improve education. On other issues, such as the environment, abortion, and a proposed constitutional amendment to ban same-sex marriages, rural residents stand out as distinctly conservative compared to other residential groups.[41]

Measuring and Tracking Public Opinion
Using science to discover what people are thinking about political issues

Long before the beginning of modern scientific polling, politicians gauged what their constituents wanted through talking and listening to them. They still learn constituent opinion from the letters, phone calls, and email messages they receive. They visit constituents, make speeches, attend meetings, and talk with community leaders and interest group representatives. Direct contact with people puts politicians in touch with concerns that could be missed entirely by a scientifically designed public opinion poll. That poll might focus on issues of national news that are on the minds of national politicians or pollsters, while citizens may be far more concerned about the building of a dam upriver from their city or about teacher layoffs in their school district.

Although public opinion polls are sometimes discounted by politicians who don't like their results, the truth is that most social scientists and political pollsters conduct public opinion surveys according to the highest standards of scientific accuracy, and their results are for the most part reliable. Informal soundings of public opinion may be useful to a politician for some purposes, but they are not very reliable for gauging how everyone in a given population thinks because they are subject to sampling problems. A sample is the portion of the population a politician or pollster surveys on an issue. Based on what that sample says, the surveyor then makes an estimation of what everyone else thinks. This may sound like hocus-pocus, but if the sample is scientifically chosen to be representative of the whole population, sampling actually works very well. Pollsters are trained in how to select a truly **random sample**—that is, one that does not overrepresent any portion of the population and whose responses can therefore be safely generalized to the whole. When a sample is not chosen scientifically and has too many people in it from one portion of the population, we say it has a problem of **sample bias**. When trying to judge public opinion from what they hear among their supporters and friendly interest groups, politicians must allow for the bias of their own sampling. If they are not effective at knowing how those they meet differ from the full public, they will get a misleading idea of public opinion.

The Quality of Opinion Polling Today

The quality of public opinion polling today is vastly improved compared to its early days in the 1930s. Today polling is big business and a relatively precise science. Political polls are actually a small portion of the marketing business, which tries to gauge what people want and are willing to buy. Many local governments also conduct surveys to find out what their citizens want and how satisfied they are with various municipal services. All polls face the same two challenges, however: getting a good sample and asking questions that yield valid results.

No sample is perfect in matching the population from which it is drawn, but it should be close. Confronted with a critic who did not trust the notion of sampling, George Gallup is said to have responded, "Okay, if you do not like the idea of a sample, then the next time you go for a blood test, tell them to take it all!" While it might seem counterintuitive, statisticians have determined that a sample of only 1,000 to 2,000 people can be very representative of the entire 300 million residents of the United States, if it is randomly drawn from that population.

Sampling error is a number that indicates how reliable the poll is; based on the size of the sample, it tells within what range the actual opinion of the whole population would fall. Typically a report of a poll will say that its "margin of error" is plus or minus 3 percent. That means that, based on sampling theory, there is a 95 percent chance that the real figure for the whole population is within 3 percent of that reported. For instance, when a poll reports a presidential approval rating of 60 percent and a 3 percent margin of error, this means that there is a 95 percent chance that between 57 and 63 percent of the population approve of the president's job performance. A poll that shows one candidate leading another by 2 percent of the projected vote is really too close to call since the 2 percent might be due to sampling error. The larger the sample, the smaller the sampling error, but samples larger than 2,000 add very little in the way of reliability.

Asking the right questions in surveys is a surprisingly tricky business. Researchers have emphasized several concerns with respect to constructing survey questions. For instance, respondents should be asked about things they know and have thought about. Otherwise, they will often try to be helpful but will give responses based on whatever cues they can pick up from the context of the interview or the particular question. Questions should not be ambiguous and should not use words that evoke strong emotional responses, like *affirmative action* or *welfare*. In addition, studies have shown that the order in which questions are asked can change the results, as can such a simple factor as the number of choices offered for responses.

Types of Polls

Many people and organizations report the results of what they claim are measures of public opinion. To make sense of this welter of claims, it is useful to know some basic polling terminology and the characteristics of different types of polls.

Conflicting Opinion
During the 1948 presidential race between Harry Truman and Thomas Dewey, the Gallup organization tried quota sampling, which attempted to predict the vote based on interviews with a certain number of people from different groups. Pollsters called the race for Dewey, but they had stopped polling a week before the election and missed out on last-minute voter decisions. Truman won, but only after some confusion.

National Polls
National polls are efforts to measure public opinion within a limited period of time using a national representative sample. The time period of interviewing may be as short as a few hours, with the results reported the next day, or extended over a period of weeks, as in academic polls. The underlying goal, however, is the same: to achieve scientifically valid measures of the knowledge, beliefs, or attitudes of the adult population. Many national polls are conducted by the media in conjunction with a professional polling organization.

Campaign Polls
Polling is an important part of candidates' efforts to win election or reelection. Most well-funded campaigns begin with a **benchmark poll** to gather baseline information

on how well the candidate is known, what issues people associate with the candidate, what issues people are concerned about, as well as assessments of the opposition, especially if the opponent is an incumbent. Benchmark polls are instrumental in designing campaign strategy.

Presidential contests and a few of the better-funded statewide races (for example, those for governor or U.S. senator) also conduct **tracking polls**. These follow changes in attitudes toward the candidates through ongoing sets of interviews. The daily samples are too small to allow reliable generalization, but when they are averaged over time, with the oldest interviews dropped as newer ones are added, they provide a dynamic view of changes in voters' preferences and perceptions. A sudden change in a tracking poll might signal that the opponent's new ads are doing damage or that interest group endorsements are having an effect. Campaign strategies can be revised accordingly. More recently the news media have undertaken tracking polls as part of their election coverage.

On election night the media commentators often "call" a race, declaring one candidate a winner, sometimes as soon as the voting booths in a state are closed but well before the official vote count has been reported. These predictions are made, in part, on the basis of **exit polls**, which are short questionnaires administered, often by a consortium of news outlets, to samples of people who have just voted in selected precincts. Exit polls focus on vote choice, a few demographic questions, some issue preferences, and evaluations of candidates. In addition to helping the networks predict the winners early, exit polls are used by network broadcasters and journalists to add explanatory and descriptive material to their election coverage.

Exit polls, however, have proved embarrassingly faulty in recent elections. In 2000, flawed data led the networks to mistakenly "call" Florida for Vice President Al Gore (which would have meant that he'd won the presidency), then to switch the call to George W. Bush, and finally, late in the evening, to conclude that the state was too close to call at all. Exit poll defenders argue that these polls are being misused by the public and the media; they are not intended to predict the elections in progress but to explain the vote after the election by providing information on what groups voted for which candidates. As a result of recent problems with these polls, networks are now relatively cautious in declaring winners without corroborating evidence from the actual vote returns. There were no mistakes in calling the states in the 2004 or 2008 presidential elections,[42] but in 2008 the pollsters took the precaution of embargoing their results until 5:00 P.M. on Election Day, in an effort to keep them out of the hands of people who didn't know how to interpret them.

Pseudo-Polls

A number of opinion studies are wrongly presented as polls. More deceptive than helpful, these pseudo-polls range from potentially misleading entertainment to outright fraud. Examples of self-selection polls include viewer or listener call-in polls and Internet polls. These polls tell you only the opinions of that portion of the media outlet's audience (self-selected in the first place by their choice of a particular outlet) who care enough to call in or click a mouse (self-selected in the second place by their willingness to expend effort).

A second and increasingly common kind of pseudo-poll is the push poll, which poses as a legitimate information-seeking effort but is really a shady campaign trick to change people's attitudes. **Push polls** present false or highly negative information, often in a hypothetical form, and ask respondents to react to it. The information, presented as if true or at least possible, can raise doubts about a candidate and even change a voter's opinion about him or her. Such polls are often conducted without any acknowledgment of who is sponsoring them (usually the opponents of the person being asked about) and at the last minute so that the candidate cannot rebut the charges being circulated. Legislation against push polling has been introduced in several state legislatures, and the practice has been condemned by the American Association of Political Consultants.[43] There is a real question, however, about whether efforts to regulate push polls can survive a First Amendment test before the Supreme Court.

New Technologies and Challenges in Polling

Technology is a pollster's friend, but it can also create unexpected challenges. In the early days of polls, surveys were done in-person, on the door stoop or in the living room. That method was superseded by telephone interviewing as almost all households got telephones and in light of the obvious efficiency of calling people on the phone versus sending interviewers to far-flung places for face-to-face interviews. With the advent of computer technology has come the substitution of computers for humans to do the interviewing. The computers dial the numbers (autodialing) and deliver recorded messages, even "interacting" by asking questions that are answered by pushing buttons on a touch-tone phone. This technology, called "robo calling," is much cheaper than using human interviewers, but it is also controversial. It is easily abused, especially when combined with push poll methods.[44] Legitimate polling firms also use robo calls and have collected more information on more political subjects than has been available in the past, such as the state-by-state results provided by SurveyUSA.[45]

Computers provide another challenge (and opportunity) for pollsters in the form of online surveys. Here we do not mean the polls that CNN or others put up asking for volunteers to punch in their opinions on some issue. Pollsters create panels of Internet users who regularly log in to deliver their opinions on matters the pollsters select. Although some critics argue that the online polls have no scientific basis, because they do not rely on strict probability samples, proponents argue that with appropriate adjustments, the Internet polls nicely match results from traditional telephone interviewing. They have the advantage of garnering fewer refusals, and for some kinds of questions, respondents to online surveys appear to be more candid in admitting to things that might be embarrassing to confess to a human interviewer.[46]

Pollsters also face a growing challenge as increasing numbers of citizens, especially younger people, rely on cell phones. The U.S. Telephone Consumer Protection

Act limits the technologies that can be used in contacting cell phone users, forbidding autodialing, for instance. Those contacted by cell phones are also more likely to refuse to answer polls. As pollsters adapt to these newer technologies, research and regulations are likely to lead to changes in contacting cell phone users.[47]

How Accurate Are Polls?

For many issues, such as attitudes toward the environment or presidential approval, we have no objective measure against which to judge the accuracy of public opinion polls. With elections, however, polls do make predictions, and we can tell by the vote count whether the polls are correct.

The record of most polls, in general, is quite good. For example, all the major polls have predicted the winner of presidential elections correctly since 1980, except in the incredibly close 2000 election. They are not correct to the percentage point, nor would we expect them to be, given the known levels of sampling error, preelection momentum shifts, and the usual 15 percent of voters who claim to remain "undecided" up to the last minute. Polls taken closer to Election Day typically become more accurate as they catch more of the late deciders.[48] Even in the 2000 presidential election, most of the polls by election eve had done a fairly good job of predicting the tightness of the race.

Citizenship and Public Opinion
Informational shortcuts that save democracy from our lack of care and attention

We have seen ample evidence that although politicians may act as if citizens are informed and attentive, only some Americans live up to our model of good citizenship, and those who do often belong disproportionately to the ranks of the well educated, the well-off, and the older portions of the population. This disparity between our ideal citizen and reality raises some provocative questions about the relationship between citizens, public opinion, and democracy. Were the founders right to limit the influence of the masses on government? Do we want less informed and coherent opinions represented in politics? Can democracy survive if it is run only by an educated elite?

Earlier in this chapter we suggested that all would not be lost for American democracy if only some of us turned out to be ideal citizens, and that it was possible to argue that although Americans as individuals might not fit the ideal, Americans as a group might behave as that ideal would predict. How is such a trick possible? The argument goes like this.

It may not be rational for all people to be deeply immersed in the minutiae of day-to-day politics. Our jobs, families, hobbies, and other interests leave us little time for in-depth study of political issues, and unless we get tremendous satisfaction from keeping up with politics (and some of us certainly do), it might be rational for us to leave the political information gathering to others. Social scientists call this idea **rational ignorance**.

This does not mean that we are condemned to make only ignorant or mistaken political decisions. Citizens are generally pretty smart. In fact, studies show that voters can behave much more intelligently than we could ever guess from their answers to surveys about politics. A great many of us use shortcuts to getting political information that serve us quite well, in the sense that they help us make the same decisions we might have made had we invested considerable time and energy in collecting that political information ourselves.[49]

Shortcuts to Political Knowledge

One shortcut is the **on-line processing** of information.[50] (*On-line* here does not refer to time spent on the Internet, as you will see.) Many of the evaluations we make of people, places, and things in our lives (including political figures and ideas) are made on the fly. We assemble impressions and reactions while we are busy leading our lives. When queried, we might not be able to explain why we like or dislike a thing or a person, and we might sound quite ignorant in the sense of not seeming to have reasons for our beliefs. But we do have reasons, and they may make a good deal of sense, even if we can't identify what they are.

A second important mental shortcut that most of us use is the **two-step flow of information**. Politicians and the media send out massive amounts of information. We can absorb only a fraction of it, and even then it is sometimes hard to know how to interpret it. In these circumstances, we tend to rely on **opinion leaders**, who are more or less like ourselves but who know more about the subject than we do.[51] Opinion leaders and followers can be identified in all sorts of realms besides politics. When we make an important purchase, say, a computer or a car, most of us do not research all the scientific data and technical specifications. We ask people who are like us, who we think should know, and whom we can trust. We compile their advice, consult our own intuition, and buy. The result is that we get pretty close to making an optimal purchase without having to become experts ourselves. The two-step flow allows us to behave as though we were very well informed without requiring us to expend all the resources that actually being informed entails.

The Rational Electorate

Politicians deal with citizens mostly in groups and only rarely as individuals. Elected officials think about constituents as whole electorates ("the people of the great state of Texas") or as members of groups (women, environmentalists, developers, workers, and so forth). Groups, it turns out, appear to be better behaved, more rational, and better informed than the individuals who make up the groups, precisely because of the sorts of shortcuts we discussed in the previous section. This doesn't seem to make sense, so perhaps a nonpolitical example will clarify what we mean.

Consider the behavior of fans at a football game. People seem to cheer at the appropriate times; they know pretty much when to boo the referees; they *oooh* and *aaaah* more or less in unison. We would say that the crowd understands the game and participates effectively in it. However, what do the individual spectators know? If we were to do a football survey, we might ask about the players' names, the teams' win-loss records, the different offensive and defensive positions, the meaning of the referees' signals, and so forth. Some fans would do well, but many would probably get only a few questions right. From the survey, we might conclude that many people in this crowd do not know football at all. But because they take their cues from others, following the behavior of those who cheer for the same team, they can act as if they know what they are doing. Despite its share of football-ignorant individuals, in the aggregate—that is, as a group—the crowd acts remarkably football-intelligent.

Similarly, if we were to ask people when national elections are held, for instance, only a handful would be able to say it is the Tuesday after the first Monday in November of evenly numbered years. Some people would guess that they occur in November, others might say in the fall sometime, and others would admit they didn't know. Based on the level of individual ignorance in this matter, it would be surprising if many people ever voted at all, since you can't vote if you don't know when Election Day is. But somehow, as a group, the electorate sorts it out, and almost everyone who is registered and wants to vote finds his or her way to the polling place on the right day. By using shortcuts and taking cues from others, the electorate behaves just as if it knew all along when the election was. More substantively, even though many voters may be confused about which candidates stand where on specific issues, groups of voters do a great job of sorting out which party or candidate best represents their interests. Members of the religious right vote for Republicans, and members of labor unions vote for Democrats, for instance. Even though there are undoubtedly quite a few confused voters in the electorate in any particular election, they tend to cancel each other out in the larger scheme of things, although understandably, some biases remain.[52] As a whole, from the politician's point of view, the electorate appears to be responsive to issues and quite rational in evaluating an incumbent's performance in office.[53]

So even though citizens do not spend a lot of time learning about politics, politicians are smart to assume that the electorate is attentive and informed. In fact, this is precisely what most of them do. For example, studies have shown that state legislators vote in accordance with the ideological preferences of their citizens, just as if the citizens were instructing them on their wishes.[54] The states with the most liberal citizens—for example, New York, Massachusetts, and California—have the most liberal policies. And the most conservative states, those in the South and the Rocky Mountains, have the most conservative policies. Other studies confirm a similar pattern in national elections.[55]

We began this chapter by asking why polling is routinely disparaged by politicians. Why don't we have more confidence in being ruled by public opinion? After all, in a democracy where the people's will is supposed to weigh heavily with our elected officials, we have uncovered some conflicting evidence. Many Americans do not model the characteristics of the ideal democratic citizen, but remember that the United States has two traditions of citizenship—one much more apolitical and self-interested than the public-spirited ideal. The reality in America is that the ideal citizen marches side by side with the more self-interested citizen, who, faced with many demands, does not put politics ahead of other daily responsibilities. But we have also argued that there are mechanisms and shortcuts that allow even some of the more apolitical and self-interested citizens to cast intelligent votes and to have their views represented in public policy. This tells us that at least one element of democracy—responsiveness of policies to public preferences—is in good working order.

We should not forget that political influence goes hand in hand with opinion formation. Those who are opinion leaders have much more relative clout than do their more passive followers. And opinion leaders are not distributed equally throughout the population. They are drawn predominantly from the ranks of the well educated and the well-off. Similarly, even though the shortcuts we have discussed allow many people to vote intelligently without taking the time to make a personally informed decision, many people never vote at all. Voters are also drawn from the more privileged ranks of American society. The poor, the young, and minorities—all the groups who are underrepresented at the voting booth—are also underrepresented in policymaking. There cannot help but be biases in such a system.[56]

▶ What's at Stake Revisited

We have argued in this chapter that public opinion is important in policymaking and that politicians respond to it in a variety of ways. But what would happen if we more or less bypassed elected officials altogether and allowed people to participate directly in national lawmaking through the use of a national referendum or initiative? What is at stake in rule by public opinion?

On the one hand, voters would seem to have something real to gain in such lawmaking reform. It would give new meaning to government "by the people," and decisions would have more legitimacy with the public. Certainly it would be harder to point the finger at those in Washington as being responsible for bad laws. In addition, as has been the experience in states with initiatives, citizens might succeed in getting legislation passed that legislators themselves refuse to vote for. Prime examples are term limits and balanced budget amendments. Term limits would cut short many congressional careers, and balanced budget amendments force politicians into hard choices about taxation and spending cuts that they prefer to avoid.

On the other side of the calculation, however, voters might be worse off. While policies like the two mentioned above clearly threaten the jobs of politicians, they also carry unintended consequences that might not be very good for the nation as a whole. Who should decide—politicians who make a career out of understanding government, or people who pay little attention to politics and current events and who vote from instinct and outrage? Politicians who have a vested interest in keeping their jobs, or the public who can provide a check on political greed and self-interest? The answer changes with the way you phrase the question, but the public might well suffer if left to its own mercy on questions of policy it does not thoroughly understand.

There is no doubt that the founders of the Constitution, with their limited faith in the people, would have rejected such a referendum wholeheartedly. Not only does it bring government closer to the people, but it wreaks havoc with their system of separation of powers and checks and balances. Popular opinion was supposed to be checked by the House and the Senate, which were in turn to be checked by the other two branches of government. Bringing public opinion to the fore upsets this delicate balance.

In addition, many scholars warn that the hallmark of democracy is not just hearing what the people want, but allowing the people to discuss and deliberate over their political choices. Home computer voting or trips to the ballot box do not necessarily permit such key interaction.[57] Majority rule without the tempering influence of debate and discussion can quickly deteriorate into majority tyranny, with a sacrifice of minority rights.

The flip side may also be true, however. Since voters tend to be those who care more intensely about political issues, supporters of a national referendum also leave themselves open to the opposite consequence of majority tyranny: the tyranny of an intense minority who care enough to campaign and vote against an issue that a majority prefer but only tepidly.

Finally, there are political stakes for politicians in such a reform. As we have already seen, the passage of laws they would not have themselves supported would make it harder for politicians to get things done. But on the positive side, a national referendum would allow politicians to avoid taking the heat for decisions that are bound to be intensely unpopular with some segment of the population. One of the reasons that national referenda are often used in other countries is to diffuse the political consequences for leaders of unpopular or controversial decisions.

Direct democracy at the national level would certainly have a major impact on American politics, but it is not entirely clear who the winners and losers would be, or even if there would be any consistent winners. The new rules would benefit different groups at different times. The American people believe they would enjoy the power, and various groups are confident they would profit, but in the long run the public interest might be damaged in terms of the quality of American democracy and the protections available to minorities. Politicians have very little to gain. If such a reform ever does come about, it will be generated not by the elite but by public interest groups, special interest groups, and reformers from outside Washington.

▶ Summary With Key Terms

The American public and politicians alike are divided about how much **public opinion** (328) should matter in democratic politics. Politicians and the media both watch public opinion, as measured in **public opinion polls** (329) very closely. Elected officials look for job security by responding to immediate public desires or by skillfully predicting future requests. The media make large investments in polls, sometimes covering public attitudes on a candidate or issue as a story in itself.

There are two competing visions of citizenship in America. The ideal democratic citizen demonstrates political knowledge, tolerates different ideas, and votes consistently. At the other extreme lies the apolitical, self-interested citizen. Most Americans fall somewhere between these extremes, but factors such as age, higher education, and improved socioeconomic status seem to contribute to behavior that is closer to the ideal.

Political socialization (336)—the transfer of fundamental democratic values from one generation to the next—is affected by demographic characteristics such as race and gender, as evidenced, for example, by the **gender gap** (340) and the **marriage gap** (340), and by life experiences such as education and religion.

Modern polling science surveys a **random sample** (345) of the population, controlling for **sample bias** (345) and keeping **sampling error** (345) as small as possible. **Benchmark polls** (346), **tracking polls** (347), and **exit polls** (347) are used in running and covering campaigns to varying degrees. Pseudo-polls like call-in polls, most Internet polls, or **push polls** (347) are used to manipulate rather than measure public opinion.

Many Americans do not measure up to the ideal of the democratic citizen, and there are grounds to argue that it may be rational for them not to do so. Despite this **rational ignorance** (350), however, much evidence supports the idea that public opinion does play a large role in government policy. While some citizens may seem apolitical and disinterested, many use rational information shortcuts like **on-line processing** (350) and the **two-step flow of information** (350), through which they get cues from **opinion leaders** (350) to make their voting decisions. Policymakers have responded by staying generally responsive to public preferences.

Explore this subject further with suggested readings, movies, and web sites at http://republic-brief.cqpress.com, where you'll also find study aids, practice quizzes, flash cards, and Internet exercises.

Chapter 11

Parties and Interest Groups

▶ What's at Stake?

Harry and Louise killed health care reform in 1994, and in 2009 President Barack Obama's chief of staff at the time, Rahm Emanuel, was determined that they wouldn't do it again.

Emanuel had been working in the Clinton White House when the insurance industry set out to stop health care reform in 1994, spending millions on TV advertising, including the infamous "Harry and Louise" commercials that featured a worried couple sitting at their kitchen table, discussing their fears over government-run health care plans. An apprehensive public was easily persuaded to share Harry and Louise's concerns, and the health care industry scored a major victory. Health care reform was dead for at least the next sixteen years.

Emanuel had watched the Clintons in 1994, and he thought he knew where they had gone wrong. President Bill Clinton had assigned his wife Hillary the task of coming up with a comprehensive health care plan. Hillary Clinton consulted experts and worked for a year before delivering a hefty plan to her husband, who in turn gave it to Congress with instructions to pass the bill. Congress, however, doesn't take that kind of instruction well. Allegedly the late senator Daniel Moynihan (whose New York seat Hillary Clinton would later win) took one look and said, "I'm not even going to read it."[1]

Members of Congress weren't the only powerful opponents of the Clinton bill. The insurance, medical, and pharmaceutical industries were all opposed and immediately spent millions on an advertising campaign to defeat it, as well as on intensive lobbying efforts to convince an already skeptical Congress to ignore the bill. It never even came up for a vote.

As far as Rahm Emanuel was concerned, the lessons learned were, first, get Congress involved from the start and, second, do something to bring the relevant interest groups to the table.

The Obama team took these lessons to heart. From the beginning, Congress invested heavily in the reform bill's design. And in March 2009, the White House invited members of all the affected industries to meet with President Obama and members of Congress. Out of the public eye the president's negotiators met with representatives of the health care industry and deals were made. For example, America's Health Insurance Plans (AHIP), an industry interest group that represents the insurance companies, agreed to sign on to a plan of universal insurance coverage for all Americans, regardless of preexisting health conditions, in exchange for the White House's agreement that any plan they endorsed would require every American who could afford it to buy insurance and would not include a public competitor to the private health insurance plans. Similarly, the representatives of the pharmaceutical industry agreed to cut drug prices by $80 billion if the administration agreed that it would not push for further cuts. Though this situation would change before the health care reform bill became law, the Obama administration had, at least initially, co-opted two of the loudest and richest voices that had brought down the Clinton health care plan.

But at what cost? Republicans had already determined that their strategy would be to deny Obama any legislative victories they could, so they were all opposed to health care reform for political, if not policy, reasons. In addition, by making deals with the health care industry, Obama, who had promised a change in the way Washington did business, alienated many in his own party. Some of the strongest criticism of his plan came from disillusioned liberals who were resentful that the bill would require them to buy insurance from private companies, and who believed that Obama had sold out the so-called "public option" and the opportunity to accrue cost savings by reducing drug costs further. The clamor of criticism nearly drowned out the victory celebration when the president finally signed the law on March 23, 2010.

Was it worth it? Was Emanuel's calculation correct that the bill would not pass at all if special interest groups torpedoed it? Was the political cost of seeming to be "consorting with the enemy" too great to bear? Just what was at stake in the Obama administration's decision to bring health groups into the reform process at an early stage?

The old adage says there is safety in numbers, but more important in politics, there is also power in numbers. In *Federalist* No. 10, James Madison wasn't worried about the odd voter getting antsy and voting for a harebrained candidate or idea. He was concerned that large numbers of voters would come to define themselves as opposed to what he thought was good for the public. He was worried about the political power of *groups* who would use the rules of politics to get what they wanted at the expense of everyone else.

And small wonder. Madison saw what happened under the Articles of Confederation, when individuals banded together to make claims on their government. Since then, we have seen innumerable examples of group power, everything from Republican attempts to restore the South after the Civil War, to the women's suffrage movement, to the NRA's efforts to limit gun control, to liberal and conservative groups' attempts to influence who sits on the Supreme Court. For many Americans, this group action is the meaning of modern democracy. In fact, we saw in earlier chapters that while some people argue that the individual voter in America cannot make a difference, many others believe in **pluralist democracy**, the idea that individuals can find their political strength only in numbers, by joining with other like-minded people to get the representation they want.

In this chapter we examine two central kinds of political groups that Americans form: parties and interest groups. Both types of groups form on the basis of common political ideas and goals, and use the system to realize those goals. The key difference is in what is at stake for the groups: political parties seek to elect their members to office in order to control government, and interest groups seek only to influence what government does. Specifically, you will learn about the role of political parties in a democracy, the American party system, the various roles interest groups play and the types of interest groups in the U.S. political system, how interest groups attempt to exert their political influence, and the resources that different interest groups bring to bear in influencing government decisions.

What Are Political Parties?
Organizations seeking to influence policy by controlling the apparatus of government

Probably because Madison hoped that political parties would not thrive, parties—unlike Congress, the presidency, the Supreme Court, and even the free press—are not mentioned in the Constitution. As we will see, in fact, many of the rules that determine the establishment and role of parties have been created by party members themselves. Although the founding documents of American politics are silent on the place of political parties, keen political observers have long appreciated the fundamental role that parties play in our system of government.[2] According to one scholar, "Political parties created democracy, and ... democracy is unthinkable save in terms of parties."[3]

The Role of Political Parties in a Democracy

Remembering that politics is about who gets what and how they get it helps us understand what parties are about. **Political parties** are organizations that seek, under a common banner, to promote their ideas and policies by gaining control of government through the nomination and election of candidates for office. In addition, parties provide support for democratic government in three crucial ways.

1. They provide a linkage between voters and elected officials, helping to tell voters what candidates stand for and providing a way for voters to hold their officials accountable for what they do in office, both individually and collectively.

2. They overcome some of the fragmentation in government that comes from separation of powers and federalism by linking members in all branches and levels of government.

3. They provide an articulate opposition to the ideas and policies of those elected to serve in government. Some citizens and critics may decry the **partisanship**, or taking of political sides, that sometimes seems to be motivated by the possibilities for party gain as much as by principle or public interest. Others, however, see partisanship as providing the necessary antagonistic relationship that keeps politicians honest and allows the best political ideas and policies to emerge.

To highlight the multiple tasks that parties perform to make democracy work and to make life easier for politicians, political scientists find it useful to divide political parties into three separate components: the party organization, the party-in-government, and the party-in-the-electorate.[4]

Party Organization

The **party organization** is what most people think of as a political party. It represents the system of central committees at the national, state, and local levels. At the top of the Democratic Party organization is the Democratic National Committee. Likewise, the Republican National Committee heads the Republican Party. Underneath these national committees are state-level party committees, and below them are county-level party committees, or county equivalents. The party organization performs the central party function of electioneering. **Electioneering** involves recruiting and nominating candidates, defining policy agendas, and getting candidates elected.

Each party's electioneering activities begin months before the general election. The first step is simply finding candidates to run. Fulfilling this responsibility is often difficult because, in many instances, the organizations must recruit candidates to run against a current officeholder—the incumbent—and incumbents are hard to beat.

The nomination phase is a formal process through which the party chooses a candidate for each elective office to be contested that year. Today, party primaries, or preliminary elections between members of the same party vying for the party's nomination, are the dominant means of choosing candidates for congressional, statewide, state legislative, and local offices. Some candidates are nominated at a convention. A **nominating convention** is a formal party gathering that is bound by a number of strict rules relating to the selection of voting participants—called *delegates*—and the nomination of candidates. The most prominent conventions are the national presidential nominating conventions for the Democratic and Republican Parties,[5] which are held the summer before the election, after the state presidential primaries. Usually the presidential nominating convention merely rubber-stamps the primary victor.

After a political party nominates its candidates, one of the party's main roles is to develop a policy agenda, which represents policies that the party's candidates agree to promote when campaigning and to pursue when governing. The development of such an agenda involves much politicking and gamesmanship as each faction of the party tries to get its views written into the party platform. Whoever wins control of the party platform has decisive input into how the campaign will proceed.

In the election phase, the role of the party changes from choosing among competing candidates within the party and developing policy agendas to getting its nominated candidates elected. Traditionally the party's role here was to "organize and mobilize" voters, but increasingly parties also provide extensive services to candidates, including fundraising, training in campaign tactics, instruction in compliance with election laws, public opinion polling, and professional campaign assistance.[6]

Party-in-Government

The **party-in-government** includes all the candidates for national, state, and local office who are elected. A key function of political parties is **governing**, or controlling government by organizing and providing leadership for the legislative and executive branches, enacting policy agendas, mobilizing support for party policy, and building coalitions.

When a party "controls" government at the national level and in the states, it means that the party determines who occupies the leadership positions in the branch of government in which it has a majority. Thus when Barack Obama won the presidency in 2008, Obama, and by extension the Democrats, controlled the top leadership positions in the executive branch of government (cabinet secretaries and undersecretaries and the White House staff). Since the Democrats enhanced the majority of the U.S. House and Senate contests they had won in 2006, their continued majority status won them the right to organize their respective houses of Congress by occupying the major leadership roles. In the Senate and the House, this meant selecting the majority leader in the Senate and the Speaker of the House, controlling committee assignments, selecting chairs of legislative committees, and having a majority of seats on each committee. When Republicans won back control of the House in 2010, they in turn selected the leaders—the Speaker, the House majority leader, and the majority whip—and took over the committee chairs. Since they didn't quite achieve a majority in the Senate, those leadership positions remained in Democratic hands.

Of course, the ultimate goal of a political party is not only to choose who occupies the leadership positions in government but also to execute its policy agenda—the party's solutions to the nation's problems. Whether the problems concern affordable health care, welfare abuse, taxes, distressed communities, low-skill jobs moving to developing countries, illegal immigrants, or the economy, each party represents an alternative vision for how to approach and solve these problems. About two-thirds of the promises of the party that controls the presidency are implemented, compared to about half of the promises of the party that does not control the presidency.[7]

Party-in-the-Electorate

The **party-in-the-electorate** represents ordinary citizens who identify with or have some feeling of attachment to one of the political parties. Public opinion surveys determine **party identification**, or party ID, by asking respondents whether they think of themselves as Democrats, Republicans, or independents. Over time, voter attachment to the two parties has declined; the percentages identifying as independents increased in the 1960s and 1970s so that today more people consider themselves independents than identify with either major party. The Democratic Party, which had a large numerical advantage among identifiers in the 1950s, is now about even with the Republicans (see Figure 11.1). Most voters who identify with one of the political parties "inherit" their party IDs from their parents, as we suggested in our discussion of political socialization in Chapter 10.[8] Party identifiers generally support the party's basic ideology and policy principles. These principles usually relate to the party's stance on the use of government to solve various economic and social problems.

Although voters do not have a strong formal role to play in the party organization, parties use identifiers as a necessary base of support during elections. In virtually every presidential election, both of the major-party candidates win the votes of an overwhelming percentage of those who identify with their respective parties. But just capturing one's **party base** is not sufficient to win a national election since neither party has a majority of the national voters. As we will see later in this chapter, candidates are often pulled between the ideological preferences of their base and the more moderate preferences of independents. Usually they try to capture those moderates during the general election campaign, but in 2004 George W. Bush took the opposite tack, focusing on appeals to his conservative activist base. Although John Kerry won more of the independent vote, the much higher turnout rate and very small number of defections among Republicans were enough to return Bush to the White House. In 2008 Republican John McCain, worried that his own independent "maverick" status would not stir enthusiasm among his base, picked social conservative Alaskan governor Sarah Palin as his running mate. Although she did get the base more excited, overall Republican turnout was still

Figure 11.1

Party Identification, 1952–2008

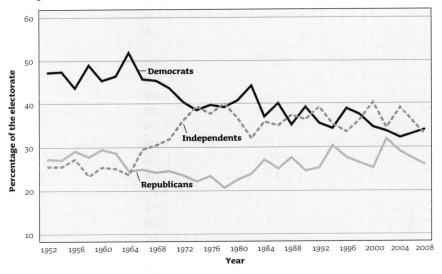

Source: American National Election Studies, University of Michigan; data made available by Inter-University Consortium for Political and Social Research.

down from 2004, and Barack Obama, with outsized turnout among young people and African Americans and an energized Democratic base, easily won the independent vote and the election.

The Responsible Party Model

Earlier we said that one of the democratic roles of parties is to provide a link between voters and elected officials, or, to use the terms we just introduced, between the party-in-the-electorate and the party-in-government. There are many ways in which parties can link voters and officials, but for the link to truly enhance democracy—that is, the control of leaders by citizens—certain conditions have to be met. Political scientists call the fulfillment of these conditions the **responsible party model**.[9]

Under the responsible party model, each party should present a coherent set of programs to the voters, consistent with its ideology and clearly different from the other party's programs, which the candidates for each party pledge to support and implement if elected. Voters should make their choices based on which party's programs most closely reflect their own ideas and hold the parties responsible for unkept promises by voting their members out of office. Each party, then, should exercise control over its elected officials to ensure that party officials are promoting and voting for its programs, thereby providing accountability to voters.

The responsible party model proposes that democracy is strengthened when voters are given clear alternatives and hold the parties responsible for keeping their promises. Voters can, of course, hold officials accountable without the assistance of parties, but it takes a good deal more of their time and attention. Furthermore, several political scientists have noted that although individuals can be held accountable for their own actions, many, if not most, government actions are the products of many officials. Political parties give us a way of holding officials accountable for what they do collectively as well as individually.[10]

The responsible party model reflects an ideal party system—one that the American two-party system rarely measures up to in reality (although other countries, notably Great Britain, do come close to the model). For example, even though voters theoretically make decisions based on each party's programs, as we will see in Chapter 12, a host of other factors, such as candidate image or evaluations of economic conditions, also influence voting behavior.[11] In addition, parties themselves do not always behave as the model dictates. For instance, American parties cannot always control candidates who refuse to support their programs. Still, the American system has evolved so that the party system today has many more of the characteristics of the responsible party model than it did a half-century ago. And although it doesn't fit the American case perfectly, the responsible party model is valuable because it underscores the importance of voters holding the parties accountable for governing and it provides a useful yardstick for understanding the character of the U.S. two-party system.

The American Party System
From party machines to effective political organizations

For James Madison, parties were just an organized version of that potentially dangerous political association, the faction. He had hopes that their influence on American politics would be minimal, but scarcely was the ink dry on the Constitution before the founders were organizing themselves into groups to promote their political views.

The History of Parties in America

In the 1790s a host of disagreements among politicians led Alexander Hamilton and John Adams to organize the Federalists, a group of legislators who supported their views. Later, Thomas Jefferson and James Madison would do the same with the Democratic-Republicans. Over the course of the next decade, these organizations expanded beyond their legislative purposes to include recruiting candidates to

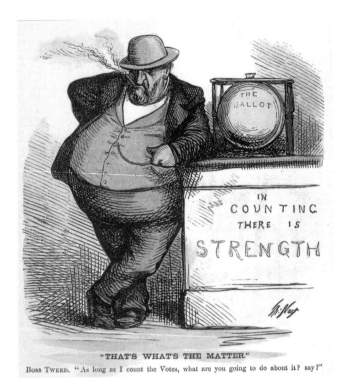

"THAT'S WHAT'S THE MATTER."

Boss Tweed. "As long as I count the Votes, what are you going to do about it? say?"

Set to Win
Party bosses like New York City's Boss Tweed controlled the political process and ruled the ballot box.

run under their party label for both Congress and the presidency. The primary focus, however, was on the party-in-government and not on the voters.[12]

In 1828 Martin Van Buren and Andrew Jackson turned the Democratic Party away from a focus on the party-in-government, creating the country's first mass-based party and setting the stage for the development of the voter-oriented party machine. **Party machines** were tightly organized party systems at the state, city, and county levels that kept control of voters by getting them jobs, helping them out financially when necessary, and in fact becoming part of their lives and their communities. This mass organization was built around one principal goal: taking advantage of the expansion of voting rights to all white men (even those without property) to elect more Democratic candidates.[13]

The Jacksonian Democrats enacted a number of party and government reforms designed to enhance the control of party leaders, known as **party bosses**, over candidates, officeholders, and campaigns. During the nomination process, the party bosses would choose the party's candidates for the general election. Winning candidates were expected to hire only other party supporters for government positions and reward only party supporters with government contracts, expanding the range of people with a stake in the party's electoral success. This system of **patronage,** which we discussed in Chapter 8, rewarded faithful party supporters with public offices, jobs, and government contracts and ensured that the party's candidates were loyal to the party or at least to the party bosses.

Because the Democratic Party machine was so effective at getting votes and controlling government, the Whig Party (1830s through 1850s), and later the Republican Party (starting in the mid-1850s), used these same techniques to organize. Party bosses and their party machines were exceptionally strong in urban areas in the East and Midwest. These urban machines, designed to further the interests of the parties themselves, had the important democratic consequence of integrating into the political process the masses of new immigrants coming into the urban centers at the turn of the twentieth century. Because parties were so effective at mobilizing voters, the average voter participation rate exceeded 80 percent in most U.S. elections prior to the 1900s.

The strength of these party machines was also their weakness. In many cases, parties would do almost anything to win, including buying votes, mobilizing new immigrants who could not speak English and were not U.S. citizens, and resurrecting dead people to vote. In addition, the whole system of patronage, based on doling out government jobs, contracts, and favors, came under attack by reformers in the early 1900s as representing favoritism and corruption. Political reforms such as **party primaries**, in which the party-in-the-electorate rather than the party bosses chose between competing party candidates for a party's nomination, and civil service reform, under which government jobs were filled on the basis of merit instead of party loyalty, did much to ensure that party machines went the way of the dinosaur.

Realignment

A striking feature of American history is that although we have not had a revolution since 1776, we have changed our political course several times and in rather dramatic ways. One of the many advantages of a democratic form of government is that dramatic changes in policy direction can be effected through the ballot box rather than through bloody revolution. Over the course of two centuries, the two-party system in the United States has been marked by twenty-five- to forty-year periods of relative stability, with one party tending to maintain a majority of congressional seats and controlling the presidency. These periods of stability are called **party eras**. Short periods of large-scale change—peaceful revolutions, as it were, signaled by one major critical election in which the majority of people shift their political allegiance from one party to another—mark the end of one party era and the beginning of another. Scholars call such shifts in party dominance a **realignment**. In these realignments, the coalitions of groups supporting the parties change. Although it is not always the case, realignments generally result in parallel changes in government policies, reflecting the policy agenda of each party's new coalition. Realignments have been precipitated by critical events like the Civil War and the Great Depression. The United States has gone through five party eras in its history.

For much of the twentieth century, the United States was in the midst of the fifth party era, a period ushered in by Franklin Roosevelt's New Deal and marked by the congressional domination of the Democratic Party. Most analysts agree that the New Deal coalition supporting the fifth party era has changed, but there is much controversy over the timing and character of that change and, in fact, about whether we have entered a new party era at all.[14] Although there have been many incremental changes, there has been no defining critical election. The dramatic but slow nature of this change can be seen in how the geographical centers of the two parties have moved since the New Deal. We used to be able to talk about the "solid Democratic South," because the southern states, though conservative on many issues, voted Democratic so as not to support the "party of Lincoln." But today the southern states are reliably Republican in presidential elections, and the Democrats' geographical strength lies in the industrial Northeast and Midwest and on the Pacific Coast.

Although these realigning changes have undoubtedly taken place, because no solid new majority has emerged, some analysts believe that we are really in a period of **dealignment**, a dissolving of the old era of party dominance, in which voters are more likely to call themselves independents and no party is clearly dominant.[15] What no one knows is whether this period of highly competitive parties is one of transition to a new party era or whether we are already in the sixth party era.

Current American party politics is thus characterized by major changes that have mobilized African Americans and other minorities into the Democratic Party and southern whites into the Republican Party, and a system in which neither party has a clear, enduring majority. This has led to a much higher incidence of divided government at the national and state levels, with the executive and legislative branches in the hands of different parties. One of the hallmarks of divided government is gridlock, or policy paralysis, as each party moves to prevent the other from enacting its policy goals. Gridlock makes it much harder to achieve the responsible party model. If neither party can accomplish its agenda because it is blocked by the other party, we do not know which one to hold accountable for the lack of government action.

What Do the American Parties Stand For?

A key feature of the responsible party model is that the parties should offer voters a choice between different visions of how government should operate. Barry Goldwater, the 1964 Republican presidential nominee, stated this more bluntly: political parties, he said, should offer "a choice, not an echo." Offering voters a choice is the primary means through which parties make representative democracy work. In many countries, particularly those with more than two parties, the choices offered by parties can range from radical communist to ultraconservative. In America, however, the ideological range of the two major parties, the Democrats and the Republicans (often also called the GOP, for "Grand Old Party"), is much narrower. In fact, among many American voters, there is a perception that the two parties do not offer real choices.

Although it may seem to voters that members of the two parties are not very different once they are elected to office, they are really quite distinct in their ideologies, their memberships, and the policies for which they stand. At least since the New Deal of the 1930s, the Democratic Party, especially outside the South, has been aligned with a liberal ideology. As we saw in Chapter 1, liberals encourage government action to solve economic and social problems but want government to stay out of their personal, religious, and moral lives, except as a protector of their basic rights. The Republican Party, on the other hand, has been associated with a conservative perspective, looking to government to provide social and moral order but demanding that the economy remain as unfettered as possible in the distribution of material resources. This is not to say that all Democrats are equally liberal or that all Republicans are equally conservative. Each party has its more extreme members and its more moderate members. Democrats and Republicans who hold their ideologies only moderately might be quite similar in terms of what they believe and stand for.

Since the 1960s the parties have become more consistent internally with respect to their ideologies. The most conservative region in the country is the South, but because of lingering resentment of the Republican Party for its role in the Civil War, the South was for decades tightly tied to the Democratic Party. In the 1960s, however, conservative southern Democratic voters began to vote for the Republican Party, and formerly Democratic politicians were switching their allegiances as well. By the 1990s the South had become predominantly Republican. This swing made the Democratic Party more consistently liberal and the Republicans more consistently conservative, and gave the party activist bases more power within each party, because they did not have to do battle with people of different ideological persuasions.

Party ideologies attract and are reinforced by different coalitions of voters. This means that the Democrats' post–New Deal liberal ideology reflects the preferences of its coalition of working- and lower-class voters, including union members, minorities, women, the elderly, and urban dwellers. The Republicans' conservative ideology reflects the preferences of upper- and middle-class whites, those who belong to evangelical and Protestant religions, and suburban voters. There is nothing inevitable about these coalitions, and they are subject to change as the parties' stances on issues change and as the opposing party offers new alternatives. Partisan differences between men and women used to be insignificant, but the gender gap we discussed in Chapter 10 has varied in recent years.

When the parties run slates of candidates for office, those candidates run on a **party platform**—a list of policy positions the party endorses and pledges its elected officials to enact. A platform is the national party's campaign promises, usually made only in a presidential election year. If the parties are to make a difference politically, their platforms have to reflect substantial differences that are consistent with their ideologies. The responsible party model requires that the parties offer distinct platforms, that voters know about them and vote on the basis of them, and that the parties ensure that their elected officials follow through in implementing them. A guide for interpreting and understanding party platforms is provided in "*Consider the Source:* Don't Be Fooled by Political Party Platforms."

Don't Be Fooled by Political Party Platforms

Think of it as an invitation to a party—so to speak. In their platforms, political parties make a broad statement about who they are and what they stand for in the hope that you will decide to join them. The excerpts below from the Democratic and Republican platforms of 2008 show differing positions on several key issues. The full text of these platforms can be found on the web sites of the parties' national committees. When you read a party's platform, keep these questions in mind:

1. Whose platform is it, and what do you know about that party's basic political positions? Understanding the basics will help you to interpret key phrases. For instance, how might the terms "family values" and "religious freedom" be defined differently in the Democratic and Republican platforms?

2. Who is the audience? Parties direct their platforms to two different groups—the party faithful and potential new supporters. For example, Democrats want to keep their traditional supporters, like union members, but they also want to broaden their appeal to the middle class and to small business owners. Republicans want to keep their base (including pro-life activists) happy but also want to attract more women in an effort to close the gender gap. How does this dual audience affect how parties portray themselves?

3. Which statements reflect values, and which are statements of fact? First, get clear about the values you are being asked to support. Parties tend to sprinkle their platforms liberally with phrases like "fundamental rights." Everybody is in favor of fundamental rights. Which ones do they actually mean, and do you consider them fundamental rights? What are the costs and benefits of agreeing to their value claims? Then evaluate the facts. Are they accurate? Check out statistics. Do they seem reasonable? If not, look them up.

4. Do you think the party can deliver on its policy proposals? What resources (money, power, and so on) would it need? Can it get them? Would enacting the promised policies achieve what the party claims it would? Who would win, and who would lose?

5. What is your reaction to the platform? Could you support it? How does it fit with your personal values and political beliefs? Is the appeal of this platform emotional? Intellectual? Ideological? Moral? Remember that party platforms are not just statements of party principles and policy proposals; they are also advertisements. Read them with all the caution and suspicion you would bring to bear on any other ad that attempts to convince you to buy, or buy into, something. Caveat emptor! (Let the buyer beware!)

Forces Drawing the Parties Apart and Pushing Them Together

Political parties in our system have a dilemma—how to keep the core ideological base satisfied while appealing to enough more moderate voters that they can win elections in diverse constituencies. In a small, homogenous district this is not likely to be a problem. Conservative Republicans and liberal Democrats can be nominated and elected and party members are happy. As constituencies get larger and more diverse, parties have a choice. They can moderate and win elections, or stay ideologically pure and lose. In other words, there are internal forces that draw the parties away from each other, to the opposite ends of the ideological spectrum, but external, electoral forces can push them together. These forces are central to understanding electoral politics in America today.

On any policy or set of policies, voters' opinions range from very liberal to very conservative. In the American two-party system, however, most voters tend to be in the middle, holding a moderate position between the two ideological extremes (see Figure 11.2). The party that appeals best to the moderate voters usually wins most of the votes. Thus even though the ideologies of the parties are distinct, the pressures related to winning a majority of votes can lead both parties to campaign on the same issue positions, making them appear more alike to voters.[16] For instance, Republicans have moved from their initial opposition to join the majority of voters in supporting Social Security, Medicare, and Medicaid. Similarly, Democrats have dropped their resistance to a balanced federal budget and have become advocates of fiscal responsibility.

Although the need to appeal to the many moderate voters in the middle of the American political spectrum has brought the two major parties together, powerful forces within the parties still keep them apart. These are the need to placate party activists and the need to raise money. The main players in a political party are often called the "party faithful," or **party activists**, people who are especially committed to the values and policies of the party and who devote more of their resources, both time and money, to the party's cause. Although these activists are not an official organ of the party, they represent its lifeblood. Compared to the average voter, party activists tend to be more ideologically extreme (more conservative or more liberal even than the average party identifier) and to care more intensely about the party's issues. They can have a significant influence on the ideological character of the party.[17]

Party activists play a key role in keeping the parties ideologically distinct, because one of their primary purposes in being active in the party is to ensure that the party advocates their issue positions (see Figure 11.2). Because they tend to be concerned with keeping the party pure, they are reluctant to compromise on these issues, even if it means losing an election.[18] Liberal activists kept the Democratic Party to the left of most Americans during the 1970s and 1980s. The only Democratic candidate who won a presidential election during that time was Jimmy Carter, in the immediate aftermath of the Watergate scandal that drove Republican Richard Nixon from office. The Democratic Party dealt with this problem by restructuring its internal

Figure 11.2

External and Internal Forces on the Parties

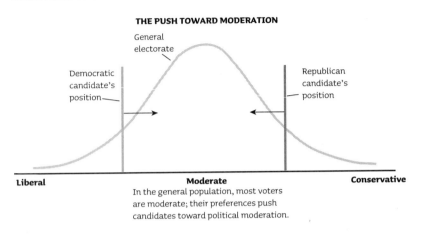

THE PUSH TOWARD MODERATION

General
electorate

Democratic
candidate's
position

Republican
candidate's
position

Liberal   Moderate   Conservative

In the general population, most voters
are moderate; their preferences push
candidates toward political moderation.

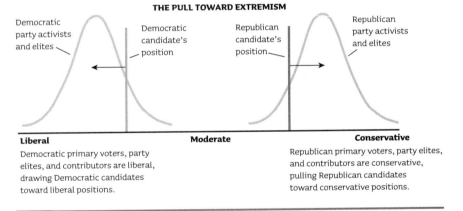

THE PULL TOWARD EXTREMISM

Democratic
party activists
and elites

Democratic
candidate's
position

Republican
candidate's
position

Republican
party activists
and elites

Liberal   Moderate   Conservative

Democratic primary voters, party
elites, and contributors are liberal,
drawing Democratic candidates
toward liberal positions.

Republican primary voters, party elites,
and contributors are conservative,
pulling Republican candidates
toward conservative positions.

politics and giving more weight to moderates like Bill Clinton and Al Gore. The
Republicans got caught in the same trap of appearing to be as conservative as their
most activist members in the religious right and, later, in the Tea Party. The Democrats were consequently able to capture the presidency by appealing to the moderate
middle—focusing on the economic problems of Americans in 1992 and appropriat-
ing and giving less extreme meaning to the label "family values" in 1996. The Republicans responded by moving to the middle in 2000, choosing in George W. Bush a
candidate who could appeal to moderate voters. In 2008 Barack Obama appealed to
moderates with his insistence that politics need not be partisan and divisive. He also
couched his economic message in terms of assistance to the middle class, another
stance that moderates found attractive. That approach, combined with his refusal to

concede to his opponent such traditionally Republican ground as foreign policy and national security, helped him win the election.

The need to please party activists gives candidates a powerful incentive to remain true to the party's causes. Candidates who moderate too much or too often risk alienating the activists who are a key component of their success. Thus, even though many nominees temper their stances to win a majority of the votes, winning candidates, mindful of their bases, tend to return to their roots once in office.[19] This means that few politicians are willing to be truly moderate and work with the other side. Since the 1980s we have seen an increased partisanship in politics, which often leads to gridlock and inaction.

Characteristics of the American Party System

Party systems vary tremendously around the world. The American party system is distinctive: it is predominantly a two-party system, it tends toward ideological moderation, it has decentralized party organizations, and its parties-in-government are undisciplined.

Two Parties

The United States has a two-party system. Throughout most of our history, in fact, the Democrats and the Republicans have been the only parties with a viable chance of winning the vast majority of elective offices. The most important reason the United States maintains a two-party system is that the rules of the system—in most cases designed by members of the two parties themselves—make it very difficult for third parties to do well on a permanent basis.[20] The U.S. Constitution prescribes a single-member-district electoral system for choosing members of Congress. This means that the candidate who receives the most votes in a defined district wins that seat and the loser gets nothing, except perhaps some campaign debt. This type of winner-take-all system creates strong incentives for voters to cast their ballots for one of the two established parties, because many voters believe that they are effectively throwing their votes away when they vote for a third-party candidate.

The United States has other legal barriers that reinforce the two-party system. In most states, state legislators from both parties have created state election laws that regulate each major party's activities, but these laws also protect the parties from competition. For example, state election laws ensure the place of both major parties on the ballot and make it difficult for third parties to gain ballot access. Many states require that potential independent or third-party candidates gather a large number of signatures before their names can be placed on the ballot. Another common state law requires a third party to have earned some minimum percentage of the votes in the previous election in order to conduct a primary to select its candidates.

As campaigns have become more dependent on money and television, both major parties have sought to limit third-party candidates' access to these vital resources. Thanks to 1974 campaign reforms, federal election laws now dictate the amount of campaign contributions that presidential candidates can receive from individuals and political action committees. These laws also provide dollar-for-dollar federal matching money for both major parties' nominees, if they agree to limit their spending to a predetermined amount. Third-party candidates cannot claim federal campaign funds until after the election is over, however, and even then their funds are limited by the percentage of past and current votes they received. In practice, they need to have gained about 5 percent or more of the national vote to be eligible for federal funds.[21] In 1992 billionaire Ross Perot funded his presidential campaign out of his own fortune, refusing the limits set by federal law and making himself ineligible to receive matching funds. This gesture, which few third-party candidates can afford to make, enabled him to receive a large enough percentage of the votes that he qualified for federal campaign funds in the 1996 election, when he did limit his spending. In addition, his party, the Reform Party, was eligible to receive such funds in 2000.

Just because the Democrats and the Republicans have dominated our party system does not mean that they have gone unchallenged. Over the years, numerous third parties have tried to alter the partisan makeup of American politics. These parties have usually arisen either to address specific issues that the major parties failed to address, like Prohibition in 1869 or the environment in 1972, or to promote ideas that were not part of the ideological spectrum covered by the existing parties, like socialist parties or the Libertarian Party. In general, third parties have sprung up from the grassroots or have broken off from an existing party (the latter are referred to as *splinter parties*). In the case of the current Tea Party movement, the new party is not actually distinct from the Republican Party (most Tea Party members identify as conservative Republicans), and as long as the Republican Party adopts most of the issues the Tea Partiers care about, they are not likely to separate and form an organized party of their own. In many cases third parties have been headed by a strong leader who carried much of the burden of the party's success on his or her shoulders. Teddy Roosevelt's Bull Moose Party (1912) and Ross Perot's Reform Party (1992) are prime examples.

Although no third-party candidate has ever won the presidency, by no means is the impact of third parties on presidential elections negligible. For example, if Ralph Nader had not run as a third-party candidate in 2000, Al Gore probably would have won the Electoral College vote as well as the popular vote. When a third-party candidate changes the results of an election in such a way, he or she is said to have played the role of a *spoiler*.

Ideological Moderation

U.S. voters must select from a limited ideological menu: the moderately conservative Republican Party and the moderately liberal Democratic Party. Neither the Democrats nor the Republicans promote vast changes in the political and economic systems. Both parties support the Bill of Rights, the Constitution and its institutions (presidency, Congress, courts, and so on), the capitalist free-enterprise system, and even basic government policies like Social Security and the Federal Reserve System. This broad agreement between the two parties in major policy areas is a reflection of public opinion. Surveys show broad public support for the basic structure and foundations of the U.S. political and economic systems. Even though, as we saw earlier, the parties do offer a real choice, they do so within the confines of the basic American political culture we discussed in Chapter 1. No communist or fascist party has ever enjoyed major electoral success in this country. It is within this agreement on the broad contours of the political system that we see clear polarization of the parties on specific issues and on the solutions to the nations' problems. On these the parties are clearly more ideologically distinct than in past decades, but still they accept the basic parameters of American politics.

Decentralized Party Organizations

In American political parties, local and state party organizations make their own decisions. They have affiliations to the national party organization but no obligation to obey its dictates other than selecting delegates to the national convention. Decision making is dispersed across the organization rather than centralized at the national level; power tends to move from the bottom up instead of from the top down. This means that local concerns and politics dominate the lower levels of the party, molding its structure, politics, and policy agendas.

Several major divisions characterize the organization of American parties. Each party has a national committee, the Republican National Committee (RNC) and the Democratic National Committee (DNC), whose members come from every state. These committees run the party business between conventions and expend enormous sums of money to get their candidates elected to office at every level. The congressional campaign committees are formed by both parties for the sole purpose of raising and distributing campaign funds for party candidates in the House and the Senate. At the more localized level, state party committees generally focus their efforts on statewide races and, to a lesser extent, state legislative contests, whereas local party organizations come together when an election approaches but are not permanently organized.

There are several reasons for the decentralized structure of American parties. One reason is that the federal electoral system makes it difficult for any national coordinating body to exercise control. Federalism also leads to decentralized parties because state laws have historically dictated the organizational structures and procedures of the state and local parties. In addition, U.S. parties lack strong organizational tools to exercise centralized control of candidates for office. In most cases, each party's candidates are chosen in direct primaries. Direct primaries, in which local party voters rather than party leaders control the nomination process, make strong centralized control an almost impossible task. When former Ku Klux Klan member David Duke ran for governor of Louisiana as a Republican in 1992, Republican leaders were outraged but powerless to stop him (he lost the election).

Changes in Party Discipline Over Time

Not only are American party organizations notable for their lack of a hierarchical (top-down) power structure, but the officials who have been elected to government from the two parties do not necessarily take their orders from the top. Party leaders have often had trouble getting their members to follow the party line, a necessary component of the responsible party model. Beginning in the 1980s, however, and perhaps best illustrated by Newt Gingrich's House Speakership (1994–1998), party discipline began to play a much stronger role in legislative politics. Gingrich made party loyalty a condition for leadership positions in committees and for his support, a pattern that continued under Speaker Dennis Hastert, R-Ill. Democrats have had more trouble holding their members to a party line, but as their frustration with President George W. Bush grew, they were more likely to vote as a block to try to stop his policies. From 2006 to 2010, Democrat Nancy Pelosi, the first woman Speaker of the House, has led the Democrats with a firm and expert hand, gaining the reputation among some as "one of the most powerful Speakers in modern history."[22] Pelosi's ability to lead the House Democrats and to pass President Obama's program was made possible by the increased ideological homogeneity within the Democratic Party, which is an important aspect of the polarized political parties of the contemporary era.[23] Following the Republican victory in 2010, it was Speaker John Boehner who faced the challenge of holding together a divided party, as Republican party discipline was challenged from within by a Tea Party coalition determined to chart its own course.

The Roles, Formation, and Types of Interest Groups

Organizing around common political goals to influence policy from outside the apparatus of government

Americans have long been addicted not only to political parties but to membership in other groups as well. As the French observer Alexis de Tocqueville noted when he traveled in America in the early 1830s, "Americans of all ages, all conditions, and all dispositions, constantly form associations. They have not only commercial and manufacturing companies, in which all take part, but associations of a thousand other kinds—religious, moral, serious, futile, general or restricted, enormous or diminutive."[24]

This tendency of Americans to form groups disturbed James Madison, who worried about the power of **factions**, or citizens united by some interest or passion that might be opposed to the common good. Most political scientists, however, have a different take on factions, which they call by the more neutral term *interest groups*. An **interest group** is an organization of individuals who share a common political goal and unite for the purpose of influencing public policy decisions.[25] We saw in Chapter 1 that interest groups play a central role in the pluralist theory of democracy, which argues that democracy is enhanced when citizens' interests are represented through group membership. Group interaction becomes a central mechanism in who gets what in American politics. It ensures that members' interests are represented, but also that no group can become too powerful.

Roles of Interest Groups

Negative images of interest groups abound in American politics and the media. Republicans speak of the Democrats as "pandering" to special interest groups like labor unions and trial lawyers, hoping to give the impression that the Democrats give special treatment to some groups at the expense of the public good. In turn, Democrats claim that the Republican Party has been captured by big business or the religious right, again suggesting that they do not have the national interest at heart but rather the specialized interests of small segments of society. In truth, interest groups have become an integral part of American politics, and neither party can afford to ignore them. They play six important roles in American politics, enhancing citizens' ability to use the system to achieve the stakes they value.[26]

> Whereas individual political action might seem futile, participation in a group can be much more effective.

1. *Representation.* Interest groups help represent their members' views to Congress, the executive branch, and administrative agencies. Representation in this case is not geographic, as it is in Congress, but rather is based on common interests. Whether an interest group represents teachers, manufacturers of baby food, people concerned with the environment, or the elderly, it ensures that its members' concerns are adequately heard in the policymaking process. The activity of persuading policymakers to support an interest group's positions is called **lobbying**.

2. *Participation.* Interest groups provide an avenue for citizen participation in politics that goes beyond voting in periodic elections. They are a mechanism for people sharing the same interests or pursuing the same policy goals to come together, pool their resources, and channel their efforts for collective action. Whereas individual political action might seem futile, participation in a group can be much more effective.

3. *Education.* One of the more important functions of interest groups is to educate policymakers regarding issues that are important to the groups.

4. *Agenda building.* Interest groups alert the proper government authorities about their issues, get the issues on the political agenda, and make those issues a high priority for action.

5. *Provision of program alternatives.* Interest groups can be effective in supplying alternative suggestions for how issues should be dealt with once they have been put on the agenda. From this mix of proposals, political actors choose a solution.[27]

6. *Program monitoring.* Once laws are enacted, interest groups keep tabs on their consequences, informing Congress and the regulatory agencies about the effects, both expected and unexpected, of federal policy.

Why Do Interest Groups Form?

Many of us can imagine public problems that we think need to be addressed. But despite our reputation as a nation of joiners, most of us never act, never organize a group, and never even join one. What makes the potential members of an interest group come together in the first place? Several conditions make organization easier. It helps if the potential members share a perception of a problem that needs to be solved or a threat to their interests that needs to be addressed. It also helps if the members have the resources—time, money, and leadership—to organize.

But even though external threats, financial resources, and effective leadership can all spur interest group formation, these factors are usually not enough to overcome what political scientists call the *problem of collective action*. Another name for this is the **free rider problem**: Why should people join a group to solve a problem when they can free ride—that is, reap the benefits of the group's actions—whether they join or not?[28] The free rider problem affects interest groups because most of the policies that these groups advocate involve the distribution of a collective good. A **collective good** is a good or benefit that, once provided, cannot be denied to others. Public safety, clean air, peace, and lower consumer prices are all examples of collective goods that can be enjoyed by anyone. When collective goods are involved, it is difficult to persuade people to join groups, because they are going to reap the benefits anyway. The larger the number of potential members involved, the more this holds true, because each member will have trouble seeing that his or her efforts will make a difference.

Many groups overcome the free rider problem by supplying **selective incentives**—benefits available to their members that are not available to the general population. They might include **material benefits**, tangible rewards that members can use. One of the most common material benefits is information. For example, many groups publish a magazine or newsletter packed with information about issues important to the group and pending legislation relevant to the group's activities. **Solidarity benefits**, which come from interaction and bonding among group members, are another type of selective incentive. For many individuals, politics is an enjoyable activity, and the social interactions occurring through group activities provide high levels of satisfaction and are a strong motivating force. Finally, **expressive benefits** are those rewards that come from doing something that you strongly believe in—essentially from the expression of your values and interests.

Group leaders often use a mixture of incentives to recruit and sustain members. Thus the National Rifle Association (NRA) recruits many of its members because they are committed to the cause of protecting an individual's right to bear arms. The NRA reinforces this expressive incentive with material incentives, such as its magazine, and solidarity incentives resulting from group fellowship. The combination of all these incentives helps make the NRA one of the strongest interest groups in Washington.

Types of Interest Groups

There are potentially as many interest groups in America as there are interests, which is to say the possibilities are endless. Therefore, it is helpful to divide these groups into different types, based on the kind of benefit they seek for their members. Here we distinguish among economic, equal opportunity, public, and government (both foreign and domestic) interest groups. Depending on the definitions they use, scholars have come up with different schemes for classifying interest groups, so don't be surprised if you come across these groups under other labels.

Economic interest groups seek to influence government for the economic benefit of their members. Generally these groups are players in the productive and professional activities of the nation. The economic benefits they seek may be higher wages, lower tax rates, bigger government subsidies, or more favorable regulations, for example. What all economic interest groups have in common is that they focus primarily on pocketbook issues. Such groups include corporations and business associations, unions and professional associations, and agricultural interest groups.

Equal opportunity interest groups organize to promote the civil rights of people who believe that their interests are not being adequately represented and protected in national politics through traditional means. Because in many cases these groups are economically disadvantaged or are afraid that they might become so, they also advocate economic rights. Equal opportunity groups believe that they are underrepresented not because of *what they do* but because of *who they are*. They may be the victims of discrimination or see themselves as threatened. These groups organize on the basis of age, race, ethnic group, gender, and sexual orientation. Membership is not limited to people who are part of the demographic group, because many people believe that promoting the interests and rights of various groups in society is in the broader interest of all. For this reason, some scholars classify these groups as public interest groups.

A **public interest group** tries to influence government to produce noneconomic benefits that cannot be restricted to the interest group's members or denied to any member of the general public. The benefits of clean air, for instance, are available to all, not just the members of the environmental group that fights for them. In a way, all interest group benefits are collective goods that all members of the group can enjoy, but public interest groups seek collective goods that are open to all members of society or, in some cases, everyone in the world.

Public interest group members are usually motivated by a view of the world that they think everyone would be better off to adopt. They believe that the benefit they seek is good for everyone, even if individuals outside their groups disagree or even reject the benefit. Although few people would dispute the value of clean air, peace, and the protection of human rights internationally, there is no such consensus about protecting the right to an abortion, the right to carry a concealed weapon, or the right to smoke marijuana. Yet public interest groups are involved in procuring and enforcing these rights for all Americans.

Because public interest groups are involved in the production of collective goods for very large populations and the incentive to contribute on an individual basis may be particularly difficult to perceive, these groups are especially vulnerable to the free rider problem. That has not stopped them from organizing, however. There are more than twenty-five hundred public interest groups in the United

States today.[29] People are drawn to a particular group because they support its values and goals; that is, expressive benefits are the primary membership draw. Although many members are initially attracted by expressive benefits, public interest groups seek to keep them active by offering material benefits and services, ranging from a free subscription to the group's magazine to discount insurance packages. Public interest groups include environmental groups, consumer groups, religious groups, Second Amendment groups, reproductive rights groups, and human rights groups.

Government interest groups—representing both foreign and domestic governments—also lobby Congress and the president. Typically some lobbyists' most lucrative contracts come from foreign governments seeking to influence foreign trade policies. In recent years, ethics rules have been initiated to prevent former government officials from working as foreign government lobbyists as soon as they leave office, but lobbying firms continue to hire them when they can because of their contacts and expertise.[30]

Domestic governments have become increasingly involved in the business of influencing federal policy. With the growing complexities of American federalism, state and local governments have an enormous stake in what the federal government does and often try to gain resources, limit the impact of policy, and otherwise alter the effects of federal law. All fifty states have government relations offices in Washington to attempt to influence federal policy directly.[31]

Interest Group Politics
Different strategies for influencing different branches of government

The term *lobbying* comes from seventeenth-century England, where representatives of special interests would meet members of the English House of Commons in the large anteroom, or lobby, outside the House floor to plead their cases.[32] Contemporary lobbying reaches far beyond the lobby of the House or the Senate, however. Interest groups contact lawmakers directly, but they no longer confine their efforts to chance meetings in the legislative lobby—or to members of the legislature. Today they target all branches of government, and the American people as well. The ranks of those who work with lobbyists also have swelled. Beginning in the 1980s, interest groups, especially those representing corporate interests, have been turning to a diverse group of political consultants, including professional Washington lobbyists, campaign specialists, advertising and media experts, pollsters, and academics. Lobbying today is a big business in its own right.

There are two main types of lobbying strategy: **direct lobbying** (sometimes called "inside lobbying"), or interaction with actual decision makers within government institutions, and **indirect lobbying** (also called "outside lobbying"), or attempts to influence public opinion and mobilize interest group members or the general public to contact their elected representatives on an issue. Some groups have resorted to more confrontational indirect methods, using political protests (often developing into full-blown social movements) to make their demands heard by policymakers. Recently, corporations and other more traditional interest groups have been combining tactics—joining conventional lobbying methods with the use of email, computerized databases, talk radio, and twenty-four-hour cable TV—to bring unprecedented pressure to bear on the voting public to influence members of government.

Direct Lobbying

Direct lobbying involves a face-to-face interaction between lobbyists and members of government. We tend to think of Congress as the typical recipient of lobbying efforts, but the president, the bureaucracy, and even the courts are also the focus of efforts to influence policy.

Lobbying Congress

When interest groups lobby Congress, they rarely concentrate on all 435 members of the House or all 100 members of the Senate. Rather, lobbyists focus their efforts on congressional committees, because that is where most bills are written and revised. Because the committee leadership is relatively stable from one Congress to the next (unless a different party wins a majority), lobbyists can develop long-term relationships with committee members and their staffs. These personal contacts, which might take place at meetings, banquets, parties, or lunches or simply in casual meetings in the hallways of Congress, are important because they represent a major means through which interest groups provide information to members of Congress. This is the most common and the most effective form of lobbying strategy.

Much of modern-day lobbying also involves the use of "hired guns," or professional lobbyists, many of them former government officials, put on retainer by a client to lobby for that client's interests. Rotating into lobbying jobs from elected or other government positions is known as passing through the **revolving door**, a concept we will encounter again in Chapter 13. It refers to public officials who leave their posts to become interest group representatives (or media figures), parlaying the special knowledge and contacts they gathered in government into lucrative salaries in the private sector. Revolving-door activity is subject to occasional attempts at regulation and frequent ethical debate, because it raises questions about whether people should be able to convert public service into private profit, and whether such an incentive draws people into public office for motives other than serving the public interest.

Interest groups also lobby congressional decision makers by providing testimony and expertise, and sometimes they even draft legislation on the many issues that policymakers cannot take the time to become expert in.[33] Information is one of the most important resources lobbyists can bring to their effort to influence Congress.

Giving money to candidates is another lobbying technique that helps interest groups gain access and a friendly ear. The 1974 Federal Election Campaign Act, which was passed in an effort to curb campaign spending abuses, sought to regulate the amount of money an interest group can give to candidates for federal office by providing for **political action committees (PACs)**, which serve as fundraisers for interest groups. There are strict limitations on how much money PACs can donate to a candidate, but a number of loopholes allow them to get around some of the restrictions.

Interest groups also attempt to bolster their lobbying efforts by forming coalitions with other interest groups. These coalitions tend to be based on single issues, and building such coalitions has become an important strategy in lobbying Congress.

Many attempts have been made to regulate the tight relationships between lobbyists and lawmakers. The difficulty, of course, is that lawmakers benefit from their relationships with lobbyists in many ways and are not enthusiastic about curtailing their opportunities to get money and support. In 1995 Congress completed its first attempt in half a century to regulate lobbying when it passed the Lobbying Disclosure Act. The act requires lobbyists to report how much they are paid, by whom, and what issues they are promoting.[34] Also in 1995, both the Senate and the House passed separate resolutions addressing gifts and travel opportunities given by interest groups to senators and representatives.[35]

These reforms have not closed the door on lavish spending by lobbyists, although initially the rule changes cast a definite chill on lobbyists' activities.[36] As lobbyists and members of Congress have learned where they can bend the rules, however, relations between them have returned to a more familiar footing. The 2005 scandals involving lobbyist Jack Abramoff touched a number of Congress members, including the powerful Republican Tom DeLay, showing that the potential for corrupt relationships between lawmakers and lobbyists is as great as ever. Partly in reaction, in September 2007, after the Democrats took back the majority in the House and the Senate in 2006, Congress passed and President Bush signed the Honest Leadership and Open Government Act, which tightened travel and gift restrictions.[37] And of course, as soon as the 2007 reform was passed, lobbying groups scrambled to find new ways to provide travel for lawmakers they wanted to influence, and ways to make free meals acceptable.[38]

Lobbying the President, the Bureaucracy, and the Courts

Lobbyists also target the president and the White House staff to try to influence policy. As with Congress, personal contacts within the White House are extremely important, and the higher up the better. The official contact point between the White House and interest groups is the Office of Public Liaison. The basic purpose of this office is to foster good relations between the White House and interest groups in order to mobilize these groups to support the administration's policies.

Whereas opportunities for lobbying the president may be somewhat limited, opportunities for lobbying the rest of the executive branch abound. Interest groups know that winning the legislative battle is only the first step. The second, and sometimes more important, battle takes place in the bureaucracy, where Congress has delegated rule-making authority to federal agencies that implement the law.[39]

Interest groups often try to gain an advantage by developing strong relations with regulating agencies. Because many of the experts on a topic are employed by the interests being regulated, it is not unusual to find lobbyists being hired by government agencies, or vice versa, in an extension of the revolving-door situation we discussed earlier. The close relationships that exist between the regulated and the regulators, along with the close relationships between lobbyists and congressional staffs, lead to the creation of iron triangles (see Chapter 8).

Interest groups try to influence government policy by challenging the legality of laws or administrative regulations in the courts. These legal tactics have been used by groups like the National Association for the Advancement of Colored People (antidiscrimination cases), the American Civil Liberties Union (freedom of speech, freedom of religion, and civil liberties cases), the Sierra Club (environmental enforcement), and Common Cause (ethics in government). Sometimes groups bring cases directly, and sometimes they file amicus curiae ("friend of the court") briefs asking the courts to rule in ways favoring their positions.

Indirect Lobbying

One of the most powerful and fastest-growing kinds of lobbying is indirect lobbying, in which lobbyists use public opinion to put pressure on politicians to do what the lobbyists want.[40] There are various ways in which interest groups use the public to lobby and influence government decision makers.

Many interest group leaders are sure that people will rally to their side once they know the "truth" about their causes, and so they set out to educate the public. They conduct extensive research to make their cases and court media attention and hire public relations firms to get their ideas across.[41] An increasingly popular way for interest groups to promote their message has been by using **issue advocacy ads**, which encourage constituents to support or oppose a certain policy or candidate without directly telling them how to vote. Such ads skirted campaign finance law that limited the money groups could spend to advocate for candidates directly, but since the 2010 Supreme Court case *Citizens United v. Federal Election Commission*, groups can raise funds and spend freely to support their favored candidates.

Groups can also get information to the public through the skillful use of the Internet, whether through carefully designed advocacy web sites and blogs, through social networks, or through web-based videos, creating messages that go "viral," spreading quickly by email and hitting targeted audiences. Internet-savvy interest groups are increasingly turning to YouTube, the video-sharing web site in place only since 2005, for a cheap and efficient way to get their message out. Lobbyists have used YouTube on behalf of such diverse interests as The Science Coalition, a group of research universities; Concerned Families for ATV Safety; and the Competitive Enterprise Institute, which lobbies against U.S. government energy standards.[42]

The point of disseminating information, hiring public relations firms, and running issue advocacy ads is to mobilize the public, motivating people to lobby politicians themselves. As you might expect, groups like AARP, the Christian Coalition, and the NRA, which are blessed with large memberships, have an advantage because they can mobilize a large contingent of citizens from all over the country to lobby representatives, senators, and the president. Generally this mobilization involves encouraging members to write letters, send email messages or faxes, or make phone calls to legislators about a pending issue.

Throughout our history, groups have turned to **social protest**—activities ranging from planned, orderly demonstrations, to strikes and boycotts, to acts of civil disobedience—when other techniques have failed to bring attention to their causes. Social protest provides a way for people to publicly express their disagreement with a government policy or action. At the same time, it often signals the strength of participants' feelings about an issue or their outrage over being closed off from more traditional avenues of political action. The media explosion of the modern age, especially the advent of the Internet, has given social protesters many more ways to find each other and organize. Social analysts also have observed that the Internet has facilitated the growth of groups like militias and white supremacist organizations that previously dwelled on the fringes of society.[43]

"Astroturf" Political Campaigns: Democratic or Elite Driven?

The indirect lobbying we have discussed is often called **grassroots lobbying**, meaning that it addresses people in their roles as ordinary citizens. It is the wielding of power from the bottom (roots) up, rather than from the top down. Most of what we refer to as grassroots lobbying, however, does not spring spontaneously from the people but is orchestrated by elites, leading some people to call it **astroturf lobbying**—indicating that it is not genuine.

Often the line between real grassroots and astroturf lobbying is blurred, however. A movement may be partly spontaneous but partly orchestrated. MoveOn is an example of a group that started out as a spontaneous expression of the popular will to lobby Congress against the impeachment of President Clinton but that spread by "word of mouse" over the Internet. Similarly, the current Tea Party movement has been, in part, the project of Dick Armey, a former Republican House majority leader whose organization, FreedomWorks, promotes low taxes and small government. FreedomWorks and several other conservative groups, as well as prominent individuals including some commentators at Fox News, have lent their organizational expertise to the Tea Partiers but deny that they are orchestrating an astroturf movement.[44] Regardless of how it started out, the Tea Party movement has certainly acquired a life and mind, perhaps several minds, of its own.

At the astroturf extreme, there was nothing spontaneous at all about the pharmaceutical industry's 2003 efforts to oppose the importation of cheaper drugs from Canada. The Pharmaceutical Research and Manufacturers Association (PhRMA), the industry's lobbying group, spent over $4 million on tactics such as persuading seniors that their access to medicine would be limited if reimportation of these American-made drugs were allowed and convincing members of a Christian advocacy group that prescription drug importation might lead to easier access to the controversial morning-after pill.[45] Such a strategy is obviously an attempt to create an opinion that might not otherwise even exist, playing on popular fears about drug availability and sentiments about abortion to achieve corporate ends.

Corporate interests seeking to take advantage of astroturf techniques employ expensive armies of lobbyists, media experts, and political strategists to conduct polls, craft multimedia advertising campaigns, and get the message out to "the people" through cable and radio talk shows, the Internet, outbound call centers, or fax machines. One media consultant has predicted that direct lobbying will become less important as indirect lobbying increases in effectiveness and popularity.[46] While indirect lobbying seems on its face to be more democratic, to the extent that it manipulates public opinion, it may in fact be less so. And as the multimedia campaigns get more and more expensive, the number of groups that can afford to participate will undoubtedly decline. Ironically, as lobbying moves away from the closed committee rooms of Congress and into the realm of what *appears* to be popular politics, it may not be any more democratic than it has been traditionally.

Interest Group Resources
Using money, leadership skills, size, and intensity to make their voices heard

Interest group success depends in large part on the resources a group can bring to the project of influencing government. The pluralist defense of interest groups is that all citizens have the opportunity to organize, and thus all can exercise equal power. But all interest groups are not created equal. Some have more money, more effective leadership, more members, or better information than others, and these resources can translate into real power differences in the high-stakes world of American politics, and consequently into real winners and losers. In this section we examine the resources that interest groups can draw on—money, leadership, membership, and information—to get what they want from government.

Money

Interest groups need money to conduct the business of trying to influence government policymakers. Money can buy an interest group the ability to put together a well-trained staff, to hire outside professional assistance, and to make campaign contributions in the hopes of gaining access to government officials. Having money does not guarantee favorable policies, but not having money just about guarantees failure.

One of the reasons money is important is that it enables an interest group to hire a professional staff, usually an executive director, assistants, and other office

Advocacy and EMILY's LIST

EMILY's List president Ellen Malcolm (center left) rubbed elbows with Michelle Obama (center right) and elected female Democratic officials during the 2008 Democratic National Convention. With the goal of placing as many qualified women into office at every level possible, EMILY's List identifies and recommends candidates to its more than 100,000 members throughout each election cycle.

support personnel. The main job of this professional staff is to take care of the group's day-to-day operations, including pursuing policy initiatives, recruiting and maintaining membership, providing membership services, and, of course, getting more money through direct mailings, telemarketing, and organizational functions. Money is important for creating an organizational infrastructure that can in turn be used to raise additional support and resources.

Money also enables the interest group to hire the services of professionals, such as a high-powered lobbying firm. Such firms have invested heavily to ensure that they have connections to members of Congress.[47] A well-endowed group also can hire a public relations firm to help shape public opinion on a particular policy.

Interest groups live by the axiom that to receive, one must give—and give a lot to important people. The maximum that any PAC can give to a congressional campaign is $5,000 for each separate election. In the 2008 cycle, PACs gave a total of $385.9 million to congressional candidates up for election, an all-time high for PAC contributions.[48] While some PACs give millions to campaigns, most PACs give less than $50,000 to candidates for each election cycle, focusing their contributions on members of the committees responsible for drafting legislation important to their groups.[49] In the wake of the *Citizens United* decision, however, considerable money can be spent by groups on a candidate's behalf, and the groups don't have to disclose the donors' identities. In the days before the 2010 midterm elections, it was apparent that, though the *Citizens United* decision made only small changes to campaign finance law, it had the psychological effect of giving a "green light" to those who wanted to spend lavishly on an election.[50]

PAC spending is usually directed toward incumbents of both parties, with incumbents in the majority party, especially committee chairs, getting the greatest share. As Figure 11.3 shows, about 80 percent of PAC contributions go to incumbent members of Congress.[51] While most PACs want to curry favor with incumbents of either party, some tend to channel their money to one party. For instance, business interests, the American Medical Association, pro-life groups, Christian groups, and the NRA tend to support Republican candidates; and labor groups, the Association of Trial Lawyers of America, the National Education Association, and environmental and pro-choice groups give primarily to Democrats.

The ability to make sizable and strategically placed campaign contributions buys an interest group access to government officials.[52] Access gives the interest group the ability to talk to a representative and members of his or her staff and to present information relevant to the policies they seek to initiate, change, or protect. Access is important because representatives have any number of competing interests vying for their time. Money is meant to oil the door hinge of a representative's

Figure 11.3

PAC Contributions to All Congressional Candidates, 2008, by Type of PAC and Candidate's Party

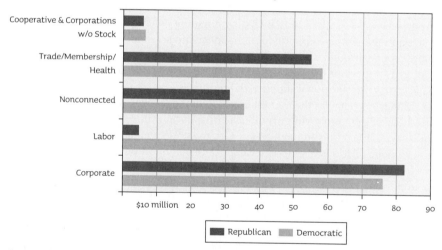

Source: Federal Election Commission press release, "Growth in PAC Financial Activity Slows," Table 2 PAC Contributions 2007–2008 Through December 31, 2008, www.fec.gov/press/press2009/20090415PAC/20090424 PAC.shtml.

office so that it swings open for the interest group. For instance, a $175,000 donation to the Republican National Committee over four years yielded a three-day private event between the donors and the Republican leadership of Congress.[53] The Clinton administration was known in its early years for allowing major donors to stay in the Lincoln bedroom of the White House. The access bought by campaign contributions is usually less blatant, but officials know who has supported their campaigns, and they are unlikely to forget it when interest groups come knocking at their doors.

The relationship between money and political influence is extremely controversial. Many critics argue that this money buys more than just access; they say it buys votes. The circumstantial evidence for this contention is strong. For instance, in the Senate deliberations on a public option in health care, which would have provided individuals with an alternative to private health care insurance, the thirty senators who supported the public option had received an average of $15,937 in contributions from the health care industry in the previous six years, compared to the $37, 322 that was received, on average, by the seventy senators who opposed it.[54]

However, in the matter of vote buying, systematic studies of congressional voting patterns are mixed. These studies show that the influence of campaign contributions is strongest in committees, where most bills are drafted. Once a bill reaches the floor of the House or the Senate, though, there is no consistent link between campaign contributions and roll-call voting.[55] This suggests that campaign contributions influence the process of creating and shaping legislation, and thus defining the policy alternatives. Nonetheless, the final outcome of a bill is determined by political circumstances that go beyond the campaign contributions of interest groups.

Leadership

Leadership is an intangible element in the success or failure of an interest group. The strong effective leadership of what one scholar has called *interest group entrepreneurs* can help a group organize even if it lacks other resources.[56] Such a leader can keep a group going when it seems to lack support from other sources. Cesar Chavez's leadership of the United Farm Workers in the mid-1950s through the early 1990s is an excellent case in point.

Membership: Size and Intensity

The size of any interest group is an important resource. For instance, with more than 40 million members, AARP can mobilize thousands of people in an attempt to influence elected officials' decisions regarding issues like mandatory retirement, Social Security, and Medicare. In addition, if an interest group's members are spread throughout the country, as are AARP's, that group can exert its influence on almost every member of Congress.

Wayne Pacelle

In the midst of one of his finest moments, Wayne Pacelle got himself thrown out of the gallery of the House of Representatives.

He was watching the vote on a budget amendment he had lobbied hard for, an amendment to cut millions of dollars of taxpayer money spent to promote the sale of U.S.-made mink coats in Italy, China, and France. He needed 218 votes to win, and everyone thought they were going to be trounced. He watched the scoreboard light up with vote after vote. When they got to 232, he couldn't help it. He let out a yell and pumped his fist. But the House frowns on emotional displays in the gallery, and out he went. Was he abashed? Hardly. "It didn't take the smile off my face," he says, grinning even now at the memory.

It was a great win, but every single triumph matters to Pacelle—it's how he feeds his spirit and keeps himself going in the face of the often daunting odds and unimaginable stories of animal abuse he confronts daily in his job as CEO of the Humane Society of the United States. Each law enacted by Congress to protect animals (fifteen in the past few years), each state bill passed (more than 150), each statewide ballot measure approved (fifteen so far), each animal life saved, each creature relieved of pain and suffering—he tallies them all. "I celebrate the positive action because it's easy to get burned out," he says. "It's easy to get demoralized. . . . And for me, I just tell people you've got to celebrate every little victory, it makes a big difference.

"For us, it's not an all-or-nothing game," he explains. "We can't solve all of the issues in the world, we never will. . . . But if we solve it for a million, or ten million, or a billion creatures, that's a 100-percent victory for each of those animals. And just that one act of merciful behavior or the shielding of an animal from abuse or cruelty can mean all the difference between a good quality of life and a miserable tormented existence for that creature."

Pacelle has felt that kind of enormous compassionate connection to animals ever since he was two or three years old. "It was a purely emotional, altruistic response that I had toward other creatures. I just saw them as powerless and I saw them as peers at that age, and they looked to me like they were composed of the same spark of life that people were."

He carried that empathy and awareness with him as he got older and, as he read philosophy and learned more about the world, he began to fit it into a broader context of what it meant to him to be a responsible citizen. He started an animal rights group in college in the 1980s, at the same time that he was active in the anti-apartheid movement to limit U.S. investment in South Africa and in protests of U.S. involvement in Central America. Ask him what the common thread is and he is clear: "I'm broadly interested in making the world a better place," he says. "That's the bottom line. Public policy is just the means to achieve the end of a more fair, a more just society."

A huge and saintly ambition, but Pacelle doesn't look like a zealot or a crusader when he says it. Actually, he looks like, well, a movie star, or a relative of a famous American political family (possessing what the *Washington Post* once called "John Kennedy, Jr. good looks"). He is polished, articulate, and funny (it must run in the family—his brother, Richard, is the funniest political scientist we know), and the animals couldn't ask for a more dedicated or committed advocate.

How has he kept that idealism and commitment in the face of the giant sums of money that Washington lobbyists traffic in these days? He may be an optimist, but he's a realist, too. "You'd be naive to think money doesn't have an impact," he says. "It does. It gains access, and it builds loyalty. But, ultimately, money is a means to an end. Money is there to have resources to deliver a message to influence voting behavior. So if you've got people who can organize around a principle and you can deliver votes based on that set of ideas, then you don't need money." Well, maybe not as much, anyway. Here are some of his thoughts:

On the positive side of lobbying:
There's a reason in Washington, D.C., that there are thousands of lobbyists and thousands of interest groups. They're not here for fun; it's not just a big party. They're here because it does make a difference and participation can have a measurable impact on public policy. I think for me, just being determined and dogged about it, just not relenting, just basically treating this as if it's a full court press all the time. . . . I mean when we're not on defense, we're on the offense. It's almost a very crusading sort of attitude. I don't like to infuse it with religious sorts of notions, but it's a powerful, ethical construct. And having enough imagination to see that things can be different. That we're not just locked into our present set of social relationships and circumstance, that we can aspire to do things better.

On keeping the republic:
No one's going to hand you a key to change everything, but if you're smart and if you're determined you can make a real difference in the world. I've seen it happen thousands and thousands of times. And anybody who tells me differently just isn't paying attention to what's going on. And don't count on somebody else to do it, you know, don't count on a group like the Humane Society of the United States to do it. When I go around and I talk to people I say, "Listen, we can help." And our staff of four hundred, we've got great experts and we do a lot of amazing stuff, but you make the difference. It's the collective action of people of conscience that really can have a meaningful impact on society. And again, the history is of people stepping up and calling themselves to action. And leadership and citizenship are such important values in this culture. And if not them, who?

The level of intensity that members exhibit in support of a group's causes also is critical. If a group's members are intensely dedicated to its causes, the group may be far stronger than its numbers would indicate. Members represent the lifeblood of an interest group because they generally fund its activities and they can be mobilized to write letters, send email messages, and engage in other forms of personal contact with legislators or administrative officials. For instance, even though a majority of Americans favor some form of gun control, they are outweighed in the political process by the intense feeling of the just over four million members of the NRA, who strongly oppose gun control.

Information

Information is one of the most powerful resources in an interest group's arsenal. Often the members of a group are the only sources of information on the potential or actual impact of a law or regulation. The long struggle to regulate tobacco is a case in point. While individuals witnessed their loved ones and friends suffering from lung disease, cancer, and heart problems, it took public health interest groups like the American Cancer Society, the Public Health Cancer Association, and the American Heart Association to conduct the studies, collect the data, and show the connection between these life-threatening illnesses and smoking. Of course, the tobacco industry and its interest group, the American Tobacco Institute, presented their own research to counter these claims. Not surprisingly, the tobacco industry's investigations showed "no causal relationship" between tobacco use and these illnesses.[57] Eventually the volume of information showing a strong relationship overwhelmed industry research suggesting otherwise. In 1998 the tobacco industry reached a settlement with states to pay millions of dollars for the treatment of tobacco-related illnesses.

Citizenship and Political Groups
Power in numbers

Defenders of pluralism believe that group formation helps give more power to more citizens, and we have seen that it certainly can enhance democratic life. Parties and interest groups offer channels for representation and participation, and they help to keep politicians accountable. Pluralists also believe that the system as a whole benefits from group politics. They argue that groups will compete with one another and ultimately must form coalitions to create a majority. In the process of forming coalitions, groups compromise on policy issues, leading to final policy outcomes that reflect the general will of the people, as opposed to the narrow interests of specific groups or individuals.[58] In this final section we examine the claims of critics who argue that the politics of groups skews democracy—gives more power to some people than to others—and particularly discriminates against segments of society that tend to be underrepresented in the first place (the poor and the young, for instance).

We have seen in this chapter that a variety of factors—money, leadership, membership, information—can make a group successful. But this raises a red flag for American democracy. In American political culture, we value political equality, which is to say the principle of one person, one vote. And as far as voting goes, this is how we practice democracy. Anyone who attempts to visit the polls twice on Election Day is turned away, no matter how rich that person is, how intensely she feels about the election, or how eloquently he begs for another vote. But policy is not made only at the ballot box. It is also made in the halls and hearing rooms of Congress, the conference rooms of the bureaucracy, corporate boardrooms, private offices, restaurants, and bars. In these places, parties and interest groups speak loudly, and since some groups are vastly more successful than others, they have the equivalent of extra votes in the policymaking process.

We are not terribly uncomfortable with the idea that interest groups with large memberships should have more power. After all, democracy is usually about counting numbers. But when it comes to the idea that the wealthy, those who feel intensely, or those who have more information have an advantage, we balk. What about the rest of us? Should we have relatively less power over who gets what because we lack these resources?

It is true that the major parties and interest groups with money have the distinct advantages of organization and access. Many critics suggest that business interests represent a small, wealthy, and united set of elites who dominate the political process,[59] and there is much evidence to support the view that business interests maintain a special relationship with government and tend to unite behind basic conservative issues (less government spending and lower taxes). Other evidence, however, suggests that business interests are often divided regarding government policies and that other factors, such as membership, can counterbalance their superior monetary resources. While corporate money may buy access, politicians ultimately depend on votes. Groups with large memberships have more voters. When a group's membership is highly motivated and numerous, it can win despite the opposition's lavish resources.[60]

Thus what helps to equalize the position of powerful groups in American politics is the willingness on the part of citizens to fight fire with fire, politics with politics, and organization with organization, an effort made more accessible with the widespread use of the Internet. It is, finally, the power of participation and democracy that can make pluralism fit the pluralists' hopes. For some groups, such as the poor, such advice may be nearly impossible to follow. Other groups left out of the system, such as the merely indifferent or young people who regard current issues as irrelevant, will pay the price of inattention and disorganization when the scorecards of interest group politics are finally tallied.

▶ What's at Stake Revisited

In this chapter we have seen that Madison's fear of factions was not unfounded. Interest groups may not be able to buy votes, per se, but they certainly can buy access and influence, and the politician who ignores them does so at his or her peril.

Having seen what happened when President Clinton failed to get the health industry groups on board, the Obama team was determined to avoid Clinton's mistakes. What was at stake for the Obama administration, for interest groups, for the political parties, and for the nation as a whole in the White House's decision to bring these groups in at the ground level in the effort to reform the country's health care system?

The stakes for the White House were huge. President Obama had made health care a signature issue of his campaign and had promised as well a new way of governing—lean, effective, bipartisan. Republicans could deny him the "bipartisan label," but he didn't want to cede ground on whether government could be an effective actor as well. Most observers agreed that if health care reform failed to pass this time around, it could be years before it had another shot. White House communications director Dan Pfeiffer said that what was on the line was whether government could still solve big problems, whereas former Senate majority leader Tom Daschle said that a failure to get the bill passed would amount to a failure to govern. The way to succeed was to get all the concerned actors on board. "The President said that having people at the table is better than having them throw stuff at the table," said Pfeiffer.[61]

For industry interest groups, the stakes were substantial as well. If they stayed outside of the process but were unable to stop health care reform, they risked being stuck with a policy they hated. And many groups agreed with one of the basic tenets of the reformers—that the status quo in health care, with its rising costs, was unsustainable. If they joined the reform effort, they could have a say in shaping the solution to the problem. America's Health Insurance Plan (AHIP), recognizing that its members would be required to cover preexisting conditions, made the "universal mandate," the condition that all who could afford it be required to buy insurance, the price of their cooperation. The drug companies were able to head off more severe cuts in drug coverage and competition from cheaper drug companies abroad by voluntarily offering to reduce costs. As *New Republic* writer Jonathan Cohn put it, for interest groups the choice was simple: you can be at the table or you can be on the menu.[62]

The value of the strategy the interest groups followed is suggested by the fate of the Republican Party, which did stay outside the process and refused to compromise. After reform passed, conservative author and former George W. Bush speechwriter David Frum criticized the Republican strategy, saying that Republican participation could have pulled the plan in a direction more consistent with conservative principles. By refusing to play at all, the Republicans ceded influence over the final product—they went for all the marbles and ended with none.[63] By getting involved early, interest groups got a good share of the marbles.

Which, of course, is what so annoyed President Obama's liberal critics. Obama gave away the store, they argued, making concessions before he had to and giving up the public option, a key element of reform near and dear to their hearts.[64] For them, what was at stake in Obama's deal-making with the health care industry was the very integrity of reform. No less than the Republicans, Democratic critics believed that to compromise was to water down their principles. Had they insisted on purity, however, there likely would have been no health care bill at all. Though the House of Representatives managed to pass a bill with a weak version of the public option without Republican support, Senate majority leader Harry Reid needed every Democrat on board, as well as independent senator Joe Lieberman of Connecticut. Lieberman tends to vote with the Democrats, but he made it clear he would not support a public option, and the legislative effort to provide it died.[65]

The *political* stakes were high for the actors, like the president, who stood to face a crippled agenda if he could not bring off the reform he had promised, and for the Republicans, who had sworn to bring Obama to his Waterloo over the issue. For the health care industry, the stakes were more substantive—how much would they have to give away to keep reform within tolerable limits? The stakes for the American people were more substantive as well. For the uninsured and the uninsurable, the stakes were the difference between regular access to quality care and a patchwork of critical care cobbled together in emergency rooms and free clinics. For all Americans, the insured as well as the uninsured, the stakes were runaway health care costs that limit our ability to spend money on other necessities, or costs brought under control, with savings ultimately reducing the federal deficit. Those on the left and the right seem to believe that, by holding out, their side could have achieved all their goals, but the truth is that American politics is about compromise, and a health care reform proposal that didn't try to incorporate multiple views and goals was probably not going to be passed at all, especially given the tenuous nature of the Democratic majority in the Senate. What was at stake in bringing the industry groups to the table in the health care reform effort was the very fate of health care in America. Whether or not the reform was strong enough to improve it remains to be seen.

▶ Summary With Key Terms

Theories of **pluralist democracy** (359) emphasize the importance of political groups, what Madison referred to as **factions** (375), in enhancing representation and helping people get what they want from the political system. Two key kinds of groups in American politics are **political parties** (360), which organize in order to seek control of government, and **interest groups** (375), whose goal is to influence government decisions.

Political parties link voters and elected officials, overcome government fragmentation, and help provide, through the promotion of **partisanship** (360), a coherent ideological opposition to the party in power. Parties have three components. The official party structure, or **party organization** (360), gets people elected to office through the process of **electioneering** (360), which includes, among other steps, the formal **nominating conventions** (361). The officials, once elected, form the **party-in-government** (361), whose job includes **governing** (361). The **party-in-the-electorate** (362) encompasses all the people whose **party identification** (362) ties them to the party, including the most active and loyal members, who form the **party base** (362). These three components come together in the **responsible party model** (363)—an ideal model of how parties can provide an essential linkage in democratic politics.

The history of parties in the United States has evolved from an age of **party machines** (365), where **party bosses** (365) controlled candidates and officeholders, partly through the practice of **patronage** (365). Reforms, including the introduction of **party primaries** (366), made the old machines obsolete by making the parties more democratic. Periods when one party has majority control of most elements of government are called **party eras** (366), signaled by a critical election and in existence until citizens switch their allegiance to another party through a political **realignment** (366). **Dealignment** (367) takes place if voters change their party ID to identify as independents instead. The parties stand for different ideologies and policies, as can be seen in their **party platforms** (368). The preferences of their bases, or **party activists** (370), make them more different, while the need to win moderate voters in national campaigns pushes them back to the middle.

Interest groups can enhance democracy by increasing citizens' opportunities for representation and participation; by educating policymakers; and by assisting in building agendas, providing program alternatives, and monitoring programs. But many groups, especially when their goals involve the provision of **collective goods** (377) accessible to all, have difficulty getting members to join and contribute to their efforts because of the **free rider problem** (377). They try to combat this problem by offering **selective incentives** (377): **material** (377), **solidarity** (377), or **expressive benefits** (377). Interest groups take several forms. Depending on the type of representation they are seeking to enhance and the kind of goals they pursue, they can be **economic interest groups** (378), **equal opportunity interest groups** (378), **public interest groups** (378), or government interest groups.

Interest groups seek to influence policymakers through an activity called **lobbying** (376). Lobbyists, many of whom work for the government at one time in a practice called the **revolving door** (380), may engage in **direct lobbying** (379), targeting Congress—through a variety of strategies including contributions to **political action committees** (381)—the president, the bureaucracy, and the Courts. **Indirect lobbying** (379) involves influencing the public to pressure lawmakers to do what the groups want. Techniques include the use of **issue advocacy ads** (382) and **social protest** (383). When such lobbying by the public is spontaneous, we call it **grassroots lobbying** (383). When it is manipulated by corporate or organized interests it is called **astroturf lobbying** (383). Interest groups' success at getting what they want can depend on their access to resources—primarily money, leadership, members, and information.

Explore this subject further with suggested readings, movies, and web sites at http://republic-brief.cqpress.com, where you'll also find study aids, practice quizzes, flash cards, and Internet exercises.

VOTE HERE

BOARD OF ELECTIONS AND ETHICS
DISTRICT OF COLUMBIA

Chapter 12

Voting, Campaigns, and Elections

▶ What's at Stake?

State of the Union addresses are well-attended affairs. In 2010, as Barack Obama stood at the podium with the Speaker of the House and the vice president sitting behind him, he looked out on an august assembly that included six black-robed members of the nation's highest court sitting in the very front rows.

Imagine the justices' surprise when the president took the highly unusual step of calling them out in front of the entire nation for a decision he said was "wrong." Targeting a ruling the Court had just handed down in a case called *Citizens United v. Federal Election Commission*, Obama said:

> Last week, the Supreme Court reversed a century of law to open the floodgates for special interests—including foreign companies—to spend without limit in our elections. Well, I don't think American elections should be bankrolled by America's most powerful interests, and worse, by foreign entities. They should be decided by the American people, and that's why I'm urging Democrats and Republicans to pass a bill that helps to right this wrong.

The *Citizens United* case reversed a significant part of the Bipartisan Campaign Reform Act of 2002 (BCRA), also

known as the McCain-Feingold Act, that had been passed after much debate in 2002. The act had prevented corporations and unions from spending money from their treasuries (as opposed to specially created political action committees) on television advertising for or against political candidates immediately before an election. While the ruling left earlier restrictions on corporate election spending in place, the majority penned a broadly worded decision that endorsed the free speech rights of corporations. The *New York Times* called it "a sharp doctrinal shift" that "will have major political and practical consequences," that would "reshape the way elections were conducted."[1]

The president's remarks were immediately controversial, starting with the words "not true" apparently mouthed by a head-shaking Justice Samuel Alito.[2] Commentators debated the propriety of the president of the United States publicly criticizing the actions of another branch of government. Some thought he had overstepped his bounds, and others argued that the words were a well-deserved rebuke of the Court.

No doubt knowing that his remarks would cause a firestorm, Obama nonetheless chose to make them in an unmistakably severe tone. Were they deserved? Was the *Citizens United* decision really that big a deal? What was at stake after all in the decision to allow corporate interests to spend without restraint in U.S. elections? We return to this question after we examine the way that elections are held, and funded, in the United States.

Although we pride ourselves on our democratic government, Americans seem to have a love-hate relationship with the idea of campaigns and voting. On the one hand, many citizens believe that elections do not accomplish anything, that elected officials ignore the wishes of the people, and that government is run for the interests of the elite rather than the many. Voters in 2008 were unusually motivated, turning out at a rate of just over 60 percent; typically only about half of the eligible electorate votes.

On the other hand, however, when it is necessary to choose a leader, whether the captain of a football team, the president of a dorm, or a local precinct chairperson, the first instinct of most Americans is to call an election. Even though there are other ways to choose leaders—picking the oldest, the wisest, or the strongest; holding a lottery; or asking for volunteers—Americans almost always prefer an election. We elect over half a million public officials in America.[3] This means we have a lot of elections—more elections more often for more officials than in any other democracy.

In this chapter we examine the complicated place of elections in American politics and American culture. You will learn about Americans' ambivalence about the vote and the reasons that only about half of the citizenry even bother to exercise what is supposed to be a precious right; how voters go about making decisions, and how this in turn influences the character of presidential elections; and the organizational and strategic aspects of running for the presidency.

Exercising the Right to Vote in America
The costs of voting and not voting

We argued in Chapter 10 that even without being well informed and following campaigns closely, Americans can still cast intelligent votes reflecting their best interests. But what does it say about the American citizen that, in a typical presidential election, barely half of the adult population votes? In off-year congressional elections, in primaries, and in many state and local elections held at different times from the presidential contest, the rates of participation drop even lower.

Who Votes and Who Doesn't?

Many political observers, activists, politicians, and political scientists worry about the extent of nonvoting in the United States.[4] When people do not vote, they have no voice in choosing their leaders, their policy preferences are not registered, and they do not develop as active citizens. Some observers fear that their abstention signals an alienation from the political process.

From survey data, we know quite a lot about who votes and who doesn't in America in terms of their age, gender, income, education, and racial and ethnic makeup:

- *Age.* Older citizens consistently vote at higher rates. For example, 69 percent of those aged 45 to 60 years reported voting in the 2008 election, compared to 51 percent of those aged 18 to 29 years. This gap of 18 percent, however, is a bit smaller than it had been in previous elections (for example, 21 percent in 2004).[5]
- *Gender.* Since 1984 women have been voting at a higher rate than men, although the differences are typically only 3 or 4 percent. For example, in the 2008 presidential election the turnout rates for women and men were 65.7 and 61.5 percent, respectively.[6]
- *Income.* The likelihood of voting goes up steadily with income. For example, in 2008 only 49 percent of those making $10,000 or less reported voting, compared to 82 percent of those earning $150,000 or more.[7]
- *Education.* Education is consistently one of the strongest predictors of turnout. For instance, in the 2008 election, only 39 percent of those with less than a high school education voted, compared to almost 72 percent of those who attended some college or got a bachelor's degree; 82.7 percent of those with advanced degrees voted.
- *Race and ethnicity.* Turnout among members of racial and ethnic minority groups has traditionally been lower than that of whites. But that changed in 2008, with an African American as the Democratic nominee. Turnout for blacks was 65 percent, virtually tied with non-Hispanic whites. Hispanic turnout increased in 2008 to 49 percent, the same level as Asians for that year.[8]

When we add these characteristics together, the differences are quite substantial. Compare, for example, the turnout among 18- to 24-year-old males with less than a high school education (only 25.5 percent) with the turnout rate for females aged 65 to 74 years with advanced degrees (87.6 percent).[9] By virtue of their different turnout rates, some groups in American society are receiving much better representation than others. The same patterns hold true and are even more pronounced for types of political engagement other than voting, such as actively working for a party or candidate in distributing literature, staffing the phone banks during a get-out-the-vote drive, or making financial contributions.[10] The upshot is that our elected officials are indebted to and hear much more from the higher socioeconomic ranks in society. They do not hear from and are not elected by the low-participation "have nots."[11]

Why Americans Don't Vote

As we have noted elsewhere, compared with other democratic nations, the United States has low voter turnout levels. Despite overall increases in education, age, and income, which generally increase the number of voters, presidential election turnout rates have barely gotten over the 60 percent mark for more than thirty years (and midterm congressional turnout rates have been much lower).[12] (See Figure 12.1.) What accounts for such low turnout rates in a country where 82 percent of adults say voting is important to democracy[13]—indeed, in a country that often prides itself on being one of the best and oldest examples of democracy in the world? The question of low and declining voter turnout in the United States poses a tremendous puzzle for political scientists, who have focused on six factors to try to explain this mystery.

Legal Obstacles

Voter turnout provides a dramatic illustration of our theme that rules make a difference in who wins and who loses in politics. The rules that govern elections vary in democracies around the world, yielding quite different rates of turnout. For example, in many other democracies, it is the government, not the individual voter, that bears the responsibility for registering citizens to vote, and in some countries—Australia, Belgium, and Italy, for example—voting is required by law. Turnout rates in these countries are high.[14] But in the United States, several election rules actually make it more difficult for voters to exercise their right to vote, not only by requiring advance registration but also by limiting voting to a single weekday when most people have to work, or simply by providing for so many elections that citizens turnout with "voter fatigue." The low turnout that results may be an accidental consequence of laws intended for other purposes, but in some cases politicians support those laws in the belief that high turnout will benefit the other party or be harmful to stable government.

A number of reform efforts have attempted to ease the burden of casting a ballot. Congress passed the National Voter Registration Act of 1993, or the **Motor Voter Bill** as it is more commonly called, which requires the states to take a more

Figure 12.1

Voter Turnout in Presidential and Midterm House Elections, 1932–2008

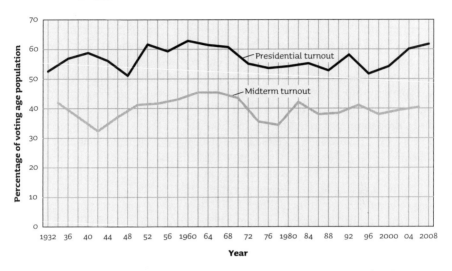

Source: Presidential data through 1976: *The New York Times Almanac*, 2005. For midterm elections through 1978, U.S. Census Bureau, 2000 Statistical Abstract; for presidential and midterm elections from 1980 on: Michael MacDonald, United States Elections Project, "Turnout 1980-2008.xls," http://elections.gmu.edu/Turnout 1980-2008.xls.

Note: The estimates here (1980–2008) exclude adults not eligible to vote (felons and non-citizens), which became a significant segment of the population in the mid-1970s. The figures for years prior to 1980 are for voting turnout as a percentage of the adult population.

active role in registering people to vote, including providing registration opportunities when applying for a driver's license or at the welfare office. In addition, some states have instituted the option to register on an election day, and Oregon has even gone as far as having its elections by mail. Each reform has marginally increased the numbers of people voting, but on the whole the results have been a disappointment to reformers. An exhaustive review of the research concluded that, even with obstacles to voting removed, "for many people, voting remains an activity from which there is virtually no gratification-instrumental, expressive, or otherwise."[15]

Politicians have been reluctant to pass major electoral reforms because of fears about whom the beneficiaries of such changes might be. The conventional wisdom is that Democrats would benefit from efforts to increase turnout because Republicans are already motivated enough to turn out under current laws, but this expectation (or fear) does not seem to have been borne out by our experience with the Motor Voter Bill. In the wake of the 2000 presidential election, and after reports of voting irregularities and long lines at the polls in the 2004 presidential election, calls for various sorts of reform have been louder and more widespread than ever, and state legislators around the country are now grappling with the issue.

Attitude Changes

Political scientists have found that some of the low voter turnout in this country is accounted for by changes over time in psychological orientations or attitudes toward politics.[16] For one thing, if people feel that they do not or cannot make a difference and that government is not responsive to their wishes, they often don't bother to vote. Lower feelings of political efficacy lead to less participation.

A second changed orientation that has proved important in explaining low turnout is partisanship. There was a distinct decline in Americans' attachments to the two major political parties in the 1960s and 1970s. With a drop in party identification came a drop in voting levels. This decline, however, has leveled off, and in recent years there has even been a slight increase in the percentage of citizens saying they identify as Democrats or Republicans. This slight increase in partisanship may have stemmed the decline in turnout that was apparent from the late 1960s through the 1980s.

Attitudes, of course, do not change without some cause; they reflect citizens' reactions to what they see in the political world. It is easy to understand why attitudes have changed since the relatively tranquil 1950s. Amid repeated scandal and increasing partisanship, our public airwaves have been dominated by negative information about and images of the leadership in Washington, D.C. The Bush administration did enjoy a period of good feeling in the aftermath of the September 11 attacks as the nation rallied against the threat of terrorism, but that dissipated as politics got back to usual. President Obama ran successfully by raising expectations for a more inclusive, cleaner, and less partisan politics. Many in the electorate bought the message of hope, and the United States saw the highest turnout levels in decades. However, while Obama was able to pass quite a bit of legislation, the deep partisan differences that divide the parties and the complexities of our economic and environmental problems dashed (the possibly unrealistic) hope of many voters. In 2010, Democratic voter turnout, especially among the young, was down, perhaps reflecting, in part, frustration with Obama's inability to change the tone as he had promised he would, and also with the continued partisanship in politics. The election of a Republican majority to the House, however, did not seem designed to reduce partisanship.

Voter Mobilization

Another factor that political scientists argue has led to lower turnout from the 1960s into the 1990s is a change in the efforts of politicians, interest groups, and especially political parties to make direct contact with people during election campaigns.[17] **Voter mobilization** includes contacting people—especially supporters—to inform them about the election and to persuade them to vote. It can take the form of making phone calls, knocking on doors, or even supplying rides to the polls. As the technology of campaigns, especially the use of television, developed and expanded in the 1980s and 1990s, fewer resources were used for the traditional shoe-leather efforts of direct contacts with voters, but solid evidence indicates that personal contacts do a

Vote Smart

Volunteer members of Project Vote Smart, liberals and conservatives alike, reach out to citizens to inform them about the voting records and backgrounds of thousands of candidates and elected officials so that voters can make informed decisions. The group accepts no funding from any organization, special interest group, or industry as part of its effort to maintain its neutral, nonbiased platform.

better job of getting out the vote than do mass mailing and telephone calls.[18] In recent campaigns, both Democrats and Republicans have increased their efforts at voter mobilization. They and a growing number of interest groups are combining computer technology with personal contacts as an integral part of their overall campaigns.[19] The increases in turnout that we have seen in the last couple of presidential elections are attributable, at least in part, to these efforts.[20]

Decrease in Social Connectedness

Some of the overall decline in voter turnout toward the end of the last century is due to larger societal changes rather than to citizen reactions to parties and political leaders. *Social connectedness* refers to the number of organizations people participate in and how tightly knit their communities and families are—that is, how well integrated they are into the society in which they live. The evidence indicates that people are increasingly likely to live alone and to be single, new to their communities, and isolated from organizations. As individuals loosen or altogether lose their ties to the larger community, they have less of a stake in participating in communal decisions—and less support for participatory activities. Lower levels of social connectedness have been an important factor in accounting for the low turnout in national elections.[21]

Generational Changes

Events occurring in the formative years of a generation continue to shape its members' orientation toward politics throughout their lives and can also account for varying turnout levels. This is different from the observation that people are more likely to vote as they get older. For instance, those age groups (cohorts) that came of age after the 1960s show much lower levels of attachment to politics, and they vote at lower rates than do their parents or grandparents. Some research suggests that generational differences account for much or most of the turnout decline at the end of the 1900s. That is, people who once voted have not stopped voting; rather they are dying and are being replaced by younger, less politically engaged voters. The result is lower turnout overall.[22] Of course, it is possible for this trend to be reversed as events and personalities politicize and mobilize new generations of citizens.

The Rational Nonvoter

A final explanation for the puzzle of low voter turnout in America considers that, for some people, not voting may be the rational choice. This explanation suggests that the question to ask is not, "Why don't people vote?" but rather, "Why does anyone vote?" The definition of *rational* means that the benefits of an action outweigh the costs. It is rational for us to do those things from which we get back more than we put in. Voting demands our resources, time, and effort. Given those costs, if someone views voting primarily as a way to influence government and sees no other benefits from it, it becomes a largely irrational act.[23] That is, no one individual's vote can change the course of an election unless the election would otherwise be a tie, and the probability of that happening in a presidential election is small (though as the 2000 election showed, it is not impossible).

For many people, however, the benefits of voting go beyond the likelihood that they will affect the outcome of the election. In fact, studies have demonstrated that turnout decisions are not really based on our thinking that our votes will determine the outcome. Rather, we achieve other kinds of benefits from voting. It feels good to do what we think we are supposed to do or to help, however little, the side or the causes we believe in. Plus, we get social rewards from our politically involved friends for voting (and avoid sarcastic remarks for not voting). These benefits accrue no matter which side wins.

Does Nonvoting Matter?

What difference does it make that some people vote and others do not? There are two ways to tackle this question. One approach is to ask whether election outcomes would be different if nonvoters were to participate. The other approach is to ask whether higher levels of nonvoting indicate that democracy is not healthy. Both questions, of course, concern important potential consequences of low participation in our elections.

Studies of the likely effects of nonvoting come up with contradictory answers. A traditional, and seemingly logical, approach is to note that nonvoters, being disproportionately poor and less educated, have social and economic characteristics that are more common among Democrats than among Republicans. Therefore, were these people to vote, we could expect that Democratic candidates would do better. Some polling results support this thinking. Pollsters asked registered voters a number of questions to judge how likely it was that they would actually vote in elections for House members. When the voting intentions of all registered voters and the subset of likely voters were compared, the likely voters were distinctly more Republican. If this were to hold true generally, we could conclude that nonvoting works to the disadvantage of Democratic candidates. One political scholar found some evidence of this for the 1980 presidential election and concluded that a much higher turnout among nonvoters would have made the election closer and that Carter might even have won reelection.[24] Similarly, when political scientists have run simulations to test whether full turnout would alter the results in elections for the U.S. Senate, the share of the vote for Democratic candidates is increased, but given that these elections are not particularly close, the extra votes would seldom change the winner of the elections.[25]

Undermining this interpretation are findings from most other presidential elections. There we find that nonvoters' preferences are quite responsive to short-term factors, so they go disproportionately for the winning candidate. Because these voters are less partisan and have less intensely held issue positions, they are moved more easily by the short-term campaign factors favoring one party or the other. In most presidential elections, nonvoters' participation would have increased the winner's margin only slightly or not changed things at all.[26] Interviews taken shortly after the two most recent presidential elections suggest that those who did not vote would have broken for the winner, Bush in 2004 and Obama in 2008.[27] The potential effects of nonvoters being mobilized, therefore, are probably not as consistently pro-Democratic as popular commentary suggests.

> The potential effects of nonvoters being mobilized . . . are probably not as consistently pro-Democratic as popular commentary suggests.

Although low turnout might not affect who wins an election, we have made it clear that elections do more than simply select leaders. How might nonvoting affect the quality of democratic life in America? Nonvoting can influence the stability and legitimacy of democratic government. The victor in close presidential elections, for example, must govern the country, but as critics often point out, as little as 25 percent of the eligible electorate may have voted for the winner. When a majority of the electorate sits out an election, the entire governmental process may begin to lose legitimacy in society at large. Nonvoting can also have consequences for the nonvoter. As we have noted, failure to participate politically can aggravate already low feelings of efficacy and produce higher levels of political estrangement. To the extent that being a citizen is an active pursuit, unhappy, unfulfilled, and unconnected citizens seriously damage the quality of democratic life for themselves and for the country as a whole.

How the Voter Decides
Many factors determine the final choice

Putting an X next to a name on a ballot or pulling a lever on a voting machine or even putting your finger on a party icon on a touch-screen monitor to register a preference would seem like a pretty simple act. But although the action itself may be simple, the decision process behind the choice is anything but. A number of considerations go into our decision about how to vote.

Partisanship and Social Group Membership

The single biggest factor accounting for how people decide to vote is *party identification*. For most citizens, party ID is stable and long term, carrying over from one election to the next in what one scholar has called "a standing decision."[28] In 2008, for example, 89 percent of those identifying with the Democratic Party voted for Barack Obama, and 90 percent of those identifying with the Republican Party voted for John McCain.[29]

Under unusual circumstances, social group characteristics can exaggerate or override traditional partisan loyalties. The 1960 election, for instance, was cast in terms of whether the nation would elect its first Catholic president. In that context, religion was especially salient, and fully 82 percent of Roman Catholics supported John Kennedy, compared to just 37 percent of Protestants—a difference of 45 percentage points. Compare that to 1976, when the Democrats ran a devout Baptist, Jimmy Carter, for president. The percentage of Catholics voting Democratic dropped to 58 percent, while Protestants voting Democratic increased to 46 percent. The difference shrank to just 12 percent.

Gender, Race, and Ethnicity

It is not clear what impact gender plays in voting decisions. In Chapter 10 we discussed the gender gap in the positions men and women take on the issues, which has generally led women to be more likely to support the Democratic candidate. Since 1964, women have been more supportive of the Democratic candidate in every presidential election but one (they were not more likely to support Carter in 1976).[30] But women do not vote monolithically; for instance, married women are more conservative than single women.

It's an open question whether the gender of a candidate affects the women's vote. In statewide races, there is some evidence Republican and independent women will cross party lines to vote for Democratic women candidates, though the opposite is not true for Republican women candidates.[31] In the Super Tuesday 2008 Democratic primaries, a larger percentage of women than men voted for Hillary Clinton in fourteen out of sixteen states.[32] However, despite the speculation that the nomination of Sarah Palin as the Republican vice presidential candidate might sway some women to support the McCain-Palin ticket, there is little evidence in the 2008 exit polls to support that idea.

African Americans have tended to vote Democratic since the civil rights movement of the 1960s. In fact, African Americans have averaged just under 90 percent of the two-party vote for the Democratic candidate in recent presidential elections (1988 to 2004).[33] The nomination of Barack Obama, the first black to receive a major party's presidential nomination, increased the solidarity of the African

American vote even further in 2008. This was evident in the Democratic primaries, where the African American vote was a major factor, with 82 percent of it going for Obama, compared to 16 percent for Hillary Clinton. Having a black presidential candidate heightened the role of race in the general election as well. African American support for the Democratic ticket reached a record 95 percent, and the gap between black and white support for the Democratic ticket was substantially larger in 2008 (52 percent) than in 2004 (37 percent).[34]

Ethnicity is less predictive of the vote than race, partly because ethnic groups in the United States become politically diverse as they are assimilated into the system. Although immigrant groups have traditionally found a home in the Democratic Party, dating back to the days when the party machine would provide the one-stop shop for new immigrants seeking jobs, homes, and social connections, recent immigrant groups include Asians and Hispanics, both of which comprise diverse ethnic communities with distinct identities and varying partisan tendencies.[35] These diverse groups tend to support the Democratic Party, but each has subgroups that are distinctly more Republican: Vietnamese, in the case of Asians, and Cubans, among Latino groups.[36] That said, in 2008, Obama received the overwhelming portion of Hispanic votes. Nationally 67 percent of Latino voters supported Obama, but this support varied by state, from 74 percent in California to 57 percent in Florida. However, this was a substantial shift in the Florida Latino vote—which is largely Cuban—from a mere 44 percent for John Kerry in 2004.

Issues and Policy

An idealized view of elections would have highly attentive citizens paying careful attention to the different policy positions offered by the candidates and then, perhaps aided by informed policy analyses from the media, casting their ballots for the candidates who best represent their preferred policy solutions. In truth, as we know by now, American citizens are not "ideal," and the role played by issues is less obvious and more complicated than the ideal model would predict.

For one thing, people are busy and, in many cases, rely on party labels to tell them what they need to know about the candidates rather than relying on the policy stances the candidates support.[37] People know where they stand on "easy" issues like capital punishment or prayer in schools, but some issues, like economic policy or health care reform, are very complicated, and many citizens tend to tune them out.[38] Adding to the complexity, the media do not generally cover issues in depth. Instead, they much prefer to focus on the horse-race aspect of elections, looking at who is ahead in the polls rather than what substantive policy issues mean for the nation.[39] As we discussed in Chapter 10, people process a lot of policy-relevant information in terms of their impressions of candidates (on-line processing) rather than as policy information. They are certainly influenced by policy information, but they cannot necessarily articulate their opinions and preferences on policy.

Although calculated policy decisions by voters are rare, policy considerations do have a real impact on voters' decisions. To see that, it is useful to distinguish between prospective and retrospective voting. The idealized model of policy voting with which we opened this section is **prospective voting**, in which voters base their decisions on what will happen in the future if they vote for a candidate—what policies will be enacted, and what values will be emphasized in policy. Prospective voting requires a good deal of information that average voters, as we have seen, do not always have or even want. While all voters do some prospective voting and, by election time, are usually aware of the candidates' major issue positions, it is primarily party activists and political elites who engage in the full-scale policy analysis that prospective voting entails.

Instead, most voters supplement their spotty policy information and interest with their evaluation of how they think the country is doing, how the economy is performing, and how well the incumbents are carrying out their jobs. They engage in **retrospective voting**, casting their votes as signs of approval or to signal their desire for change.[40] In presidential elections, this means that voters consistently look back at the state of the economy, at perceived successes or failures in foreign policy, and at domestic issues like education, gun control, or welfare reform. In 1980 Ronald Reagan skillfully focused on voter frustration in the presidential debate by asking voters this question: "Next Tuesday, all of you will go to the polls, and stand there in the polling place and make a decision. I think when you make that decision it might be well if you would ask yourself, are you better off than you were four years ago?"[41] Politicians have been reprising that question ever since. In 2008 the situation was more complicated, as no incumbent was running, but nonetheless Democrat Barack Obama tried to make the election a retrospective referendum on the Bush years, tying Republican John McCain to Bush's record whenever he could. But in the 2010 midterm elections Republicans managed to turn the strategy back on Obama, pegging the stubbornly bad economy to his policies and tapping into voter angst about the economy to turn Democrats out of office.

Retrospective voting is considered to be "easy" decision making as opposed to the more complex decision making involved in prospective voting because one only has to ask, "How have things been going?" as a guide to whether to support the current party in power. Retrospective voting is also seen as a useful way of holding politicians accountable, not for what they said or are saying in a campaign, but for what they or members of their party in power *did*. Some scholars believe that this type of voting is all that is needed for democracy to function well.[42] In practice, voters combine these two voting strategies, deciding partly on what candidates promise to do and partly on what incumbents have done.

The Candidates

In addition to considerations of party, personal demographics, and issues, voters also base their decisions on judgments about candidates as individuals. What goes into voters' images of candidates?

Some observers have claimed that voters view candidate characteristics much as they would a beauty or personality contest. There is little support, however, for the notion that voters are won over merely by good looks or movie-star qualities. Consider, for example, that Richard Nixon almost won against John Kennedy, who had good looks, youth, and a quick wit in his favor. Then, in 1964, the awkward, gangly Lyndon Johnson defeated the much more handsome and articulate Barry Goldwater in a landslide. In contrast, ample evidence indicates that voters form clear opinions about candidate qualities that are relevant to governing. These include trustworthiness, competence, experience, and sincerity. Citizens also make judgments about the ability of the candidates to lead the nation and to withstand the pressures of the presidency. Ronald Reagan, for example, was admired widely for his ability to stay above the fray of Washington politics and to see the humor in many situations. He appeared, to most Americans, to be in control. By contrast, his predecessor, Jimmy Carter, seemed overwhelmed by the job.

The 2008 campaign allowed voters to develop quite distinct images of Barack Obama and John McCain. Many more agreed that McCain "has the right experience to be president" (54 percent versus 36 percent for Obama). However, this potential advantage was trumped by Obama's success with his "change" theme. Fifty-four percent agreed that Obama "can bring the kind of change the country needs," compared to just 39 percent who felt that statement applied to McCain. Voters also perceived differences in temperament. Obama achieved a substantial advantage on having "a better personality and temperament to be president" (55 percent to McCain's 37 percent). One of the many things that made Ronald Reagan popular was the slogan "It's morning again in America," which symbolized for many his optimistic outlook for the country. On this dimension, when voters were asked which candidate "is more optimistic," Obama fared very well, with 62 percent of respondents (versus 30 percent for McCain).[43] It is no surprise that Obama stuck with the theme of "change you can believe in," while McCain tried to convince voters to put more weight on experience and service to the country.

Presidential Campaigns
The long, expensive road to the White House

Being president of the United States is undoubtedly a difficult challenge, but so is getting the job in the first place. It is a long, expensive, and grueling "road to the White House," as the media like to call it.

Getting Nominated

Each of the major parties (and the minor parties, too) needs to come up with a single viable candidate from the long list of party members with ambitions to serve in the White House. How the candidate is chosen will determine the sort of candidate chosen. Remember, in politics the rules are always central to shaping the outcome. Prior to 1972, primary election results were mostly considered "beauty contests" because their results were not binding. But since 1972, party nominees for the presidency have been chosen in primaries, taking the power away from the party elite and giving it to the activist members of the party who care enough to turn out and vote in the party primaries.

The Pre-primary Season

It is hard to say when a candidate's presidential campaign actually begins. Potential candidates may begin planning and thinking about running for the presidency in childhood. Bill Clinton is said to have wanted to be president since high school, when he shook President Kennedy's hand. At one time or another, many people in politics consider going for the big prize, but there are several crucial steps between wishful thinking and actually running for the nomination. Candidates vary somewhat in their approach to the process, but most of those considering a run for the White House follow similar steps.

Potential candidates usually test the waters unofficially. They talk to friends and fellow politicians to see just how much support they can count on, and they often leak news of their possible candidacy to the press to see how it is received in the media. This period of jockeying for money, lining up top campaign consultants, generating media buzz, and getting commitments of potential support from party and interest group notables even before candidates announce they are running is called the **invisible primary**. If these efforts have positive results, candidates file with the Federal Election Commission (FEC) to set up a committee to receive funds so that they can officially explore their prospects. The formation of an *exploratory committee* can be exploited as a media event by the candidate, using the occasion to get free publicity for the launching of the still-unannounced campaign. Candidates then need to acquire a substantial war chest to pay for the enormous expenses of running for the nomination. With the money in the bank, the potential candidate must use the pre-primary season to position himself or herself as a credible prospect with the media. It is no coincidence that in the last eight elections, the parties' nominees have all held prominent government offices and have entered the field with some media credibility. Incumbents especially have a huge advantage here. The final step of the pre-primary season is the official announcement of candidacy. Like the formation of the exploratory committee, this statement is part of the campaign itself. Promises are made to supporters, agendas are set, media attention is captured, and the process is under way.

Primaries and Caucuses

The actual fight for the nomination takes place in the state party caucuses and primaries in which delegates to the parties' national conventions are chosen. In a **party caucus**, grassroots members of the party in each community gather in selected locations to discuss the current candidates. They then vote for delegates from that locality who will be sent to the national convention, or who will go on to larger caucuses at the state level to choose the national delegates. Attending a caucus is time consuming, and other than in the 2004 Iowa caucus, where the turnout doubled from its 2000 level, participation rates are frequently in the single digits.[44] However, 2008 marked a big change, with most states setting records for primary and caucus turnout, especially on the Democratic side, where the heated nomination battle between Barack Obama and Hillary Clinton sparked unusual levels of interest. Most states still hold primary elections, but in recent years there has been a trend toward caucuses, the method used in fifteen states.[45]

The most common device for choosing delegates to the national conventions is the **presidential primary**. Primary voters cast ballots that send to the conventions those delegates who are committed to voting for a particular candidate. Presidential primaries can be either open or closed, depending on the rules the state party organizations adopt, and these can change from year to year. Any registered voter may vote in an **open primary**, regardless of party affiliation. At the polling place, the voter chooses the ballot of the party whose primary he or she wants to vote in. Only registered party members may vote in a **closed primary**. A subset of this type of primary is the semi-open primary, open only to registered party members and those not registered as members of another party.

The Democrats also send elected state officials, including Democratic members of Congress and governors, to their national conventions. Some of these officials are "superdelegates," able to vote as free agents, but the rest must reflect the state's primary vote.[46]

The parties' primary rules differ not only in terms of whom they allow to vote but also in how they distribute delegates among the candidates. The Democrats generally use a method of proportional representation, in which the candidates get the percentage of delegates equal to the percentage of the primary vote they win (provided they get at least 15 percent). Republican rules run from proportional representation, to winner take all (the candidate with the most votes gets all the delegates, even if he or she does not win an absolute majority), to direct voting for delegates (the delegates are not bound to vote for a particular candidate at the convention), to the absence of a formal system (caucus participants may decide how to distribute the delegates).

State primaries also vary in the times at which they are held, with various states engaged in **front-loading**, vying to hold their primaries first in order to gain maximum exposure in the media and power over the nomination. By tradition and state law, the Iowa caucuses and the New Hampshire primary are the first contests for delegates. As a result, they get tremendous attention, from both candidates and the media—much more than their contribution to the delegate count would justify. This is why in 1998 other states began moving their primaries earlier in the season.[47] The process of moving primary dates up continued in 2008 so that on February 5, twenty-four states plus American Samoa had their primaries and caucuses in an event that some termed "tsunami Tuesday."

The consequence of such front-loading is that candidates must have a full war chest and be prepared to campaign nationally from the beginning. Traditionally, winners of early primaries could use that success to raise more campaign funds to continue the battle. With the primaries stacked at the beginning, however, this becomes much harder. When the winner can be determined within weeks of the first primary, it is less likely that a dark horse, or unknown candidate, can emerge. The process favors well-known, well-connected, and especially well-funded candidates. Again, incumbents have an enormous advantage here. The heavily front-loaded primary has almost no defenders, but it presents a classic example of the problems of collective action that politics cannot always solve.[48] No single state has an incentive to hold back and reduce its power for the good of the whole; each state is driven to maximize its influence by strategically placing its primary early in the pack.

In most of the crowded primaries in recent years there has been a clear **front-runner**, a person whom many assume will win the nomination before the primaries even begin. Early front-runner status is positive because it means the candidate has raised significant money, has a solid organization, and receives more media coverage than his or her opponents. But success in primaries comes not just from getting a majority of the votes but also from being perceived as a winner, and front-runners are punished if they fail to live up to lofty expectations—the fate shared by Republican Rudy Giuliani and Democrat Hillary Clinton in 2008. The goal for all the other candidates is to attack the front-runner so as to drive down his or her support, while maneuvering into position as the chief alternative. Then, if the front-runner stumbles, as often happens, each of the attacking candidates hopes to emerge from the pack.

Generally a candidate's campaign strategy becomes focused on developing **momentum**, the perception by the press, the public, and the other candidates in the field that one is on a roll, and that polls, primary victories, endorsements, and funding are all coming one's way. Since all candidates in a primary are from the same party, voters cannot rely on partisanship as a cue in making up their minds. Considerations of electability—which candidate has the best chance to triumph in November—are important as voters decide whom to support, and here candidates who seem to have momentum can have an advantage (see Figure 12.2). Developing momentum helps to distinguish one's candidacy in a crowded field and is typically established in the early primaries.

The Convention

Since 1972, delegates attending the national conventions have not had to decide who the parties' nominees would be. However, two official actions continue to take place at the conventions. First, as we discussed in Chapter 11, the parties hammer out and approve their platforms, the documents in which parties set out their distinct issue positions. Second, the vice presidential candidate is named officially. The choice of the vice president is up to the presidential nominee. Traditionally, the choice was made to balance the ticket (ideologically, regionally, or even, when Democrat Walter Mondale chose Geraldine Ferraro in 1984, by gender). Bill Clinton's choice of Al Gore was a departure from this practice, as he tapped a candidate much like himself—a Democratic moderate from a southern state. In 2000 George W. Bush picked

Figure 12.2

Preferences for 2008 Democratic Presidential Candidates

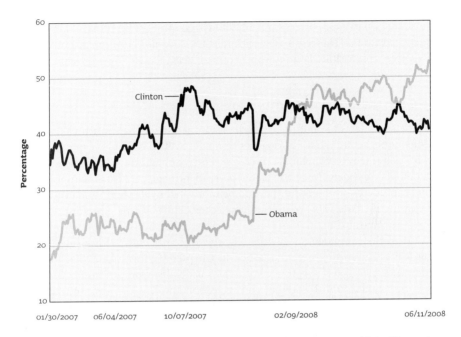

Clinton

Obama

01/30/2007 06/04/2007 10/07/2007 02/09/2008 06/11/2008

Source: Real Clear Politics, "RCP Poll Average: Democratic Presidential Nomination," www.realclearpolitics.com/epolls/2008/president/us/democratic_presidenti al_nomination-191.html.

Dick Cheney, a man whose considerable experience in the federal government was expected to offset Bush's relative lack of it. In 2004 liberal Bostonian Kerry returned to the regional and ideological balancing principle, choosing moderate North Carolina senator John Edwards as his running mate, though he broke with tradition by announcing his choice three weeks before his party's convention.

In 2008 Barack Obama chose Delaware senator Joe Biden as his running mate, going for an experienced hand with foreign policy background to shore up his own record. Democrats applauded his pick of Biden as one who would balance the ticket and showcased Obama's own judgment and decision-making skills. They had barely finished cheering their new nominee, however, when John McCain upstaged Obama with his own pick, Alaska governor Sarah Palin, who he felt would bolster his maverick credentials, help him energize his base, and bolster his standing with women. The choice was immediately controversial; wildly popular with religious conservatives, it was viewed with surprise and skepticism by Democrats and media commentators. There is no clear evidence that the vice presidential choice has significant electoral consequences, but the presidential nominees weigh it carefully nonetheless. If nothing else, the caliber of the nominee's choice for vice president is held to be an indication of the kind of appointments the nominee would make if elected.

Although their actual party business is limited, the conventions still provide the nominee with a "convention bump" in the polls. The harmonious coverage, the enthusiasm of party supporters, and even the staged theatrics seem to have a positive impact on viewers. The result is that candidates have usually, though not always, experienced a noticeable rise in the polls immediately following the conventions.

The General Election Campaign

After the candidates are nominated in late summer, there is a short break, at least for the public, before the traditional fall campaign. When the campaign begins, the goal of each side is to convince supporters to turn out and to get undecided voters to choose its candidate. Most voters, the party identifiers, will usually support their party's candidate, although they need to be motivated by the campaign to turn out and cast their ballots. Most of the battle in a presidential campaign is for the **swing voters**, the one-third or so of the electorate who have not made up their minds at the start of the campaign and who are open to persuasion by either side. As one would expect given the forces described in Chapter 11, this means that for both parties the general election strategy differs considerably from the strategy used to win a primary election. To win the general election, the campaigns move away from the sharp ideological tone used to motivate the party faithful in the primaries and "run to the middle" by making less ideological appeals.

In the general campaign, each side seeks to get its message across, to define the choice in terms that give its candidate the advantage. This massive effort to influence the information to which citizens are exposed requires a clear strategy, which begins with a plan for winning the states where the candidate will be competitive.

The Electoral College

Because our founders feared giving too much power to the volatile electorate, we do not actually vote for the president and vice president in presidential elections. Rather, we cast our votes in November for electors (members of the **Electoral College**), who in turn vote for the president in December. The Constitution provides for each state to have as many electoral votes as it does senators and representatives in Congress. Thus Alaska has three electoral votes (one for each of the state's U.S. senators and one for its sole member of the House of Representatives). By contrast, California has fifty-five electoral votes (two senators and fifty-three representatives). In addition, the Twenty-third Amendment gave the District of Columbia three electoral votes. There are 538 electoral votes in all; 270 are needed to win the presidency.

Electors are generally activist members of the party whose presidential candidate carried the state. In December, following the election, the electors meet and vote in their state capitals. In the vast majority of cases, they vote as expected, but

The Most Votes

In the 2000 presidential election, Al Gore won the popular vote, but George W. Bush received the most Electoral College votes, giving him the presidency. The Electoral College works on a mostly winner-take-all basis that three times in the course of our electoral history has not reflected the popular vote.

there are occasional "faithless electors" who vote for their own preferences. The results of the electors' choices in the states are then sent to the Senate, where the ballots are counted when the new session opens. If no candidate achieves a majority in the Electoral College, the Constitution calls for the House of Representatives to choose from the top three electoral vote winners. In this process, each state has one vote. Whenever the vote goes to the House, the Senate decides on the vice president, with each senator having a vote. This has happened only twice (the last time was in 1824), although some observers of the 2000 election speculated that that election, too, could have been decided in the House of Representatives if Florida's election had not been decided in the courts.

The importance of the Electoral College is that all the states but Maine and Nebraska operate on a winner-take-all basis. Thus the winner in California, even if he or she has less than half of the popular vote, wins all of the state's fifty-five electoral votes. Similarly, the loser in California may have won 49 percent of the popular vote but gets nothing in the Electoral College. It is possible, then, for the popular vote winner to lose in the Electoral College. This has happened only three times in our history, most recently in 2000, when Bush received an Electoral College majority even though Gore won the popular vote by more than half a million votes. Usually, however, the opposite happens: the Electoral College exaggerates the candidate's apparent majority. The 2008 election is typical of this exaggeration of the victory margin in the Electoral College. Obama got 52.9 percent of the popular vote, but his majority in the Electoral College was 67.8 percent. This exaggeration of the winning margin has the effect of legitimizing the winner's victory and allowing him to claim that he has a *mandate*—a broad popular endorsement—even if he won by a small margin of the popular vote.

The rules of the Electoral College give greater power to some states over others. The provision that all states get at least three electoral votes in the Electoral College means that citizens in the smaller states get proportionately greater representation in the Electoral College. Alaska, for example, sent one elector to the Electoral College for every 223,000 people, while California had one elector for every 645,000 residents.

However, this "advantage" is probably offset by the practice of winner take all, which focuses the candidates' attention on the largest states with the biggest payoff in electoral votes, especially the competitive or "battleground" states. Small states with few electoral votes or those that are safely in the corner of one party or the other are ignored (although California, a reliably Democratic state, still received sixty visits from McCain, forty-one of them for fundraising purposes).[49] Perennial battlegrounds get the most candidate attention. Ohio, for instance, saw forty-two campaign visits by McCain and forty-five by Obama. Indiana, until 2008 a safely Republican state, had rarely seen a presidential candidate in person or even in a commercial. But following his strong primary campaign in Indiana, Obama showed some strength in the Hoosier State (which neighbors his home state of Illinois) and targeted it with visits and heavy media advertising. The McCain campaign assumed that Indiana was safe for them and largely ignored it until it was too late. Indiana saw little of McCain, but a lot of Barack Obama, and he won the state by less than 1 percent and received all eleven of its electoral votes, turning it blue for the first time since 1964.

Over the years hundreds of bills have been introduced in Congress to reform or abolish the Electoral College, an especially urgent project for many Democrats after the 2000 election.[50] Major criticisms of the current system include the claims that the Electoral College is undemocratic because it is possible for the popular winner not to get a majority of the electoral votes, that in a very close contest the popular outcome could be dictated by a few "faithless electors" who vote their conscience rather than the will of the people of their states, and that the Electoral College distorts candidates' campaign strategies. The winner-take-all provision in all but two states puts a premium on a few large competitive states, which get a disproportionate share of the candidates' attention.

Few people deny the truth of these charges, and hardly anyone believes that if we were to start all over, the current Electoral College would be chosen as the best way to elect a president. Nevertheless, all the proposed alternatives also have problems or at least face serious criticisms.

Who Runs the Campaign?

Running a modern presidential campaign has become a highly specialized profession. Most presidential campaigns are led by an "amateur," a nationally prestigious chairperson who may serve as an adviser and assist in fundraising. However, the real work of the campaign is done by the professional staff the candidate hires. These may be people the candidate knows well and trusts, or they may be professionals who sign on for the duration of the campaign and then move on to another (see the *Profiles in Citizenship* in this chapter, on James Carville). Campaign work at the beginning of the twenty-first century is big business.

Some of the jobs include not only the well-known ones of campaign manager and strategist but also more specialized components tailored to the modern campaign's emphasis on information and money. For instance, candidates need to hire research teams to prepare position papers on issues so that the candidate can answer any question posed by potential supporters and the media. But researchers also engage in the controversial but necessary task of **oppo research**—delving into the background and vulnerabilities of the opposing candidate with an eye to exploiting his or her weaknesses. Central to the modern campaign's efforts to get and control the flow of information are pollsters and focus group administrators, who are critical for testing the public's reactions to issues and strategies. Media consultants try to get free coverage of the campaign whenever possible and to make the best use of the campaign's advertising dollars by designing commercials and print advertisements.

Candidates also need advance teams to plan and prepare their travel agendas, to arrange for crowds (and the signs they wave) to greet the candidates at airports, and even to reserve accommodations for the press. Especially in the primaries, staff devoted to fundraising are essential to ensure the constant flow of money necessary to grease the wheels of any presidential campaign. They work with big donors and engage in direct-mail campaigns to solicit money from targeted groups. Finally, of course, candidates need to hire a legal team to keep their campaigns in compliance with the regulations of the FEC and to file the required reports. In general, campaign consultants are able to provide specialized technical services that the parties' political committees cannot.[51]

Presenting the Candidate

An effective campaign begins with a clear understanding of how the candidate's strengths fit with the context of the times and the mood of the voters. To sell a candidate effectively, the claims to special knowledge, competence, or commitment must be credible.[52] As the campaigns struggle to control the flow of information about their candidates and influence how voters see their opponents, oppo research comes into play, sometimes complete with focus groups and poll testing. In fact, oppo research has become a central component in all elections, leading to the negative campaigning so prevalent in recent years.[53] Research on one's opponent, however, cannot compensate for the failure to define oneself in clear and attractive terms.

The Issues

Earlier we indicated that issues matter to voters as they decide how to vote. This means that issues must be central to the candidate's strategy for getting elected.

James Carville

James Carville found his calling and his salvation in his love affair with politics. "You know, I was never that great at anything," he says in that manic Louisiana drawl familiar to anyone who has watched the movie *The War Room* or seen him on CNN. "The only thing I was great at was being kind of, you know, a horrible student—a worse than bad lawyer. I sat in my office one day and said if I had to hire a lawyer I wouldn't hire me."

But the man loved politics—had done so since he was a kid, when larger-than-life figures walked the Louisiana landscape of his youth, people like Gov. Earl Long ("There's a great man! He's my guy!") and characters called "Pinhead Willie," "Coozan Dud," and "Wild Bill, Big Bad Bill Dodd." Ask him if politics was a big deal in his family when he was growing up in Carville, Louisiana (a town named for his postmaster grandfather), and he gives a single-word answer: "Huge."

So politics was the path he chose to get himself away from lawyering. He set up as a political consultant, finding the pace of electoral politics perfectly suited to his personal occupational challenges ("I have pretty serious attention problems and dyslexia and the whole dictionary of fashionable childhood diseases"). It was a life made to measure for him: "You're really determining something that profoundly matters to people all across the spectrum and it's something that, if you're like me and you've got a lot of energy left over—if you're a sprinter, not a distance runner—it's perfect. And you know at the end of the day if you've won or lost. How can you beat it? There's nothing that could be more fun."

With his brilliant mind and intuitive understanding of politics, Carville ran a couple of winning Pennsylvania campaigns and caught the attention of Bill Clinton in his 1992 run for the presidency. Carville headed up the Little Rock "War Room" and kept attention focused on the campaign's famous mantra—"It's the Economy, Stupid." Of course, Clinton won—and now Carville was at the top of his game. "And there was a time—it certainly passed—there was a time in my life where if I had to hire a political consultant I would have hired me. Now that's a great feeling. . . . And it was particularly great on the heels of knowing that I was a bad lawyer. It's not a very satisfying way to go through life, being bad and not liking what you do."

Carville's life must be superbly satisfying now. No longer running campaigns (he says he has become a victim of his own success, drawing more attention than the candidates he would work for), he is still active in the Democratic Party, appearing frequently as a commentator on television and with his wife, Republican Mary Matalin, on the lecture circuit.

Matalin was working for the first president Bush when she and Carville met (they ran opposing campaigns in 1992), and she has worked for Vice President Dick Cheney since that time. If you think "politics makes strange bedfellows," read their book, *All's Fair: Love, War and Running for President,* to see just how strange.

With the high-octane life their parents lead, it would seem that politics could hardly help being as "huge" for their two kids as it was for Carville (although he says since it's "the family business," they are not too impressed).

But it's hard to imagine that they will remain wholly unmoved by their father's powerful feelings about politics. Nobody could be. Leafing though a book of photographs of his beloved Louisiana, James Carville talks about politics with the passion and reverence of a man recalling a first love. His voice gets hushed with the intensity of his memories, reading passages out loud and getting so eager to share the stories that he impulsively gives us the book to keep.

Impulsive and emotional, Carville may be, but when it comes to assessing the day-to-day stake of politics, he is a sharp-eyed realist. He knows powerful people would prefer us to check out and let them have their way. "All these decisions are going to get made—doesn't matter whether you're involved in them," he says. "The school's going to go on, somebody's going to have the hiring policy, somebody's going to decide the curriculum, the hospitals are going to get built, somebody's going to have to decide where they are, who gets served, etc., etc. . . . the taxes are going to get collected. Whatever. Okay. Now what a lot of powerful people would like to tell you is, you don't worry your pretty little head with that. We'll take care of all these things and you don't need to, you know, you just have a couple of beers and eat some Doritos and watch the game."

He is amazed that people fall for the idea that they can't figure out complex issues. "None of this stuff is impenetrable. The only way that the political golden rule operates—that those who have got the gold make the rules—is if it's by default"— that is, if people fail to pay attention. More Carville wisdom:

On why politics matters:
There's a lot of things you can say about politics and politicians . . . some are corrupt and some are liars . . . but the one thing you can't say is that what they do doesn't matter. Because it matters profoundly. From where you put the intersection, to the park, to the taxes, to the bonds, you name it. Abortion, euthanasia, it doesn't matter. On a sliding scale of does the bridge get built or not, all of this is decided by politicians. So every criticism that a young person has of politics is valid until they get to the point that it doesn't matter. Then that's where the whole argument completely falls apart. Right on its face.

On keeping the republic:
The first thing we need to do is remove this thing that participating in public affairs in whatever form you want to is some kind of chore. I don't think it really is. I think it's kind of a privilege and it's fun. . . . I tell young people you have the right not to participate, but don't confuse the right to do something with the right thing to do. They are two distinct things. I think the biggest thing that young people can do is, when it comes to this, be guided by your passion. . . . It's a hell of a lot of fun. And it's a really fascinating thing. And you learn a lot. But the biggest thing you do is you actually get to make a difference.

From the candidate's point of view, there are two kinds of issues to consider when planning a strategy: valence issues and position issues.

Valence issues are policy matters on which the voters and the candidates share the same preference. These are what we might call "motherhood and apple pie" issues, because no one opposes them. Everyone is for a strong, prosperous economy; for America having a respected leadership role in the world; for fighting terrorism; for thrift in government; and for a clean environment. Similarly, everyone opposes crime and drug abuse, government waste, political corruption, and immorality.

Position issues have two sides. On abortion, there are those who are pro-life and those who are pro-choice. On military engagements such as Vietnam or Iraq, there are those who favor pursuing a military victory and those who favor just getting out. Many of the hardest decisions for candidates are on position issues: although a clear stand means that they will gain some friends, it also guarantees that they will make some enemies. Realistic candidates, who want to win as many votes as possible, try to avoid being clearly identified with the losing side of important position issues. One example is abortion. Activists in the Republican Party fought to keep their strong pro-life plank in the party platform in 2000. However, because a majority of the electorate is opposed to the strong pro-life position, George W. Bush seldom mentioned the issue during the campaign, even though one of his first acts as president was to cut federal funding to overseas groups that provide abortions or abortion counseling. John McCain, needing to solidify his Republican base in 2008, was more explicit about his party's pro-life stance, and it appeared to cost him with independent voters. It was Barack Obama who tried to find a middle ground, encouraging Democrats to add to their platform a commitment to policy that would reduce the need for abortion by reducing unwanted pregnancies and that would assist women who wanted to choose adoption as an option.

When a candidate or party does take a stand on a difficult position issue, the other side often uses it against them as a wedge issue. A **wedge issue** is a position issue on which the parties differ and that proves controversial within the ranks of a particular party. For a Republican, an anti–affirmative action position is not dangerous, since few Republicans actively support affirmative action. For a Democrat, though, it is a very dicey issue, because liberal party members endorse it but more moderate members do not. An astute strategy for a Republican candidate is to raise the issue in a campaign, hoping to drive a wedge between the Democrats and to recruit to his or her side the Democratic opponents of affirmative action.

The idea of **issue ownership** helps to clarify the role of policy issues in presidential campaigns. Because of their past stands and performance, each of the parties is widely perceived as better able to handle certain kinds of problems. For instance, the Democrats are seen as better able to deal with the economy while the Republicans are held to be more effective at foreign policy. The voter's decision then is not so much evaluating positions on those issues, but rather deciding which problem is more important. In 2008, when the economy foundered as a result of the subprime mortgage crisis, it benefited Barack Obama since voters believed his party was better able to cope.[54] From the candidate's point of view, the trick is to convince voters that the election is about the issues that his or her party "owns." Sometimes a party will try to take an issue that is "owned" by the other party and redefine it in order to claim ownership of it. Bush did this successfully in 2000 with the education issue, just as Clinton reversed the advantage Republicans usually held on crime.[55]

Because valence issues are relatively safe, candidates stress them at every opportunity. They also focus on the position issues that their parties "own" or on which they have majority support. This suggests that the real campaign is not about debating positions on issues—how to reduce the deficit or whether to restrict abortion—but about which issues should be considered. Issue campaigning is to a large extent about setting the agenda.

The Media

It is impossible to understand the modern political campaign without appreciating the pervasive role of the media. Even though many voters tend to ignore campaign ads—or at least they tell survey interviewers that they do—we know that campaign advertising matters. It has increased dramatically with the rise of television as people's information source of choice. Studies show that advertising provides usable information for voters. Political ads can heighten the loyalty of existing supporters, and they can educate the public about what candidates stand for and what issues candidates believe are most important. Ads also can be effective in establishing the criteria on which voters choose between candidates. Although **negative advertising** may turn off some voters and give the perception that politics is an unpleasant business, the public accepts accurate attacks on the issues. As long as it does not go too far, an attack ad that highlights negative aspects of an opponent's record actually registers more quickly and is remembered more frequently and longer by voters than are positive ads.[56] Experts suggested that requiring candidates to appear in their own ads would discourage negativity, but that doesn't seem to be the case. For instance, by early October 2008, nearly all the ads run by Republican John McCain were negative. Although only 35 percent of Barack Obama's advertising was negative, the fact that he was outspending McCain by running more ads meant that the gap wasn't as large as those numbers would indicate.[57]

Because paid media coverage is so expensive, a campaign's goal is to maximize opportunities for free coverage while controlling, as much as possible, the kind of coverage they get. The major parties' presidential candidates are accompanied by a substantial entourage of reporters who need to file stories on a regular basis, not only for the nation's major newspapers and television networks but also to keep reporters and commentators on the cable news stations like CNN, MSNBC, and Fox busy. These media have substantial influence in setting the agenda—determining which issues are important and, hence, which candidates' appeals will resonate with voters.[58] As a result, daily campaign events are planned more for the press and the demands of the evening news than for the actual in-person audiences, who often seem to function primarily as a backdrop for the candidates' efforts to get favorable airtime each day. The campaigns also field daily conference calls with reporters to attack their opponents and defend their candidates and to try to control, or "spin," the way they are covered. In 2008 a strategy for getting on the news without spending a lot of money was to produce negative "web ads" designed for Internet circulation, which, if catchy enough, could get endless coverage by the networks, the cable stations, and the blogs.

Although the candidates want the regular exposure, they do not like the norms of broadcast news, which they see as perpetuating horse-race journalism, focusing on who is ahead rather than on substantive issues.[59] In addition, the exhausting nature of campaigns, and the mistakes and gaffes that follow, are a source of constant concern because of the media's tendency to zero in on them and replay them endlessly. The relationship between the campaigns and the media is testy. Each side needs the other, but the candidates want to control the message, and the media want stories that are "news"—controversies, changes in the candidates' standings, or stories of goofs and scandals. We discuss the complex relationship between the media and the candidates at greater length in Chapter 13.

Candidates in recent elections have turned increasingly to "soft news" and entertainment programming to get their messages across. Candidates have been especially effective in appealing across party lines to reach the less engaged voters in the soft news formats. Many 2008 candidates, including John McCain, Barack Obama, Ron Paul, and Hillary Clinton appeared on *Saturday Night Live,* Comedy Central's *The Daily Show With Jon Stewart,* and *The Colbert Report* (even Michelle Obama made a stop at both of these). Such appearances give the candidates more unedited airtime and allow them to evade the hard news tendency to interpret all events in horse-race terms.

In 2008 the Internet came into its own as a source of news. Mainstream media outlets like the *New York Times,* the *Washington Post, Time* magazine, and the major networks maintained blogs that joined independent bloggers like Josh Marshall of Talkingpointsmemo.com and National Review Online in updating campaign news and poll results throughout the day. And with everyone having a cell phone camera or a video camera in his or her pocket, YouTube helped to transform the electoral landscape as well. A recorded gaffe or misstatement by a candidate or a campaign surrogate could go viral—reaching millions of viewers with the quick clicks of many mouses. Politicians accustomed to a more conventional way of campaigning were often caught in the YouTube trap. Bill Clinton, for instance, campaigning for his wife in the Democratic primary, was several times captured on tape saying something ill-advised that spread quickly before he could attempt damage control. Even the more media-savvy Obama found a tape of his words about frustrated voters becoming bitter, spoken at what he thought was a closed fundraiser, making the Internet and then the mainstream media rounds at lightning speed.

Presidential Debates

Since 1976 the presidential debates have become one of the major focal points of the campaign. The first televised debate was held in 1960 between Sen. John Kennedy and Vice President Richard Nixon. The younger and more photogenic Kennedy came out on top in those televised debates, but interestingly, those who heard the debates on the radio thought that Nixon did a better job.[60] In general, leading candidates find it less in their interest to participate in debates because they have more to lose and less to win, and so for years debates took place on a sporadic basis.

In the past twenty-five years, however, media and public pressure have all but guaranteed that at least the major-party candidates will participate in debates, although the number, timing, and format of the debates are renegotiated for each presidential election season. Recent elections have generated two or three debates, with a debate among the vice presidential contenders worked in as well. Third-party candidates, who have the most to gain from the free media exposure and the legitimacy that debate participation confers on a campaign, lobby to be included but rarely are. Ross Perot was invited in 1992 because both George Bush and Bill Clinton hoped to woo his supporters. Ralph Nader and Pat Buchanan were shut out of all three debates in 2000.

Do the debates matter? Detailed statistical studies show, not surprisingly, that many of the debates have been standoffs. However, some of the debates, especially those identified with significant candidate errors or positive performances, have moved vote intentions 2 to 4 percent, which in a close race could be significant.[61] In addition, there is a good deal of evidence, including from 2004, that citizens learn about the candidates and their issue positions from the debates.[62] In 2008, with Barack Obama an unknown quantity to many voters, the debates helped to introduce him to the general electorate in a way that voters found reassuring, and media "insta-polls" unanimously proclaimed him the winner over John McCain in all three. Interest in the debates varies with how much suspense surrounds the outcome of the election. When the seat is open or the candidates are less well known, more people are likely to watch the debates.[63] The presidential debates in 2008 were unusually important. Many Americans were relatively unfamiliar with the candidates, especially with Obama, who was new on the national scene and the target of rumors that made him seem unusual and foreign. But in the debates he displayed a calm demeanor and deliberative tone that reassured viewers and undercut John McCain's arguments that Obama was "too risky" or "too liberal."

Money

Winning—or even losing—a presidential campaign involves serious money. The presidential candidates in 2008 spent a total of $1.3 billion, more than double what was spent by the presidential candidates in 2004, which had doubled what was spent in 2000. The data in Figure 12.3 show this striking upward trend, which came about despite significant fundraising limits put into place by BCRA.

This torrent of cash is used to cover the costs of all of the activities just discussed: campaign professionals, polling, travel for the candidates and often their wives (along with the accompanying staff and media), and the production and purchase of media advertising. Of course, the 2008 expenditures easily topped these, breaking all previous records.[64] Where does all this money come from?

Government matching funds are given, in the primary and general election campaigns, to qualified presidential candidates who choose to accept it and to

Figure 12.3

Increase in Total Spending in Presidential Campaigns, 1976–2008

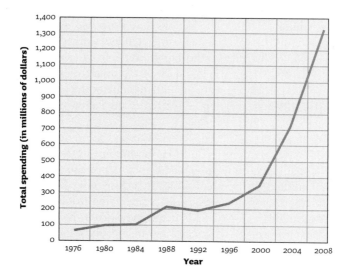

Source: Center for Responsive Politics, "Presidential Fund-raising and Spending, 1976–2008," www.opensecrets.org/preso8/totals.php?cycle=2008, and "Banking on Becoming President," http://opensecrets.org/preso8/index.php.

spend only that money. The funds come from citizens who have checked the box on their tax returns that sends $3 ($6 on joint returns) to fund presidential election campaigns. The idea behind the law is to more easily regulate big money influence on campaign finances, ensure a fair contest, and free up candidates to communicate with the public. For primary elections, if a candidate raises at least $5,000 in each of twenty states and agrees to abide by overall spending limits (about $50 million in 2008), as well as state-by-state limits, the federal government matches every contribution up to $250.

This same fund fully finances both major-party candidates' general election campaigns and subsidizes the two national party nominating conventions. John McCain opted to participate in the 2008 federal campaign financing and faced a spending limit of $84.1 million. Barack Obama chose not to participate in the general election federal financing, arguing that by relying on small donors, his campaign was essentially publicly funded anyway. This meant that his campaign had to raise all the funds it would spend rather than receiving the federal subsidy, but it also meant that the Obama campaign was not limited in the amount it could spend. If presidential candidates accept this public funding, and Obama is the first major-party candidate not to have done so for the general election campaign, they may not raise any other funds or use any leftover funds raised during the primary campaign. Third parties that received at least 5 percent of the vote in the previous presidential campaign may also collect public financing. Unlike the two major parties, however, the money a third party receives depends on the number of votes the party received in the previous election. Ross Perot was eligible to receive $29 million for his 1996 presidential campaign after his party won 19 percent of the vote in 1992, while the two major parties received $61.8 million each.[65]

Hard money refers to the funds given *directly* to candidates by individuals, political action committees (PACs), the political parties, and the government. The spending of hard money is under the control of the candidates, but its collection is governed by the rules of the Federal Election Campaign Act (FECA) of 1972, 1974, and its various amendments. This act established the FEC and was intended to stop the flow of money from, and the influence of, large contributors by outlawing contributions by corporations and unions, and by restricting contributions from individuals. The campaign finance reform bill passed in 2002 actually raised the hard money limits. Under that law, individuals can give a federal candidate up to $2,300 per election and can give a total of $108,200 to all federal candidates and parties in a two-year election cycle.[66] The limit on the parties' hard money contributions to candidates was held to be unconstitutional in a 1999 Colorado district federal court decision but was later upheld in a five-to-four Supreme Court decision.[67]

However, in the 2010 decision in *Citizens United v Federal Election Commission*,[68] which we discussed in the *What's at Stake?* feature that opened this chapter, the Supreme Court struck down a provision of the McCain-Feingold Act that prohibited corporations (and by implication unions and interest groups) from sponsoring broadcast ads for or against specific candidates. Corporations and unions are thus free to engage in broadcast campaigns, although provisions requiring disclosure and limitations on direct contributions to candidates were retained. Experts disagreed about the likely consequences of the far-reaching decision, but mirroring the Court's five-to-four breakdown on the ruling, it was generally decried by liberals and supported by conservatives.[69]

Soft money is unregulated money collected by parties and interest groups in unlimited amounts to spend on party-building activities, get-out-the-vote drives, voter education, or issue position advocacy. Prior to the passage of campaign reform in 2002, as long as the money was not spent to tell people how to vote or coordinated with a specific candidate's campaign, the FEC could not regulate soft money. This allowed corporate groups, unions, and political parties to raise unlimited funds often used for television and radio advertising, especially in the form of issue advocacy ads. As we discussed in Chapter 11, **issue advocacy ads** are television or radio commercials during an election campaign that promote a particular issue, usually by attacking the character, views, or position of the candidate the group running the ad wishes to defeat. The courts have considered these ads protected free speech and have held that individuals and organizations could not be stopped from spending money to express their opinions about issues, or even candidates, so long as they did not explicitly tell viewers how to vote.

Most observers thought that BCRA would remove unregulated money from campaigns and curb negative advertising. While it limited the spending of PACs and parties, new groups, called 527 groups after the loophole (section 527) in the Internal Revenue Code that allows them to avoid the regulations imposed by BCRA, sprang up in their stead (see Chapter 11). Like groups that raised and spent soft money prior to BCRA, 527s can raise unlimited funds for issue advocacy or voter mobilization so long as they do not openly promote any candidate or openly try to defeat any particular candidate. BCRA does forbid all groups, even 527s, from running such ads funded by soft money within sixty days of a general election or thirty days of a primary election.

The 2010 *Citizens United* case loosened the regulations further, lifting the sixty-day limit. For upcoming elections it appears that interest groups, corporations, and unions will have greater leeway in how and when they campaign for candidates. Even so, they are still limited in making direct (hard money) contributions; most of their efforts will be as independent expenditures (efforts that cannot be coordinated with the candidates' campaigns). Moreover, it can be argued that the new decision will not affect our elections in a major way as these entities found plenty of ways to attempt to influence campaigns under the old laws. In any case, given that such contributors do not share a single common ideology or set of issue preferences, some observers argue that any effects will largely cancel each other out. Only with the unfolding of future elections will we know for sure.[70]

Getting Out the Vote

The voter mobilization efforts we discussed earlier in this chapter are an increasingly important part of any presidential campaign. As we noted, in the 1980s and 1990s, such efforts concentrated mostly on television advertising. Parties have not decreased their television advertising, but they have found that increasing their volunteer corps on the ground, in conjunction with the efforts of sympathetic interest groups (unions and liberal groups for Democrats, Christian conservative groups for Republicans), is a successful strategy for mobilizing voters. In an analysis of the 2002 midterm elections, Republicans found that they could turn out 2 to 3 percent more of their voters by having precinct chairs knock on doors than by using advertising and phone calling alone.[71] Today mobilization efforts combine old-school door-to-door campaigning with modern technology,[72] including the use of vast computer databases to tell volunteers whose doors to knock on.[73] The Obama ground game, using volunteers for contacting voters and mobilizing supporters, exceeded by a wide margin anything that had been done in the past and dwarfed the McCain campaign's efforts. Rather than sending in staff and volunteers in the last couple of weeks of the campaign, the Obama campaign had paid staff and dozens, even hundreds of offices, and millions of volunteers across all of the battleground states. One high-level Republican campaign official said of it, "This is the greatest ground game they've ever put together. It's scary."[74] It set a new model for effective campaigns: engaging everyday citizens as integral parts of the campaigns rather than just as spectators and voters.

Interpreting Elections

After the election is over, when the votes are counted, and we know who won, it would seem that the whole election season is finally finished. In reality, the outcomes of our collective decisions cry for interpretation. Probably the most important interpretation is the one articulated by the victor. The winning candidate in presidential elections inevitably claims an **electoral mandate**, maintaining that the people want the president to do the things he campaigned on and that the election is all about the voters' preference for his leadership and policy programs. Presidents who can sell the interpretation that their election to office is a ringing endorsement of their policies can work with Congress from a favored position. To the extent that the president is able to sell his interpretation, he will be more successful in governing. In contrast, the losing party will try to argue that its loss was due to the characteristics of its candidate or specific campaign mistakes. Party members will, predictably, resist the interpretation that the voters rejected their message and their vision for the nation.

The media also offer their interpretations. In fact, research shows that of the many possible explanations that are available, the mainstream media quickly—in just a matter of weeks—hone in on an agreed-upon standard explanation of the election.[75] In 2000 the media, in explaining the closeness of the race, focused on how much more likable voters found George W. Bush, despite the majority's agreement with Al Gore on the issues, and on what they claimed to be Gore's badly run campaign. In 2004 the media quickly decided that though the nation was closely divided, moral values voters in red states put Bush over the top. In 2008 the media story was that President Bush's rock-bottom approval ratings were dragging McCain down and that, with the economy in collapse, the Republican was facing insurmountable odds while the voters were hungry for change. The media, assisted by the left-leaning blogosphere, also maintained that Obama had run a reasonably positive campaign, but that McCain and Palin were stirring up anger and mob-like sentiments with their insinuations that Obama was "un-American" and "risky." These explanations offer parts of the truth, but they oversimplify reality and do not give us a complete understanding of the complex decisions made by the American electorate.

Citizenship and Elections
Do too many informed voters lead to too much conflict?

At the beginning of this chapter, we acknowledged that the American citizen does not bear a strong resemblance to the ideal citizen of classic democratic theory. Nothing we have learned here leads us to think otherwise, but that does not mean that Americans are doomed to an undemocratic future. Scholars who conducted the earliest studies of voting based on survey research were surprised at the low levels of interest most citizens showed in presidential election campaigns. These studies of the 1944 and 1948 presidential elections found that most citizens had their minds made up before the campaigns began and that opinions changed only slightly in response to the efforts of the parties and candidates. These studies found that, instead of people relying on new information coming from the campaigns, they voted according to the groups they belonged to. Income, occupation, religion, and similar factors structured whom people talked to, what they learned, and how they voted. The authors concluded that democracy is probably safer without a single type of citizen who matches the civics ideal of high levels of participation, knowledge, and commitment.[76]

In this view, such high levels of involvement would indicate a citizenry fraught with conflict. Intense participation comes with intense commitment and strongly held positions, which make for an unwillingness to compromise. This revision of the call for classic "good citizens" holds that our democratic polity is actually better off when it has lots of different types of citizens: some who care deeply, are highly informed, and participate intensely; many more who care moderately, are a bit informed, and participate as much out of duty to the process as commitment to one party or candidate; and some who are less aware of politics until some great issue or controversy awakens their political slumber.

The virtue of modern democracy in this *political specialization view* is that citizens play different roles and that together these combine to form an electoral system that has the attributes we prefer: it is reasonably stable; it responds to changes of issues and candidates, but not too much; and the electorate as a whole cares, but not so intensely that any significant portion of the citizenry will challenge the results of an election. Its most obvious flaw is that it is biased against the interests of those who are least likely to be activist or pluralist citizens—the young, the poor, the uneducated, and minorities.[77]

▶ What's at Stake Revisited

When, during his 2010 State of the Union address, President Obama criticized the Supreme Court's *Citizens United* ruling, he was expressing a sentiment held widely by Democrats. By contrast, Republicans generally hailed the Court's decision that corporations' campaign spending was protected speech as a good thing. Congressional Democrats later attempted to make the spending of corporate money on elections more transparent through legislation they called the Disclose Act. The act would have required corporations to make public who they are and how they spend their money, but it was defeated by a Republican filibuster in the Senate.

We have seen that reforming campaign finance law has been a tough job for Congress, one that they have tried to accomplish more than once without great success. The McCain-Feingold Act was a bipartisan effort to rein in campaign spending, but the issue continues to divide Americans along partisan lines. Why is the spending of corporate money on campaigns such a hot-button issue in American politics? Who stands to win and who to lose?

Democrats say that everyday Americans have a stake in the matter, that corporations have too much influence in American electoral politics, and that corporate dollars swamp the preferences of ordinary citizens. In their view, regular Americans lose when they cannot summon equal resources to fight political battles.[78] Of course, Democratic politicians themselves have a stake as well. Since the Democratic Party tends not to support big business, those unlimited corporate dollars are more likely to go toward promoting their Republican opponents, as the midterm election campaign in 2010 made clear. Naturally they'd like the playing field evened out.

By the same token, Republicans will be winners here because that corporate money most often serves their electoral interests. They claim broader stakes, however, arguing that something fundamental is at risk here. In their view, the *Citizens United* decision is a victory for free speech and corporate freedom from government regulation. As Senate minority leader Mitch McConnell, R-Ky., put it, "For too long, some in this country have been deprived of full participation in the political process. With this monumental decision, the Supreme Court took an important step in the direction of restoring the First Amendment rights of these groups by ruling that the Constitution protects their right to express themselves about political candidates and issues up until Election Day."[79]

In truth, this is not just a partisan issue because Republicans and Democrats are both right—the issue is about unequal power and it is about fundamental freedoms. As long as the Supreme Court equates the right to spend money to promote a political cause to be equivalent to the right to free speech, Americans will have to grapple with the real consequence that some people will be able to speak very much more loudly than others. Whether this violates the rights of ordinary Americans or whether limiting such spending violates the rights of corporations (and whether corporations are indeed entitled to the same rights as individuals) are issues that are not cut and dried even for the Court, as the five-to-four vote in *Citizens United* makes clear.

▶ Summary With Key Terms

Voting enhances the quality of democratic life by legitimizing the outcomes of elections. However, American voter turnout levels are typically among the lowest in the world and may endanger American democracy. Factors such as age, income, education, and race affect whether a person is likely to vote, as do legal obstacles (though measures like the **Motor Voter Bill** [400] try to overcome these), varying levels of **voter mobilization** (402), and attitudinal changes.

Candidates and the media often blur issue positions, and voters realistically cannot investigate policy proposals on their own. Therefore, voters make a decision by considering party identification and peer viewpoints, prominent issues, employing elements of both **prospective voting** (408) and **retrospective voting** (408) as well as candidate image.

The "road to the White House" is long, expensive, and grueling. It begins with planning and early fundraising, a sort of **invisible primary** (410) stage, and develops into more active campaigning during the **presidential primary** (411)—where primaries may be **open** (411) or **closed** (411)—and **party caucus** (410) phase, a period considerably shortened these days due to the practice of **front-loading** (411). Candidates want to be perceived to have **momentum** (412) in the race, but being considered the **front-runner** (412) has both advantages and disadvantages. Each party's choice of a candidate is announced officially at the party conventions, and the general election campaign is launched after Labor Day.

The general election campaign is shaped by the battle for large states with significant votes in the **Electoral College** (414) and the quest to find and convert **swing voters** (414). Professional staff run the campaign—coordinating activities, engaging in **oppo research** (417), managing the media and running ads, including **negative advertising** (421). An essential part of campaign strategy is the consideration of issues—**valence issues** (420) on which most candidates agree; **position issues** (420) on which they differ; **wedge issues** (420), which can be used against the other side; and **issue ownership** (420), which can give one party or the other an edge. Raising and spending money is also a key part of campaigns. Campaign money can be in the form of **government matching funds** (423) given to candidates of the major parties and to candidates of the minor parties who performed well in the previous election, **hard money** (425) donations collected by the candidates, or **soft money** (425) collected by parties and interest groups. Soft money, used for get-out-the-vote efforts and the funding of **issue advocacy ads** (425), was supposed to be regulated by campaign finance legislation in 2002, but loopholes have allowed it to flourish in a different form. All this campaign activity is geared toward winning the election, so the victorious candidate can claim an **electoral mandate** (427).

Explore this subject further with suggested readings, movies, and web sites at http://republic-brief.cqpress.com, where you'll also find study aids, practice quizzes, flash cards, and Internet exercises.

VOTE
HERE

BOARD OF ELECTIONS AND ETHICS
DISTRICT OF COLUMBIA

Chapter 13

The Media

▶ What's at Stake?

Portions of this *What's at Stake?* were written on the author's iPhone, when inspiration struck at a moment when she was away from her computer. She emailed them to herself, and later pasted them into the document she was writing. When, still away from her desk, she needed to check a source, she looked up the book on Amazon.com, downloaded it to the Kindle on her phone, and did a little research, highlighting the material she needed to come back to. All news sources and most of the research for this chapter were accessed over the Internet. The one thing you can guarantee about this technology, some of which would have seemed downright astounding a year or two before, is that by the time this book comes out it will seem like no big deal at all. We are in the midst of a media revolution, and the only thing we know for sure is that things will change, quickly and inevitably. Hang on for the ride.

For anyone born after the 1960s, it might sound laughable, but news used to enter the average American's life at only a couple of neatly defined and very predictable points during the day. The local morning paper arrived before dawn, there to be read over coffee and breakfast. The afternoon paper (yes, most cities had two papers back then) was waiting for you when you came home from work. Big city papers like the *New York Times* and the *Washington Post* were available only to those who lived in New York or Washington, D.C., unless you ordered a copy of the paper to be mailed to you at great expense, arriving several days late (no FedEx, no overnight delivery).

In 1960 the evening news came on all three TV stations at 7:30 P.M., and TV-owning America (87 percent of households in 1960) got their last news of the day from Chet Huntley and David Brinkley on NBC, John Daly on ABC, or Douglas Edwards on CBS (Edwards was to be followed two years later by Walter Cronkite, also known as "Uncle Walter," the most trusted face in news). That was pretty much it for news in 1960s America, unless a special event (a space shot, for instance) or a tragedy (like JFK's assassination) occurred that required a special bulletin.

That was then. Fifty years later, readership of newspapers is way, way down. Whereas a third of Americans bought a daily paper in 1941, only 13 percent did so in 2009.[1] Figures released in October 2009 showed circulation down nearly 11 percent in the previous six months alone.[2] Most towns have only one paper, if they have any at all. Meanwhile, in addition to the three original networks, which continue to broadcast news as well as a variety of programming, there are now more than a dozen television stations around the world that are devoted to nothing but news, 24–7, many of which can be accessed from the United States. In addition, there are hundreds of talk radio stations around the country, and of course there is the glorious, chaotic marketplace of ideas and information called the Internet.

Today we take for granted that we can access most information sources not only from newspapers, magazines, books, radios, and the television, but also from our computers. More portably, we can be linked to the world of information from our phones, our electronic books, and our wireless notebooks, which we can use to read the news, follow a blog, download a book, or watch a movie.

Carry around a newspaper? Why on earth would we want to do that?

A web site called newspaperdeathwatch.com, dedicated to "chronicling the decline of newspapers and the rebirth of journalism," keeps tabs on the papers that have ceased publication or moved to a print-online hybrid or simply an online existence, among them, the *Tucson Citizen,* the *Rocky Mountain News,* the *Baltimore Examiner,* the *Seattle Post-Intelligencer,* the *Detroit News/Free Press,* the *Christian Science Monitor.* You can check it out yourself to see the latest list of the dead and dying.[3]

As we leave the decade of the 2000s, it is not unusual to hear people say that the day of the print media is over. If you are feeling inclined to irony, you can Google "the newspaper is dead" and you will get tens of thousands of hits, with all people insisting (1) that it is true, (2) that it isn't, (3) that it matters, and (4) that it doesn't. In further irony, many of the most thriving news web sites—online journals like the *Drudge Report* and the *Huffington Post* that traffic in "breaking news"—are often merely linking to the reporting of others—often to reporting done by those same dinosaur newspapers whose deaths they are quick to proclaim.

What's the truth here? Is the newspaper an anachronism, a dinosaur left over from another era, or an essential institution whose demise is unimaginable? A writer at *LA Observed,* an online site that touts its independent reporting and commentary, jumped in with both feet: "Not that I'm happy about this, but I'll say it. Newspapers don't matter. Otherwise people would be reading them."[4] Less cavalierly, a journalist writing in *USA Today* (one of the endangered papers), speculated recently that "[s]ometime soon, millions of people may find themselves unwittingly involved in a test that could profoundly change their daily routines, local economies and civic lives. They'll have to figure out how to keep up with City Hall, their neighborhoods and their kids' schools—as well as store openings, new products and sales—without a 170-year-old staple of daily life: a local newspaper."[5]

Does it matter? No less a grand thinker than Thomas Jefferson said, "The basis of our governments being the opinion of the people, the very first object should be to keep that right; and were it left to me to decide whether we should have a government without newspapers or newspapers without a government, I should not hesitate a moment to prefer the latter."[6] Are newspapers that fundamental? Can a democratic world survive without newsprint? Just what is at stake in the declining importance of the American newspaper?

It's hard to imagine anyone today voting for a presidential candidate without checking out the candidate's web site or Facebook page, seeing him give a speech on streaming video, following her on Twitter, or watching a fundraising pitch on YouTube. But most of those who voted for George Washington for president, or for Abraham Lincoln, had never even heard the voice of the candidate they chose, and they might have had only a vague idea of what the candidate looked like. While photographs of Lincoln were available, only portraits, sketches, or cartoons of Washington could reach voters. And while Franklin Roosevelt's voice reached millions in his radio "fireside chats," and his face was widely familiar to Americans from newspaper and magazine photographs, his video image was restricted to newsreels that had to be viewed in the movie theater. Not until the advent of television in the mid–twentieth century were presidents, senators, and representatives beamed in to the living rooms of Americans, and their smiling, moving images made a part of the modern culture of American politics.

Fast forward fifty years. The electronic age in which we live today has made politics immediate and personal in a way that could only leave even these later politicians stunned and bemused. Our information-oriented culture means we are bombarded 24–7 with news flashes, sound bites, web ads, blog posts, commercials, comedy routines, text messages, podcasts, and requests to join networks of those who want our friendship and support. Politicians scramble to stay on top of electronic innovations that continually shape and alter the political world. President George W. Bush's use of the words "internets" and "the Google" signaled his discomfort with the changing electronic world, much as his father's unfamiliarity with a grocery scanner revealed his, eight years before. Barack Obama's confident use of networking strategies and text messaging in his campaign for the presidency put him at an advantage over his older and less tech-savvy opponent, John McCain.

Democracy demands that citizens be informed about their government, that they be able to criticize it, deliberate about it, and change it if it doesn't do their will. Information, in a very real sense, is power. Information must be available, and it must be disseminated widely. This was fairly easy to accomplish in the direct democracy of ancient Athens, where the small number of citizens were able to meet together and debate the political issues of the day. Because their democracy was direct and they were, in effect, the government, there was no need for anything to mediate *between* them and government, to keep them informed, to publicize candidates for office, to identify issues, and to act as a watchdog for their democracy.

In some ways our democratic political community is harder to achieve today. We don't know most of our fellow citizens personally, we cannot directly discover the issues ourselves, and we have no idea what actions our government takes to deal with issues unless the media tell us. We are dependent on the **mass media** to connect us to our government and to create the only real space we have for public deliberation of issues. But increasing technological developments make possible ever-newer forms of political community and more immediate access to information. Networking sites like Facebook, LinkedIn, and Twitter allow people to reach out and interact socially, and politicians have not been shy about using such strategies to create networks of supporters. Chat rooms and blogs allow people with common interests to find each other from the far reaches of the world, and allow debate and discussion on a scale never before imagined.

Ross Perot, third-party presidential candidate in 1992 and 1996, talked of the day when we would all vote electronically on individual issues from our home computers. If we have not yet arrived at that day of direct democratic decision making, changes in the media are nonetheless revolutionizing the possibilities of democracy, much as the printing press and television did earlier, bringing us closer to the Athenian ideal of political community in cyberspace, if not in real space.

In this chapter you will learn about this powerful entity called the media as we focus on the sources of the information we get, the historical development of the ownership of the American media and its implications for the political news we get, and the role of journalists themselves—who they are and what they believe, and the link between the media and politics.

Where Do We Get Our Information?
Increasingly from a combination of sources

In a recent study, most Americans (84 percent) reported that they enjoyed keeping up with the news, and a bare majority (52 percent) even enjoyed it a lot. Young people were less likely to feel this way—only a third of those aged 18–24 fell into the "a lot" category, compared to nearly two-thirds of those aged 50 and older—but even a majority of them enjoyed the news at least somewhat.[7] Even though about 80 percent of Americans will get some news on a given day, only 34 percent say they get it from reading a newspaper (down from 48 percent ten years earlier). Television news watchers are holding steady at about 57 percent of the public, but radio listeners have dropped to 35 percent, down from 49 percent ten years ago. The news source that shows growth is the Internet—37 percent of the public gets some news online, up from only 13 percent in 1998. Many of those who do get their news online combine the Internet with more traditional sources.[8]

Given the myriad sources of information that Americans now confront, it is not surprising that all news-getters are not the same. The Pew Research Center, which surveys Americans' news-getting behavior every two years, divides Americans into four groups: Traditionalists, Integrators, Net-Newsers, and Disengaged. The Traditionalists (just under half of Americans) stick to network news as their primary source. They tend to be older and less well educated. The Integrators, about a quarter of the public, get their news from television (cable as well as the networks) but also go online for news daily. On the whole they are well educated, well-to-do, and middle aged. Net-Newsers, as their name suggests, get more news online than from other sources. Although they amount to only 13 percent of the public, they tend to be well educated, well off, and younger. The Disengaged group is relatively small (14 percent of the public); they tend to be younger, less educated, and by far the least informed about American politics.[9]

Despite the fact that most of the American public is exposed to some news, and some people are exposed to quite a lot of it, levels of political information in this country are not high. In one study, only about half of the public could correctly answer questions about domestic politics and public figures.[10] These politically informed people are not evenly distributed throughout the population, either. Older Americans, those with more education, and men were more likely to answer the questions correctly.[11]

Newspapers and Magazines

American newspaper readership is currently at a historical low, and is also lower than in most other industrialized nations (see Figure 13.1).[12] Today only about a dozen cities have more than one daily paper. But several major newspapers—the *Wall Street Journal, USA Today,* the *New York Times,* the *Washington Post,* and the *Los Angeles Times*—have achieved what amounts to national circulation, providing even residents of single-daily cities with an alternative. Those major papers gather their own news, and some smaller papers that cannot afford to station correspondents around the world can subscribe to their news services. Practically speaking, this means that most of the news that Americans read on a daily basis comes from very few sources: these outlets or wire services like the Associated Press or Reuters.

Newspapers cover political news, of course, but many other subjects also compete with advertising for space in a newspaper's pages. Business, sports, entertainment (movies and television), religion, weather, book reviews, comics, crossword puzzles, advice columns, classified ads, and travel information are just some of the content that most newspapers provide in an effort to woo readers, although increasingly many of these are available online. Craigslist, for instance, has done much to make the classified sections of newspapers redundant, and some observers argue the site is at least partly responsible for making newspapers an endangered

Figure 13.1

U.S. Newspaper Circulation Compared to Other Countries

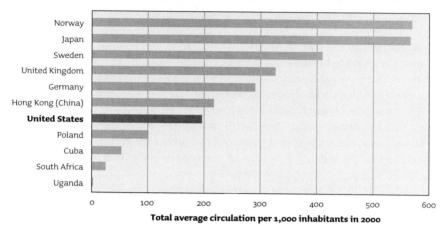

Total average circulation per 1,000 inhabitants in 2000

Source: Harold W. Stanley and Richard G. Niemi, *Vital Statistics on American Politics, 2005–2006* (Washington, D.C.: CQ Press, 2005), 174–175.

species.[13] Generally the front section and especially the front page are reserved for major current events, but these need not be political in nature. Business deals, sporting events, and even sensational and unusual weather conditions can push politics farther back in the paper.

Magazines can often be more specialized than newspapers. While the standard weekly news magazines (*Newsweek, Time,* and *U.S. News & World Report*) carry the same eclectic mix of subjects as major newspapers, they can also offer more comprehensive news coverage because they do not need to meet daily deadlines, giving them more time to develop a story. These popular news magazines tend to be middle of the road in their ideological outlook. Other magazines appeal specifically to liberal readers—for instance, the *New Republic* and *Nation*—or to conservatives—for instance, the *National Review* and the *American Spectator.*

Radio

The decline in the number of newspapers that began in the early 1900s was probably due in part to the emergence of radio. Although radios were expensive at first, one in six American families owned one by 1926,[14] and the radio had become a central part of American life. Not only was radio news more up-to-the-minute, it was also more personal. For example, Franklin Roosevelt used his fireside chats to sell his New Deal policies directly to the public, without having to go through the reporters he viewed as hostile to his ideas.[15] Today 99 percent of American households own at least one radio,[16] and more than 11,000 radio stations offer entertainment and news shows through commercial networks and their local affiliates. There are also two noncommercial networks, National Public Radio and Public Radio International, funded in small part by the U.S. government but also by private donations from corporations and individuals.

Television

The impact of radio on the American public, however dramatic initially, cannot compare with the effects of television. American ownership of television sets skyrocketed from 9 percent of households in 1950 to 98 percent in 1975, a statistic that continues to hold firm. In fact, 40 percent of American households today own three or more television sets, and more than two-thirds receive cable or satellite transmission. Politicians were quick to realize that, like radio, television allowed them to reach a broad audience without having to deal with print reporters and their adversarial questions. The Kennedy administration was the first to make real use of television, a medium that was well suited to the young media-savvy president. And it was television that brought the nation together in a community of grief when Kennedy was assassinated. Television carried the Vietnam War (along with its protesters) and the civil rights movement into Americans' homes, and the images that it created helped build popular support to end the war abroad and segregation at home. Television can create global as well as national communities, an experience many Americans shared as they sat captive before their television sets in the days following the terrorist attacks on New York and Washington, D.C., in 2001.

There are many television shows whose primary subject is politics. Many cable stations and C-SPAN, sometimes called "America's Town Hall," offer news around the clock, although not all the news concerns politics. Weekend shows like *Meet the Press* highlight the week's coverage of politics, and cable news shows frequently showcase debates between liberals and conservatives on current issues. Some stations, such as the music channel MTV, direct their political shows to a specific age group (here, young people), and others, like *America's Voice,* to those holding particular ideologies (conservatism, in this case).

Like radio, television has its call-in talk shows. And politics is often the subject of the jokes on such shows as *Saturday Night Live, The Daily Show With Jon Stewart, The Colbert Report, Late Show With David Letterman,* and *The Tonight Show.* Sometimes the line between fun and fact gets blurred, as when in 2003 Democratic senator John Edwards announced his candidacy for the presidency on Stewart's show, prompting Stewart to say, "I guess I should probably tell you now that we're a fake show. So, I want you to know that this may not count." Since 2000 the major presidential candidates and their wives have regularly sat down to chat with Larry King, Leno, Letterman, and even Oprah Winfrey. In late October 2010, just days before the midterm elections, President Barack Obama sat down with Jon Stewart for an interview, and days later Stewart and Stephen Colbert held a rally in Washington, D.C.—a merger of Stewart's "The Rally to Restore Sanity" and Colbert's "The March to Keep Fear Alive." Clearly meant to be spoofs on the angry conservative Tea Party rallies and Glenn Beck's "Restoring Honor" rally, they were taken seriously enough by real news organizations that most forbade their reporters from attending unless they were there in a political capacity on the grounds that these were political events.[17]

The Internet

The most recent new medium to revolutionize the way we get political news is the Internet, or the web (for World Wide Web), which connects home or business computers to a global network of sites that provide printed, audio, and visual information on any topic you can imagine. In 2010 some 80 percent of American adults used the Internet, over 66 percent had a broadband connection at home, and 60 percent went online wirelessly from their laptops or phones.[18] Sixty-one percent of Americans in 2010 said they got some news from the Internet on a typical day—more than five times the number from a decade ago, and 25 percent did so from their phones. Fifty-nine percent of adult Americans say they get their news from a combination of on- and offline sources. Twenty-eight percent of Americans have a customizable web page that feeds them news, and 37 percent of Internet users have socially interacted with others concerning the news—creating it, commenting on it, or disseminating it through social networking sites like Facebook or Twitter.[19] It is not too much to say that the Internet is revolutionizing the way we get information.

All the major newspapers and the Associated Press have web sites, usually free, where all or most of the news in their print versions can be found. Many magazines and journals are also available online. By searching for the topics we want and connecting to links with related sites, we can customize our web news. Politics buffs can bypass nonpolitical news, and vice versa. True political junkies can go straight to the source: the federal government makes enormous amounts of information available at its www.whitehouse.gov and www.senate.gov sites.

In addition to traditional media outlets that provide online versions, the web offers myriad other sources of information. Online sources like *Slate, Salon, Politico,* the *Huffington Post,* and the *Drudge Report* exist solely on the Internet and may or may not adopt the conventions, practices, and standards of the more traditional media. Web logs, or **blogs**, have become increasingly popular as well. Blogs—online journals that can be set up by anyone with a computer and an Internet connection—can be personal, political, cultural, or anything in between; they run the gamut from individual diaries to investigative journalism. In fact, anyone can put up a blog or a web page and distribute information on any topic. This makes the task of using the information on the web challenging. It gives us access to more information than ever before, but the task of sorting and evaluating that information is solely our own responsibility (see *Consider the Source* in Chapter 5).

Not only does the web provide information, but it is also interactive to a degree that far surpasses talk radio or television. The social networking sites Facebook, LinkedIn, and Twitter, as well as many other web sites and blogs, have chat rooms or discussion opportunities where all sorts of information can be shared, topics debated, and people met. Although this can allow the formation of communities based on specialized interests or similar views, it can also make it very easy for people with fringe or extreme views to find each other and organize.[20] In 2008, political campaigns took advantage of online technology and social networking principles to organize, raise funds, and get out the vote. It was Democratic senator Barack Obama's early use of the Internet for his campaign, borrowing from the innovative 2004 campaign of Howard Dean, that gave him an edge over Sen. Hillary Clinton in the presidential primaries. The Internet has the potential to increase the direct participation of citizens in political communities and political decisions, though the fact that not all Americans have access to the web means that multiple classes of citizenship could form.

Who Owns the Media, and How Does That Affect Our News?
From government control to corporate control

The ownership structure of the American media has changed dramatically since the days of the nation's founding. The media have gone from dependence on government for their very existence to massive corporate ownership that seems to rival government for its sheer power and influence on the citizenry.

The Early American Press: Dependence on Government

In its earliest days, the press in America was dependent on government officials for its financial, and sometimes political, survival. Under those circumstances, the press could hardly perform either the watchdog function of checking up on government or the democratic function of empowering citizens. It served primarily to empower government or, during the Revolution, the patriots who had seized control of many of the colonial presses.

Andrew Jackson, elected in 1824, carried the patronage of the press to new lengths. Like his predecessors, he offered friendly papers the opportunity to print government documents and denied it to his critics. But Jackson's administration heralded an age of mass democracy. Voter turnout doubled between 1824 and 1828.[21] People were reading newspapers in unheard-of numbers, and those papers were catering to their new mass audiences with a blunter and less elite style than they had used in the past.

Growing Media Independence

The newspapers after Jackson's day were characterized by larger circulations, which drew more advertising and increased their financial independence. As newspapers sought to increase their readership, they began to offer more politically impartial news coverage in the hope that they would not alienate potential readers. This effort to be objective, which we see as a journalistic virtue today, came about at least partly as the result of the economic imperatives of selling newspapers to large numbers of people who do not share the same political views.

Prior to 1833, newspapers had been expensive; a year's subscription cost more than the average weekly wages of a skilled worker.[22] But in that year, the *New York Sun* began selling papers at only a penny a copy. Its subject matter was not an intellectual treatment of complex political and economic topics but rather more superficial political reporting of crime, human interest stories, humor, and advertising. As papers began to appeal to mass audiences rather than partisan supporters, they left behind their opinionated reporting and strove for more objective, "fairer" treatment of their subjects that would be less likely to alienate the readers and the advertisers on whom they depended for their livelihood. This isn't to say that newspaper editors stayed out of politics, but they were not seen as being in the pocket of one of the political parties, and the news they printed was seen as evenhanded. In 1848 the Associated Press was organized as a wire service to collect foreign news and distribute it to member papers in the United States. This underscored the need for objectivity in political reporting so that the news would be acceptable to a variety of papers.[23]

After the Civil War the need for newspapers to appeal to a mass audience resulted in the practice of *yellow journalism,* the effort to lure readers with sensational reporting on topics like sex, crime, gossip, and human interest. Newspapers became big business in the United States. The irony, of course, is that sensationalism did win new readers and allowed papers to achieve independence from parties and politicians, even as they were criticized for lowering the journalistic standards.

The Media Today: Concentrated Corporate Power

Today the media continue to be big business but on a scale undreamed of by such early entrepreneurs as Joseph Pulitzer and William Randolph Hearst. No longer does a single figure dominate a paper's editorial policy; rather, all of the major circulation newspapers in this country, as well as the national radio and television stations, are owned by major conglomerates. Often editorial decisions are matters of corporate policy, not individual judgment. Interestingly, journalists freed themselves from the political masters who ruled them in the early years of this country, only to find themselves just as thoroughly dominated by the corporate bottom line.

The modern media get five times as much of their revenue from advertising as from circulation. Logic dictates that the advertisers will want to spend their money where they can get the biggest bang for their buck: the papers with the most readers and the stations with the largest audiences. Because advertisers go after the most popular media outlets, competition is fierce, and outlets that cannot promise advertisers wide enough exposure fail to get the advertising dollars and go out of business. Competition drives out the weaker outlets, corporations seeking to maximize market share gobble up smaller outlets, and to retain viewers, they all stick to the formulas that are known to produce success. What this means for the media world today is that there are fewer and fewer outlets, they are owned by fewer and fewer corporations, and the content they offer is more and more the same.[24]

In fact, today ten corporations, among them Time-Warner, Disney, National Amusements (owner of both Viacom and CBS Corporation), News Corporation Limited, and General Electric, own the major national newspapers, the leading news magazines, the national television networks including CNN and other cable stations, as well as publishing houses, movie studios, telephone companies, entertainment firms, and other multimedia operations. Most of these corporations are also involved in other businesses, as their familiar names attest. These giant corporations cross national lines, forming massive global media networks, controlled by a handful of corporate headquarters. Media critic Ben Bagdikian calls these media giants a "new communications cartel within the United States," with the "power to surround every man, woman, and child in the country with controlled images and words, to socialize each new generation of Americans, to alter the political agenda of the country."[25] What

> [T]oday . . . there are fewer and fewer media outlets, they are owned by fewer and fewer corporations, and the content they offer is more and more the same.

troubles him and other critics is that many Americans don't know that most of the news and entertainment comes from just a few corporate sources and are unaware of the consequences that this corporate ownership structure has for all of us.

What does the concentrated corporate ownership of the media mean to us as consumers of the news? We should be aware of at least four major consequences. First, there is a **commercial bias** in the media today toward what will increase advertiser revenue and audience share. People tune in to watch scandals and crime stories, so extensive coverage of nonnewsworthy events like the O.J. Simpson trial in the 1990s and, more recently, the lingering scandal over Michael Jackson's death appear relentlessly on the front pages of every newspaper in the country, not just the gossip-hungry tabloids but also the more sober *New York Times* and *Wall Street Journal*. Journalistic judgment and ethics are often at odds with the imperative to turn a profit.

Second, the effort to get and keep large audiences, and to make way for increased advertising, means a reduced emphasis on political news. This is especially true at the local level, which is precisely where the political events that most directly affect most citizens occur.[26]

Third, the content of the news we get is lightened up and dramatized to keep audiences tuned in.[27] As in the days of yellow journalism, market forces encourage sensational coverage of the news. Television shows often capitalize on the human interest in dramatic reenacts of news events, with a form of journalism that has come to be called *infotainment* because of its efforts to make the delivery of information more attractive by dressing it up as entertainment. To compete with such shows, the mainstream network news broadcasts increase the drama of their coverage as well.

Finally, the corporate ownership of today's media means that the media outlets frequently face conflicts of interest in deciding what news to cover or how to cover it. As one critic asks, how can NBC's anchor report critically on nuclear power without crossing the network's corporate parent, General Electric, or ABC give fair treatment to Disney's business practices?[28] And with Rupert Murdoch's News Corporation giving a million dollars to the Republican Governors Association in 2010, who would be surprised at the Republican-friendly coverage of News Corporation's news operations like Fox News, the *New York Post,* and the *Wall Street Journal.*[29] In fact, 33 percent of newspaper editors in America said they would not feel free to publish news that might harm their parent company,[30] a statistic that should make us question what is being left out of the news we receive.

The corporate media monopoly affects the news we get in serious ways. Citizens have some alternative news options, but few are truly satisfactory as a remedy, and all require more work than switching on the television in the evening. One alternative is public radio and television. Sometimes, then, publicly owned media may be "freer" than privately owned media if they allow producers to escape the commercial culture in which most media shows exist. The United States has public radio and television networks, but they are not subsidized by the government at sufficient levels to allow them complete commercial freedom. Rather, they are funded by a combination of government assistance and private or corporate donations. These donations sound very much like commercials when announced at the start and finish of programming and could arguably affect the content of the shows.

Another choice for citizens is the *alternative press.* Born of the counterculture and antiwar movement in the 1960s, these local weekly papers, like the (New York) *Village Voice* and the *SF* (San Francisco) *Weekly* were intended to offer a radical alternative to the mainstream media. Usually free and dependent on advertising, these papers have lost their radical edge and become so profitable that, in an ironic turn of events, they themselves are now getting bought up by chains like New Times, Inc.[31] Rejecting the alternative press as too conventional, there is now even an "alternative to the alternative press" aimed at a younger audience and coveted by advertisers.[32]

A final, but rapidly growing, alternative to the mainstream corporate media is, of course, the Internet. The Internet offers myriad sources for political news. Although, as we saw in *Consider the Source* in Chapter 5, it takes time and effort to figure out which of these sources are accurate and trustworthy—and in many cases the news options on the web are dominated by the same corporate interests as are the rest of the media—the Internet provides a way for the motivated individual to get around the biases of the mainstream media and to customize the news in a way that was previously impossible. Not only are there news feeds and web portals that allow users to get the news they want, when they want it, but the growing number of blogs presents news readers with a new and independent option for finding news online— one that allows them to go around the corporate barriers in their quest for news. Although in 2008 only 10 percent of the public reported regularly reading blogs for information about current events and politics, that remains a huge number of

Internet Reporting

The Internet has proven to be a rapidly growing alternative to mainstream corporate media, as evidenced by bloggers receiving their own lounge at the 2008 Democratic National Convention. News feeds, web portals, and blogs can serve as independent sources for information on current events and politics.

Americans who are logging on to get their political news from this alternative source.[33] In addition, the growing number of cell phone users offers another way for people to access customized news, with owners of smart phones notable for their heavy news consumption.[34] The fact that these tech-savvy news readers are disproportionately well educated and young suggests that America's news-reading habits may be changing dramatically, and that the web may come closer to realizing its potential for offering a truly democratic, practical, and "free" alternative to the corporate-produced news we now receive.

Regulation of the Broadcast Media

The media in America are almost entirely privately owned, but they do not operate without some public control. Although the principle of freedom of the press keeps the print media almost free of restriction (see Chapter 4), the broadcast media have been treated differently. In the early days of radio, great public enthusiasm for the new medium resulted in so many radio stations that signal interference threatened to damage the whole industry. Broadcasters asked the government to impose some order, which it did with the passage of the Federal Communications Act, creating the Federal Communications Commission (FCC), an independent regulatory agency, in 1934.

Because access to the airwaves was considered a scarce resource, the government acted to ensure that radio and television serve the public interest by representing a variety of viewpoints. Accordingly, the 1934 bill contained three provisions designed to ensure fairness in broadcasting.

The *equal time rule* means that if a station allows a candidate for office to buy or use airtime outside of regular news broadcasts, it must allow all candidates that opportunity. On its face, this provision seems to give the public a chance to hear from candidates of all ideologies and political parties, but in actuality, it often has the reverse effect. Confronted with the prospect of allowing every candidate to speak, no matter how slight the chance of his or her victory and how small an audience is likely to tune in, many stations instead opt to allow none to speak at all. This rule has been suspended for purposes of televising political debates. Minor-party candidates may be excluded and may appeal to the FCC if they think they have been unfairly left out.

The *fairness doctrine* extended beyond election broadcasts; it required that stations give free airtime to issues that concerned the public and to opposing sides when controversial issues were covered. Like the equal time rule, this had the effect of encouraging stations to avoid controversial topics. The FCC ended the rule in the 1980s, and when Congress tried to revive it in 1987, President Ronald Reagan vetoed the bill, claiming it led to "bland" programming.[35]

The *right of rebuttal* says that individuals whose reputations are damaged on the air have a right to respond. This rule is not enforced strictly by the FCC and the courts, however, for fear that it would quell controversial broadcasts, as the other two rules have done.

All these rules remain somewhat controversial. Politicians would like to have the rules enforced because they help them to air their views publicly. Theoretically, the rules should benefit the public, though as we have seen, they often do not. Media owners see these rules as forcing them to air unpopular speakers who damage their ratings and as limiting their abilities to decide station policy. They argue that given all the cable and satellite outlets, access to broadcast time is no longer such a scarce resource and that the broadcast media should be subject to the same legal protections as the print media.

Many of the limitations on station ownership that the original act established were abolished with the 1996 Telecommunications Act in order to open up competition and promote diversity in media markets. The act failed to reign in the media giants, however, and, in fact, ended up facilitating mergers that concentrated media ownership even more. The law permits ownership of multiple stations as long as they do not reach more than 35 percent of the market, and nothing prevents the networks themselves from reaching a far larger market through their collective affiliates. The 1996 legislation also opened up the way for ownership of cable stations by network owners, and it allows cable companies to offer many services previously supplied only by telephone companies. The overall effect of this deregulation has been to increase the possibilities for media monopoly dramatically.

As of now, the Internet remains unregulated. Some users want the government to create and enforce a policy of *net neutrality* that would ensure that telecommunication companies cannot use their control over Internet access to restrict or limit content with price discrimination, and to keep the Internet unfettered and open to innovation. Opponents believe that such a policy would reduce incentives for companies to innovate. In 2007 the Federal Trade Commission declined to recommend regulation, issuing a report disparaging the subject of regulation generally and arguing that the industry is a young one and the effects of regulation on consumers and providers are unknown.[36] In 2008 several net neutrality bills were introduced in Congress; the "netroots," such as the posters at *Daily Kos*, are strongly in favor, and the telecom and cable companies are opposed.[37]

Who Are the Journalists?
Gatekeepers deciding what news gets covered and how

Corporate ownership does not tell the whole story of modern journalism. Although the mass media are no longer owned primarily by individuals, individuals continue to be the eyes, ears, nose, and legs of the business. Journalists are people who discover, report, edit, and publish the news in newspapers and magazines and on radio, television, and the Internet. They decide, in large part, the details about what news gets covered and how. In carrying out this journalistic function, they act as **gatekeepers**. Not all journalists share this enormous power equally. Managers of the wire services, which determine which news gets sent on to their members; editors, who decide which stories should be covered or which parts of a story should be cut; and even reporters, who decide how to pitch a story, are all gatekeepers, though to varying degrees. To understand the powerful influence the media exert on American politics, we need to move beyond the ownership structure to the question of who American journalists are and how they do their jobs.

Who Chooses Journalism?

The vast majority of journalists in this country (just over two-thirds) work in the print media, and about one-third are in broadcast journalism. Journalists live throughout the country, although those with more high-powered jobs tend to be concentrated in the Northeast. The statistics regarding journalists—85 percent white and 67 percent male—do not reflect the U.S. population as a whole, though they are a closer match to the portion of the labor force that holds college degrees.

Does this demographic profile of journalism make any difference? Does a population need to get its news from a group of reporters that mirrors its own gender, ethnic, and religious characteristics in order to get an accurate picture of what is going on? Not surprisingly, this question generates controversy among journalists. Some insist that the personal profile of a journalist is irrelevant to the quality of his or her news coverage, but evidence suggests that the life experiences of journalists do influence their reporting. For instance, most mainstream media focus on issues of concern to white middle-class America and reflect the values of that population, at the expense of minority issues and the concerns of poor people. General reporting also emphasizes urban rather than rural issues and concentrates on male-dominated sports. Women journalists, on the other hand, tend to report more on social issues that are of more concern to women.[38]

What Journalists Believe: Is There an Ideological Bias in the Media?

It is not the demographic profile of journalists, but their ideological profile—that is, the political views they hold—that concerns many observers. Political scientists know that the more educated people are, the more liberal their views tend to be, and because professional journalists are a well-educated lot on the whole, their views tend to be to the left of the average American's, particularly on social issues[39] (see Table 13.1). Women and minority journalists in particular are more liberal than the general population and are more likely to vote Democratic, though of course there are Republicans and independents in the profession as well.[40]

Still, despite the fact that they have ideological inclinations of their own, most members of the so-called "mainstream media" in the United States strive to leave their values outside the newsroom and to do objective work. Indeed, studies show that there is no discernible overall ideological bias in the media. To the extent that some outlets are slightly tilted to the left, they are offset by others that lean slightly to the right.[41] Most journalists, aware that their values are more liberal than the average American's, try hard to keep their coverage of issues balanced. Some Democratic candidates for president have even accused the press of being harder on them to compensate for their personal preferences.[42] In addition to this sort of self-restraint, the liberal tendencies of many journalists are tempered by the undoubtedly conservative nature of news ownership and management we have already discussed. The editorial tone of most papers is conservative; however, in the run-up to the 2008 presidential election, Barack Obama beat John McCain in endorsements 287 to 159 (see Figure 13.2 on page 450).[43]

Interestingly, despite the studies showing no discernible partisan bias in the media, people today, both liberals and conservatives, tend to perceive a bias against their own views, especially to the extent that they talk with others with like views about that bias.[44] Until the mid-1980s, citizens were not convinced that there was an ideological bias in the media—55 percent believed that the media were basically accurate and only 45 percent thought the press was biased in its reporting. Today large percentages are skeptical about the media sources they follow—both print and broadcast.[45]

Not surprisingly, the rise in the perception that the media are biased coincides with the growth of a more partisan tone in the media. A concerted conservative effort to bring what they believe is a much needed balance to the news has resulted in a host of talk radio shows, including those of Rush Limbaugh and Glenn Beck,

Table 13.1

Political Party Identification of U.S. Journalists Compared With U.S. Adult Population (percentage in each group)

Political Leanings	Journalists			
	1971	1982–1983	1992	2002
Democrat	35.5	38.5	44.1	37.0
Republican	25.7	18.8	16.4	18.6
Independent	32.5	39.1	34.4	33.5
Other/don't know/refused	6.3	3.7	5.1	10.5

Political Leanings	U.S. Adult Population			
	1971	1982–1983	1992	2002
Democrat	43.0	45.0	34.0	32.0
Republican	28.0	25.0	33.0	31.0
Independent	29.0	30.0	31.0	32.0
Other/don't know/refused	–	–	3.0	5.0

Sources: David H. Weaver et al., *The American Journalist in the 21st Century* (Mahwah, N.J.: Lawrence Erlbaum Associates, 2006); Gallup/CNN/USA Today survey, July 29–31, 2002.

the Fox News Channel on TV, and the online *Drudge Report,* to join already-existing conservative media outlets like the *Wall Street Journal* editorial page. The rise of the conservative media has led to what two scholars call a conservative "echo chamber," "a self-protective enclave hospitable to conservative beliefs" that "reinforces the views of these outlets' like-minded audience members, helps them maintain ideological coherence, protects them from counterpersuasion, reinforces conservative values and dispositions . . . and distances listeners, readers, and viewers from 'liberals' in general and Democrats in particular."[46]

The increasing effectiveness of this Republican media machine has led liberals, especially after media coverage of the Clinton impeachment, the 2000 election recount, the swift-boating of John Kerry, and the rise of the Tea Party movement, to argue that the media is biased against them.[47] Their response, in the form of shows—like *Countdown With Keith Olbermann* and the *Rachel Maddow Show* on MSNBC; and the online *Huffington Post* (among other blogs and liberal web sites)— now contributes a powerful liberal voice, but one nowhere near as effective politically as the conservative voice already in place. This is due partly to the different

Figure 13.2

Newspaper Endorsements of Presidential Candidates, 1932–2008

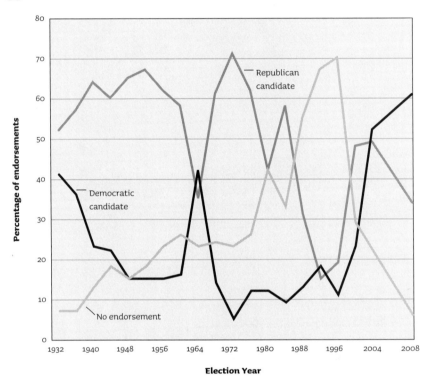

Source: Harold W. Stanley and Richard G. Niemi, *Vital Statistics on American Politics, 2009–2010* (Washington, D.C.: CQ Press, 2010), Table 14.7.

values that conservatives and liberals bring to the table. Liberals can't settle on a single truth to promote and often argue as much among themselves as with their ideological opponents. Conservatives, on the other hand, are more willing to silence their own party members who don't conform to the conservative ideal they believe Ronald Reagan embodied.[48]

When Americans, most of whom hold moderate views somewhere in the political center, listen to these overtly partisan media sources, it is no wonder that they perceive the media as biased in one direction or another. In 2010, at his "Rally to Restore Sanity and/or Fear," held on the Washington Mall, comedian Jon Stewart blasted what he called the "24-hour political pundit perpetual panic conflictinator," accusing cable news outlets on both sides of demonizing each other so severely that they were creating a political environment where compromise and cooperation are well nigh impossible.

The Growth of the Washington Press Corps

From a news-gathering perspective, America is organized into beats, identifiable areas covered by reporters who become familiar with their territories, get to know the sources of their stories, and otherwise institutionalize their official bit of journalistic "turf." Typical beats include the police, politics, business, education, and sports, and these can be broken down into even more specialized areas, such as the White House, Congress, and the Supreme Court.

The beat system is well entrenched in American journalism, and at the top echelon of American journalists are those who cover the national political beat in Washington. National politics takes place in Washington—not just the interactions of Congress, the president, and the courts but also the internal workings of political parties and the rival lobbying of interest groups, including states, major corporations, and other national organizations. For a political reporter, Washington is the coveted place to be.

As the *Washington Post*'s David Broder points out, the concentration of politics, politicians, and reporters in Washington leads to "a complex but cozy relationship between journalists and public officials."[49] Washington journalists share an interest in politics with politicians, they have similar educations, they often make about the same amount of money, and they are in many ways natural colleagues and friends. So much do journalists and politicians have in common that they often exchange jobs with ease, in a trend that Broder calls the "revolving door."

The **revolving door**, like the practice we discussed in Chapter 11, refers to the practice of journalists taking positions in government and then returning to journalism again, or vice versa, perhaps several times over. Consequently some journalists have insider knowledge and access that can enhance their reporting, but they are open to criticisms of conflict of interest and lack of objectivity. The number of prominent journalists who have gone through this revolving door is legion, including such notables as George Stephanopoulos, a Clinton adviser who now hosts *Good Morning America* on ABC; Karl Rove, President George W. Bush's political adviser who is now a commentator on Fox; and the late Tony Snow, who went from a career in television to being Bush's press secretary, to name only a few.[50]

The Media and Politics
Manipulating information to influence who gets what and how

As we have seen, the American media make up an amazingly complex institution. Once primarily a nation of print journalism, the United States is now in the grip of the electronic media. Television has changed the American political landscape, and now the Internet promises, or threatens, to do the same. Privately owned, the media have a tendency to represent the corporate interest, but that influence is countered to some extent by the professional concerns of journalists. Still, some of those at the upper levels of the profession, those who tend to report to us on national politics, have very close links with the political world they cover, and this too influences the news we get. What is the effect of all this on American politics?

The Shaping of Public Opinion

We have already looked at the question of bias in the media and noted that not only is there a corporate or commercial bias, but that Americans are also increasingly convinced that the news media are ideologically biased. Political scientists acknowledge that ideological bias may exist, but they conclude that it isn't so much that the media tell us what to think as that they tell us what to think *about*. These scholars have documented four kinds of media effects on our thinking: agenda setting, priming, framing, and persuasion by professional communicators.[51]

Most of us get most of our news from television, but television is limited in which of the many daily political events it can cover. As political scientists Shanto Iyengar and Donald Kinder say, television news is "news that matters,"[52] which means that television reporters perform the function of agenda setting. When television reporters choose to cover an event, they are telling us that out of all the events happening, this one is important, and we should pay attention. The agenda-setting role of the media is not the last word, however. Often the media will be fascinated with an event that simply fails to resonate with the public. Despite extensive media coverage of President Clinton's affair with White House intern Monica Lewinsky in 1998, public opinion polls continued to show that the public did not think it was an issue worthy of the time the media spent on it.

Closely related to agenda setting, **priming** refers to the ways that the media influence how people and events should be evaluated by things they emphasize as important. The theory of priming says that if the media are constantly emphasizing crime, then politicians, and particularly the president, will be evaluated on how well they deal with crime. If the media emphasize the environment, then that will become the relevant yardstick for evaluation. In effect, according to this concept, the media not only tell us what to think about but how to think about those things. Priming has been supported with empirical evidence,[53] although it is clearly not in effect all the time on all the issues.

A third media effect on our thinking is called **framing**. Just as a painting's appearance can be altered by changing its frame, a political event can look different to us depending on how the media frame it—that is, what they choose to emphasize in their coverage. For example, people view a war differently depending on whether the coverage highlights American casualties or military victories. The important point about framing is that how the media present a political issue or event may affect how the public perceives that issue, whether they see it as a problem, and who they view as responsible for solving it.

Finally, some political scientists argue that the media affect public opinion because viewers, who often don't have the time or background to research the issues themselves, sometimes change their minds to agree with trusted newscasters and expert sources.[54] Familiar with this phenomenon, when President Lyndon Johnson heard popular CBS news anchor Walter Cronkite take a stand against American involvement in Vietnam, he told an aide it was "all over." Predicting that the public would follow the lead of one of the most trusted figures in America, he knew there would be little support for a continued war effort. Often, however, especially in the age of cable news and multiple broadcast choices, the communicators on whom the media rely are not revered figures like "Uncle Walter," but people who regularly pass through the revolving door and whose objectivity cannot be taken for granted.

The effects of agenda setting, priming, framing, and expert persuasion should not be taken to mean that we are all unwitting dupes of the media. In the first place, these are not iron-clad rules; they are tendencies that scholars have discovered and confirmed with experimentation and public opinion surveys. That means that they hold true for many but not all people. Members of the two major political parties, for instance, are less affected by agenda setting than are independents, perhaps because the latter do not have a party to rely on to tell them what is important.[55]

Second, we bring our own armor to the barrage of media effects we face regularly. We all filter our news watching through our own ideas, values, and distinct perspectives. Scholars who emphasize that audiences are active, not passive, consumers of the media say that people counter the effects of the media by setting their own agendas and processing the news in light of those agendas. That is, viewers exercise **selective perception**; they filter information through their own values and interests, thereby determining the news items they will pay attention to, the items they will remember, and the items they will forget.[56] If people do not seem to be well informed on the issues emphasized by the media, it may be that they do not see them as having an effect on their lives. The point is that, as consumers, we do more than passively absorb the messages and values provided by the media.

The Portrayal of Politics as Conflict and Image

In addition to shaping public opinion, the media also affect politics by their tendency to portray complex and substantive political issues as questions of personal image and contests between individuals. Rather than examining the details and nuances of policy differences, the media tend to focus on image and to play up personalities and conflicts even when their readers and viewers say they want something quite different. The effect of this approach, according to some researchers, is to make politics seem negative and to increase popular cynicism.

Horse-race journalism refers to the media's tendency to see politics as competition between individuals. Rather than report on the policy differences between politicians or the effects their proposals will have on ordinary Americans, today's media tend to report on politics as if it were a battle between individual gladiators or a game of strategy and wit but not substance. This sort of journalism not only

Don't Be Fooled by the Media

As we have seen in this chapter, many forces are working to make the citizen's job difficult when it comes to getting, following, and interpreting the news. But forewarned is forearmed, and the knowledge you have gained can turn you into the savviest of media consumers. Journalist Carlin Romano says, "What the press covers matters less in the end than how the public reads. Effective reading of the news requires not just a key—a Rosetta stone by which to decipher current clichés—but an activity, a regimen."[1] When you read the paper, watch the news, listen to the radio, or surf the Internet, try to remember to ask yourself the following questions. This will be a lot more work than just letting the words wash over you or pass before your eyes, but as a payoff you will know more and be less cynical about politics; you will be less likely to be manipulated, either by the media or by more knowledgeable friends and family; and, as a bonus, you will be a more effective, sophisticated, and satisfied citizen. Here are the questions. Keep a copy in your wallet.

1. **Who owns this media source?** Look at the page in newspapers and magazines that lists the publisher and editors. Take note of radio and television call letters. See if the source is owned by one of the media conglomerates. Look to see who takes credit for a web site. What could be this owner's agenda? Is it corporate, political, ideological? How might that agenda affect the news?

2. **Who is this journalist (reporter, anchor person, webmaster, etc.)?** Does he or she share the characteristics of the average American or of the media elite? How might that affect his or her perspective on the news? Has he or she been in politics? In what role? How might that affect how he or she sees current political events? Some of this information might be hard to find at first, but if a particular journalist appears to have a special agenda, it might be worth the extra research to find out.

3. **Is the writer doing reporting or commentary?** Straight reporting is an objective offering of the facts, with some analysis to help you interpret what those facts mean. Commentary inserts the writer's opinion of the facts, and reflects the writer's values. At one time, reporting was found throughout the newspaper or news broadcast, and commentary was saved for the op-ed pages or a special segment of the broadcast. These days the line is blurred somewhat in the traditional news and is almost invisible in many online news sources or on specialty news sources like Fox. Both kinds of news stories can be useful, but the reader needs to be wary when opinion is injected or when it frames the facts. Use the tips in "*Consider the Source:* Don't be Fooled by the Op-Ed Pages" (see Chapter 3) to be a savvy consumer of opinion journalism.

4. **What is the news of the day?** How do the news stories covered by your source (radio, TV, newspaper, magazine, or web) compare to the stories covered elsewhere? Why are these stories covered and not others? Who makes the decisions? How are the stories framed? Are positive or negative aspects emphasized? What standards do the journalists suggest you use to evaluate the story—that is, what standards do they seem to focus on?

5. **What issues are involved?** Can you get beyond the "horse race"? For instance, if reporters are focusing on the delivery of a politician's speech and her opponent's reactions to it, try to get a copy of the speech to read for yourself. Check the web or a source like the *New York Times.* Similarly, when the media emphasize conflict, ask yourself what underlying issues are involved. Look for primary (original) sources whenever possible, ones that have not been processed by the media for you. If conflicts are presented as a choice between two sides, ask yourself if there are other sides that might be relevant.

6. **Who are the story's sources?** Are they "official" sources? Whose point of view do they represent? Are their remarks attributed to them, or are they speaking "on background" (anonymously)? Such sources frequently show up as "highly placed administration officials" or "sources close to the senator." Why would people not want their names disclosed? How should that affect how we interpret what they say? Do you see the same sources appearing in many stories in different types of media? Have these sources been through the "revolving door"? Are they pundits? What audience are they addressing?

7. **Is someone putting spin on this story?** Is there visible news management? Is the main source the politician's press office? Is the story based on a leak? If so, can you make a guess at the motivation of the leaker? What evidence supports your guess? What is the spin? That is, what do the politician's handlers want you to think about the issue or event?

8. **Who are the advertisers?** How might that affect the coverage of the news? What sorts of stories might be affected by the advertisers' presence? Are there potential stories that might hurt the advertiser?

9. **What are the media doing to get your attention?** Is the coverage of a news event detailed and thorough, or is it "lightened up" to make it faster and easier for you to process? If so, what are you missing? What is on the cover of the newspaper or magazine? What is the lead story on the network? How do the media's efforts to get your attention affect the news you get? Would you have read or listened to the story if the media had not worked at getting your attention?

10. **What values and beliefs do you bring to the news?** What are your biases? Are you liberal? Conservative? How do your current life experiences affect your political views or priorities? How do these values, ideas, and experiences affect how you see the news, what you pay attention to, and what you skip? List all the articles or stories you tuned out, and ask yourself why you did so. Can you find a news source that you usually disagree with, that you think is biased or always wrong? Read it now and again. It will help you keep your perspective and ensure that you get a mix of views that will keep you thinking critically. We are challenged not by ideas we agree with but by those that we find flawed. Stay an active media consumer.

---

1. Carlin Romano, "What? The Grisley Truth About Bare Facts," in Robert Karl Manoff and Michael Schudson, eds., *Reading the News* (New York: Pantheon Books, 1986), 78.

shows politics in the most negative light, as if politicians cared only to score victories off one another in a never-ending fight to promote their own self-interests, but it also ignores the concerns that citizens have about politics.

As journalist James Fallows points out, when citizens are given a chance to ask questions of politicians, they focus on all the elements of politics that touch their lives: taxes, wars, Social Security, student loans, education, and welfare.[57] But journalists focus on questions of strategy, popularity, and relative positioning in relation to real or imagined rivals. The obsession with who is winning makes the coverage of campaigns, or of partisan battles in Congress, or of disputes between the president and Congress far more trivial than it needs to be, and far less educational to the American public. (*"Consider the Source:* Don't Be Fooled by the Media" will help you get beyond the horse-race coverage in much of today's media.)

Television is primarily an entertainment medium and, by its nature, one that is focused on image: what people look like, what they sound like, and how an event is staged and presented. Television, and to some extent its competitors in the print media, concentrates on doing what it does well: giving us pictures of politics instead of delving beneath the surface. This has the effect of leading us to value the more superficial aspects of politics, even if only subconsciously. An early and telling example was the 1960 presidential debate between Richard Nixon and John Kennedy, when the younger, better-looking Kennedy presented a more presidential image than the swarthy and sweating Nixon and won both the debate and the election. Combine this emphasis on image with horse-race journalism, and the result is a preoccupation with appearance and strategy at the cost of substance.

The words of politicians are being similarly reduced to the audio equivalent of a snapshot, the **sound bite**. A sound bite is a short block of speech by a politician that makes it on the news. These are often played repetitively and can drown out the substance of the message a politician wishes to convey. Occasionally they can come back to haunt a politician, too, as did George H. W. Bush's famous 1988 promise, "Read my lips, no new taxes," broken in 1992 when, as president, he did, in fact, support a tax hike. The amount of time that the electronic media devote to the actual words a politician utters is shrinking. In 2000 the average length for a sound bite from a presidential candidate on the nightly network news was 7.3 seconds, down from 10 seconds in 1992 and 42 seconds in 1968.[58] Journalists use the extra time to interpret what we have heard and often to put it into the horse-race metaphor.[59]

Reporters also tend to concentrate on developing scandals to the exclusion of other, possibly more relevant, news events. At the end of the summer of 2008, when former Democratic candidate John Edwards revealed that he had had an affair with a campaign staffer, media attention immediately and obsessively focused on Edwards, who had been out of the race for months, rather than the two candidates, Obama and McCain, who were still contending for the presidency. Political scientist Larry Sabato refers to this behavior as a **feeding frenzy**: "the press coverage attending any political event or circumstance where a critical mass of journalists leap to cover the same embarrassing or scandalous subject and pursue it intensely, often excessively, and sometimes uncontrollably."[60] When the scandal is relevant to the job that a politician is doing, as was Watergate or the more recent Jack Abramoff lobbying scandal, then the feeding frenzy may yield useful information for the public, but often it focuses on personal scandals that are easier for people to understand and prove a distraction from the news people need to know.

Political scientist Thomas Patterson attributes the phenomenon of the feeding frenzy to a growing negativity and increased cynicism among members of the media. He argues that it is not a liberal or a conservative bias among reporters that we ought to worry about. Rather, it is their antigovernment views, focusing on the adversarial and negative aspects of politics to the exclusion of its positive achievements, that foster a cynical view of politics among the general public. Most presidents and presidential candidates are treated by the press as fundamentally untrustworthy, when in fact most do precisely what they say they are going to do. Since it takes time and energy to investigate all the claims that a president or a candidate makes, the media evaluate political claims not with their own careful scrutiny but with statements from political opponents. This makes politics appear endlessly adversarial and, as Patterson says, replaces investigative journalism with attack journalism.[61]

A consequence of the negative content of political coverage is that voters' opinions of candidates have sunk, and citizen dissatisfaction with the electoral process has risen.[62] Not only is the public becoming more cynical about the political world, but it is also becoming more cynical about the media. A recent public opinion poll showed that half or more of the American public now thinks that the news is too biased, sensationalized, and manipulated by special interests and that reporters offer too many of their own opinions, quote unnamed sources, and are negative.[63] But another consequence, and one that may somewhat alleviate the first, is that, as we have noted, new forms of the media are opening up to supplement or even replace the older ones. Television talk shows, radio call-in shows, and other outlets that involve public input and bypass the adversarial questions and negative comments of the traditional media allow the public, in some ways, to set the agenda. In fact, a study of the 1992 election showed that television talk shows focused more on substantive policy issues and presented more balanced and positive images of the candidates than did the mainstream media.[64]

Politics as Public Relations

There is no doubt that the media portray politics in a negative light, that news reporting emphasizes personality, superficial image, and conflict over substantive policy issues. Some media figures argue, however, that this is not the media's fault, but rather the responsibility of politicians and their press officers who are so obsessed with their own images on television that they limit access to the media, speak only in prearranged sound bites, and present themselves to the public in carefully orchestrated "media events."[65] Media events are designed to limit the ability of reporters to put their own interpretation on the occasion.

'... Political campaigns have become so simplistic and superficial...
In the 20 seconds we have left, could you explain why?

THE CHRISTIAN SCIENCE MONITOR

The rules of American politics that require a politician to have high public approval to maximize his or her clout, mean that politicians have to try to get maximum exposure for their ideas and accomplishments while limiting the damage the media can do with their intense scrutiny, investigations, and critical perspectives. This effort to control the media can lead to an emphasis on short-term gain over long-term priorities and the making of policy decisions with an eye to their political impact—a tendency that has come to be known as the **permanent campaign**.[66] A first-rate example of how the permanent campaign drove events in the George W. Bush administration can be found in *What Happened: Inside the Bush White House and Washington's Culture of Deception,* the memoirs of Bush's former press secretary Scott McClellan.[67]

News management describes the chief mechanism of the permanent campaign—the efforts of a politician's staff—media consultants, press secretaries, pollsters, campaign strategists, and general advisers—to control the news about the politician. The staff want to put their own issues on the agenda, determine for themselves the standards by which the politician will be evaluated, frame the issues, and supply the sources for reporters, so that they will put their client, the politician, in the best possible light. In contemporary political jargon, they want to put a **spin**, or an interpretation, on the news that will be most flattering to the politician whose image is in their care. To some extent, modern American politics has become a battle between the press and the politicians and among the politicians themselves to control the agenda and the images that reach the public. It has become a battle of the "spin doctors."

The techniques of news management can include tightly controlling the information released by the politician's office, limiting access to the politician, constructing an elaborate communications bureaucracy, making a concerted effort to bypass the Washington press corps and go directly to the public, prepackaging the news in sound-bite-size pieces, and using strategic **leaks**, that is, secretly revealing confidential information to the press.[68]

Not all presidential administrations are equally accomplished at using these techniques of news management, of course. Nixon was successful, at least in his first administration, and Reagan's has been referred to as a model of public relations.[69] Clinton did not manage the media effectively in the early years of his first administration; consequently, he was at the mercy of a frustrated and an annoyed press corps. Within a couple of years, however, the Clinton staff had become much more skilled and, by his second administration, was adeptly handling scandals that would have daunted more seasoned public relations experts.

The George W. Bush administration did a superb job of news management, especially in Bush's first term. For instance, most of Bush's public events were open only to Bush supporters; where there was audience interaction, he received questions only from those who endorsed his programs and goals. In addition, in 2005 it was revealed that the Bush administration had paid several journalists to report favorably on the president's policies, and the administration expanded a Clinton-era program of government-produced videos touting administration achievements that are distributed to local television stations, which show them as actual news.[70] The Government Accountability Office has said that such videos may be "covert propaganda" and cannot be made if they do not disclose who made them, but the Department of Justice and the Office of Management and Budget has said that the agencies may ignore that finding.[71] Finally, reporters who could be trusted to ask supportive questions were favored in White House news briefings and press conferences.[72] Supporters defended the Bush White House's news management strategy as efficient and praiseworthy. Critics, on the other hand, claimed that the White House has become a "propaganda machine" to serve the president's political goals.[73]

All indications in the first two years of Barack Obama's administration are that it will be as disciplined as Bush's was. During the presidential campaign, the Obama camp was famous for avoiding leaks and controlling their message, and although that perfect discipline has not been maintained in the White House, it is still remarkably free of public infighting and leaks. Obama's press secretary, Robert Gibbs, is a senior adviser to the president and has uncommon access and a dedication to protecting his interests.[74] One difference between the Obama administration and its predecessors is the elaborate electronic communication network they have set up, which allows them to talk directly to supporters and to bypass the traditional media if they want to.

There is a real cost to the transformation of politics into public relations, no matter whose administration is engaging in the practice (and, with varying degrees of expertise, they all do). Not only does the public suffer from not getting the straight story to evaluate government policies that affect their lives, but politicians must spend time and energy on image considerations that do not really help them serve the public. And the people who are skilled enough at managing the press to get elected to office have not necessarily demonstrated any leadership skills. The skills required by an actor and a statesperson are not the same, and the current system may encourage us to choose the wrong leaders for the wrong reasons and discourage the right people from running at all.

Reduction in Political Accountability

A final political effect of the media, according to some scholars, is a reduction in political accountability. **Political accountability** is the very hallmark of democracy: political leaders must answer to the public for their actions. If our leaders do something we do not like, we can make them bear the consequences of their actions by voting them out of office. The threat of being voted out of office is supposed to encourage them to do what we want in the first place.

Some political scientists, however, argue that Americans' reliance on television for their news has weakened political accountability and thus democracy as well.[75] Their arguments are complex but compelling. First, they say that television has come to reduce the influence of political parties, since it allows politicians to take their message directly to the people. Parties are no longer absolutely necessary to mediate politics—that is, to provide a link between leaders and the people—but parties have traditionally been a way to keep politicians accountable. Second, television covers politicians as individuals, and as individuals they have incentives to take credit for what the public likes and to blame others for what the public doesn't like. And because they are covered as individuals, they have little reason to form coalitions to work together. Third, television, by emphasizing image and style, allows politicians to avoid taking stances on substantive policy issues; the public often does not know where they stand and cannot hold them accountable. Finally, the episodic way in which the media frame political events makes it difficult for people to discern what has really happened politically and whose responsibility it is.

The result is that the modern media, and especially television, have changed the rules of politics. Today it is harder for citizens to know who is responsible for laws, policies, and political actions and harder to make politicians behave responsibly.

Citizenship and the Media
Growing citizen access increases participation but
blurs lines of journalism

We have been unable to talk about the media in this chapter without talking about citizenship. Citizens have been a constant "who" in our analysis because the media exist, by definition, to give information to citizens and to mediate their relationship to government. But if we evaluate the traditional role of the media with respect to the public, the relationship that emerges is not a particularly responsive one. Almost from the beginning, control of the American media has been in the hands of an elite group, whether party leaders, politicians, wealthy entrepreneurs, or corporate owners. Financial concerns have meant that the media in the United States have been driven more by profit motive than by public interest. Not only are ownership and control of the media far removed from the hands of everyday Americans, but the reporting of national news is done mostly by reporters who do not fit the profile of those "average" citizens and whose concerns often do not reflect the concerns of their audience.

Citizens' access to the media has been correspondingly remote. The primary role available to them has been passive: that of reader, listener, or watcher. The power they wield is the power of switching newspapers or changing channels, essentially choosing among competing elites, but this is not an active participatory role. While freedom of the press is a right technically held by all citizens, there is no right of access to the press; citizens have difficulty making their voices heard, and of course most do not even try. Members of the media holler long and loud about their right to publish what they want, but only sporadically and briefly do they consider their obligations to the public to provide the sort of information that can sustain a democracy. If active democracy requires a political community in which the public can deliberate about important issues, it would seem that the American media are failing miserably at creating that community.

But as we see in this chapter's *What's at Stake?* feature, the media are in flux and although the future of the print media is in question, some of the **new media** that are replacing it are remarkably more open and responsive. The term *new media* refers to the high-tech outlets that have sprung up to compete with traditional newspapers, magazines, and network news. Some of these outlets, such as cable news, specialized television programs, and Internet news, allow citizens to get fast-breaking reports of events as they occur and even to customize the news that they get. Talk radio and call-in television shows—new uses of the "old" media—allow citizen interaction, as do Internet chat rooms and other online forums. Many web sites allow users to give their opinions of issues in unscientific straw polls. Some analysts speculate that it is only a matter of time until we can all vote on issues from our home computers. The one thing that these new forms of media have in common is that they bypass the old, making the corporate journalistic establishment less powerful than it was but perhaps giving rise to new elites and raising new questions about participation and how much access we really want citizens to have.

One of the most significant developments in the new media is the proliferation of blogs. It is truly citizen journalism—the cyber-equivalent of giving everyday people their own printing presses and the means to publish their views. While blogs can be on any subject, the ones that interest us here are the ones that focus on politics and media criticism. As is true of any unregulated media source, there is a good deal of inaccurate and unsubstantiated information in the so-called blogosphere. There is no credentialing process for bloggers, they are not usually admitted to the

White House or other official news conferences unless they also report for a more traditional media outlet, and they generally lack the resources required to do a great deal of investigative reporting.

But blogs can also do many things their more mainstream brethren cannot, and there is some truly first-rate journalism to be found on blogs. Since bloggers are not (usually) indebted to deep corporate pockets, they can hold the mainstream media accountable, but in turn it is the job of the consumer to scrutinize the reporting of bloggers as scrupulously as they do the rest of the media. There is no substitute for critical evaluation of the news, but blogs are a media form that is truly independent, open, and democratic in a way that no other media source can be.

▶ What's at Stake Revisited

In this chapter we have seen that the world of information has undergone enormous, one might almost say revolutionary, change in the last half century, and the roller coaster ride hasn't come to an end. There are so many new ways to get information that the real challenge seems to be processing it and evaluating it. Worrying about the fate of something as old fashioned as a newspaper seems almost beside the point.

But what is at stake in the impending demise of newspapers as a business model is more than it might seem on its face. The issue is not about newspapers per se—but about the news they report. As Clay Shirky, an Internet expert and writer, says, "Society doesn't need newspapers. What we need is journalism."[76] By this he means information, well researched and objective, about the world we live in, about the things our elected officials are doing in our name, about the consequences of the public choices we make.

Journalism has traditionally been paid for by newspapers that have either had their own news bureaus around the world or subscribed to and supported a news service like the Associated Press. The money they paid for news-gathering came from advertisers who paid their rates because they had no other way to reach their markets. Now that those advertisers have multiple, cheap outlets in which to market their wares, newspapers, and thus journalism, are in danger. But journalism today is also in danger from forces within. As we have seen, the mainstream media, the conventional media of which print is the backbone, are concentrated in corporate ownership and driven by their quest for advertising dollars to simplify and "dummy down" the news, often becoming uncomfortably close to their sources in the process. The quality of journalism has been threatened by more than the decline of the print media.

Shirky argues that we are in the midst of a revolution, "where the old stuff gets broken faster than the new stuff is put in its place,"[77] so we don't know what journalism will look like in a new, post-newspaper age. But Shirky thinks it's a mistake to assume that we aren't transitioning to such an age, that those who proclaim loudly that the old newspaper model can be saved are whistling past the graveyard, refusing to acknowledge that printing presses are costly to run and that the model of newspaper-centered news is obsolete in a world where the Internet makes it impossible for them to charge for or to retain control over the work they do.

And as we saw, some observers, such as journalist Dan Gillmor, believe that the revolution is bringing positive changes—that a powerful, citizen-driven journalism is taking the place of a complacent, ratings-driven corporate journalism, that information is gathered and disseminated in real time with multiple researchers on the job to correct and assist each other, a sort of Wikipedia journalism, perhaps.[78] This is the model, for instance, of *Atlantic Monthly* blogger Andrew Sullivan, who "live blogged" the Iranian uprising in 2009, passing on to his readers information tweeted to him from the front lines—information that could not have been easily gathered even with a news bureau in Tehran. Sullivan would agree with Gillmor, arguing that blogging is "the first journalistic model that actually harnesses rather than exploits the true democratic nature of the web."[79]

For Sullivan, the demise of the old media and the rise of the new is a positive development, making him more hopeful for democracy, not less. He says,

> But what distinguishes the best of the new media is what could still be recaptured by the old: the mischievous *spirit* of journalism and free, unfettered inquiry. Journalism has gotten too pompous, too affluent, too self-loving, and too entwined with the establishment of both wings of American politics to be what we need it to be.
>
> We need it to be fearless and obnoxious, out of a conviction that more speech, however much vulgarity and nonsense it creates, is always better than less speech. In America, this is a liberal spirit in the grandest sense of that word—but also a conservative one, since retaining that rebelliousness is tending to an ancient American tradition, from the Founders onward.[80]

Shirky is optimistic, as well:

> For the next few decades, journalism will be made up of overlapping special cases. Many of these models will rely on amateurs as researchers and writers. Many of these modes will rely on sponsorship or grants or endowments instead of revenues. Many of these models will rely on excitable 14-year-olds distributing the results. Many of these models will fail. No one experiment is going to replace what we are now losing with the demise of news on paper, but over time, the collection of new experiments that do might give us the journalism we need.[81]

And then again, they may not—Shirky's optimism does not seem misplaced in light of the work of writers such as Gillmor and Sullivan, but the truth is that what's at stake in the end of the newspaper model may be the very information we need to make the intelligent decisions that allow democracy to thrive. The jury is out on this one, but the open, innovative nature of the medium allows each of us to engage in the experimentation and work that might bring the answers. The late media critic Marshall McLuhan wrote in the 1960s that "the medium is the message." In the Internet age, that has the potential to be true as never before.

▶ Summary With Key Terms

Mass media (436) are forms of communication—such as television, radio, web sites and **blogs** (440), newspapers, and magazines—that reach large public audiences. More media outlets and more information mean that Americans must devote ever-increasing time, effort, and money to sort out what is relevant to them.

Media ownership can influence the kind of news we get. Early political parties and candidates created newspapers to advocate their issues. When newspapers suddenly became cheap and thus accessible to the general public in the 1830s, papers aimed for objectivity as a way to attract more readers. Later, newspaper owners used sensationalist reporting to sell more newspapers and gain independence from political interests. Today's media, still profit driven, are now owned by a few large corporate interests, creating a **commercial bias** (443) in the news we get. The 1934 Federal Communications Act, which created the Federal Communications Commission, imposed order on multiple media outlets and attempted to serve the public interest through three provisions: the equal time rule, the fairness doctrine, and the right of rebuttal.

Journalists, as **gatekeepers** (447), have great influence over news content and presentation, but public skepticism of the media has increased in recent decades. Some critics believe the homogeneous background of journalists—mostly male, white, well educated, with northeastern roots—biases the press, as does their predominantly liberal ideology. Others claim that the **revolving door** (451), the practice of journalists taking government positions but later returning to reporting, severely damages news objectivity.

The media influences politics by shaping public opinion through agenda setting, **priming** (452), **framing** (452), and persuasion, although citizens have their own armor against this influence, called **selective perception** (453). Journalists also tend to reduce politics to conflict and image, especially through the widespread practice of **horse-race journalism** (453), the frequent use of **sound bites** (456), and the **feeding frenzy** (456) they engage in at the whiff of scandal. Politicians respond by turning politics into public relations, running what amounts to a **permanent campaign** (458), by mastering the techniques of **news management** (458), attempting to control with **spin** (458) and the judicious use of **leaks** (459) any news that affects them. The result of this complex relationship between the media and politicians is a reduction in **political accountability** (460).

Because the media play such a central role in democracy, the degree to which they fail to provide relevant, objective information about government is worrying. The growing use of the **new media** (461), including blogs, has the potential to restore journalism to its more traditional watchdog and information-provider role.

Explore this subject further with suggested readings, movies, and web sites at http://republic-brief.cqpress.com, where you'll also find study aids, practice quizzes, flash cards, and Internet exercises.

...es in the energy and credit marke...

...equities.

...nergy prices continued their lon...

Tough time

...like making... ...Global supply...

Chapter 14

Domestic and Foreign Policy

▶ What's at Stake?

In the spring and summer of 2010, Americans watched, horrified, as oil gushed into the Gulf of Mexico from a ruined oil rig, the *Deepwater Horizon,* leased by British Petroleum off the coast of Louisiana. It was the worst offshore oil spill in U.S. history. For weeks, and then months, the oil company and the U.S. government were stymied in their efforts to stem the leak by a lack of technology, equipment, and know-how. As TV commentators covered the wreckage in the Gulf, they turned time and again to a question of just how horrified we really were. Would the vision of oil-soaked birds and dead fish do anything to quench America's seemingly insatiable thirst for oil? Would it encourage us to be more frugal in our consumption of fossil fuels and spur us to invest more in alternative sources of energy?

Not really. In a country like the United States, where so much development took place after the invention of the automobile, we can't get along without our cars, and as an auto-dependent nation, we're at the mercy of gas prices, which have climbed in recent years to well over $2.00 or even $3.00 a gallon. Many factors can cause gas prices to rise, but a central one is the availability of oil: oil prices account for roughly half the cost of gasoline.[1] Most of the oil we use in the United States comes from outside the country. In early 2008, 66 percent came from abroad and that figure is expected to rise by an additional two-thirds by 2025.[2]

How do we insulate ourselves from the vagaries of the oil market? Should we develop alternative sources of energy, build hybrid cars, brew up fuel from corn or other common resources, or just encourage Americans to use less gas, perhaps by carpooling or biking to work? Conservationists insist that we are devoting far too little time and money to promoting such environmentally friendly solutions.[3] Others argue, however, that the answer is much more straightforward and obvious—we should simply look for more oil on our own shores.

The question of whether we should offset that dependence by pursuing more domestic sources of oil—via offshore drilling or drilling in the Arctic National Wildlife Refuge (ANWR)—has long been a hot-button issue in American politics. Although the Deepwater Horizon oil spill changed public opinion about offshore drilling, the public remained closely divided on the issue.[4] And while a majority had opposed drilling in ANWR, as gas prices rose, so did approval of tapping our Alaskan reserves.[5] Highlighting the divisive nature of the issue, support for drilling broke down along party lines: during the 2008 presidential campaign the Republican position was summed up by the chant "Drill, Baby, Drill"; the Democrats' view, by a less catchy determination to do no such thing. President Obama, seeking to bridge the gap, made the development of alternate forms of energy a priority for his administration, but he also supported the growth of offshore drilling as an interim measure until those alternate sources could be tapped.

The case of ANWR, a massive amount of land in Alaska that is the nation's largest wildlife preserve, provides a good example of the political challenges involved in trying to augment our oil supply at home. Environmentalists have battled with advocates of drilling in ANWR for more than thirty years, beginning in the Carter administration. In 1995 Congress approved drilling, only to have President Clinton veto the measure. The election of George W. Bush in 2000 provided drilling advocates with their best chance to date to remove restrictions in ANWR. Although President Bush made opening up ANWR a key legislative priority through both his terms in office, these attempts were consistently controversial and ultimately thwarted.

Concerned interest groups have lined up on both sides of the issue, spending millions to convince lawmakers to see things their way. Arctic Power, an organization whose members include ExxonMobil and which has been endorsed by the Alaska state legislature, has been at the forefront of the pro-drilling fight, as have been the Alaska Chamber of Commerce and the International Brotherhood of Teamsters. On the other side, the U.S. Public Interest Research Group opposes drilling, as does the Sierra Club and smaller groups like the Alaska Wilderness League.[6] Those supporting drilling in ANWR were energized in 2008 with Sen. John McCain's choice of then–Alaska governor Sarah Palin as his running mate. Though McCain disagreed with the policy, Palin has been a vocal advocate of drilling in her state. Why has the effort to open drilling in Alaska been so hard fought, and why do its foes remain so bitterly opposed? What exactly is at stake in the battle over drilling for oil here at home? We return to these questions after we look more closely at the policymaking process and at environmental policymaking, in particular.

"The quality of this air is horrible," we say as we gasp for breath while jogging in a local park. "Someone ought to *do* something about this."

"It's intolerable that homeless people are allowed to sleep in the public library. Why doesn't somebody *do* something?"

"How tragic that so many young children don't have health care. Can't anyone *do* anything about it?"

When we utter such cries of disgust, frustration, or compassion, we are not calling on the heavens to visit us with divine intervention. Usually the general somebody/anybody we call on for action is our government, and what government *does* or doesn't *do*, at the end of the day, is called public policy. In fact, public policy has been a focus of discussion throughout this book. When we ask what's at stake, as we do throughout this book, the *what* is almost always a government action or policy. The study of public policy is inseparable from the study of American politics.

In this chapter we focus specifically on what public policy is and how the parts of government we have studied come together to create it. But government is not something "out there," something external to us. We have seen in this book that in many ways American government is very responsive to us as citizens, either individually as voters or collectively as interest groups. While we do not dictate the details, the broad outlines of American public policy are largely what we say they should be. In some policy areas, such as social welfare reform and crime policy, politicians have responded to public opinion by limiting welfare and getting tougher on criminals. In other areas, notably Social Security and health care, politicians have responded to the powerful demands of organized interest groups. In still other policy areas, primarily economic policy, some of the political decisions have been taken out of the hands of elected officials precisely because these individuals tend to respond to what voters and interest groups want, or what they imagine they want.

In this chapter we look at the who, what, and how of American policymaking—who makes it, who benefits, and who pays, and how different sets of rules or incentive structures shape the policy that is produced and help to determine the winners and losers. You will learn about what policy is, who makes it, and how it is made, as well as about specific domestic policy areas—social policy such as Social Security, welfare, and health care policy, and economic policy such as fiscal, monetary, and tax policy—and the less familiar world of foreign policy.

Making Public Policy
How government attempts to solve collective problems

Our lives are regulated by policies that influence nearly everything we do. For example, many stores have a no-return *policy* on sales merchandise. Restaurant owners alert customers to their *policy* toward underdressed diners with the sign "No shirt, no shoes, no service." Your college or university may have a *policy* requiring a minimum grade point average for continued enrollment.

These are private, nongovernmental policies, adopted by individuals, businesses, or organizations to solve problems and to advance individual or group interests. Stores want to sell their new merchandise, not last season's leftovers; restaurant owners want a certain clientele to dine in their establishments; and institutions of higher education want to maintain standards and give students an incentive to excel. The problems of the clothing store, the restaurant, and the university are straightforward. Addressing these problems with a policy is pretty easy. Creating public policies, however, is more difficult than creating policies on merchandise returns, dining attire, and acceptable grades.

Public policy is a government plan of action to solve a problem that people share collectively or that they cannot solve on their own. That is not to say that the intended problem is always solved, or that the plan might not create more and even worse problems. Sometimes government's plan of action is to do nothing; that is, it may be a plan of *in*action, with the expectation (or hope) that the problem will go away on its own, or in the belief that it is not or should not be government's business to solve it. Some issues may be so controversial that policymakers would rather leave them alone, confining the scope of a policy debate to relatively "safe" issues.[7] But, by and large, we can understand public policy as a purposeful course of action intended by public officials to solve a public problem.[8] When that problem occurs here in the United States, we say that the government response is domestic policy; when it concerns our relations with other nations, we call it foreign policy.

Solving Public Problems

Public policies differ from the restaurant's "No shirt, no shoes, no service" policy because they are designed to solve common problems, not to address the concerns of a single business or institution. We think of problems as public when they cannot be handled by individuals, groups, businesses, or other actors privately, or when they directly or indirectly affect many citizens. Public problems might include the need for collective goods that individuals alone cannot or will not produce, such as highways, schools, and welfare. Public problems can include harm caused to citizens by the environment, foreign countries, dangerous products, or each other. Sometimes the very question of whether or not a problem is public becomes the subject of political debate. When people suggest that government ought to do something about violent crime, or about drug use, or about poor school quality, they are suggesting that government should create a policy to address a public problem.

Government can address public problems directly, by building schools, prisons, or highways, for example, but a great deal of public problem solving entails offering incentives to individuals or groups to get them to behave the way government wants them to behave. In other words, public policy can encourage or discourage behaviors in order to solve a problem that already exists or to avoid creating a future problem. For instance, government has an interest in having well-educated, property-owning citizens, since the conventional wisdom is that such people are more stable and more likely to obey the laws—in short, to be good citizens. Consequently, government policy encourages students to go to college by offering low-interest college loans and generous tax credits. It encourages homeownership in the same way. These various forms of federal assistance provide incentives for us to behave in a certain way to avoid creating the problem of an uneducated, rootless society.

Difficulties in Solving Public Problems

Despite the good intentions of policymakers, however, public problems can be difficult to solve. First, as we have already suggested, people have different ideas about what constitutes a problem in the first place. The definition of a public problem is not something that can be looked up in a book. It is the product of the values and beliefs of political actors and, consequently, is frequently the subject of passionate debate. Even something that seems to be as obviously problematic as poverty can be controversial. To people who believe that poverty is an inevitable though unfortunate part of life, or to those who feel that poor people should take responsibility for themselves, poverty may not be a problem requiring a public solution.

A second reason that solving public problems can be hard is that solutions cost money—often a lot of money. Finding the money to address a new problem usually requires shifting it out of existing programs or raising taxes. With an eye toward the next election, politicians are reluctant to spend tax dollars to support new initiatives. This is especially true when these new initiatives are not widely supported by citizens, which is often the case with policies that take money from some citizens in order to benefit others, such as welfare policy.

Public problems can also be difficult to solve because often their solutions generate new problems. Policies tough on crime can jam up the courts and slow the criminal justice system. Policies to help the poor can create dependence on government among the disadvantaged. And environmental policies can impair a business's ability to compete. Often the problems caused by policy require new policies to solve them in turn.

A final reason that problems can be hard to solve has to do with their complexity. Seldom are there easy answers to any public dilemma. Even when policymakers can agree on a goal, they often lack sufficient knowledge about how to get there. Competing solutions may be proposed, with no one knowing definitively which will best solve the problem. And some public problems may in reality be multiple problems with multiple causes—further muddying the effort to find adequate solutions. Policymaking in the American context is made even more complex by the federal system. Whose responsibility is it to solve a given problem—the federal, state, or local government's?

Types of Public Policy

In an effort to make sense of all the policies in contemporary politics, some political scientists divide them into types—redistributive, distributive, or regulatory—depending on who benefits and who pays, what the policy tries to accomplish, and

Table 14.1

Types of Policy

Type of policy	Policy goal	Who promotes this policy?	Who benefits? (Wins)	Who pays? (Loses)	Examples
Redistributive	To help the have-nots in society	Public interest groups, officials motivated by values	Disadvantaged citizens	Middle- and upper-class taxpayers	Medicaid; food stamps
Distributive	To meet the needs of various groups	Legislators and interest groups	Members of interest groups and the legislators they support	All taxpayers	Homeowners' tax deductions; veterans' benefits; anticrime policies; education reform
Regulatory	To limit or control actions of individuals or groups	Public interest groups	Public	Targeted groups	Environmental policy

how it is made.[9] Although this classification, summarized in Table 14.1, is not perfect (it turns out, for instance, that sometimes a policy can fit into more than one category), it does help us to think about policy in a coherent way.

Redistributive policies attempt to shift wealth, income, and other resources from the "haves" to the "have-nots." Like Robin Hood, government acting through redistributive policies seeks to help its poorer citizens. The U.S. government's income tax policy is redistributive because it is based on a progressive tax rate. People who earn more pay a higher percentage of their incomes to the federal government in taxes. (The progressivity of the income tax, however, is tempered by other elements of the U.S. tax code.) Programs such as Medicaid or **food stamps** are redistributive policies because they shift dollars away from people with relatively larger incomes to people with smaller or no incomes. As we see later in this chapter, U.S. social welfare policy is largely redistributive. Health care policy in the United States is also redistributive, since the government, through taxation, provides for the cost of health care for some of those who cannot afford it.

Redistributive policies are generally politically difficult to put in place because they have to take resources away from the affluent segments of society who are most likely to be politically active, to vote regularly, and to contribute to political campaigns or interest groups. These attentive constituents individually or collectively contact their congressional representatives to express their views. In contrast, the recipients of redistributive policies, far lower on the socioeconomic scale, tend to vote less often and lack the resources to donate to political campaigns or form interest groups. Their causes may be taken up by public interest groups, professional organizations representing social workers, or legislators who believe that it is government's job to help the needy. In the battle of who gets what in politics, policies that redistribute wealth are relatively rare because the people who must pay for the policy are better equipped than the poor to fight political battles.

Distributive policies, on the other hand, are much easier to make, because the costs are not perceived to be borne by any particular segment of the population. Tax deductions for interest on home mortgage payments, agriculture price supports, interstate highway policies, federal grants for higher education, even programs that provide for parks and recreation are examples of distributive policies. The common feature of distributive policies is that while they provide benefits to a recognizable group (such as homeowners or the families of college students), the costs are widely distributed. In other words, all taxpayers foot the bill.

Regulatory policies differ from redistributive and distributive policies in that they are designed to restrict or change the behavior of certain groups or individuals. While redistributive and distributive policies work to increase assistance to particular groups, regulatory policies tend to do just the opposite. They limit the actions of the regulatory target group—the group whose behavior government seeks to control. Most environmental policies, for example, are regulatory in nature. Business owners face myriad air emission limitations and permit requirements that must be met in order to avoid government sanctions, including the possibility of civil fines or a criminal trial. Since the groups being regulated frequently have greater resources at their disposal than the groups seeking the regulation (often public interest groups), the battle to regulate business can be lopsided.

The politics surrounding the creation of regulatory policies are highly confrontational. The "losers" in regulatory policy are often the target groups. Business doesn't want to pay for environmental controls, nor do manufacturers want to be monitored for compliance by government. By contrast, interest groups representing the beneficiaries of the policy argue just as strongly for the need for regulatory control. To continue our environmental policy example, the Environmental Defense Fund and the American Lung Association are repeat players in policy developments under the Clean Air Act. These groups have frequently sued the U.S. Environmental Protection Agency to compel it to lower the acceptable levels of airborne pollutants.[10]

Who Makes Policy?

All the political actors we have studied in this book have a hand in the policymaking process. Government actors inside the system—members of Congress, the president, the courts, and bureaucrats—are involved, as are actors outside the system—interest groups, the media, and members of the public themselves.

Policies are usually created by members of Congress in the form of one or more new laws. Sometimes what we think of as a single policy is really a bundle of several laws or amendments to laws. Environmental policy and social welfare policy are prime examples of bundles of programs and laws. National environmental policy is included in more than a dozen laws, among them the Clean Air Act, the Clean Water Act, and the Safe Drinking Water Act. Social welfare policy consists of more than direct financial assistance to poor families. Also included are programs that subsidize food purchases, provide day-care for children, and offer job training and education for the parents.

The role of Congress in creating and legitimating policy through its laws is critically important to understanding national public policy. As we discussed in Chapter 6, members of Congress are often most attentive to what their constituencies and the interest groups that support their campaigns want. Nonetheless, many members of Congress also follow their own values and consciences when making difficult political decisions.

The president may also create policy, perhaps by putting an issue on the public agenda, by including it (or not) in his budget proposal, by vetoing a law made by Congress, or by issuing an executive order that establishes a new policy or augments an existing one. Executive orders sometimes make profound changes in policy. One such executive order created affirmative action. When Congress passed the Civil Rights Act in 1964 banning employment discrimination against women and minorities, the law did not require that employers actively seek to employ persons within these protected classes. Arguing that America must seek "equality as a fact and equality as a result," President Johnson issued executive orders requiring federal contractors to develop affirmative action programs to promote the hiring and advancement of minorities and women.

Government bureaucracies at the federal, state, or local level may also create or enhance policy through their power to regulate. Administrative agencies are crucial to the policymaking process, helping to propose laws, lobbying for their passage, making laws of their own under authority delegated from Congress, and implementing laws. Moreover, agencies have enormous control over policy simply by how they enforce it.

Finally, the courts are policymakers as well. We saw in Chapter 9 that the Supreme Court has been responsible for some of the major changes in policy direction in this country with respect to business regulation, civil rights, and civil liberties, to name just a few. When the courts rule on what the government can or should do (or not do), they are clearly taking an active policymaking role. In addition, they are often asked to rule on the implementation of policy decisions made elsewhere in the government, on affirmative action, for example, or welfare policy, or education.

National policies are best thought of as packages made by several actors. Congress passes a law that establishes a policy. In turn, federal or state agencies respond by writing regulations and working with individuals and groups who are affected by the policy. The president may want to emphasize (or deemphasize) a policy in several ways. He may publicize the new policy through public statements—most notably the State of the Union address. The president may issue formal (executive orders) or informal instructions to agencies that highlight policy goals. So, although a law may initially establish a plan of action for a public problem, policies tend to evolve over time and contain many elements from all branches of government. Taken as a whole, these various components (laws, regulations, executive orders, agency actions, and so on) form the government's policy.

Steps in the Policymaking Process

Political scientists have isolated five steps that most policymakers follow in the process of trying to solve a public problem. Figure 14.1 illustrates the policymaking process.

Figure 14.1

The Policymaking Process

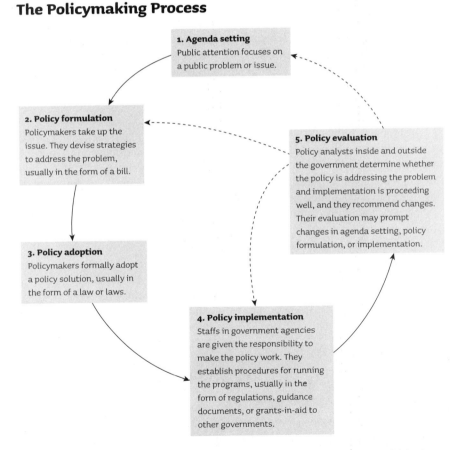

Policymaking begins with agenda setting and ends with policy evaluation, which often cycles back to the creation of new policy initiatives.

The first step in creating policy is *agenda setting*. Agenda setting occurs when problems come to the attention of people who can address them (usually members of Congress). These problems can be brought to Congress' attention by individual members, the president, interest groups, the media, or public opinion polls.

The second step in the policymaking process is called *policy formulation*. At this step, several competing solutions to the policy problem or objective are developed and debated in Congress. These alternative strategies often take the form of bills, perhaps proposed by the president or an administrative agency, that are introduced into Congress and sent to committees for deliberation.

If a preferred policy alternative emerges from the policy formulation stage, it must be legitimized through formal governmental action, referred to as the *policy adoption* stage. Policies—some trivial, some enormously important—are continually being adopted by all three branches of government through congressional legislation, executive order, agency regulation, or court ruling.

Once policies are adopted they must be put into practice. During the *policy implementation* stage, federal or state agencies interpret the policy by writing regulations, creating guidance documents, or drafting memorandums of agreement with other agencies. Agency staff meet with the beneficiaries of the policy, staff in other departments, citizens, and interest groups in an attempt to devise a workable plan for putting the policy into action. Implementation of public policy is neither easy nor guaranteed, however; those charged with implementing it can often derail the policy by not enforcing it.

The last step in the policymaking process is to evaluate the policy. *Policy evaluation* requires the policy analyst to ask several fundamental questions. Does the policy, as currently constructed, address the initial public problem? Does it represent a reasonable use of public resources? Would other strategies be more effective? Has it produced any undesirable effects?

Policy evaluation is conducted inside government by agencies such as the U.S. Government Accountability Office, the Congressional Budget Office, the Office of Management and Budget, and the Congressional Research Service. Congress also conducts oversight hearings in which agencies that implement programs report their progress toward policy goals. Groups outside government also evaluate policy to determine whether the desired outcomes are being achieved. Some of these groups are nonpartisan and are funded by philanthropic organizations.

Social Policy
Government efforts to improve citizens' lives

In the United States we have public policies to address every imaginable public problem, from transportation, to crime, to education. We can't discuss every public policy in this short chapter, but we can zero in on a few in order to give you a clearer idea of how the policy process works—who the actors are, what they want, and how they go about getting it.

Social policies are primarily distributive and redistributive policies that seek to improve the quality of citizens' lives. They focus on a variety of quality-of-life problems—most of them centered on the problem of improving people's standards of living. As we will see, social policies can benefit people at all levels of income and wealth, but most frequently they deal with the issue of poverty.

Poverty is a particularly difficult issue for societies to deal with because there is no universally accepted understanding of who is poor. In fact, defining poverty is itself a policy decision made by the government through the agency of the Census Bureau, which determines the poverty threshold, or the poverty line for American families.

Whether they address poverty by ignoring it and leaving the issue to private charities or by building an extensive welfare state, all societies have a policy on how to take care of the economically vulnerable. One way to address the problem is with **social welfare policies**, government programs that provide for the needs of those who cannot, or sometimes will not, provide for themselves—needs for shelter, food and clothing, jobs, education, old age care, and medical assistance. Most social welfare policies are redistributive; they transfer resources, in the form of financial assistance or essential services, from those with resources to those without. Policies such as these are usually **means-tested programs**; that is, beneficiaries must prove that they lack the necessary means to provide for themselves, according to the government's definitions of eligibility. As we said earlier, redistributive programs can be politically divisive and can open the way to partisan battle.

A second way societies deal with the problem of caring for the economically vulnerable is through **social insurance programs** that offer benefits in exchange for contributions made by citizens to offset future economic need. Social Security is an example of a social insurance program. While welfare policies are usually designed to be temporary solutions for helping the poor, social insurance programs cover longer-range needs. Social insurance programs are distributive because everyone pays, but only a certain segment of the population—in the case of Social Security, the elderly—receives benefits.

Although both welfare and Social Security were originally designed to aid the needy—poor children in the first case and the elderly poor in the second—they have evolved in different directions because of who is involved and how they go about trying to get what they want from the system. Today the differences are substantial.

Social Security is a hugely popular program whose benefit levels are guarded zealously, while welfare has been reformed to end its thirty-year guarantee that no American child would go hungry. Social Security promises a lifetime of benefits to recipients, even though most draw far more money out of the system than they ever put in, while welfare laws now limit recipients to two years at a time in the program, with a lifetime total of five years. Why the differences? The answer lies in the identity of the beneficiaries of the two programs and those who pay for them (the *who*), what the two programs try to accomplish (the *what*), and the politics under which each policy is produced (the *how*). In this section we look at each of these elements more closely.

Social Security

Social Security was born in the midst of the Great Depression, when so many older Americans found themselves facing an impoverished retirement that Franklin Roosevelt's New Deal administration passed the Social Security Act in 1935. Social Security provides what is essentially a guaranteed pension for workers. Lyndon Johnson's amendment to the act added health care benefits for the elderly in the form of Medicare. These programs have brought financial security to many retired people, but they are costly programs, especially as the baby boomer generation approaches retirement age.

Social Security is a social insurance program: people contribute to Social Security during their working lives in order to receive benefits when they retire. Consequently most people see Social Security in a positive light—as if they are receiving something they have earned and to which they are entitled, not a government handout. As we will see, that is only part of the story.

On its face, Social Security looks very different from the social welfare programs in which income or resources are transferred from one group to another. Recipients contribute a portion of their income, matched by their employers, directly into a fund for Social Security. Their Social Security contribution appears on their paycheck as a withholding called FICA (Federal Insurance Contributions Act). Current workers pay the Social Security of current retirees, with any leftover money going into the Social Security Trust Fund. When workers retire they receive monthly checks from the Social Security Administration, based on how much money they have paid into the system.

So Social Security looks like an insurance program, and as we noted earlier that's what we call it. But Social Security differs from real insurance in critical ways. Insurance allows us to pool our resources with others to cover the uncertainties of life—illness, accidents, and the like. Those of us who are lucky end up subsidizing those of us who aren't. But we will all get old (at least we hope we will), and we will all receive Social Security benefits, so there will be no lucky retirees subsidizing the lives of unlucky retirees. Social Security has to pay for all of us so that it is really more like a forced savings plan than an insurance plan. The government requires that we save our money each month so that we can draw on it in our retirement.

But if Social Security is a forced savings account, it is a magical one indeed because it never runs out as long as we or our spouses are alive. We continue to receive payments long after we've gotten back the money we put in, even including the interest we might have earned had our money been in a real savings account. And since there is no means-test for Social Security, not only poor recipients but also billionaires can continue to collect this direct subsidy from taxpayers.

So far this system has worked because the number of people in the workforce has been able to cover the retirement expenses of those leaving it. The Social Security Trust Fund has gotten fat because the pool of workers has grown faster than the pool of retirees. But by 2017 that will change as the number of baby boomer retirees grows and the fund has to be tapped to pay their benefits. This means that the federal government, which has been borrowing the money, will need to pay it back, with interest. If nothing is done to change the way Social Security works (for example, by cutting benefits, increasing Social Security taxes, or raising the retirement age), the Social Security Board of Trustees estimates that the trust fund will run out of money by the year 2041 and that the only funds available to pay retirees' benefits will be the money simultaneously paid in by current workers. Social Security recipients would receive only about 74 percent of the benefits they are owed, according to the current promise of the program.[11]

Unless the law changes that promise, the government will have to pay benefits whether or not the money is there. This is because Social Security is an **entitlement program**, which means that benefits must be paid to people who are entitled to receive them. Funding entitlement programs is nondiscretionary for government: once the entitlement is created, recipients who qualify must

Retirement Security

The Social Security program was part of Franklin Roosevelt's New Deal program. Promoting it as a social insurance program that you paid in to and from which you later received earnings made it seem less like a government handout and more like an investment in future financial security.

receive their benefits. Entitlements comprise an increasing share of the federal budget. By 2007 entitlement spending was almost 55 percent of the budget, and it continues to grow.

Many older Americans continue to need the economic protection that Social Security provides, but the system is not sustainable into the indefinite future in its present form. It could be made sustainable but the remedies we just discussed — cutting benefit levels, increasing taxes, or raising the retirement age—are politically unpalatable. If they were enacted, people would have to pay more or get less or both, and no one wants to do those things.

Social Security has been shielded from hard decisions by AARP, a powerful organization of older Americans that protects the interests of retirees. After the

2004 election, however, George W. Bush claimed that he had won a mandate for change and he proposed that people be allowed to invest some portion of the Social Security taxes they pay in private stock market accounts. Critics argued that Bush's plan would not actually save the program, however, and might spell its end, and public opinion polls showed that the majority of Americans agreed with the critics.[12] Confronted with falling approval ratings due to the Iraq war, high oil prices, and other domestic misfortunes, Bush let his proposal drop. Social Security continues to face a solvency crisis in the not-too-distant future.

Welfare Policy in the United States

Social Security is a program designed to protect people's long-term financial futures; it is not designed to alleviate poverty in the short term. In fact, through the greater part of our history, poverty was not considered a public problem requiring government action. It was not until the Great Depression of 1929 forced large numbers of previously successful working- and middle-class people into poverty that the public view shifted and citizens demanded that government step in. Today the American government tries to improve the quality of life for its poorest citizens through social welfare policies, focusing particularly on economic security for children.

The same New Deal **Social Security Act** that guaranteed pensions for older Americans included a program called Aid to Families With Dependent Children (AFDC), based on the commitment that no child would ever go hungry in America. AFDC was a means-tested program that provided benefits for families with children who could demonstrate need, to keep the children fed and to tide over the adults until they could find work and provide for their children themselves. The federal government contributed more than half the AFDC payments, and the states supplied the balance, managed the program, and determined who was eligible and how much they received. Even though states retained a role, with AFDC, for the first time, the federal government assumed responsibility for the economic well-being of its citizens.

It is important to note, however, what AFDC did not promise. Assistance here was primarily to dependent children—their parents were aided only secondarily, and the intention was to get them back to work. We had not become a society that easily accepted the notion that the haves are responsible for the have-nots. Redistributive policies that transfer money from the working person to children might seem acceptable; policies that subsidize able-bodied adults, much less so. The United States has never kept pace with the western European welfare states that have promised their citizens security from cradle to grave (or from womb to tomb, as some observers have put it more graphically). American welfare policy has had far more limited aspirations, and even those have been controversial. By the 1990s even liberals were clamoring for reform of a welfare system that seemed to have lost sight of its ideals and that, rather than propping up people until they could return to work, produced a culture of dependency that became increasingly difficult for recipients to escape.

At the center of the controversy was AFDC. By 1996 over four million families were receiving aid, and the majority of AFDC recipients in the 1990s were young unmarried mothers (aged nineteen to thirty), unemployed, residing in central cities.[13] AFDC had been designed to raise above the poverty line those families hurt by economic downturns. President Roosevelt and the New Deal architects believed that the government should provide some temporary support when the economy slumped. Opponents of AFDC posed the question: how long is "temporary"?

AFDC was criticized because it contained no work requirements and set no time limits for remaining on welfare. As a redistributive program, it seemed to transfer money from a hard-working segment of the population to one that did nothing to earn it. Public opinion polls showed that many Americans believed that welfare recipients were unwilling to work, living off the generosity of hard-working taxpayers. Since lower-income people are less likely to organize for political purposes, welfare recipients put up no coordinated defense of their benefits. While Republicans had traditionally been more critical of welfare policy, even some Democrats began to heed the calls of their constituents for welfare reform, arguing that the welfare system created disincentives for recipients to become productive members of society. On August 22, 1996, President Clinton signed the Personal Responsibility and Work Opportunity Reconciliation Act, fulfilling his promise to "end welfare as we know it."

With Clinton's signature, AFDC was replaced by the **Temporary Assistance to Needy Families (TANF)** block grant to state governments. This reform gives states greater control over how they spend their money but caps the amount that the federal government will pay for welfare. The law requires work in exchange for time-limited benefits. Most recipients must find a job within two years of going on welfare and cannot stay on the welfare rolls for more than a total of five years altogether or less, depending on the state. Moreover, many states cap family benefits when an additional child is born to a family on welfare. The 1996 legislation expired in October 2002 and had to be renewed by Congress. After a lengthy and contentious reauthorization process, Congress finally enacted changes to TANF three years later in the Deficit Reduction Act of 2005. The reforms enacted in the Deficit Reduction Act increased further the work focus of the TANF program, by increasing the proportion of recipients who must be working and by defining more narrowly what counts as "work."[14] More than a decade after the heated debates surrounding its adoption, the controversy over welfare reform has waned. Few observers dispute that the program has successfully reduced the welfare rolls—the U.S. Department of Health and Human Services reports that, from August 1996 to October 2009, the number of welfare recipients fell from 12.2 million to around 4.3 million (see Figure 14.2). Most states met their 2004 goals in putting 50 percent of single parents to work for thirty hours per week and 90 percent of two-parent families to work for thirty-five hours per week. But some critics argue that even when jobs are found, wages are so low that many people are unable to lift their families out of poverty.[15] The inadequacy of work as a means of raising low-wage workers out of poverty is even more pronounced in the current economic climate characterized by high unemployment. These challenges were the focus of a recent national

Figure 14.2

Percentage of the Population Receiving Welfare (AFDC and TANF), 1960–2010

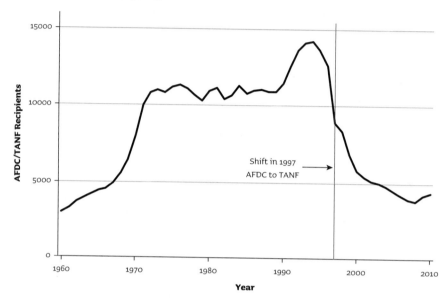

Source: Data obtained from U.S. Department of Health and Human Services, Administration for Children and Families, Office of Family Assistance, www.acf.hhs.gov/programs/ofa/data-reports/index.htm#tanfdata.

poverty conference in which one expert reported, "We have a work-based safety net without work. We're really in a pickle."[16]

TANF is not the only policy designed to solve the problem of poverty in the United States. In 2009, expenditures for food assistance totaled almost $79 billion—a nearly 30 percent increase from the previous year. In fact, 2009 saw the largest increase in demand for food assistance in thirty-four years.[17] The largest food assistance program is the **Supplemental Nutrition Assistance Program (SNAP)**, previously called the Food Stamp program. In 2009, 33.7 million Americans participated in SNAP each month—with more than one in ten Americans participating at any given time during the year.[18] SNAP provides low-income families with vouchers to purchase food (typically dispersed via an electronic system using a plastic card similar to a bank card). For most poor families, SNAP benefits are only part of the food budget. Families also spend some of their own cash to buy enough food for the month. The amount of SNAP benefits that households receive is indexed to family income. In 2009, these benefits averaged $124 per person, which is 23 percent higher than in the previous year.

Another approach to poverty policy in the United States is Head Start, a major component of Lyndon Johnson's War on Poverty. The program provides preschool education for low-income children and assistance and education to pregnant women. Head Start is a different approach to helping the poor; it aims at making welfare unnecessary by giving low-income children many of the advantages that their more affluent peers take for granted, and that can be significant in determining one's chances in life. Head Start prepares children for elementary school by putting them in environments that encourage learning and help them develop social skills. Most people agree with the goal of Head Start, but much controversy exists over how successful the program has been. Because of the increasing costs[19] and perceived limited return on the investment, conservatives often recommend scaling back Head Start.

Health Care

In 2010 Congress passed and President Obama signed the Patient Protection and Affordable Care Act, which will increase access to health insurance and make it more affordable for most Americans by 2014. Even so, the United States stands out among industrialized nations as the only one that doesn't have a universal health care system guaranteeing minimum basic care to all. Ironically, of those nations, it also spends the most on health care. Public opinion polls have shown that health care reform consistently ranks as one of the most important concerns of the public. A 2007 poll asking about people's chief concerns and priorities for Congress identified "reducing health care costs" as a top priority; only improving the education system and preventing terrorist attacks ranked higher.[20] Indeed, an estimated 47 million Americans, or 15.8 percent of the population, were without coverage in 2006.[21]

Before health care reform was passed in 2010, the federal government's only role in health care was confined to the provision of Medicare and Medicaid. Like Social Security, Medicare is a social insurance program designed to help the elderly pay their medical costs. Like TANF, Medicaid is a means-tested welfare program to assist the poor—especially children—with their medical costs. Between these two programs, many Americans have been left uninsured, either unable to provide insurance for themselves, or willing to gamble that they will not need it.

Signed into law by President Johnson in 1965 as an amendment to the Social Security Act, **Medicare** extended health care coverage to virtually all Americans who are over sixty-five, disabled, or suffering from permanent kidney failure. The idea was that workers would pay a small Medicare tax (collected as a payroll tax like FICA) while they were healthy in order to receive medical health insurance when they retired.

As the population ages and lives longer, and as medical costs skyrocket, Medicare has become an extraordinarily expensive program. Medicare is the nation's fourth most expensive program, and the trustees for the Medicare Trust Fund estimate that full benefit payments can be made only until 2020, twenty-one years before the Social Security Trust Fund is expected to experience a shortfall.[22]

Because of this, many people argue that the urgent crisis for policymakers is Medicare rather than Social Security.[23]

In 2003 Congress passed and President Bush signed the Medicare Modernization Act, which provided the elderly with prescription drug coverage under Medicare for the first time and gave private insurance companies a much greater role in the program. Democrats criticized the cost of the program (estimated to be $724 billion over the next ten years), argued that the plan gave too much power to health maintenance organizations (HMOs), and attacked Bush for not allowing the importation of less expensive drugs from Canada, claiming that the plan is a windfall for the pharmaceutical industry.

Medicaid was also enacted as an amendment to the Social Security Act in 1965, as part of President Johnson's Great Society program. A federally sponsored program that provides free medical care to the poor, Medicaid is funded jointly by the national and state governments and covers hospitalization, prescription drugs, doctors' visits, and long-term nursing care.

Rising medical costs are a concern to state and national policymakers who worry about the states' ability to continue to fund Medicaid, a program that costs states around one-fourth of their budgets. Because of these rising costs, President Bush recommended scaling back the number of people eligible for Medicaid as well as the expenses that would be covered under the program. According to Bush, these changes would have saved the government $60 billion over ten years.[24] But governors from both parties were concerned that the reductions would add to the budget deficits of the states, which would have to pick up the costs of the cuts. Others believed Bush's proposal would reduce the number of poor people covered under Medicaid. Because of these concerns, the Senate refused to back Bush's proposed cuts.

The problems with Medicare and Medicaid give some clues about why U.S. policymakers have consistently hesitated to create a national health care system to serve all Americans. Fears of excessive government control, large costs, and inefficient services have doomed reform efforts. Proponents of universal health care find it difficult to eliminate the perception that government control will harm the quality and raise the cost of health care services. The rise of HMOs in the 1990s has raised hopes that the phenomenal costs can be controlled and health care standards maintained. However, in response to HMOs, doctors frequently lament the loss of autonomy and patients complain of diminishing quality of care and ever-rising costs.[25]

In 2004 John Kerry ran for president with a plan to insure all Americans.[26] Voters generally thought Kerry would handle health care better than would Bush, but the public seemed more concerned about national security issues and Kerry was narrowly defeated.[27] By 2008, however, health care had returned to the national agenda. It was a major point of discussion in the Democratic primary race between Hillary Clinton and Barack Obama, and continued into the general election. As the economy worsened in the fall of 2008, polls consistently showed that the public considered Obama better able to handle the issue of health care than John McCain.

Nonetheless, rising health care costs for everyone and concern over the high number of Americans who had no health care insurance at all made federal health care reform a key issue in the 2008 election, both in the Democratic primary campaign and later in the general election. Although Obama, an advocate of making health insurance available to all, won the presidency, there was no guarantee that health care reform would proceed as he had hoped. The economic crash of 2008 and the expensive financial bailout and stimulus plans made spending money on social programs much less attractive to politicians. Even so, the Obama administration continued to push health care reform as its primary domestic policy priority. Adopting lessons from failed efforts to reform our nation's complex health care insurance and delivery system, Obama did not propose the creation of a single-payer or unified national health care plan like those in Europe. Instead, he endorsed a range of separate policy changes that he argued would combine together to expand access to health insurance, slow the growth of health care costs, and provide more patient protections—particularly for the hard-to-insure such as those with preexisting conditions.[28]

After a contentious yearlong debate, a massive reform bill—the Patient Protection and Affordable Care Act—was signed into law in March 2010. It did not include a public option, a proposed government-sponsored health insurance plan that would compete with the plans offered by private health insurance companies, because the Speaker of the House and the Senate majority leader were unable to put together a winning coalition to vote for its inclusion. However, the bill includes many provisions aimed at expanding insurance coverage through requirements that employers with fifty or more employees must provide health insurance and that most Americans outside that system purchase health insurance for themselves. To make these mandates affordable, the bill expands Medicaid to more low-income individuals and provides subsidies and tax credits to individuals and small businesses to reduce the burden of insurance premiums.

The reform bill also creates state-based American Health Benefit Exchanges and Small Business Health Options Exchanges, which will serve as vehicles for individuals and small businesses to purchase qualified health insurance in a competitive market. These exchanges will be administered by a government agency or nonprofit organization—under governance of the states. Additionally, Consumer Operated and Oriented Plans (CO-OPs) programs will allow for the creation of nonprofit, member-run health insurance companies in all fifty states.[29] The various elements of the health care reform bill will be phased in gradually over the next five to ten years.

The hard-won victory for the Democrats was made more difficult by the refusal of any Republican to support the bill and by the death of longtime health care reform advocate Sen. Ted Kennedy of Massachusetts. After a grueling battle in the House and the subsequent legislative maneuvers required to align the House bill with the Senate version, the public was frustrated with the partisan debate. Although Republicans decried the bill and insisted they would work to repeal it, Democrats scrambled to get some key provisions into effect before the 2010 midterm elections so that voters could see what the reforms might mean in their lives. Though experts

▶ Health Care Reform Implementation Highlights of Provisions by Year

2010

- Coverage for young adults is expanded to allow them to stay on their parents' plan until age twenty-six.
- Tax credits that help small businesses provide insurance benefits to workers are made available.
- Those uninsured because of a preexisting condition can buy coverage through a Pre-Existing Condition Insurance Plan.

2011

- Health care premium costs decrease because 85 percent of premiums must be spent on health care, not administrative costs.
- The Center for Medicare and Medicaid Innovation and the Children's Health Insurance Program (CHIP) target improvements in health care quality and efficiency.
- The Independent Payment Advisory Board explores new measures to reduce health care costs and expand quality care.

2012

- Integrated health systems will be fostered for better communication and collaboration with doctors engaged in patient care.
- Paperwork and administrative costs will be reduced by shifting to secure, electronic records.

2013

- Preventive health coverage will be expanded through new funding of state Medicare programs.

2014

- Individuals and small businesses will be able to buy health insurance directly through a Health Insurance Exchange, a competitive insurance marketplace for qualified plans. Members of Congress will also begin to receive their health insurance through Exchanges.
- Individuals who can afford it will be required to obtain basic health insurance coverage (if not already covered) or to pay a fee to offset the costs of caring for uninsured Americans. Exemptions will be available to those who can't afford to pay.
- Annual cap on the amount of coverage that an individual may receive will be eliminated.
- Reforms will prohibit the denial of the sale of health insurance due to preexisting conditions.
- The small business insurance tax credit will increase.

2015

- Physician payments will be tied to the quality of care physicians provide.

Source: "Understanding the Affordable Care Act, Timeline: What's Changing and When," Health-Care.gov, www.healthcare.gov/law/timeline/index.html#event1-pane.

said the bill would mean long-term savings for the health care system, a recession-weary nation, tired of government spending and leery of giving too much power to federal officials, remained skeptical in the months before the election.[30]

Middle-Class and Corporate Welfare

Social policies include not only what we typically think of as welfare—programs to assist the poor—but also programs that increase the quality of life for the middle class. Clearly this is true of the social insurance programs of Social Security and Medicare, which go to all contributors, rich and poor, in amounts that generally exceed their contributions. But a number of other distributive policies benefit workers, middle-class homeowners, students, and members of the military. These policies help a particular group in society at the expense of all taxpayers by giving that group a subsidy. **Subsidies** are financial incentives such as cash grants, tax deductions, or price supports given by the government to corporations, individuals, or other governments usually to encourage certain activities or behaviors (such as homeownership or going to college). Even though these subsidies are designed to achieve government's ends, they have long since fallen into the category of benefits to which groups feel entitled.

Among the subsidies that benefit groups we wouldn't typically associate with social welfare policies are those that support education. A well-educated citizenry is a valuable asset for a nation, and government uses subsidies in a number of ways to try to achieve one. For instance, the federal government provides funds to local school systems for certain types of educational programs, provides direct student loans and guarantees loans made to students by private lenders such as banks and credit unions, and provides some relief to families with dependents in college by allowing taxpayers tax credits as long as their adjusted gross income is below a certain amount.

Another kind of subsidy that benefits the middle class encourages homeownership through the mortgage interest tax deduction, which allows homeowners to deduct the cost of their mortgage interest payments from their taxable income. Because homeowners must meet a certain income level to receive this tax break, the policy in effect helps only taxpayers in the middle- and upper-class income brackets. A similar government program provides student and home mortgage loans to veterans and those currently serving in the military.

Finally, U.S. corporations are also beneficiaries of social subsidies. According to some analysts, an estimated $170 billion is funneled to American corporations through direct federal subsidies and tax breaks each year.[31] Many subsidies are linked to efforts to create jobs. However, there is little oversight for many of these programs, and there are many instances of subsidies going to companies that are downsizing or—in the case of many high-tech companies—moving jobs overseas. Business leaders also claim that subsidies for research and development are needed to keep American companies afloat in the global marketplace. The biggest winners are agribusiness, the oil industry, and energy plants.

Economic Policy
Promoting the nation's financial stability

Another kind of public policy is **economic policy**, which addresses the problem of economic security, not for some particular group or segment of society, but for society itself. In Chapter 1 we said that the United States has an economic system of regulated capitalism. That is, the U.S. economy is a market system in which the government intervenes to protect rights and make procedural guarantees. All the different strategies that government officials, both elected and appointed, employ today to solve economic problems, to protect economic rights, and to provide procedural guarantees to help the market run smoothly are called economic policy.

For much of our history, policymakers have felt that government should pursue a hands-off economic policy, in effect letting the market take care of itself, guided only by the laws of supply and demand. This attitude was in keeping with a basic tenet of capitalism, which holds that the economy is already regulated by millions of individual decisions made each day by consumers and producers in the market. The Great Depression of the 1930s, however, changed the way government policymakers viewed the economy. Since that economic disaster, the goal of economic policymakers has been to even out the dramatic cycles of inflation and recession without undermining the vitality and productivity of a market-driven economy.

Fiscal Policy and Monetary Policy

Even before the stock market crash of 1929 that precipitated the Great Depression, economic reformers had begun to question the ability of the unregulated market to guard the public interest. They argued that some government intervention in the economy might be necessary—not only to improve the public welfare and protect people from the worst effects of the business cycle but also to increase the efficiency of the market itself. Such intervention could take one of two forms: fiscal policy, which enables government to regulate the economy through its powers to tax and spend, or monetary policy, which allows government to manage the economy by controlling the money supply through the regulation of interest rates (the cost of borrowing money). Each of these strategies, as we will see, has political advantages and costs, and both play an important role in contemporary economic policy.

One of the strongest advocates of government action in the 1930s was British economist John Maynard Keynes (pronounced "canes"), who argued that government can and should step in to regulate the economy by using **fiscal policy**—the government's power to tax and spend. According to Keynes, government could stimulate a lagging economy by putting more money into it (increasing government spending and cutting taxes) or cool off an inflationary economy by taking money out (cutting spending and raising taxes).

Keynes argued, contrary to most other economists at the time, that achieving a **balanced budget** in the national economy—in which government spends no more money than it brings in through taxes and revenues—is not essential. Rather, for Keynes, **deficits** (shortfalls due to the government spending more in a year than it takes in) and **surpluses** (extra funds because government revenues are greater than its expenditures) were tools to be utilized freely to fine-tune the economy.

The Keynesian strategy of increasing government spending during recessionary periods and cutting back during expansionary periods gradually became the primary tool of economic policy in the period between 1930 and the 1970s. Franklin Roosevelt used it to lead the country out of the Depression in the 1930s, and subsequent presidents made fiscal policy the foundation of their economic programs until the late 1970s, when the economy took a turn that fiscal policy seemed unable to manage. During this period the U.S. economy was characterized by inflation and, *at the same time,* unemployment. Keynesian theory was unable to explain this odd combination of economic events, and economists and policymakers searched for new theories to help guide them through this difficult economic period.

Many people looking at the high inflation and growing unemployment of the 1970s began to turn to monetary policy as a way to manage the economy. **Monetary policy** regulates the economy by controlling the money supply (the sum of all currency on hand in the country plus the amount held in checking accounts) by manipulating **interest rates**. The monetarists believed that the high inflation of the 1970s was caused by too much money in the economy, and they advocated cutting back on the supply by raising interest rates to take some money out of circulation. When money is scarce (and interest rates are high), people borrow less because it costs more; thus they spend less and drive down aggregate demand. When there is a lot of money, people can borrow it cheaply—that is, at low interest rates—and they are more likely to spend it, raising aggregate demand. By raising and lowering interest rates, government can regulate the cycles of the market economy just as it does by taxing and spending. As a tool of economic policy, however, monetary policy can be somewhat hard to control. Small changes can have big effects. Reducing the money supply might lower inflation, but too great a reduction can also cause a recession, which is what happened in the early 1980s. Changes need to be made in narrow increments rather than in broad sweeps.

Today policymakers use a combination of fiscal and monetary policy to achieve economic goals, and the highs and lows of boom and bust have been tempered greatly. Fluctuations in inflation, unemployment, and gross domestic product continue to occur, but they lack the punishing ferocity of the earlier unregulated period. The two kinds of policy are not equally easy for government to employ, however. Most significantly, unlike the heavily political tools of fiscal policy, the instruments of monetary policy are removed from the political arena and are wielded by actors who are not subject to electoral pressures.

We can thank the politicians of the early twentieth century for divorcing monetary policy from politics. Controlling interest rates is a regulatory policy that would generate heavy lobbying from businesses and corporations, which have a huge stake in the cost of money. Realizing that Congress and the president could

Don't be Fooled by Economic Indicators

Keeping up with the economy, in good times or bad, can be a challenge, especially when politicians are trying to persuade you to see things their way. As one guide to understanding the economy put it, "Economic figures can be manipulated to demonstrate almost anything."[1] Politicians are wont to spin those figures to support their arguments and to attract voters to their side.

Critical consumers of politics have some tools available to help them sort through the political spin and figure out how the economy is doing. Objective measures of the economy are of two kinds: *coincident economic indicators* help us understand how the economy is currently functioning, and *leading economic indicators* predict how it will look in the future. Coincident economic indicators include such variables as employment, personal income, and industrial production. Leading economic indicators focus on variables that indicate a reemergence from a recession and growth in the economy, like consumer confidence, stock market prices, and "big-ticket purchases" such as automobiles and homes. Understanding these two kinds of economic indicators can help us figure out how the economy is really doing and can arm us against the persuasive words of politicians.

Here we examine just a few of literally dozens of these variables. You can find the most recent data from these leading economic indicators and others at www.economicindicators.gov. For a more complete guide to understanding a wide range of economic indicators, you might want to consult a reference book, such as *The Economist's Guide to Economic Indicators*.[2]

- **Real GDP.** The real gross domestic product (GDP) is the total economic activity in constant prices. Because of inflation, it is important to put all prices on the same scale. In other words, to see how much the economy has grown from 2000 to 2010, you would want to convert 2010 dollars into 2000 dollars. Because real GDP uses constant prices, it is a useful measure to track economic growth over time. A real GDP growth of around 3 percent per year is a good sign for the American economy.[3] A rise in real GDP shows that production and consumption are increasing.
- **Unemployment.** The unemployment rate is the percentage of the labor force (defined as those aged sixteen and older) that is out of work. An unemployment rate of 5 percent or less is generally considered to be a sign of a strong economy and a growing GDP. However, the unemployment rate can be misleading because it includes only people who are available for and actively seeking work. Therefore, the real percentage of those unemployed is usually higher than the unemployment rate because some people are not actively seeking jobs.
- **Personal income and personal disposable income.** Personal income is an individual's income received from many sources but primarily from wages and salaries. It also includes interest, dividends, and Social Security. Personal disposable income is a person's income after taxes and fees are deducted. A growth rate of 3 percent per year is considered to be a healthy increase in personal income, although growth should be steady. Too rapid an increase in personal income can lead to inflation.[4] These two measures predict the ability of citizens to consume and save.
- **Consumer spending.** The amount of goods that people are buying is another way to measure the health of the economy because it is the key factor in the increase or

decrease of the GDP. One way to measure consumer spending is by the Department of Labor's Consumer Expenditure Survey, which asks American consumers questions about their buying habits on items such as food, apparel, housing, and entertainment. Consumer spending accounts for approximately 70 percent of the GDP and has a big impact on job growth.[5]

- **Stock market price indexes.** A stock market price index measures the overall change in stock prices of corporations traded on U.S. stock markets. There are many different stock market price indexes, including the New York Stock Exchange (NYSE) Composite Index, the NASDAQ Composite Index, and the Dow Jones Industrial Average Index. The Dow Jones Industrial Average Index, for instance, provides the average price per share of thirty large companies' stocks on the NYSE. The NYSE Composite Index covers the prices of approximately 2,900 companies listed on the NYSE. A strongly performing stock market affects consumer and investment spending. If the stock market is performing well, people are more optimistic about the economy and are more likely to buy or invest.
- **Home and motor vehicle sales.** The purchases of these major items are good indicators of consumer demand, as well as of construction and manufacturing activity. The number of homes and motor vehicles sold can change depending on the time of year (for example, car sales are likely to increase when companies decrease prices to sell older models to make way for the new models), which makes it a smart idea to take two or three months together and compare that with similar periods of previous years.

To avoid being duped, ask yourself the following questions when you hear these indicators bandied about by a politician with an agenda. They may help you become a critical consumer of economic information.

- **Whose numbers are they?** Who is reporting the numbers? Is it a government agency? A political party? A business or consumer group? A newspaper? How might the source influence the interpretation of the numbers?
- **What were the expectations?** As important as the actual numbers is whether the numbers met the expectations of economic forecasters. An increase of 50,000 new jobs might seem like positive growth, but not if forecasters projected an increase of 250,000. (Also ask yourself who the forecasters are, and what agenda they might have.)
- **Are the numbers affected by seasonality?** Consumer spending and sales rise and fall at certain times of the year. For example, few people are building houses in the winter, which means that a decline in the number of home sales from August to December does not necessarily mean a drop-off in the economy. For seasonal variables it is best to compare numbers to previous years.

---

1. *The Economist's Guide to Economic Indicators: Making Sense of Economics,* 5th ed. (Princeton, N.J.: Bloomberg Press, 2003), 1.

2. Ibid.

3. Ibid, 47.

4. Ibid, 85.

5. Norman Frumkin, *Guide to Economic Indicators,* 3rd ed. (Armonk, N.Y.: M. E. Sharpe, 2000).

probably not agree on interest rates any more effectively than on taxes, spending, or anything else, Congress established the **Federal Reserve System** in 1913, as an independent commission, to control the money supply. The Fed, as it is known, is a system of twelve federal banks, run by a Board of Governors. The Fed chairman is appointed by the president and serves a four-year term that overlaps the president's term of office. The Fed controls the supply of money by controlling the interest rates at which banks borrow money, by limiting the amount the banks have to hold in reserve, and by buying government securities.

Monetary policy, while subject to its own challenges, can at least avoid the political pitfalls that those making fiscal policy must regularly watch out for. This is primarily because fiscal policymakers, as elected officials, try to respond to their constituents' demands or what they anticipate their constituents' demands will be. For instance, most of us do not want our taxes increased even if it means that the national economy will be better off, and we may threaten to punish politicians who try to raise them.

Fiscal policy is made by Congress and the president through the budget process. Government budgets are where we find the clearest indications, in black and white, of politics—who gets what, and who pays for it. The government budget process also exemplifies the conflict we discussed in Chapter 6 between the needs for lawmaking and the electoral imperatives of representation. Members of Congress and the president, as lawmakers, have an interest in maintaining a healthy economy and should be able to agree on appropriate levels of taxes and spending to see that the economy stays in good shape. But as elected leaders they are also accountable to constituencies and committed to ideological or partisan goals. From a politician's perspective the budget is a pie to be divided and fought over.

The preparation of the president's budget begins over a year before it is submitted to Congress by the Office of Management and Budget (OMB). OMB acts as the president's representative and negotiates for months with the agencies and departments in fashioning a budget that reflects the president's priorities but at the same time does not inflame entrenched constituencies.

Congress's job is to approve the budget, but it does not accept everything that the president requests. Members' ability to use fiscal policy in a responsible way is hampered by the desire to increase spending for the folks back home at the same time that they are disinclined to raise their taxes. Caught as they are between the demands of lawmaking and representation, and their own divergent ideological goals, they are unable to use the budget as a very effective tool of fiscal policy.

Increased spending without corresponding tax increases, of course, raises the federal deficit; and interest payments on the money we borrow to pay the deficit constrain our future choices. In the 1990s the deficit problem disappeared briefly when, due in large part to general national economic prosperity and cooperation between President Clinton and the Fed, the federal government balanced its budget and began to run a surplus in 1998.[32] Politically this changed the process dramatically. National politicians now began to debate which priorities should be the target of government spending.

The problem of how to spend the surplus, however, was short lived. The 2001 tax cut, promised by George W. Bush in his campaign and passed by a Republican-led House and Senate soon after he became president, cut sharply into the surplus. As economic growth slowed and the prosperity of the 1990s began to wind down, government revenues dropped from earlier estimates, shrinking the anticipated surplus further. To help stimulate the economy, the president endorsed additional tax cuts in 2003, which further contributed to the rising deficit. Finally, the wars in Afghanistan and Iraq had cost the government over $500 billion during the Bush administration (headed toward $1 trillion by 2010). By mid-2002 the deficit had returned.[33]

It was destined to grow quickly. With economic disaster on the immediate horizon, the Bush administration oversaw the passage of the Troubled Assets Relief Program (TARP) in October 2008 to bail out financial institutions deemed "too big to fail." Much of the funds had been repaid by 2010, but the cost of the program was still about $30 billion, although it might ultimately end up making a profit for the government.[34] The American Recovery and Reinvestment Act of 2009 (commonly known as the stimulus bill) added nearly $900 billion of spending on tax relief for individuals and businesses, extensions of unemployment insurance, infrastructure development, and various other projects designed in the Keynesian economic tradition to kick the economy into gear. Supporters of these efforts to soften the blow of economic recession and jumpstart the economy claimed that TARP and the stimulus package headed off a much worse decline in the economy. Detractors from the right argued that they simply bailed out big corporations while leaving the taxpayers to pay a mounting load of debt, whereas critics on the left asserted that the stimulus needed to be even bigger than it was.[35] The nonpartisan Congressional Budget Office, however, estimated that the program was on track to meeting the goal of saving 3.5 million jobs by the end of 2010.[36]

With the 2010 deficit projected to be $1.3 trillion (just below the record $1.42 trillion of 2009), the issues of spending and taxing were back at the heart of partisan battles as the 2010 midterm elections approached.[37] Republicans declared the stimulus bill a failure because it hadn't created enough jobs to pump up the economy, saying further that a recession was no time for government to spend money. They deplored the recklessness of running up the deficit by spending, while insisting that the Bush tax cuts, scheduled to lapse in 2010, be made permanent.[38] The Democrats, on the other hand, argued that a recession was the very time that government should spend money and demanded an end to the Bush tax cuts for the top 2 percent of the population.[39]

The American public is quite concerned about the large budget deficit and the increasing national debt, but it is not necessarily willing to make sacrifices in spending to combat these problems. According to one poll, 89 percent of the public said that reducing the budget deficit was a "top priority" or "important" problem for the country, but 47 percent also wanted to see more spending to help the economy recover.[40] Without popular pressure to curtail spending and balance the budget, politicians are unlikely to make the hard choices such action would entail.

Tax Policy

Technically, taxation is part of the federal budgetary process. The U.S. government takes in a lot of money in taxes every year, estimated to be $2.7 trillion in 2008.[41] The largest single source of revenue for the federal government is individual federal income taxes. The next largest is contributions to social insurance, the largest component of which is Social Security by far, with funds coming equally from our paychecks and employers.

Personal income taxes in the United States are **progressive taxes**, which means that people with higher incomes not only pay more taxes but they also pay at a higher rate. Taxes are paid on all the income an individual or household receives, including wage and salary income, interest and dividends, rents on property owned, and royalties. Everyone is subject to the same rate of taxation for some base amount, and incomes over that amount are subject to progressively higher percentages of tax. The range of taxable income at each tax bracket determines your marginal tax rate. For example, if you are in a 35 percent tax bracket, it does not mean that you pay 35 percent of all your income in taxes, but that you pay 35 percent on everything you make above the tax bracket beneath you—and a lower percentage on the income made under that base amount.

Other taxes are called **regressive taxes**, even if they are fixed percentages, because they take a higher proportion of income from a poor person's income than from those who are well-off. Sales taxes are often argued to be regressive, particularly when they are levied on necessities like food and electricity. Furthermore, poor people spend a higher portion of their incomes on consumables that are subject to the sales tax; the wealthy, in contrast, spend a significant portion of their income on investments, stocks, or elite education for their children, which are not subject to sales taxes. Other regressive taxes include excise taxes and Social Security taxes.

The two parties have very different ideas about what kinds of tax should be levied on whom. In general, Democrats focus on easing the tax burden on lower-income groups in the name of fairness and equity. As a matter of fiscal policy, they tend to want to put money into the hands of workers and the working poor on the assumption that this will translate quickly into consumer spending, which increases demand and stimulates the whole economy. This is the "trickle-up" strategy. Give benefits to those with less, and let the effects percolate upward throughout the economic system.

In contrast, Republicans focus more on lowering the high rates of taxation on those with larger incomes. Their sentiments are motivated by a different view of fairness; those who make more money should have the freedom to keep it. Republicans argue that the wealthy are more likely to save or invest their extra income (from a tax break), thus providing businesses with the capital they need to expand—an argument that some call supply-side economics. Not only do they believe that the rate of taxation on the top tax brackets should be reduced, but they argue for a reduction in the **capital gains tax**, the tax levied on the returns that people earn from capital investments, like the profits from the sale of stocks or a home. The notion here is that if wealthy people are taxed at lower rates, they will invest and spend more, the economy will prosper, and the benefits will "trickle down" to the rest of

Figure 14.3

U.S. Federal Budget Deficit/Surplus

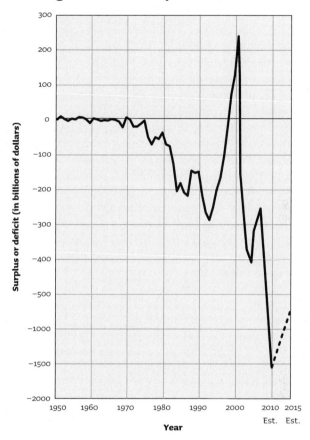

The budget deficit is the amount by which government spending exceeds tax revenues. If tax revenue is greater than government spending, a budget surplus results. In the 1970s and 1980s the United States ran larger budget deficits (in the billions), only to have the trend reversed in the mid-1990s. The surplus did not survive long, however, as the nation slid back into deficit territory in 2002. Stimulus spending in 2009–2010 added to the deficit, but budget estimates show it recovering in the future.

Source: Office of Management and Budget, Historical Tables, "Table 1.1—Summary of Receipts, Outlays and Surpluses and Deficits" and "Table 7.1—Federal Debt at the End of Year: 1940–2015," www.whitehouse.gov/omb/budget/Historicals/.

the members of society. The debate between trickle-up and trickle-down theories of taxation represents one of the major partisan battles in Congress, and not only reveals deep ideological divisions between the parties but also demonstrates the very real differences in the constituencies to which they respond.

As all tax-paying Americans know, the system of tax regulations—known as the tax code—is extremely complex. The complexity stems in part from the fact that you don't pay tax on your entire salary. Many expenses are deductible, that is, you can subtract them from your salary before you calculate the tax you owe. To pay no more taxes than you should, you need to be aware of all the deductions you can take—for instance, for mortgage interest, interest on college loans, business expenses, and charitable contributions. Furthermore, the government often gives tax benefits to promote certain behaviors. Businesses might receive tax credits if they buy environmentally friendly equipment, or farmers might be able to write off the expenses of a new tractor. Knowing which deductions you are entitled to can save you hundreds or thousands of dollars at tax time.

The tax code is so frustrating to so many taxpayers that politicians periodically propose reforms to make filing taxes easier and, they argue, fairer. After his reelection in 2004, for instance, President Bush made reforming the tax code a central piece of his second term. Perhaps the most common change proposed by tax reform groups is the institution of a **flat tax**. Under a flat tax, all people would pay the same percentage of their incomes in taxes, regardless of how much money they made or what their expenses were. According to advocates, the plan would vastly simplify the tax code and almost everyone would be able to file their taxes on their own.

However, much more is at stake here than just making it easier to file taxes; there are ideological reasons for a flat tax as well. Recall that we said earlier that progressive taxes are redistributive policies. As a result, wealthier people pay a greater percentage of their salary in taxes. Not only do conservatives argue against this redistribution on grounds of fairness, but advocates of lower, flatter taxes usually align with the conservative notion of limited government. In their eyes, government is providing too many unnecessary services—cutting taxes would force the government to shrink for lack of resources.

Another option proposed occasionally is a national sales tax—otherwise known as a **consumption tax**. Currently all but five states have their own sales tax, but a national tax would apply in addition to these sales taxes. Under such a plan, the national income tax would be abolished and people would be taxed not on what they earn but on what they spend. Again, proponents argue that a consumption tax would simplify the tax code. European countries have a version of a consumption tax called a **value-added tax** (**VAT**). Unlike the consumption tax proposed in the United States, where the tax is implemented at the point of sale, the VAT is levied at each stage of production based on the value added to the product at that stage.

The adoption of either a flat income tax or a consumption tax would dramatically simplify tax-paying for Americans, but there is significant resistance to implementing these reforms. Some opponents argue that the taxes are unfair to the less well-off because they are regressive. Other opponents of reforming the current tax code fear that such reforms will seriously reduce donations to charitable organizations. Although many Americans would like to see the tax code made less complex, few can agree on how to make this happen because, for all their complaints, no one really wants to give up the advantages they have under the current system.

Economic Regulatory Policy

Whereas fiscal policies tend to be redistributive in nature, most economic policy, including monetary policy, is regulatory. A regulatory policy is designed to restrict or change the behavior of certain groups or individuals. Government can regulate business in the interests of consumer safety, for instance, or to impose environmental standards and to limit the impact industry might have on the environment. When it comes to the American system of regulated capitalism, economic regulatory policy aims to protect economic rights and make procedural guarantees. So far we have been discussing government's role in regulating the markets to even out the highs and lows and encourage the growth of prosperity. Government can also intervene for other purposes as well.

Economic regulation can be an extremely controversial issue in a capitalist economy. Those who favor it argue that the market, left to its own devices, can be unfair and unpredictable, wreaking havoc in individual lives and having the potential for systemwide disaster. They point to problems such as the subprime mortgage crisis in 2008, in which thousands of loans were made to high-risk homebuyers without adequate background checks. When the economy soured, foreclosures soared as buyers could not make their home payments. The crisis extended to legions of other homeowners facing declining property values and to failing mortgage companies and the collapse of some of the largest financial corporations on Wall Street.[42] Opponents of regulation argue that when industries face more regulation, it increases their costs of production, which in turn makes prices rise and limits consumer choice.

Both sides often cite the classic example of the airline industry to make their point. In 1938 the government began to make laws determining how the airline industry would run, on the grounds that it was a new industry in need of regulation and a public utility. The Civil Aeronautics Board was established to set prices, determine routes, and set up schedules while ensuring the airlines earned a fair rate of return. By the 1970s the system was bogged down in bureaucratic rules. Flying was not easily accessible to many Americans; airfares were expensive because competition was limited, parts of the country had no easy air service, and consumers were unhappy. Under President Jimmy Carter, the process of **deregulation**—the removal of excessive regulations in order to improve economic efficiency—was begun, to be completed by Congress in 1978. Under deregulation, airfares dropped, new routes opened, low-cost airlines started up, and scheduling became more flexible.

Proponents of deregulation insist that the increased efficiency is reason enough to reduce regulation. At the same time, opponents point to the costs of deregulation—bankruptcies that left many airline workers unemployed and without pensions, and continuing labor problems as the remaining airlines struggled to stay in business.[43] In general, because it helps some groups and hurts others, the issue of regulation remains controversial in American politics. Both political parties tend to support making business more efficient by removing excessive regulations, but Republicans, with their closer ties to business, tend to push for more deregulation, whereas Democrats, with a traditional alliance with labor, push for less.

Following the collapse of the subprime mortgage market in 2008, however—a crisis brought on in part by lack of regulation in the first place—Congress passed, and President Obama signed, a financial reform bill in 2010. Called the Dodd-Frank Bank Reform bill, it establishes a consumer protection agency, sets in place some banking reform, and increases federal oversight and control over derivatives trading, the financial instrument that allowed mortgage speculation and that brought down such financial giants as AIG.[44] The bill's so-called Volcker rule prevents banks from speculating with their own money. The bill was criticized by the left as not going far enough to control the excesses on Wall Street and by the right as going too far and inhibiting the free play of capital. That it was passed at all under the partisan conditions of 2010 politics in America is notable itself, but the Dodd-Frank bill is not a dramatic change in the way banks do business. As the *Wall Street Journal* wrote after the bill passed, "From the beginning, lawmakers opted against a dramatic reshaping of the country's financial architecture. Instead, they moved to create new layers of regulation to prevent companies from taking on too much risk."[45]

Foreign Policy
Dealing with issues that cross national borders

Foreign policy is official U.S. policy designed to solve problems that take place between us and actors outside our borders. It is crucial to our domestic tranquility; without a strong and effective foreign policy, our security as a rich and peaceful country could be blown away in a heartbeat. Our foreign policy is almost always carried out for the good of American citizens or in the interest of national security. Even foreign aid, which seems like giving away American taxpayers' hard-earned money to people who have done nothing to deserve it, is part of a foreign policy to stabilize the world, to help strengthen international partnerships and alliances, and to keep Americans safe. Similarly, humanitarian intervention, like the NATO (North Atlantic Treaty Organization) military action in Kosovo in 1999, is ultimately conducted to support our values and the quality of life we think other nations ought to provide for their citizens.

> Foreign policy exists to support American interests, but determining what American interests are can be very difficult.

Many politicians have tried to encourage Americans to turn their backs on the rest of the world, promoting a foreign policy called **isolationism**, which holds that Americans should put themselves and their problems first and not interfere in global concerns. The United States has tried to pursue an isolationist policy before, perhaps most notably after World War I, but this experiment was largely seen as a failure. Most recently, the events of September 11 have put to rest the fiction that what happens "over there" is unrelated to what is happening "over here." In opposition to isolationism, **interventionism** holds that to keep the republic safe, we must be actively engaged in shaping the global environment and be willing to intervene in order to shape events. The United States has had a long history of interventionism—in the Americas and Asia in the 1800s, in World Wars I and II, and, since September 11, in the Middle East.

Foreign policy exists to support American interests, but determining what American interests are can be very difficult. In crisis situations, as we will see, foreign policy decisions are often made in secret. When situations are not critical, however, foreign policy decisions are made in the usual hubbub of American politics. Here, as we know, many actors with competing interests struggle to make their voices heard and to get policy to benefit themselves. Foreign policy, just like domestic policy, is about who gets what, and how they get it. The difference is that in foreign policy the stakes can be a matter of life and death, and we have far less control over the other actors involved.

Understanding Foreign Policy

The outward focus of foreign policy separates it from domestic policy, although sometimes the distinction between "foreign" and "domestic" is not so clear. Consider, for example, how environmental policy in America can have foreign repercussions. American industries located on the border with Canada have been the source of some tensions between the two countries because pollution from U.S. factories is carried into Canada by prevailing winds. This pollution can damage forests and increase the acidity of lakes, killing fish and harming other wildlife. Environmental regulations are largely a domestic matter, but because pollution is not confined to the geography of the United States, the issue takes on unintended international importance. Still, foreign policy is generally understood to be intentionally directed at external actors and the forces that shape these actions.

External actors can include many different entities. They could be other countries—sovereign bodies with governments and territories, like Mexico or the Republic of Ireland. **Intergovernmental organizations**—bodies that have countries as members, such as the United Nations, which has 192 member countries; NATO, which has 26 members from North America and Europe; the Organization of Petroleum Exporting Countries (OPEC), which has 12 member countries from Africa, Asia, the Middle East, and Latin America; and the European Union (EU), which has 27 members from across Europe and 4 more waiting to join—are also the focus of foreign policy interactions, as are **nongovernmental organizations**, or NGOs. NGOs are organizations that focus on specific issues and whose members are private individuals or groups from around the world. Greenpeace (environmental), Amnesty International (human rights), International Committee of the Red Cross (humanitarian relief), and Doctors Without Borders (medical care) are all NGOs. U.S. foreign policy also can be directed toward other nongovernmental groups, such as **multinational corporations**—large companies that do business in multiple countries and that often wield tremendous economic power, like Nike or General Motors. Miscellaneous other actors—groups that do not fit the other categories, including those that have a "government" but no territory, like the Middle

East's Palestinians or Ireland's Irish Republican Army, and groups that have no national ties, such as terrorist groups like al Qaeda—often have much at stake in U.S. foreign policy, too.

American foreign policy toward these actors falls into three broad categories.[46] **Crisis policy** deals with emergency threats to our national interests or values. Such situations often come as a surprise, and the use of force is one way to respond.[47] **Strategic policy** lays out the basic U.S. stance toward another country or a particular problem. **Structural defense policy** focuses largely on the policies and programs that deal with defense spending and military bases. These policies usually focus on, for example, buying new aircraft for the air force and navy or deciding which military bases to consolidate or close down.

The Post–Cold War Setting of American Foreign Policy

Before we can hope to have a clear understanding of contemporary American foreign policy, a historical note is in order. At the end of World War II, when the common purpose of fighting Adolf Hitler and ending German fascism no longer held the United States and the Soviet Union in an awkward alliance, the tensions that existed between the two largest and strongest superpowers in global politics began to bubble to the surface. Nearly all of Europe was divided between allies of the Soviets and allies of the United States, a division seen most graphically in the splitting of postwar Germany into a communist East and a capitalist West.

For nearly fifty years following World War II, tensions between the two superpowers shaped U.S. foreign policy and gave it a predictable order. The **Cold War**, waged between the United States and the Soviet Union from 1945 to 1989, was a bitter global competition between democracy and authoritarianism, capitalism and communism. It never erupted into a "hot" war of military action due in large part to the deterrent effect provided by a policy of "mutual assured destruction." Each side spent tremendous sums of money on nuclear weapons to make sure it had the ability to wipe out the other side. During this era, American foreign policy makers pursued a policy of **containment**, in which the United States tried to prevent the Soviet Union from expanding its influence, especially in Europe.

But as dangerous as the world was during the Cold War, it seemed easy to understand, casting complicated issues into simple choices of black and white. Countries were either with us or against us: they were free societies or closed ones, had capitalist or communist economies, were good or bad. Although the world was hardly that simple, it seemed that way to many people, and much of the complexity of world politics was glossed over—or perhaps bottled up—only to explode after the end of the Cold War in 1989.[48]

In 1991 the Soviet Union finally fell apart, to be replaced by more than a dozen independent states. Although most Westerners hailed the fall of the Soviet Union as an end to the tensions that kept the Cold War alive, Russia (one of the states of the former USSR) still holds the Soviet nuclear arsenal, and its citizens still project considerable fear and hostility toward the United States. Recently, anti-American sentiment has grown there, especially as efforts at Russian economic reform have been accompanied by suffering, deprivation, and economic humiliation, and as the Western military alliance, NATO, has enlarged by absorbing members of the former Soviet alliance.

This "new world order," or post–Cold War era, has eluded easy description in terms of global organization and threats to the United States, especially in the days since September 11, 2001.[49] Who is likely to be our most dangerous adversary? What threats must we prepare for? How much should we spend on military preparedness? Are we the world's policeman, a global banker, or a humanitarian protector? We have experimented with all of these roles in the past decade.[50] In September 2002 President George W. Bush opened the door to a new foreign policy approach when he asserted that the role of the United States was to maintain its military supremacy and take preemptive action against hostile and threatening states. The president also said that the United States would make no distinction between terrorist groups that threaten or attack the United States and countries that harbor those groups. In identifying an "axis of evil" of Iran, Iraq, and North Korea, President Bush set out a vision of American foreign policy that was rooted in taking active steps to promote democracy and to use force, alone if necessary, to eliminate perceived threats before they could more fully develop. This **Bush Doctrine** joined a long list of presidential foreign policy doctrines that have tried to define and protect U.S. interests in the world. Although there is not yet an "Obama Doctrine," the current president's approach has been markedly different from his predecessor's. Obama has emphasized diplomatic over military solutions, keeping communications channels with our enemies open and trying to find common interests on which to build. Although Obama has pulled troops out of Iraq, a war he opposed from the start, he has ramped up the war effort in Afghanistan in the hopes of creating a stable system there that won't provide cover to those who wish our country harm.

Who Makes Foreign Policy?

Consider the following headlines: "U.S. Opens Relations With China" and "U.S. Attacks al Qaeda Base in Afghanistan." They make it sound as if a single actor—the United States—makes foreign policy. Even as a figure of speech, this is misleading in two important ways. First, the image of the United States as a single actor suggests that the country acts with a single, united mind, diverting our attention from the political reality of conflict, bargaining, and cooperation that takes place *within* the government over foreign policy.[51] Second, it implies that all foreign policies are essentially the same—having the same goals and made by the same actors and processes. Our earlier description of the three different policy types indicates that this is not so; and, in fact, as we will see, each type of policy is made by different actors in different political contexts.

The political dynamics behind crisis policy, for instance, are dominated by the president and the small group of advisers around the Oval Office. Congress tends

Foreign Policy

Secretary of State Hillary Clinton and President Barack Obama visited Cairo, Egypt, in June 2009 to promote better relations between the United States and the Muslim world. The president relies on numerous advisers to help craft the nation's foreign security policy, which is by and large carried out by diplomats and bureaucrats.

not to be much engaged in crisis policy but often watches with the rest of the public (and the world) as presidents and their advisers decide how to respond to international crises. The choice of going to war in Iraq in 2003, for example, was made by President Bush and a number of key government policymakers around him.

Strategic policy tends to be formulated in the executive branch but usually deep in the bureaucracy rather than at the top levels. This gives interest groups and concerned members of Congress opportunities to lobby for certain policies. The public usually learns about these policies (and responds to and evaluates them) once they are announced by the president. The U.S. policy of containment of communism in the 1940s, for example, was developed mostly in the State Department and was then approved by President Harry Truman.[52]

Finally, structural defense policy, which often starts in the executive branch, is crafted largely in Congress, whose members tend to have their fingers on the pulses of their constituents, with much input from the bureaucracy and interest groups. When a plan to build and deploy a new fighter jet is developed, for example, it is made with coordination between Congress and the Defense Department—usually with members of Congress keeping a close eye on how their states and districts will fare from the projects.

Clearly a variety of actors are involved in making different types of foreign policy. What they all have in common is that they are officially acting on behalf of the federal government. It is not official foreign policy when New York City and San Francisco impose economic sanctions on Burma, or when private citizens like former president Jimmy Carter or the Reverend Jesse Jackson attempt to help resolve conflicts in Africa or Serbia.[53]

The President and the Executive Branch

As we saw in Chapter 7, the president is the chief foreign policy maker. The president is more likely to set the foreign policy agenda than other actors in American politics because of his constitutional powers, the informal powers that come with this high-profile job, and the chief executive's opportunities to communicate directly with the public.

The president sits at the top of a large pyramid of executive agencies and departments that assist him in making foreign policy (see Figure 14.4). If he does not take time to manage the agencies, other individuals may seize the opportunity to interpret foreign policy in terms of their own interests and goals. In a sense, the president provides a check on the power of the executive agencies, and without his leadership, foreign policy can drift. President Ronald Reagan didn't pay a lot of attention to foreign affairs, and so staff members in the National Security Council began to make foreign policy themselves. The result was the Iran-contra affair in the mid-1980s.

The **National Security Council (NSC)** is part of the president's inner circle, the Executive Office of the President. It was created in 1947 by the National Security Act to advise the president on matters of foreign policy and is coordinated by the national security adviser. By law the NSC includes the president, vice president, secretary of state, and secretary of defense. Additionally, the director of national intelligence (who is also the head of the Central Intelligence Agency) and the chairman of the Joint Chiefs of Staff (the head of the commanders of the military services) sit as advisers to the NSC. Beyond this, the president has wide discretion to decide what the NSC will look like and how he will use it by appointing other members and deciding how the council will function.

In addition to the NSC, several executive departments and agencies play a critical role in foreign policy making. The **Department of State** is charged with managing foreign affairs. It is often considered to be "first among equals" in its position relative to the other departments because it was the first department established by the Constitution in 1789. The State Department is headed by the secretary of state, who is part of the president's cabinet and fulfills a variety of foreign policy roles, including maintaining diplomatic and consular posts around the world, sending delegates and missions (groups of government officials) to a variety of international organization meetings, and negotiating treaties and executive agreements with other countries. Among the employees of the State Department are the foreign service officers, the most senior of which are the U.S. ambassadors.

The second major department involved in foreign policy is the **Department of Defense**, headquartered in the Pentagon. The main job of this department is to

Figure 14.4

Key Foreign Policy Agencies

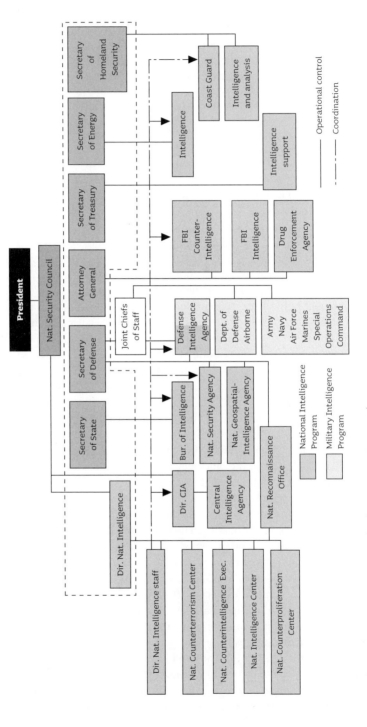

Source: Mark Lowenthal, Intelligence, 4th ed. (Washington, D.C.: CQ Press, 2009).

manage American soldiers and their equipment in order to protect the United States. The Defense Department is headed by the secretary of defense, whose job in part is to advise the president on defense matters and who, it is important to note, is a civilian.

The **Joint Chiefs of Staff** (**JCS**) is part of the Defense Department. This group consists of the senior military officers of the armed forces: the army and navy chiefs of staff, the chief of naval operations, and the commandant of the marine corps. The chairman is selected by the president. The JCS advises the secretary of defense, although the chair also may offer advice directly to the president and is responsible for managing the armed forces of the United States.

Another executive actor in foreign policy making is the **intelligence community**, which comprises several government agencies and bureaus. This community's job is to collect, organize, and analyze information. Information can be gathered in a number of ways, from the mundane (such as reading foreign newspapers) to the more clandestine (for instance, spying both by human beings and through surveillance satellites). Until 2004 the community was coordinated by the director of central intelligence, who was also the head of the **Central Intelligence Agency** (**CIA**). In the wake of many studies and hearings about the events leading up to September 11, as well as current security concerns, President Bush signed legislation that alters how the intelligence community is managed. The job of the director of central intelligence was limited to directing the CIA. The job of coordinating the entire network of agencies now falls to the newly created **director of national intelligence**.

In addition to the State Department, the Defense Department, and the intelligence community, other departments have roles to play in foreign policy. For instance, the Treasury Department and the Commerce Department are concerned with America's foreign economic policy, and the Department of Agriculture is interested in promoting American agricultural products abroad.

Congress

As we saw in Chapter 6, Congress has a variety of constitutional roles in making foreign policy, including the power to make treaties, to declare war, and to appropriate money, to name just a few. But Congress faces obstacles in its efforts to play an active role in foreign policy. It must deal with the considerable powers of the president, for instance, and it is more oriented toward domestic than foreign affairs, given the ever-present imperative of reelection. Congressional organization also can hamper Congress' role in foreign policy. The fragmentation of Congress, the slow speed of deliberation, and the complex nature of many foreign issues can make it difficult for Congress to play a big role, particularly in fast-moving foreign events.

The foreign policy tension between the president and Congress is illustrated by the complex issues surrounding the use of military force. The president is in charge of the armed forces, but only Congress can declare war. Presidents try to get around the power of Congress by committing troops to military actions that do not have the official status of a war, but this can infuriate legislators. Presidents have sent troops abroad without a formal declaration of war on a number of occasions—for example, to Korea (1950), the Dominican Republic (1965), Vietnam (1965), Lebanon (1982), Grenada (1983), Panama (1989), the Persian Gulf (1990), Afghanistan (2001), and Iraq (2003). As the United States became more involved in the Vietnam War, however, Congress became increasingly unhappy with the president's role. When, in the early 1970s, public opinion against the war became increasingly vocal, Congress turned on the commander-in-chief, passing the War Powers Act of 1973 over President Richard Nixon's veto. The act includes the following provisions:

1. The president must inform Congress of the introduction of forces into hostilities or situations where imminent involvement in hostilities is clearly indicated by the circumstances.

2. Troop commitments by the president cannot extend past sixty days without specific congressional authorization.

3. Any time American forces become engaged in hostilities without a declaration of war or specific congressional authorization, Congress can direct the president to disengage such troops by a concurrent resolution of the two houses of Congress.

The War Powers Act has not stopped presidents from using force abroad, however. Chief executives have largely sidestepped the act through a simple loophole: they don't make their reports to Congress exactly as the act requires, and therefore they never trigger the sixty-day clock. They generally report "consistent with but not pursuant to" the act, a technicality that allows them to satisfy Congress' interest in being informed without tying their hands by starting the clock.

Despite its difficulties in enforcing the War Powers Act, Congress has tried to play a fairly active role in foreign policy making, sometimes working with the president and sometimes at odds with him. The calculation for Congress is fairly straightforward: let the president pursue risky military strategies. If he succeeds, take credit for staying out of his way. If he fails, blame him for not consulting and for being "imperial." Either way, Congress wins.

How Do We Define a Foreign Policy Problem?

The actors we have just discussed work in a very distinctive political environment that helps them decide when a foreign situation constitutes a problem and when it should be acted on. Most foreign policy is either action to correct something we don't like in the world or reaction to world events. America could try to meddle in almost any country's affairs and could react to almost anything that happens in the world. How do policymakers in Washington, members of the media, and average Americans decide what is sufficiently important to Americans and American interests to require a foreign policy? What makes the United States act or react?

The answer is complex. First, a distinctive American approach to foreign policy has developed over the years that reflects America's view of its global role, its values, and its political goals. For instance, American foreign policy makers are divided about the United States' role in the world: should it be an interventionist actor, or should it focus on problems closer to home and leave the global community to solve its own problems? A second tension comes from the question of whether U.S. foreign policy should be driven by moral concerns (doing what is right—for instance, with respect to human rights) or by practical concerns (ignoring what is right in favor of what is expedient—for instance, ensuring U.S. access to foreign oil or other natural resources). A final tension arises from the conflict between the desire of the United States to promote its own national security and economic growth and its desire to promote the spread of democracy in the world. Because of inherent tensions among these roles, values, and goals, our country's approach to defining foreign policy problems is not always consistent.

Foreign policy also is shaped by politics. The political context in which American foreign policy is forged involves the actors we have just met, in combination with pressures both global and domestic. Global pressures involve the actions of other nations, over which we have no control other than brute force, and international organizations, like the United Nations and NATO. Other global pressures concern economic issues. In an increasingly interdependent global economy, ups and downs in one country tend to reverberate throughout the world. Foreign policy makers are influenced by these international forces, but also by domestic pressures. Just as in domestic policy, the media, public opinion, and interest groups weigh in and try to influence what policymakers do. To the extent that the policymakers are elected officials, these domestic actors can carry considerable weight.

Citizenship and Policy
The influence of the public's opinions on policymaking

In this book we have discussed elite, pluralist, and participatory theories of democracy. This chapter has shown that each theory explains some aspect of policymaking in the United States. Clearly some foreign policy and domestic policy are the products of a closely guarded elite policymaking process that could not be less democratic at its core. Foreign policy, especially when dealing with crisis situations, takes place in secrecy, with the details kept even from other policymakers at the elite level. Monetary policy is designed specifically to protect the economy from the forces of democracy—from the short-term preferences of citizens and the eagerness of elected officials to give citizens what they want. Other policy areas, like Social Security policy, are very pluralistic. Even though society as a whole might be better off with more stringent rules concerning who gets what from Social Security, older Americans, in the guise of AARP, have lobbied successfully to maintain the generous and universal benefits that make Social Security so expensive. But the power of political groups does not negate the power of citizens. Individual Americans, in their roles as voters and participants in public opinion polls, have a decisive influence on policymaking, both domestic and foreign. Although they may not participate in the sense of getting deeply involved in the process themselves, there is no doubt that politicians respond to their preferences in creating public policy.

As we saw in Chapter 10, public opinion matters in politics. State legislators, for instance, vote in accordance with the ideological preferences of their constituents.[54] States with more liberal citizens, such as New York, Massachusetts, and California, have more liberal policies, and more conservative states, like those in the South and the Rocky Mountains, have more conservative state policies. Other studies have found a similar pattern in national elections.[55] What these findings tell us is that for all the cynicism in politics today, when it comes to who gets what, when, and how, American democracy works to a remarkable degree.

▶ What's at Stake Revisited

The public debate over offshore drilling that followed the disaster on the *Deepwater Horizon* in 2010 only underscored the controversial nature of drilling at home that was already deeply familiar to the advocates of drilling in the Arctic National Wildlife Refuge. With soaring gas prices and growing public concern, the issue of drilling in ANWR had returned to the federal agenda two years before the *Deepwater Horizon* spill, in May 2008, when President Bush again asked Congress to allow oil and natural gas drilling in the refuge. But the Democratic-controlled Senate voted 56 to 42 against the proposal, with opponents refusing to consider tapping new domestic sources of oil as part of a broad energy approach.[56] Under the plan pushed by President Bush, drilling would occur in roughly 1.5 million acres of the 19-million-acre refuge. Why so much fuss over a small slice of land inhabited by 256 people?[57] What was at stake in drilling in ANWR?

For the oil industry, the policy was a win-win proposition. According to one estimate by the American Petroleum Institute, the land in question could produce 1.5 million barrels of oil a day for twenty years (roughly the amount of oil the U.S. imports from Saudi Arabia), reduce the trade deficit by $19 billion annually, and create thousands of new jobs.[58]

Drilling advocates claimed that the environmental impact of drilling would be minimal. They argued that the land where the drilling would take place is limited: "Production would come from a portion of ANWR consisting of only 2,000 acres, an area about the size of a regional airport in a refuge the size of South Carolina."[59] They were not convinced that wildlife would be adversely affected, especially with the new techniques of directional drilling that would be used, which makes it possible to drill in virtually any direction for miles.[60] From the perspective of supporters of the drilling, what's not to like about a policy that produces so much oil and is good for the economy?

Plenty, say the environmentalists. Although the drilling would only occur in roughly 8 percent of the refuge, opponents argued that it will degrade air and water quality and destroy the pristine land that is home to many animals, including migratory birds, caribou, polar bears, and oxen. Furthermore, they disputed the American Petroleum Institute's projections on the amount of oil available in the refuge, arguing that it contains a six-month supply of oil at the most and will never supply more than 2 percent of the national demand.[61] Critics are also concerned about setting dangerous precedents, that drilling in ANWR would potentially lead to greater support for offshore drilling, especially in places such as the waters off California's coast. Finally, they claim that drilling offers short-term gain at the cost of developing the alternative resources that could solve our energy problems for the long haul. According to drilling opponents, instead of searching for more oil, the United States should focus on lowering oil consumption by continuing to produce more fuel-efficient vehicles and developing alternative sources of energy.[62] These same arguments arose again in the aftermath of the *Deepwater Horizon* oil spill.

The deeper philosophical issues here go beyond the issues we see on the surface. What is interesting about the fundamental stakes in the ANWR drilling issue, and in fact in environmental policy generally, is how it turns our conventional definitions of liberal and conservative on their heads. Here it is conservatives who argue for progress and change and put their faith in technology to solve the problems of the future and liberals who argue that we should preserve our traditional ways, slow down, consider consequences, and not act rashly.

For proponents of drilling, it is about a philosophy of economic development, progress, and profit-making. From their perspective, it is silly not to use the resources we have at hand, and they claim that those objecting are not the people who live in Alaska, who stand to gain financially, but do-gooder environmentalists who use the "protect the land" argument at the expense of developing land that will be beneficial to the country. For opponents, on the other hand, the core issues are long-term planning versus short-term indulgence. They fear that drilling will distract us from what we ought to be focusing on, conservation and technology to make us independent of foreign oil in the future. Drilling today (and possibly tomorrow, if precedent is set) allows us to remain SUV-driving gasaholics, addicted to a resource we will eventually run out of, damaging not only our own lives but those of our children as well. For now, anyway, the balance of power in Washington sides with the former, and the disasters like the *Deepwater Horizon* spill put environmentalists in the unenviable position of being able to test empirically whether their gloomy prognostications of environmental catastrophe come true.

► Summary With Key Terms

Public policy (470) is a government plan of action to solve problems that people share collectively or that they cannot solve by themselves. Policies that address these problems can be **redistributive policies** (472), which shift resources from those who have them to those who do not; **distributive policies** (473), which use the resources of all to benefit a segment of society; or **regulatory policies** (473), which seek to modify the behavior of groups or individuals.

Public policy is made by actors in all branches and levels of government. The policymaking process involves agenda setting, policy formulation, policy adoption, policy implementation, and policy evaluation.

Social policies (477) are mostly redistributive and distributive policies that work to improve individuals' quality of life. They include **social welfare policies** (477), usually **means-tested programs** (477) directed toward those who cannot care for themselves, and **social insurance programs** (477), like **Social Security** (478), that offer benefits in exchange for contributions. Social Security is currently in financial straits because it is an **entitlement program** (479) whose benefits must be paid whether or not the money is there. The older Americans who receive those benefits are well-organized politically. Social welfare programs are easier to reform because poor people do not organize effectively to defend their interests, and in 1996 the guarantees of the **Social Security Act of 1935** (478) were eliminated with the advent of **Temporary Assistance to Needy Families (TANF)** (481). Other social welfare policies include the **Supplemental Nutrition Assistance Program (SNAP)** (482) and Head Start. Social policy also covers health care policy, including **Medicare** (483) and **Medicaid** (484), and various programs that supply **subsidies** (487) to citizens and corporations to encourage behaviors that the government values, like buying a home, going to college, and providing jobs.

Economic policy (488) refers to government strategies to provide for the health of the economy as a whole and solve economic problems. One of its main tools is **fiscal policy** (488), which involves regulating the ups and downs of the economy through government's power to tax and spend. Practitioners of fiscal policy believe that it is not necessary for government to pursue a **balanced budget** (488) but that **deficits** (489) and **surpluses** (489) are tools to be used strategically to help regulate the economy. A second tool of economic policy is **monetary policy** (489), which tries to regulate the economy by controlling the money supply through manipulation of **interest rates** (489). Congress is the main agent of fiscal policy, which means that it is often subject to political pressure. Monetary policy, made by the **Federal Reserve System** (492), is much more insulated from politics.

Part of the nation's tax policy, federal income taxes are **progressive taxes** (494), meaning that people with more income are taxed at a higher rate; other taxes are **regressive taxes** (494), meaning that they impose a greater burden on the less well-off. Conservatives in the United States would rather have fewer progressive taxes and seek to eliminate the **capital gains tax** (494) on investments altogether. Liberals prefer the wealthy to bear a larger share to lighten the load on the poor. Current proposals for reforming the tax code include a **flat tax** (496) and a **consumption tax** (496) such as a **value-added tax (VAT)** (496). Although Democrats and Republicans disagree on what exactly its role should be, government also seeks to keep the economy healthy through regulatory policy, including **deregulation** (497).

Foreign policy (498) is designed to solve problems between us and foreign actors. Sometimes the United States has tried to ignore the rest of the world, a policy known as **isolationism** (498), but more often it has tried to reach its goals by engaging other nations with a more active policy of **interventionism** (498). The actors the United States engages with are many other countries, **intergovernmental organizations** (499), **nongovernmental organizations** (499), and **multinational corporations** (499), among others. Foreign policies can be **crisis policy** (500), dealing with emergency threats; **strategic policy** (500), dealing with our basic stance to a foreign actor or problem; or **structural defense policy** (500), dealing with defense and military issues. Throughout the latter half of the twentieth century, our foreign policy was defined by the **Cold War** (500) with the Soviet Union, in which we pursued a policy of **containment** (500) to limit the USSR's influence. Our policy in a post–Cold War era is more difficult to define, as the threats to us are not necessarily from other nations but from groups like al Qaeda.

American foreign policy is made by a variety of actors—executive, legislative, and judicial—acting on behalf of the federal government. The president is the chief foreign policy maker, with the assistance of a huge network of federal agencies, among them the **National Security Council** (503), the **Department of State** (503), the **Department of Defense** (503), the **Joint Chiefs of Staff** (505), and the **intelligence community** (505), including the **Central Intelligence Agency (CIA)** (505) and the **director of national intelligence** (505). With different constitutional responsibilities, the president and Congress often wrangle for control over foreign policy, most recently over what has come to be known as the **Bush Doctrine** (501).

Explore this subject further with suggested readings, movies, and web sites at http://republic-brief.cqpress.com, where you'll also find study aids, practice quizzes, flash cards, and Internet exercises.

Appendix Material

APPENDIX 1

Articles of Confederation

Articles of Confederation and perpetual Union between the states of New Hampshire, Massachusetts-bay Rhode Island and Providence Plantations, Connecticut, New York, New Jersey, Pennsylvania, Delaware, Maryland, Virginia, North Carolina, South Carolina and Georgia.

ARTICLE I

The Stile of this Confederacy shall be "The United States of America".

ARTICLE II

Each state retains its sovereignty, freedom, and independence, and every power, jurisdiction, and right, which is not by this Confederation expressly delegated to the United States, in Congress assembled.

ARTICLE III

The said States hereby severally enter into a firm league of friendship with each other, for their common defense, the security of their liberties, and their mutual and general welfare, binding themselves to assist each other, against all force offered to, or attacks made upon them, or any of them, on account of religion, sovereignty, trade, or any other pretense whatever.

ARTICLE IV

The better to secure and perpetuate mutual friendship and intercourse among the people of the different States in this Union, the free inhabitants of each of these States, paupers, vagabonds, and fugitives from justice excepted, shall be entitled to all privileges and immunities of free citizens in the several States; and the people of each State shall free ingress and regress to and from any other State, and shall enjoy therein all the privileges of trade and commerce, subject to the same duties, impositions, and restrictions as the inhabitants thereof respectively, provided that such restrictions shall not extend so far as to prevent the removal of property imported into any State, to any other State, of which the owner is an inhabitant; provided also that no imposition, duties or restriction shall be laid by any State, on the property of the United States, or either of them.

If any person guilty of, or charged with, treason, felony, or other high misdemeanor in any State, shall flee from justice, and be found in any of the United States, he shall, upon demand of the Governor or executive power of the State from which he fled, be delivered up and removed to the State having jurisdiction of his offense.

Full faith and credit shall be given in each of these States to the records, acts, and judicial proceedings of the courts and magistrates of every other State.

ARTICLE V

For the most convenient management of the general interests of the United States, delegates shall be annually appointed in such manner as the legislatures of each State shall direct, to meet in Congress on the first Monday in November, in every year, with a power reserved to each State to recall its delegates, or any of them, at any time within the year, and to send others in their stead for the remainder of the year.

No State shall be represented in Congress by less than two, nor more than seven members; and no person shall be capable of being a delegate for more than three years in any term of six years; nor shall any person, being a delegate, be capable of holding any office under the United States, for which he, or another for his benefit, receives any salary, fees or emolument of any kind.

Each State shall maintain its own delegates in a meeting of the States, and while they act as members of the committee of the States.

In determining questions in the United States in Congress assembled, each State shall have one vote.

Freedom of speech and debate in Congress shall not be impeached or questioned in any court or place out of Congress, and the members of Congress shall be protected in their persons from arrests or imprisonments, during the time of their going to and from, and attendence on Congress, except for treason, felony, or breach of the peace.

ARTICLE VI

No State, without the consent of the United States in Congress assembled, shall send any embassy to, or receive any embassy from, or enter into any conference, agreement, alliance or treaty with any King, Prince or State; nor shall any person holding any office of profit or trust under the United States, or any of them, accept any present, emolument, office or title of any kind whatever from any King, Prince or foreign State; nor shall the United States in Congress assembled, or any of them, grant any title of nobility.

No two or more States shall enter into any treaty, confederation or alliance whatever between them, without the consent of the United States in Congress assembled, specifying accurately the purposes for which the same is to be entered into, and how long it shall continue.

No State shall lay any imposts or duties, which may interfere with any stipulations in treaties, entered into by the United States in Congress assembled, with any King, Prince or State, in pursuance of any treaties already proposed by Congress, to the courts of France and Spain.

No vessel of war shall be kept up in time of peace by any State, except such number only, as shall be deemed necessary by the United States in Congress assembled, for the defense of such State, or its trade; nor shall any body of forces be kept up by any State in time of peace, except such number only, as in the judgement of the United States in Congress assembled, shall be deemed requisite to garrison the forts necessary for the defense of such State; but every State shall always keep up a well-regulated and disciplined militia, sufficiently armed and accoutered, and shall provide and constantly have ready for use, in public stores, a due number of filed pieces and tents, and a proper quantity of arms, ammunition and camp equipage.

No State shall engage in any war without the consent of the United States in Congress assembled, unless such State be actually invaded by enemies, or shall have received certain advice of a resolution being formed by some nation of Indians to invade such State, and the danger is so imminent as not to admit of a delay till the United States in Congress assembled can be consulted; nor shall any State grant commissions to any ships or vessels of war, nor letters of marque or reprisal, except it be after a declaration of war by the United States in Congress assembled, and then only against the Kingdom or State and the subjects thereof, against which war has been so declared, and under such regulations as shall be established by the United States in Congress assembled, unless such State be infested by pirates, in which case vessels of war may be fitted out for that occasion, and kept so long as the danger shall continue, or until the United States in Congress assembled shall determine otherwise.

ARTICLE VII

When land forces are raised by any State for the common defense, all officers of or under the rank of colonel, shall be appointed by the legislature of each State respectively, by whom such forces shall be raised, or in such manner as such State shall direct, and all vacancies shall be filled up by the State which first made the appointment.

ARTICLE VIII

All charges of war, and all other expenses that shall be incurred for the common defense or general welfare, and allowed by the United States in Congress assembled, shall be defrayed out of a common treasury, which shall be supplied by the several States in proportion to the value of all land within each State, granted or surveyed for any person, as such land and the buildings and improvements thereon shall be estimated according to such mode as the United States in Congress assembled, shall from time to time direct and appoint.

The taxes for paying that proportion shall be laid and levied by the authority and direction of the legislatures of the several States within the time agreed upon by the United States in Congress assembled.

ARTICLE IX

The United States in Congress assembled, shall have the sole and exclusive right and power of determining on peace and war, except in the cases mentioned in the sixth article—of sending and receiving ambassadors—entering into treaties and alliances, provided that no treaty of commerce shall be made whereby the legislative power of the respective States shall be restrained from imposing such imposts and duties on foreigners, as their own people are subjected to, or from prohibiting the exportation or importation of any species of goods or commodities whatsoever—of establishing rules for deciding in all cases, what captures on land or water shall be legal, and in what manner prizes taken by land or naval forces in the service of the United States shall be divided or appropriated—of granting letters of marque and reprisal in times of peace—appointing courts for the trial of piracies and felonies commited on the high seas and establishing courts for receiving and determining finally appeals in all cases of captures, provided that no member of Congress shall be appointed a judge of any of the said courts.

The United States in Congress assembled shall also be the last resort on appeal in all disputes and differences now subsisting or that hereafter may arise between two or more States concerning boundary, jurisdiction or any other causes whatever; which authority shall always be exercised in the manner following. Whenever the legislative or executive authority or lawful agent of any State in controversy with another shall present a petition to Congress stating the matter in question and praying for a hearing, notice thereof shall be given by order of Congress to the legislative or executive authority of the other State in controversy, and a day assigned for the appearance of the parties by their lawful agents, who shall then be directed to appoint by joint consent, commissioners or judges to constitute a court for hearing and determining the matter in question: but if they cannot agree, Congress shall name three persons out of each of the United States, and from the list of such persons each party shall alternately strike out one, the petitioners beginning, until the number shall be reduced to thirteen; and from that number not less than seven, nor more than nine names as Congress shall direct, shall in the presence of Congress be drawn out by lot, and the persons whose names shall be so drawn or any five of them, shall be commissioners or judges, to hear and finally determine the controversy, so always as a major part of the judges who shall hear the cause shall agree in the determination: and if either party shall neglect to attend at the day appointed, without showing reasons, which Congress shall judge sufficient, or being present shall refuse to strike, the Congress shall proceed to nominate three persons out of each State, and the secretary of Congress shall strike in behalf of such party absent or refusing; and the judgement and sentence of the court to be appointed, in the manner before prescribed, shall be final and conclusive; and if any of the parties shall refuse to submit to the authority of such court, or to appear or defend their claim or cause, the court shall nevertheless proceed to pronounce sentence, or judgement, which shall in like manner be final and decisive, the judgement or sentence and other proceedings being in either case transmitted to Congress, and lodged among the acts of Congress for the security of the parties concerned: provided that every commissioner, before he sits in judgement, shall take an oath to be administered by one of the judges of the supreme or superior court of the State, where the cause shall be tried, 'well and truly to hear and determine the matter in question, according to the best of his judgement, without favor, affection or hope of reward': provided also, that no State shall be deprived of territory for the benefit of the United States.

All controversies concerning the private right of soil claimed under different grants of two or more States, whose jurisdictions as they may respect such lands, and the States which passed such grants are adjusted, the said grants or either of them being at the same time claimed to have originated antecedent to such settlement of jurisdiction, shall on the petition of either party to the Congress of the United States, be finally determined as near as may be in the same manner as is before prescribed for deciding disputes respecting territorial jurisdiction between different States.

The United States in Congress assembled shall also have the sole and exclusive right and power of regulating the alloy and value of coin struck by their own authority, or by that of the respective States—fixing the standards of weights and measures throughout the United States—regulating the trade and managing all affairs with the Indians, not members of any of the States, provided that the legislative right of any State within its own limits be not infringed or violated—establishing or regulating post offices from one State to another, throughout all the United States, and exacting such postage on the papers passing through the same as may be requisite to defray the expenses of the said office—appointing all officers of the land forces, in the service of the United States, excepting regimental officers—appointing all the officers of the naval forces, and commissioning all officers whatever in the service of the United States—making rules for the government and regulation of the said land and naval forces, and directing their operations.

The United States in Congress assembled shall have authority to appoint a committee, to sit in the recess of Congress, to be denominated 'A Committee of the States', and to consist of one delegate from each State; and to appoint such other committees and civil officers as may be necessary for managing the general affairs of the United States under their direction—to appoint one of their members to preside, provided that no person be allowed to serve in the office of president more than one year in any term of three years; to ascertain the necessary sums of money to be raised for the service of the United States, and to appropriate and apply the same for defraying the public expenses—to borrow money, or emit bills on the credit of the United States, transmitting every half-year to the respective States an account of the sums of money so borrowed or emitted—to build and equip a navy—to agree upon the number of land forces, and to make requisitions from each State for its quota, in proportion to the number of white inhabitants in such State; which requisition shall be binding, and thereupon the legislature of each State shall appoint the regimental officers, raise the men and cloath, arm and equip them in a solid-like manner, at the expense of the United States; and the officers and men so cloathed, armed and equipped shall march to the place appointed, and within the time agreed on by the United States in Congress assembled. But if the United States in

Congress assembled shall, on consideration of circumstances judge proper that any State should not raise men, or should raise a smaller number of men than the quota thereof, such extra number shall be raised, officered, cloathed, armed and equipped in the same manner as the quota of each State, unless the legislature of such State shall judge that such extra number cannot be safely spread out in the same, in which case they shall raise, officer, cloath, arm and equip as many of such extra number as they judge can be safely spared. And the officers and men so cloathed, armed, and equipped, shall march to the place appointed, and within the time agreed on by the United States in Congress assembled.

The United States in Congress assembled shall never engage in a war, nor grant letters of marque or reprisal in time of peace, nor enter into any treaties or alliances, nor coin money, nor regulate the value thereof, nor ascertain the sums and expenses necessary for the defense and welfare of the United States, or any of them, nor emit bills, nor borrow money on the credit of the United States, nor appropriate money, nor agree upon the number of vessels of war, to be built or purchased, or the number of land or sea forces to be raised, nor appoint a commander in chief of the army or navy, unless nine States assent to the same: nor shall a question on any other point, except for adjourning from day to day be determined, unless by the votes of the majority of the United States in Congress assembled.

The Congress of the United States shall have power to adjourn to any time within the year, and to any place within the United States, so that no period of adjournment be for a longer duration than the space of six months, and shall publish the journal of their proceedings monthly, except such parts thereof relating to treaties, alliances or military operations, as in their judgement require secrecy; and the yeas and nays of the delegates of each State on any question shall be entered on the journal, when it is desired by any delegates of a State, or any of them, at his or their request shall be furnished with a transcript of the said journal, except such parts as are above excepted, to lay before the legislatures of the several States.

ARTICLE X

The Committee of the States, or any nine of them, shall be authorized to execute, in the recess of Congress, such of the powers of Congress as the United States in Congress assembled, by the consent of the nine States, shall from time to time think expedient to vest them with; provided that no power be delegated to the said Committee, for the exercise of which, by the Articles of Confederation, the voice of nine States in the Congress of the United States assembled be requisite.

ARTICLE XI

Canada acceding to this confederation, and adjoining in the measures of the United States, shall be admitted into, and entitled to all the advantages of this Union; but no other colony shall be admitted into the same, unless such admission be agreed to by nine States.

ARTICLE XII

All bills of credit emitted, monies borrowed, and debts contracted by, or under the authority of Congress, before the assembling of the United States, in pursuance of the present confederation, shall be deemed and considered as a charge against the United States, for payment and satisfaction whereof the said United States, and the public faith are hereby solemnly pledged.

ARTICLE XIII

Every State shall abide by the determination of the United States in Congress assembled, on all questions which by this confederation are submitted to them. And the Articles of this

Confederation shall be inviolably observed by every State, and the Union shall be perpetual; nor shall any alteration at any time hereafter be made in any of them; unless such alteration be agreed to in a Congress of the United States, and be afterwards confirmed by the legislatures of every State.

And Whereas it hath pleased the Great Governor of the World to incline the hearts of the legislatures we respectively represent in Congress, to approve of, and to authorize us to ratify the said Articles of Confederation and perpetual Union. Know Ye that we the undersigned delegates, by virtue of the power and authority to us given for that purpose, do by these presents, in the name and in behalf of our respective constituents, fully and entirely ratify and confirm each and every of the said Articles of Confederation and perpetual Union, and all and singular the matters and things therein contained: And we do further solemnly plight and engage the faith of our respective constituents, that they shall abide by the determinations of the United States in Congress assembled, on all questions, which by the said Confederation are submitted to them. And that the Articles thereof shall be inviolably observed by the States we respectively represent, and that the Union shall be perpetual.

In Witness whereof we have hereunto set our hands in Congress. Done at Philadelphia in the State of Pennsylvania the ninth day of July in the Year of our Lord One Thousand Seven Hundred and Seventy-Eight, and in the Third Year of the independence of America.

Agreed to by Congress 15 November 1777
In force after ratification by Maryland, 1 March 1781

APPENDIX 2

Declaration of Independence

In Congress, July 4, 1776,
The Unanimous Declaration of
the Thirteen United States of America,

On June 11, 1776, the responsibility to "prepare a declaration" of independence was assigned by the Continental Congress, meeting in Philadelphia, to five members: John Adams, Benjamin Franklin, Thomas Jefferson, Robert Livingston, and Roger Sherman. Impressed by his talents as a writer, the committee asked Jefferson to compose a draft. After modifying Jefferson's draft the committee turned it over to Congress on June 28. On July 2 Congress voted to declare independence; on the evening of July 4, it approved the Declaration of Independence.

When in the Course of human events, it becomes necessary for one people to dissolve the political bands which have connected them with another, and to assume among the Powers of the earth, the separate and equal station to which the Laws of Nature and of Nature's God entitle them, a decent respect to the opinions of mankind requires that they should declare the causes which impel them to the separation.

We hold these truths to be self-evident, that all men are created equal, that they are endowed by their Creator with certain unalienable Rights, that among these are Life,

Liberty and the pursuit of Happiness. That to secure these rights, Governments are instituted among Men, deriving their just powers from the consent of the governed. That whenever any form of Government becomes destructive of these ends, it is the Right of the People to alter or to abolish it, and to institute new Government, laying its foundation on such principles and organizing its powers in such form, as to them shall seem most likely to effect their Safety and Happiness. Prudence, indeed, will dictate that Government long established should not be changed for light and transient causes; and accordingly all experience hath shown, that mankind are more disposed to suffer, while evils are sufferable, than to right themselves by abolishing the forms to which they are accustomed. But when a long train of abuses and usurpations, pursuing invariably the same Object evinces a design to reduce them under absolute Despotism, it is their right, it is their duty, to throw off such Government, and to provide new Guards for their future security. Such has been the patient sufferance of these Colonies; and such is now the necessity which constrains them to alter their former Systems of Government. The history of the present King of Great Britain is a history of repeated injuries and usurpations, all having in direct object the establishment of an absolute Tyranny over these States. To prove this, let Facts be submitted to a candid world.

He has refused his Assent to Laws, the most wholesome and necessary for the public good.

He has forbidden his Governors to pass Laws of immediate and pressing importance, unless suspended in their operation till his Assent should be obtained; and when so suspended, he has utterly neglected to attend to them.

He has refused to pass other Laws for the accommodation of large districts of people, unless those people would relinquish the right of Representation in the Legislature, a right inestimable to them and formidable to tyrants only.

He has called together legislative bodies at places unusual, uncomfortable, and distant from the depository of their Public Records, for the sole purpose of fatiguing them into compliance with his measures.

He has dissolved Representative Houses repeatedly, for opposing with manly firmness his invasions on the rights of the people.

He has refused for a long time, after such dissolutions, to cause others to be elected; whereby the Legislative Powers, incapable of Annihilation, have returned to the People at large for their exercise; the State remaining in the mean time exposed to all the dangers of invasion from without, and convulsions within.

He has endeavored to prevent the population of these States; for that purpose obstructing the Laws of Naturalization of Foreigners; refusing to pass others to encourage their migration hither, and raising the conditions of new Appropriations of Lands.

He has obstructed the Administration of Justice, by refusing his Assent to Laws for establishing Judiciary Powers.

He has made Judges dependent on his Will alone, for the tenure of their offices, and the amount and payment of their salaries.

He has erected a multitude of New Offices, and sent hither swarms of Officers to harass our People, and eat out their substance.

He has kept among us, in times of peace, Standing Armies without the Consent of our legislature.

He has affected to render the Military independent of and superior to the Civil Power.

He has combined with others to subject us to a jurisdiction foreign to our constitution, and unacknowledged by our laws; giving his Assent to their acts of pretended legislation:

For quartering large bodies of armed troops among us:

For protecting them, by a mock Trial, from Punishment for any Murders which they should commit on the Inhabitants of these States:

For cutting off our Trade with all parts of the world:

For imposing taxes on us without our Consent:

For depriving us in many cases, of the benefits of Trial by Jury:

For transporting us beyond Seas to be tried for pretended offences:

For abolishing the free System of English Laws in a neighbouring Province, establishing therein an Arbitrary government, and enlarging its Boundaries so as to render it at once an example and fit instrument for introducing the same absolute rule into these Colonies:

For taking away our Charters, abolishing our most valuable Laws, and altering fundamentally the Forms of our Governments:

For suspending our own Legislature, and declaring themselves invested with Power to legislate for us in all cases whatsoever.

He has abdicated Government here, by declaring us out of his Protection and waging War against us.

He has plundered our seas, ravaged our Coasts, burnt our towns, and destroyed the lives of our people.

He is at this time transporting large armies of foreign mercenaries to compleat the works of death, desolation and tyranny, already begun with circumstances of Cruelty & perfidy scarcely parallel in the most barbarous ages, and totally unworthy the Head of a civilized nation.

He has constrained our fellow Citizens taken Captive on the high Seas to bear Arms against their Country, to become the executioners of their friends and Brethren, or to fall themselves by their Hands.

He has excited domestic insurrections amongst us, and has endeavoured to bring on the inhabitants of our frontiers, the merciless Indian Savages, whose known rule of warfare, is an undistinguished destruction of all ages, sexes and conditions.

In every stage of these Oppressions We have Petitioned for Redress in the most humble terms: Our repeated Petitions have been answered only by repeated injury. A Prince, whose character is thus marked by every act which may define a Tyrant, is unfit to be the ruler of a free People.

Nor have We been wanting in attention to our British brethren. We have warned them from time to time of attempts by their legislature to extend an unwarrantable jurisdiction over us. We have reminded them of the circumstances of our emigration and settlement here. We have appealed to their native justice and magnanimity, and we have conjured them by the ties of our common kindred to disavow these usurpations, which would inevitably interrupt our connections and correspondence. They too have been deaf to the voice of justice and of consanguinity. We must, therefore, acquiesce in the necessity, which denounces our Separation, and hold them, as we hold the rest of mankind, Enemies in War, in Peace Friends.

We, therefore, the Representatives of the United States of America, in General Congress, Assembled, appealing to the Supreme Judge of the world for the rectitude of our intentions, do, in the Name, and by Authority of the good People of these Colonies, solemnly publish and declare, That these United Colonies are, and of Right ought to be Free and Independent States; that they are Absolved from all Allegiance to the British Crown, and that all political connection between them and the State of Great Britain, is and ought to be totally dissolved; and that as Free and Independent States, they have full Power to levy War, conclude Peace, contract Alliances, establish Commerce, and to do all other Acts and Things which Independent States may of right do. And for the support of this Declaration, with a firm reliance on the Protection of Divine Providence, we mutually pledge to each other our Lives, our Fortunes and our sacred Honor.

APPENDIX 3

Constitution of the United States

The United States Constitution was written at a convention that Congress called on February 21, 1787, for the purpose of recommending amendments to the Articles of Confederation. Every state but Rhode Island sent delegates to Philadelphia, where the convention met that summer. The delegates decided to write an entirely new constitution, completing their labors on September 17. Nine states (the number the Constitution itself stipulated as sufficient) ratified by June 21, 1788.

The Framers of the Constitution included only six paragraphs on the Supreme Court. Article III, Section 1, created the Supreme Court and the federal system of courts. It provided that "[t]he judicial power of the United States, shall be vested in one supreme Court," and whatever inferior courts Congress "from time to time" saw fit to establish. Article III, Section 2, delineated the types of cases and controversies that should be considered by a federal—rather than a state—court. But beyond this, the Constitution left many of the particulars of the Supreme Court and the federal court system for Congress to decide in later years in judiciary acts.

We the People of the United States, in Order to form a more perfect Union, establish Justice, insure domestic Tranquility, provide for the common defence, promote the general Welfare, and secure the Blessings of Liberty to ourselves and our Posterity, do ordain and establish this Constitution for the United States of America.

ARTICLE I

Section 1. All legislative Powers herein granted shall be vested in a Congress of the United States, which shall consist of a Senate and House of Representatives.

Section 2. The House of Representatives shall be composed of Members chosen every second Year by the People of the several States, and the Electors in each State shall have the Qualifications requisite for Electors of the most numerous Branch of the State Legislature.

No Person shall be a Representative who shall not have attained to the age of twenty five Years, and been seven Years a Citizen of the United States, and who shall not, when elected, be an Inhabitant of that State in which he shall be chosen.

[Representatives and direct Taxes shall be apportioned among the several States which may be included within this Union, according to their respective Numbers, which shall be determined by adding to the whole Number of free Persons, including those bound to Service for a Term of Years, and excluding Indians not taxed, three fifths of all other Persons.][1] The actual Enumeration shall be made within three Years after the first Meeting of the Congress of the United States, and within every subsequent Term of ten Years, in such Manner as they shall by Law direct. The Number of Representatives shall not exceed one for every thirty Thousand, but each State shall have at Least one Representative; and until such enumeration shall be made, the State of New Hampshire shall be entitled to chuse three, Massachusetts eight, Rhode-Island and Providence Plantations one, Connecticut five, New-York six, New Jersey four, Pennsylvania eight, Delaware one, Maryland six, Virginia ten, North Carolina five, South Carolina five, and Georgia three.

When vacancies happen in the Representation from any State, the Executive Authority thereof shall issue Writs of Election to fill such Vacancies.

The House of Representatives shall chuse their Speaker and other Officers; and shall have the sole Power of Impeachment.

Section 3. The Senate of the United States shall be composed of two Senators from each State, [chosen by the Legislature thereof,]² for six Years; and each Senator shall have one Vote.

Immediately after they shall be assembled in Consequence of the first Election, they shall be divided as equally as may be into three Classes. The Seats of the Senators of the first Class shall be vacated at the Expiration of the second Year, of the second Class at the Expiration of the fourth Year, and of the third Class at the Expiration of the sixth Year, so that one third may be chosen every second Year; [and if Vacancies happen by Resignation, or otherwise, during the Recess of the Legislature of any State, the Executive thereof may make temporary Appointments until the next Meeting of the Legislature, which shall then fill such Vacancies.]³

No Person shall be a Senator who shall not have attained to the Age of thirty Years, and been nine Years a Citizen of the United States, and who shall not, when elected, be an Inhabitant of that State for which he shall be chosen.

The Vice President of the United States shall be President of the Senate, but shall have no Vote, unless they be equally divided.

The Senate shall chuse their other Officers, and also a President pro tempore, in the Absence of the Vice President, or when he shall exercise the Office of President of the United States.

The Senate shall have the sole Power to try all Impeachments. When sitting for that Purpose, they shall be on Oath or Affirmation. When the President of the United States is tried, the Chief Justice shall preside: And no Person shall be convicted without the Concurrence of two thirds of the Members present.

Judgment in Cases of Impeachment shall not extend further than to removal from Office, and disqualification to hold and enjoy any Office of honor, Trust or Profit under the United States: but the Party convicted shall nevertheless be liable and subject to Indictment, Trial, Judgment and Punishment, according to Law.

Section 4. The Times, Places and Manner of holding Elections for Senators and Representatives, shall be prescribed in each State by the Legislature thereof; but the Congress may at any time by Law make or alter such Regulations, except as to the Places of chusing Senators.

The Congress shall assemble at least once in every Year, and such Meeting shall [be on the first Monday in December],⁴ unless they shall by Law appoint a different Day.

Section 5. Each House shall be the Judge of the Elections, Returns and Qualifications of its own Members, and a Majority of each shall constitute a Quorum to do Business; but a smaller Number may adjourn from day to day, and may be authorized to compel the Attendance of absent Members, in such Manner, and under such Penalties as each House may provide.

Each House may determine the Rules of its Proceedings, punish its Members for disorderly Behaviour, and, with the Concurrence of two thirds, expel a Member.

Each House shall keep a Journal of its Proceedings, and from time to time publish the same, excepting such Parts as may in their Judgment require Secrecy; and the Yeas and Nays of the Members of either House on any question shall, at the Desire of one fifth of those Present, be entered on the Journal.

Neither House, during the Session of Congress, shall, without the Consent of the other, adjourn for more than three days, nor to any other Place than that in which the two Houses shall be sitting.

Section 6. The Senators and Representatives shall receive a Compensation for their Services, to be ascertained by Law, and paid out of the Treasury of the United States. They shall in all Cases, except Treason, Felony and Breach of the Peace, be privileged from Arrest during their Attendance at the Session of their respective Houses, and in going to and returning from the same; and for any Speech or Debate in either House, they shall not be questioned in any other Place.

No Senator or Representative shall, during the Time for which he was elected, be appointed to any civil Office under the Authority of the United States, which shall have been created, or the Emoluments whereof shall have been encreased during such time; and no Person holding any Office under the United States, shall be a Member of either House during his Continuance in Office.

Section 7. All Bills for raising Revenue shall originate in the House of Representatives; but the Senate may propose or concur with Amendments as on other Bills.

Every Bill which shall have passed the House of Representatives and the Senate, shall, before it become a Law, be presented to the President of the United States; If he approve he shall sign it, but if not he shall return it, with his Objections to that House in which it shall have originated, who shall enter the Objections at large on their Journal, and proceed to reconsider it. If after such Reconsideration two thirds of that House shall agree to pass the Bill, it shall be sent, together with the Objections, to the other House, by which it shall likewise be reconsidered, and if approved by two thirds of that House, it shall become a Law. But in all such Cases the Votes of both Houses shall be determined by yeas and Nays, and the Names of the Persons voting for and against the Bill shall be entered on the Journal of each House respectively. If any Bill shall not be returned by the President within ten Days (Sundays excepted) after it shall have been presented to him, the Same shall be a Law, in like Manner as if he had signed it, unless the Congress by their Adjournment prevent its Return, in which Case it shall not be a Law.

Every Order, Resolution, or Vote to which the Concurrence of the Senate and House of Representatives may be necessary (except on a question of Adjournment) shall be presented to the President of the United States; and before the Same shall take Effect, shall be approved by him, or being disapproved by him, shall be repassed by two thirds of the Senate and House of Representatives, according to the Rules and Limitations prescribed in the Case of a Bill.

Section 8. The Congress shall have Power To lay and collect Taxes, Duties, Imposts and Excises, to pay the Debts and provide for the common Defence and general Welfare of the United States; but all Duties, Imposts and Excises shall be uniform throughout the United States;

To borrow Money on the credit of the United States;

To regulate Commerce with foreign Nations, and among the several States, and with the Indian Tribes;

To establish an uniform Rule of Naturalization, and uniform Laws on the subject of Bankruptcies throughout the United States;

To coin Money, regulate the Value thereof, and of foreign Coin, and fix the Standard of Weights and Measures;

To provide for the Punishment of counterfeiting the Securities and current Coin of the United States;

To establish Post Offices and post Roads;

To promote the Progress of Science and useful Arts, by securing for limited Times to Authors and Inventors the exclusive Right to their respective Writings and Discoveries;

To constitute Tribunals inferior to the supreme Court;

To define and punish Piracies and Felonies committed on the high Seas, and Offences against the Law of Nations;

To declare War, grant Letters of Marque and Reprisal, and make Rules concerning Captures on Land and Water;

To raise and support Armies, but no Appropriation of Money to that Use shall be for a longer Term than two Years;

To provide and maintain a Navy;

To make Rules for the Government and Regulation of the land and naval Forces;

To provide for calling forth the Militia to execute the Laws of the Union, suppress Insurrections and repel Invasions;

To provide for organizing, arming, and disciplining, the Militia, and for governing such Part of them as may be employed in the Service of the United States, reserving to the States respectively, the Appointment of the Officers, and the Authority of training the Militia according to the discipline prescribed by Congress;

To exercise exclusive Legislation in all Cases whatsoever, over such District (not exceeding ten Miles square) as may, by Cession of particular States, and the Acceptance of Congress, become the Seat of the Government of the United States, and to exercise like Authority over all Places purchased by the Consent of the Legislature of the State in which the Same shall be, for the Erection of Forts, Magazines, Arsenals, dock-Yards, and other needful Buildings;—And

To make all Laws which shall be necessary and proper for carrying into Execution the foregoing Powers, and all other Powers vested by this Constitution in the Government of the United States, or in any Department or Officer thereof.

Section 9. The Migration or Importation of such Persons as any of the States now existing shall think proper to admit, shall not be prohibited by the Congress prior to the Year one thousand eight hundred and eight, but a Tax or duty may be imposed on such Importation, not exceeding ten dollars for each Person.

The Privilege of the Writ of Habeas Corpus shall not be suspended, unless when in Cases of Rebellion or Invasion the public Safety may require it.

No Bill of Attainder or ex post facto Law shall be passed.

No Capitation, or other direct, Tax shall be laid, unless in Proportion to the Census or Enumeration herein before directed to be taken.[5]

No Tax or Duty shall be laid on Articles exported from any State.

No Preference shall be given by any Regulation of Commerce or Revenue to the Ports of one State over those of another; nor shall Vessels bound to, or from, one State, be obliged to enter, clear, or pay Duties in another.

No Money shall be drawn from the Treasury, but in Consequence of Appropriations made by Law; and a regular Statement and Account of the Receipts and Expenditures of all public Money shall be published from time to time.

No Title of Nobility shall be granted by the United States: And no Person holding any Office of Profit or Trust under them, shall, without the Consent of the Congress, accept of any present, Emolument, Office, or Title, of any kind whatever, from any King, Prince, or foreign State.

Section 10. No State shall enter into any Treaty, Alliance, or Confederation; grant Letters of Marque and Reprisal; coin Money; emit Bills of Credit; make any Thing but gold and silver Coin a Tender in Payment of Debts; pass any Bill of Attainder, ex post facto Law, or Law impairing the Obligation of Contracts, or grant any Title of Nobility.

No State shall, without the Consent of the Congress, lay any Imposts or Duties on Imports or Exports, except what may be absolutely necessary for executing its inspection Laws: and the net Produce of all Duties and Imposts, laid by any State on Imports or Exports, shall be for the Use of the Treasury of the United States; and all such Laws shall be subject to the Revision and Controul of the Congress.

No State shall, without the Consent of Congress, lay any Duty of Tonnage, keep Troops, or Ships of War in time of Peace, enter into any Agreement or Compact with another State, or with a foreign Power, or engage in War, unless actually invaded, or in such imminent Danger as will not admit of delay.

ARTICLE II

Section 1. The executive Power shall be vested in a President of the United States of America. He shall hold his Office during the Term of four Years, and, together with the Vice President, chosen for the same Term, be elected, as follows:

Each State shall appoint, in such Manner as the Legislature thereof may direct, a Number of Electors, equal to the whole Number of Senators and Representatives to which the State may be entitled in the Congress: but no Senator or Representative, or Person holding an Office of Trust or Profit under the United States, shall be appointed an Elector.

[The Electors shall meet in their respective States, and vote by Ballot for two Persons, of whom one at least shall not be an Inhabitant of the same State with themselves. And they shall make a List of all the Persons voted for, and of the Number of Votes for each; which List they shall sign and certify, and transmit sealed to the Seat of the Government of the United States, directed to the President of the Senate. The President of the Senate shall, in the Presence of the Senate and House of Representatives, open all the Certificates, and the Votes shall then be counted. The Person having the greatest Number of Votes shall be the President, if such Number be a Majority of the whole Number of Electors appointed; and if there be more than one who have such Majority, and have an equal Number of Votes, then the House of Representatives shall immediately chuse by Ballot one of them for President; and if no Person have a Majority, then from the five highest on the list the said House shall in like Manner chuse the President. But in chusing the President, the Votes shall be taken by States, the Representation from each State having one Vote; A quorum for this Purpose shall consist of a Member or Members from two thirds of the States, and a Majority of all the States shall be necessary to a Choice. In every Case, after the Choice of the President, the Person having the greatest Number of Votes of the Electors shall be the Vice President. But if there should remain two or more who have equal Votes, the Senate shall chuse from them by Ballot the Vice President.][6]

The Congress may determine the Time of chusing the Electors, and the Day on which they shall give their Votes; which Day shall be the same throughout the United States.

No Person except a natural born Citizen, or a Citizen of the United States, at the time of the Adoption of this Constitution, shall be eligible to the Office of President; neither shall any Person be eligible to that Office who shall not have attained to the Age of thirty five Years, and been fourteen Years a Resident within the United States.

In Case of the Removal of the President from Office, or of his Death, Resignation, or Inability to discharge the Powers and Duties of the said Office,[7] the Same shall devolve on the Vice President, and the Congress may by Law provide for the Case of Removal, Death,

Resignation or Inability, both of the President and Vice President, declaring what Officer shall then act as President, and such Officer shall act accordingly, until the Disability be removed, or a President shall be elected.

The President shall, at stated Times, receive for his Services, a Compensation, which shall neither be encreased nor diminished during the Period for which he shall have been elected, and he shall not receive within that Period any other Emolument from the United States, or any of them.

Before he enter on the Execution of his Office, he shall take the following Oath or Affirmation:—"I do solemnly swear (or affirm) that I will faithfully execute the Office of President of the United States, and will to the best of my Ability, preserve, protect and defend the Constitution of the United States."

Section 2. The President shall be Commander in Chief of the Army and Navy of the United States, and of the Militia of the several States, when called into the actual Service of the United States; he may require the Opinion, in writing, of the principal Officer in each of the executive Departments, upon any Subject relating to the Duties of their respective Offices, and he shall have Power to grant Reprieves and Pardons for Offences against the United States, except in Cases of Impeachment.

He shall have Power, by and with the Advice and Consent of the Senate, to make Treaties, provided two thirds of the Senators present concur; and he shall nominate, and by and with the Advice and Consent of the Senate, shall appoint Ambassadors, other public Ministers and Consuls, Judges of the supreme Court, and all other Officers of the United States, whose Appointments are not herein otherwise provided for, and which shall be established by Law: but the Congress may by Law vest the Appointment of such inferior Officers, as they think proper, in the President alone, in the Courts of Law, or in the Heads of Departments.

The President shall have Power to fill up all Vacancies that may happen during the Recess of the Senate, by granting Commissions which shall expire at the End of their next Session.

Section 3. He shall from time to time give to the Congress Information of the State of the Union, and recommend to their Consideration such Measures as he shall judge necessary and expedient; he may, on extraordinary Occasions, convene both Houses, or either of them, and in Case of Disagreement between them, with Respect to the Time of Adjournment, he may adjourn them to such Time as he shall think proper; he shall receive Ambassadors and other public Ministers; he shall take Care that the Laws be faithfully executed, and shall Commission all the Officers of the United States.

Section 4. The President, Vice President and all civil Officers of the United States, shall be removed from Office on Impeachment for, and Conviction of, Treason, Bribery, or other high Crimes and Misdemeanors.

ARTICLE III

Section 1. The judicial Power of the United States, shall be vested in one supreme Court, and in such inferior Courts as the Congress may from time to time ordain and establish. The Judges, both of the supreme and inferior Courts, shall hold their Offices during good Behaviour, and shall, at stated Times, receive for their Services, a Compensation, which shall not be diminished during their Continuance in Office.

Section 2. The judicial Power shall extend to all Cases, in Law and Equity, arising under this Constitution, the Laws of the United States, and Treaties made, or which shall be made, under their Authority;—to all Cases affecting Ambassadors, other public Ministers and

Consuls;—to all Cases of admiralty and maritime Jurisdiction;—to Controversies to which the United States shall be a Party;—to Controversies between two or more States;—between a State and Citizens of another State;[8]—between Citizens of different States;—between Citizens of the same State claiming Lands under Grants of different States, and between a State, or the Citizens thereof, and foreign States, Citizens or Subjects.[8]

In all Cases affecting Ambassadors, other public Ministers and Consuls, and those in which a State shall be Party, the supreme Court shall have original Jurisdiction. In all the other Cases before mentioned, the supreme Court shall have appellate Jurisdiction, both as to Law and Fact, with such Exceptions, and under such Regulations as the Congress shall make.

The Trial of all Crimes, except in Cases of Impeachment, shall be by Jury; and such Trial shall be held in the State where the said Crimes shall have been committed; but when not committed within any State, the Trial shall be at such Place or Places as the Congress may by Law have directed.

Section 3. Treason against the United States, shall consist only in levying War against them, or in adhering to their Enemies, giving them Aid and Comfort. No Person shall be convicted of Treason unless on the Testimony of two Witnesses to the same overt Act, or on Confession in open Court.

The Congress shall have Power to declare the Punishment of Treason, but no Attainder of Treason shall work Corruption of Blood, or Forfeiture except during the Life of the Person attainted.

ARTICLE IV

Section 1. Full Faith and Credit shall be given in each State to the public Acts, Records, and judicial Proceedings of every other State. And the Congress may by general Laws prescribe the Manner in which such Acts, Records and Proceedings shall be proved, and the Effect thereof.

Section 2. The Citizens of each State shall be entitled to all Privileges and Immunities of Citizens in the several States.

A Person charged in any State with Treason, Felony, or other Crime, who shall flee from Justice, and be found in another State, shall on Demand of the executive Authority of the State from which he fled, be delivered up, to be removed to the State having Jurisdiction of the Crime.

[No Person held to Service or Labour in one State, under the Laws thereof, escaping into another, shall, in Consequence of any Law or Regulation therein, be discharged from such Service or Labour, but shall be delivered up on Claim of the Party to whom such Service or Labour may be due.][9]

Section 3. New States may be admitted by the Congress into this Union; but no new State shall be formed or erected within the Jurisdiction of any other State; nor any State be formed by the Junction of two or more States, or Parts of States, without the Consent of the Legislatures of the States concerned as well as of the Congress.

The Congress shall have Power to dispose of and make all needful Rules and Regulations respecting the Territory or other Property belonging to the United States; and nothing in this Constitution shall be so construed as to Prejudice any Claims of the United States, or of any particular State.

Section 4. The United States shall guarantee to every State in this Union a Republican Form of Government, and shall protect each of them against Invasion; and on Application of the Legislature, or of the Executive (when the Legislature cannot be convened) against domestic Violence.

ARTICLE V

The Congress, whenever two thirds of both Houses shall deem it necessary, shall propose Amendments to this Constitution, or, on the Application of the Legislatures of two thirds of the several States, shall call a Convention for proposing Amendments, which, in either Case, shall be valid to all Intents and Purposes, as Part of this Constitution, when ratified by the Legislatures of three fourths of the several States, or by Conventions in three fourths thereof, as the one or the other Mode of Ratification may be proposed by the Congress; Provided [that no Amendment which may be made prior to the Year One thousand eight hundred and eight shall in any Manner affect the first and fourth Clauses in the Ninth Section of the first Article; and][10] that no State, without its Consent, shall be deprived of its equal Suffrage in the Senate.

ARTICLE VI

All Debts contracted and Engagements entered into, before the Adoption of this Constitution, shall be as valid against the United States under this Constitution, as under the Confederation.

This Constitution, and the Laws of the United States which shall be made in Pursuance thereof; and all Treaties made, or which shall be made, under the Authority of the United States, shall be the supreme Law of the Land; and the Judges in every State shall be bound thereby, any Thing in the Constitution or Laws of any State to the Contrary notwithstanding.

The Senators and Representatives before mentioned, and the Members of the several State Legislatures, and all executive and judicial Officers, both of the United States and of the several States, shall be bound by Oath or Affirmation, to support this Constitution; but no religious Test shall ever be required as a Qualification to any Office or public Trust under the United States.

ARTICLE VII

The Ratification of the Conventions of nine States, shall be sufficient for the Establishment of this Constitution between the States so ratifying the Same.

Done in Convention by the Unanimous Consent of the States present the Seventeenth Day of September in the Year of our Lord one thousand seven hundred and Eighty seven and of the Independence of the United States of America the Twelfth. IN WITNESS whereof We have hereunto subscribed our Names,

George Washington, President and
deputy from Virginia, and
thirty-eight other delegates.

[The language of the original Constitution, not including the Amendments, was adopted by a convention of the states on September 17, 1787, and was subsequently ratified by the states on the following dates: Delaware, December 7, 1787; Pennsylvania, December 12, 1787; New Jersey, December 18, 1787; Georgia, January 2, 1788; Connecticut, January 9, 1788; Massachusetts, February 6, 1788; Maryland, April 28, 1788; South Carolina, May 23, 1788; New Hampshire, June 21, 1788.

Ratification was completed on June 21, 1788.

The Constitution subsequently was ratified by Virginia, June 25, 1788; New York, July 26, 1788; North Carolina, November 21, 1789; Rhode Island, May 29, 1790; and Vermont, January 10, 1791.]

Amendments

AMENDMENT I

(First ten amendments ratified December 15, 1791.)

Congress shall make no law respecting an establishment of religion, or prohibiting the free exercise thereof; or abridging the freedom of speech, or of the press; or the right of the people peaceably to assemble, and to petition the Government for a redress of grievances.

AMENDMENT II

A well regulated Militia, being necessary to the security of a free State, the right of the people to keep and bear Arms, shall not be infringed.

AMENDMENT III

No Soldier shall, in time of peace be quartered in any house, without the consent of the Owner, nor in time of war, but in a manner to be prescribed by law.

AMENDMENT IV

The right of the people to be secure in their persons, houses, papers, and effects, against unreasonable searches and seizures, shall not be violated, and no Warrants shall issue, but upon probable cause, supported by Oath or affirmation, and particularly describing the place to be searched, and the persons or things to be seized.

AMENDMENT V

No person shall be held to answer for a capital, or otherwise infamous crime, unless on a presentment or indictment of a Grand Jury, except in cases arising in the land or naval forces, or in the Militia, when in actual service in time of War or public danger; nor shall any person be subject for the same offence to be twice put in jeopardy of life or limb; nor shall be compelled in any criminal case to be a witness against himself, nor be deprived of life, liberty, or property, without due process of law; nor shall private property be taken for public use, without just compensation.

AMENDMENT VI

In all criminal prosecutions, the accused shall enjoy the right to a speedy and public trial, by an impartial jury of the State and district wherein the crime shall have been committed, which district shall have been previously ascertained by law, and to be informed of the nature and cause of the accusation; to be confronted with the witnesses against him; to have compulsory process for obtaining witnesses in his favor, and to have the Assistance of Counsel for his defence.

AMENDMENT VII

In Suits at common law, where the value in controversy shall exceed twenty dollars, the right of trial by jury shall be preserved, and no fact tried by a jury, shall be otherwise re-examined in any Court of the United States, than according to the rules of the common law.

AMENDMENT VIII

Excessive bail shall not be required, nor excessive fines imposed, nor cruel and unusual punishments inflicted.

AMENDMENT IX

The enumeration in the Constitution, of certain rights, shall not be construed to deny or disparage others retained by the people.

AMENDMENT X

The powers not delegated to the United States by the Constitution, nor prohibited by it to the States, are reserved to the States respectively, or to the people.

AMENDMENT XI *(Ratified February 7, 1795)*

The Judicial power of the United States shall not be construed to extend to any suit in law or equity, commenced or prosecuted against one of the United States by Citizens of another State, or by Citizens or Subjects of any Foreign State.

AMENDMENT XII *(Ratified June 15, 1804)*

The Electors shall meet in their respective states and vote by ballot for President and Vice-President, one of whom, at least, shall not be an inhabitant of the same state with themselves; they shall name in their ballots the person voted for as President, and in distinct ballots the person voted for as Vice-President, and they shall make distinct lists of all persons voted for as President, and of all persons voted for as Vice-President, and of the number of votes for each, which lists they shall sign and certify, and transmit sealed to the seat of the government of the United States, directed to the President of the Senate;—The President of the Senate shall, in the presence of the Senate and House of Representatives, open all the certificates and the votes shall then be counted;—The person having the greatest number of votes for President, shall be the President, if such number be a majority of the whole number of Electors appointed; and if no person have such majority, then from the persons having the highest numbers not exceeding three on the list of those voted for as President, the House of Representatives shall choose immediately, by ballot, the President. But in choosing the President, the votes shall be taken by states, the representation from each state having one vote; a quorum for this purpose shall consist of a member or members from two-thirds of the states, and a majority of all the states shall be necessary to a choice. [And if the House of Representatives shall not choose a President whenever the right of choice shall devolve upon them, before the fourth day of March next following, then the Vice-President shall act as President, as in the case of the death or other constitutional disability of the President.—][11] The person having the greatest number of votes as Vice-President, shall be the Vice-President, if such number be a majority of the whole number of Electors appointed, and if no person have a majority, then from the two highest numbers on the list, the Senate shall choose the Vice-President; a quorum for the purpose shall consist of two-thirds of the whole number of Senators, and a majority of the whole number shall be necessary to a choice. But no person constitutionally ineligible to the office of President shall be eligible to that of Vice-President of the United States.

AMENDMENT XIII *(Ratified December 6, 1865)*

Section 1. Neither slavery nor involuntary servitude, except as a punishment for crime whereof the party shall have been duly convicted, shall exist within the United States, or any place subject to their jurisdiction.

Section 2. Congress shall have power to enforce this article by appropriate legislation.

AMENDMENT XIV *(Ratified July 9, 1868)*

Section 1. All persons born or naturalized in the United States, and subject to the jurisdiction thereof, are citizens of the United States and of the State wherein they reside. No State shall make or enforce any law which shall abridge the privileges or immunities of citizens of the United States; nor shall any State deprive any person of life, liberty, or property, without due process of law; nor deny to any person within its jurisdiction the equal protection of the laws.

Section 2. Representatives shall be apportioned among the several States according to their respective numbers, counting the whole number of persons in each State, excluding Indians not taxed. But when the right to vote at any election for the choice of electors for President and Vice President of the United States, Representatives in Congress, the Executive and Judicial officers of a State, or the members of the Legislature thereof, is denied to any of the male inhabitants of such State, being twenty-one years of age,[12] and citizens of the United States, or in any way abridged, except for participation in rebellion, or other crime, the basis of representation therein shall be reduced in the proportion which the number of such male citizens shall bear to the whole number of male citizens twenty-one years of age in such State.

Section 3. No person shall be a Senator or Representative in Congress, or elector of President and Vice President, or hold any Office, civil or military, under the United States, or under any State, who, having previously taken an oath, as a member of Congress, or as an officer of the United States, or as a member of any State legislature, or as an executive or judicial officer of any State, to support the Constitution of the United States, shall have engaged in insurrection or rebellion against the same, or given aid or comfort to the enemies thereof. But Congress may by a vote of two-thirds of each House, remove such disability.

Section 4. The validity of the public debt of the United States, authorized by law, including debts incurred for payment of pensions and bounties for services in suppressing insurrection or rebellion, shall not be questioned. But neither the United States nor any State shall assume or pay any debt or obligation incurred in aid of insurrection or rebellion against the United States, or any claim for the loss or emancipation of any slave; but all such debts, obligations and claims shall be held illegal and void.

Section 5. The Congress shall have power to enforce, by appropriate legislation, the provisions of this article.

AMENDMENT XV *(Ratified February 3, 1870)*

Section 1. The right of citizens of the United States to vote shall not be denied or abridged by the United States or by any State on account of race, color, or previous condition of servitude.

Section 2. The Congress shall have power to enforce this article by appropriate legislation.

AMENDMENT XVI *(Ratified February 3, 1913)*

The Congress shall have power to lay and collect taxes on incomes, from whatever source derived, without apportionment among the several States, and without regard to any census or enumeration.

AMENDMENT XVII *(Ratified April 8, 1913)*

The Senate of the United States shall be composed of two Senators from each State, elected by the people thereof, for six years; and each Senator shall have one vote. The electors in each

State shall have the qualifications requisite for electors of the most numerous branch of the State legislatures.

When vacancies happen in the representation of any State in the Senate, the executive authority of such State shall issue writs of election to fill such vacancies: Provided, That the legislature of any State may empower the executive thereof to make temporary appointments until the people fill the vacancies by election as the legislature may direct.

This amendment shall not be so construed as to affect the election or term of any Senator chosen before it becomes valid as part of the Constitution.

AMENDMENT XVIII *(Ratified January 16, 1919)*

Section 1. After one year from the ratification of this article the manufacture, sale, or transportation of intoxicating liquors within, the importation thereof into, or the exportation thereof from the United States and all territory subject to the jurisdiction thereof for beverage purposes is hereby prohibited.

Section 2. The Congress and the several States shall have concurrent power to enforce this article by appropriate legislation.

Section 3. This article shall be inoperative unless it shall have been ratified as an amendment to the Constitution by the legislatures of the several States, as provided in the Constitution, within seven years from the date of the submission hereof to the States by the Congress.[13]

AMENDMENT XIX *(Ratified August 18, 1920)*

The right of citizens of the United States to vote shall not be denied or abridged by the United States or by any State on account of sex.

Congress shall have power to enforce this article by appropriate legislation.

AMENDMENT XX *(Ratified January 23, 1933)*

Section 1. The terms of the President and Vice President shall end at noon on the 20th day of January, and the terms of Senators and Representatives at noon on the 3d day of January, of the years in which such terms would have ended if this article had not been ratified; and the terms of their successors shall then begin.

Section 2. The Congress shall assemble at least once in every year, and such meeting shall begin at noon on the 3d day of January, unless they shall by law appoint a different day.

Section 3.[14] If, at the time fixed for the beginning of the term of the President, the President elect shall have died, the Vice President elect shall become President. If a President shall not have been chosen before the time fixed for the beginning of his term, or if the President elect shall have failed to qualify, then the Vice President elect shall act as President until a President shall have qualified; and the Congress may by law provide for the case wherein neither a President elect nor a Vice President elect shall have qualified, declaring who shall then act as President, or the manner in which one who is to act shall be selected, and such person shall act accordingly until a President or Vice President shall have qualified.

Section 4. The Congress may by law provide for the case of the death of any of the persons from whom the House of Representatives may choose a President whenever the right of choice shall have devolved upon them, and for the case of the death of any of the persons from whom the Senate may choose a Vice President whenever the right of choice shall have devolved upon them.

Section 5. Sections 1 and 2 shall take effect on the 15th day of October following the ratification of this article.

Section 6. This article shall be inoperative unless it shall have been ratified as an amendment to the Constitution by the legislatures of three-fourths of the several States within seven years from the date of its submission.

AMENDMENT XXI *(Ratified December 5, 1933)*

Section 1. The eighteenth article of amendment to the Constitution of the United States is hereby repealed.

Section 2. The transportation or importation into any State, Territory, or possession of the United States for delivery or use therein of intoxicating liquors, in violation of the laws thereof, is hereby prohibited.

Section 3. This article shall be inoperative unless it shall have been ratified as an amendment to the Constitution by conventions in the several States, as provided in the Constitution, within seven years from the date of the submission hereof to the States by the Congress.

AMENDMENT XXII *(Ratified February 27, 1951)*

Section 1. No person shall be elected to the office of the President more than twice, and no person who has held the office of President, or acted as President, for more than two years of a term to which some other person was elected President shall be elected to the office of the President more than once. But this Article shall not apply to any person holding the office of President when this Article was proposed by the Congress, and shall not prevent any person who may be holding the office of President, or acting as President, during the term within which this Article becomes operative from holding the office of President or acting as President during the remainder of such term.

Section 2. This article shall be inoperative unless it shall have been ratified as an amendment to the Constitution by the legislatures of three-fourths of the several States within seven years from the date of its submission to the States by the Congress.

AMENDMENT XXIII *(Ratified March 29, 1961)*

Section 1. The District constituting the seat of Government of the United States shall appoint in such manner as the Congress may direct:
A number of electors of President and Vice President equal to the whole number of Senators and Representatives in Congress to which the District would be entitled if it were a State, but in no event more than the least populous State; they shall be in addition to those appointed by the States, but they shall be considered, for the purposes of the election of President and Vice President, to be electors appointed by a State; and they shall meet in the District and perform such duties as provided by the twelfth article of amendment.

Section 2. The Congress shall have power to enforce this article by appropriate legislation.

AMENDMENT XXIV *(Ratified January 23, 1964)*

Section 1. The right of citizens of the United States to vote in any primary or other election for President or Vice President, for electors for President or Vice President, or for Senator or Representative in Congress, shall not be denied or abridged by the United States or any State by reason of failure to pay any poll tax or other tax.

Section 2. The Congress shall have power to enforce this article by appropriate legislation.

AMENDMENT XXV *(Ratified February 10, 1967)*

Section 1. In case of the removal of the President from office or of his death or resignation, the Vice President shall become President.

Section 2. Whenever there is a vacancy in the offie of the Vice President, the President shall nominate a Vice President who shall take office upon confirmation by a majority vote of both Houses of Congress.

Section 3. Whenever the President transmits to the President pro tempore of the Senate and the Speaker of the House of Representatives his written declaration that he is unable to discharge the powers and duties of his office, and until he transmits to them a written declaration to the contrary, such powers and duties shall be discharged by the Vice President as Acting President.

Section 4. Whenever the Vice President and a majority of either the principal officers of the executive departments or of such other body as Congress may by law provide, transmit to the President pro tempore of the Senate and the Speaker of the House of Representatives their written declaration that the President is unable to discharge the powers and duties of his office, the Vice President shall immediately assume the powers and duties of the office as Acting President.

Thereafter, when the President transmits to the President pro tempore of the Senate and the Speaker of the House of Representatives his written declaration that no inability exists, he shall resume the powers and duties of his office unless the Vice President and a majority of either the principal officers of the executive departments or of such other body as Congress may by law provide, transmit within four days to the President pro tempore of the Senate and the Speaker of the House of Representatives their written declaration that the President is unable to discharge the powers and duties of his office. Thereupon Congress shall decide the issue, assembling within forty-eight hours for that purpose if not in session. If the Congress, within twenty-one days after receipt of the latter written declaration, or, if Congress is not in session, within twenty-one days after Congress is required to assemble, determines by two-thirds vote of both Houses that the President is unable to discharge the powers and duties of his office, the Vice President shall continue to discharge the same as Acting President; otherwise, the President shall resume the powers and duties of his office.

AMENDMENT XXVI *(Ratified July 1, 1971)*

Section 1. The right of citizens of the United States, who are eighteen years of age or older, to vote shall not be denied or abridged by the United States or by any State on account of age.

Section 2. The Congress shall have power to enforce this article by appropriate legislation.

AMENDMENT XXVII *(Ratified May 7, 1992)*

No law varying the compensation for the services of the Senators and Representatives shall take effect, until an election of Representatives shall have intervened.

Notes:

1. The part in brackets was changed by section 2 of the Fourteenth Amendment.
2. The part in brackets was changed by the first paragraph of the Seventeenth Amendment.

3. The part in brackets was changed by the second paragraph of the Seventeenth Amendment.
4. The part in brackets was changed by section 2 of the Twentieth Amendment.
5. The Sixteenth Amendment gave Congress the power to tax incomes.
6. The material in brackets was superseded by the Twelfth Amendment.
7. This provision was affected by the Twenty-fifth Amendment.
8. These clauses were affected by the Eleventh Amendment.
9. This paragraph was superseded by the Thirteenth Amendment.
10. Obsolete.
11. The part in brackets was superseded by section 3 of the Twentieth Amendment.
12. See the Nineteenth and Twenty-sixth Amendments.
13. This amendment was repealed by section 1 of the Twenty-first Amendment.
14. See the Twenty-fifth Amendment.

APPENDIX 4

Federalist No. 10

The Same Subject Continued: The Union as a Safeguard Against Domestic Faction and Insurrection.

From the New York Packet
Friday, November 23, 1787.
Author: James Madison

To the People of the State of New York:

AMONG the numerous advantages promised by a wellconstructed Union, none deserves to be more accurately developed than its tendency to break and control the violence of faction. The friend of popular governments never finds himself so much alarmed for their character and fate, as when he contemplates their propensity to this dangerous vice. He will not fail, therefore, to set a due value on any plan which, without violating the principles to which he is attached, provides a proper cure for it. The instability, injustice, and confusion introduced into the public councils, have, in truth, been the mortal diseases under which popular governments have everywhere perished; as they continue to be the favorite and fruitful topics from which the adversaries to liberty derive their most specious declamations. The valuable improvements made by the American constitutions on the popular models, both ancient and modern, cannot certainly be too much admired; but it would be an unwarrantable partiality, to contend that they have as effectually obviated the danger on this side, as was wished and expected. Complaints are everywhere heard from our most considerate and virtuous citizens, equally the friends of public and private faith, and of public and personal liberty, that our governments are too unstable, that the public good is disregarded in the conflicts of rival parties, and that measures are too often decided, not according to the rules of justice and the rights of the minor party, but by the superior force of an interested and overbearing majority. However anxiously we may wish that these complaints had no foundation, the evidence, of known facts will not permit us to deny that they are in some degree true. It will be found, indeed, on a candid review of our situation, that some of the distresses under which we labor have been erroneously charged on the operation of our governments; but it will be found, at the same time, that other causes will not alone account for many of our heaviest misfortunes; and, particularly, for that prevailing and increasing distrust of public engagements, and alarm for private rights, which are echoed from one end of the continent to the other. These must be chiefly, if not wholly, effects of the unsteadiness and injustice with which a factious spirit has tainted our public administrations.

By a faction, I understand a number of citizens, whether amounting to a majority or a minority of the whole, who are united and actuated by some common impulse of passion, or of interest, adversed to the rights of other citizens, or to the permanent and aggregate interests of the community.

There are two methods of curing the mischiefs of faction: the one, by removing its causes; the other, by controlling its effects.

There are again two methods of removing the causes of faction: the one, by destroying the liberty which is essential to its existence; the other, by giving to every citizen the same opinions, the same passions, and the same interests.

It could never be more truly said than of the first remedy, that it was worse than the disease. Liberty is to faction what air is to fire, an aliment without which it instantly expires. But it could not be less folly to abolish liberty, which is essential to political life, because it nourishes faction, than it would be to wish the annihilation of air, which is essential to animal life, because it imparts to fire its destructive agency.

The second expedient is as impracticable as the first would be unwise. As long as the reason of man continues fallible, and he is at liberty to exercise it, different opinions will be formed. As long as the connection subsists between his reason and his self-love, his opinions and his passions will have a reciprocal influence on each other; and the former will be objects to which the latter will attach themselves. The diversity in the faculties of men, from which the rights of property originate, is not less an insuperable obstacle to a uniformity of interests. The protection of these faculties is the first object of government. From the protection of different and unequal faculties of acquiring property, the possession of different degrees and kinds of property immediately results; and from the influence of these on the sentiments and views of the respective proprietors, ensues a division of the society into different interests and parties.

The latent causes of faction are thus sown in the nature of man; and we see them everywhere brought into different degrees of activity, according to the different circumstances of civil society. A zeal for different opinions concerning religion, concerning government, and many other points, as well of speculation as of practice; an attachment to different leaders ambitiously contending for pre-eminence and power; or to persons of other descriptions whose fortunes have been interesting to the human passions, have, in turn, divided mankind into parties, inflamed them with mutual animosity, and rendered them much more disposed to vex and oppress each other than to co-operate for their common good. So strong is this propensity of mankind to fall into mutual animosities, that where no substantial occasion presents itself, the most frivolous and fanciful distinctions have been sufficient to kindle their unfriendly passions and excite their most violent conflicts. But the most common and durable source of factions has been the various and unequal distribution of property. Those who hold and those who are without property have ever formed distinct interests in society. Those who are creditors, and those who are debtors, fall under a like discrimination. A landed interest, a manufacturing interest, a mercantile interest, a moneyed interest, with many lesser interests, grow up of necessity in civilized nations, and divide them into different classes, actuated by different sentiments and views. The regulation of these various and interfering interests forms the principal task of modern legislation, and involves the spirit of party and faction in the necessary and ordinary operations of the government.

No man is allowed to be a judge in his own cause, because his interest would certainly bias his judgment, and, not improbably, corrupt his integrity. With equal, nay with greater reason, a body of men are unfit to be both judges and parties at the same time; yet what are many of the most important acts of legislation, but so many judicial determinations, not indeed concerning the rights of single persons, but concerning the rights of large bodies of citizens? And what are the different classes of legislators but advocates and parties to the causes which they determine? Is a law proposed concerning private debts? It is a question to which the creditors are parties on one side and the debtors on the other. Justice ought to hold the balance between them. Yet the parties are, and must be, themselves the judges; and the most numerous party, or, in other words, the most powerful faction must be expected to prevail. Shall domestic manufactures be encouraged, and in what degree, by restrictions on foreign manufactures? are questions which would be differently decided by the landed and the manufacturing classes, and probably by neither with a sole regard to justice and the public good. The apportionment of taxes on the various descriptions of property is an act which seems to require the most exact impartiality; yet there is, perhaps, no legislative act in which greater opportunity and temptation are given to a predominant party to trample on the rules of justice. Every shilling with which they overburden the inferior number, is a shilling saved to their own pockets.

It is in vain to say that enlightened statesmen will be able to adjust these clashing interests, and render them all subservient to the public good. Enlightened statesmen will not always be at the helm. Nor, in many cases, can such an adjustment be made at all without taking into view indirect and remote considerations, which will rarely prevail over the immediate interest which one party may find in disregarding the rights of another or the good of the whole.

The inference to which we are brought is, that the CAUSES of faction cannot be removed, and that relief is only to be sought in the means of controlling its EFFECTS.

If a faction consists of less than a majority, relief is supplied by the republican principle, which enables the majority to defeat its sinister views by regular vote. It may clog the administration, it may convulse the society; but it will be unable to execute and mask its violence under the forms of the Constitution. When a majority is included in a faction, the form of popular government, on the other hand, enables it to sacrifice to its ruling passion or interest both the public good and the rights of other citizens. To secure the public good and private rights against the danger of such a faction, and at the same time to preserve the spirit and the form of popular government, is then the great object to which our inquiries are directed. Let me add that it is the great desideratum by which this form of government can be rescued from the opprobrium under which it has so long labored, and be recommended to the esteem and adoption of mankind.

By what means is this object attainable? Evidently by one of two only. Either the existence of the same passion or interest in a majority at the same time must be prevented, or the majority, having such coexistent passion or interest, must be rendered, by their number and local situation, unable to concert and carry into effect schemes of oppression. If the impulse and the opportunity be suffered to coincide, we well know that neither moral nor religious motives can be relied on as an adequate control. They are not found to be such on the injustice and violence of individuals, and lose their efficacy in proportion to the number combined together, that is, in proportion as their efficacy becomes needful.

From this view of the subject it may be concluded that a pure democracy, by which I mean a society consisting of a small number of citizens, who assemble and administer the government in person, can admit of no cure for the mischiefs of faction. A common passion or interest will, in almost every case, be felt by a majority of the whole; a communication and concert result from the form of government itself; and there is nothing to check the inducements to sacrifice the weaker party or an obnoxious individual. Hence it is that such democracies have ever been spectacles of turbulence and contention; have ever been found incompatible with personal security or the rights of property; and have in general been as short in their lives as they have been violent in their deaths. Theoretic politicians, who have patronized this species of government, have erroneously supposed that by reducing mankind to a perfect equality in their political rights, they would, at the same time, be perfectly equalized and assimilated in their possessions, their opinions, and their passions.

A republic, by which I mean a government in which the scheme of representation takes place, opens a different prospect, and promises the cure for which we are seeking. Let us examine the points in which it varies from pure democracy, and we shall comprehend both the nature of the cure and the efficacy which it must derive from the Union.

The two great points of difference between a democracy and a republic are: first, the delegation of the government, in the latter, to a small number of citizens elected by the rest; secondly, the greater number of citizens, and greater sphere of country, over which the latter may be extended.

The effect of the first difference is, on the one hand, to refine and enlarge the public views, by passing them through the medium of a chosen body of citizens, whose wisdom may best discern the true interest of their country, and whose patriotism and love of justice will be least likely to sacrifice it to temporary or partial considerations. Under such a regulation, it may well happen that the public voice, pronounced by the representatives of the people, will be more consonant to the public good than if pronounced by the people themselves, convened for the purpose. On the other hand, the effect may be inverted. Men of factious tempers, of local prejudices, or of sinister designs, may, by intrigue, by corruption, or by other means, first obtain the suffrages, and then betray the interests, of the people. The question resulting is, whether small or extensive republics are more favorable to the election of proper guardians of the public weal; and it is clearly decided in favor of the latter by two obvious considerations:

In the first place, it is to be remarked that, however small the republic may be, the representatives must be raised to a certain number, in order to guard against the cabals of a few; and that, however large it may be, they must be limited to a certain number, in order to guard against the confusion of a multitude. Hence, the number of representatives in the two cases not being in proportion to that of the two constituents, and being proportionally greater in the small republic, it follows that, if the proportion of fit characters be not less in the large than in the small republic, the former will present a greater option, and consequently a greater probability of a fit choice.

In the next place, as each representative will be chosen by a greater number of citizens in the large than in the small republic, it will be more difficult for unworthy candidates to practice with success the vicious arts by which elections are too often carried; and the suffrages of the people being more free, will be more likely to centre in men who possess the most attractive merit and the most diffusive and established characters.

It must be confessed that in this, as in most other cases, there is a mean, on both sides of which inconveniences will be found to lie. By enlarging too much the number of electors, you render the representatives too little acquainted with all their local circumstances and lesser interests; as by reducing it too much, you render him unduly attached to these, and too little fit to comprehend and pursue great and national objects. The federal Constitution forms a happy combination in this respect; the great and aggregate interests being referred to the national, the local and particular to the State legislatures.

The other point of difference is, the greater number of citizens and extent of territory which may be brought within the compass of republican than of democratic government; and it is this circumstance principally which renders factious combinations less to be dreaded in the former than in the latter. The smaller the society, the fewer probably will be the distinct parties and interests composing it; the fewer the distinct parties and interests, the more frequently will a majority be found of the same party; and the smaller the number of individuals composing a majority, and the smaller the compass within which they are placed, the more easily will they concert and execute their plans of oppression. Extend the sphere, and you take in a greater variety of parties and interests; you make it less probable that a majority of the whole will have a common motive to invade the rights of other citizens; or if such a common motive exists, it will be more difficult for all who feel it to discover their own strength, and to act in unison with each other. Besides other impediments, it may be remarked that, where there is a consciousness of unjust or dishonorable purposes, communication is always checked by distrust in proportion to the number whose concurrence is necessary.

Hence, it clearly appears, that the same advantage which a republic has over a democracy, in controlling the effects of faction, is enjoyed by a large over a small republic,—is enjoyed by the Union over the States composing it. Does the advantage consist in the substitution of representatives whose enlightened views and virtuous sentiments render them superior to local prejudices and schemes of injustice? It will not be denied that the representation of the Union will be most likely to possess these requisite endowments. Does it consist in the greater security afforded by a greater variety of parties, against the event of any one party being able to outnumber and oppress the rest? In an equal degree does the increased variety of parties comprised within the Union, increase this security. Does it, in fine, consist in the greater obstacles opposed to the concert and accomplishment of the secret wishes of an unjust and interested majority? Here, again, the extent of the Union gives it the most palpable advantage.

The influence of factious leaders may kindle a flame within their particular States, but will be unable to spread a general conflagration through the other States. A religious sect may degenerate into a political faction in a part of the Confederacy; but the variety of sects dispersed over the entire face of it must secure the national councils against any danger from that source. A rage for paper money, for an abolition of debts, for an equal division of property, or for any other improper or wicked project, will be less apt to pervade the whole body of the Union than a particular member of it; in the same proportion as such a malady is more likely to taint a particular county or district, than an entire State.

In the extent and proper structure of the Union, therefore, we behold a republican remedy for the diseases most incident to republican government. And according to the degree of pleasure and pride we feel in being republicans, ought to be our zeal in cherishing the spirit and supporting the character of Federalists.

PUBLIUS.

APPENDIX 5

Federalist No. 51

*The Structure of the Government Must Furnish
the Proper Checks and Balances Between the Different
Departments*

From the New York Packet.
Friday, February 8, 1788.
Author: James Madison

To the People of the State of New York:

TO WHAT expedient, then, shall we finally resort, for maintaining in practice the necessary partition of power among the several departments, as laid down in the Constitution? The only answer that can be given is, that as all these exterior provisions are found to be inadequate, the defect must be supplied, by so contriving the interior structure of the government as that its several constituent parts may, by their mutual relations, be the means of keeping each other in their proper places. Without presuming to undertake a full development of this important idea, I will hazard a few general observations, which may perhaps place it in a clearer light, and enable us to form a more correct judgment of the principles and structure of the government planned by the convention.

In order to lay a due foundation for that separate and distinct exercise of the different powers of government, which to a certain extent is admitted on all hands to be essential to the preservation of liberty, it is evident that each department should have a will of its own; and consequently should be so constituted that the members of each should have as little agency as possible in the appointment of the members of the others. Were this principle rigorously adhered to, it would require that all the appointments for the supreme executive, legislative, and judiciary magistracies should be drawn from the same fountain of authority, the people, through channels having no communication whatever with one another. Perhaps such a plan of constructing the several departments would be less difficult in practice than it may in contemplation appear. Some difficulties, however, and some additional expense would attend the execution of it. Some deviations, therefore, from the principle must be admitted. In the constitution of the judiciary department in particular, it might be inexpedient to insist rigorously on the principle: first, because peculiar qualifications being essential in the members, the primary consideration ought to be to select that mode of choice which best secures these qualifications; secondly, because the permanent tenure by which the appointments are held in that department, must soon destroy all sense of dependence on the authority conferring them.

It is equally evident, that the members of each department should be as little dependent as possible on those of the others, for the emoluments annexed to their offices. Were the executive magistrate, or the judges, not independent of the legislature in this particular, their independence in every other would be merely nominal. But the great security against a gradual concentration of the several powers in the same department, consists in giving to those who administer each department the necessary constitutional means and personal motives to resist encroachments of the others. The provision for defense must in this, as in all other cases, be made commensurate to the danger of attack. Ambition must be made to counteract ambition. The interest of the man must be connected with the constitutional rights of the place. It may be a reflection on human nature, that such devices should be necessary to control the abuses of government. But what is government itself, but the greatest of all reflections on human nature? If men were angels, no government would be necessary. If angels were to govern men, neither external nor internal controls on government would be necessary. In framing a government which is to be administered by men over men, the great difficulty lies in this: you must first enable the government to control the governed; and in the next place oblige it to control itself.

A dependence on the people is, no doubt, the primary control on the government; but experience has taught mankind the necessity of auxiliary precautions. This policy of supplying, by opposite and rival interests, the defect of better motives, might be traced through the whole system of human affairs, private as well as public. We see it particularly displayed in all the subordinate distributions of power, where the constant aim is to divide and arrange the several offices in such a manner as that each may be a check on the other that the private interest of every individual may be a sentinel over the public rights. These inventions of prudence cannot be less requisite in the distribution of the supreme powers of the State. But it is not possible to give to each department an equal power of self-defense. In republican government, the legislative authority necessarily predominates. The remedy for this inconveniency is to divide the legislature into different branches; and to render them, by different modes of election and different principles of action, as little connected with each other as the nature of their common functions and their common dependence on the society will admit. It may even be necessary to guard against dangerous encroachments by still further precautions. As the weight of the legislative authority requires that it should be thus divided, the weakness of the executive may require, on the other hand, that it should be fortified.

An absolute negative on the legislature appears, at first view, to be the natural defense with which the executive magistrate should be armed. But perhaps it would be neither altogether safe nor alone sufficient. On ordinary occasions it might not be exerted with the requisite firmness, and on extraordinary occasions it might be perfidiously abused. May not this defect of an absolute negative be supplied by some qualified connection between this weaker department and the weaker branch of the stronger department, by which the latter may be led to support the constitutional rights of the former, without being too much detached from the rights of its own department? If the principles on which these observations are founded be just, as I persuade myself they are, and they be applied as a criterion to the several State constitutions, and to the federal Constitution it will be found that if the latter does not perfectly correspond with them, the former are infinitely less able to bear such a test.

There are, moreover, two considerations particularly applicable to the federal system of America, which place that system in a very interesting point of view. First. In a single republic, all the power surrendered by the people is submitted to the administration of a single government; and the usurpations are guarded against by a division of the government into distinct and separate departments. In the compound republic of America, the power surrendered by the people is first divided between two distinct governments, and then the portion allotted to each subdivided among distinct and separate departments. Hence a double security arises to the rights of the people. The different governments will control each other, at the same time that each will be controlled by itself. Second. It is of great importance in a republic not only to guard the society against the oppression of its rulers, but to guard one part of the society against the injustice of the other part. Different interests necessarily exist in different classes of citizens. If a majority be united by a common interest, the rights of the minority will be insecure.

There are but two methods of providing against this evil: the one by creating a will in the community independent of the majority that is, of the society itself; the other, by comprehending in the society so many separate descriptions of citizens as will render an unjust combination of a majority of the whole very improbable, if not impracticable. The first method prevails in all governments possessing an hereditary or self-appointed authority. This, at best, is but a precarious security; because a power independent of the society may as well espouse the unjust views of the major, as the rightful interests of the minor party, and may possibly be turned against both parties. The second method will be exemplified in the federal republic of the United States. Whilst all authority in it will be derived from and dependent on the society, the society itself will be broken into so many parts, interests, and classes of citizens, that the rights of individuals, or of the minority, will be in little danger from interested combinations of the majority.

In a free government the security for civil rights must be the same as that for religious rights. It consists in the one case in the multiplicity of interests, and in the other in the multiplicity of sects. The degree of security in both cases will depend on the number of interests and sects; and this may be presumed to depend on the extent of country and number of people comprehended under the same government. This view of the subject must particularly recommend a proper federal system to all the sincere and considerate friends of republican government, since it shows that in exact proportion as the territory of the Union may be formed into more circumscribed Confederacies, or States oppressive combinations of a majority will be facilitated: the best security, under the republican forms, for the rights of every class of citizens, will be diminished: and consequently the stability and independence of some member of the government, the only other security, must be proportionately increased. Justice is the end of government. It is the end of civil society. It ever has been and ever will be pursued until it be obtained, or until liberty be lost in the pursuit. In a society under the forms of which the stronger faction can readily unite and oppress the weaker, anarchy may as truly be said to reign as in a state of nature, where the weaker individual is not secured against the violence of the stronger; and as, in the latter state, even the stronger individuals are prompted, by the uncertainty of their condition, to submit to a government which may protect the weak as well as themselves; so, in the former state, will the more powerful factions or parties be gradually induced, by a like motive, to wish for a government which will protect all parties, the weaker as well as the more powerful.

It can be little doubted that if the State of Rhode Island was separated from the Confederacy and left to itself, the insecurity of rights under the popular form of government within such narrow limits would be displayed by such reiterated oppressions of factious majorities that some power altogether independent of the people would soon be called for by the voice of the very factions whose misrule had proved the necessity of it. In the extended republic of the United States, and among the great variety of interests, parties, and sects which it embraces, a coalition of a majority of the whole society could seldom take place on any other principles than those of justice and the general good; whilst there being thus less danger to a minor from the will of a major party, there must be less pretext, also, to provide for the security of the former, by introducing into the government a will not dependent on the latter, or, in other words, a will independent of the society itself. It is no less certain than it is important, notwithstanding the contrary opinions which have been entertained, that the larger the society, provided it lie within a practical sphere, the more duly capable it will be of self-government. And happily for the REPUBLICAN CAUSE, the practicable sphere may be carried to a very great extent, by a judicious modification and mixture of the FEDERAL PRINCIPLE.

PUBLIUS.

APPENDIX 6

Presidents, Vice Presidents, Speakers, and Chief Justices, 1789–2010

President/Vice President	Congress	Speaker of the House	Chief Justice of the United States
George Washington[1] (1789–1797)	1st	Frederick A.C. Muhlenberg, Pa.	John Jay (1789–1795)
John Adams	2nd	Jonathan Trumbull, F-Conn.	John Rutledge (1795)
	3rd	Muhlenberg	Oliver Ellsworth (1796–1800)
	4th	Jonathan Dayton, F-N.J.	
John Adams, F (1797–1801)	5th	Dayton	Ellsworth
Thomas Jefferson, D-R	6th	Theodore Sedgwick, F-Mass.	John Marshall (1801–1835)
Thomas Jefferson, D-R (1801–1809)	7th	Nathaniel Macon, D-N.C.	Marshall
Aaron Burr (1801–1805)	8th	Macon	
George Clinton (1805–1809)	9th	Macon	
	10th	Joseph B. Varnum, Mass.	
James Madison, D-R (1809–1817)	11th	Varnum	Marshall
George Clinton[2] (1809–1812)	12th	Henry Clay, R-Ky.	
Elbridge Gerry[2] (1813–1814)	13th	Clay/Langdon Cheves, D-S.C.	
	14th	Clay	
James Monroe, D-R (1817–1825)	15th	Clay	Marshall
Daniel D. Tompkins	16th	Clay/John W. Taylor, D-N.Y.	
	17th	Philip P. Barbour, D-Va.	
	18th	Clay	
John Quincy Adams, D-R (1825–1829)	19th	Taylor	Marshall
John C. Calhoun	20th	Andrew Stevenson, D-Va.	
Andrew Jackson, D (1829–1837)	21st	Stevenson	Marshall
John C. Calhoun[3] (1829–1832)	22nd	Stevenson	Roger B. Taney (1836–1864)

President/Vice President	Congress	Speaker of the House	Chief Justice of the United States
Martin Van Buren (1833–1837)	23rd	Stevenson/John Bell, W-Tenn.	
	24th	James K. Polk, D-Tenn.	
Martin Van Buren, D (1837–1841) Richard M. Johnson	25th	Polk	Taney
	26th	Robert M.T. Hunter, D-Va.	
William Henry Harrison,[2] W (1841) John Tyler			Taney
John Tyler, W (1841–1845)	27th	John White, W-Ky.	Taney
	28th		John W. Jones, D-Va.
James K. Polk, D (1845–1849) George M. Dallas	29th	John W. Davis, D-Ind.	Taney
	30th	Robert C. Winthrop, W-Mass.	
Zachary Taylor,[2] W (1849–1850) Millard Fillmore	31st	Howell Cobb, D-Ga.	Taney
Millard Fillmore, W (1850–1853)	31st	Cobb	Taney
	32nd		Linn Boyd, D-Ky.
Franklin Pierce, D (1853–1857) William R. King[2] (1853)	33rd	Boyd	Taney
	34th	Nathaniel P. Banks, R-Mass.	
James Buchanan, D (1857–1861) John C. Breckinridge	35th	James L. Orr, D-S.C.	Taney
	36th	William Pennington, R-N.J.	
Abraham Lincoln,[2] R (1861–1865) Hannibal Hamlin (1861–1865) Andrew Johnson,[4] D (1865)	37th	Galusha A. Grow, R-Pa.	Taney
	38th	Schuyler Colfax, R-Ind.	Salmon P. Chase (1864–1873)
Andrew Johnson, D (1865–1869)	39th	Colfax	Chase
	40th	Colfax/Theodore M. Pomeroy, R-N.Y.	
Ulysses S. Grant, R (1869–1877) Schuyler Colfax (1869–1873) Henry Wilson[2] (1873–1875)	41st	James G. Blaine, R-Maine	Chase
	42nd	Blaine	Morrison R. Waite (1874–1888)
	43rd	Blaine	
	44th	Michael C. Kerr, D-Ind./ Samuel J. Randall, D-Pa.	

President/Vice President	Congress	Speaker of the House	Chief Justice of the United States
Rutherford B. Hayes, R (1877–1881) William A. Wheeler	45th 46th	Randall Randall	Waite
James A. Garfield,[2] R (1881) Chester A. Arthur			Waite
Chester A. Arthur, R (1881–1885)	47th 48th	Joseph Warren Keifer, R-Ohio John G. Carlisle, D-Ky.	Waite
Grover Cleveland, D (1885–1889) Thomas A. Hendricks[2] (1885)	49th 50th	Carlisle Carlisle	Waite Melville W. Fuller (1888–1910)
Benjamin Harrison, R (1889–1893) Levi P. Morton	51st 52nd	Thomas Brackett Reed, R-Maine Charles F. Crisp, D-Ga.	Fuller
Grover Cleveland, D (1893–1897) Adlai E. Stevenson	53rd 54th	Crisp Reed	Fuller
William McKinley,[2] R (1897–1901) Garret A. Hobart[2] (1897–1899) Theodore Roosevelt (1901)	55th 56th	Reed David B. Henderson, R-Iowa	Fuller
Theodore Roosevelt, R (1901–1909) Charles W. Fairbanks (1905–1909)	57th 58th 59th 60th	Henderson Joseph G. Cannon, R-Ill. Cannon Cannon	Fuller
William Howard Taft, R (1909–1913) James S. Sherman[2] (1909–1912)	61st 62nd	Cannon James B. "Champ" Clark, D-Mo.	Fuller Edward D. White (1910–1921)
Woodrow Wilson, D (1913–1921) Thomas R. Marshall	63rd 64th 65th 66th	Clark Clark Clark Frederick H. Gillett, R-Mass.	White

President/Vice President	Congress	Speaker of the House	Chief Justice of the United States
Warren G. Harding,[2] R (1921–1923) Calvin Coolidge	67th	Gillett	William Howard Taft (1921–1930)
Calvin Coolidge, R (1923–1929) Charles G. Dawes (1925–1929)	68th 69th 70th	Gillett Nicholas Longworth, R-Ohio Longworth	Taft
Herbert C. Hoover, R (1929–1933) Charles Curtis	71st 72nd	Longworth John Nance Garner, D-Texas	Taft Charles Evans Hughes (1930–1941)
Franklin D. Roosevelt,[2] D (1933–1945) John Nance Garner (1933–1941) Henry A. Wallace (1941–1945) Harry S. Truman (1945)	73rd 74th 75th 76th 77th 78th 79th	Henry T. Rainey, D-Ill. Joseph W. Byrns, D-Tenn./William B. Bankhead, D-Ala. Bankhead Bankhead/Sam Rayburn, D-Texas Rayburn Rayburn Rayburn	Hughes Harlan F. Stone (1941–1946)
Harry S. Truman, D (1945–1953) Alben W. Barkley (1949–1953)	79th 80th 81st 82nd	Rayburn Joseph W. Martin Jr., R-Mass. Rayburn Rayburn	Stone Frederick M. Vinson (1946–1953)
Dwight D. Eisenhower, R (1953–1961) Richard Nixon	83rd 84th 85th 86th	Martin Rayburn Rayburn Rayburn	Vinson Earl Warren (1953–1969)
John F. Kennedy,2 D (1961–1963) Lyndon B. Johnson	87th 88th	Rayburn/John W. McCormack, D-Mass. McCormack	Warren
Lyndon B. Johnson, D (1963–1969)	88th	McCormack	Warren

President/Vice President	Congress	Speaker of the House	Chief Justice of the United States
Hubert H. Humphrey (1965–1969)	89th	McCormack	
	90th	McCormack	
Richard Nixon,[3] R (1969–1974)	91st	McCormack	Warren
Spiro T. Agnew[3] (1969–1973)	92nd	Carl Albert, D-Okla.	Warren E. Burger (1969–1986)
Gerald R. Ford[5] (1973–1974)	93rd	Albert	
Gerald R. Ford, R (1974–1977)	93rd	Albert	Burger
Nelson A. Rockefeller[5]	94th	Albert	
Jimmy Carter, D (1977–1981)	95th	Thomas P. O'Neill Jr., D-Mass.	Burger
Walter F. Mondale	96th	O'Neill	
Ronald Reagan, R (1981–1989)	97th	O'Neill	Burger
George Bush	98th	O'Neill	William Rehnquist (1986–2005)
	99th	O'Neill	
	100th	Jim Wright, D-Texas	
George H. W. Bush, R (1989–1993)	101st	Wright/Thomas S. Foley, D-Wash.	Rehnquist
Dan Quayle	102nd	Foley	
Bill Clinton, D (1993–2001)	103rd	Foley	Rehnquist
Al Gore	104th	Newt Gingrich, R-Ga.	
	105th	Gingrich	
	106th	J. Dennis Hastert, R-Ill.	
George W. Bush, R (2001–2009)	107th	J. Dennis Hastert, R-Ill.	Rehnquist
Richard B. Cheney	108th	Hastert	John Roberts
	109th	Hastert	(2005–)
	110th	Nancy D. Pelosi, D-Ca.	
Barack H. Obama (2009–)	111th	Pelosi	Roberts
Joseph R. Biden	112th	John Boehner, R-Ohio	

Notes: The vice president's term or party is noted when it differs from that of the president. Key to abbreviations: D—Democrat; D-R—Democratic-Republican; F—Federalist; R—Republican; W—Whig.

1. Washington belonged to no formal party.

2. Died in office.

3. Resigned from office.

4. Democrat Johnson and Republican Lincoln ran under the Union Party banner in 1864.

5. Appointed to office.

Notes

Chapter 1

1. Frank Rich, "It Still Felt Good the Morning After," *New York Times,* November 9, 2008.
2. Emily Hoban Kirby and Kei Kawashima-Ginsberg, "The Youth Vote in 2008," www.civic youth.org/PopUps/FactSheets/FS_youth_Voting_2008_updated_6.22.pdf.
3. Center for Information & Research on Civic Learning and Engagement, "Youth Turnout Rate Rises to at Least 52%," November 7, 2008, www.civicyouth.org/?p=323#comments.
4. E. J. Dionne, *Why Americans Hate Politics* (New York: Simon & Schuster, 1991), 354, 355.
5. Harold D. Lasswell, *Politics: Who Gets What, When, How* (New York: McGraw-Hill, 1938).
6. Joseph A. Schumpeter, *Capitalism, Socialism, and Democracy,* 3rd ed. (New York: Harper Colophon Books, 1950), 269–296.
7. Robert A. Dahl, *Pluralist Democracy in the United States* (Chicago: Rand McNally, 1967).
8. Carole Pateman, *Participation and Democratic Theory* (New York: Cambridge University Press, 1970).
9. Bruce E. Johansen, *Forgotten Founders: Benjamin Franklin, the Iroquois and the Rationale for the American Revolution* (Ipswich, Mass.: Gambit, Inc., 1982).
10. For an explanation of this view, see, for example, Russell L. Hanson, *The Democratic Imagination in America: Conversations With Our Past* (Princeton: Princeton University Press, 1985), 55–91; and Gordon Wood, *The Creation of the American Republic, 1776–1787* (New York: Norton, 1969).
11. E. J. Dionne Jr., *Why Americans Hate Politics* (New York: Simon & Schuster, 1991), 354, 355.
12. *Graham v. Richardson,* 403 U.S. 532 (1971).
13. See, for instance, Nicole Cusano, "Amherst Mulls Giving Non-Citizens Right to Vote," *Boston Globe,* October 26, 1998, B1; "Casual Citizenship?" editorial, *Boston Globe,* October 31, 1998, A18.
14. Daniel M. Shea, Director of Allegheny College's Center for Political Participation in Meadville, Pa., cited in Bryan Bender, "Turnout Was Strong, But Maintaining Interest Is Key, *Boston Globe,* November 5, 2004, A6.
15. Mark Carreau, "America Responds," *Houston Chronicle,* September 22, 2001, A26; Bronwen Maddox, "America Feels the Draft," *Times* (London), October 4, 2001; Chuck Haga, "Rules for Draft Changed Since Vietnam," *Minneapolis Star Tribune,* September 19, 2001, 11A.
16. "GOP Warns Rock the Vote About 'Malicious' Draft-Themed Campaign," *Chicago Sun-Times,* November 4, 2004, 50.

Chapter 2

1. David Barstow, "Tea Party Lights Fuse for Rebellion on Right," *New York Times,* February 15, 2010, www.nytimes.com/2010/02/16/us/politics/16teaparty.html?emc=eta1.
2. Richard A. Serrano, "Uneasy in Oklahoma: Fifteen Years After the McVeigh Bombing, Anger at Washington and Talk of a State Militia," *Los Angeles Times,* April 18, 2010.

3. Toni Lucy, "Anti-Government Forces Still Struggle to Recover From Oklahoma City Fallout," *USA Today*, May 9, 2000, 9A; Evan Thomas and Eve Conant, "Hate: Antigovernment Extremists Are on the Rise—and On the March," *Newsweek*, April 19, 2010.
4. Mark Guarino, "Hutaree Militia Arrests Point to Tripling of Militias Since 2008," *Christian Science Monitor*, March 29, 2010, www.csmonitor.com/USA/Justice/2010/0329/Hutaree-militia-arrests-point-to-tripling-of-militias-since-2008.
5. There are many good illustrations of this point of view. See, for example, Gordon Wood, *The Creation of the American Republic, 1776–1787* (New York: Norton, 1969); Lawrence Henry Gipson, *The Coming of the Revolution, 1763–1775* (New York: Harper Torchbooks, 1962); Bernard Bailyn, *The Ideological Origins of the American Revolution* (Cambridge, Mass.: Belknap, 1967); and Jack P. Greene, ed., *The Reinterpretation of the American Revolution, 1763–1789* (New York: Harper and Row, 1968).
6. Cited in John L. Moore, *Speaking of Washington* (Washington, D.C.: Congressional Quarterly Press, 1993), 102–103.
7. John Locke, *Second Treatise of Government*, C. B. Macpherson, ed. (Indianapolis, Ind.: Hackett, 1980), 31
8. Donald R. Wright, *African Americans in the Colonial Era* (Arlington Heights, Ill.: Harlan Davidson, 1990), 122.
9. Ibid., 152.
10. Mary Beth Norton, et al., *A People and a Nation* (Boston: Houghton Mifflin, 1994), 159.
11. Robert Darcy, Susan Welch, and Janet Clark, *Women, Elections, and Representation* (Lincoln: University of Nebraska Press, 1994), 8.
12. See, for example, Sally Smith Booth, *The Women of '76* (New York: Hastings House, 1973); and Charles E. Claghorn, *Women Patriots of the American Revolution: A Biographical Dictionary* (Metuchen, N.J.: Scarecrow Press, 1991).
13. Carl Holliday, *Woman's Life in Colonial Days* (Boston: Cornhill, 1922), 143.
14. Wood, *Creation of the American Republic*, 398–399.
15. Ibid., 404.
16. Alexander Hamilton, James Madison, and John Jay, *The Federalist Papers*, Clinton Rossiter, ed. (New York: New American Library, 1961), 84.
17. James Madison, *Notes of Debates in the Federal Convention of 1787* (New York: Norton, 1969), 86.
18. Baron de Montesquieu, *The Spirit of the Laws*, Thomas Nugent, trans. (New York: Hafner Press, 1949), 152.
19. There are many collections of Anti-Federalist writings. See, for example, W. B. Allen and Gordon Lloyd, eds., *The Essential Antifederalist* (Lanham, Md.: University Press of America, 1985); Cecilia Kenyon, ed., *The Antifederalists* (Indianapolis, Ind.: Bobbs-Merrill, 1966); and Ralph Ketcham, *The Anti-Federalist Papers and the Constitutional Convention Debates* (New York: New American Library, 1986).
20. Clinton Rossiter, "Introduction," in Hamilton, Madison, and Jay, *Federalist Papers*, vii.
21. Hamilton, Madison, and Jay, *Federalist Papers*, 322.
22. Ketcham, *Anti-Federalist Papers*, 14.
23. Carl Hulse, "Recalling 1995 Bombing, Clinton Sees Parallels," *New York Times*, April 16, 2010.

Chapter 3

1. Stephanie Armour, "Employers Grapple With Medical Marijuana Use: Ethical, Liability Issues Rise as More States Make It Legal," *USA Today,* April 17, 2007, 1B.
2. *Gonzales v. Raich* 545 U.S. 1 (2005).
3. Jerry Seper, "DEA Raids Medical Marijuana Centers," *Washington Times,* January 19, 2007, A9.

4. Carrie Johnson, "U.S. Eases Stance on Medical Marijuana," *Washington Post,* October 20, 2009.
5. For a full explanation of the bakery metaphors, see Morton Grodzins, *The American System* (Chicago: Rand-McNally, 1966). A more updated discussion of federalism can be found in Joseph Zimmerman, *Contemporary American Federalism: The Growth of National Power* (New York: Praeger, 1992).
6. Thomas Bodenheimer, "The Oregon Health Plan: Lessons for the Nation (First of Two Parts)," *New England Journal of Medicine,* August 28, 1997, 651–655; "The Oregon Health Plan: Lessons for the Nation (Second of Two Parts)," *New England Journal of Medicine,* September 4, 1997, 720–723.
7. James Dao, "Red, Blue and Angry All Over," *New York Times,* January 16, 2005.
8. *McCulloch v. Maryland,* 4 Wheat. 316 (1819).
9. *Gibbons v. Ogden,* 9 Wheat. 1 (1824).
10. *Cooley v. Board of Wardens of Port of Philadelphia,* 53 U.S. (12 How.) 299 (1851).
11. *Dred Scott v. Sanford,* 60 U.S. 393 (1857).
12. *Pollock v. Farmer's Loan and Trust Co.,* 1157 U.S. 429 (1895).
13. *Lochner v. New York,* 198 U.S. 45 (1905).
14. *Hammer v. Dagenhart,* 247 U.S. 251 (1918).
15. John Kincaid, "State-Federal Relations: Dueling Policies," in *The Book of the States 2008* (Lexington, Ky.: The Council of State Governments, 2008), 19.
16. *Garcia v. San Antonio Metropolitan Transit Authority,* 469 U.S. 528 (1985).
17. U.S. Advisory Commission on Intergovernmental Relations, *Federal Regulation of State and Local Governments: The Mixed Record of the 1980s* (Washington, D.C.: U.S. Government Printing Office, July 1993), 3.
18. Kincaid, "State-Federal Relations: Dueling Policies."
19. Morris Fiorina, *Congress: Keystone of the Washington Establishment,* 2nd ed. (New Haven: Yale University Press, 1989); John E. Chubb, "Federalism and the Bias for Centralization," in John E. Chubb and Paul E. Peterson, eds., *The New Directions in American Politics* (Washington, D.C.: Brookings Institution, 1985), 273–306.
20. *Statistical Abstract of the United States, 2010,* Table 419. Washington, D.C.: U.S. Bureau of the Census.
21. David Walker, *The Rebirth of Federalism* (Chatham, N.J.: Chatham House, 1995), 139, 224.
22. Quote from Rochelle L. Stanfield, "Holding the Bag," *National Journal,* September 9, 1995, 2206.
23. Walker, *The Rebirth of Federalism,* 232–234; Kincaid, "State-Federal Relations: Dueling Policies."
24. Priscilla M. Regan, "Opposition to REAL ID Act at the State Level: Privacy, Immigration or Unfunded Mandates," prepared for delivery at the annual meeting of the American Political Science Association, Boston, Massachusetts, August 28–31, 2008; Department of Homeland Security, "REAL ID Final Rule," www.dhs.gov/files/laws/gc_1172765386179.shtm.
25. Martha Derthick, "Madison's Middle Ground in the 1980s," *Public Administration Review* (January–February 1987): 66–74.
26. U.S. Advisory Commission on Intergovernmental Relations, *Federal Mandate Relief for State, Local, and Tribal Governments* (Washington, D.C.: U.S. Government Printing Office, January 1995), 18.
27. *South Dakota v. Dole,* 483 U.S. 203 (1987).
28. U.S. Advisory Commission on Intergovernmental Relations, *Federal Regulation of State and Local Governments.*
29. John Maggs, "Hizzoner, the Pizza Man," *National Journal,* November 21, 1998, 2796–2798.
30. Jacob Sullum, "The Power to Regulate Anything," *Los Angeles Times,* April 22, 2008.
31. Warren Richey, "Showdown Over Medical Marijuana," *Christian Science Monitor,* November 29, 2004.

Chapter 4

1. "Mr. Cuccinelli's Witch Hunt: Virginia's Attorney General Declares War on Academic Freedom and Climate Reality," *Washington Post,* Editorial, May 7, 2010, www.washingtonpost.com/wp-dyn/content/article/2010/05/06/AR2010050605936.html.
2. Lawrence Biemiller, "U. of Virginia Asks Court to Halt Attorney General's Demand for Documents," *Chronicle of Higher Education,* May 27, 2010, http://chronicle.com/article/U-of-Virginia-Asks-Court-to/65721/?sid=at&utm_source=at&utm_medium=en; "Mr. Cuccinelli's Witch Hunt."
3. "Petition to Set Aside Civil Investigative Demands Issued to the University of Virginia," May 27, 2010, www.virginia.edu/uvatoday/newsRelease.php?id=12022.
4. Rosalind S. Helderman, "U-Va Urged to Fight Cuccinelli Subpoena in Probe of Scientist; Climate Researchers Are Victims of Political Assault, Many Say," *Washington Post,* May 9, 2010.
5. Ann Bowman and Richard Kearney, *State and Local Government,* 3rd ed. (Boston: Houghton Mifflin, 1996), 39.
6. David M. O'Brien, *Constitutional Law and Politics,* vol. 2 (New York: Norton, 1995), 300.
7. *Barron v. The Mayor and City Council of Baltimore,* 7 Peters 243 (1833).
8. *Chicago, Burlington & Quincy Railroad Co. v. Chicago,* 166 U.S. 226 (1897).
9. *Gitlow v. New York,* 268 U.S. 652 (1925), cited in David M. O'Brien, *Constitutional Law and Politics,* vol. 2 (New York: Norton, 1991), 304.
10. Peter Irons, *Brennan vs. Rehnquist: The Battle for the Constitution* (New York: Knopf, 1994), 116.
11. O'Brien, *Constitutional Law and Politics,* 646.
12. Irons, *Brennan vs. Rehnquist,* 137.
13. *Abington School District v. Schempp,* 374 U.S. 203, 83 S. Ct. 1560 (1963).
14. Ibid.; *Murray v. Curlett,* 374 U.S. 203 (1963).
15. *Engel v. Vitale,* 370 U.S. 421, 82 S. Ct. 1261 (1962).
16. *Epperson v. Arkansas,* 393 U.S. 97 (1968).
17. *Lemon v. Kurtzman,* 403 U.S. 602, 91 S. Ct. 2105 (1971).
18. O'Brien, *Constitutional Law and Politics,* 661.
19. *Cantwell v. Connecticut,* 310 U.S. 296 (1940).
20. *Minersville School District v. Gobitis,* 310 U.S. 586 (1940).
21. *West Virginia State Board of Education v. Barnette,* 319 U.S. 624 (1943).
22. *McGowan v. Maryland,* 36 U.S. 420 (1961); *Two Guys From Harrison-Allentown, Inc., v. McGinley,* 366 U.S. 582 (1961); *Gallagher v. Crown Kosher Super Market of Massachusetts,* 366 U.S. 617 (1961); *Braunfield v. Brown,* 366 U.S. 599 (1961).
23. *Sherbert v. Verner,* 374 U.S. 398 (1963).
24. *Employment Division, Department of Human Resources v. Smith,* 494 U.S. 872 (1990).
25. *City of Boerne v. Flores,* 521 U.S. 507 (1997).
26. *Gonzales v. O Centro Espirata Beneficente Uniao do Vegetal,* 546 U.S. 418 (2006).
27. John L. Sullivan, James Piereson, and George Marcus, *Political Tolerance and American Democracy* (Chicago: University of Chicago Press, 1982), 203.
28. O'Brien, *Constitutional Law and Politics,* 373; Samuel Walker, *In Defense of American Liberties: A History of the ACLU* (New York: Oxford University Press, 1990), 14.
29. *Schenck v. United States,* 249 U.S. 47 (1919); *Debs v. United States,* 249 U.S. 211 (1919); *Frowerk v. United States,* 249 U.S. 204 (1919); *Abrams v. United States,* 250 U.S. 616 (1919).
30. *Brandenburg v. Ohio,* 395 U.S. 444 (1969).
31. *United States v. O'Brien,* 391 U.S. 367 (1968).
32. *Tinker v. Des Moines,* 393 U.S. 503 (1969).
33. *Street v. New York,* 394 U.S. 576 (1969).
34. *Texas v. Johnson,* 491 U.S. 397 (1989).

35. *United States v. Eichman,* 110 S.Ct. 2404 (1990).
36. *Virginia v. Black,* 538 U.S. 343 (2003).
37. *National Association for the Advancement of Colored People v. Alabama,* 357 U.S. 449 (1958).
38. *Sheldon v. Tucker,* 364 U.S. 516 (1960).
39. *Heart of Atlanta Motel v. United States,* 379 U.S. 241 (1964).
40. *Roberts v. United States Jaycees,* 468 U.S. 609 (1984).
41. *Jacobellis v. Ohio,* 378 U.S. 476 (1964).
42. *Miller v. California,* 413 U.S. 15 (1973).
43. *Cohen v. California,* 403 U.S. 15 (1971).
44. *Chaplinsky v. New Hampshire,* 315 U.S. 568 (1942).
45. *Terminello v. Chicago,* 337 U.S. 1 (1949).
46. *Cohen v. California,* 403 U.S. 15 (1971).
47. *Doe v. University of Michigan,* 721 F.Supp. 852 (E.D. Mich. 1989); *UMW Post v. Board of Regents of the University of Wisconsin,* 774 F.Supp. 1163, 1167, 1179 (E.D. Wis. 1991).
48. *R.A.V. v. City of St. Paul,* 60 LW 4667 (1992).
49. *Near v. Minnesota,* 283 U.S. 697 (1930).
50. *New York Times Company v. United States,* 403 U.S. 670 (1971).
51. *New York Times v. Sullivan,* 376 U.S. 254 (1964).
52. *Sheppard v. Maxwell,* 385 U.S. 333 (1966).
53. *Nebraska Press Association v. Stuart,* 427 U.S. 539 (1976).
54. *Reno v. ACLU,* 521 U.S. 1113 (1997).
55. *Ashcroft v. ACLU,* 124 S. Ct. 2783 (2004).
56. *United States v. American Library Association, Inc.,* 539 U.S. 194 (2003).
57. Pamela LiCalzi O'Connell, "Compressed Data: Law Newsletter Has to Sneak Past Filters," *New York Times,* April 2, 2001, C4.
58. Jeffery Seligno, "Student Writers Try to Duck the Censors by Going On-line," *New York Times,* June 7, 2001, G6.
59. Robert J. Spitzer, *The Politics of Gun Control* (Chatham, N.J.: Chatham House, 1995), 47, 49.
60. *United States v. Lopez,* 514 U.S. 549 (1995); *Printz v. United States,* 521 U.S. 898 (1997).
61. *United States v. Cruikshank,* 92 U.S. 542 (1876); *Presser v. Illinois,* 116 U.S. 252 (1886); *Miller v. Texas,* 153 U.S. 535 (1894); *United States v. Miller,* 307 U.S. 174 (1939).
62. *Printz v. United States,* 521 U.S. 898 (1997).
63. Warren Richey, "Supreme Court Asserts Broad Gun Rights," *Christian Science Monitor,* June 27, 2008.
64. Adam Liptak, "Justices Extend Firearm Rights in 5-to-4 Ruling," *New York Times,* June 28, 2010, www.nytimes.com/2010/06/29/us/29scotus.html.
65. Robert Barnes and Dan Eggen, "Supreme Court Affirms Fundamental Right to Bear Arms," *Washington Post,* June 29, 2010.
66. Fredrick Kunkle, "Virginia Gun-rights Enthusiasts Celebrate Virginia Law on Firearms in Bars," *Washington Post,* July 3, 2010.
67. *Olmstead v. United States,* 277 U.S. 438 (1928).
68. *Katz v. United States,* 389 U.S. 347 (1967).
69. *Berger v. State of New York,* 388 U.S. 41 (1967).
70. Eric Lichtblau and Scott Shane, "Basis for Spying in U.S. Is Doubted," *New York Times,* January 7, 2006, A1.
71. *Skinner v. Railway Labor Executive Association,* 489 U.S. 602 (1989).
72. *Veronia School District v. Acton,* 515 U.S. 646 (1995).
73. *Weeks v. United States,* 232 U.S. 383 (1914).
74. *Wolf v. Colorado,* 338 U.S. 25 (1949).
75. *Mapp v. Ohio,* 367 U.S. 643 (1961).
76. *United States v. Calandra,* 414 U.S. 338 (1974).
77. *United States v. Janis,* 428 U.S. 433 (1976).

78. *Massachusetts v. Sheppard,* 468 U.S. 981 (1984); *United States v. Leon,* 468 U.S. 897 (1984); *Illinois v. Krull,* 480 U.S. 340 (1987).

79. *Herring v. United States,* No. 07–513. Argued October 7, 2008—Decided January 14, 2009.

80. *Miranda v. Arizona,* 382 U.S. 925 (1965); *Dickerson v. United States,* 530 U.S. 428, 120 S. Ct. 2326; 2000 U.S. LEXIS 4305.

81. *Johnson v. Zerbst,* 304 U.S. 458 (1938).

82. *Gideon v. Wainwright,* 372 U.S. 335 (1963).

83. *Ross v. Moffitt,* 417 U.S. 600 (1974); *Murray v. Giarratano,* 492 U.S. 1 (1989).

84. *Atkins v. Georgia* 536 U.S. 304 (2002). *Roper v. Simmons,* 543 U.S. 551 (2005). *Kennedy v. Louisiana,* No. 07–343. Argued April 16, 2008—Decided June 25, 2008; modified October 1, 2008.

85. *Furman v. Georgia,* 409 U.S. 902 (1972); *Jackson v. Georgia,* 409 U.S. 1122 (1973); *Branch v. Texas,* 408 U.S. 238 (1972).

86. *Gregg v. Georgia,* 428 U.S. 153 (1976); *Woodson v. North Carolina,* 428 U.S. 280 (1976); *Roberts v. Louisiana,* 428 U.S. 325 (1976).

87. *McClesky v. Zant,* 111 S. Ct. 1454 (1991).

88. *Baze v. Rees,* 553 U.S. ___ (2008).

89. Jack Hitt, "The Moratorium Gambit," *New York Times Magazine,* December 9, 2001, 82.

90. Keith Richburg, "New Jersey Approves Abolition of Death Penalty," *Washington Post,* December 14, 2007, A3.

91. Frank Newport, "In U.S., Two-Thirds Continue to Support Death Penalty," October, 13, 2009, www.gallup.com/poll/123638/In-U.S.-Two-Thirds-Continue-Support-Death-Penalty .aspx.

92. *Griswold v. Connecticut,* 391 U.S. 145 (1965).

93. *Roe v. Wade,* 410 U.S. 113 (1973).

94. *Harris v. McRae,* 448 U.S. 297 (1980).

95. See, for example, *Webster v. Reproductive Health Services,* 492 U.S. 4090 (1989); *Rust v. Sullivan,* 111 S. Ct. 1759 (1991); and *Gonzales v. Carhart,* 550 U.S. 124 (2007).

96. Lydia Saad, "U.S. Abortion Attitudes Closely Divided," August 4, 2009, www.gallup.com/ poll/122033/U.S.-Abortion-Attitudes-Closely-Divided.aspx.

97. *Bowers v. Hardwick,* 478 U.S. 186 (1986).

98. *Lawrence v. Texas,* 539 U.S. 558 (2003).

99. *Romer v. Evans,* 517 U.S. 620 (1996).

100. Cruzan by *Cruzan v. Director, Missouri Department of Health,* 497 U.S. 261 (1990).

101. Frank Newport, "The Terri Schiavo Case in Review: Support for Her Being Allowed to Die Consistent," April 1, 2005, www.gallup.com.

102. "Mr. Cuccinelli's Witch Hunt."

103. See the American Association of University Professors, "1940 Statement of Principles on Academic Freedom and Tenure," www.aaup.org/AAUP/pubsres/policydocs/contents/ 1940statement.htm.

104. Kelly Simmons, "Students Fight Alleged Political Prejudice," *Atlanta Journal-Constitution,* March 24, 2004, 1B.

105. Simmons, "Students Fight Alleged Political Prejudice."

Chapter 5

1. Patrick Healy and Jeff Zeleny, "Obama and Clinton Tangle at Debate," *New York Times,* January 22, 2008, www.nytimes.com/2008/01/22/us/politics/22dems.html?partner=rssnyt &emc=rss.

2. Mark Mellman, "Can a Woman or a Black Man Win?" *Los Angeles Times,* February 3, 2008, www.latimes.com/news/opinion/commentary/la-op-mellman3feb03,0,2099860.story.

3. Katharine Q. Seelye and Julie Bosman, "Media Charged With Sexism in Clinton Coverage," *New York Times*, June 13, 2008, www.nytimes.com/2008/06/13/us/politics/13women.html?partner=rssnyt.

4. Andy Barr, "Davis Apologizes for Calling Obama 'Boy,'" *The Hill*, April 14, 2008, http://thehill.com/leading-the-news/davis-apologizes-for-calling-obama-boy-2008-04-14.html.

5. Eugene Robinson, "An Inarticulate Kickoff," *Washington Post*, February 2, 2007, A15.

6. Jake Tapper, "Bubba: Obama Is Just Like Jesse Jackson," *Political Punch*, January 26, 2008, http://blogs.abcnews.com/politicalpunch/.

7. Kathy Kiely and Jill Lawrence, "Clinton Makes Case for Wide Appeal," *USA Today*, May 8, 2008, www.usatoday.com/news/politics/election2008/2008-05-07-clintoninterview_N.htm.

8. Sean Wilentz, "Race Man," *The New Republic*, February 27, 2008.

9. Kathy Kiely, "These Are America's Governors. No Blacks. No Hispanics," *USA Today*, January 21, 2002, 1A.

10. David M. O'Brien, *Constitutional Law and Politics*, vol. 2 (New York: Norton, 1991), 1265.

11. American Civil Liberties Union, "Felon Enfranchisement and the Right to Vote," www.aclu.org/votingrights/exoffenders/index.html.

12. Scholars are divided about Lincoln's motives in issuing the Emancipation Proclamation; whether he genuinely desired to end slavery or merely used political means to shorten the war is hard to tell at this distance. Donald G. Nieman, *Promises to Keep: African-Americans and the Constitutional Order, 1776 to the Present* (New York: Oxford University Press, 1991), 55.

13. Bernard A. Weisberger, *Many Papers, One Nation* (Boston: Houghton Mifflin Company, 1987), 200.

14. Nieman, *Promises to Keep*, 107.

15. *The Civil Rights Cases*, 109 U.S. 3 (1883).

16. *Plessy v. Ferguson*, 163 U.S. 537 (1896).

17. *Brown v. Board of Education of Topeka (I)*, 347 U.S. 483 (1954).

18. *Brown v. Board of Education of Topeka (II)*, 349 U.S. 294 (1955).

19. *Gayle v. Browder*, 352 U.S. 903 (1956).

20. *Heart of Atlanta Motel, Inc. v. United States*, 379 U.S. 241 (1964); *Katzenbach v. McClung*, 379 U.S. 294 (1964); *Harper v. Virginia Board of Elections*, 383 U.S. 663 (1966).

21. Nieman, *Promises to Keep*, 179.

22. Ibid., 180.

23. *Swann v. Charlotte-Mecklenberg Board of Education*, 402 U.S. 1 (1971).

24. *Milliken v. Bradley*, 418 U.S. 717 (1974).

25. "*Brown v. Board*'s Goals Unrealized," *Atlanta Journal-Constitution*, May 16, 2004, 6C; Gary Orfield and Chungmei Lee, "*Brown* at 50: King's Dream or *Plessy*'s Nightmare?" report conducted by the Harvard Civil Rights Project, 2004, www.civilrightsproject.harvard.edu/research/reseg04/brown50.pdf.

26. *Regents of the University of California v. Bakke*, 438 U.S. 265 (1978).

27. *Patterson v. McLean Credit Union*, 491 U.S. 164 (1989).

28. *Wards Cove Packing, Inc., v. Atonio*, 490 U.S. 642 (1989).

29. *City of Richmond v. J. A. Croson*, 488 U.S. 469 (1989).

30. Pew Research Center for People and the Press, "Public Backs Affirmative Action but Not Minority Preferences," June 2, 2009, www.pewresearch.org/pubs/1240/sotomayor-supreme-court-affirmative-action-minority-preferences.

31. *Gratz v. Bollinger*, 539 U.S. 244 (2003).

32. *Grutter v. Bollinger*, 539 U.S. 306 (2003).

33. Carmen DeNavas-Walt, Bernadette D. Proctor, and Jessica C. Smith, "Income, Poverty, and Health Insurance Coverage in the United States, 2008: Poverty in the United States," U.S. Census Bureau, www.census.gov/prod/2009pubs/p60-236.pdf.

34. Ford Fessenden, "Examining the Vote: The Patterns," *New York Times*, November 12, 2001, A17.

35. National Conference of Black Mayors, "About Us," www.ncbm.org/aboutncbm/index.html.
36. CNNPolitics.com, "Poll: 76 Percent Say U.S. Ready for Black President," April 4, 2008, http://edition.cnn.com/2008/POLITICS/04/03/poll.black.president/index.html.
37. "Voter Turnout Increases by 5 Million in 2008 Presidential Election U.S. Census Reports," July 20, 2009, www.census.gov/press-release/www/releases/archives/voting/013995.html.
38. Pew Research Center for the People and the Press, "Blacks Upbeat About Black Progress, Prospects," January 12, 2010, www.people-press.org/reports/576.
39. Kathy Kiely, "National Elite Political Circles Lack Minorities," *USA Today Online,* January 21, 2002.
40. J. Bretting and B. Morris, "Fry-Bread Federalism Revisited: A Model of American Indian Intergovernmental Relations," paper presented at the 2005 annual meeting of the Western Political Science Association, Oakland, CA.
41. "American Indians by the Numbers: From the U.S. Census Bureau," www.infoplease.com/spot/aihmcensus1.html; DeNavas-Walt, Proctor, and Smith, "Income, Poverty, and Health Insurance Coverage in the United States, 2008: Poverty in the United States."
42. William Roller, "Groups Aim to Boost Native American Graduation Rate," *Yuma Sun,* January 12, 2009, www.yumasun.com/news/evidenced-47067-crisis-says.html.
43. National Indiana Gaming Commission, "Gaming Revenue Reports," www.nigc.gov/Default.aspx?tabid=67.
44. Adrian Sainz, "Indian Gambling Revenues Up in 2006, But Growth Slows," *North County Times,* June 28, 2007; National Indian Gaming Commission, "Tribal Gaming Revenues (in thousands) by Region, Fiscal Year 2003 and 2002," n.d., www.nigc.gov/nigc/tribes/tribaldata2003/gamerevenue.jsp.
45. Pew Hispanic Center, "Statistical Portrait of Hispanics in the United States, 2008," Table 1, http://pewhispanic.org/factsheets/factsheet.php?FactsheetID=58.
46. Pew Hispanic Center, "Latinos by Country of Origin," http://pewhispanic.org.
47. Mark Falcoff, "Our Language Needs No Law," *New York Times,* August 5, 1996.
48. Douglas R. Hess and Jody Herman, "Representational Bias in the 2008 Electorate," November 2009, www.projectvote.org.
49. U.S. Census Bureau, "Hawaii: ACS Demographic and Housing Estimates: 2006–2008," American Community Survey; U.S. Census Bureau, "California: ACS Demographic and Housing Estimates: 2006–2008," American Community Survey.
50. Christine Nifong, "Hispanics and Asians Change the Face of the South," *Christian Science Monitor,* August 6, 1996.
51. *Hirabayashi v. United States,* 320 U.S. 81 (1943); *Korematsu v. United States,* 323 U.S. 214 (1944).
52. Data from harvard.edu, mit.edu, stanford.edu, and berkeley.edu.
53. DeNavas-Walt, Proctor, and Smith, "Income, Poverty, and Health Insurance Coverage in the United States, 2008."
54. Lena H. Sun, "Getting Out the Ethnic Vote," *Washington Post,* October 7, 1996, B5; K. Connie Kang, "Asian Americans Slow to Flex Their Political Muscle," *Los Angeles Times,* October 31, 1996, A18.
55. Ibid.
56. Sun, "Getting Out the Ethnic Vote," B5.
57. See Paula D. McClain and Joseph Stewart Jr., *Can We All Get Along?* 3rd ed. (Boulder: Westview, 2003), 78.
58. Eleanor Flexner, *Century of Struggle: The Woman's Rights Movement in the United States* (New York: Atheneum, 1973), 148–149.
59. Nancy E. McGlen and Karen O'Connor, *Women's Rights: The Struggle for Equality in the 19th and 20th Centuries* (New York: Praeger, 1983), 272–273.
60. Flexner, *Century of Struggle,* 296.
61. Jane Mansbridge, *Why We Lost the ERA* (Chicago: University of Chicago Press, 1986), 13.
62. *Reed v. Reed,* 404 U.S. 71 (1971); *Craig v. Boren,* 429 U.S. 190 (1976).

63. Shelley Donald Coolidge, "Flat Tire on the Road to Pay Equity," *Christian Science Monitor,* April 11, 1997, 9; National Committee on Pay Equity, "The Wage Gap Over Time: In Real Dollars, Women See a Continuing Gap," www.pay-equity.org/info-time.html.

64. *Ledbetter v. Goodyear Tire & Rubber Co.,* 550 U.S. 618 (2007).

65. Barbara Noble, "At Work: And Now the Sticky Floor," *New York Times,* November 22, 1992, 23.

66. Kenneth Gray, "The Gender Gap in Yearly Earnings: Can Vocational Education Help?" Office of Special Populations' Brief, University of California, Berkeley, vol. 5, no. 2.

67. Center for American Women and Politics, "Women in Elective Office 2010," www.cawp .rutgers.edu/fast_facts/index.php; "Women Mayors in U.S. Cities 2009, www.cawp .rutgers.edu/fast_facts/levels_of_office/Local-WomenMayors.php.

68. Siena Research Institute, "Do You Think the United States Is Ready for a Woman President in 2008?" February 22, 2005, www.siena.edu/sri/firstwomanpresident/fwp_release_final_ sans.pdf.

69. Center for American Women and Politics, "Women in Elective Office 2010," www.cawp .rutgers.edu/fast_facts/index.php.

70. Gary F. Moncrief, Peverill Squire, and Malcom F. Jewell, *Who Runs for the Legislature* (New York: Prentice-Hall), 98–99.

71. Center for Women and Politics, "Women Candidates for Governor 1970–2008," www .cawp.rutgers.edu/fast_facts/elections/documents/canwingov_histlst.pdf; CNNPolitics. com, ElectionCenter 2008, www.cnn.com/ELECTION/2008/results/full/.

72. Kristin Eliasberg, "Making a Case for the Right to Be Different," *New York Times,* June 16, 2001, B11.

73. *Bowers v. Hardwick,* 478 U.S. 186 (1986).

74. *Romer v. Evans,* 115 S. Ct. 1092 (1996).

75. *Lawrence v. Texas,* 539 U.S. 558 (2003).

76. *Goodridge v. Dep't of Pub. Health,* 440 Mass. 309 (2003).

77. Center for Responsive Politics, "Human Rights Campaign," www.opensecrets.org/orgs/ all_summary.php?id=D000000158&nid=1276.

78. Nathaniel Frank, "What the Changes to DADT Mean: The Good, the Bad and the Politi- cally Dangerous," *Huffington Post,* March 25, 2010, www.huffingtonpost.com/nathaniel- frank/what-the-changes-to-dadt_b_513665.html.

79. David M. Herszenhorn and Carl Hulse, "House Votes to Allow 'Don't Ask, Don't Tell' Repeal," *New York Times,* May 27, 2010. www.nytimes.com/2010/05/28/us/politics/28tell .html?scp=1&sq=Don%27t%20Ask%20Don%27t%20Tell%20Senate&st=cse.

80. PoliticalTicker, "CNN Poll: Nearly 8 in 10 Favor Gays in the Military," CNN Politics, May 25, 2010, http://politicalticker.blogs.cnn.com/2010/05/25/cnn-poll-nearly-8-in-10-favor-gays- in-the-military/?fbid=podlhA70hYs; Pew Research Center for the People and the Press, "Less Opposition to Gay Marriage, Adoption, and Military Service," Survey Reports, March 22, 2006, http://people-press.org/report/273/less-opposition-to-gay-marriage-adoption- and-military-service.

81. Pew Forum on Religion and Public Life, "Public Opinion on Gay Marriage: Opponents Consistently Outnumber Supporters," July 9, 2009, http://pewforum.org/gay-marriage- and-homosexuality/public-opinion-on-gay-marriage-opponents-consistently-outnumber- supporters.aspx#3.

82. *Massachusetts Board of Retirement v. Murgia,* 427 U.S. 307 (1976).

83. Ibid.; *Vance v. Bradley,* 440 U.S. 93 (1979); *Gregory v. Ashcroft,* 501 U.S. 452 (1991).

84. *Alabama v. Garrett,* 531 U.S. 356 (2001).

85. Hillary Clinton, "Hillary's Remarks in Washington, DC," June 7, 2008, www.hillaryclinton .com.

86. Eugene Robinson, "What He Overcame," *Washington Post,* June 6, 2008, A19.

87. MLDB, "Just a Second, Obama Is Speaking," *Daily Kos,* July 25, 2008, www.dailykos .com/storyonly/2008/7/25/93510/1800/555/556771.

Chapter 6

1. Katherine Seelye, "Fighting Health Care Overhaul, and Proud of It," *New York Times,* August 30, 2009, www.nytimes.com/2009/08/31/us/politics/31demint.htm?scp=4&sq=Obama%20Waterloo%20DeMint&st=cse.
2. Ryan Grim, "Pelosi: End the Filibuster," *The Huffington Post,* July 1, 2010, www.huffingtonpost.com/2010/07/01/pelosi-end-the-filibuster_n_632851.html.
3. David Herszenhorn, "How the Filibuster Became the Rule," *New York Times,* December 3, 2007, www.nytimes.com/2007/12/02/weekinreview/02herszenhorn.html?scp=1&sq=McConnell%20umpteenth&st=cse.
4. John R. Hibbing and Elizabeth Theiss-Morse, *Congress as Public Enemy* (New York: Cambridge University Press, 1995), chs. 2, 3.
5. Glenn R. Parker and Roger H. Davidson, "Why Do Americans Love Their Congressmen So Much More Than Their Congress?" *Legislative Studies Quarterly,* 4 (February 1979): 52–61.
6. Heinz Eulau and Paul D. Karps, "The Puzzle of Representation: Specifying Components of Responsiveness," *Legislative Studies Quarterly* 2 (1977): 233–254.
7. Gary Jacobson, *The Politics of Congressional Elections,* 4th ed. (New York: Longman, 1997), ch. 8.
8. Ross K. Baker, *House and Senate* (New York: Norton, 1989).
9. Lyle Denniston, "GAO Sues for Access to Cheney Records," *Boston Globe,* February 23, 2002, A1; Adam Cohen, "Bush v. Congress: The Looming Battle of Executive Privilege," *New York Times,* April 10, 2007, 20; Bruce Fein, "Restoring Congressional Oversight," *Washington Times,* November 28, 2006; Sheryl Gay Stolberg, "Bush Moves Toward Showdown With Congress on Executive Privilege," *New York Times,* June 29, 2007, 23.
10. Charles Cameron, Albert Cover, and Jeffrey Segal, "Senate Voting on Supreme Court Nominations," *American Political Science Review* 84 (1990): 525–534.
11. *Baker v. Carr,* 396 U.S. 186 (1962); *Wesberry v. Sanders,* 376 U.S. 1 (1964).
12. Karen Mills, "Census 2000 Brief: Congressional Apportionment" (Washington, D.C.: U.S. Census Bureau, July 2001), www.census.gov/prod/2001pubs/c2kbr01–7.pdf.
13. Roger H. Davidson and Walter J. Oleszek, *Congress and Its Members,* 9th ed. (Washington, D.C.: CQ Press, 2004), 48.
14. Charles Cameron, David Epstein, and Sharyn O'Halloran, "Do Majority–Minority Districts Maximize Substantive Black Representation in Congress?" *American Political Science Review* 90 (December 1996): 794–812; Kevin Hill, "Does the Creation of Majority Black Districts Aid Republicans? An Analysis of the 1992 Congressional Election in Eight Southern States," *Journal of Politics* 57 (May 1995): 384–401; D. Lublin, "Racial Redistricting and African-American Representation: A Critique of 'Do Majority-Minority Districts Maximize Substantive Black Representation in Congress?'" *American Political Science Review* 93 (1999): 183–186.
15. Holly Idelson, "Court Takes a Hard Line on Minority Voting Blocs," *CQ Weekly Report,* July 1, 1995, 4, 5, web version.
16. *Shaw v. Reno,* 509 U.S. 630 (1993); *Miller v. Johnson,* 115 S. Ct. 2475 (1995).
17. *Shaw v. Hunt,* 116 S. Ct. 1894 (1996); *Bush v. Vera,* 116 S. Ct. 1941 (1996); *Hunt v. Cromartie et al.,* 532 U.S. 534 (2001).
18. Peter Urban, "Congress Gets Lavish Benefits," *Connecticut Post,* January 16, 2005; Debra J. Saunders, "Perks of Office" [editorial], *San Francisco Chronicle,* November 19, 2000, 9.
19. Norman J. Ornstein, Thomas E. Mann, and Michael J. Malbin, *Vital Statistics on Congress, 2001–2002* (Washington, D.C.: AEI Press, 2002), 69; Davidson and Oleszek, *Congress and Its Members,* 60; Peter E. Harrell, "A Slightly Redder Hue," *CQ Weekly,* November 6, 2004, 2621–2625; "Table 1–15 Mean Turnover in the House of Representatives from Various Causes, by Decade and my Party System, 1789–2008," *Vital Statistics on American Politics* Online Edition, CQ Press Electronic Library. Originally published in

Harold W. Stanley and Richard G. Niemi, *Vital Statistics on American Politics 2007–2008* (Washington, D.C.: CQ Press, 2008).

20. Calculated by the authors from "Table 1–19, Incumbent Reelection Rates: Representatives, Senators, and Governors, General Elections, 1960–2008," *Vital Statistics on American Politics* Online Edition.

21. Calculated by the authors from Campaign Finance Institute data table, "Expenditures of House Incumbents and Challengers, by Election Outcome, 1974–2008*," www.cfinst .org/pdf/vital/VitalStats_t3.pdf.

22. "Table 1–19, Incumbent Reelection Rates: Representatives, Senators, and Governors, General Elections, 1960–2008," *Vital Statistics on American Politics* Online Edition.

23. Harold Stanley and Richard Niemi, *Vital Statistics on American Politics,* 5th ed. (Washington, D.C.: Congressional Quarterly Press, 1995).

24. Edward R. Tufte, *Political Control of the Economy* (Princeton: Princeton University Press, 1978); Robert S. Erikson, "The Puzzle of the Midterm Loss," *Journal of Politics* 50 (November 1988): 1011–1029; Robert S. Erikson and Gerald C. Wright, "Voters, Candidates, and Issues in Congressional Elections," in Lawrence Dodd and Bruce Oppenheimer, eds., *Congress Reconsidered,* 9th ed. (Washington, D.C.: CQ Press, 2005), 71–96.

25. Glenn Parker, *Characteristics of Congress: Patterns in Congressional Behavior* (Englewood Cliffs, N.J.: Prentice Hall, 1989), 17–18, ch. 9.

26. Davidson and Oleszek, *Congress and Its Members,* 155–156.

27. Leroy Rieselbach, *Congressional Reform in the Seventies* (Morristown, N.J.: General Learning Press, 1977); Leroy Rieselbach, *Congressional Reform* (Washington, D.C.: Congressional Quarterly Press, 1986).

28. Ed Gillespie and Bob Schellhas, eds., *Contract With America: The Bold Plan by Rep. Newt Gingrich, Rep. Dick Armey and the House Republicans to Change the Nation* (New York: Random House, 1994); James G. Gimpel, *Legislating the Revolution* (Boston: Allyn & Bacon, 1996).

29. Perry Bacon Jr., "Don't Mess With Nancy Pelosi," *Time,* August 27, 2006.

30. Edward Epstein, "Her Key to the House," *CQ Weekly,* October 29, 2007, 3158.

31. Edward Epstein, "Pelosi's Action Plan for Party Unity," *CQ Weekly,* March 30, 2009, 706.

32. Davidson and Oleszek, *Congress and Its Members,* 193.

33. Mathew McCubbins and Thomas Schwartz, "Congressional Oversight Overlooked: Police Patrols Versus Fire Alarms," *American Journal of Political Science* (February 1984): 165–179.

34. Barbara Sinclair, "Party Leaders and the New Legislative Process," in Dodd and Oppenheimer, eds., *Congress Reconsidered,* 6th ed., 229–245.

35. Jonathan Cohn, "Dems 'Almost Certain' to Bypass Conference," *The New Republic* Online, January 3, 2010, www.tnr.com/blog/the-treatment/exclusive-dems-almost-certain-bypass-conference.

36. Davidson and Oleszek, *Congress and Its Members,* 204.

37. Steven Smith and Eric Lawrence, "Party Control of Committees in the Republican Congress," in Dodd and Oppenheimer, eds., *Congress Reconsidered,* 6th ed., 163–192.

38. Davidson and Oleszek, *Congress and Its Members,* 219–220.

39. Barbara Sinclair, *The Transformation of the U.S. Senate* (Baltimore: Johns Hopkins University Press, 1989).

40. Roger H. Davidson, Walter J. Oleszek, and Frances E. Lee, eds. *Congress and Its Members,* 11th ed. (Washington, D.C.: CQ Press, 2008), 276.

41. John Stewart, "A Chronology of the Civil Rights Act of 1964," in Robert Loevy, ed., *The Civil Rights Act of 1964: The Passage of the Law That Ended Racial Segregation* (Albany: SUNY Press, 1997), 358.

42. Ibid., 358–360.

43. Barbara Sinclair, "The New World of U.S. Senators," in Dodd and Oppenheimer, eds., *Congress Reconsidered,* 8th ed., 11; Richard Beth and Stanley Bach, "Filibusters and

Cloture in the Senate," *Congressional Research Service,* March 28, 2003, www.senate.gov/reference/resources/pdf/RL30360.pdf.

44. Emily Pierce, "Cloture, Filibusters Spur Furious Debate," *Roll Call,* March 5, 2008; U.S. Senate Virtual Reference Desk, "Cloture Motions—110th Congress," www.senate.gov/pagelayout/reference/cloture_motions/110.htm.

45. Donald R. Matthews and James A. Stimson, *Yeas and Nays* (New York: Wiley, 1975).

46. Richard Smith, "Interest Group Influence in the U.S. Congress," *Legislative Studies Quarterly* 20 (February 1995): 89–140.

47. Parker and Davidson, "Why Do Americans Love Their Congressmen So Much More Than Their Congress?"; Richard F. Fenno Jr., "If, as Ralph Nader Says, Congress Is 'the Broken Branch,' How Come We Love Our Congressmen So Much?" in Norman J. Ornstein, ed., *Congress in Change* (New York: Praeger, 1975), 277–287.

48. Hibbing and Theiss-Morse, *Congress as Public Enemy.*

49. John R. Hibbing and Elizabeth Theiss-Morse, "Civics Is Not Enough: Teaching Barbarics in K–12," *Political Science & Politics* 29 (1996): 157.

50. Grim, "Pelosi: End the Filibuster."

51. Herszenhorn, "How the Filibuster Became the Rule."

52. Ibid.

Chapter 7

1. Charlie Savage, "Bush Shuns Patriot Act," *Boston Globe,* March 24, 2006, A1.

2. Ibid.

3. Ibid.

4. Charlie Savage, "Bush Challenges Hundreds of Laws," *Boston Globe,* April 30, 2006, www.boston.com.

5. Philip Cooper, cited in Savage, "Bush Challenges Hundreds of Laws."

6. Jack Goldsmith, cited in Savage, "Bush Challenges Hundreds of Laws."

7. Bruce Miroff, "Monopolizing the Public Space: The President as a Problem for Democratic Politics," in Bruce Miroff, Raymond Seidelman, and Todd Swanstrom, eds., *Debating Democracy* (Boston: Houghton Mifflin, 1997), 294–303.

8. Brian Montopoli, "Seven Republicans All for Special Prosecutor in Sestak Case," CBS News *Political Hotsheet,* May 26, 2010, www.cbsnews.com/8301–503544_162–20006072–503544.html; Jeffrey T. Kuhner, "Impeach the President?" *Washington Times,* March 19, 2010, www.washingtontimes.com/news/2010/mar/19/impeach-the-president/.

9. Robert DiClerico, *The American President,* 4th ed. (Englewood Cliffs, N.J.: Prentice Hall, 1995), 374; Susan Milligan, "Democrats Scuttle Proposal to Impeach Bush: Move Avoids House Debate," *Boston Globe,* June 12, 2008, A5.

10. Joseph A. Pika and John Anthony Maltese, *The Politics of the Modern Presidency,* 6th ed. (Washington, D.C.: CQ Press, 2004), 3; Jeffrey K. Tulis, "The Two Constitutional Presidencies," in Michael Nelson, ed., *The Presidency and the Political System* (Washington, D.C.: Congressional Quarterly Press, 1995), 91–123.

11. Johnson and James M. McCormick, "The Making of International Agreements: a Reappraisal of Congressional Involvement," *Journal of Politics* 40 (1978): 468–478.

12. Joseph J. Schatz, "With a Deft and Light Touch, Bush Finds Ways to Win," *CQ Weekly,* December 11, 2004, 2900–2904; and calculated by authors from Thomas, http://thomas.loc.gov/home/treaties/treaties.html.

13. D. Roderick Kiewiet and Mathew D. McCubbins, "Presidential Influence on Congressional Appropriations Decisions," *American Political Science Review* 32 (1988): 713–736.

14. Schatz, "With a Deft and Light Touch, Bush Finds Ways to Win."

15. Peter Baker, "A Veto From Obama Does Not Stop Presses," *The Caucus,* December 20, 2009, http://thecaucus.blogs.nytimes.com/2009/12/30/a-veto-from-obama-does-not-stop-presses/.

16. Adam L. Warber, *Executive Orders and the Modern Presidency: Legislating From the Oval Office* (Boulder, Colo.: Lynne Rienner Publishers, 2006); William G. Howell, *Power Without Persuasion: The Politics of Direct Presidential Action* (Princeton: Princeton University Press, 2003).

17. Peter Baker, "Obama Making Plans to Use Executive Power," *New York Times,* February 12, 2010, www.nytimes.com/2010/02/13/us/politics/130bama.html.

18. Robert A. Carp, Ronald Stidham, and Kenneth L. Manning, *Judicial Process in America,* 6th ed. (Washington, D.C.: CQ Press, 2004), 168.

19. Amy Goldstein, "Civil Rights Organizations Question Nominee Elena Kagan's Record on Race," *Washington Post,* June 27, 2010.

20. Charlie Savage, "Obama Backers Fear Opportunities to Reshape Judiciary Are Slipping Away," *New York Times,* November 14, 2009, www.nytimes.com/2009/11/15/us/politics/15judicial.html?scp=3&sq=Obama%20judicial%20appointments&st=cse.

21. Gerald Boyd, "White House Hunts for a Justice, Hoping to Tip Ideological Scales," *New York Times,* June 30, 1987; Alan I. Abramowitz and Jeffrey A. Segal, *Senate Elections* (Ann Arbor: University of Michigan Press, 1992), 1–6.

22. Russell Wheeler, "Prevent Federal Court Nomination Battles: De-Escalating the Conflict Over the Judiciary," Brookings Institution Working Paper, 2008, www.brookings.edu/~/media/Files/Projects/Opportunity08/PB_JudicialPolicy_Wheeler.ashx.

23. David Plotz, "Advise and Consent (Also, Obstruct, Delay, and Stymie): What's Still Wrong With the Appointments Process," *Slate,* March 19, 1999, www.slate.com/StrangeBedfellow/99–03–19/StrangeBedfellow.asp.

24. Rebecca Mae Salokar, *The Solicitor General: The Politics of Law* (Philadelphia: Temple University Press, 1992), 29.

25. Bob Woodward, *Shadow: Five Presidents and the Legacy of Watergate* (New York: Simon & Schuster, 1999), 212–217.

26. *In re Neagle,* 135 U.S. 546 (1890); *In re Debs,* 158 U.S. 564 (1895); *United States v. Curtiss-Wright Export Corp.,* 299 U.S. 304, 57 S. Ct. 216 (1936); *Youngstown Sheet & Tube v. Sawyer,* 343 U.S. 579 (1952).

27. Lyn Ragsdale, *Presidential Politics* (Boston: Houghton Mifflin, 1993), 55.

28. *Historical Statistics of the United States: Colonial Times to 1970* (Washington, D.C.: U.S. Government Printing Office, 1975).

29. *Inaugural Addresses of the United States* (Washington, D.C.: U.S. Government Printing Office, 1982), quoted in Ragsdale, *Presidential Politics,* 71.

30. Suzanne Bilyeu, "FDR: How He Changed America—and Still Affects Your Life Today," *New York Times Upfront,* January 14, 2008.

31. Arthur M. Schlesinger Jr., *The Imperial Presidency* (Boston: Mariner Books, 2004).

32. Richard Nixon interview with David Frost, May 20, 1977, cited in Charles Savage, *Takeover: The Return of the Imperial Presidency and the Subversion of American Democracy* (New York: Little, Brown, 2007), 21.

33. Dana Milbank, "Cheney Refuses Records' Release; Energy Showdown With GAO Looms," *Washington Post,* January 28, 2002, A1.

34. Terry Moe, "Presidents, Institutions, and Theory," in George C. Edwards III, John H. Kessel, and Bert A. Rockman, eds., *Researching the Presidency: Vital Questions, New Approaches* (Pittsburgh: University of Pittsburgh Press, 1993), 370.

35. See, for example, Peter Jamison, "Obama 'Even Worse' Than Bush on Secret Wiretapping Case, Says S.F. Lawyer," *The Snitch,* April 1, 2010, http://blogs.sfweekly.com/thesnitch/2010/04/obama_wiretap_ruling.php; Editorial, "We Can't Tell You," *New York Times,* April 3, 2010, www.nytimes.com/2010/04/04/opinion/04sun1.html.

36. Peter M. Shane, "The Ambivalent Presidency? Executive Power Under the Obama Administration," *Executive Watch,* May 5, 2009, http://executivewatch.net/2009/05/05/the-ambivalent-adminstration-executive-power-under-the-obama-administration/; Charlie

Savage, "Obama's Use of a Bush Tactic Riles Congress," *New York Times,* August 8, 2009, www.nytimes.com/2009/08/09/us/politics/09signing.html?_r=1&hpw.

37. Jeffrey Tulis, *The Rhetorical Presidency* (Princeton: Princeton University Press, 1987).
38. Ibid.
39. George Edwards III, *The Strategic President: Persuasion and Opportunity in Presidential Leadership* (Princeton: Princeton University Press, 2009).
40. Samuel Kernell, *Going Public: New Strategies of Presidential Leadership,* 2nd ed. (Washington, D.C.: Congressional Quarterly Press, 1996).
41. Barbara Hinckley, *The Symbolic Presidency* (London: Routledge, 1990), ch. 2.
42. See Hedrick Smith, *The Power Game: How Washington Works* (New York: Random House, 1988), 405–406, for similar reports on the Nixon and Reagan administrations.
43. Lee Sigelman, "Gauging the Public Response to Presidential Leadership," *Presidential Studies Quarterly* 10 (summer 1980): 427–433; James A. Stimson, "Public Support for American Presidents: A Cyclical Model," *Public Opinion Quarterly* 40 (spring 1976): 1–21; Michael MacKuen, "Political Drama, Economic Conditions, and the Dynamics of Presidential Popularity," *American Journal of Political Science* 27 (February 1983): 165–192.
44. John R. Hibbing, and Elizabeth Theiss-Morse, *Stealth Democracy: Americans' Beliefs About How Government Should Work* (New York: Cambridge University Press, 2002).
45. Paul Brace and Barbara Hinckley, *Follow the Leader: Opinion Polls and the Modern Presidents* (New York: Basic Books, 1992), ch. 5.
46. Ibid., ch. 6.
47. Neustadt, *Presidential Power and the Modern Presidents,* 50–72.
48. James L. Sundquist, "Needed: A Political Theory for a New Era of Coalition Government in the United States," *Political Science Quarterly* 103 (winter 1988–1989): 613–635.
49. "Vote Studies: Presidential Support Definitions," *Congressional Quarterly Weekly Report,* December 21, 1996, 3455.
50. Shawn Zeller, "Historic Success, at No Small Cost," *CQ Weekly,* January 11, 2010, 112, http://library.cqpress.com/cqweekly/file.php?path=/files/wr20100111–02prezsupport-cht1new1.pdf.
51. David Mayhew, *Divided We Govern: Party Control, Lawmaking, and Investigations, 1946–1990* (New Haven: Yale University Press, 1991).
52. Terry Moe, "Presidents, Institutions, and Theory," in George C. Edwards III, John H. Kessel, and Bert A. Rockman, eds., *Researching the Presidency: Vital Questions, New Approaches* (Pittsburgh: University of Pittsburgh Press, 1993), 370.
53. Ibid.
54. The President's Committee on Administrative Management, *Report of the Committee* (Washington, D.C.: U.S. Government Printing Office, 1937).
55. Jane Meyer and Doyle MacManus, *Landslide: The Unmaking of the President, 1984–1988* (Boston: Houghton Mifflin, 1988).
56. Tom Hamburger and Christi Parsons, "President Obama's Czar System Concerns Some," *Los Angeles Times,* March 5, 2009; Zachary Coile, "Obama's Big Task: Managing the Best, Brightest," *San Francisco Chronicle,* January 11, 2009.
57. White House, "2010 Annual Report to Congress on White House Staff," www.whitehouse.gov/briefing-room/disclosures/annual-records/2010.
58. James P. Pfiffner, *The Modern Presidency,* 2nd ed. (New York: St. Martin's, 1998), 91.
59. Harold Relyea, "Growth and Development of the President's Office," in David Kozak and Kenneth Ciboski, eds., *The American Presidency* (Chicago: Nelson Hall, 1985), 135; Pfiffner, *The Modern Presidency,* 122.
60. Sid Frank and Arden Davis Melick, *The Presidents: Tidbits and Trivia* (Maplewood, N.J.: Hammond, 1986), 103.
61. Timothy Walch, ed., *At the President's Side: The Vice-Presidency in the Twentieth Century* (Columbia: University of Missouri Press, 1997), 45.

62. Ann Devroy and Stephen Barr, "Reinventing the Vice Presidency: Defying History, Al Gore Has Emerged as Bill Clinton's Closest Political Advisor," *Washington Post National Weekly Edition,* February 27–March 5, 1995, 6–7.

63. Perry Bacon Jr., "Biden Sees Vice President's Role as 'Advisor in Chief,' Aides Say," *Washington Post,* November 5, 2008, A31.

64. Michelle Obama, "As Barack's First Lady, I Would Work to Help Working Families and Military Families," *U.S. News & World Report,* October 1, 2008.

65. Robert K. Murray and Tim H. Blessing, "The Presidential Performance Study: A Progress Report," *Journal of American History* 70 (December 1983): 535–555.

66. Jon R. Bond and Richard Fleisher, *The President in the Legislative Arena* (Chicago: University of Chicago Press, 1990); George C. Edwards III, *Presidential Influence in Congress* (San Francisco: Freeman, 1980).

67. James David Barber, *The Presidential Character,* 4th ed. (Englewood Cliffs, N.J.: Prentice Hall, 1992).

68. See Michael Nelson, "James David Barber and the Psychological Presidency," in David Pederson, ed., *The "Barberian" Presidency: Theoretical and Empirical Readings* (New York: Peter Lang, 1989), 93–110; Alexander George, "Assessing Presidential Character," *World Politics* (January 1974): 234–283; Jeffrey Tulis, "On Presidential Character," in Jeffrey Tulis and Joseph Bessette, eds., *The Presidency and the Constitutional Order* (Baton Rouge: Louisiana State University Press, 1981).

69. Joseph Califano, *A Presidential Nation* (New York: Norton, 1975), 184–188.

70. Joel Achenbach, "In a Heated Race, Obama's Cool Won the Day," *Washington Post,* November 6, 2008, A47.

71. Savage, "Bush Shuns Patriot Act."

72. Jonathan Weisman, "'Signing Statements' Study Finds Administration Has Ignored Laws," *Washington Post,* June 19, 2007, A4.

73. Charlie Savage, "Obama's Embrace of a Bush Tactic Riles Congress," *New York Times,* August 8, 2009, www.nytimes.com/2009/08/09/us/politics/09signing.html?sq=Obama%20signing%20statements&st=cse&adxnnl=1&scp=1&adxnnlx=1279886452-NLooqWZTPbH429iBCM50mg.

74. Quoted in Savage, "Bush Shuns Patriot Act."

Chapter 8

1. Organic Trade Association, "U.S. Organic Product Sales Reach $26.6 Billion in 2009," Press Release, April 22, 2010, www.organicnewsroom.com/2010/04/us_organic_product_sales_reach_1.html.

2. Dann Denny, "Defining 'Organic,'" *Bloomington Herald Times,* April 16, 1998, D1.

3. Marian Burros, "Eating Well: U.S. Proposal on Organic Food Gets a Grass-Roots Review," *New York Times,* March 25, 1998, F10.

4. Gene Kahn, "National Organic Standard Will Aid Consumers," *Frozen Food Age* 47 (September 1998): 18.

5. Burros, "Eating Well," F10.

6. H. H. Gerth and C. Wright Mills, eds., *From Max Weber* (New York: Oxford University Press, 1946), 196–199.

7. Herbert Kaufman, "Emerging Conflicts in the Doctrines of Public Administration," *American Political Science Review* 50 (December 1956): 1057–1073.

8. Morris P. Fiorina, *Congress: Keystone of the Washington Establishment* (New Haven: Yale University Press, 1977).

9. Bureau of Labor Statistics, *Career Guide to Industries, 2010–2011 Edition,* www.bls.gov/oco/cg/cgs041.htm.

10. Kenneth J. Meier, *Politics and the Bureaucracy: Policymaking in the Fourth Branch of Government* (Pacific Grove, Calif.: Brooks/Cole, 1993), 18.

11. Ibid., 18–24.
12. William G. Howell and David E. Lewis, "Agencies by Presidential Design," *The Journal of Politics* 64 (2002): 1095–114.
13. Dennis D. Riley, *Controlling the Federal Bureaucracy* (Philadelphia: Temple University Press, 1987), 139–142.
14. Kenneth J. Meier, *Politics and the Bureaucracy: Policymaking in the Fourth Branch of Government,* 5th ed. (Pacific Grove, Calif.: Brooks/Cole, 2007), 78.
15. *U.S. News & World Report,* February 11, 1980, 64.
16. David E. Lewis, "The Adverse Consequences of the Politics of Agency Design for Presidential Management in the United States: The Relative Durability of Insulated Agencies," *British Journal of Political Science* 34 (2004): 377–404.
17. John B. Judis, "The Quiet Revolution: Obama Has Reinvented the State in More Ways Than You Can Imagine," *New Republic,* February 1, 2010, www.tnr.com/article/politics/the-quiet-revolution.
18. U.S. Office of Personnel Management, "Federal Civilian Workforce Statistics," *The Fact Book, 2007 Edition,* www.opm.gov/feddata/factbook/2007/2007FACTBOOK.pdf.
19. Meier, *Politics and the Bureaucracy,* 177–181.
20. Donald F. Kettl, *System Under Stress: Homeland Security and American Politics* (Washington, D.C.: CQ Press, 2004), 48.
21. "The 9/11 Commission Report: Final Report of the National Commission on Terrorist Attacks Upon the United States, Executive Summary," www.c-span.org/pdf/911final reportexecsum.pdf.
22. Quoted in Kettl, *System Under Stress,* 53.
23. Catherine Rampell, "Whistle-blowers Tell of Cost of Conscience," *USA Today,* November 24, 2006, p 13A; Peter Eisler, "Whistle-blowers' Rights Get Second Look; Bills to Strengthen Protections Now Have Better Chance to Pass, Backers Say," *USA Today,* March 15, 2010, 6A.
24. Terry Moe, "The President's Cabinet," in James Pfiffner and Roger J. Davidson, eds., *Understanding the Presidency,* 3rd ed. (New York: Longman, 2003), 208.
25. Office of Personnel Management, *Federal Workforce Statistics: The Fact Book, 2003 Edition* (Washington, D.C.: Office of Personnel Management, 2003), 10, www.opm.gov/feddata/03factbk.pdf.
26. Francis E. Rourke, *Bureaucracy, Politics and Public Policy,* 3rd ed. (Boston: Little, Brown, 1984), 106.
27. Albert B. Crenshaw, "Cash Flow," *Washington Post,* June 28, 1998, H1.
28. Anthony E. Brown, *The Politics of Airline Regulation* (Knoxville: University of Tennessee Press, 1987).
29. David E. Lewis, "Staffing Alone: Unilateral Action and the Politicization of the Executive Office of the President, 1988–2004," *Presidential Studies Quarterly* 35 (2005): 496–514.
30. Charlie Savage, "Bush Aide Admits Hiring Boasts; Says He Broke No Rules Giving Jobs to Conservatives," *Boston Globe,* June 6, 2007, A9; Charlie Savage, "Scandal Puts Spotlight on Christian Law School; Grads Influential in Justice Dept.," *Boston Globe,* April 8, 2007, A1; Eric Lipton, "Colleagues Cite Partisan Focus by Justice Officials," *New York Times,* May 12, 2007, A1.
31. Judis, "The Quiet Revolution."
32. Riley, *Controlling the Federal Bureaucracy,* ch. 2.
33. Harold Seidman and Robert Gilmour, *Politics, Position, and Power: From the Positive to the Regulatory State,* 4th ed. (New York: Oxford University Press, 1986), 3.
34. Quoted in Riley, *Controlling the Federal Bureaucracy,* 43.
35. Edmund L. Andrews, "Blowing the Whistle on Big Oil," *New York Times,* December 3, 2006.
36. Quoted in Jason DeParle, "Minerals Service Had a Mandate to Produce Results," *New York Times,* August 7, 2010.

37. Center for Responsive Politics, "Oil and Gas," www.opensecrets.org/industries/indus .php?ind=e01.

38. Hugh Heclo, "Issue Networks and the Executive Establishment," in Anthony King, ed., *The New American Political System* (Washington, D.C.: American Enterprise Institute, 1978), 87–124.

39. Deborah Zabarenko, "Environmental Group to Sue U.S. Over Oil Permits," Reuters, May 14, 2010, www.reuters.com/article/idUSTRE64D64320100515.

40. Thomas E. Mann, Molly Reynolds, and Peter Hoey, "Is Congress on the Mend?" *New York Times,* April 28, 2007.

41. Felicity Barringer, "Limits on Logging are Reinstated," *The New York Times,* July 16, 2009, www.nytimes.com/2009/07/17/science/earth/17forest.html?_r=1&ref=earth.

42. Matthew Crenson and Francis E. Rourke, "By Way of Conclusion: American Bureaucracy Since World War II," in Louis Galambois, ed., *The New American State: Bureaucracies and Policies Since World War II* (Baltimore: Johns Hopkins University Press, 1987), 137–177.

43. Charles Lane, "High Court Rejects Detainee Tribunals: 5 to 3 Ruling Curbs President's Claim of Wartime Power," *Washington Post,* June 30, 2006, A1; Robert Barnes, "Justices Say Detainees Can Seek Release," *Washington Post,* June 13, 2008, A1.

Chapter 9

1. This list is based loosely on the discussion of the functions of law in James V. Calvi and Susan Coleman, *American Law and Legal Systems* (Upper Saddle River, N.J.: Prentice Hall, 1997), 2–4; Steven Vago, *Law and Society* (Upper Saddle River, N.J.: Prentice Hall, 1997), 16–20; and Lawrence Baum, *American Courts: Process and Policy,* 2nd ed. (Boston: Houghton Mifflin, 1998), 4–5.

2. Alexander Hamilton, James Madison, and John Jay, *The Federalist Papers,* ed. Clinton Rossiter (New York: New American Library, 1961).

3. *Marbury v. Madison,* 5 U.S. (1 Cranch) 137 (1803).

4. *Dred Scott v. Sanford,* 19 How. 393 (1857).

5. Lawrence Baum, *The Supreme Court,* 8th ed. (Washington, D.C.: CQ Press, 2004), 170, 173.

6. Lawrence Baum, *The Supreme Court,* 5th ed. (Washington, D.C.: CQ Press, 1995), 22–24.

7. Joan Biskupic, "Making a Mark on the Bench," *Washington Post National Weekly Edition,* December 2–8, 1996, 31.

8. Ibid.

9. Sheldon Goldman, Sara Schiavoni, and Elliot Slotnick, "George W. Bush's Judicial Philosophy: Mission Accomplished," *Judicature* 92 (May/June 2009): 283.

10. David G. Savage, "Conservative Courts Likely Bush Legacy," *Los Angeles Times,* January 2, 2008, A11.

11. Doug Kendall, "The Bench in Purgatory: The New Republican Obstructionism on Obama's Judicial Nominees," *Slate,* October 26, 2009, www.slate.com/id/2233309/.

12. David M. O'Brien, "Ironies and Disappointments: Bush and Federal Judgeships," in Colin Campbell and Bert Rockman, eds., *The George W. Bush Presidency* (Washington, D.C.: CQ Press, 2004), 139–143.

13. Manu Raju, "Republicans Warn Obama on Judges," *Politico,* March 2, 2009, www.politico .com/news/stories/0309/19526.html.

14. Greg Gordon, "Federal Courts, Winner Will Make a Mark on the Bench," *Minneapolis Star Tribune,* September 27, 2004, 1A.

15. Gallup Organization, *Polls, Topics & Trends: Trust in Government,* various dates through 2004, www.gallup.com/poll/content/?ci=5392&pg=1; Linda Greenhouse, "The Nation: Vote Count Omits a Verdict on the Court," *New York Times,* November 18, 2001, sec. 4, 4.

16. Although the president has no official "list" of criteria, scholars are mostly agreed on these factors. See, for instance, Henry J. Abraham, *The Judiciary* (New York: New York University Press, 1996), 65–69; Lawrence Baum, *American Courts,* 4th ed. (Boston:

Houghton Mifflin, 1998), 105–106; Philip Cooper and Howard Ball, *The United States Supreme Court: From the Inside Out* (Upper Saddle River, N.J.: Prentice Hall, 1996), 49–60; and Thomas G. Walker and Lee Epstein, *The Supreme Court of the United States* (New York: St. Martin's Press, 1993), 34–40.

17. Baum, *American Courts*, 4th ed., 105.
18. From the filmstrip *This Honorable Court* (Washington, D.C.: Greater Washington Educational Telecommunications Association, 1988), program 1.
19. Ibid.
20. Peter Baker, "Kagan Nomination Leaves Longing on the Left," *New York Times*, May 10, 1010, www.nytimes.com/2010/05/11/us/politics/11nominees.html?scp=1&sq=Elena%20Kagan%201iberal&st=cse.
21. Baum, *American Courts*, 4th ed., 105.
22. Walker and Epstein, *The Supreme Court of the United States*, 40.
23. Sonia Sotomayor, "A Latina Judge's Voice," address at U.C. Berkeley, October 26, 2001, www.berkeley.edu/news/media/releases/2009/05/26_sotomayor.shtml.
24. Baum, *The Supreme Court*, 8th ed., 103.
25. U.S. Supreme Court, "2009 Year-End Report on the Federal Judiciary," www.supremecourt.gov/publicinfo/year-end/2009year-endreport.pdf.
26. Cooper and Ball, *The United States Supreme Court*, 104.
27. Ibid., 134.
28. Walker and Epstein, *The Supreme Court of the United States*, 90.
29. Ibid., 91–92.
30. Ibid., 129–130.
31. Adam Cohen, "Psst . . . Justice Scalia . . . You Know, You're an Activist Too," *New York Times*, April 19, 2005, web version.
32. What follows is drawn from the excellent discussion in Cohen, "Psst . . . Justice Scalia," 131–139.
33. Baum, *The Supreme Court*, 8th ed., 82.
34. Max Lerner, *Nine Scorpions in a Bottle: Great Judges and Cases of the Supreme Court* (New York: Arcade Publishing, 1994).
35. Philip J. Cooper, *Battles on the Bench: Conflict Inside the Supreme Court* (Lawrence: University Press of Kansas, 1995), 42–46.
36. For a provocative argument that the Court does not, in fact, successfully produce significant social reform and actually damaged the civil rights struggles in this country, see Gerald N. Rosenberg, *The Hollow Hope: Can Courts Bring About Social Change?* (Chicago: University of Chicago Press, 1991).
37. *Marbury v. Madison* (1803).
38. *Martin v. Hunter's Lessee*, 14 U.S. 304 (1816).
39. *McCulloch v. Maryland*, 4 Wheat. 316 (1819).
40. *Gibbons v. Ogden*, 9 Wheat. 1 (1824).
41. *Lochner v. New York*, 198 U.S. 45 (1905).
42. *Hammer v. Dagenhart*, 247 U.S. 251 (1918).
43. *Adkins v. Children's Hospital*, 261 U.S. 525 (1923).
44. *Dred Scott v. Sanford*, 19 How. 393 (1857).
45. *Plessy v. Ferguson*, 163 U.S. 537 (1896).
46. *Brown v. Board of Education*, 347 U.S. 483 (1954).
47. For example, *Mapp v. Ohio*, 367 U.S. 643 (1961); *Gideon v. Wainwright*, 372 U.S. 335 (1963); and *Miranda v. Arizona*, 382 U.S. 925 (1965).
48. *Baker v. Carr*, 396 U.S. 186 (1962).
49. *Roe v. Wade*, 410 U.S. 113 (1973).
50. *Citizens United v. Federal Election Commission*, 558 U.S. ___ (2010).
51. Maria Puente, "Poll: Blacks' Confidence in Police Plummets," *USA Today*, March 21, 1995, 3A.

52. Michael Tonry, "Racial Politics, Racial Disparities, and the War on Crime," *Crime and Delinquency* (1994): 475–494.

53. John H. Langbein, "Money Talks, Clients Walk," *Newsweek,* April 17, 1995, 32.

54. Legal Services Corporation, "Fact Sheet: What Is LSC?" www.lsc.gov/about/lsc.php.

55. Linda Greenhouse, "Bush v. Gore: A Special Report," *New York Times,* February 20, 2001.

Chapter 10

1. Mike Gravel, "Philadelphia II: National Initiatives," *Campaigns and Elections* (Dec. 1995/ Jan. 1996): 2.

2. According to a September 1994 Roper poll, 76 percent favor a national referendum.

3. Survey by Fox News and Opinion Dynamics, May 24–May 25, 2000. Retrieved from the iPOLL database, The Roper Center for Public Opinion Research, University of Connecticut, www.ropercenter.uconn.edu/ipoll.html.

4. "Exchange With Reporters in Waco, Texas, August 7, 2001," Public Papers of the Presidents: George W. Bush—2001, vol. 2, p. 945. U.S. Government Printing Office via GPO Access.

5. Joshua Green, "The Other War Room," *Washington Monthly,* April 2002, 16.

6. Matt Bai, "Rove's Way," *New York Times Magazine,* October 20, 2002, 56.

7. V. O. Key Jr., *Public Opinion and American Democracy* (New York: Knopf, 1961), 7.

8. John Kingdon, *Congressmen's Voting Decisions,* 2nd ed. (New York: Harper & Row, 1981), ch. 2.

9. Gary C. Jacobson, "The War, the President, and the 2006 Midterm Congressional Elections," paper presented at the annual meeting of the Midwest Political Science Association, Chicago, April 12–15, 2007.

10. Many works repeat this theme of the uninformed and ignorant citizen. See, for example, Bernard Berelson, Paul F. Lazarsfeld, and William N. McPhee, *Voting: A Study of Opinion Formation in a Presidential Campaign* (Chicago: University of Chicago Press, 1954); Angus Campbell, Philip E. Converse, Warren E. Miller, and Donald E. Stokes, *The American Voter* (New York: Wiley, 1960); W. Russell Neuman, *The Paradox of Mass Politics* (Cambridge: Harvard University Press, 1986); and Michael X. Delli Carpini and Scott Keeter, *What Americans Know About Politics and Why It Matters* (New Haven: Yale University Press, 1996).

11. These data come from Delli Carpini and Keeter, *What Americans Know About Politics,* 70–75.

12. 2008 American National Election Studies, www.electionstudies.org.

13. John Marzulli and Michael Saul, "A Disturbing Wave of Hatred: Anti-Muslim, Anti-Arab Incidents in City, Nation," New York *Daily News,* September 19, 2001.

14. Herbert McClosky and Alida Brill, *Dimensions of Tolerance* (New York: Russell Sage Foundation, 1983), 50.

15. Ibid.

16. M. Kent Jennings and Richard G. Niemi, *The Political Character of Adolescence* (Princeton: Princeton University Press, 1974); Robert C. Luskin, John P. McIver, and Edward Carmines, "Issues and the Transmission of Partisanship," *American Journal of Political Science* 33 (May 1989): 440–458; Erikson and Tedin, *American Public Opinion,* 5th ed., 127–128; Christopher H. Achen, "Parental Socialization and Rational Party Identification," *Political Behavior* 24 (June 2002): 151–170.

17. Jennings and Niemi, *The Political Character of Adolescence,* 41.

18. Shirley Engle and Anna Ochoa, *Education for Democratic Citizenship: Decision Making in the Social Studies* (New York: Teacher's College of Columbia University, 1988).

19. Kenneth D. Wald, Dennis E. Owen, and Samuel S. Jill Jr., "Political Cohesion in Churches," *Journal of Politics* 52 (1990): 197–215; Robert Huckfeldt, Paul Allen Beck, Russell J. Dalton, and Jeffrey Levine, "Political Environments, Cohesive Social Groups, and the Communication of Public Opinion," *American Journal of Political Science* 39 (1995):

1025–1054; David C. Leege, Kenneth D. Wald, Brian S. Krueger, and Paul D. Mueller, *The Politics of Cultural Differences: Social Change and Voter Mobilization in the Post-New Deal Period* (Princeton: Princeton University Press, 2002).

20. Elisabeth Noelle-Neumann, *The Spiral of Silence: Public Opinion, Our Social Skin* (Chicago: University of Chicago Press, 1984).

21. Wald, Owen, and Jill, "Political Cohesion in Churches"; Huckfeldt, Beck, Dalton, and Levine, "Political Environments"; Leege, Wald, Krueger, and Mueller, *The Politics of Cultural Differences.*

22. National Election Studies, 1958–2000; various polls from the Roper Center, 1994–2004. Yearly averages calculated by the authors with separate averages for 2001 (before and after September 11).

23. General Social Survey, 2002.

24. Campbell et al., *The American Voter;* Donald P. Green, Bradley Palmquist, and Eric Schickler, *Partisan Hearts and Minds: Political Parties and the Social Identities of Voters* (New Haven: Yale University Press, 2002).

25. Larry M. Bartels, "Beyond the Running Tally: Partisan Bias in Political Perceptions," *Political Behavior* 24 (June 2002).

26. CBS News Poll, February 2–4, 2009. Telephone survey of 864 respondents. Calculated by the authors. Data were obtained from the Roper Center.

27. M. J. Hetherington, "Resurgent Mass Partisanship: The Role of Elite Polarization," *American Political Science Review* 95 (2001): 619–631; Alan L. Abramowitz, *The Disappearing Center: Engaged Citizens, Polarization, and American Democracy* (New Haven: Yale University Press, 2010).

28. National Election Studies, 2004; General Social Survey, 2002; Norman H. Nie, Jane Junn, and Kenneth Stehlik-Barry, *Education and Democratic Citizenship in America* (Chicago: University of Chicago Press, 1996). For more on the effects of education, see Delli Carpini and Keeter, *What Americans Know About Politics,* 188–189; Robert S. Erikson and Kent L. Tedin, *American Public Opinion: Its Origins, Content, and Impact,* 7th ed. (New York: Pearson Longman, 2005), 152–159; and Herbert H. Hyman, Charles R. Wright, and John Shelton Reed, *The Enduring Effects of Education* (Chicago: University of Chicago Press, 1975). But for a dissenting view that formal education is just a mask for intelligence and native cognitive ability, see Robert Luskin, "Explaining Political Sophistication," *Political Behavior* 12 (1990): 3298–3409.

29. Christine L. Day, *What Older Americans Think: Interest Groups and Aging Policy* (Princeton: Princeton University Press, 1990).

30. Scott Helman, "Obama Strikes Chord With Generation Next: Campaign Targets Youth Vote in Ind.," *Boston Globe,* May 3, 2008; Cynthia Burton and Joseph A. Gambardello, "Turnout for N.J. Primary Highest in Half a Century," *Philadelphia Inquirer,* February 7, 2008.

31. Data from CBS/*New York Times* polls.

32. Erikson and Tedin, *American Public Opinion,* 5th ed., 208–212.

33. Based on authors' analysis of the 1996 and 2000 Voter News Service Election Day exit polls.

34. Lee Sigelman and Susan Welch, *Black Americans' Views of Racial Equality—The Dream Deferred* (Cambridge: Cambridge University Press, 1991).

35. Katherine Tate, "Black Political Participation in the 1984 and 1988 Presidential Elections," *American Political Science Review* 85 (December 1991): 1159–1176.

36. Wendy K. Tam Cho, "Asians—a Monolithic Voting Bloc?" *Political Behavior* 17 (1995): 223–249; Rodolfo O. De La Garza, *Latino Voices: Mexican, Puerto Rican, and Cuban Perspectives on American Politics* (Boulder: Westview Press, 1992).

37. Data from CBS/*New York Times* polls, 2000–2004. Calculated by the authors.

38. Frank Newport, "Mormons Most Conservative Major Religious Group in U.S.," www.gallup.com/poll/125021/mormons-conservative-major-religious-group.aspx.

39. Ibid.
40. Robert S. Erikson, Gerald C. Wright, and John P. McIver, *Statehouse Democracy* (New York: Cambridge University Press, 1993), 18.
41. General Social Survey, 2000; for gay marriage, ABC News/*Washington Post* poll, March 2004.
42. Adam Lisberg, "Exit Polls Out of Whack: Early Numbers Told Wrong Story," New York *Daily News*, November 4, 2002, 11; "Evaluation of Edison/Mitofsky Election System 2004," prepared by Edison Media Research and Mitofsky International for the National Election Pool (NEP), January 19, 2005.
43. "Pollsters Seek AAPC Action," *Campaigns and Elections* (July 1996): 55.
44. William Saletan, "Phoning It In," *Slate,* December 7, 2007, www.slate.com/iod/2179395/.
45. SurveyUSA home page, www.surveyusa.com.
46. David Sanders, Harold D. Clarke, Marianne C. Stewart, and Paul Whiteley, "Does Mode Matter for Modeling Political Choice? Evidence From the 2005 British Election Study," *Political Analysis* 15 (2007): 257–285; Robert P. Berrens, Alok K. Bohara, Hank Jenkins-Smith, Carol Silva, and David L. Weimer, "The Advent of Internet Surveys for Political Research: A Comparison of Telephone and Internet Samples," *Political Analysis* 11 (2003): 1–22; Taylor Humphrey, "The Case for Publishing (Some) Online Polls," *Polling Report*, January 15, 2007; Linchiat Chang and Jon A. Krosnick, "National Surveys via RDD Telephone Interviewing Versus the Internet," *Public Opinion Quarterly* 73 (2009): 641–678.
47. J. Michael Brick, Pat D. Brick, Sarah Dipko, Stanley Presser, Clyde Tucker, and Yangyang Yuan, "Cell Phone Survey Feasibility in the U.S.: Sampling and Calling Cell Numbers Versus Landline Numbers," *Public Opinion Quarterly* 71 (spring 2007): 23–39. See the special issue of *Public Opinion Quarterly* (winter 2007) for perspectives on the challenges of cell phones for surveys.
48. Robert S. Erikson and Kent Tedin, *American Public Opinion,* 5th ed. (Boston: Allyn & Bacon, 1995), 42–47.
49. Research suggests that use of information shortcuts does allow the electorate to make decisions that are more in line with their values than if they did not have such shortcuts; see Samuel Popkin, *The Reasoning Voter* (Chicago: University of Chicago Press, 1991); and Paul Sniderman, Richard Brody, and Philip Tetlock, *Reasoning and Choice: Exploration in Political Psychology* (New York: Cambridge University Press, 1991). However, this is not the same as saying that if fully informed, everyone would make the same decision as they do without information. Indeed, information really does count; see Larry Bartels, "Uninformed Votes: Information Effects in Presidential Elections," *American Journal of Political Science* 40 (February 1996): 194–230; and Scott Althaus, "Information Effects in Collective Preferences," *American Political Science Review* 92 (September 1998): 545–558.
50. Milton Lodge, Kathleen McGraw, and Patrick Stroh, "An Impression-Driven Model of Candidate Evaluation," *American Political Science Review* 82 (June 1989): 399–419.
51. Berelson, Lazarsfeld, and McPhee, *Voting,* 109–115.
52. Larry M. Bartels, "Uninformed Votes: Information Effects in Presidential Elections," *American Journal of Political Science* 40 (1996): 194–230.
53. Gerald C. Wright, "Level of Analysis Effects on Explanations of Voting," *British Journal of Political Science* 18 (July 1989): 381–398; Popkin, *The Reasoning Voter;* Benjamin Page and Robert Shapiro, *The Rational Public* (Chicago: University of Chicago Press, 1993).
54. Erikson, Wright, and McIver, *Statehouse Democracy,* 18.
55. Michael B. MacKuen, Robert S. Erikson, and James A. Stimson, "Macropartisanship," *American Political Science Review* 89 (December 1989): 1125–1142.
56. Larry M. Bartels, *Unequal Democracy: The Political Economy of the New Gilded Age* (Princeton: Princeton University Press, 2008), ch. 9; Martin Gilens, "Inequality and Democratic Responsiveness," *Public Opinion Quarterly* 69 (2005): 778–896.
57. Jean Bethke Elshtain, "A Parody of True Democracy," *Christian Science Monitor,* August 13, 1992, 18.

Chapter 11

1. PBS, "Obama's Deal," Part I, *Frontline*, www.pbs.org/wgbh/pages/frontline/obamasdeal/.
2. See, for example, James Bryce, *The American Commonwealth*, vol. 2 (Chicago: Sergel, 1891), pt. 3.
3. E. E. Schattschneider, *Party Government* (New York: Holt, Rinehart and Winston, 1942), 1.
4. This definition and the following discussion are based on Frank Sorauf, *Party Politics in America* (Boston: Little, Brown, 1964), ch. 1; and V. O. Key, *Politics, Parties, and Pressure Groups*, 5th ed. (New York: Corwell, 1964).
5. The discussion of national conventions is based on David Price, *Bring Back the Parties* (Washington, D.C.: Congressional Quarterly Press, 1984), chs. 6 and 7; and Leon D. Epstein, *Political Parties in the American Mold* (Madison: University of Wisconsin Press, 1986), ch. 4.
6. C. P. Cotter, J. L. Gibson, J. F. Bibby, and R. J. Huckshorn, *Party Organizations in American Politics* (New York: Praeger, 1984); John J. Coleman, "Resurgent or Just Busy? Party Organizations in Contemporary America," in John Green and Daniel Shea, eds., *The State of the Parties*, 2nd ed. (Lanham, Md.: Rowman and Littlefield, 1996), ch. 2.
7. Gerald Pomper with Susan Lederman, *Elections in America*, 2nd ed. (New York: Longman, 1980), 145–150, 167–173.
8. Richard G. Niemi and M. Kent Jennings, "Issues of Inheritance in the Formation of Party Identification," *American Journal of Political Science* 35 (1991): 970–988.
9. The discussion of the responsible party model is based on Austin Ranney, *The Doctrine of the Responsible Party Government* (Urbana: University of Illinois Press, 1962), chs. 1 and 2; and Frank J. Sorauf and Paul Allen Beck, *Party Politics in America*, 6th ed. (Glenview, Ill.: Scott, Foresman, 1988), ch. 16.
10. Morris P. Fiorina, "The Decline of Collective Responsibility in American Politics," *Daedalus* 109 (summer 1980): 24–45; John H. Aldrich, *Why Parties: The Origin and Transformation of Party Politics in America* (Chicago: University of Chicago Press, 1995), 3.
11. Sorauf and Beck, *Party Politics in America*, 6th ed., 454.
12. Aldrich, *Why Parties*, 69.
13. This discussion of the Jacksonian Democrats and machine politics and patronage is based on Aldrich, *Why Parties*, ch. 4; Epstein, *Political Parties in the American Mold*, 134–143; and Sorauf and Beck, *Party Politics in America*, 6th ed., 83–91.
14. Marjorie Randon Hershey, *Party Politics in America*, 11th ed. (New York: Longman, 2004), 130–135.
15. William H. Flanigan and Nancy H. Zingale, *Political Behavior of the American Electorate*, 9th ed. (Washington, D.C.: Congressional Quarterly Press, 1998), 59–66.
16. Anthony Downs, *An Economic Theory of Democracy* (New York: Harper and Row, 1957).
17. James L. Gibson and Susan E. Scarrow, "State Organizations in American Politics," in Eric M. Uslaner, ed., *American Political Parties: A Reader* (Itasca, Ill.: Peacock, 1993), 234.
18. James Q. Wilson, *The Amateur Democrat: Club Politics in Three Cities* (Chicago: University of Chicago Press, 1965).
19. Gerald C. Wright and Michael B. Berkman, "Candidates and Policy in U.S. Senatorial Elections," *American Political Science Review* 80 (1986): 576–590.
20. This section is based on Alan Ware, *Political Parties and Party Systems* (Oxford: Oxford University Press, 1996).
21. L. Sandy Maisel, *Parties and Elections in America*, 2nd ed. (New York: McGraw-Hill, 1993), ch. 10; Price, *Bring Back the Parties*, 284.
22. Michelle Cottle, "House Broker," *New Republic*, June 11, 2008, www.tnr.com.
23. John Aldrich and David Rohde, "The Logic of Conditional Party Government: Revisiting the Electoral Connection," in L. Dodd and B. I. Oppenheimer, eds., *Congress Reconsidered*, 7th ed. (Washington, D.C.: CQ Press, 2001).
24. Alexis de Tocqueville, *Democracy in America*, Richard D. Heffner, ed. (New York: New American Library, 1956), 198.

25. This definition is based on Jeffrey M. Berry, *The Interest Group Society,* 3rd ed. (New York: Longman, 1997); and David Truman, *The Governmental Process,* 2nd ed. (New York: Knopf, 1971).
26. Berry, *The Interest Group Society,* 6–8; John W. Kingdon, *Agendas, Alternatives, and Public Policy* (Boston: Little, Brown, 1984).
27. Kingdon, *Agendas, Alternatives, and Public Policy.*
28. Mancur Olson Jr., *The Logic of Collective Action* (New York: Schocken, 1971).
29. Allan J. Cigler and Anthony J. Nowns, "Public Interest Entrepreneurs and Group Patrons," in Allan J. Cigler and Burdett A. Loomis, eds., *Interest Group Politics,* 4th ed. (Washington, D.C.: Congressional Quarterly Press, 1995), 77–78.
30. Pamela Fessler, "Ethics Standards Announced," *Congressional Quarterly Weekly Report,* December 12, 1992, 3792; Allison Mitchell, "A New Form of Lobbying Puts Public Face on Private Interests," *New York Times on the Web,* September 30, 1998.
31. Beverly A. Cigler, "Not Just Another Special Interest: Intergovernmental Representation," in Cigler and Loomis, eds., *Interest Group Politics,* 4th ed., 134–135.
32. William Safire, *Safire's New Political Dictionary* (New York: Random House, 1993), 417–418.
33. See Diana M. Evans, "Lobbying the Committee: Interest Groups and the House Public Works and Transportation Committee," in Allan J. Cigler and Burdett A. Loomis, eds., *Interest Group Politics,* 3rd ed. (Washington, D.C.: Congressional Quarterly Press, 1991), 264–265. For a graphic example of this practice, see Michael Weisskopf and David Maraniss, "Forging an Alliance for Deregulation; Rep. DeLay Makes Companies Full Partners in the Movement," *Washington Post,* March 12, 1995, A1.
34. Adam Clymer, "Congress Passes Bill to Disclose Lobbyists' Roles," *New York Times,* November 30, 1995, 1.
35. Adam Clymer, "Senate, 98–0, Sets Tough Restriction on Lobbyist Gifts," *New York Times,* July 29, 1995, 1; "House Approves Rule to Prohibit Lobbyists' Gifts," *New York Times,* November 17, 1995, 1.
36. David S. Cloud, "Three-Month-Old Gift Ban Having Ripple Effect," *Congressional Quarterly Weekly Report,* March 23, 1996, 777–778.
37. Jeff Zeleny and David D. Kirkpatrick, "House, 411–8, Passes a Vast Ethics Overhaul," *New York Times,* August 1, 2007, www.nytimes.com.
38. Ibid.
39. See Douglas Yates, *Bureaucratic Democracy* (Cambridge: Harvard University Press, 1982), ch. 4.
40. Samuel Kernell, *Going Public: New Strategies of Presidential Leadership* (Washington, D.C.: Congressional Quarterly Press, 1986), 34.
41. Berry, *The Interest Group Society,* 121–122.
42. Cindy Skrzycki, "The Newest Lobbying Tool: Underwear," *Washington Post,* May 29, 2007, D1.
43. Susan Dodge and Becky Beaupre, "Internet Blamed in Spread of Hate," Chicago *Sun-Times,* July 6, 1999, 3; Jennifer Oldham, "Wiesenthal Center Compiles List of Hate-Based Web Sites," *Los Angeles Times,* December 18, 1999, A1; Victor Volland, "Group Warns of Hate on Internet," *St. Louis Post-Dispatch,* October 22, 1997, 8A; Becky Beaupre, "Internet Pumps Up the Volume of Hatred," *USA Today,* February 18, 1997, 6A.
44. Chris Good, "The Tea Party Movement: Who's In Charge?" *The Atlantic,* April 13, 2009, www.theatlantic.com/politics/archive/2009/04/the-tea-party-movement-whos-in-charge/13041/.
45. Mark Brunswick, "Prescription Politics; Drug Lobby Intensifies Fight on Price Controls and Imports," Minneapolis *Star Tribune,* November 16, 2003, 1A; Jim VandeHei and Juliet Eilperin, "Drug Firms Gain Church Group's Aid; Claim About Import Measure Stirs Anger," *Washington Post,* July 23, 2003, A01.
46. Mike Murphy, quoted in Alison Mitchell, "A New Form of Lobbying Puts Public Face on Private Interest," *New York Times,* September 30, 1998, A1.

47. Bill McAllister, "Rainmakers Making a Splash," *Washington Post*, December 4, 1997, A21.

48. Federal Election Commission, "Growth in PAC Financial Activity Slows," April 24, 2009, http://fec.gov/press/press2009/20090415PAC/20090424PAC.shtml.

49. Federal Election Commission, "PAC's Grouped by Total Spent," April 13, 2005, www.fec.gov/press/press2005/20050412pac/groupbyspending2004.pdf; Richard L. Hall and Frank W. Wayman, "Buying Time: Money Interests and the Mobilization of Bias in Congressional Committees," *American Political Science Review* 84 (1990): 797–820.

50. Michael Luo, "Money Talks Louder than Ever in Midterms," *New York Times*, October 7, 2010, www.nytimes.com/2010/10/08/us/politics/08donate.html?scp=1&sq=Luo%20Money%20talks%2010uder&st=cse; *Citizens United v Federal Election Commission*, 558 U.S. 50 (2010).

51. Jeffrey H. Birnbaum, "To Predict Losers in a Power Shift, Follow the Money," *Washington Post*, October 16, 2006, D1.

52. Andrew Bard Schmookler, "When Money Talks, Is It Free Speech?" *Christian Science Monitor*, November 11, 1997, 15; Nelson W. Polsby, "Money Gains Access. So What?" *New York Times*, August 13, 1997, A19.

53. Sara Fritz, "Citizen Lobby's Call to Arms," *International Herald-Tribune*, January 4–5, 1997; Katharine Q. Seelye, "G.O.P.'s Reward for Top Donors: 3 Days With Party Leaders," *New York Times*, February 20, 1997, A6.

54. "Senators Supporting Public Option Received Half as Much Money from Health Insurers," October 9, 2009, http://maplight.org/senators-supporting-public-option-got-half-as-much-money-from-health-insurers.

55. See John R. Wright, *Interest Groups and Congress* (Boston: Allyn and Bacon, 1996), 136–145; "Contributions, Lobbying, and Committee Voting in the U.S. House of Representatives," *American Political Science Review* 84 (1990): 417–438; Richard L. Hall and Frank W. Wayman, "Buying Time: Money Interests and the Mobilization of Bias in Congressional Committees," *American Political Science Review* 84 (1990): 797–820.

56. Robert Salisbury, "An Exchange Theory of Interest Groups," *Midwest Journal of Political Science* 13 (1969): 1–32.

57. A. Lee Fritscheler and James M. Hoefler, *Smoking and Politics*, 5th ed. (Upper Saddle River, N.J.: Prentice Hall, 1996), 20–35.

58. Truman, *The Governmental Process*, 2nd ed., 519.

59. See C. Wright Mills, *The Power Elite* (New York: Oxford University Press, 1956); G. William Domhoff, *The Powers That Be* (New York: Vintage, 1979).

60. The problem is that a relatively small number of groups have large memberships. Labor unions, some environmental groups like the Sierra Club, some social movements revolving around abortion and women's rights, and the NRA currently have large memberships spread across a number of congressional districts.

61. PBS, "Obama's Deal," Part I.

62. PBS, "Obama's Deal," Part II, *Frontline*, www.pbs.org/wgbh/pages/frontline/obamasdeal/.

63. David Frum, "Waterloo," *FrumForum*, March 21, 2010, www.frumforum.com/waterloo.

64. Jane Hamsher, "We Want the Public Option," *The Guardian*, September 9, 2009, www.guardian.co.uk/commentisfree/cifamerica/2009/sep/08/healthcare-public-option-barack-obama; David Dayen, "The Deal With the Hospital Industry to Kill the Public Option," October 5, 2010, http://news.firedoglake.com/2010/10/05/the-deal-with-the-hospital-industry-to-kill-the-public-option/.

65. Jonathan Cohn, "How They Did It, Part Four," *New Republic*, May 25, 2010, www.tnr.com/article/politics/75147/ow-they-did-it-part-four.

Chapter 12

1. Adam Liptak, "Justices, 5–4, Reject Corporate Spending Limit," *New York Times*, January 21, 2010. www.nytimes.com/2010/01/22/us/politics/22scotus.html?scp=1&sq=Citizens%20United&st=cse.

2. Linda Greenhouse, "Justice Alito's Reaction," *New York Times* online, January 27, 2010. http://opinionator.blogs.nytimes.com/2010/01/27/justice-alitos-reaction/?scp=2&sq=Obama%20Citizens%20United&st=cse.

3. Gerald Pomper, *Elections in America* (New York: Dodd, Mead, 1970), 1.

4. Steven J. Rosenstone and John Mark Hansen, *Mobilization, Participation, and Democracy in America* (New York: Macmillan, 1993); Ruy A. Teixeira, *The Disappearing American Voter* (Washington, D.C.: Brookings Institution, 1992); Raymond E. Wolfinger and Steven J. Rosenstone, *Who Votes?* (New Haven: Yale University Press, 1980); Richard J. Timpone, "Structure, Behavior, and Voter Turnout in the United States," *American Political Science Review* 92 (March 1998): 145–158.

5. Michael MacDonald, "2008 Current Population Survey Voting and Registration Supplement," United States Elections Project, http://elections.gmu.edu/CPS_2008.html.

6. U.S. Bureau of the Census, Current Population Survey Report, "Voting and Registration in the Election of November 2008—Detailed Tables," Table 1, www.census.gov/hhes/www/socdemo/voting/publications/p20/2008/tables.html.

7. Ibid., Table 8.

8. Current Population Reports, "Voting and Registration in the Election of November 2008," www.census.gov/prod/2010pubs/p20–562.pdf.

9. Calculated by the authors from U.S. Census Bureau, "Voting and Registration in the Election of November 2008—Detailed Tables," www.census.gov/hhes/www/socdemo/voting/publications/p20/2008/tables.html.

10. Sidney Verba, Kay Lehman Schlozman, and Henry E. Brady, *Voice and Equality: Civic Voluntarism in American Politics* (Cambridge: Harvard University Press, 1995).

11. Kay Lehman Schlozman, Sidney Verba, and Henry E. Brady, "Civic Participation and the Inequality Problem," in Theda Skocpol and Morris P. Fiorina, eds., *Civic Engagement in American Democracy* (New York: Russell Sage, 1999); Henry E. Brady, Kay Lehman Schlozman, and Sidney Verba, "Prospecting for Participants: Rational Expectations and the Recruitment of Political Activists," *The American Political Science Review* 93 (1999): 153–168.

12. Richard Brody, "The Puzzle of Political Participation in America," in Anthony King, ed., *The New American Political System* (Washington, D.C.: American Enterprise Institute, 1978), 287–324.

13. Stephen Knack, "Drivers Wanted: Motor Voter and the Election of 1996," *PS: Political Science & Politics* (June 1999): 237–243.

14. International Institute for Democracy and Electoral Assistance, "Turnout in the World, Country by Country Performance," 2005, www.idea.int/vt/survey/voter_turnout_pop2.cfm.

15. Benjamin Highton, "Voter Registration and Turnout in the United States," *Perspectives on Politics* 2 (2004): 507–515.

16. Teixeira, *The Disappearing American Voter,* ch. 2; Paul R. Abramson, John H. Aldrich, and David W. Rohde, *Change and Continuity in the 1998 Elections* (Washington, D.C.: Congressional Quarterly Press, 1999).

17. Rosenstone and Hansen, *Mobilization, Participation, and Democracy in America.*

18. Alan S. Gerber and Donald P. Green, "The Effects of Canvassing, Direct Mail, and Telephone Contact on Voter Turnout: A Field Experiment," *American Political Science Review* 94 (2000): 653–663.

19. Jeff Mapes, "National Parties Try Personal Touch," *Oregonian,* December 23, 2003, A01; Sharon Schmickle and Greg Gordon, "Vying for Voters," Minneapolis *Star Tribune,* October 31, 2004, 13A; Thomas B. Edsall, "Labor Targets Nonunion Voters; $20 Million Turnout Effort Expands Effort to Regain Influence," *Washington Post,* February 27, 2003.

20. Gerald Pomper, "The Presidential Election: The Ills of American Politics After 9/11," in Michael Nelson, ed., *The Elections of 2004* (Washington, D.C.: CQ Press), 46.

21. Teixeira, *The Disappearing American Voter,* 36–50; Robert Putnam, *Bowling Alone: The Collapse and Revival of American Community* (New York: Simon and Schuster, 2000), 31–47.

22. Warren E. Miller and Merrill J. Shanks, *The New American Voter* (Cambridge: Harvard University Press, 1996); Kevin Chen, *Political Alienation and Voting Turnout in the United States, 1969–1988* (Pittsburgh: Mellon Research University Press, 1992).

23. Anthony Downs, *An Economic Theory of Democracy* (New York: Harper and Row, 1957), 260–276.

24. John Petrocik, "Voter Turnout and Electoral Preference: The Anomalous Reagan Elections," in Kay Lehman Schlozman, ed., *Election in America* (Boston: Allen and Unwin, 1987), 239–260.

25. Jack Citrin, Eric Schickler, and John Sides, "What If Everyone Voted? Simulating the Impact of Increased Turnout in Senate Elections," *American Journal of Political Science* 47 (January 2003): 75–90.

26. Petrocik, "Voter Turnout and Electoral Preference," 243–251; Stephen Earl Bennett and David Resnick, "The Implications of Nonvoting for Democracy in the United States," *American Journal of Political Science* 34 (August 1990): 795.

27. Calculated by the authors from the 2004 and 2008 Pre- and Post-American National Election Studies.

28. V. O. Key Jr., *The Responsible Electorate: Rationality in Presidential Voting, 1936–1960* (Cambridge: Harvard University Press, 1966); Miller and Shanks, *The New American Voter*, 1996.

29. Calculated by the authors from the National Election Study, 2004 Pre-Post Study, Version 20050131 (Advance Release), January 31, 2005.

30. CNN Election Center, 2008, www.cnn.com/election/2008/results/polls/#usp00p1.

31. Eric Plutzer and John Zipp, "Identity Politics, Partisanship and Voting for Women Candidates," *Public Opinion Quarterly* 60 (1996): 30–57.

32. Center for American Women and Politics, "Proportions of Women and Men Who Voted for Hillary Clinton in the Super Tuesday Races of February 5, 2008, www.cawp.rutgers.edu/fast_facts/voters/documents/SuperTuesday_Clinton.pdf.

33. Calculated from Harold W. Stanley and Richard G. Niemi, *Vital Statistics on American Politics, 2007–2008* (Washington, D.C.: CQ Press, 2008), 127.

34. These figures are taken from the media exit polls for the 2004 and 2008 presidential elections.

35. Wendy K. Tam, "Asians—A Monolithic Voting Bloc? *Political Behavior* 17 (1995): 223–249; Pie-Te Lein, M. Margaret Conway, and Janelle Wong, *The Politics of Asian-Americans: Diversity and Community* (New York: Routledge, 2004); Atiya Kai Stokes, "Latino Group Consciousness and Political Participation," *American Politics Research* 41 (2003): 361–378; Benjamin Highton and Arthur L. Burris, "New Perspectives on Latino Voter Turnout in the United States," *American Politics Research* 30 (2002): 285–306.

36. Pei-Te Lien, Christian Collet, Janelle Wong, and S. Karthick Ramakrishnan, "Asian Pacific American Public Opinion and Participation," *PS: Political Science and Politics* 34 (2001): 628; David L. Leal, Matt A. Barreto, Jongho Lee, and Rodolofo O. De la Graza, "The Latino Vote in the 2004 Election," *PS: Political Science and Politics* 38 (2005): 41–49.

37. Downs, *An Economic Theory of Democracy*.

38. Edward Carmines and James Stimson, "Two Faces of Issue Voting," *American Political Science Review* 74 (March 1980): 78–91.

39. James Fallows, "Why Americans Hate the Media," *Atlantic Monthly*, February 1996, 45–64.

40. Morris P. Fiorina, *Retrospective Voting in American National Elections* (New Haven: Yale University Press, 1981).

41. "The Candidates' Confrontation: Excerpts From the Debate," *Washington Post*, October 30, 1980, A14.

42. Fiorina, *Retrospective Voting in American National Elections*; Benjamin I. Page, *Choice and Echoes in Presidential Elections* (Chicago: University of Chicago Press, 1978).

43. CNN/Opinion Research Corporation poll, October 17–19, 2008; national poll of likely voters and ABC News/*Washington Post* poll, October 16–18, 2008; both polls accessed via http://pollingreport.com/wh08.htm.

44. Thomas R. Marshall, "Turnout and Representation: Caucuses Versus Primaries," *American Journal of Political Science* 22 (1978): 169–182; Gerald C. Wright, "Rules and the Ideological Character of Primary Electorates," in Steven S. Smith and Melanie J. Springer, eds., *Reforming the Presidential Nomination Process* (Washington, D.C.: Brookings Institution Press, 2009).

45. Barry Burden, "The Nominations: Technology, Money, and Transferable Momentum," in Michael Nelson, ed., *The Elections of 2004* (Washington, D.C.: CQ Press), 21–22.

46. Rhodes Cook, "Steps to the Nomination: Earlier Voting in 1996 Forecasts Fast and Furious Campaigns," *Congressional Quarterly Weekly*, August 19, 1995, 24487.

47. Burden, "The Nominations," 21.

48. Jack Germond and Jules W. Witcover, "Front-Loading Folly: A Dash to Decision, at a Cost in Deliberation," *Baltimore Sun*, March 22, 1996.

49. Calculated by the authors from the *Washington Post* Campaign Tracker, http://projects.washingtonpost.com/2008-presidential-candidates/tracker/.

50. Sholomo Slonim, "The Electoral College at Philadelphia," *Journal of American History* 73 (June 1986): 35.

51. Robin Kolodny and Angela Logan, "Political Consultants and the Extension of Party Goals," *PS: Political Science & Politics* (June 1998): 155–159.

52. Patrick Sellers, "Strategy and Background in Congressional Campaigns," *American Political Science Review* 92 (March 1998): 159–172.

53. Ruth Shalit, "The Oppo Boom," *New Republic,* January 3, 1994, 16–21; Adam Nagourney, "Researching the Enemy: An Old Political Tool Resurfaces in a New Election," *New York Times,* April 3, 1996, D20.

54. For other examples, see John Petrocik, "Issue Ownership in Presidential Elections, With a 1980 Case Study," *American Journal of Political Science* 40 (August 1996): 825–850.

55. David B. Holian, "He's Stealing My Issues! Clinton's Crime Rhetoric and the Dynamics of Issue Ownership," *Political Behavior* 26 (2004): 95–124.

56. Kathleen Hall Jamieson, "Shooting to Win; Do Attack Ads Work? You Bet—and That's Not All Bad," *Washington Post,* September 26, 2004, B1.

57. Wisconsin Advertising Project, "Facts About Tone of Presidential Advertising Campaign From the Wisconsin Advertising Project," press release, October, 16, 2008, http://wiscadproject.wisc.edu/wiscads_release_101608.pdf.

58. Shanto Iyengar and Donald Kinder, *News That Matters: Television and American Opinion* (Chicago: University of Chicago Press, 1987); James N. Druckman, "Priming the Vote: Campaign Effects in a U.S. Senate Election," *Political Psychology* 25 (4): 577–594.

59. Thomas Patterson, *Out of Order* (New York: Knopf, 1993); Fallows, 45–64.

60. Elihu Katz and Jacob Feldman, "The Debates in Light of Research," in Sidney Kraus, ed., *The Great Debates* (Bloomington: Indiana University Press, 1962), 173–223.

61. Thomas Holbrook, "Campaigns, National Conditions, and U.S. Presidential Elections," *American Journal of Political Science* 38 (1994): 986–992; John Geer, "The Effects of Presidential Debates on the Electorate's Preferences for Candidates," *American Politics Quarterly* 16 (1988): 486–501; David Lanoue, "The 'Turning Point': Viewers' Reactions to the Second 1988 Presidential Debate," *American Politics Quarterly* 19 (1991): 80–89.

62. David Lanoue, "One That Made a Difference: Cognitive Consistency, Political Knowledge, and the 1980 Presidential Debate," *Public Opinion Quarterly* 56 (summer 1992): 168–184; Carol Winkler and Catherine Black, "Assessing the 1992 Presidential and Vice Presidential Debates: The Public Rationale," *Argumentation and Advocacy* 30 (fall 1993): 77–87; Lori McKinnon, John Tedesco, and Lynda Kaid, "The Third 1992 Presidential Debate: Channel and Commentary Effects," *Argumentation and Advocacy* 30 (fall 1993): 106–118; Mike Yawn, Kevin Ellsworth, and Kim Fridkin Kahn, "How a Presidential Primary Debate

Changed Attitudes of Audience Members," *Political Behavior* 20 (July 1998): 155–164; Annenberg Public Policy Center, "Voters Learned Positions on Issues Since Presidential Debates," NAES04 National Annenberg Election Survey, 2005, www.naes04.0rg.

63. Scott Keeter, "Public Opinion and the Election," in Gerald Pomper, ed., *The Election of 1996* (Chatham, N.J.: Chatham House, 1997), 127; drawn from polls done by the Pew Research Center and the Times Mirror Center.

64. OpenSecrets.org, "Banking on Becoming President" and "U.S. Election Will Cost $5.3 Billion, Center for Responsive Politics Predicts," www.opensecrets.org/pres08/index.php.

65. Federal Election Commission, "Chapter Two: Presidential Public Funding," 2005, www .fec.gov/info/arch2.htm.

66. Federal Election Commission, "Contribution Limits Chart 2007–08," www.fec.gov/pages/ brochures/contriblimits.shtml.

67. Susan Glasser, "Court's Ruling in Colorado Case May Reshape Campaign Finance; Limits on Political Parties' 'Hard Money' Spending Nullified," *Washington Post*, March 28, 1999, A6; *FEC v. Colorado Republican Federal Campaign Committee*, 121 S. Ct. 2351, 2371 (2001).

68. 558 U.S. 50 (2010).

69. "How Corporate Money Will Reshape Politics: Restoring Free Speech in Elections," *New York Times*, January 21, 2010, http://roomfordebate.blogs.nytimes.com/2010/01/21/ how-corporate-money-will-reshape-politics.

70. "The Court's Blow to Democracy," *New York Times*, January 21, 2010; Warren Richey, "Supreme Court: Campaign-Finance Limits Violate Free Speech," *Christian Science Monitor*, January 21, 2010; John Samples and Ilya Shapiro, "Supreme Court: Free Speech for All," *Washington Examiner*, January 21, 2010.

71. Les Blumenthal, "Down to the Wire; Canvassers Set a Frenetic Pace to Get Out the Vote," *Sacramento Bee*, October 25, 2004, A1.

72. Blumenthal, "Down to the Wire."

73. Marjorie Hershey, "The Constructed Explanation: Interpreting Election Results in the 1984 Presidential Race," *Journal of Politics* 54 (November 1992): 943–976.

74. George Stephanopolulos, "It's a Whole Different Game," *George's Bottom Line*, http:// blogs.abcnews.com/george/2008/10/its-a-whole-dif.html.

75. Marjorie Hershey, "The Constructed Explanation: Interpreting Election Results in the 1984 Presidential Race," *Journal of Politics* 54 (November 1992): 943–976.

76. Bernard Berelson, Paul Lazarsfeld, and William N. McPhee, *Voting* (Chicago: University of Chicago Press, 1954), ch. 10.

77. Sidney Verba, Kay Lehman Schlozman, Henry Brady, and Norman H. Nie, "Race, Ethnicity and Political Resources: Participation in the United States," *British Journal of Political Science* 23 (1993): 453–497.

78. Katrina vanden Heuvel, "Citizens United Aftershocks," *Washington Post*, August 25, 2010, www.washingtonpost.com/wp-dyn/content/article/2010/08/24/AR2010082405642 .html?hpid=opinionsbox1.

79. Chris Good, "Citizens United Decision: Republicans Like It, Liberals Don't," *The Atlantic*, January 21, 2010, www.theatlantic.com/politics/archive/2010/01/citizens-united-decision-republicans-like-it-liberals-dont/33935/.

Chapter 13

1. Frank Ahrens, "The Accelerating Decline of Newspapers," *Washington Post*, October 27, 2009, www.washingtonpost.com/wp-dyn/content/article/2009/10/26/AR200910260 3272.html.

2. Richard Perez-Pena, "U.S. Newspaper Circulation Falls 10%," *New York Times*, October 26, 2009, www.nytimes.com/2009/10/27/business/media/27audit.html?scp=1&sq=Audit Bureau 0f Circulations&st=cse.

3. Newspaper Death Watch, http://newspaperdeathwatch.com.
4. T. J. Sullivan, "Newspapers Don't Matter," *LA Observed,* December 15, 2008, www.laobserved.com/intell/2008/12/newspapers_dont_matter.php.
5. David Lieberman, "Extra! Extra! Are Newspapers Dying?" *USA Today,* March 18, 2009, www.usatoday.com/printedition/money/20090318/newspapers18_cv.art.htm.
6. Thomas Jefferson to Edward Carrington, 1787, ME 6:57, Thomas Jefferson on Politics and Government, http://etext.virginia.edu/jefferson/quotations/jeff1600.htm.
7. Pew Research Center, "Audience Segments in a Changing News Environment: Key News Audiences Now Blend Online and Traditional Sources," Pew Research Center Biennial News Consumption Survey, August 17, 2008, p. 31, http://people-press.org/reports/pdf/444.pdf.
8. Ibid., 7, 21.
9. Ibid., 3–5.
10. Pew Research Center for the People and the Press, "The Times Mirror News Interest Index: 1989–1995," www.people-press.org.
11. Pew Research Center, "Audience Segments in a Changing News Environment," 44.
12. Ben H. Bagdikian, *The Media Monopoly,* 5th ed. (Boston: Beacon Press, 1997), 203.
13. Philip Weiss, "A Guy Named Craig: How a Schlumpy IBM Refugee Found You Your Apartment, Your Boyfriend, Your New Couch, Your Afternoon Sex Partner—and Now Finds Himself Killing Your Newspaper," *New York Magazine,* January 8, 2006, http://nymag.com/nymetro/news/media/internet/15500/.
14. Richard Davis, *The Press and American Politics: The New Mediator* (Upper Saddle River, N.J.: Prentice Hall, 1996), 60.
15. Ibid., 67.
16. Harold W. Stanley and Richard G. Niemi, *Vital Statistics on American Politics–1997* (Washington, D.C.: Congressional Quarterly Press, 1998), 47.
17. See, for example, Dana Davis Rehm, "Why Can't NPR Staff Go to 'Rally to Restore Sanity' or 'March to Keep Fear Alive?'" October 13, 2010, www.npr.org/blogs/thisisnpr/2010/10/13/130549777/why-can-t-npr-staff-go-to-stewart-s-rally-to-restore-sanity-or-colbert-s-march-to-keep-fear-alive.
18. Pew Internet, "Home Broadband 2010," August 11, 2010, www.pewinternet.org/Press-Releases/2010/Home-Broadband-2010.aspx; "Mobile Access 2010," July 7, 2010, www.pewinternet.org/Press-Releases/2010/Mobile-Access-2010.aspx.
19. Pew Research Center, "The New News Landscape: Rise of the Internet," March 1, 2010, http://pewresearch.org/pubs/1508/internet-cell-phone-users-news-social-experience.
20. Robert Marquand, "Hate Groups Market to the Mainstream," *Christian Science Monitor,* March 6, 1998, 4.
21. Davis, *The Press and American Politics,* 27.
22. Michael Emery and Edwin Emery, *The Press and America* (Upper Saddle River, N.J.: Prentice Hall, 1988), 115.
23. David Broder, *Behind the Front Page* (New York: Simon & Schuster, 1987), 134–135.
24. Bagdikian, *The Media Monopoly,* xv.
25. Ibid., ix
26. Robert Entman, *Democracy Without Citizens* (New York: Oxford University Press, 1989), 110–111.
27. Walter Goodman, "Where's Edward R. Murrow When You Need Him?" *New York Times,* December 30, 1997, E2.
28. Mark Crispin Miller, "Free the Media," *Nation,* June 3, 1996, 9.
29. Neil King Jr. and Louise Radnofsky, "News Corp. Gives $1 Million to GOP," *Wall Street Journal* online, August 18, 2010, http://online.wsj.com/article/SB20001424052748703824304575435922310302654.html.
30. Bagdikian, *The Media Monopoly,* 217.
31. David Armstrong, "Alternative, Inc.," *In These Times,* August 21, 1995, 14–18.

32. Jeff Gremillion, "Showdown at Generation Gap," *Columbia Journalism Review* (July–August 1995): 34–38.
33. Pew Research Center, "Audience Segments in a Changing News Environment," 26.
34. Ibid., 61–62.
35. Doris Graber, *Mass Media and American Politics,* 5th ed. (Washington, D.C.: Congressional Quarterly Press, 1997), 62.
36. Federal Trade Commission, "Broadband and Connectivity Competition Policy," June 2007, www.ftc.gov/reports/broadband/v070000report.pdf.
37. "Democracy and the Web," editorial, *New York Times,* May 19, 2008, www.nytimes.com.
38. Graber, *Mass Media and American Politics,* 95–96.
39. William Schneider and I. A. Lewis, "Views on the News," *Public Opinion Quarterly* (August–September 1985): 6.
40. David H. Weaver and G. Cleveland Wilhoit, *The American Journalist in the 1990s* (Mahwah, N.J.: Erlbaum Associates, 1996), 15–19.
41. Dave D'Alessio and Mike Allen, "Media Bias in Presidential Elections: A Meta-Analysis," *Journal of Communication* (autumn 2000): 133–156.
42. Mark Hertsgaard, *On Bended Knee: The Press and the Reagan Presidency* (New York: Farrar, Straus & Giroux, 1988), 3.
43. Greg Mitchell and Dexter Hill, "Final Friday Tally of Newspaper Endorsements—Obama in Landslide, at 287 to 159," *Editor and Publisher,* November 7, 2008, www.editorandpublisher.com.
44. William P. Eveland Jr. and Dhavan V. Shah, "The Impact of Individual and Interpersonal Factors on Perceived News Media Bias," *Political Psychology* (2003): 101.
45. Pew Research Center, "Audience Segments in a Changing News Environment," 56.
46. Kathleen Hall Jamieson and Joseph N. Cappella, "Preface," in *Echo Chamber: Rush Limbaugh and the Conservative Media Elite* (New York: Oxford University Press, 2008).
47. Michael Calderone, "How Dems Grew to Hate the Liberal Media," August 24, 2008, www.politico.com.
48. Jamieson and Cappella, "Preface."
49. Broder, *Behind the Front Page,* 148.
50. Dom Bonafede, "Crossing Over," *National Journal,* January 14, 1989, 102; Michael Kelly, "David Gergen, Master of the Game," *New York Times Magazine,* October 31, 1993, 64ff.; Jonathan Alter, "Lost in the Big Blur," *Newsweek,* June 9, 1997, 43.
51. Shanto Iyengar, *Is Anyone Responsible?* (Chicago: University of Chicago Press, 1991), 2.
52. Shanto Iyengar and Donald R. Kinder, *News That Matters* (Chicago: University of Chicago Press, 1987).
53. Ibid.
54. Benjamin I. Page, Robert Y. Shapiro, and Glenn R. Dempsey, "What Moves Public Opinion?" *American Political Science Review* (March 1987): 23–43. The term "professional communicator" is used by Benjamin Page, *Who Deliberates? Mass Media in Modern Democracy* (Chicago: University of Chicago Press, 1996), 106–109.
55. Iyengar and Kinder, *News That Matters,* 93.
56. W. Russell Neuman, Marion R. Just, and Ann N. Crigler, *Common Knowledge: News and the Construction of Political Meaning* (Chicago: University of Chicago Press, 1996), 106–119.
57. James Fallows, "Why Americans Hate the Media," *Atlantic Monthly,* February 1996, 16, web version.
58. Center for Media and Democracy, "Sound Bites Get Shorter," *O'Dwyer's PR Newsletter,* November 11, 2000, www.prewatch.org/node/384.
59. Thomas E. Patterson, *Out of Order* (New York: Vintage Books, 1994), 74.
60. Larry J. Sabato, *Feeding Frenzy: How Attack Journalism Has Transformed American Politics* (New York: Free Press, 1991), 6.
61. Patterson, *Out of Order,* 245.

62. Ibid., 23.
63. Judith Valente, "Do You Believe What Newspeople Tell You?" *Parade Magazine,* March 2, 1997, 4.
64. S. Robert Lichter and Richard E. Noyes, *Good Intentions Make Bad News: Why Americans Hate Campaign Journalism* (Lanham, Md.: Rowman and Littlefield, 1995), xix.
65. Walter Cronkite, "Reporting Political Campaigns: A Reporter's View," in Doris Graber, Denis McQuail, and Pippa Norris, eds., *The Politics of News, The News of Politics* (Washington, D.C.: Congressional Quarterly Press, 1998), 57–69.
66. Joe Klein, "The Perils of the Permanent Campaign," *Time,* October 30, 2005.
67. Scott McClellan, *What Happened: Inside the Bush White House and Washington's Culture of Deception* (New York: Public Affairs, 2008).
68. Stephen Hess, *News and Newsmaking* (Washington, D.C.: Brookings Institution, 1996), 68–90.
69. Dana Milbank, "Bush Courts Regional Media," *Washington Post,* October 14, 2003, A4.
70. Anne Kornblut, "Administration Is Warned About Its Publicity Videos," *New York Times,* February 19, 2005, 11.
71. David Barstow and Robin Stein, "Under Bush, a New Age of Prepackaged News," *New York Times,* March 13, 2005, 1.
72. Johanna Neuman, "An Identity Crisis Unfolds in a Not-So-Elite Press Corps," *Los Angeles Times,* February 25, 2005, 18.
73. Jack Shafer, "The Propaganda President: George W. Bush Does His Best Kim Jong-il," *Slate,* February 3, 2005, www.slate.msn.com/id/2113052.
74. Jeff Zeleny, "Robert Gibbs," *New York Times,* November 6, 2008.
75. Stephen Ansolabehere, Roy Beyr, and Shanto Iyengar, *The Media Game: American Politics in the Television Age* (New York: Macmillan, 1993); Iyengar, *Is Anyone Responsible?*
76. Clay Shirky, "Newspapers and Thinking the Unthinkable," March 13, 2009, www.shirky.com/weblog/2009/03/newspapers-and-thinking-the-unthinkable/.
77. Ibid.
78. Dan Gillmor, *We the Media: Grassroots Journalism By the People, For the People* (Sebastopol, Calif.: O'Reilly Media, 2008).
79. Andrew Sullivan, "A Blogger Manifesto: Why Online Weblogs Are One Future for Journalism," *The Sunday Times of London,* February 24, 2002.
80. Andrew Sullivan, "Happy 4th," *The Daily Dish,* July 4, 2010, http://andrewsullivan.theatlantic.com/the_daily_dish/2010/07/happy-4th.html.
81. Clay Shirky, "Newspapers and Thinking the Unthinkable."

Chapter 14

1. Barbara Hagenbaugh, "Oil Drilling Up, But Impact May Be Slight," *USA Today,* May 31, 2005, 4B.
2. Energy Information Administration, "Data on US Field Production and Imports January and February 2008," http://tonto.eia.doe.gov/dnav/pet/pet_sum_crdsnd_adc_mbbl_m.htm; Mark Clayton, "Can Hybrids Save US From Foreign Oil?" *Christian Science Monitor,* May 19, 2005, www. csmonitor.com/2005/0519/p14s01-sten.html.
3. "Vote on Arctic Drilling Heads in Wrong Direction," *San Antonio Express-News,* March 18, 2005, 6B.
4. Jeffrey M. Jones, "Americans Divided on Increased Coastal Oil Drilling," Gallup.com, May 28, 2010, www.gallup.com/poll/137885/americans-divided-increased-coastal-oil-drilling.aspx.
5. The Pew Research Center or the People and the Press, "As Gas Prices Pinch, Support for Energy Exploration Rises," July 1, 2008, http://people-press.org/report/433/gas-prices.
6. Courtney Mabeus, "Boiling Oil: The Money Behind the Debate Over Drilling in the Arctic National Wildlife Refuge," *Capital Eye,* March 17, 2005, www.capitaleye.org/inside.asp?ID=160.

7. Peter Bachrach and Morton S. Baratz, "The Two Faces of Power," *American Political Science Review* 56 (December 1962): 948.
8. This definition of public policy is based on the one offered by James E. Anderson, *Public Policymaking: An Introduction* (Boston: Houghton Mifflin, 1997), 9.
9. Theodore Lowi, "American Business, Public Policy Case Studies, and Political Theory," *World Politics* (July 1964): 677–715.
10. For a discussion of the effect of lawsuits on air emission standards, see Robert Percival, Alan Miller, Christopher Schroeder, and James Leape, *Environmental Regulation: Law, Science and Policy*, 2nd ed. (Boston: Little, Brown, 1996).
11. Social Security Administration, "A Summary of the 2005 Annual Reports," www.ssa.gov/OACT/TRSUM/trsummary.html.
12. Robert J. Shiller, "American Casino: The Promise and Perils of Bush's 'Ownership Society.'" *Atlantic Monthly*, March 2005, 33–34; "Insuring America," *New Republic,* February 28, 2005, 9; Joel Havemann, "One Person's Fix Is Another's Flaw," *Los Angeles Times,* May 1, 2005, A22; "The Risks in Personal Accounts," *Washington Post,* February 20, 2005, B6.
13. U.S. Census Bureau, *Statistical Brief: Mothers Who Receive AFDC Payments: Fertility and Socioeconomic Characteristics* (Washington, D.C.: U.S. Department of Commerce, Economics and Statistics Administration, March 1995).
14. Center for Law and Social Policy, *Implementing the TANF Changes in the Deficit Reduction Act,* 2nd ed., www.cbpp.org/2–9–07tanf.htm.
15. Peter Edelman, "The True Purpose of Welfare Reform," *New York Times,* May 29, 2002, A21.
16. Jason DeParle, "Slumping Economy Tests System Tied to Jobs," *New York Times,* May 1, 2009, www.nytimes.com/2009/06/01/us/politics/01poverty.html.
17. U.S. Drug Administration, "Food Assistance Landscape, FY 2009; Annual Report, 2010," www.ers.usda.gov/Publications/EIB6–7/EIB6–7.pdf.
18. Ibid.
19. U.S. Department of Health and Human Services, "Head Start Program Fact Sheet," 2005, www.acf.hhs.gov/programs/hsb/research/2005.htm.
20. Pew Research Center, January 2007 poll, www.publicagenda.org/issues/pcc_detail.cfm?issue_type=healthcare&list=1.
21. U.S. Census Bureau, "Income, Poverty, and Health Insurance Coverage in the United States: 2005," www.census.gov/prod/2007pubs/p60–233.pdf.
22. Social Security Administration, "A Summary of the 2005 Annual Reports," www.ssa.gov/OACT/TRSUM/trsummary.html.
23. Murray Light, "Medicare Reform Being Neglected," *Buffalo News,* March 6, 2005, H3.
24. Joel Havemann and Maura Reynolds, "He Pitched, No One Swung," *Los Angeles Times,* April 30, 2005, A14.
25. Daniel Weintraub, "A Possible Antidote to Rising Health Care Costs," *Sacramento Bee,* November 23, 2004, B7; Stephanie Armour and Julie Appleby, "As Health Care Costs Rise, Workers Shoulder Burden," *USA Today,* October 21, 2003, C1.
26. Bob Kemper, "Campaign at Full Bore; Bush Says Kerry Health Care Plan Too Expensive," *Atlanta Journal-Constitution,* October 22, 2004, 4C.
27. Henry J. Kaiser Family Foundation, "Health Care and the 2004 Elections," September 2004, www.kff.org/kaiserpolls/7167.cfm.
28. "Obama's Health Care Speech," CBS News, September 9, 2009, www.cbsnews.com/stories/2009/09/09/politics/main5299229.shtml.
29. "Focus on Health Reform: Summary of New Health Reform Law," Kaiser Family Foundation, www.kff.org/healthreform/upload/8061.pdf.
30. Michael Crowley, "Will Health Reform Be a Key Factor in Midterms?" *Time,* August 20, 2010, www.time.com/time/politics/article/0,8599,2011907,00.html.
31. Robert McIntyre, "Your Federal Tax Dollars at Work," *American Prospect,* May 20, 2002.

32. George Hager, "End of Deficit Era Marks Beginning of Battle Over Surpluses," *Washington Post,* September 30, 1998, C10.

33. "2008 U.S. Budget Deficit Bleeding Red Ink; First 4 Months of Budget Year at Nearly $88B, Double Amount Recorded for Same 2007 Period," CBS News, February 12, 2008, www.cbsnews.com/stories/2008/02/12/national/main3822385.shtml.

34. Tobin Harshaw, "Will TARP Turn to Gold?" *New York Times,* October 1, 2010.

35. Paul Krugman, "That 30's Show," *New York Times,* July 2, 2009, www.nytimes.com/2009/07/03/opinion/03krugman.html.

36. Lori Montgomery, "Report Gives Stimulus Package High Marks," *Washington Post,* October 1, 2010.

37. Ibid.

38. David Leonhardt, "Imagining a Deficit Plan from Republicans," *New York Times,* September 28, 2010, www.nytimes.com/2010/09/29/business/economy/291eonhardt.html?scp=1&sq=REpublican%20pledge&st=cse.

39. Al Hunt, "Democrats Relish Battle Over High-Income Tax Cuts," *Bloomberg News,* August 1, 2010, www.bloomberg.com/news/2010–08–01/democrats-relish-fight-over-big-income-tax-cuts-commentary-by-albert-hunt.html.

40. Pew Research Center for the People and the Press, "Deficit Concerns Rise, But Solutions Are Elusive," March 10, 2010, http://pewresearch.org/pubs/1519/deficit-concerns-rise-little-support-for-spending-cuts.

41. Office of Management and Budget, *Budget of the United States Government, Fiscal Year 2009, Historical Tables,* "Table 1.1," www.whitehouse.gov/omb/budget/fy2009/pdf/hist.pdf.

42. David Leonhardt, "Can't Grasp Credit Crisis? Join the Club," *New York Times,* March 19, 2008, A1; Robert Gavin, "Frank Urges Overhaul of Business Regulations," *Boston Globe,* March 21, 2008, C3; Paul Davidson, "Mortgage Brokers Fall on Tough Times; Many Now Victims of a Crisis They May Have Played Role In," *USA Today,* August 31, 2007, 1B; Joe Nocera, "On Wall St., A Problem of Denial," *New York Times,* September 15, 2008, www.nytimes.com.

43. Michael Maynard, "Navigating Turbulent Skies," *New York Times,* October 10, 2004, sect. 5, 4; Matthew L. Wald, "Advances in Airplanes Are Mostly Invisible," *New York Times,* May 18, 2003, sect. 5, 3; Agis Salpukas, "Future of Airline Deregulation," *New York Times,* May 8, 1982, sect. 2, 29; Leslie Wayne, "The Airlines Stacked Up in Red Ink," *New York Times,* February 14, 1982, sect. 3, 1.

44. Andrew Leonard, "The Dodd-Frank Bank Reform Bill: A Deeply Flawed Success," Salon, June 25, 2010, www.salon.com/technology/how_the_world_works/2010/06/25/the_dodd_frank_bank_reform_bill.

45. Damian Paletta, "U.S. Lawmakers Reach Accord on New Finance Rules," *Wall Street Journal,* June 25, 2010, http://online.wsj.com/article/SB10001424052748703615104575328020013164184.html?mod=djemalertNEWS.

46. Randall B. Ripley and Grace A. Franklin, *Congress, the Bureaucracy, and Public Policy,* 5th ed. (Belmont, Calif.: Wadsworth, 1991).

47. See Charles F. Hermann, *Crises in Foreign Policy* (Indianapolis: Bobbs-Merrill, 1969); Michael Brecher, "A Theoretical Approach to International Crisis Behavior," *Jerusalem Journal of International Relations* 3, nos. 2–3 (1978): 5–24.

48. See John Lewis Gaddis, *Strategies of Containment* (New York: Oxford University Press, 1982).

49. John Lewis Gaddis, *The United States and the End of the Cold War* (New York: Oxford University Press, 1992); Richard Ned Lebow and Thomas Risse-Kappen, eds., *International Relations Theory and the End of the Cold War* (New York: Columbia University Press, 1995).

50. See, for example, Richard N. Haass, *The Reluctant Sheriff: The United States After the Cold War* (New York: Council on Foreign Relations Press, 1997).

51. See Graham Allison, *Essence of Decision* (New York: HarperCollins, 1971); Helen V. Milner, *Interest, Institutions, and Information: Domestic Politics and International Relations* (Princeton: Princeton University Press, 1997).
52. See "X" (George F. Kennan), "The Sources of Soviet Conduct," *Foreign Affairs,* July 25, 1947, 566–582.
53. See, for example, Michael H. Shuman, "Dateline Main Street: Local Foreign Policies," *Foreign Policy* 65 (winter 1986/87): 154–174.
54. Robert S. Erikson, Gerald C. Wright, and John P. McIver, *Statehouse Democracy* (New York: Cambridge University Press, 1993).
55. James A. Stimson, Michael B. MacKuen, and Robert S. Erikson, *American Political Science Review* 89 (1995): 543–565.
56. Carl Hulse and Steven Lee Myers, "Congress Votes to Stop Stockpiling Oil," *New York Times,* May 14, 2008, www.nytimes.com/2008/05/14/business/140il.html?scp=1&sq=Arctic+National+Wildlife+Refuge&st=nyt.
57. The city of Kaktovik's web page, www.kaktovik.com.
58. Julie Cart and Ralph Vartabedian, "Refuge Has Long Been a Major Environmental Battleground," *Los Angeles Times,* March 17, 2005.
59. Paul Mirengoff, "Trading Places: Have Republicans Replaced Democrats as the Party of Pragmatism?" *Daily Standard,* March 21, 2005.
60. Jonah Goldberg, "Ugh, Wilderness!" *National Review Online,* March 18, 2005.
61. Cart and Vartabedian.
62. Michael T. Klare, "Arctic Drilling Is No Energy Answer," *Los Angeles Times,* April 3, 2005, M5.

Glossary

accommodationists supporters of government nonpreferential accommodation of religion (4)

accountability the principle that bureaucratic employees should be answerable for their performance to supervisors, all the way up the chain of command (8)

administrative law law established by the bureaucracy, on behalf of Congress (9)

advanced industrial democracy a system in which a democratic government allows citizens a considerable amount of personal freedom and maintains a free-market (though still usually regulated) economy (1)

affirmative action a policy of creating opportunities for members of certain groups as a substantive remedy for past discrimination (5)

agency capture process whereby regulatory agencies come to be protective of and influenced by the industries they were established to regulate (8)

allocative representation congressional work to secure projects, services, and funds for the represented district (6)

amendability the provision for the Constitution to be changed, so as to adapt to new circumstances (2)

amicus curiae briefs "friend of the court" documents filed by interested parties to encourage the court to grant or deny certiorari or to urge it to decide a case in a particular way (9)

analysis understanding how something works by breaking it down into its component parts (1)

anarchy the absence of government and laws (1)

Anti-Federalists advocates of states' rights who opposed the Constitution (2)

appeal a rehearing of a case because the losing party in the original trial argues that a point of law was not applied properly (9)

appellate jurisdiction the authority of a court to review decisions made by lower courts (9)

Articles of Confederation the first constitution of the United States (1777) creating an association of states with weak central government (2)

astroturf lobbying indirect lobbying efforts that manipulate or create public sentiment, "astroturf" being artificial grassroots (11)

authoritarian capitalism a system in which the state allows people economic freedom, but maintains stringent social regulations to limit noneconomic behavior (1)

authoritarian governments systems in which the state holds all power over the social order (1)

authority power that is recognized as legitimate (1)

balanced budget a budget in which expenditures equal revenues (14)

benchmark poll initial poll on a candidate and issues on which campaign strategy is based and against which later polls are compared (10)

bicameral legislature legislature with two chambers (2, 6)

Bill of Rights a summary of citizen rights guaranteed and protected by a government; added to the Constitution as its first ten amendments in order to achieve ratification (2)

bills of attainder laws under which specific persons or groups are detained and sentenced without trial (4)

black codes a series of laws in the post–Civil War South designed to restrict the rights of former slaves before the passage of the Fourteenth and Fifteenth Amendments (5)

block grant federal funds provided for a broad purpose, unrestricted by detailed requirements and regulations (3)

blogs web logs, or online journals, that can cover any topic, including political analysis (13)

boycotts refusals to buy certain goods or services as a way to protest policy or force political reform (5)

bureaucracy an organization characterized by hierarchical structure, worker specialization, explicit rules, and advancement by merit (8)

bureaucratic culture the accepted values and procedures of an organization (8)

bureaucratic discretion bureaucrats' use of their own judgment in interpreting and carrying out the laws of Congress (8)

Bush Doctrine policy that supports preemptive attacks as a legitimate tactic in the U.S. war on state-sponsored terrorism (14)

busing achieving racial balance by transporting students to schools across neighborhood boundaries (5)

cabinet a presidential advisory group selected by the president, made up of the vice president, the heads of the federal executive departments, and other high officials to whom the president elects to give cabinet status (7)

capital gains tax a tax levied on the returns that people earn from capital investments, like the profits from the sale of stocks or a home (14)

capitalist economy an economic system in which the market determines production, distribution, and price decisions and property is privately owned (1)

casework legislative work on behalf of individual constituents to solve their problems with government agencies and programs (6)

categorical grant federal funds provided for a specific purpose, restricted by detailed instructions, regulations, and compliance standards (3)

Central Intelligence Agency (CIA) the government organization that oversees foreign intelligence-gathering and related classified activities (14)

checks and balances the principle that allows each branch of government to exercise some form of control over the others (2)

chief administrator the president's executive role as the head of federal agencies and the person responsible for the implementation of national policy (7)

chief foreign policy maker the president's executive role as the primary shaper of relations with other nations (7)

chief of staff the person who oversees the operations of all White House staff and controls access to the president (7)

citizen advisory council a citizen group that considers the policy decisions of an agency; a way to make the bureaucracy responsive to the general public (8)

citizens members of a political community having both rights and responsibilities (1)

civil laws laws regulating interactions between individuals; violation of a civil law is called a tort (9)

civil liberties individual freedoms guaranteed to the people primarily by the Bill of Rights (4)

civil rights citizenship rights guaranteed to the people (primarily in the Thirteenth, Fourteenth, Fifteenth, Nineteenth, and Twenty-sixth Amendments) and protected by the government (4, 5)

civil service nonmilitary employees of the government who are appointed through the merit system (8)

clear and present danger test rule used by the courts that allows language to be regulated only if it presents an immediate and urgent danger (4)

clientele groups groups of citizens whose interests are affected by an agency or a department and who work to influence its policies (8)

closed primaries primary elections in which only registered party members may vote (12)

cloture a vote to end a Senate filibuster; requires a three-fifths majority, or sixty votes (6)

coattail effect the added votes received by congressional candidates of a winning presidential party (6)

Cold War the half-century of competition and conflict after World War II between the United States and the Soviet Union (and their allies) (14)

collective good a good or service that, by its very nature, cannot be denied to anyone who wants to consume it (11)

commander-in-chief the president's role as the top officer of the country's military establishment (7)

commercial bias the tendency of the media to make coverage and programming decisions based on what will attract a large audience and maximize profits (13)

common law tradition a legal system based on the accumulated rulings of judges over time, applied uniformly—judge-made law (9)

communist democracy a utopian system in which property is communally owned and all decisions are made democratically (1)

communitarians those who favor a strong substantive government role in the economy and the social order in order to realize their vision of a community of equals (1)

compelling state interest a fundamental state purpose, which must be shown before the law can limit some freedoms or treat some groups of people differently (4)

concurrent powers powers that are shared by both the federal and state governments (3)

concurring opinions documents written by justices expressing agreement with the majority ruling but describing different or additional reasons for the ruling (9)

confederal systems governments in which local units hold all the power (3)

confederation a government in which independent states unite for common purpose, but retain their own sovereignty (2)

conference committees temporary committees formed to reconcile differences in House and Senate versions of a bill (6)

congressional oversight efforts by Congress, especially through committees, to monitor agency rule making, enforcement, and implementation of congressional policies (6, 8)

conservatives people who generally favor limited government and are cautious about change (1)

constituency the voters in a state or district (6)

constitution the rules that establish a government (2)

Constitutional Convention the assembly of fifty-five delegates in the summer of 1787 to recast the Articles of Confederation; the result was the U.S. Constitution (2)

constitutional law law stated in the Constitution or in the body of judicial decisions about the meaning of the Constitution handed down in the courts (9)

consumption tax a plan in which people are taxed not on what they earn but on what they spend (14)

containment the U.S. Cold War policy of preventing the spread of communism (14)

cooperative federalism the federal system under which the national and state governments share responsibilities for most domestic policy areas (3)

Council of Economic Advisors organization within the EOP that advises the president on economic matters (7)

courts institutions that sit as neutral third parties to resolve conflicts according to the law (9)

criminal laws laws prohibiting behavior the government has determined to be harmful to society; violation of a criminal law is called a crime (9)

crisis policy foreign policy, usually made quickly and secretly, that responds to an emergency threat (14)

critical thinking analysis and evaluation of ideas and arguments based on reason and evidence (1)

cycle effect the predictable rise and fall of a president's popularity at different stages of a term in office (7)

dealignment a trend among voters to identify themselves as independents rather than as members of a major party (11)

Declaration of Independence the political document that dissolved the colonial ties between the United States and Britain (2)

de facto discrimination discrimination that is the result not of law but rather of tradition and habit (5)

deficits shortfalls in the budget due to the government spending more in a year than it takes in (14)

de jure discrimination discrimination arising from or supported by the law (5)

democracy government that vests power in the people (1)

Department of Defense the executive department charged with managing the country's military personnel, equipment, and operations (14)

Department of State the executive department charged with managing foreign affairs (14)

departments one of the major subdivisions of the federal government, represented in the president's cabinet (8)

deregulation the elimination of regulations in order to improve economic efficiency (14)

devolution the transfer of powers and responsibilities from the federal government to the states (3)

direct lobbying direct interaction with public officials for the purpose of influencing policy decisions (11)

director of national intelligence overseer and coordinator of the activities of the many agencies involved in the production and dissemination of intelligence information in the U.S. government, as well as the president's main intelligence adviser (14)

dissenting opinions documents written by justices expressing disagreement with the majority ruling (9)

distributive policies policies funded by the whole taxpayer base that address the needs of particular groups (14)

divided government political rule split between two parties: one controlling the White House and the other controlling one or both houses of Congress (7)

dual federalism the federal system under which the national and state governments are responsible for separate policy areas (3)

due process of law guarantee that laws will be fair and reasonable and that citizens suspected of breaking the law will be treated fairly (4)

economic conservatives those who favor a strictly procedural government role in the economy and the social order (1)

economic interest groups groups that organize to influence government policy for the economic benefit of their members (11)

economic liberals those who favor an expanded government role in the economy but a limited role in the social order (1)

economic policy all the different strategies that government officials employ to solve economic problems (14)

economics production and distribution of a society's material resources and services (1)

electioneering the process of getting a person elected to public office (11)

Electoral College an intermediary body that elects the president (2, 12)

electoral mandate the perception that an election victory signals broad support for the winner's proposed policies (12)

elite democracy a theory of democracy that limits the citizens' role to choosing among competing leaders (1)

English-only movements efforts to make English the official language of the United States (5)

entitlement program a federal program that guarantees benefits to qualified recipients (14)

enumerated powers of Congress congressional powers specifically named in the Constitution (Article I, Section 8) (3)

equal opportunity interest groups groups that organize to promote the civil and economic rights of underrepresented or disadvantaged groups (11)

Equal Rights Amendment constitutional amendment passed by Congress but *never ratified* that would have banned discrimination on the basis of gender (5)

establishment clause the First Amendment guarantee that the government will not create and support an official state church (4)

evaluation assessing how well something works or performs according to a particular standard or yardstick (1)

exclusionary rule rule created by the Supreme Court that evidence illegally seized may not be used to obtain a conviction (4)

executive the branch of government responsible for putting laws into effect (2)

executive agreement a presidential arrangement with another country that creates foreign policy without the need for Senate approval (7)

Executive Office of the President, or EOP collection of nine organizations that help the president with policy and political objectives (7)

executive orders clarifications of congressional policy issued by the president and having the full force of law (7, 9)

exit polls election-related questions asked of voters right after they vote (10)

ex post facto laws laws that criminalize an action *after* it occurs (4)

expressive benefits selective incentives that derive from the opportunity to express values and beliefs and to be committed to a greater cause (11)

factions groups of citizens united by some common passion or interest and opposed to the rights of other citizens or to the interests of the whole community (2, 11)

fascist government an authoritarian government in which policy is made for the ultimate glory of the state (1)

federalism a political system in which power is divided between the central and regional units (2, 3)

The Federalist Papers a series of essays written in support of the Constitution to build support for its ratification (2)

Federalists supporters of the Constitution who favored a strong central government (2)

Federal Register publication containing all federal regulations and notifications of regulatory agency hearings (8)

Federal Reserve System independent commission that controls the money supply through a system of twelve federal banks (14)

feeding frenzy excessive press coverage of an embarrassing or scandalous subject (13)

fighting words speech intended to incite violence (4)

filibuster a practice of unlimited debate in the Senate in order to prevent or delay a vote on a bill (6)

fiscal policy economic policy in which government regulates the economy through its powers to tax and spend (14)

flat tax a tax system in which all people pay the same percentage of their income (14)

food stamps a program that provides assistance to the poor to help them buy food (14)

foreign policy a country's official positions, practices, and procedures for dealing with actors outside its borders (14)

framing process through which the media emphasize particular aspects of a news story, thereby influencing the public's perception of the story (13)

freedom of assembly the right of the people to gather peacefully and to petition government (4)

Freedom of Information Act (FOIA) 1966 law that allows citizens to obtain copies of most public records (8)

free exercise clause the First Amendment guarantee that citizens may freely engage in the religious activities of their choice (4)

free rider problem the difficulty groups face in recruiting when potential members can gain the benefits of the group's actions whether they join or not (11)

French and Indian War a war fought between France and England, and allied Indians, from 1754 to 1763; resulted in France's expulsion from the New World (2)

front-loading the process of scheduling presidential primaries early in the primary season (12)

front-runner the leading candidate and expected winner of a nomination or an election (12)

gatekeepers journalists and media elite who determine which news stories are covered and which are not (13)

gender gap the tendency of men and women to differ in their political views on some issues (10)

gerrymandering redistricting to benefit a particular group (6)

Gibbons v. Ogden Supreme Court ruling (1824) establishing national authority over interstate business (3)

going public a president's strategy of appealing to the public on an issue, expecting that public pressure will be brought to bear on other political actors (7)

governing activities directed toward controlling the distribution of political resources by providing executive and legislative leadership, enacting agendas, mobilizing support, and building coalitions (11)

government a system or organization for exercising authority over a body of people (1)

government corporations companies created by Congress to provide to the public a good or service that private enterprise cannot or will not profitably provide (8)

government matching funds money given by the federal government to qualified presidential candidates in the primary and general election campaigns (12)

grandfather clauses provisions exempting from voting restrictions the descendants of those able to vote in 1867 (5)

grassroots lobbying indirect lobbying efforts that spring from widespread public concern (11)

Great Compromise the constitutional solution to congressional representation: equal votes in the Senate, votes by population in the House (2)

habeas corpus the right of an accused person to be brought before a judge and informed of the charges and evidence against him or her (4)

hard money campaign funds donated directly to candidates; amounts are limited by federal election laws (12)

Hatch Act 1939 law limiting the political involvement of civil servants in order to protect them from political pressure and keep politics out of the bureaucracy (8)

head of government the political role of the president as leader of a political party and chief arbiter of who gets what resources (7)

head of state the apolitical, unifying role of the president as symbolic representative of the whole country (7)

honeymoon period the time following an election when a president's popularity is high and congressional relations are likely to be productive (7)

horse-race journalism the media's focus on the competitive aspects of politics rather than on actual policy proposals and political decisions (13)

House Rules Committee the committee that determines how and when debate on a bill will take place (6)

ideologies sets of beliefs about politics and society that help people make sense of their world (1)

immigrants citizens or subjects of one country who move to another country to live or work (1)

imminent lawless action test rule used by the courts that restricts speech only if it is aimed at producing or is likely to produce imminent lawless action (4)

incorporation Supreme Court action making the protections of the Bill of Rights applicable to the states (4)

incumbency advantage the electoral edge afforded to those already in office (6)

independent agencies government organizations independent of the departments but with a narrower policy focus (8)

independent regulatory boards and commissions government organizations that regulate various businesses, industries, or economic sectors (8)

indirect lobbying attempts to influence government policymakers by encouraging the general public to put pressure on them (11)

individualism belief that what is good for society is based on what is good for individuals (1)

inherent powers presidential powers implied but not explicitly stated in the Constitution (7)

institutions organizations in which governmental power is exercised (1)

intelligence community the agencies and bureaus responsible for obtaining and interpreting information for the government (14)

interest group an organization of individuals who share a common political goal and unite for the purpose of influencing government decisions (11)

interest rates the cost of borrowing money calculated as a percentage of the money borrowed (14)

intergovernmental organizations bodies, such as the United Nations, whose members are countries (14)

intermediate standard of review standard of review used by the Court to evaluate laws that make a quasisuspect classification (5)

interventionism a foreign policy view that the United States should actively engage in the affairs of other nations in order to try to shape events in accordance with U.S. interests (14)

invisible primary early attempts to raise money, line up campaign consultants, generate media attention, and get commitments for support even before candidates announce they are running (12)

iron triangles the phenomenon of a clientele group, congressional committee, and bureaucratic agency cooperating to make mutually beneficial policy (8)

issue advocacy ads advertisements that support issues or candidates without telling constituents how to vote (11, 12)

issue networks complex systems of relationships between groups that influence policy, including elected leaders, interest groups, specialists, consultants, and research institutes (8)

issue ownership the tendency of one party to be seen as more competent in a specific policy area (12)

isolationism a foreign policy view that nations should stay out of international political alliances and activities, and focus on domestic matters (14)

Jim Crow laws southern laws designed to circumvent the Thirteenth, Fourteenth, and Fifteenth Amendments and to deny blacks rights on bases other than race (5)

Joint Chiefs of Staff the senior military officers from four branches of the U.S. armed forces (14)

joint committees combined House-Senate committees formed to coordinate activities and expedite legislation in a certain area (6)

judicial activism view that the courts should be lawmaking, policymaking bodies (9)

judicial interpretivism a judicial approach holding that the Constitution is a living document and that judges should interpret it according to changing times and values (9)

judicial power the power to interpret laws and judge whether a law has been broken (2)

judicial restraint view that the courts should reject any active lawmaking functions and stick to judicial interpretations of the past (9)

judicial review power of the Supreme Court to rule on the constitutionality of laws (2, 9)

jurisdiction a court's authority to hear certain cases (9)

leaks confidential information secretly revealed to the press (13)

legislative agenda the slate of proposals and issues that representatives think it worthwhile to consider and act on (6)

legislative liaison executive personnel who work with members of Congress to secure their support in getting a president's legislation passed (7)

legislature the body of government that makes laws (2)

legitimate accepted as "right" or proper (1)

***Lemon* test** three-pronged rule used by the courts to determine whether the establishment clause is violated (4)

libel written defamation of character (4)

liberals people who generally favor government action and view change as progress (1)

libertarians those who favor a minimal government role in any sphere (1)

literacy tests tests requiring reading or comprehension skills as a qualification for voting (5)

lobbying interest group activities aimed at persuading policymakers to support the group's positions (11)

majority party the party with the most seats in a house of Congress (6)

Marbury v. Madison the landmark case that established the U.S. Supreme Court's power of judicial review (9)

marriage gap the tendency for married people to hold political opinions that differ from those of people who have never married (10)

mass media means of conveying information to large public audiences cheaply and efficiently (13)

material benefits selective incentives in the form of tangible rewards (11)

McCulloch v. Maryland Supreme Court ruling (1819) confirming the supremacy of national over state government (3)

means-tested programs social programs whose beneficiaries qualify by demonstrating need (14)

Medicaid a federally sponsored program that provides medical care to the poor (14)

Medicare the federal government's health insurance program for the elderly and disabled (14)

midterm loss the tendency for the presidential party to lose congressional seats in off-year elections (6)

***Miller* test** rule used by the courts in which the definition of *obscenity* must be based on local standards (4)

minimum rationality test standard of review used by the Court to evaluate laws that make a nonsuspect classification (5)

momentum the widely held public perception that a candidate is gaining electoral strength (12)

monarchy an authoritarian government with power vested in a king or queen (1)

monetary policy economic policy in which government regulates the economy by manipulating interest rates to control the money supply (14)

Motor Voter Bill legislation allowing citizens to register to vote at the same time they apply for a driver's license or other state benefit (12)

multinational corporations large companies that do business in multiple countries (14)

National Association for the Advancement of Colored People (NAACP) an interest group founded in 1910 to promote civil rights for African Americans (5)

national lawmaking the creation of policy to address the problems and needs of the entire nation (6)

National Security Council (NSC) organization within the executive office of the president that provides foreign policy advice to the president (7, 14)

naturalization the legal process of acquiring citizenship for someone who has not acquired it by birth (1)

necessary and proper clause constitutional authorization for Congress to make any law required to carry out its powers (3)

negative advertising campaign advertising that emphasizes the negative characteristics of opponents rather than one's own strengths (12)

neutral competence the principle that bureaucracy should be depoliticized by making it more professional (8)

New Jersey Plan a proposal at the Constitutional Convention that congressional representation be equal, thus favoring the small states (2)

new media high-tech outlets that have sprung up to compete with traditional newspapers, magazines, and network news (13)

news management the efforts of a politician's staff to control news about the politician (13)

nominating convention formal party gathering to choose candidates (11)

nongovernmental organizations organizations comprising individuals or interest groups from around the world focused on a special issue (14)

normative describes beliefs or values about how things should be or what people ought to do rather than what actually is. (1)

nullification declaration by a state that a federal law is void within its borders (3)

Office of Management and Budget organization within the EOP that oversees the budgets of departments and agencies (7)

oligarchy rule by a small group of elites (1)

on-line processing the ability to receive and evaluate information as events happen, allowing us to remember our evaluation even if we have forgotten the specific events that caused it (10)

open primaries primary elections in which eligible voters do not need to be registered party members (12)

opinion the written decision of the court that states the judgment of the majority (9)

opinion leaders people who know more about certain topics than we do and whose advice we trust, seek out, and follow (10)

oppo research investigation of an opponent's background for the purpose of exploiting weaknesses or undermining credibility (12)

original jurisdiction the authority of a court to hear a case first (9)

pardoning power a president's authority to release or excuse a person from the legal penalties of a crime (7)

participatory democracy a theory of democracy that holds that citizens should actively and directly control all aspects of their lives (1)

partisanship loyalty to a political cause or party (11)

party activists the "party faithful"; the rank-and-file members who actually carry out the party's electioneering efforts (11)

party base members of a political party who consistently vote for that party's candidates (11)

party bosses party leaders, usually in an urban district, who exercised tight control over electioneering and patronage (11)

party caucus local gathering of party members to choose convention delegates (12)

party eras extended periods of relative political stability in which one party tends to control both the presidency and Congress (11)

party identification voter affiliation with a political party (11)

party-in-government members of the party who have been elected to serve in government (11)

party-in-the-electorate ordinary citizens who identify with the party (11)

party machines mass-based party systems in which parties provided services and resources to voters in exchange for votes (11)

party organization the official structure that conducts the political business of parties (11)

party platform list of policy positions a party endorses and pledges its elected officials to enact (11)

party polarization greater ideological (liberal versus conservative) differences between the parties and increased ideological consensus within the parties (6)

party primary nomination of party candidates by registered party members rather than party bosses (11)

patronage system in which successful party candidates reward supporters with jobs or favors (8, 11)

Pendleton Act 1883 civil service reform that required the hiring and promoting of civil servants to be based on merit, not patronage (8)

permanent campaign the idea that governing requires a continual effort to convince the public to sign onto the program, requiring a reliance on consultants and an emphasis on politics over policy (13)

pluralist democracy a theory of democracy that holds that citizen membership in groups is the key to political power (1, 11)

pocket veto presidential authority to kill a bill submitted within ten days of the end of a legislative session by not signing it (6)

police power the ability of the government to protect its citizens and maintain social order (4)

policy entrepreneurship practice of legislators becoming experts and taking leadership roles in specific policy areas (6)

policy representation congressional work to advance the issues and ideological preferences of constituents (6)

political accountability the democratic principle that political leaders must answer to the public for their actions (13)

political action committee (PAC) the fundraising arm of an interest group (11)

political correctness the idea that language shapes behavior and therefore should be regulated to control its social effects (4)

political culture the broad pattern of ideas, beliefs, and values about citizens and government held by a population (1)

political party a group of citizens united by ideology and seeking control of government in order to promote their ideas and policies (11)

political socialization the process by which we learn our political orientations and allegiances (10)

politics who gets what, when, and how; a process of determining how power and resources are distributed in a society without recourse to violence (1)

poll taxes taxes levied as a qualification for voting (5)

popular sovereignty the concept that the citizens are the ultimate source of political power (1)

popular tyranny the unrestrained power of the people (2)

pork barrel public works projects and grants for specific districts paid for by general revenues (6)

position issues issues on which the parties differ in their perspectives and proposed solutions (12)

power the ability to get other people to do what you want (1)

power to persuade a president's ability to convince Congress, other political actors, and the public to cooperate with the administration's agenda (7)

precedent a previous decision or ruling that, in common law tradition, is binding on subsequent decisions (9)

presidential primary an election by which voters choose convention delegates committed to voting for a certain candidate (12)

presidential style image projected by the president that represents how he would like to be perceived at home and abroad (7)

presidential veto a president's authority to reject a bill passed by Congress; may be overridden only by a two-thirds majority in each house (7)

priming the way in which the media's emphasis on particular characteristics of people, events, or issues influences the public's perception of those people, events, or issues (13)

prior restraint censorship of or punishment for the expression of ideas before the ideas are printed or spoken (4)

Privacy Act of 1974 a law that gives citizens access to the government's files on them (8)

procedural due process procedural laws that protect the rights of individuals who must deal with the legal system (9)

procedural guarantees government assurance that the rules will work smoothly and treat everyone fairly, with no promise of particular outcomes (1)

procedural laws laws that establish how laws are applied and enforced—how legal proceedings take place (9)

progressive taxes taxes whose rates increase with income (14)

prospective voting basing voting decisions on well-informed opinions and consideration of the future consequences of a given vote (12)

public interest groups groups that organize to influence government to produce collective goods or services that benefit the general public (11)

public opinion the collective attitudes and beliefs of individuals on one or more issues (10)

public opinion polls scientific efforts to estimate what an entire group thinks about an issue by asking a smaller sample of the group for its opinion (10)

public policy a government plan of action to solve a problem (14)

push polls polls that ask for reactions to hypothetical, often false, information in order to manipulate public opinion (10)

racial gerrymandering redistricting to enhance or reduce the chances that a racial or ethnic group will elect members to the legislature (6)

racism institutionalized power inequalities in society based on the perception of racial differences (5)

random samples samples chosen in such a way that any member of the population being polled has an equal chance of being selected (10)

ratification the process through which a proposal is formally approved and adopted by vote (2)

rational ignorance the state of being uninformed about politics because of the cost in time and energy (10)

realignment substantial and long-term shift in party allegiance by individuals and groups, usually resulting in a change in policy direction (11)

reapportionment a reallocation of congressional seats among the states every ten years, following the census (6)

Reconstruction the period following the Civil War during which the federal government took action to rebuild the South (5)

redistributive policies policies that shift resources from the "haves" to the "have-nots" (14)

redistricting process of dividing states into legislative districts (6)

red tape the complex procedures and regulations surrounding bureaucratic activity (8)

refugees individuals who flee an area or country because of persecution on the basis of race, nationality, religion, group membership, or political opinion (1)

regressive taxes taxes that require poor people to pay a higher proportion of their income than do the well off (14)

regulated capitalism a market system in which the government intervenes to protect rights and make procedural guarantees (1)

regulations limitations or restrictions on the activities of a business or individual (8)

regulatory policies policies designed to restrict or change the behavior of certain groups or individuals (14)

representation the efforts of elected officials to look out for the interests of those who elect them (6)

republic a government in which decisions are made through representatives of the people (1)

responsible party model party government when four conditions are met: clear choice of ideologies, candidates pledged to implement ideas, party held accountable by voters, and party control over members (11)

retrospective voting basing voting decisions on reactions to past performance; approving the status quo or signaling a desire for change (12)

revolving door the tendency of public officials, journalists, and lobbyists to move between public and private sector (media, lobbying) jobs (11, 13)

roll call voting publicly recorded votes on bills and amendments on the floor of the House or Senate (6)

Rule of Four the unwritten requirement that four Supreme Court justices must agree to grant a case certiorari in order for the case to be heard (9)

rules directives that specify how resources will be distributed or what procedures govern collective activity (1)

sample bias the effect of having a sample that does not represent all segments of the population (10)

sampling error a number that indicates within what range the results of a poll are accurate (10)

sedition speech that criticizes the government (4)

segregation the practice and policy of separating races (5)

select committee a committee appointed to deal with an issue or problem not suited to a standing committee (6)

selective incentives benefits that are available only to group members as an inducement to get them to join (11)

selective incorporation incorporation of rights on a case-by-case basis (4)

selective perception the phenomenon of filtering incoming information through personal values and interests (13)

senatorial courtesy tradition of granting senior senators of the president's party considerable power over federal judicial appointments in their home states (7, 9)

seniority system the accumulation of power and authority in conjunction with the length of time spent in office (6)

separationists supporters of a "wall of separation" between church and state (4)

separation of powers the institutional arrangement that assigns judicial, executive, and legislative powers to different persons or groups, thereby limiting the powers of each (2)

Shays's Rebellion a grassroots uprising (1787) by armed Massachusetts farmers protesting foreclosures (2)

social conservatives those who endorse limited government control of the economy but considerable government intervention to realize a traditional social order; based on religious values and hierarchy rather than equality (1)

social contract the notion that society is based on an agreement between government and the governed in which people agree to give up some rights in exchange for the protection of others (1)

social democracy a hybrid system combining a capitalist economy and a government that supports equality (1)

social insurance programs programs that offer benefits in exchange for contributions (14)

socialist economy an economic system in which the state determines production, distribution, and price decisions and property is government owned (1)

social liberals those who favor greater control of the economy and the social order to bring about greater equality and to regulate the effects of progress (1)

social order the way we organize and live our collective lives (1)

social policies distributive and redistributive policies that seek to improve the quality of citizens' lives (14)

social protest public activities designed to bring attention to political causes, usually generated by those without access to conventional means of expressing their views (11)

Social Security a social insurance program under which individuals make contributions during working years and collect benefits in retirement (14)

Social Security Act the New Deal Act that created AFDC, Social Security, and unemployment insurance (14)

social welfare policies public policies that seek to meet the basic needs of people who are unable to provide for themselves (14)

soft money unregulated campaign contributions by individuals, groups, or parties that promote general election activities but do not directly support individual candidates (12)

solicitor general Justice Department officer who argues the government's cases before the Supreme Court (7, 9)

solidarity benefits selective incentives related to the interaction and bonding among group members (11)

sound bite a brief, snappy excerpt from a public figure's speech that is easy to repeat on the news (13)

Speaker of the House the leader of the majority party who serves as the presiding officer of the House of Representatives (6)

spin an interpretation of a politician's words or actions, designed to present a favorable image (13)

spoils system the nineteenth-century practice of rewarding political supporters with public office (8)

standing committees permanent committees responsible for legislation in particular policy areas (6)

State of the Union address a speech given annually by the president to a joint session of Congress and to the nation announcing the president's agenda (7)

statutory laws laws passed by a state or the federal legislature (9)

strategic policy foreign policy that lays out a country's basic stance toward international actors or problems (14)

strict constructionism a judicial approach holding that the Constitution should be read literally, with the framers' intentions uppermost in mind (9)

strict scrutiny a heightened standard of review used by the Supreme Court to assess the constitutionality of laws that limit some freedoms or that make a suspect classification (5)

structural defense policy foreign policy dealing with defense spending, military bases, and weapons procurement (14)

subjects individuals who are obliged to submit to a government authority against which they have no rights (1)

subsidy financial incentive given by the government to corporations, individuals, or other governments (14)

substantive guarantees government assurance of particular outcomes or results (1)

substantive laws laws whose content, or substance, defines what we can or cannot do (9)

sunshine laws legislation opening the process of bureaucratic policymaking to the public (8)

supremacy clause constitutional declaration (Article VI) that the Constitution and laws made under its provisions are the supreme law of the land (3)

surpluses the extra funds available because government revenues are greater than its expenditures (14)

suspect classifications classifications, such as race, for which any discriminatory law must be justified by a compelling state interest (5)

swing voters the approximately one-third of the electorate who are undecided at the start of a campaign (12)

symbolic representation efforts of members of Congress to stand for American ideals or identify with common constituency values (6)

Temporary Assistance to Needy Families (TANF) a welfare program of block grants to states that encourages recipients to work in exchange for time-limited benefits (14)

theocracy an authoritarian government that claims to draw its power from divine or religious authority (1)

Three-fifths Compromise the formula for counting five slaves as three people for purposes of representation that reconciled northern and southern factions at the Constitutional Convention (2, 11)

totalitarian government a system in which absolute power is exercised over every aspect of life (1)

tracking polls ongoing series of surveys that follow changes in public opinion over time (10)

treaties formal agreements with other countries; negotiated by the president and requiring approval by two-thirds of the Senate (7)

two-step flow of information the process by which citizens take their political cues from more well-informed opinion leaders (10)

unfunded mandate a federal order mandating that states operate and pay for a program created at the national level (3)

unitary system government in which all power is centralized (3)

valence issues issues on which most voters and candidates share the same position (12)

value-added tax (VAT) a consumption tax levied at each stage of production, based on the valued added to the product at that stage (14)

values central ideas, principles, or standards that most people agree are important (1)

veto override reversal of a presidential veto by a two-thirds vote in both houses of Congress (6)

Virginia Plan a proposal at the Constitutional Convention that congressional representation be based on population, thus favoring the large states (2)

voter mobilization a party's efforts to inform potential voters about issues and candidates and persuade them to vote (12)

wedge issue a controversial issue that one party uses to split the voters in the other party (12)

whistleblowers individuals who publicize instances of fraud, corruption, or other wrongdoing in the bureaucracy (8)

White House Office the approximately four hundred employees within the EOP who work most closely and directly with the president (7)

writ of certiorari formal request by the U.S. Supreme Court to call up the lower court case it decides to hear on appeal (9)

Index

References in bold typeface denote defined terms. References ending with "f" or "t" denote figures or tables. References in italic typeface denote illustrations or photos.

Age
  discrimination by, 149, 180–181
  drinking age, 79
  ideologies and, 339–340
  interest groups focusing on, 378
  news awareness and, 433–434, 436–437
  political orientation and, 339–340
  of presidential candidates, 229
  voter turnout and, 403–404
Age Discrimination Act of 1967, 180
Agencies, 194, 269f, 281–282. *See also*
    Bureaucracy; Executive/executive branch
Agency capture, **282**
Agenda setting
  by Congress, 212
  by interest groups, 376
  by media, 452
  in policymaking, 475f, 476
  by political parties, 361
Agricultural interest groups, 378
Agriculture, Department of
  agricultural interests and, 268, 282
  foreign policy and, 505
  organic foods standards and, 261–262, 290
AHIP (America's Health Insurance Plans),
    358, 392
AIDS, discrimination and, 180, 181
Aid to Families with Dependent Children
    (AFDC), 99, 480–481, 482f
AIM (American Indian Movement), 164
Airline deregulation, 282, 497
Airline travel, security screenings, 109
Alaska
  Arctic National Wildlife Refuge in, 468,
    508–509
  electoral votes of, 414, 416
Alaska Chamber of Commerce, 468
Alaska Wilderness League, 468
Alcohol use, testing for, 131
Alien and Sedition Act of 1798, 118
Aliens. *See* Immigrants/immigration
Alito, Samuel, 129, *300,* 312, 398
Allocative representation, **190**
All's Fair: Love, War, and Running for President
    (Carville & Matalin), 418
Alternative press, 444
AMA (American Medical Association), 386
Amendability, 66–68, **67**
Amendments to Constitution. *See also specific*
    amendments
  Bill of Rights as, 70–71
  procedures for, 67f
American Association for the Advancement of
    Science, 106
American Association of Political Consultants,
    348
American Association of University Professors,
    106, 141

American Bar Association, 134, 307, 311
American Cancer Society, 390
American Civil Liberties Union (ACLU)
  on death penalty cases, 134
  lobbying by, 382
  Virginia, 106
American Enterprise Institute, 48
American Health Benefit Exchanges, 485
American Heart Association, 390
American Indian Movement (AIM), 164
American Indians. *See* Native Americans
American Lung Association, 473
American Medical Association (AMA), 386
American Petroleum Institute, 508, 509
American Recovery and Reinvestment Act of
    2009, 98, 493
American Samoa, presidential primary in, 411
American Spectator (magazine), 438
Americans with Disabilities Act of 1990, 181
America's Health Insurance Plans (AHIP), 358,
    392
Amicus curiae briefs, 234, **318,** 319, 382
Amtrak (National Railroad Passenger
    Corporation), 271
Analysis, **31**
  academic research and, 140
  policy evaluation and, 210
  political, 32
  prospective voting and, 408
Anarchy, 13f, **14**
Animal rights, interest groups focused
    on, 388
Anthony (Susan B.) Amendment, 172, 173
Anti-Federalists, **57**
  balance of power debates, 78, 88
  Bill of Rights and, 110
  ratification of Constitution and, 68–71
Antislavery movement, 52
ANWR. *See* Arctic National Wildlife Refuge
AP. *See* Associated Press
Appeals (legal), **304**
Appeals courts, 303–304, 305–306
Appellate jurisdiction, **303**–304
Appointments, presidential
  bureaucracy and, 280–281, 283
  of federal district court judges, 233–234,
    306–309, 308–309t
  Senate approval of, 193t, 195, 234, 313–314
  of Supreme Court justices, 233–234
Apportionment, 196–197
Approval ratings
  for Congress, 191, 216–217
  for president, 241–242, 241f
Arctic National Wildlife Refuge (ANWR) and oil
    drilling, 468, 508–509
Arctic Power, 468
Aristotle, 4
Armey, Dick, 383

political accountability, **460**
presidency and, 257–258
separation of powers and, **65**–66, 66*f*
Cheney, Dick
as (G. W.) Bush's vice presidential choice, 412–413
Matalin and, 418
on modern presidency, 238–239
as vice president, 252
Chief administrator, **230**
Chief executive. *See also* Executive/executive branch
Bush (G. W.) image of, 255
Constitution on, 63, 194, 225, 230
foreign policy and, 503
War Powers Act and, 506
Chief foreign policy maker, **230**
Chief of staff, **250**
Child labor laws, 90
Child Online Protection Act, 127
Children. *See also* Education and schools
welfare and, 482–483
Children's Internet Protection Act, 127
China
founding celebrations in, 45
immigrants from, 167
socialism in, 11
Christian Coalition
on abortion rights, 137
public mobilization by, 383
on separation of church and state, 114
Christian Right. *See also* Religious right
gay rights and, 179
on gays in military, 179
Chu, Steven, *283*
Church and state. *See also* Christian Coalition; Christian Right
separation of, 112–117
CIA. *See* Central Intelligence Agency
Cities. *See* Local governments
Citizen advisory councils, **289**
Citizen involvement, 20
Citizen journalism. *See* Blogs
Citizens, **16**. *See also* Citizenship; Individuals; Public opinion
activist, 6–7
bureaucracy and, 289
civil liberties and, 139–140
Congress and, 216–217
Constitution and, 110
courts and, 322–323
elections and, 427–428
expectations of president, 225–228
federalism effects on, 86
foreign policy and, 507–508
founding of U.S. and, 72
ideal democratic vs. apolitical, self-interested, 329, 331

on ideological media bias, 448
interest groups and, 390–391
media and, 461–462
native-born and naturalized, 21–23
policy implementation and, 476
political skill of, 3
power and rights of, 108–109
presidency and, 256–257
public opinion and, 349–351
responsibilities, 16–18, 327
rights of, 16–18
role in democracy, 16–18, 329–331
values of, 331–335
Citizenship, 19–23. *See also* Citizenship profiles
for African Americans, 111
civil rights and, 182
contemporary views of, 20–21
dual, 22
federalism and, 101–102
Madison's vision of, 19–20
political systems and, 11–18, 36–37
of president, 229
public interest and, 19–21, 37–38
public opinion and, 349–352
qualifications for, 21
self-interested, 19–21, 37–38
as status, 21–23
views of, 19–21
Citizenship and Immigration Services, U.S. (USCIS), 22–23
Citizenship profiles
Benjamin, Tiffany, 6–7
Carville, James, 418–419
Daniels, Mitch, 80–82
Emanuel, Rahm, 248–251
Feingold, Russ, 200–201
Gingrich, Newt, 48–49
Maher, Bill, 120–121
O'Connor, Sandra Day, 316–317
Pacelle, Wayne, 388–389
purpose of, 36
Citizens United v. Federal Election Commission (2010), 382, 385–386, 397–398, 425–426, 428–429
City of. *See name of city*
Civic journalism, 461–462
Civil Aeronautics Board, airline deregulation and, 282, 497
Civil disobedience, 383. *See also* Demonstrations, as social protest
Civil justice system, equal access to, 323
Civil laws, **298**
Civil liberties, **107**–108. *See also* Equal rights
Bill of Rights and, 25
individual vs. collective rights and, 139–140
national security and, 109
Smith and McCarran Acts and, 119

Civil rights, **107**–108, **147**. *See also* Equal rights
  interest groups focused on, 378
  national protection for, 90–91
  for Native Americans, 163–165
  substantive vs. procedural equality and, 151
Civil Rights Act of 1875, 154
Civil Rights Act of 1964, 158, 214, 474
Civil Rights Act of 1991, 160, 176
Civil rights movement, 156–160
Civil service, **264**. *See also* Bureaucracy
  Pendleton Act of 1883, **264**
  political appointees and, 280–281
Civil Service Reform Act of 1883, 264
Civil War
  blacks in America after, 152–154
  national domination of states and, 88, 89
  newspapers and, 442
  realignment and, 366, 368
  slavery and, 152
Clean Air Act of 1970, 473, 474
Clean Water Act of 1972, 474
Clear and present danger test, **119**
Clientele groups, **267**–268. *See also* Constituents/
    constituencies
  interagency politics, 281
  iron triangles and, 287
  issue networks and, 287
Climate change research, 105–106
Clinton, Bill
  as active-positive president, 255
  antiterrorism and, 45
  approval ratings, 256–257
  on Arctic National Wildlife Refuge, 468
  block grants under, 99
  cabinet of, 246
  campaign contributors and, 387
  Congress and, 245
  divided government under, 245
  DLC and, 32
  economy and, 242
  election of 1992 and, 418
  election of 2008 and, 146
  Emanuel as policy adviser for, 248
  expectations of president and, 227
  federal court judges appointed by, 306
  gays in military and, 179
  Gore as vice presidential choice of, 412
  health care reform proposal of, 357–358, 392
  honeymoon period for, 241
  impeachment of, 192, 229, 383, 449
  Internet effect on campaigning and, 422
  Kennedy (J.F.), handshake with, 410
  moderate ideology of, 371
  modern presidency and, 238
  National Performance Review and, 285
  Native American sacred sites and, 165
  news management by, 459
  pardons by, 235

party ideology and, 371
polls conducted for, 328
presidential style of, 255–256
public opinion of behavior of, 452
signing statements, use of, 224
Supreme Court and, 312
Supreme Court appointments by, 234
televised presidential debates and, 423
time in office, 227
Unfunded Mandate Act and, 100
vetoes by, 231
vice president of, 252
welfare reform under, 481
Clinton, Hillary Rodham
  Comedy Central appearance by, 422
  as first lady, 253–254
  gender of voters and, 406
  health care and, 357–358
  nomination battle of 2008 election and, 411,
      412, 413*f*, 441
  as presidential candidate, 145–147, 182–183
  race of voters and, 407
  as secretary of state, 246, *502*
  soft news and entertainment programs use
      by, 422
Closed primaries, **411**
Cloture, **214**–215
CLUES (mnemonic), for critical thinking, 35–36
CNN (television network), 348, 443
Coalitions, of interest groups, 381
Coalition to Stop Gun Violence, 128
Coattail effect, **199**
Coercive Acts (1774), 50
Cohn, Jonathan, 392
Coincident economic indicators, 490
Colbert, Stephen, 439–440
The Colbert Report (TV show), 422, 439
Cold War, 267, **500**–501
Cole, Tom, 165
Collective action, problem of
  deliberation and, 21
  front-loading in presidential primaries and,
      411–412
  interest groups and, 376, 377
Collective benefits, 139–140. *See also* Society
Collective good, **377**
Colonial America. *See also* Founding period
  Great Britain and, 47
  press ownership during, 441
Colorado
  gay rights in, 138, 178
  marijuana, medical use, 77
  women's suffrage in, 173
Columnists, critical reading of, 92–93
Commander-in-chief, 63, **230**. *See also* President/
    presidency
Commerce, Department of, 268, 505
Commercial bias, **443**

Delegates to party nominating conventions, 411
DeMint, Jim, 187
Democracy/democracies, **15**. *See also specific types*
  as American value, 25
  bureaucracy and, 264–265
  in congressional politics, public dissatisfaction
    with, 216–217
  dangers of, 19
  direct, 327, 353
  education, role of, 338–339, 339*f*
  foreign policy and, 207
  law, role of, 296
  models and theories of, 15–16
  nonvoters and, 404–405
  origins in America, 18–21
  political parties, role of, 360–363
  political systems compared, 13*f*
  public opinion and, 109
  republic vs. pure, 19, 70
  theories of, 15–16
  tolerance in, 333–334
  voting in, 399–405
Democratic Leadership Conference (DLC),
  31–32, 33*f*
Democratic National Committee (DNC),
  360, 374
Democrats/Democratic Party
  African Americans and, 341, 367, 406–407
  economic liberals and, 31
  ideological placement of, 30*f*, 33*f*, 202–203,
    372–373
  interest groups and, 386
  nominating convention of 2000 in Los
    Angeles, 6–7
  nomination battle of 2008 election and, 413*f*
  in 112th Congress, 202
  organization, 360
  patronage and, 362
  platform (2008), 369
  presidential primaries of, 145–147, 411, 413*f*
  during Reconstruction, 153
  Republican Party vs., 367–368
  social liberals and, 31
  on tax reform, 494
  two-party system and, 372
Demographics. *See also* Diversity
  of families, 481
  of income gap by race and education level,
    161, 162*f*
  of journalists, 447–448, 449*t*
  of National Governors Association, 147
  of political parties, 368
  of Senate, 147
  of voter turnout, 399–400
Demonstrations, as social protest, 50, *156*,
  157, 383
Departments of government, 246–247, **268**.
  See also specific departments

Depressions. *See* Great Depression
Deregulation, 282, **497**
Detainees at Guantánamo Bay, due process rights
  for, 238, 288
Devolution, **78**, 94
Dewey, Thomas, *346*
Dionne, E. J., 21
Direct democracy
  of ancient Athens, 436
  responsibilities of, 327, 353
  technology and, 433–435
Direct lobbying, **379**–382
  of bureaucracy, 381–382
  of Congress, 380–381
  of courts, 381–382
  of president, 381–382
Director of national intelligence, **505**
Disabled persons, discrimination against, 181
Discrimination. *See also* Racism
  affirmative action and, 159–160
  by age, 149, 180–181
  AIDS and, 180, 181
  against Asians, 167
  de jure and de facto, 157–160
  equality and, 25, 26
  against gays and lesbians, 178–180
  against immigrants, 23
  against people with disabilities, 181
  resistance to, 157–158
  against women, 149, 175–176. *See also*
    Gender gap
Disney Corporation, 443, 444
Dissenting opinions, Supreme Court, **320**
Distributive policies, 472*t*, **473**, 477
District courts, 305. *See also* Courts
District of Columbia. *See* Washington, D.C.
Districts, congressional, 196–198
Diversity. *See also* Demographics
  among Asian Americans, 167
  among Hispanics, 165
  of cabinet members, 246
  of race and gender in 112th Congress, 202
Divided government, **243**
  dealignment and, 367
  partisanship and, 243–245, 244*f*
Divorce, 172. *See also* Marriage
DLC. *See* Democratic Leadership Conference
DNA testing, 135
DNC. *See* Democratic National Committee
Doctors Without Borders, 499
Dodd, Chris, 146
Dodd-Frank Bank Reform bill (2010), 498
Dole, Elizabeth, 145
DOMA (Defense of Marriage Act of 1996), 179
Domestic economic policy. *See* Economic policy
Domestic government, 379
Domestic policy. *See* Public policy
Dominican Republic, undeclared war in, 506

founders' ambitions for, 4
growth in and strengthening of, 87–88
judicial branch of, 63–64
legislature of, 61–62
local governments, 82–83
Native Americans and, 163–164
organizational chart of, 269*f*
party control of, 361–362
politics and, 5
president as head of, 227–228
presidential reorganization of, 284–285
rules and institutions, 5–8
social order and, 27, 28
trust in, 3
women in, 176–177
Government Accountability Office (GAO), 210, 459, 476
Government corporations, 269*f*, **271**
Government matching funds, 372–373, **423–424**
Governors
    African American, 161
    Hispanic, 166
    women, 177
Grandfather clauses, **153**
Grand Old Party (GOP), 367. *See also* Republicans/Republican Party
Grants, 96–99, 96*t*
Grassroots lobbying, 262, **383–384**
Gravel, Mike, 328
Great Britain. *See also* United Kingdom
    colonial separation from, 47–53
    New World dominance by, 47
Great Compromise, **59**, 196
Great Depression
    economic policy and, 488
    presidency and, 236–237
    Social Security and, 478
    welfare programs and, 480
Great Law of Peace, 18
Great Society, 237, 484. *See also* Johnson, Lyndon B.
Greenpeace, 499
Grenada, undeclared war in, 506
Gridlock, political, 367
Griles, J. Steven, 286
Griswold v. Connecticut (1965), 136, 311
Gross domestic product (GDP), 490–491
GRS (General Revenue Sharing), 98
Guam and American citizenship, 21
Guantánamo Bay detainees, 238, 288
Gulf of Mexico off-shore drilling disaster (2010), 194, 212, 286–287, 467, 508–509
Gulf War. *See* Persian Gulf War
Gun control laws, 128–129

Habeas corpus, **110**
Hamdan v. Rumsfeld (2006), 238

Hamdi v. Rumsfeld (2004), 238
Hamilton, Alexander. *See also Federalist Papers*
    on Bill of Rights, 70–71
    election of 2000 and, 293
    Federalist Party and, 364
    on judiciary, 64, 301
    on strong executive, 62
Hamilton, John, 7
Hammer v. Dagenhart (1918), 90
Hancock, John, 50
Handgun Control, Inc., 128
Hard money, **425**
Hardwick, Michael, 138
Harlan, John Marshall (1877–1911), 154
Harlan, John Marshall (1955–1971), 124
"Harry and Louise" ads, 357
Hastert, Dennis, 206, 375
Hatch Act of 1939, **264**
Hate crime laws, 125
Head of government, **227–228**. *See also* President/presidency
Head of state, **227**
Head Start, 483
Health and Human Services, Department of, 271, 481
Health care policy
    history of, 483–487
    opposition to reform efforts, 43, 357–358
    passage of Patient Protection and Affordable Care Act of 2010, 187–188, 357–358, 392–393
    as redistributive policy, 472
Health maintenance organizations (HMOs), 484
Hearst, William Randolph, 442
Henry, Patrick, 71, 107
Hierarchy, bureaucratic, 263
Higher education, affirmative action in, 159–160
Hispanics
    disenfranchisement in election of 2000, 161
    diversity among, 165
    education and schools of, 165–166
    English-only movement and, 166
    as illegal immigrants, 165–166
    income of, 161, 162*f*
    in 112th Congress, 202
    political preferences of, 342–343
    as presidential candidates, 145–146
    rights denied to, 165–167
    voting in 2008 election, 407
Hitler, Adolf, 500
HMO (Health maintenance organizations), 484
Hobbes, Thomas, 5, 18, 295
Holder, Eric, 147
Holmes, Oliver Wendell, 119
Homeland security
    foreign policy and, 504*f*
    select committee on, 208

Social liberals, 28, **29,** 30*f*, 31
Social networking. *See also* Internet
  Facebook, 435, 436, 440
  LinkedIn, 436, 440
  Twitter, 435, 436, 440
Social order, **4,** 27, 28
Social policies, 476–487, **477**
  health care. *See* Health care policy
  Social Security, 478–480
  welfare policy, 480–483
Social protests, **383**
Social Security, **478**–480
  citizen advisory councils and, 289
  contributions to, as regressive tax, 494
  New Deal and, 90
  as social insurance program, 477, 478, *479*
Social Security Act of 1935, 478, **480**
Social Security Administration, 267, 270, 478
Social Security Trust Fund, 478, 483
Social welfare policies, 474, **477**. *See also* Welfare
Society
  rights of individuals vs., 109
  role of law in, 296
Sodomy laws, 138, 178
Soft money, **425**
Solicitor general, **234, 318**
Solidary benefits, **377**
Sons of Liberty, 44, 50
Sotomayor, Sonia, 166, 234, *300,* 312, 313
Sound bites, **456,** 459
Sources, journalist's, 433–435
Sources of information
  bureaucratese language, 275, 276–279
  critical thinking about, 35–36
  economic indicators, 490–491
  media, 454–455
  op-ed pages, 92–93
  party platforms, 369
  for political scientists, 32
  public opinion polls, 332–333
  textbooks, 45–46
South (southern states). *See also specific states*
  civil rights movement in, 155, 157–158
  filibusters by senators from, 214
  party identification in, 367
  political parties in, 368
  Three-fifths Compromise and, 60
South Dakota, on unfunded mandates for federal
  highway funds, 100
Southern Christian Leadership Conference, 157
Southwest Voter Registration Education Project,
  167
Sovereignty
  of Native Americans, 163–164
  popular, 15
  of states under Articles of Confederation,
    54, 55
Soviet Union

Cold War and, 500
  former, socialism in, 10, 11
  former, totalitarianism in, 12
Spanish Empire, 47
Spanish language. *See also* Hispanics
  English-only movement and, 165–166
Speaker of the House, 203, **204,** 205, 229
Special interests. *See* Interest groups
Specialization, bureaucratic, 263, 275
Speech, freedom of. *See also* Expression,
    freedom of
  corporations, 398, 429
  speech codes, 125
  students and, 125
  symbolic, 122–123
  Tea Party demonstrators, *27*
  tolerance about, 334
Speech codes, 125
Spin, **458**–459
The Spirit of the Laws (Montesquieu), 65
Spoils system, **264**
Staff. *See also* Bureaucracy; Executive Office of
    the President (EOP)
  congressional, 209–210
  of interest groups, 384–385
  presidential campaign, 416–417
  White House staff, **247,** 247–252
Stamp Act of 1765, 50
Standing committees, **207**–208
Stare decisis, 297, 319
State courts, 303*f*, 304–305
State Department, 267, **503,** 504*f*, 505
State of the Union address, 63, **231,** 397
State party committees, 374
States. *See also* Devolution; Governors
  balance of power with national government,
    78–79, 88–91
  Bill of Rights and, 110–112, 112*t*
  censorship and speech limitations by, 119
  congressional strategies for influencing policy
    in, 95–101, 96*t*
  constitutional powers of, 83, 84*f*
  direct democracy in, 327
  election laws and two-party system of, 372
  ERA ratification and, 175
  federalism effects on, 86
  large vs. small under Constitution, 57–59
  marijuana, medical use, 102
  sovereignty under Articles of Confederation,
    54, 55
  women in government of, 176–177
  women's rights movement and, 172–174
Statutory laws, **299**
Steele, Michael, 342
Stephanopoulos, George, 451
Stevens, John Paul, 294, 324
Stewart, Jon, 422, 439–440, 450
Stewart, Potter, 123

Stimulus plan, economic, 88, 493
Stock market price indexes, 491
Stonewall riot (1969), 179
Strategic policy, **500,** 502
Straw polls, Internet, 461
Strict constructionism, **311,** 319
Strict scrutiny test, **149,** 175, 197
Structural defense policy, **500,** 502
Student newspapers, Internet publication of, 127
Student Nonviolent Coordinating Committee, 159
Students for Academic Freedom, 141
Stupak, Bart, 137
Subjects, people as, **16**
Subprime mortgage crisis, 497
Subsidies, **487**
Substantive guarantees, **10,** 151
Substantive laws, **297**
Succession, presidential order of, 63, 229
Suffrage. *See* Voting rights
The Suffragist (magazine), *172*
Sugar Act of 1764, 50
Suicide, assisted, 139
Sullivan, Andrew, 463
Sunshine laws, **289**
Superdelegates, 411
Super Tuesday, 406
Supplemental Nutrition Assistance Program (SNAP), **482**
Supply side economics, 494
Supremacy clause, **83**
Supreme Court. *See also* Justices
  on abortion rights, 321, *321*
  on affirmative action, 160
  on age discrimination, 180
  on Americans with Disabilities Act, 181
  on Bill of Rights, 111
  on busing, 159–160
  checks and balances and, 65, 66*f*
  choosing which cases to hear, 314–315, 315*f,* 318
  composition of, 313
  Constitution on, 63, 66*f*
  decision-making process, 318–320
  dissenting opinions, **320**
  federalism and, 88–91
  on Florida recount in election of 2000, 293–294
  founders on, 64
  on gun rights and Second Amendment, 129
  ideology and, 311–312
  incorporation of Bill of Rights into states' obligations, 111
  interest groups and, 319
  on Internet censorship, 127
  judicial interpretation by, 311–312
  on majority-minority districts, 197
  on marijuana, medical uses of, 78
  on Native American issues, 165

on necessary and proper clause, 83
political effects of decisions, 320–321
politics and, 310–321
on privacy, 136–137
on religious freedom, 115–117
on rights of accused, 130
on right to die, 139
on sedition laws, 119
selection of, 310–314
on self-incrimination, 132–133
on separation of church and state, 114–115
on states' rights, 83
Surpluses, budgetary, **489,** 492–493, 495*f*
Surveillance, electronic, 109, 131
SurveyUSA, 348
Susan B. Anthony Amendment, 172, 173
Suspect classifications, 149, **149,** 150*t,* 175
Sweden. *See* Scandinavia
Swift Boat Veterans for Truth, 449
Swing voters, **414**
Switzerland, federalism in, 86
Symbolic representation, **191**
Symbolic speech, 122–123

Talkingpointsmemo.com, 422
Talk radio, 461. *See also* Radio
TANF. *See* Temporary Assistance to Needy Families
Taxation. *See also specific types*
  under Articles of Confederation, 54
  citizenship obligation and, 139
  of English colonies, 50
  of immigrants, 22
  middle class, social welfare policies for, 487
  policies on, 494–496
  as redistributive policy, 472
  Three-fifths Compromise and, 60
  voting rights and, 47
Tax code reform, 496
Tea Act of 1763, 50
Tea Party movement, 27, 43–45, 72, 373, 383, 449
Technology. *See also* Internet; Social networking
  campaigns, use by, 441
  censorship and Internet, 126–127
  news transmission using, 433–435
  oil drilling and, 509
  polling and, 329, 348
  voter mobilization and, 402–403, 426
Telecommunications Act of 1996, 446
Telephone Consumer Protection Act of 1991, 348
Television. *See also* Cable television
  image emphasis of, 456
  as news source, 434, 435, 439–440
  ownership of, 443, 446
  political accountability and, 460
  public, 444
  regulation of, 445–447
  talk shows, 457, 461

Profile Sources

Chapter 1: Tiffany Benjamin spoke with Christine Barbour in March 2005.

Chapter 2: Newt Gingrich talked with Christine Barbour on March 21, 2005.

Chapter 3: Mitch Daniels spoke with Christine Barbour and Gerald Wright on April 12, 2005.

Chapter 4: Bill Maher talked with Christine Barbour and Gerald Wright on May 9, 2005.

Chapter 6: Senator Russ Feingold spoke with Christine Barbour and Gerald Wright on August 19, 2005.

Chapter 7: Rahm Emanuel talked with Christine Barbour and Gerald Wright on May 17, 2005.

Chapter 9: Sandra Day O'Connor spoke with Christine Barbour on March 3, 2005.

Chapter 11: Wayne Pacelle talked with Christine Barbour on March 10, 2005.

Chapter 12: James Carville spoke with Christine Barbour and Gerald Wright on June 21, 2005.

Illustration Credits